INQUIRY

INQUIRY

A Cross-Curricular Reader

EDITED BY

LYNN Z. BLOOM
University of Connecticut, Storrs

EDWARD M. WHITE
California State University, San Bernardino

A BLAIR PRESS BOOK

PRENTICE HALL, ENGLEWOOD CLIFFS, NJ 07632

Library of Congress Cataloging-in-Publication Data
Inquiry : a cross-curricular reader / edited by Lynn Z. Bloom, Edward M. White.
    p.   cm.
    "A Blair Press book."
    Includes bibliographical references and index.
    1. College readers.   2. English language—Rhetoric.
   3. Interdisciplinary approach in education.   I. Bloom, Lynn Z.
   II. White, Edward M. (Edward Michael).
   PE1417.I56   1993
   808'.0427—dc20   92-29509
                                                  CIP

Cover photo: John Petry
Cover design: Richard Stalzer Associates, Ltd.
Prepress buyer: Herb Klein
Manufacturing buyer: Robert Anderson/Patrice Fraccio

Acknowledgments appear on pages 689–692, which constitute a continuation of the copyright page.

Blair Press
The Statler Building
20 Park Plaza, Suite 1113
Boston, MA 02116-4399

© 1993 by Prentice-Hall, Inc.
A Simon & Schuster Company
Englewood Cliffs, NJ 07632

Printed in the United States

10 9 8 7 6 5 4 3 2

ISBN 0-13-466137-0

Prentice-Hall International (UK) Limited, *London*
Prentice-Hall of Australia Pty., Limited, *Sydney*
Prentice-Hall of Canada Inc., *Toronto*
Prentice-Hall of Hispanoamericana, S.A., *Mexico*
Prentice-Hall of India Private Limited, *New Dehli*
Prentice-Hall of Japan, Inc., *Tokyo*
Simon & Schuster Asia Pte. Ltd., *Singapore*
Editoria Prentice-Hall do Brasil, Ltda., *Rio de Janeiro*

PREFACE

The title of this book, *Inquiry*, reflects the process at its heart. In *Inquiry*, a wide variety of writers are searching, from a wide range of academic and social perspectives, for answers to important questions. The book, in fact, is filled with questions: questions define and organize the chapters, stimulate thought before and after the readings, and call for connections at the chapters' ends. Inquiry is by definition a process of asking questions and trying out answers. Active reading demands the same kind of process. So does writing. Our hope is that students using this book will produce writing that is worth the reading because it will be writing based on inquiry. Long after the course using *Inquiry* is a memory, the process of inquiry, so central to reading and writing, should remain in students' minds.

Organization

Good questions are at the heart of good reading and writing. Thus this book focuses upon on six major questions of perennial interest:

1. How do I know who I am?
2. How do I know what I know?
3. What is really important?
4. What is a good idea?
5. What can we learn from the past?
6. What will the future be like?

These questions differ significantly from many questions posed to students: they have no right answers. The questions are intended to stimulate thought, to encourage critical examination of what others have to say, to develop independent ideas. Each chapter's readings show important writers—from Plato to Laurel Thatcher Ulrich, from Frederick Douglass to Shirley Brice Heath—approaching the central question, from many different fields of study and from many different social perspectives. Students pursuing the ideas the questions suggest will be considering their own views in the light of what these other writers have had to say.

The central question of each chapter is subdivided into three more specific subquestions. Thus Chapter 1—"How Do I Know Who I Am?"—has three groups of readings centered on the following subquestions: (1) What Is My Physical Self? (2) Who Am I in Relation to Others? and (3) How Does My Writing Relate to My Self? The readings grouped under each subquestion present different approaches to the topic, different perspectives and positions. Active readers will need to examine not only the readings but their own lives for possible answers, perspectives, parallels.

Readings

Because inquiry is by definition open to many methods of pursuit, and many individual perspectives, we have included a wide variety of authors taking differing approaches to the specific chapter questions. In our choice of readings, we have been particularly attentive to the various discourse communities that make up the American university. Although some readings do not fit neatly into such categories, of course, and some fit approximately into several, we think that almost every student will find some readings in or very close to his or her major field of study. Close to half of the readings are from the humanities, including philosophic and reflective writing and such literature as autobiography, fiction, humor, and poetry. Many of the readings are from the social and behavioral sciences, including anthropology, economics, history, political science, psychology, and sociology. Likewise, the natural sciences are well represented, with readings from astronomy, physics, biology, chemistry, environmental studies, computer science, and medicine. We have consulted with our colleagues in a variety of disciplines to ensure cross-curricular perspectives, but we have included only readings appropriate to our audience of undergraduate students.

Inquiry also represents the diversity of American culture. Almost half of our authors are women, and we have strong representation from many of the ethnic communities that make up the United States today. Issues of ethnicity and gender recur throughout, as is appropriate for a book whose opening chapter asks, "How Do I Know Who I Am?"

Chapter Introductions

The introduction to each of the six chapters provides background for the question and subquestions, an overview of that chapter's readings, a discussion of a specific rhetorical concept for writers, and preliminary discussion/writing questions. Each of these four sections has a distinct purpose.

"Why Consider This Question?" opens each chapter introduction by discussing the meaning of the chapter question. For example, the second chapter asks, "How Do I Know What I Know?"—very different from alternative versions of the question such as "What Do I Know?" We begin each introduction by emphasizing the complexity and challenge of its central question, which governs not only the choice of reading selections but the direction of all the other questions in the chapter.

The second section of each introduction presents the three subquestions that shape the chapter, with brief commentary about each reading. Here, we give an overview of the contents to come and discuss how the readings relate to one another and to the chapter's questions.

Because rhetorical concepts are best taught in context, as a way of addressing the reading and writing problems that emerge from engagement with a text, the third section of each introduction defines and exemplifies a rhetorical concept appropriate to the chapter question. Notice how the sequence of six rhetorical concepts, each loosely related to the central question of its chapter, covers the rhetorical issues associated with most college writing courses:

1. Writing for an Audience
2. Writing as a Means of Learning: The Writing Processes
3. Definition
4. Argument and Evidence
5. Use of Sources
6. Discourse Communities

The "Questions for Discovery and Discussion" that conclude each introduction ask students to begin thinking about the central question of the chapter in light of what they already know. Students who discuss or write about the question prior to their reading are in a better position to read actively; the readings become encounters with the ways other writers have dealt with the same ideas and issues.

Questions

The "Responding to Reading" questions that follow each reading are meant to be used for discussion or writing. Some of these are designed to deepen understanding of the particular reading, while others ask students to make connections between that reading and other readings, or between that reading and their own lives. At the end of each chapter are "Questions for Reflection and Writing," pertinent to the entire chapter, that ask students to consider the ways the selections have enriched and deepened their own thoughts. In keeping with the concept of inquiry, the book contains over four hundred questions of one sort or another; our hope is that every instructor will find ample materials for discussion and writing, whatever the level of the students and goals of the class.

Headnotes

We have taken special care with the headnotes that precede readings. Each headnote provides a ready biographical reference to the author, concise, incisive, and humanizing, and it contains key concepts and terms associated with that author's work. The headnote also serves as an introduction to the reading, identifying its significant intellectual and rhetorical features and providing a lead-in to the "Responding to Reading" questions that follow.

Alternative Ways to Use This Book

The movement from chapter to chapter is a natural one, outward, from self to future. Nonetheless, instructors using this book may want to make reading and writing assignments in a different order. Our purpose was to create a textbook that would present a clear curriculum but that would also allow a considerable amount of flexibility to instructors with different levels of students, different curricular goals, and different amounts of class time. Instructors interested in grouping the selections by field of study or by rhetorical concept will find alternative listings at the back of the book to support such rearrangements. We know that many instructors share our belief that inquiry must lie behind both reading and writing, and we urge these colleagues to use the book imaginatively, to ask their own questions, to explore their own answers.

Acknowledgments

No book, even a collaborative work, is the product of its authors alone. Over the years we have listened to many voices, our teachers, our students, and a host of writers—some of whom appear in this book, others whose thinking informs more generally our culture and our profession. Specifically, colleagues who have read and commented on *Inquiry*, in various drafts, include Laura Brady, West Virginia University; Christine Cetrulo, University of Kentucky; Kristine Hansen, Brigham Young University; Susie Paul Johnson, Auburn University, Montgomery; and Laura Stokes, University of California, Davis. Martin Bloom and Volney White aided our collaboration at long and short distance, cheerfully providing the comforts of home on East and West coasts. Research assistants Katherine Heenan, Thomas Moore, and Ning Yu, of the University of Connecticut, have helped *Inquiry* come out on time, with accuracy. Leslie Cavaliere and LeeAnn Einert of Blair Press likewise made our work easier and better. We reserve special thanks for Nancy Perry, publisher of Blair Press and editor *par excellence*. She has helped us keep our balance between vision and revision, writing and respite and writing again. And, three years after we started, we are still friends. These short sentences say a lot.

Lynn Z. Bloom   Edward M. White
University of Connecticut   California State University
Storrs, Connecticut   San Bernardino, California

Contents

Chapter 1

How Do I Know Who I Am?   7

What Is My Physical Self?   19

Who Am I in Relation to Others?   57

CHAPTER 2

HOW DO I KNOW WHAT I KNOW? 113

Chapter 3

What Is Really Important?   225

How Do We Develop a Sense of Values?   236

What Does Nature Mean?   265

How Do We Resolve Conflicts in Values?   301

CHAPTER 4

WHAT IS A GOOD IDEA?   340

Chapter 5

Chapter 6

WHAT IS THE FUTURE OF THE FAMILY? 577

WILL WAR SHAPE THE FUTURE? 627

HOW CAN WE THINK AND SPEAK ABOUT THE FUTURE? 657

INQUIRY

Introduction

We write, as we read, for a variety of reasons. We also write for a variety of audiences. In saying "I write for myself and strangers," Gertrude Stein identifies two sets of readers, the author and everyone else. She also implies two major areas of concern for any writer—the need to preserve material for oneself and the need to communicate it to others. Yet no matter what we say or how we say it, we are reacting to what is in the world, reacting on paper, in our minds, and in our hearts. What we write provides some point of view or interpretation for ourselves, our friends, teachers, prospective employers, strangers. Even something as seemingly arbitrary as a list is rarely random. We choose what to put on the list (our friends, say, on a Christmas card list), what to leave off (no longer friends), and how to arrange it (in alphabetical order or from the most to the least important in case we run out of time, or stamps).

Sometimes we write simply to *list facts*, for our own reference or others': people to invite to a party; things to do today or to be put off till tomorrow. Or we write to *record or summarize others' opinions and our own reactions to events, experiences, reading:* class notes, a reading journal, or a travel diary. At times we write to *convey information:* directions on how to get downtown or to Bali ("You can get there from here!"); instructions on how to assemble a bicycle or write a computer program; recipes for pasta, potpourri, or the perfect friendship. Or we write to *clarify or interpret information or ideas:* letters to friends and family, final examinations, job applications.

This book emphasizes *writing as thinking, or inquiry.* Novelist E. M. Forster described his own writing as a process of inquiry, "How do I know what I think until I see what I say?" Writing about the

1

ideas of others enables us not only to understand what they mean but also to focus our own thoughts. Does the author make sense? What are the essay's main points? Subordinate points? Does its organization reinforce the logic or help the argument to flow? What are the illustrations or supporting information? Does the author tell me something I did not know before? Enable me to see the issue in new ways? Shake up beliefs I have taken for granted? Make me angry, delighted, or inspired to protest the way things are and want to change the world?

Inquiry also raises other questions. Will the issue still look the same if I compare one author with another? Or another? Where do I now stand on the issue? And why? Through sorting out the implications, wrestling with the ideas, reacting, reaffirming, or taking issue with them, it is possible to enter into a dialogue, spoken or written, with the authors in this book, individually or in combination. As we do so, we are forced to think, to try out ideas, to take a stand. We can find out why we are right, where we are wrong, or what are the implications of our thinking. And so we become authors ourselves.

Writing as inquiry has a number of significant features:

- Writing as inquiry needs *a question worth asking*, an issue worth exploring as a starting place. But such value may start only in the mind of the beholder; millions of apples fell, insignificantly, before Isaac Newton asked what principle this implied. Through writing, the question's significance emerges to writer and readers alike.

- Writing as inquiry is *thought in action*. As your ideas develop, you can expect to make a number of drafts, in your head or on paper. Writing as inquiry is never really finished, since one's thinking is continually in process. Any given draft of a paper, even the "final" one, shows where one's thinking is at the time.

- Writing as inquiry requires writers *to have a voice and point of view* of their own; it can never merely report what others have said.

- Writing as inquiry cannot occur in a vacuum. It requires *taking other people's ideas, research, speculations, and disagreements into account*, whether one discounts, disagrees with, or incorporates them into one's own writing.

- Writing as inquiry ultimately *requires a controlling idea or thesis, whether it is stated overtly or implied*. What point (or points) do you want to make? Can you make your point most effectively through an argument that marhsalls facts and other evidence selected to lead to an apparently inevitable conclusion? ("We should/should not sacrifice market efficiency to protect the environment.") Or will another mode of writing work better—a narration, a poem, a satire, a parody? (Does Woody Allen *really* mean that college graduates have only a choice of disasters ahead of them?)

At the heart of *Inquiry* is the premise that *a good question can lead to all sorts of answers.* A good question has intellectual vitality; to answer it may lead to a fundamental understanding about human nature, the quality of life, or the importance of one value or set of values over another. Or it may lead to still more questions, some with answers, some that represent stages in an ongoing dialogue that can never be fully resolved. As editors of this book, we think it is more important to ask exciting questions and explore their possibilities than to define the issues so narrowly that they lead to predictable, safe discussions. Therefore we have organized this book around six major questions. That these questions have provoked a variety of lively discussions is indicated by the essays that follow each topic and that resonate with others throughout the book. The questions are:

1. How do I know who I am?
2. How do I know what I know?
3. What is really important?
4. What is a good idea?
5. What can we learn from the past?
6. What will the future be like?

These issues have not yet been resolved, and may never be, but they provide a wealth of opportunity for you to express your own point of view, which is, after all, the basic task for every writer. Joan Didion claims that all writers are fundamentally subversive, that they approach the subject, and their readers saying, *"Listen to me. See it my way. Change your mind."*

We invite you to participate in this subversive activity. A good way to start your inquiry is by doing some exploratory writing about the given questions as you begin to think about it, before you do much reading. Each chapter introduction presents a few writing topics to help you focus on the subject. Your thinking, and writing, will be more interesting if you keep the questions as complex (and messy) as they really are; avoid making them overly simple in search of tidy answers. For example, if you change "How do I know who I am?" into "Who am I?", the revised question, can be much less complicated than the first. *"How* do I know who I am?" asks you to focus on how people come to understand themselves and the human condition. That is, the questions in *Inquiry* are concerned with the nature of learning about an issue ("What does it mean to be a member of the human race, or of a particular gender?") rather than on exploring or finding a specific answer applicable only to a single individual. Writing at this stage, before you have read much on the subject, can help you start thinking about the subject, asking questions that will be addressed as you read further in the chapter or elsewhere in *Inquiry*.

The chapter introductions, with their discussions of the central chapter question, explanations of related rhetorical issues, and exploratory writing assignments, are followed by clusters of readings arranged around three subquestions related to the chapter questions. The subquestions allow us to focus the selections on specific issues that generate debate and to illustrate how writers from various scholarly perspectives think about the issues. Space limitations allow us to include in *Inquiry* only a few of the many ways of looking at a subject. So we have chosen the writings of major thinkers and influential commentators, people who write well and whose work can be understood by general readers. In addition, we have sought writers whose disagreements will lead to continuing debate by those working with the book. The questions following each selection and at the end of each chapter ask not only for careful reading but also for connections, comparisons, contrasts, and inquiry.

In order to consider writing as inquiry, you will need to undertake reading as inquiry. As with writing, it is possible to read in many different ways. Sometimes we read passively, to memorize information—French verb tenses or vital statistics. Sometimes we read essentially to be able to understand the author's subject matter (What *is* DNA, anyway?) or point of view (What are the effects of working mothers on families?). Such reading is valuable, but *Inquiry* expects you to go beyond accepting, uncritical ways of reading. Although you will need to read carefully, it should also be with a keen and critical mind. You will be looking for the writer's underlying—and often unstated—definitions and assumptions; you will be examining the evidence and testing it against what you know and what other writers claim. As you form your own opinions, test and challenge the ideas in each essay. Since many of the essays disagree with each other, you will not be able simply to accept what one authority has to say without taking into account conflicting points of view. You will need to understand why they differ, what the grounds for differences are, and what you find of value in each—and what you reject. Write in the margins of this book; argue with the authors; and notice when, where, and why they disagree with one another. Only strong, active readers can become strong, active writers.

None of the writers you read in *Inquiry* has the last word. You have that privilege—and that responsibility. You might consider your writing as an *evolving interpretation*, a series of drafts that enable you to think through the questions and possible answers raised by your reading. As you write you will incorporate some of the ideas or perspectives you have read, dispute others, give some opinions and evidence greater weight than others, dismiss still others out of hand. As you bring later reading and thinking to bear on the issues, your own inquiry should become more knowledgeable than your initial writing was, more complicated—and possibly more certain. You may find the question itself to be more interesting than any of the available answers. When Gertrude Stein was dying, her lifelong companion, Alice B. Toklas, is said to have asked, "What is the answer?" To which Stein replied, "What is the question?" To be able to ask good questions, as you read and as you write, is ultimately to understand the importance of inquiry in all learning.

1

How Do I Know Who I Am?

"A biography is considered complete if it merely accounts for six or seven selves, whereas a person may have as many thousand."

VIRGINIA WOOLF

Why Consider This Question?

We are our most fascinating subjects, for thinking about and for writing. Living intimately with ourselves as we do, we seldom seek to escape or transcend the self but rather strive to know ourselves more fully. Indeed, "know thyself" might be the motto of our contemporary society. But, what is that self we are to know? If each of us has a core self, what is it? Our genetic makeup remains constant but old photographs of ourselves, as babies or even five years ago, reveal changes that may overwhelm the continuities—the "family" build, or ears, or set of the smile.

Who is this self we seek to understand, this changing entity that takes its coloration and configuration from changing contexts? Because that self shifts in significant ways according to the roles we choose or have assigned to us throughout our lives, the person we are in class is both the same as and different from the person with the same name, same size and shape outside of class. Who is the version of our self who lives in our dorm room or apartment, holds down a job after class, plays music, watches TV, cooks, swims, hangs out with friends? Is the self who votes the same self that pays taxes, worships, makes love (or war)? Who are, or will we be, when and if we marry, become parents, in-laws, adults with elderly parents, ourselves aged?

7

Will our selves be determined by our roles, our jobs, our personalities—and chance and luck—or some combination of these?

How, indeed, do we know when we have attained even a partial understanding of the numerous selves that, like Benjamin Franklin's many roles as tradesman, businessman, author, publisher, public citizen, inventor, scholar, statesman, husband, father, and flirt, comprise our essence? By what means can we come to even the limited self-understanding that we will have to live with? One way is by reading others' explorations of themselves. Because we understand what we read, in part, through analogy with our own lives, as we learn about others we can come to understand ourselves.

To examine the question, "How do I know who I am?" this chapter focuses on three clusters of writings that explore the physical self, the social self, and the self that is both expressed and created through writing. As these writings make clear, these selves are inextricably intertwined. For instance, the physical self, male or female, black, white or some other racial "color," is as much a construct of social interpretation and language as of one's genetic constitution.

What Is My Physical Self?

Contemporary Americans are concerned with having perfect health and obsessed with having perfect bodies. Many of us have in mind an ideal of what we should look like, even if that ideal is an unreal image constructed and reinforced by the media. We spend considerable effort, worry, and money in trying to make our bodies attain the ideal that fewer than five percent conform to naturally.

If we don't like the way we look, for whatever reason, we can change it. We can exercise and diet for a fit or muscular or slender body. We can curl, straighten, or bleach our hair, shave it off, wear wigs. We can tan and tattoo our skin; straighten our teeth; surgically pare our noses, bellies, and buttocks; use steroids or other drugs to increase our strength, height, fighting spirit; even alter our sex, or cure congenital defects of our offspring in utero. We want to believe that these changes are for the better, notwithstanding the existence of skin cancer, anorexia, bulimia, sterility, and other potentially devastating consequences.

Once we have made these changes, with their innumerable surface manifestations that send messages to those who see us (Do blondes *really* have more fun?), are we the same people underneath? Well, yes and no, say the authors in this chapter as they consider the question, "What is my physical self?" All, however, take issue with the conventional conception of the self as an autonomous, coherent, unchanging entity. Even our mature brains can grow in size and capability in response to stimulating experiences, say biologists Robert Ornstein and Richard Thompson, reporting on their research in "Learning and Brain Growth." Our skin, too, is not necessarily the same from one season to the next, as John Updike shows in "At War with My Skin." It may even put our inner selves in conflict with our outer surfaces.

Our physical selves gain meaning from the social and political contexts in which we live. Many people contend that even gender does not automatically carry with it a cluster of distinctively "male" or "female" characteristics unless society affirms what these are. Maxine Hong Kingston's Tang Ao of "On Discovery," transformed through bound feet, pierced ears, diet, and dress from "male" to "female," is a case in point. In "On Being Female, Black, and Free," Margaret Walker disagrees with the notion that society determines the meaning of gender, claiming the reverse—that her gender has social meaning and controls how she fulfills the roles of daughter, sister, sweetheart, wife, mother, grandmother, even writer. In "The Men We Carry in Our Minds," Scott Russell Sanders also examines the interrelation of class, race, and expectations of gender. Working class men—miners, truck drivers, factory workers—says Sanders, "labored with their bodies," wore them out, and died early; "only women lived into old age." Walker, however, disputes the idea that women have advantages; "being female, black, and poor" was a triple disadvantage that restricted her and other black women to the bottom of American society.

All the essays in this section demonstrate that, in some way, the shape and condition of one's body reflect the possessor's state of mind. And when change occurs, mutation does not have to mean mutilation; it can be a source of new and powerful self-definition, as Nancy Mairs demonstrates in "On Being a Cripple." Here she breaks the taboos of reticence, propriety, and social expectations to face publicly the "brutal truth" of her life as a victim of multiple sclerosis. "As a cripple, I swagger." The unconventional perspectives of Mairs, Sanders, and Walker, like the more familiar views of Kingston and Updike, challenge readers' comfortable assumptions about body shape, size, condition, gender, class, and race; they question their readers' values and shake them up.

Who Am I in Relation to Others?

To be human is to be inextricably involved with other people. In John Donne's view of the integration of humanity, no man, or woman, "is an island, entire of itself." All of us are assigned, and assume, particular roles that are continually changing in response to the way others play their parts: child, parent, student, friend, lover, spouse, in-law, someone at work or at play, or citizen—of a community, a state, a country, the world.

As citizens or residents of the United States, our expectations are influenced by the ideal of the American dream—work hard and you will succeed, not as the member of a team but as an individual making an extraordinary personal effort. Benjamin Franklin's adage, "Early to bed, early to rise, makes a man healthy, wealthy, and wise," is one expression of the American dream; "Arriving at Moral Perfection," from his *Autobiography,* is another. In the fashion of innumerable advice-givers on whom Americans dote, Franklin shows the American people how-to-do-it and how to keep score—a record of their successes and failures—both characteristic American preoccupations. He implies that his system of attaining moral perfection will be successful if faithfully followed. In "Resurrection," Frederick Douglass explains how he singlehandedly fought his way out of slavery, defying his overseer with strength, intelligence, and ingenuity. Only then was he able to become an independent human being; his fate was literally in his own hands, as he explains throughout his autobiography.

But even in this land of opportunity, not everyone will be as successful as Benjamin Franklin or Frederick Douglass. The American dream is too often contradicted by the reality of monotonous, back-breaking work that leads nowhere and pays little, as Scott Russell Sanders shows. Some people tailor their expectations to the reality rather than the dream. In "I Just Wanna Be Average," Mike Rose shows how high schools slot students into particular tracks, academic and vocational. "Students will float to the mark you set," he says. If a curriculum does not free its students to aspire to the best, they may "just wanna be average," no better or worse than anyone else, and no different.

How Does My Writing Relate to My Self?

All writing involves some representation of the writer. The writer must decide what to include or leave out and how to arrange the items—a reflection not only of taste but also of a way to order the world. While lists merely hint at the writer behind them, other writings reveal their authors more explicitly—diaries, letters, personal essays, self-sketches, autobiographies. Like snapshots, each writing "frames" the writer, highlighting some features, shadowing others, and cropping out others altogether. As writers, we choose the image and we choose our frame. To the extent that we can, we try to control how readers will respond to the self or selves we have presented.

When writers discuss the ways in which their writing expresses profoundly moving experiences, they disclose an intimate relationship between their words and themselves. In "Why I Write: Making No Become Yes," Elie Wiesel explains how surviving the Holocaust influenced his career as a writer; he is "duty-bound to give meaning" to his survival, to justify each moment of his life and to transmit that experience to his readers. Not to transmit a profound experience, he says, is to betray it.

Literacy is a paramount value in our society. A democracy not only empowers its citizens through enabling them to read and write, but initiates them into the prevailing culture. Thus literacy can impart group meanings as well as individual ones. Shirley Brice Heath, ethnographer and linguist, explores the "Literate Traditions" in an Appalachian small town that determine why and how and what children learn to read and write. In Trackton, literacy is a social activity; "authority in the written word does not rest in the words themselves, but in the meanings which are negotiated through the experiences of the group." Richard Rodriguez provides a case history of his own literacy in "Aria," analyzing his bicultural childhood as a Mexican-American who spoke Spanish at home and English in school. Through this personal example, he argues against bilingual education; rather than being taught first in their native language and then in English, school children should be taught in English right from the start to give them the "public identity" they will need as American citizens. In "The Need to Say It," Patricia Hampl shows how important it was for her, as a child, to become literate. As a budding writer, she wrote letters for her immigrant Czech grandmother, an important practice for becoming a professional writer herself who could preserve the culture of her ethnic heritage and make the "personal world" public.

But the social levels of meaning can be oppressive as well as constructive. In "Being a Man," Paul Theroux, a novelist and travel writer, criticizes the uncomfortable American expectation that male writers must behave in stereotypical macho ways—bullfighting, arm wrestling, elephant shooting—before their work will be taken seriously.

The authors in this section define themselves through the aspects of their lives that they choose to emphasize in their writing. In all cases, their individual presentations transcend the personal and demonstrate their connections with others: families, members of their community or culture, the human race. As writers, we can understand from these examples how to use writing not only to discover who we are but also to disclose some of our various selves to readers, who interpret our experiences and point of view through analogy with their own.

Rhetorical Issues: Writing for an Audience

"I write for myself and strangers," said Gertrude Stein, making explicit the implicit principle that guides the writing of most skilled authors, professional or otherwise. In contrast, "I write for myself alone" or "I write for myself and people who know and love me" appears to guide the composition of many less skilled writers who are unaware of or indifferent to what outside readers need to know to understand their writing.

The Audience

Writers aware of an audience ask themselves such questions as, "Who would want to read this?" "Why?" "So what?" Although the questions may sound cynical, the answers are not. Unless your writing is deliberately private, you can expect others to read it. The audience may be specific and predetermined, such as your teacher, boss, or friends. Or it may be the "strangers" to whom Gertrude Stein referred, anyone who might want to read your work or an imaginary reader to keep in mind as you write. No writer can anticipate everything that a reader will bring to a given work but you will need to consider some characteristics of your anticipated readers, for instance, their level of knowledge, cultural heritage, values, and biases. And you will have to consider the same features about yourself as a writer, in order to ensure the intended reception for your writing. We return to this matter of audience in Chapter 6, but for now consider what it means to share your inquiry with others.

Knowledge, general and specialized: An important consideration is, How much do the readers already know about the subject? What else do they need to know in order to understand what I'm saying? What background information will I need to supply? What terms must I define? How simple or technical, general or specialized can my language be? In addition to common sense and common knowledge, do you expect your readers to know as much as an eighth grader (the reading level of many American newspapers), a high school graduate, or a college student? Does your reader have a hobbyist's interests or a professional-level education in a specialized field on which you are writing? Do you expect your readers to know more about the subject than you do (as would a teacher reading your exam), less, the same amount?

Your expectations will determine how simple or complicated to make your thoughts and your language, which terms to define, and how much background information and other explanations to include. However, even if you are explaining something elementary, you can avoid condescension by treating your readers as collaborators in the process of gaining an understanding, rather than as a lecture audience. For a good example, notice how Shirley Brice Heath helps us see how the children of Trackton learn to read.

Cultural heritage: If you are an American writing for other Americans, you can assume some aspects of a common cultural heritage. You will not need to explain Oprah or the Alamo or Washington—as long as it is clear whether you are talking about George or Booker T., the District of Columbia, or the state. If you are a typical member of the group for which you are writing, you can use yourself as a reference point. Assume that what you know and take for granted your audience will also understand (whether pom-pom girls or Prohibition, Elvis Presley or the Promised Land). What is strange or difficult for you will be likely to present problems for your readers.

Values: All of us hold values, whether or not we explicitly label them as such. We may openly or subtly approve of (or reject) marriage, having children, equal employment opportunities for minorities and women, regular exercise, suburban living, and a host of other aspects of our lives that we take for granted—or question. Our values unavoidably influence the way we treat a topic; even when we try to be even-handed, it is hard not to speak more glowingly of what we approve than of what we disapprove ("Vote the rascals out!" "Never! They're the noble leaders I know and love!") To accommodate divergent views, try to imagine your subject as some disparate readers might. Suppose you were writing on dual career marriages. What would a feminist—man or woman—assume about these? Would a traditional male agree with any of the feminist's assumptions about the role of each wage-earner? Each partner's responsibilities as a parent? As a member of a household? If so, what might be the points of agreement? Of disagreement? Would any of these views coincide with those of a traditional female—over 40? Between 25–40? Under 25? Each aspect of the issue can assume a different perspective, as revealed in the essays on "What Is the Future of the Family" in the first section of Chapter 6.

Persona

All writers speak through a *persona,* the mask or created character they invent to talk to their readers. Readers often believe that because a piece of writing sounds personal—if the author uses *I* or appears as a conspicuous character in the work—it is unaltered autobiography. Nothing could be farther from the truth; because a piece of writing intended for an external audience is as carefully cultivated as a well-tended garden—planted, arranged, pruned, weeded, and shaped to accommodate the aims of both writer and audience.

When scientists write about the natural world, for instance, the authorial persona may be self-effacing, subdued. But even here an authorial character is present through the tone of voice, the presentation of data, and the organization—someone who is authoritative, rigorous, keen-minded, logical, and yet who cares deeply about the subject. This persona is "scientific"—but with a heart— see Rachel Carson and William Warner (Chapter 5) or Carl Sagan (Chapter 6).

Writing that seems to be more personal, where the writer's persona more closely and conspicuously corresponds to the author's real life, is also shaped to enhance the author's aims. As Joan Didion says in "Why I Write" (Chapter 3), all writing is "the act of saying *I*, of imposing yourself upon other people, of saying *listen to me, see it my way, change your mind*." In "On Being a Cripple," Nancy Mairs compels an audience of physically-abled people to experience her version of what it means to be a "cripple," the word she chooses to define herself instead of "disabled," "handicapped," or "differently able." Her persona is quite different from both the objective medical textbook definitions of multiple sclerosis as a collection of symptoms, and the smiling-through-tears public persona that often characterizes poster children. Mairs shows herself in action, grotesque ("one arm bent in front of me, the fingers curled into a claw"), clumsy (dropping cans, falling over backward in a public toilet), and fearful of others' pity ("always the terror that people are kind to me only because I'm a cripple"). In exposing her frailties, admitting that she is grouchy and surly, and in laughing at herself, Mairs gives her readers permission to regard her on the same human terms as they regard themselves. In forcing her audience to confront her illness head on, as she does, without evasive delicacy, Mairs forces them to understand it on her terms, in her way. This deeply human persona is no less shaped and crafted than the scientific one.

We have only to think of the different selves we present in our letters to different people, even on the same subject, to realize how we select and shape evidence, mood, motives, and foreground and background information to render the same experience in different ways on different occasions. As victims of discrimination, Margaret Walker, Frederick Douglass, Elie Wiesel, and Richard Rodriguez offer very different presentations of their subject. If you were to write as a victim of discrimination, for instance, how would you tell your story to your grandparents, your best friends (male or female), your English teacher, a court of law, the local newspapers? Depending on what you chose to emphasize and suppress, you would probably be a somewhat diferent character in each account. Your purpose, your audience, and the type of story you decide to tell—a sermon, a cautionary tale, a plea for sympathy or social action, even a joke—would determine whether you presented yourself as a hero, either bold or unassuming; a victim of circumstances; a rebel bent on revenge; or the embodiment of noble forgiveness.

The language of your writing should reinforce your persona, the self you present to your audience. If you are writing informally, imagine yourself composing a letter to a friend; the friendly, casual, conversational tone incorporating contractions, your everyday vocabulary, and the first person will resemble your actual conversations with that person. If you want to sound more formal, you will choose a less intimate approach to your subject; longer sentences and the more technical vocabulary that you would find in specialized writings on the subject will communicate your seriousness.

Finding a Focus

All writing intended for an audience needs to have a focus; readers cannot be expected to come along for the ride until you have decided where you are going. The focus of a paper, like a camera's focus, sharpens one's perspective on a subject, confines it within identifiable boundaries, and presents the resulting interpretation for the readers' response. See it my way, the writer promises the reader; keep that image of the focused picture in mind no matter what your other "takes" on the subject may be.

As you examine your subject from all the possible perspectives to find just the right angle, you will be looking for ways to make it your own. Think of your subject as a problem and the paper you write as offering one or more ways of clarifying, solving the problem. When examining a subject area as a problem, you could look at it in some of the following ways.

- *Define the problem.* What is it? What major issue(s) does it contain? Are there any minor issues or other ways of subdividing a large or vague subject to make it more manageable? Suppose you want to write about discrimination—a broad topic. What about it? One major issue might be whether legislation can effectively address or remedy the problem. But first you would need to define and explain the kind of discrimination —religious, racial, gender, or whatever.

- *Explain the key terms pertinent to the problem.* Sometimes a clarification of terms focuses or even resolves the issue. What exactly do you mean by discrimination? Giving a minority candidate or a woman preferential treatment in hiring, for instance? Just what does "preferential treatment" mean? Or "affirmative action"? Are these synonyms? Do they have the same meaning in all circumstances?

- *Explain the problem.* What are the causes of the problem? What are its short-term and long-term effects? Is there disagreement over the alleged causes or effects? If so, what is the disagreement? For instance, does affirmative action undercut either a merit or a seniority system of hiring and retention? Does it lead to the stereotyping of minorities? Or does it enhance equal opportunity?

- *What is the solution to the problem?* Are there alternative solutions? Can the problem be resolved at all? Would preferential treatment in hiring actually solve the problems it is intended to remedy? Or would it lead to earlier firings ("last hired, first fired") or to reverse discrimination suits? Are other solutions feasible or only ways of perpetuating inequality?

- *Which solutions are most necessary? Desirable? Feasible? Likely to be put into effect?* Why? How can the possible solutions be effected? Are there conflicts, actual or potential, among the alternatives? What is the relation of a quota system to merit hiring or retention?

- *Which individuals or groups favor which solutions?* Why? Which stand(s) to gain or lose the most from which solutions? Why? Whose views should be given precedence? Under what circumstances?

- *What will be the consequences of any given solution?* On what basis can you predict these? Will they be permanent? Temporary? Are they contingent on still other factors, controllable or uncontrollable?

- *Are some consequences preferable to others?* On what basis? Ethical? Political? Social? Economic? Religious? Expediency?

Here are some other perspectives from which to examine your subject. For instance, you might consider its *static* or *dynamic characteristics.* If you regard something as static, you will be treating it at a particular moment in time. Although that might be possible with an object, such as a car, anything that involves policy, values, or activity, for instance affirmative action, is a dynamic part of a process that changes over time, space, and circumstances. Is the "desegregation" of the 1960s, manifested through integrated schools and lunch counters, the same as affirmative action of the 1990s, giving women in the military the right to front line combat or employees who test HIV positive for AIDS the right to keep this information confidential? You could consider the dynamics of the subject in relation to the various ways you view it, from *psychological, chronological, or physical distance.* Would you have seen affirmative action differently when you were a child from the way you do now as an adult? How close you are to the subject will undoubtedly affect your views; familiarity breeds understanding. If you or people you know have been the victims of discrimination, these experiences will probably be more important—the more recently or profoundly, the more memorable.

It is also useful to consider your subject from the perspective of *figure/ground.* How does the issue appear in isolation? How does it appear in relation to others like itself? In relation to things different from itself? To what extent is it influenced by its context? And, perhaps most importantly, how has the process of your thinking about the subject changed your views even as you contemplated it? How can you compel your readers to care about the subject as much as you do—and to see it your way?

Finally, writing for an audience is a human relationship, not all that different from the other human relationships you engage in all of the time. You want to remain aware of your audience and of how you present yourself and your ideas to that audience. Your choice and use of words tell your readers who you are.

QUESTIONS FOR DISCOVERY AND DISCUSSION

1. Compose three brief descriptions of yourself, from your own point of view.

A. Describe yourself physically, so precisely that a stranger in the room could pick you out from everyone else in the room.

B. Now describe yourself as a member of your family or some other group.

C. Then describe the person you would like to be ten years from now. Notice that you will be creating this person through your writing.

D. Review your three descriptions and find the relationship among them. For what audience have you written? Who are you? How do you know who you are?

2. Compose three brief descriptions of yourself, from an outside point of view.

A. Describe yourself as might someone who has just met you for the first time.

B. Follow this with a description of yourself as you appear to most people who know you.

C. Then, describe yourself the way your best friend or your favorite family member would.

D. Review your three descriptions and reflect on what they say about you. How do they relate to your responses to question 1? Have you written for the same audience? How do other people know who you are?

WHAT IS MY PHYSICAL SELF?

On Discovery

MAXINE HONG KINGSTON

Maxine Hong Kingston's *Woman Warrior: Memories of a Girlhood Among Ghosts* (1975) was in 1990 "the most widely taught book by a living writer in U.S. colleges and universities." In a recent interview she commented on the subject of her writing: "My family is more imaginative and brave than most people. They've had more adventures, more triumphs and defeats. They've traveled half-way round the world. They're people with big lives. And I guess I think this about all Chinese people: They have an amazing amalgam of practicality and imagination. Maybe that's the Chinese spirit—to embody those two wildly different world views."

"On Discovery," from Kingston's second book, *China Men* (1980), expresses the dual vision of this Chinese-American writer who was born in 1940 in Stockton, California, educated in Chinese and American schools, and holds a B.A. from the University of California at Berkeley. At home she spoke Chinese, her only language until she started first grade. She also learned Chinese customs from stories exchanged in her parents' laundry. As this passage from *Woman Warrior* illustrates, discrimination against women pervades the traditional Chinese culture, such as the selling of girls into slavery: "Eight-year-olds were about twenty dollars. Five-year-olds were ten dollars and up. Two-year-olds were about five dollars. Babies were free."

Kingston's writing reflects her experience with both racial and sexual stereotyping. Tang Ao's transformation in the Land of Women, as recounted in "On Discovery," presents a contemporary interpretation of the values embedded in traditional roles of Chinese men and women. Although on one level Kingston's writings can be read as a feminist protest against sex discrimination in China, on other levels they can be seen as a celebration of the complexity, vitality, and endurance of the ancient Chinese culture in contemporary America, with women as vigorous participants.

Once upon a time, a man, named Tang Ao, looking for the Gold 1
Mountain, crossed an ocean, and came upon the Land of Women. The women immediately captured him, not on guard against ladies. When they asked Tang Ao to come along, he followed; if he had had male companions, he would've winked over his shoulder.

"We have to prepare you to meet the queen," the women said. 2
They locked him in a canopied apartment equipped with pots of makeup, mirrors, and a woman's clothes. "Let us help you off with

your armor and boots," said the women. They slipped his coat off his shoulders, pulled it down his arms, and shackled his wrists behind him. The women who kneeled to take off his shoes chained his ankles together.

A door opened, and he expected to meet his match, but it was only two old women with sewing boxes in their hands. "The less you struggle, the less it'll hurt," one said, squinting a bright eye as she threaded her needle. Two captors sat on him while another held his head. He felt an old woman's dry fingers trace his ear; the long nail on her little finger scraped his neck. "What are you doing?" he asked. "Sewing your lips together," she joked, blackening needles in a candle flame. The ones who sat on him bounced with laughter. But the old women did not sew his lips together. They pulled his earlobes taut and jabbed a needle through each of them. They had to poke and probe before puncturing the layers of skin correctly, the hole in the front of the lobe in line with the one in back, the layers of skin sliding about so. They worked the needle through—a last jerk for the needle's wide eye ("needle's nose" in Chinese). They strung his raw flesh with silk threads; he could feel the fibers. 3

The women who sat on him turned to direct their attention to his feet. They bent his toes so far backward that his arched foot cracked. The old ladies squeezed each foot and broke many tiny bones along the sides. They gathered his toes, toes over and under one another like a knot of ginger root. Tang Ao wept with pain. As they wound the bandages tight and tighter around his feet, the women sang footbinding songs to distract him: "Use aloe for binding feet and not for scholars." 4

During the months of a season, they fed him on women's food: the tea was thick with white chrysanthemums and stirred the cool female winds inside his body; chicken wings made his hair shine; vinegar soup improved his womb. They drew the loops of thread through the scabs that grew daily over the holes in his earlobes. One day they inserted gold hoops. Every night they unbound his feet, but his veins had shrunk, and the blood pumping through them hurt so much, he begged to have his feet re-wrapped tight. They forced him to wash his used bandages, which were embroidered with flowers and smelled of rot and cheese. He hung the bandages up to dry, streamers that dropped and draped wall to wall. He felt embarrassed; the wrappings were like underwear, and they were his. 5

One day his attendants changed his gold hoops to jade studs and strapped his feet to shoes that curved like bridges. They plucked out each hair on his face, powdered him white, painted his eyebrows like a moth's wings, painted his cheeks and lips red. He served a meal at the queen's court. His hips swayed and his shoulders swiveled 6 because of his shaped feet. "She's pretty, don't you agree?" the diners said, smacking their lips at his dainty feet as he bent to put dishes before them.

In the Women's Land there are no taxes and no wars. Some   7 scholars say that the country was discovered during the reign of Empress Wu (A.D. 694–705), and some say earlier than that, A.D. 441, and it was in North America.

RESPONDING TO READING

Key words: discovery identity gender minority power race rights transformation

Rhetorical concepts: analogy comparison/contrast definition fiction myth narrative/example process story

1. By what process(es) is Tang Ao transformed from a man to a woman, physically, psychologically, and socially?
2. What is Tang Ao's personality like before, during, and after this process? Why does he willingly submit to his captors, even to the painful process of foot binding?
3. What definition of woman emerges from this parable? Why is this definition a feminist protest? Against what? What else does the parable protest?
4. Is this parable fair to men? Does it, or any parable or other literary work, have to be fair, to provide equal representation of all likely stands on an issue?
5. How does the reader of a parable know to read the work not as a literal truth, but as analogous to real life? In what way does Kingston let her readers know they are reading a parable rather than a literally true story?

On Being Female, Black, and Free
MARGARET WALKER

Margaret Walker wrote this essay for the first volume of Janet Sternburg's *The Writer on Her Work* (1981), a collection of essays by distinguished women writers on why and how they write. In her piece, Walker explores the indelible effects of her gender, race, and social class on her life and work. Not only have these factors determined what she did and how she did it, but they also have irrevocably shaped her vision of her career as a writer and her commitment to it: "I believe absolutely in the power of my black mind to create, to write, to speak, to witness truth, and to be heard."

Walker was born in Birmingham, Alabama, in 1915; she earned a B.A. from Northwestern University in 1935 (where she "went hungry unless friends fed me") and, thirty years later, a Ph.D. from the

University of Iowa. For over thirty years she taught English at Jackson State College and directed the Institute for the Study of the History, Life, and Culture of Black Peoples. She was the mainstay of her family, supporting her disabled husband and their four children on a salary that never exceeded six thousand dollars a year. A writer since early childhood, she published *For My People*, a book of poetry, in 1942, and a historical novel *Jubilee*, in 1966, a fictional slave narrative celebrating a heroic woman who grows into the maturity and freedom that Walker so values.

My birth certificate reads female, Negro, date of birth and place. 1 Call it fate or circumstance, this is my human condition. I have no wish to change it from being female, black, and free. I like being a woman. I have a proud black heritage, and I have learned from the difficult exigencies of life that freedom is a philosophical state of mind and existence. The mind is the only place where I can exist and feel free. In my mind I am absolutely free.

My entire career of writing, teaching, lecturing, yes, and raising 2 a family is determined by these immutable facts of my human condition. As a daughter, a sister, a sweetheart, a wife, a mother, and now a grandmother, my sex or gender is preeminent, important, and almost entirely deterministic. Maybe my glands have something to do with my occupation as a creative person. About this, I am none too sure, but I think the cycle of life has much to do with the creative impulse and the biorhythms of life must certainly affect everything we do.

Creativity cannot exist without the feminine principle, and I am 3 sure God is not merely male or female but He-She—our Father-Mother God. All nature reflects this rhythmic and creative principle of feminism and femininity: the sea, the earth, the air, fire, and all life whether plant or animal. Even as they die, are born, grow, reproduce, and grow old in their cyclic time, so do we in lunar, solar, planetary cycles of meaning and change.

Ever since I was a little girl I have wanted to write and I have 4 been writing. My father told my mother it was only a puberty urge and would not last, but he encouraged my early attempts at rhyming verses just the same, and he gave me the notebook or daybook in which to keep my poems together. When I was eighteen and had ended my junior year in college, my father laughingly agreed it was probably more than a puberty urge. I had filled the 365 pages with poems.

Writing has always been a means of expression for me and for 5 other black Americans who are just like me, who feel, too, the need for freedom in this "home of the brave, and land of the free." From the first, writing meant learning the craft and developing the art.

Going to school had one major goal, to learn to be a writer. As early as my eighth year I had the desire, at ten I was trying, at eleven and twelve I was learning, and at fourteen and fifteen I was seeing my first things printed in local school and community papers. I have a copy of a poem published in 1930 and an article with the caption, "What Is to Become of Us?" which appeared in 1931 or 1932. All of this happened before I went to Northwestern.

I spent fifteen years becoming a poet before my first book ap- 6 peared in 1942. I was learning my craft, finding my voice, seeking discipline as life imposes and superimposes that discipline upon the artist. Perhaps my home environment was most important in the early stages—hearing my mother's music, my sister and brother playing the piano, reading my father's books, hearing his sermons, and trying every day to write a poem. Meanwhile, I found I would have to start all over again and learn how to write prose fiction in order to write the novel I was determined to create to the best of my ability and thus fulfill my promise to my grandmother. A novel is not written exactly the same way as a poem, especially a long novel and a short poem. The creative process may be basically the same—that is, the thinking or conceptualization—but the techniques, elements, and form or craft are decidedly and distinctively different.

It has always been my feeling that writing must come out of living, 7 and the writer is no more than his personality endures in the crucible of his times. As a woman, I have come through the fires of hell because I am a black woman, because I am poor, because I live in America, and because I am determined to be both a creative artist and maintain my inner integrity and my instinctive need to be free.

I don't think I noticed the extreme discrimination against women 8 while I was growing up in the South. The economic struggle to exist and the racial dilemma occupied all my thinking until I was more than an adult woman. My mother had undergone all kinds of discrimination in academia because of her sex; so have my sisters. Only after I went back to school and earned a doctorate did I begin to notice discrimination against me as a woman. It seems the higher you try to climb, the more rarefied the air, the more obstacles appear. I realize I had been naïve, that the issues had not been obvious and that as early as my first employment I felt the sting of discrimination because I am female. . . .

And then I began looking through the pages of books of American 9 and English literature that I was teaching, trying in vain to find the works of many women writers. I have read so many of those great women writers of the world—poets, novelists, and playwrights: Sigrid Undset and Selma Lagerlof, Jane Austen, George Sand, George Eliot, and Colette. All through the ages women have been writing

and publishing, black and white women in America and all over the
world. A few women stand out as geniuses of their times, but those
are all too few. Even the women who survive and are printed, published, taught, and studied in the classroom fall victim to negative
male literary criticism. Black women suffer damages at the hands of
every male literary critic, whether he is black or white. Occasionally
a man grudgingly admits that some woman writes well, but only
rarely.

Despite severe illness and painful poverty, and despite jobs that   10
always discriminated against me as a woman—never paying me equal
money for equal work, always threatening or replacing me with a
man or men who were neither as well educated nor experienced but
just men—despite all these examples of discrimination I have managed to work toward being a self-fulfilling, re-creating, reproducing
woman, raising a family, writing poetry, cooking food, doing all the
creative things I know how to do and enjoy. But my problems have
not been simple; they have been manifold. Being female, black, and
poor in America means I was born with three strikes against me. I
am considered at the bottom of the social class-caste system in these
United States, born low on the totem pole. If "a black man has no
rights that a white man is bound to respect," what about a black
woman?

Racism is so extreme and so pervasive in our American society   11
that no black individual lives in an atmosphere of freedom. The world
of physical phenomena is dominated by fear and greed. It consists of
pitting the vicious and the avaricious against the naïve, the hunted,
the innocent, and the victimized. Power belongs to the strong, and
the strong are BIG in more ways than one. No one is more victimized
in this white male American society than the black female.

There are additional barriers for the black woman in publishing,   12
in literary criticism, and in promotion of her literary wares. It is an
insidious fact of racism that the most highly intellectualized, sensitized white person is not always perceptive about the average black
mind and feeling, much less the creativity of any black genius. Racism
forces white humanity to underestimate the intelligence, emotion,
and creativity of black humanity. Very few white Americans are conscious of the myth about race that includes the racial stigmas of inferiority and superiority. They do not understand its true economic
and political meaning and therefore fail to understand its social purpose. A black, female person's life as a writer is fraught with conflict,
competitive drives, professional rivalries, even danger, and deep frustrations. Only when she escapes to a spiritual world can she find
peace, quiet, and hope of freedom. To choose the life of a writer, a
black female must arm herself with a fool's courage, foolhardiness,

and serious purpose and dedication to the art of writing, strength of will and integrity, because the odds are always against her. The cards are stacked. Once the die is cast, however, there is no turning back.

In the first place, the world of imagination in which the writer 13 must live is constantly being invaded by the enemy, the mundane world. Even as the worker in the fires of imagination finds that the world around her is inimical to intellectual activity, to the creative impulse, and to the kind of world in which she must daily exist and also thrive and produce, so, too, she discovers that she must meet that mundane world head-on everyday on its own terms. She must either conquer or be conquered.

A writer needs certain conditions in which to work and create 14 art. She needs a piece of time; a peace of mind; a quiet place; and a private life.

Early in my life I discovered I had to earn my living and I would 15 not be able to eke out the barest existence as a writer. Nobody writes while hungry, sick, tired, and worried. Maybe you can manage with one of these but not all four at one time. Keeping the wolf from the door has been my full-time job for more than forty years. Thirty-six of those years I have spent in the college classroom, and nobody writes to full capacity on a full-time teaching job. My life has been public, active, and busy to the point of constant turmoil, tumult, and trauma. Sometimes the only quiet and private place where I could write a sonnet was in the bathroom, because that was the only room where the door could be locked and no one would intrude. I have written mostly at night in my adult life and especially since I have been married, because I was determined not to neglect any members of my family; so I cooked every meal daily, washed dishes and dirty clothes, and nursed sick babies.

I have struggled against dirt and disease as much as I have against 16 sin, which, with my Protestant and Calvinistic background, was always to be abhorred. Every day I have lived, however, I have discovered that the value system with which I was raised is of no value in the society in which I must live. This clash of my ideal with the real, of my dream world with the practical, and the mystical inner life with the sordid and ugly world outside—this clash keeps me on a battlefield, at war, and struggling, even tilting windmills. Always I am determined to overcome adversity, determined to win, determined to be me, myself at my best, always female, always black, and everlastingly free. I think this is always what the woman writer wants to be, herself, inviolate, and whole. Shirley Chisholm, who is also black and female, says she is unbossed and unbought. So am I, and I intend to remain that way. Nobody can tell me what to write because nobody owns me and nobody pulls my strings. I have not been writing to make money or earn my living. I have taught school as my vocation. Writing is my life, but it is an avocation nobody can buy. In this respect I believe I am a free agent, stupid perhaps, but *me* and still free. . . .

Enough for a time about being female and black. What about 17 freedom? The question of freedom is an essential subject for any writer. Without freedom, personal and social, to write as one pleases and to express the will of the people, the writer is in bondage. This bondage may seem to be to others outside oneself but closely related by blood or kinship in some human fashion; or this bondage may appear to be to the inimical forces of the society that so impress or repress that individual.

For the past twenty years or longer I have constantly come into 18 contact with women writers of many different races, classes, nationalities, and degrees. . . .

For the nonwhite woman writer, whether in Africa, Asia, Latin 19 America, the islands of the Caribbean, or the United States, her destiny as a writer has always seemed bleak. Women in Africa and Asia speak of hunger and famine and lack of clean water at the same time that their countries are riddled with warfare. Arab women and Jewish women think of their children in a world that has no hope of peace. Irish women, Protestant and Catholic, speak of the constant threat of bombs and being blown to bits. The women of southern Africa talk of their lives apart from their husbands and their lives in exile from their homelands because of the racial strife in their countries. A Turkish woman speaks of the daily terrorism in her country, of combing the news each evening to see if there are names known on the list of the murdered.

I have read the works of scores of these women. I saw Zora Neale 20 Hurston when I was a child and I know what a hard life she had. I read the works of a dozen black women in the Harlem Renaissance, who despite their genius received only a small success. Langston Hughes translated Gabriela Mistral, and I read her before she won the Nobel Prize for Literature. Hualing Nieh Engle tells of her native China, and my friends in Mexico speak of the unbelievable poverty of their people. Each of these internationally known women writers is my sister in search of an island of freedom. Each is part of me and I am part of her.

Writing is a singularly individual matter. At least it has historically 21 been so. Only the creative, original individual working alone has been considered the artist working with the fire of imagination. Today, this appears no longer to be the case. In America, our affluent, electronic, and materialistic society does not respect the imaginative writer regardless of sex, race, color, or creed. It never thought highly of the female worker, whether an Emily Dickinson or Amy Lowell, Phillis

Wheatley, or Ellen Glasgow. Our American society has no respect for the literary values of intellectual honesty nor for originality and creativity in the sensitive individual. Books today are managed, being written by a committee and promoted by the conglomerate, corporate structures. Best sellers are designed as commodities to sell in the marketplace before a single word is written. Plastic people who are phony writers pretending to take us into a more humanistic century are quickly designated the paper heroes who are promoted with super-HYPE. Do I sound bitter? A Black Woman Writer who is free? Free to do what? To publish? To be promoted? Of what value is freedom in a money-mad society? What does freedom mean to the racially biased and those bigots who have deep religious prejudices? What is my hope as a woman writer?

I am a black woman living in a male-oriented and male-dominated 22 white world. Moreover, I live in an American Empire where the financial tentacles of the American Octopus in the business-banking world extend around the globe, with the multinationals and international conglomerates encircling everybody and impinging on the lives of every single soul. What then are my problems? They are the pressures of a sexist, racist, violent, and most materialistic society. In such a society life is cheap and expendable; honor is a rag to be scorned; and justice is violated. Vice and money control business, the judicial system, government, sports, entertainment, publishing, education, and the church. Every other arm of this hydra-headed monster must render lip service and yeoman support to extend, uphold, and perpetuate the syndicated world-system. The entire world of the press, whether broadcast or print journalism, must acquiesce and render service or be eliminated. And what have I to do with this? How do I operate? How long can I live under fear before I too am blown to bits and must crumble into anonymous dust and nonentity?

Now I am sixty-three. I wish I could live the years all over. I am 23 sure I would make the same mistakes and do all the things again exactly the same way. But perhaps I might succeed a little more; and wistfully I hope, too, I might have written more books.

What are the critical decisions I must make as a woman, as a 24 writer? They are questions of compromise, and of guilt. They are the answers to the meaning and purpose of all life; questions of the value of life lived half in fear and half in faith, cringing under the whip of tyranny or dying, too, for what one dares to believe and dying with dignity and without fear. I must believe there is more wisdom in a righteous path that leads to death than an ignominious path of living shame; that the writer is still in the avant-garde for Truth and Justice, for Freedom, Peace, and Human Dignity. I must believe that women are still in that humanistic tradition and I must cast my lot with them.

Across the world humanity seems in ferment, in war, fighting over land and the control of people's lives; people who are hungry, sick, and suffering, most of all fearful. The traditional and historic role of womankind is ever the role of the healing and annealing hand, whether the outworn modes of nurse, and mother, cook, and sweetheart. As a writer these are still her concerns. These are still the stuff about which she writes, the human potential, the human destiny. Her place, let us be reminded, is anywhere she chooses to be, doing what she has to do, creating, healing, and always being herself. Female, Black, and Free, this is what I always want to be.

RESPONDING TO READING

Key words: class   discovery   freedom   gender   identity   minority racism   rights   transformation   writing

Rhetorical concepts: autobiography   definition   explanation illustration   meditation   narrative/example

1.   What are Walker's definitions of each of her title terms, "female," "black," "free"? What examples from her life does she use to define these?
2.   How does she see these as interrelated, in her life, her work, and her writing?
3.   In order for this essay to function as an argument, Walker anatomizes (describes in detail) her life and uses it as an argument against race, gender, and class discrimination. Show where and how she does this. To what extent is she justified in generalizing from her individual example?
4.   How can Walker say that "writing is a singularly individual matter" when she bases so much of her argument on factors beyond the individual's control (race, gender, and class background)?
5.   Who is the audience for such statements as "Very few white Americans are conscious of the myth about race that includes the racial stigmas of inferiority and superiority"? How does Walker expect her audience to respond to the tone of her assertions? Walker wrote this over a decade ago; are her assertions accurate, and relevant today for contemporary readers, including not only whites, but Asians and Hispanics?

The Men We Carry in Our Minds

SCOTT RUSSELL SANDERS

"We learn who we will be from the people we carry in our minds," says Scott Russell Sanders, born in 1945, under "the sign of the mushroom cloud." Although he was educated at Brown (B.A. 1967) and Cambridge (Ph.D. 1971) universities, the men he knew when he was a young child on a "scrape-dirt farm" in Tennessee—steel workers, carpenters, miners—"labored with their bodies," and when they got home at night "they looked as though somebody had been whipping them." White collar workers—bankers, doctors, brokers—were from an alien world. The women in his childhood were the ones interested in art, music, literature, the only people enjoying "a sense of ease and grace." Sanders's career choice and subjects for writing emerged from this life. His efforts against the Vietnam war, nuclear weapons, and American militarization are a reaction to what he learned as an adolescent on the grounds of the Ohio Arsenal, where his father supervised production lines that loaded explosives into artillery shells, land mines, and bombs.

During his career at Indiana University, where he has taught since 1971, Sanders has published over a dozen books, including literary criticism, a biography, two novels, and two volumes of science fiction. Recently, he has been writing personal essays, collected in *Secrets of the Universe: Scenes from the Journey Home* (1991) and *The Paradise of Bombs* (1987), which includes "The Men We Carry in Our Minds." This essay captures Sanders's characteristic focus on "the fierce, tangled relations between parent and child, between man and woman," and his interpretation of the values these relationships imply.

This must be a hard time for women," I say to my friend Anneke.   1
"They have so many paths to choose from, and so many voices calling them."

"I think it's a lot harder for men," she replies.   2

"How do you figure that?"   3

"The women I know feel excited, innocent, like crusaders in a   4
just cause. The men I know are eaten up with guilt."

We are sitting at the kitchen table drinking sassafras tea, our hands   5
wrapped around the mugs because this April morning is cool and drizzly. "Like a Dutch morning," Anneke told me earlier. She is Dutch herself, a writer and midwife and peacemaker, with the round face and sad eyes of a woman in a Vermeer painting who might be waiting for the rain to stop, for a door to open. She leans over to sniff a sprig of lilac, pale lavender, that rises from a vase of cobalt blue.

"Women feel such pressure to be everything, do everything," I   6
say. "Career, kids, art, politics. Have their babies and get back to the office a week later. It's as if they're trying to overcome a million years' worth of evolution in one lifetime."

"But we help one another. We don't try to lumber on alone, like   7
so many wounded grizzly bears, the way men do." Anneke sips her tea. I gave her the mug with owls on it, for wisdom. "And we have this deep-down sense that we're in the *right*—we've been held back,

passed over, used—while men feel they're in the wrong. Men are the ones who've been discredited, who have to search their souls."

I search my soul. I discover guilty feelings aplenty—toward the   8
poor, the Vietnamese, Native Americans, the whales, an endless list of debts—a guilt in each case that is as bright and unambiguous as a neon sign. But toward women I feel something more confused, a snarl of shame, envy, wary tenderness, and amazement. This muddle troubles me. To hide my unease I say, "You're right, it's tough being a man these days."

"Don't laugh." Anneke frowns at me, mournful-eyed, through   9
the sassafras steam. "I wouldn't be a man for anything. It's much easier being the victim. All the victim has to do is break free. The persecutor has to live with his past."

How deep is that past? I find myself wondering after Anneke has   10
left. How much of an inheritance do I have to throw off? Is it just the beliefs I breathed in as a child? Do I have to scour memory back through father and grandfather? Through St. Paul? Beyond Stone-henge and into the twilit caves? I'm convinced the past we must contend with is deeper even than speech. When I think back on my childhood, on how I learned to see men and women, I have a sense of ancient, dizzying depths. The back roads of Tennessee and Ohio where I grew up were probably closer, in their sexual patterns, to the campsites of Stone Age hunters than to the genderless cities of the future into which we are rushing.

The first men, besides my father, I remember seeing were black   11
convicts and white guards, in the cottonfield across the road from our farm on the outskirts of Memphis. I must have been three or four. The prisoners wore dingy gray-and-black zebra suits, heavy as canvas, sodden with sweat. Hatless, stooped, they chopped weeds in the fierce heat, row after row, breathing the acrid dust of boll-weevil poison. The overseers wore dazzling white shirts and broad shadowy hats. The oiled barrels of their shotguns flashed in the sunlight. Their faces in memory are utterly blank. Of course those men, white and black, have become for me an emblem of racial hatred. But they have also come to stand for the twin poles of my early vision of manhood—the brute toiling animal and the boss.

When I was a boy, the men I knew labored with their bodies.   12
They were marginal farmers, just scraping by, or welders, steelwork-ers, carpenters; they swept floors, dug ditches, mined coal, or drove trucks, their forearms ropy with muscle; they trained horses, stoked furnaces, built tires, stood on assembly lines wrestling parts onto cars and refrigerators. They got up before light, worked all day long what-ever the weather, and when they came home at night they looked as

though somebody had been whipping them. In the evenings and on weekends they worked on their own places, tilling gardens that were lumpy with clay, fixing broken-down cars, hammering on houses that were always too drafty, too leaky, too small.

The bodies of the men I knew were twisted and maimed in ways 13 visible and invisible. The nails of their hands were black and split, the hands tattooed with scars. Some had lost fingers. Heavy lifting had given many of them finicky backs and guts weak from hernias. Racing against conveyor belts had given them ulcers. Their ankles and knees ached from years of standing on concrete. Anyone who had worked for long around machines was hard of hearing. They squinted, and the skin of their faces was creased like the leather of old work gloves. There were times, studying them, when I dreaded growing up. Most of them coughed, from dust or cigarettes, and most of them drank cheap wine or whiskey, so their eyes looked bloodshot and bruised. The fathers of my friends always seemed older than the mothers. Men wore out sooner. Only women lived into old age.

As a boy I also knew another sort of men, who did not sweat and 14 break down like mules. They were soldiers, and so far as I could tell they scarcely worked at all. During my early school years we lived on a military base, an arsenal in Ohio, and every day I saw GIs in the guardshacks, on the stoops of barracks, at the wheels of olive drab Chevrolets. The chief fact of their lives was boredom. Long after I left the Arsenal I came to recognize the sour smell the soldiers gave off as that of souls in limbo. They were all waiting—for wars, for transfers, for leaves, for promotions, for the end of their hitch—like so many braves waiting for the hunt to begin. Unlike the warriors of older tribes, however, they would have no say about when the battle would start or how it would be waged. Their waiting was broken only when they practiced for war. They fired guns at targets, drove tanks across the churned-up fields of the military reservation, set off bombs in the wrecks of old fighter planes. I knew this was all play. But I also felt certain that when the hour for killing arrived, they would kill. When the real shooting started, many of them would die. This was what soldiers were *for*, just as a hammer was for driving nails.

Warriors and toilers: those seemed, in my boyhood vision, to be 15 the chief destinies for men. They weren't the only destinies, as I learned from having a few male teachers, from reading books, and from watching television. But the men on television—the politicians, the astronauts, the generals, the savvy lawyers, the philosophical doctors, the bosses who gave orders to both soldiers and laborers— seemed as remote and unreal to me as the figures in tapestries. I could no more imagine growing up to become one of these cool, potent creatures than I could imagine becoming a prince.

A nearer and more hopeful example was that of my father, who 16 had escaped from a red-dirt farm to a tire factory, and from the assembly line to the front office. Eventually he dressed in a white shirt and tie. He carried himself as if he had been born to work with his mind. But his body, remembering the earlier years of slogging work, began to give out on him in his fifties, and it quit on him entirely before he turned sixty-five. Even such a partial escape from man's fate as he had accomplished did not seem possible for most of the boys I knew. They joined the Army, stood in line for jobs in the smoky plants, helped build highways. They were bound to work as their fathers had worked, killing themselves or preparing to kill others.

A scholarship enabled me not only to attend college, a rare enough 17 feat in my circle, but even to study in a university meant for the children of the rich. Here I met for the first time young men who had assumed from birth that they would lead lives of comfort and power. And for the first time I met women who told me that men were guilty of having kept all the joys and privileges of the earth for themselves. I was baffled. What privileges? What joys? I thought about the maimed, dismal lives of most of the men back home. What had they stolen from their wives and daughters? The right to go five days a week, twelve months a year, for thirty or forty years to a steel mill or a coal mine? The right to drop bombs and die in war? The right to feel every leak in the roof, every gap in the fence, every cough in the engine, as a wound they must mend? The right to feel, when the lay-off comes or the plant shuts down, not only afraid but ashamed?

I was slow to understand the deep grievances of women. This 18 was because, as a boy, I had envied them. Before college, the only people I had ever known who were interested in art or music or literature, the only ones who read books, the only ones who ever seemed to enjoy a sense of ease and grace were the mothers and daughters. Like the menfolk, they fretted about money, they scrimped and made-do. But, when the pay stopped coming in, they were not the ones who had failed. Nor did they have to go to war, and that seemed to me a blessed fact. By comparison with the narrow, ironclad days of fathers, there was an expansiveness, I thought, in the days of mothers. They went to see neighbors, to shop in town, to run errands at school, at the library, at church. No doubt, had I looked harder at their lives, I would have envied them less. It was not my fate to become a woman, so it was easier for me to see the graces. Few of them held jobs outside the home, and those who did filled thankless roles as clerks and waitresses. I didn't see, then, what a prison a house could be, since houses seemed to me brighter, handsomer places than any factory. I did not realize—because such things were never spoken of—how often women suffered from men's bullying. I did learn about the wretchedness of abandoned wives, single mothers, widows; but I also learned about the wretchedness of lone men. Even then I could see how exhausting it was for a mother to cater all day to the needs of young children. But if I had been asked, as a boy, to choose between tending a baby and tending a machine, I think I would have chosen the baby. (Having now tended both, I know I would choose the baby.)

So I was baffled when the women at college accused me and my   19 sex of having cornered the world's pleasures. I think something like my bafflement has been felt by other boys (and by girls as well) who grew up in dirt-poor farm country, in mining country, in black ghettos, in Hispanic barrios, in the shadows of factories, in Third World nations—any place where the fate of men is as grim and bleak as the fate of women. Toilers and warriors. I realize now how ancient these identities are, how deep the tug they exert on men, the undertow of a thousand generations. The miseries I saw, as a boy, in the lives of nearly all men I continue to see in the lives of many—the body-breaking toil, the tedium, the call to be tough, the humiliating powerlessness, the battle for a living and for territory.

When the women I met at college thought about the joys and   20 privileges of men, they did not carry in their minds the sort of men I had known in my childhood. They thought of their fathers, who were bankers, physicians, architects, stockbrokers, the big wheels of the big cities. These fathers rode the train to work or drove cars that cost more than any of my childhood houses. They were attended from morning to night by female helpers, wives and nurses and secretaries. They were never laid off, never short of cash at month's end, never lined up for welfare. These fathers made decisions that mattered. They ran the world.

The daughters of such men wanted to share in this power, this   21 glory. So did I. They yearned for a say over their future, for jobs worthy of their abilities, for the right to live at peace, unmolested, whole. Yes, I thought, yes yes. The difference between me and these daughters was that they saw me, because of my sex, as destined from birth to become like their fathers, and therefore as an enemy to their desires. But I knew better. I wasn't an enemy, in fact or in feeling. I was an ally. If I had known, then, how to tell them so, would they have believed me? Would they now?

RESPONDING TO READING

Key words: class discovery gender growing up identity
memory power striving

Rhetorical concepts: anecdote autobiography
comparison and contrast definition illustration

1.   Who are "The Men We Carry in Our Minds"? Why has Sanders chosen this title for his essay?
2.   Sanders categorizes three types of men: "toilers," "warriors," and the men who "ran the world." What differences among them does he identify? Have they any similarities? What connections does Sanders make between social class, self-image, and life expectations?
3.   Why does Sanders carry these particular images in his mind? Does he expect other male readers to share the same images with the same connotations as he has? Does Sanders expect women readers to carry the same images as male readers? Why or why not?
4.   Identify some of the physical images Sanders uses, such as "forearms ropy with muscle," and "the skin of their faces was creased like the leather of old work gloves," and show how he relates his interpretation of men's bodies to his interpretation of their lives.
5.   Is this truly an era of equal opportunities for women and men, and equal expectations of both? If so, will men no longer "wear out sooner"? Will "only women live into old age"?

Learning and Brain Growth
ROBERT ORNSTEIN and RICHARD F. THOMPSON

Richard Thompson (born 1930) has had an academic career since earning a doctorate in physiological psychology at the University of Wisconsin in 1956. He has been a professor and physiological and psychological researcher at the University of Oregon, Harvard, the University of California, Irvine, and since 1985 at the University of Southern California. His work in neurophysiology, cerebral cortex and behavior, and the neural basis of learning has earned numerous awards.

Robert Ornstein (born 1930), also a psychologist, was educated at Queens College (B.A. 1964) and Stanford (Ph.D. 1968). Currently president of the Langley Porter [psychoanalytic] Institute, since 1969 he has also taught medical psychology at the University of California, San Francisco. His numerous writings include *The Psychology of Consciousness* (1977), *The Healing Brain* (with David Sobel, 1987), and *New World, New Mind: Moving Towards Conscious Evolution* (with Paul Ehrlich, 1989).

"Learning and Brain Growth," from Ornstein and Thompson's

book, *The Amazing Brain* (1984), is a good example of how scientists explain the complex phenomena discovered in the course of their research to a nonspecialized audience. The authors explain that brains are as varied and distinctive as people's faces. Like the rest of one's body, the brain needs adequate nutrition to develop properly. It also grows significantly in response to a stimulating environment with new and challenging things to think about, but it remains smaller in an impoverished, boring context. Likewise, atmospheric conditions can not only affect one's mood, they can influence brain growth, as well. The language here is nontechnical; the explanations apply what is familiar to the readers (infant babbling, playing with toys) to what is not (brain weight and brain growth).

It seemed a straightforward job. All one of the authors (Robert   1
Ornstein) was trying to do was to measure the different sizes of the cortex in several brains, to get an idea of the size of the different areas of the brain underneath the skull. He didn't realize how much there was to be discovered by actually looking at real brains. What was most striking was this: like most people, the author's idea of what the brain is came from anatomical drawings, the models he had seen, and the sample brains he had dissected. But as he worked in the laboratory day after day, he began to realize that each brain was distinct. One had characteristic bulges here, one there, one a large occipital lobe, another a small temporal lobe. In fact, people's brains are as different as their faces.

Faces have, of course, some regularity: the eyes are above the   2
nose, the nose is above the mouth, both are above the jaw. But within this regularity there are wide variations: some faces have large noses, some have small eyes. So it is with the brain. The specific features in the brain are different in different individuals. How the brain develops, how it grows and changes within a person's lifetime, and even how it changes within a day is an area just beginning to be explored. We may not think for long of "the brain" as exactly the same in all people. Some of the recent discoveries cited here will make that idea impossible. . . .

Humans are born extraordinarily immature, and the human brain   3
develops largely in the outside world. So environmental conditions play a greater role in the brain development of humans than in that of any other primate.

It is commonly thought that at birth the neurons begin to make   4
connections and that these connections increase as we age and acquire experience. However, the opposite appears to be the case: there may be many *more* connections and nerve cells in the brain of an infant than in an elderly adult. Development seems to be more a matter of "pruning" those original connections than of making any new ones. Consider this about infant babbling: in the first weeks of life, a baby

utters almost every sound of every known language. Later on, the
infant loses the ability to make sounds that are not in the language
he has learned to speak. There may be an enormous potential of sound
patterns available to us at birth, but we learn only a few of them. The
brain may be "set up" to do many different things, such as to learn
the thousands of languages available to humans, only a few of which
we actually do learn.

However, the growth of the brain depends on an adequate early   5
environment. Severe malnutrition may cause inadequate brain development, a smaller brain than normal, and severe mental retarda-
tion. In a long series of experiments, rats deprived of normal food in
infancy show distortions in brain structure, and even shrinkage of
certain brain structures. Cells from "deprived" ones look shriveled
compared to normal cells. The brain, somewhat like a muscle, then,
can grow in response to certain experience—the neurons themselves
become larger.

Some of the most revolutionary evidence has come from a series   6
of studies over the last twenty years from work initiated by Mark
Rosenzweig and continued by Marion Diamond at the University of
California at Berkeley. They study rat brains so that they can control
the genetic background. Rats have a fairly short gestation period—
twenty-one days—and they have, most beneficially for these purposes, a smooth cerebral cortex. The dog brain is folded, the cat brain
is folded, but the rat brain has yet to fold, and that's one of its beauties
for making chemical and anatomical measurements—the smooth-sur-
face cerebral cortex allows one to deal with uniform pieces of tissues.

All the animals are in "standard colony" conditions for prelimi-   7
nary measures, which means that there are three rats to a small cage
and water and food are provided. Besides standard colonies, the experiment involves ones with environments enriched with "toys," or
objects to play with, and ones with impoverished conditions, in which
there is little stimulation and movement is restricted by cage size. The
enriched condition in the postnatal rat consists of twelve rats living
together with toys. Every day the experimenters change the objects
from a standard pool. If they don't change them, the animals become
bored, just as we all do when we've sat too long receiving the same
type of stimulus. In the impoverished environment, the rat lives by
himself and has no toys; he can see, smell, and hear the other rats
but does not play with them.

Typically, Diamond selects three brother rats; one goes into en-   8
riched, one into standard colony, and one into impoverished environment. Even in young adults a year old, the enriched environment
will cause an increase in the actual *weight* of the brain—about 10
percent in most cases. At first most scientists didn't believe the results,
but the evidence has now convinced virtually everyone.

Although their work was revolutionary enough, Diamond and   9
her colleagues were curious to see if they could produce the same
result in the brains of very old rats. They put four very old rats in
with eight of the young to see whether the stimulating effect of associating young rats with old would result in measurable changes in
the brain. It turned out that the old rats enjoyed living with the young
more than the young enjoyed living with the old. The brain growth
of the rats confirmed this result. *Each* old rat's brain grew 10 percent
while living with the young rats. The young rats' brains did not grow
at all while living with the old. Why didn't the young rats' brains
grow while the old rats' brains did? A clue may be found in the
different responses of the old and young to the experimental situation.
Each day when one of the experimenters went to change their toys,
the old rats would come to see what toys were available, while the
young remained sleeping in the back. So it appears, says Diamond,
that there is some sort of hierarchy when the young live with the old;
the old dominate. Marion Diamond often jokes that this is why old
professors continue to be excited and live to be a hundred—because
they are dealing with young people, who are essentially like the young
rats. And everybody knows that it is the young students who are
sleeping in the back of the lecture hall.

An analysis of the brain growth showed that the specific changes 10
in the brain took place in the dendrites of each nerve cell, which
thickened with stimulating experiences. It is as if the forest of nerve
cells became literally enriched, and the density of the branches increased; this is what produced a bigger brain.

Not only specific experiences can affect brain growth. Such con- 11
ditions as increasing negative ionization of the air (the kind of
"charged" air found on mountaintops, near waterfalls, or at the sea),
when introduced by a negative ion generator to Diamond's rat colonies, produced the same changes in brain growth. So, not only do
friends and stimulating experiences get into your head and brain, but
so might the fresh air of mountaintops, waterfalls, and other places
where the ion concentration (both positive and negative) is greater.
The ions can also change the chemical composition of the neurotrans-
mitters, and can elevate or suppress mood, something almost everyone knows who has noted the exhilaration of the mountains, or the
depression with a Santa Ana wind.

RESPONDING TO READING

Key words: biology   discovery   growing up   identity   science

Rhetorical concepts: analogy   cause and effect   definition
explanation   illustration   induction   process   research report

1.   Did you know that "people's brains are as different as their faces"? What evidence do Ornstein and Thompson present to support this assertion?
2.   What is the relation between "pruning" and brain growth? Between nutrition and brain growth?
3.   Analogies between what is familiar to readers and what is unfamiliar are often used to explain concepts (scientific or other) to an audience. Find some examples in this essay and discuss how they enhance your understanding of learning and brain growth.
4.   Diamond's research on learning and brain growth in old and young rats leads her to joke that "this is why old professors continue to be excited and live to be a hundred—because they are dealing with young people, who are essentially like the young rats" she has studied. Are you convinced by her analogy? Her research results?
5.   A novel (Barbara Harris, *Who Is Julia?* NY: D. McKay, 1972) and a film with the same title hinge on "brain transplant," one person's brain being put in another person's body. Consider the question: is the resulting identity that of the body or that of the brain? To what degree are you your brain?

On Being a Cripple
NANCY MAIRS

Nancy Mairs (born 1943), chose as the epigraph to her book, *Remembering the Bone House* (1989), a quotation from Gaston Bachelard's *The Poetics of Space:* "Not only our memories, but the things we have forgotten are 'housed.' Our soul is an abode. And by remembering 'houses' and 'rooms,' we learn to 'hide' within ourselves." In conceiving of her self, body and soul, as a "bone house," Mairs writes about her life as framed and determined by her body.

As she reveals in *Plaintext* (1986), the collection of essays she wrote when earning her doctorate in creative writing at the University of Arizona, Mairs is afflicted with multiple sclerosis. In addition, she has been plagued by allergies, headaches, clinical depression, infections, and fatigue that made her feel as if her bones were changing "from porous calcium to solid granite." Nevertheless, as "On Being a Cripple," from *Plaintext,* makes clear, Mairs's illness governs but does not dominate her life. In this essay, as in some of her other writings, this utterly candid writer presents herself as bitchy, whiny, self-indulgent—but with a redeeming sense of wry humor. We ultimately come to admire her gritty and abrasive personality, but with difficulty, for she succeeds in making her life just as hard for her readers as it has been for her.

To escape is nothing. Not to escape is nothing.
                                      Louise Bogan

The other day I was thinking of writing an essay on being a   1
cripple. I was thinking hard in one of the stalls of the women's room
in my office building, as I was shoving my shirt into my jeans and
tugging up my zipper. Preoccupied, I flushed, picked up my book
bag, took my cane down from the hook, and unlatched the door. So
many movements unbalanced me, and as I pulled the door open I fell
over backward, landing fully clothed on the toilet seat with my legs
splayed in front of me: the old beetle-on-its-back routine. Saturday
afternoon, the building deserted, I was free to laugh aloud as I wrig-
gled back to my feet, my voice bouncing off the yellowish tiles from
all directions. Had anyone been there with me, I'd have been still and
faint and hot with chagrin. I decided that it was high time to write
the essay.

First, the matter of semantics. I am a cripple. I choose this word   2
to name me. I choose from among several possibilities, the most common of which are "handicapped" and "disabled." I made the choice
a number of years ago, without thinking, unaware of my motives for
doing so. Even now, I'm not sure what those motives are, but I recognize that they are complex and not entirely flattering. People—
crippled or not—wince at the word "cripple," as they do not at "handicapped" or "disabled." Perhaps I want them to wince. I want them
to see me as a tough customer, one to whom the fates/gods/viruses
have not been kind, but who can face the brutal truth of her existence
squarely. As a cripple, I swagger.

But, to be fair to myself, a certain amount of honesty underlies   3
my choice. "Cripple" seems to me a clean word, straightforward and
precise. It has an honorable history, having made its first appearance
in the Lindisfarne Gospel in the tenth century. As a lover of words,
I like the accuracy with which it describes my condition: I have lost the
full use of my limbs. "Disabled," by contrast, suggests any incapac-
ity, physical or mental. And I certainly don't like "handicapped,"
which implies that I have deliberately been put at a disadvantage, by
whom I can't imagine (my God is not a Handicapper General), in order
to equalize chances in the great race of life. These words seem to me
to be moving away from my condition, to be widening the gap between
word and reality. Most remote is the recently coined euphemism
"differently abled," which partakes of the same semantic hopefulness
that transformed countries from "undeveloped" to "underdeveloped," then to "less developed," and finally to "developing" nations.
People have continued to starve in those countries during the shift.
Some realities do not obey the dictates of language.

Mine is one of them. Whatever you call me, I remain crippled.   4
But I don't care what you call me, so long as it isn't "differently abled,"
which strikes me as pure verbal garbage designed, by its ability to

describe anyone, to describe no one. I subscribe to George Orwell's thesis that "the slovenliness of our language makes it easier for us to have foolish thoughts." And I refuse to participate in the degeneration of the language to the extent that I deny that I have lost anything in the course of this calamitous disease; I refuse to pretend that the only differences between you and me are the various ordinary ones that distinguish any one person from another. But call me "disabled" or "handicapped" if you like. I have long since grown accustomed to them; and if they are vague, at least they hint at the truth. Moreover, I use them myself. Society is no readier to accept crippledness than to accept death, war, sex, sweat, or wrinkles. I would never refer to another person as a cripple. It is the word I use to name only myself.

I haven't always been crippled, a fact for which I am soundly ⁵ grateful. To be whole of limb is, I know from experience, infinitely more pleasant and useful than to be crippled; and if that knowledge leaves me open to bitterness at my loss, the physical soundness I once enjoyed (though I did not enjoy it half enough) is well worth the occasional stab of regret. Though never any good at sports, I was a normally active child and young adult. I climbed trees, played hopscotch, jumped rope, skated, swam, rode my bicycle, sailed. I despised team sports, spending some of the wretchedest afternoons of my life, sweaty and humiliated, behind a field-hockey stick and under a basketball hoop. I tramped alone for miles along the bridle paths that webbed the woods behind the house I grew up in. I swayed through countless dim hours in the arms of one man or another under the scattered shot of light from mirrored balls, and gyrated through countless more as Tab Hunter and Johnny Mathis gave way to the Rolling Stones, Creedence Clearwater Revival, Cream. I walked down the aisle. I pushed baby carriages, changed tires in the rain, marched for peace.

When I was twenty-eight I started to trip and drop things. What ⁶ at first seemed my natural clumsiness soon became too pronounced to shrug off. I consulted a neurologist, who told me that I had a brain tumor. A battery of tests, increasingly disagreeable, revealed no tumor. About a year and a half later I developed a blurred spot in one eye. I had, at last, the episodes "disseminated in space and time" requisite for a diagnosis: multiple sclerosis. I have never been sorry for the doctor's initial misdiagnosis, however. For almost a week, until the negative results of the tests were in, I thought that I was going to die right away. Every day for the past nearly ten years, then, has been a kind of gift. I accept all gifts.

Multiple sclerosis is a chronic degenerative disease of the central ⁷ nervous system, in which the myelin that sheathes the nerves is somehow eaten away and scar tissue forms in its place, interrupting the nerves' signals. During its course, which is unpredictable and un-controllable, one may lose vision, hearing, speech, the ability to walk, control of bladder and/or bowels, strength in any or all extremities, sensitivity to touch, vibration, and/or pain, potency, coordination of movements—the list of possibilities is lengthy and yes, horrifying. One may also lose one's sense of humor. That's the easiest to lose and the hardest to survive without.

In the past ten years, I have sustained some of these losses. Characteristic of MS are sudden attacks, called exacerbations, followed by remissions, and these I have not had. Instead, my disease has been slowly progressive. My left leg is now so weak that I walk with the aid of a brace and a cane; and for distances I use an Amigo, a variation on the electric wheelchair that looks rather like an electrified kiddie car. I no longer have much use of my left hand. Now my right side is weakening as well. I still have the blurred spot in my right eye. Overall, though, I've been lucky so far. My world has, of necessity, been circumscribed by my losses, but the terrain left me has been ample enough for me to continue many of the activities that absorb me: writing, teaching, raising children and cats and plants and snakes, reading, speaking publicly about MS and depression, even playing bridge with people patient and honorable enough to let me scatter cards every which way without sneaking a peek.

Lest I begin to sound like Pollyana, however, let me say that I don't like having MS. I hate it. My life holds realities—harsh ones, some of them—that no right-minded human being ought to accept without grumbling. One of them is fatigue. I know of no one with MS who does not complain of bone-weariness; in a disease that presents an astonishing variety of symptoms, fatigue seems to be a common factor. I wake up in the morning feeling the way most people do at the end of a bad day, and I take it from there. As a result, I spend a lot of time *in extremis* and, impatient with limitation, I tend to ignore my fatigue until my body breaks down in some way and forces rest. Then I miss picnics, dinner parties, poetry readings, the brief visits of old friends from out of town. The offspring of a puritanical tradition of exceptional venerability, I cannot view these lapses without shame. My life often seems a series of small failures to do as I ought.

I lead, on the whole, an ordinary life, probably rather like the one I would have led had I not had MS. I am lucky that my predilections were already solitary, sedentary, and bookish—unlike the world-famous French cellist I have read about, or the young woman I talked with one long afternoon who wanted only to be a jockey. I had just begun graduate school when I found out something was wrong with me, and I have remained, interminably, a graduate student. Perhaps I would not have if I'd thought I had the stamina to return to a full-time job as a technical editor; but I've enjoyed my studies.

In addition to studying, I teach writing courses. I also teach med-   11 ical students how to give neurological examinations. I pick up free-lance editing jobs here and there. I have raised a foster son and sent him into the world, where he has made me two grandbabies, and I am still escorting my daughter and son through adolescence. I go to Mass every Saturday. I am a superb, if messy, cook. I am also an enthusiastic laundress, capable of sorting a hamper full of clothes into five subtly differentiated piles, but a terrible housekeeper. I can do italic writing and, in an emergency, bathe an oil-soaked cat. I play a fiendish game of Scrabble. When I have the time and the money, I like to sit on my front steps with my husband, drinking Amaretto and smoking a cigar, as we imagine our counterparts in Leningrad and make sure that the sun gets down once more behind the sharp childish scrawl of the Tucson Mountains.

This lively plenty has its bleak complement, of course, in all the   12 things I can no longer do. I will never run again, except in dreams, and one day I may have to write that I will never walk again. I like to go camping, but I can't follow George and the children along the trails that wander out of a campsite through the desert or into the mountains. In fact, even on the level I've learned never to check the weather or try to hold a coherent conversation: I need all my attention for my wayward feet. Of late, I have begun to catch myself wondering how people can propel themselves without canes. With only one usable hand, I have to select my clothing with care not so much for style as for ease of ingress and egress, and even so, dressing can be laborious. I can no longer do fine stitchery, pick up babies, play the piano, braid my hair. I am immobilized by acute attacks of depression, which may or may not be physiologically related to MS but are certainly its logical concomitant.

These two elements, the plenty and the privation, are never pure,   13 nor are the delight and wretchedness that accompany them. Almost every pickle that I get into as a result of my weakness and clumsiness—and I get into plenty—is funny as well as maddening and sometimes painful. I recall one May afternoon when a friend and I were going out for a drink after finishing up at school. As we were climbing into opposite sides of my car, chatting, I tripped and fell, flat and hard, onto the asphalt parking lot, my abrupt departure interrupting him in mid-sentence. "Where'd you go?" he called as he came around the back of the car to find me hauling myself up by the door frame. "Are you all right?" Yes, I told him, I was fine, just a bit rattly, and we drove off to find a shady patio and some beer. When I got home an hour or so later, my daughter greeted me with "What have you done to yourself?" I looked down. One elbow of my white turtleneck with the green froggies, one knee of my white trousers, one white kneesock were blood-soaked. We peeled off the clothes and inspected the damage, which was nasty enough but not alarming. That part wasn't funny: The abrasions took a long time to heal, and one got a little infected. Even so, when I think of my friend talking earnestly, suddenly, to the hot thin air while I dropped from his view as though through a trap door, I find the image as silly as something from a Marx Brothers movie.

I may find it easier than other cripples to amuse myself because 14 I live propped up by the acceptance and the assistance and, sometimes, the amusement of those around me. Grocery clerks tear my checks out of my checkbook for me, and sales clerks find chairs to put into dressing rooms when I want to try on clothes. The people I work with make sure I teach at times when I am least likely to be fatigued, in places I can get to, with the materials I need. My students, with one anonymous exception (in an end-of-the-semester evaluation), have been unperturbed by my disability. Some even like it. One was immensely cheered by the information that I paint my own fingernails; she decided, she told me, that if I could go to such trouble over fine details, she could keep on writing essays. I suppose I became some sort of bright-fingered muse. She wrote good essays, too.

The most important struts in the framework of my existence, of 15 course, are my husband and children. Dismayingly few marriages survive the MS test, and why should they? Most twenty-two- and nineteen-year-olds, like George and me, can vow in clear conscience, after a childhood of chickenpox and summer colds, to keep one another in sickness and in health so long as they both shall live. Not many are equipped for catastrophe: the dismay, the depression, the extra work, the boredom that a degenerative disease can insinuate into a relationship. And our society, with its emphasis on fun and its association of fun with physical performance, offers little encouragement for a whole spouse to stay with a crippled partner. Children experience similar stresses when faced with a crippled parent, and they are more helpless, since parents and children can't usually get divorced. They hate, of course, to be different from their peers, and the child whose mother is tacking down the aisle of a school auditorium packed with proud parents like a Cape Cod dinghy in a stiff breeze jolly well stands out in a crowd. Deprived of legal divorce, the child can at least deny the mother's disability, even her existence, forgetting to tell her about recitals and PTA meetings, refusing to accompany her to stores or church or the movies, never inviting friends to the house. Many do.

But I've been limping along for ten years now, and so far George 16
and the children are still at my left elbow, holding tight. Anne and
Matthew vacuum floors and dust furniture and haul trash and rake
up dog droppings and button my cuffs and bake lasagne and Toll
House cookies with just enough grumbling so I know that they don't
have brain fever. And far from hiding me, they're forever dragging
me by racks of fancy clothes or through teeming school corridors, or
welcoming gaggles of friends while I'm wandering through the house
in Anne's filmy pink babydoll pajamas. George generally calls before
he brings someone home, but he does just as many dumb thankless
chores as the children. And they all yell at me, laugh at some of my
jokes, write me funny letters when we're apart—in short, treat me
as an ordinary human being for whom they have some use. I think
they like me. Unless they're faking. . . .

Faking. There's the rub. Tugging at the fringes of my conscious- 17
ness always is the terror that people are kind to me only because I'm
a cripple. My mother almost shattered me once, with that instinct
mothers have—blind, I think, in this case, but unerring nonetheless—
for striking blows along the fault-lines of their children's hearts, by
telling me, in an attack of my selfishness, "We all have to make al-
lowances for you, of course, because of the way you are." From the
distance of a couple of years, I have to admit that I haven't any idea
just what she meant, and I'm not sure that she knew either. She was
awfully angry. But at the time, as the words thudded home, I felt my
worst fear, suddenly realized. I could bear being called selfish: I am.
But I couldn't bear the corroboration that those around me were doing
in fact what I'd always suspected them of doing, professing fondness
while silently putting up with me because of the way I am. A cripple.
I've been a little cracked ever since.

Along with this fear that people are secretly accepting shoddy 18
goods comes a relentless pressure to please—to prove myself worth
the burdens I impose, I guess, or to build a substantial account of
goodwill against which I may write drafts in times of need. Part of
the pressure arises from social expectations. In our society, anyone
who deviates from the norm had better find some way to compensate.
Like fat people, who are expected to be jolly, cripples must bear their
lot meekly and cheerfully. A grumpy cripple isn't playing by the rules.
And much of the pressure is self-generated. Early on I vowed that,
if I had to have MS, by God I was going to do it well. This is a class
act, ladies and gentlemen. No tears, no recriminations, no faint-heart-
edness.

One way and another, then, I wind up feeling like Tiny Tim, 19
peering over the edge of the table at the Christmas goose, waving my
crutch, piping down God's blessing on us all. Only sometimes I don't

want to play Tiny Tim. I'd rather be Caliban, a most scurvy monster. Fortunately, at home no one much cares whether I'm a good cripple or a bad cripple as long as I make vichyssoise with fair regularity. One evening several years ago, Anne was reading at the dining-room table while I cooked dinner. As I opened a can of tomatoes, the can slipped in my left hand and juice spattered me and the counter with bloody spots. Fatigued and infuriated, I bellowed, "I'm so sick of being crippled!" Anne glanced at me over the top of her book. "There now," she said, "do you feel better?" "Yes," I said, "yes, I do." She went back to her reading. I felt better. That's about all the attention my scurviness ever gets.

Because I hate being crippled, I sometimes hate myself for being 20 a cripple. Over the years I have come to expect—even accept—attacks of violent self-loathing. Luckily, in general our society no longer connects deformity and disease directly with evil (though a charismatic once told me that I have MS because a devil is in me) and so I'm allowed to move largely at will, even among small children. But I'm not sure that this revision of attitude has been particularly helpful. Physical imperfection, even freed of moral disapprobation, still defies and violates the ideal, especially for women, whose confinement in their bodies as objects of desire is far from over. Each age, of course, has its ideal, and I doubt that ours is any better or worse than any other. Today's ideal woman, who lives on the glossy pages of dozens of magazines, seems to be between the ages of eighteen and twenty-five; her hair has body, her teeth flash white, her breath smells minty, her underarms are dry; she has a career but is still a fabulous cook, especially of meals that take less than twenty minutes to prepare; she does not ordinarily appear to have a husband or children; she is trim and deeply tanned; she jogs, swims, plays tennis, rides a bicycle, sails, but does not bowl; she travels widely, even to out-of-the-way places like Finland and Samoa, always in the company of the ideal man, who possesses a nearly identical set of characteristics. There are a few exceptions. Though usually white and often blonde, she may be black, Hispanic, Asian, or Native American, so long as she is unusually sleek. She may be old, provided she is selling a laxative or is Lauren Becall. If she is selling a detergent, she may be married and have a flock of strikingly messy children. But she is never a cripple.

Like many women I know, I have always had an uneasy relation- 21 ship with my body. I was not a popular child, largely, I think now, because I was peculiar: intelligent, intense, moody, shy, given to unexpected actions and inexplicable notions and emotions. But as I entered adolescence, I believed myself unpopular because I was homely: my breasts too flat, my mouth too wide, my hips too narrow, my clothing never quite right in fit or style. I was not, in fact, particularly ugly, old photographs inform me, though I was well off the ideal; but I carried this sense of self-alienation with me into adulthood, where it regenerated in response to the depredations of MS. Even with my brace I walk with a limp so pronounced that, seeing myself on the videotape of a television program on the disabled, I couldn't believe that anything but an inchworm could make progress humping along like that. My shoulders droop and my pelvis thrusts forward as I try to balance myself upright, throwing my frame into a bony S. As a result of contractures, one shoulder is higher than the other and I carry one arm bent in front of me, the fingers curled into a claw. My left arm and leg have wasted into pipe-stems, and I try always to keep them covered. When I think about how my body must look to others, especially to men, to whom I have been trained to display myself, I feel ludicrous, even loathsome.

At my age, however, I don't spend much time thinking about my   22 appearance. The burning egocentricity of adolescence, which assures one that all the world is looking all the time, has passed, thank God, and I'm generally too caught up in what I'm doing to step back, as I used to, and watch myself as though upon a stage. I'm also too old to believe in the accuracy of self-image. I know that I'm not a hideous crone, that in fact, when I'm rested, well dressed, and well made up, I look fine. The self-loathing I feel is neither physically nor intellectually substantial. What I hate is not me but a disease.

I am not a disease.   23

And a disease is not—at least not singlehandedly—going to de-   24 termine who I am, though at first it seemed to be going to. Adjusting to a chronic incurable illness, I have moved through a process similar to that outlined by Elizabeth Kübler-Ross in *On Death and Dying*. The major difference—and it is far more significant than most people recognize—is that I can't be sure of the outcome, as the terminally ill cancer patient can. Research studies indicate that, with proper medical care, I may achieve a "normal" life span. And in our society, with its vision of death as the ultimate evil, worse even than decrepitude, the response to such news is, "Oh well, at least you're not going to *die*." Are there worse things than dying? I think that there may be.

I think of two women I know, both with MS, both enough older   25 than I to have served me as models. One took to her bed several years ago and has been there ever since. Although she can sit in a high-backed wheelchair, because she is incontinent she refuses to go out at all, even though incontinence pants, which are readily available at any pharmacy, could protect her from embarrassment. Instead, she stays at home and insists that her husband, a small quiet man, a retired civil servant, stay there with her except for a quick weekly foray to the supermarket. The other woman, whose illness was diagnosed when she was eighteen, a nursing student engaged to a young doctor, finished her training, married her doctor, accompanied him to Germany when he was in the service, bore three sons and a daughter, now grown and gone. When she can, she travels with her husband; she plays bridge, embroiders, swims regularly; she works, like me, as a symptomatic-patient instructor of medical students in neurology. Guess which woman I hope to be.

At the beginning, I thought about having MS almost incessantly. 26 And because of the unpredictable course of the disease, my thoughts were always terrified. Each night I'd get into bed wondering whether I'd get out again the next morning, whether I'd be able to see, to speak, to hold a pen between my fingers. Knowing that the day might come when I'd be physically incapable of killing myself, I thought perhaps I ought to do so right away, while I still had the strength. Gradually I came to understand that the Nancy who might one day lie inert under a bedsheet, arms and legs paralyzed, unable to feed or bathe herself, unable to reach out for a gun, a bottle of pills, was not the Nancy I was at present, and that I could not presume to make decisions for that future Nancy, who might well not want in the least to die. Now the only provision I've made for the future Nancy is that when the time comes—and it is likely to come in the form of pneumonia, friend to the weak and the old—I am not to be treated with machines and medications. If she is unable to communicate by then, I hope she will be satisfied with these terms.

Thinking all the time about having MS grew tiresome and intru- 27 sive, especially in the large and tragic mode in which I was accustomed to considering my plight. Months and even years went by without catastrophe (at least without one related to MS), and really I was awfully busy, what with George and children and snakes and students and poems, and I hadn't the time, let alone the inclination, to devote myself to being a disease. Too, the richer my life became, the funnier it seemed, as though there were some connection between largesse and laughter, and so my tragic stance began to waver until, even with the aid of a brace and cane, I couldn't hold it for very long at a time.

After several years I was satisfied with my adjustment. I had 28 suffered my grief and fury and terror, I thought, but now I was at ease with my lot. Then one summer day I set out with George and the children across the desert for a vacation in California. Part way to Yuma I became aware that my right leg felt funny. "I think I've had an exacerbation," I told George. "What shall we do?" he asked. "I think we'd better get the hell to California," I said, "because I don't know whether I'll ever make it again." So we went on to San Diego and then to Orange, and up the Pacific Coast Highway to Santa Cruz, across to Yosemite, down to Sequoia and Joshua Tree, and so back over the desert to home. It was a fine two-week trip, filled with friends and fair weather, and I wouldn't have missed it for the world, though I did in fact make it back to California two years later. Nor would there have been any point in missing it, since in MS, once the symptoms have appeared, the neurological damage has been done, and there's no way to predict or prevent that damage.

The incident spoiled my self-satisfaction, however. It renewed my 29 grief and fury and terror, and I learned that one never finishes adjusting to MS. I don't know now why I thought one would. One does not, after all, finish adjusting to life, and MS is simply a fact of my life—not my favorite fact, of course—but as ordinary as my nose and my tropical fish and my yellow Mazda station wagon. It may at any time get worse, but no amount of worry or anticipation can prepare me for a new loss. My life is a lesson in losses. I learn one at a time.

And I had best be patient in the learning, since I'll have to do it 30 like it or not. As any rock fan knows, you can't always get what you want. Particularly when you have MS. You can't, for example, get cured. In recent years researchers and the organizations that fund research have started to pay MS some attention even though it isn't fatal; perhaps they have begun to see that life is something other than a quantitative phenomenon, that one may be very much alive for a very long time in a life that isn't worth living. The researchers have made some progress toward understanding the mechanism of the disease: It may well be an autoimmune reaction triggered by a slow-acting virus. But they are nowhere near its prevention, control, or cure. And most of us want to be cured. Some, unable to accept incurability, grasp at one treatment after another, no matter how bizarre: megavitamin therapy, gluten-free diet, injections of cobra venom, hypothermal suits, lymphocytopharesis, hyperbaric chambers. Many treatments are probably harmless enough, but none are curative.

The absence of a cure often makes MS patients bitter toward their 31 doctors. Doctors are, after all, the priests of modern society, the new shamans, whose business is to heal, and many an MS patient roves from one to another, searching for the "good" doctor who will make him well. Doctors too think of themselves as healers, and for this reason many have trouble dealing with MS patients, whose disease in its intransigence defeats their aims and mocks their skills. Too few doctors, it is true, treat their patients as whole human beings, but the reverse is also true. I have always tried to be gentle with my doctors, who often have more at stake in terms of ego than I do. I may be frustrated, maddened, depressed by the incurability of my disease, but I am not diminished by it, and they are. When I push myself up from my seat in the waiting room and stumble toward them, I incarnate the limitation of their powers. The least I can do is refuse to press on their tenderest spots.

This gentleness is part of the reason that I'm not sorry to be a 32 cripple. I didn't have it before. Perhaps I'd have developed it anyway— how could I know such a thing?—and I wish I had more of it, but I'm glad of what I have. It has opened and enriched my life enormously, this sense that my frailty and need must be mirrored in others, that in searching for and shaping a stable core in a life wrenched by change and loss, change and loss, I must recognize the same process, under individual conditions, in the lives around me. I do not deprecate such knowledge, however I've come by it.

All the same, if a cure were found, would I take it? In a minute. 33 I may be a cripple, but I'm only occasionally a loony and never a saint. Anyway, in my brand of theology God doesn't give bonus points for a limp. I'd take a cure; I just don't need one. A friend who also has MS startled me once by asking, "Do you ever say to yourself, 'Why me, Lord?' " "No, Michael, I don't," I told him, "because whenever I try, the only response I can think of is 'Why not?' " If I could make a cosmic deal, who would I put in my place? What in my life would I give up in exchange for sound limbs and a thrilling rush of energy? No one. Nothing. I might as well do the job myself. Now that I'm getting the hang of it.

RESPONDING TO READING

Key words: family   freedom   identity   loss   medicine
minority   power   striving   transformation

Rhetorical concepts: anecdote   autobiography   comparison and contrast
definition   humor   illustration   meditation   narration/example

1.   Why does Mairs deliberately label herself a "cripple" (paragraphs 2–4) and reject the more euphemistic alternatives of "disabled," "handicapped," "differently abled"? Why does she use that loaded word in her title?
2.   Identify some of the many illustrations that Mairs uses to define "being a cripple." Given the fact that these physical difficulties and failures represent a condition that will only get worse, how do you account for the essay's essentially positive, affirmative attitude ("I'm not sorry to be a cripple," paragraph 32)?
3.   Throughout the essay, Mairs makes numerous comparisons and contrasts, overt and implied, between being crippled and "whole of limb." Why is it important for her to let her readers know that she "was a normally active child and young adult" (paragraph 5), and that she actively functions in a variety of roles, as friend, wife, mother, writer, teacher?

4.   Mairs is very candid about her body ("When I think about how my body must look to others, especially to men . . . I feel ludicrous, even loathsome," paragraph 21), even though she is careful not to equate her body with her illness ("I am not a disease," paragraph 23.) Might her "uneasy relationship" with her physical condition be a mirror of Americans' general dissatisfaction with their bodies? Is this as true of adults as of teenagers, of men as well as women? What features of American society contribute to this dissatisfaction?

5.   "On Being a Cripple" shows the positive as well as the negative consequences of being different, and how many of those differences can be transcended, in spirit and in action. If you have ever felt sufficiently different from your peers to be uncomfortable or isolated, write a definition of "On Being Different" in which you discuss the positive as well as the negative consequences. If you can generalize from your individual experience, do so.

At War with My Skin

JOHN UPDIKE

Novelist John Updike, born in Shillington, Pennsylvania in 1932, has been called "the Andrew Wyeth of American writers." The comparison implies an affinity of subject (ordinary men and women in everyday activities), technique (realistic, exacting, and highly detailed), and location (rural and small-town settings in Pennsylvania). Updike has used such characters and setting in his best-known series, novels that chronicle the life of former high school basketball star Harry "Rabbit" Angstrom, an automobile salesman with an unsatisfying marriage and an uneasy relationship to middle age: *Rabbit, Run* (1960), *Rabbit Redux* (1971), the Pulitzer prize-winning *Rabbit is Rich* (1981), and *Rabbit at Rest* (1990). "I like middles," says Updike of his middle-American subject, "It is in middles that extremes clash, where ambiguity relentlessy rules."

"At War with My Skin" discusses a middle-level concern—a source of intermittent discomfort, not a matter of life or death. It is a chapter from Updike's *Self-Consciousness: Memoirs* (1989), an autobiography written to counteract "the threat of someone wanting to write my biography, to take my life, my lode of ore and heap of memories, from me!" He aimed to write in a "mode of impersonal egoism a specimen life, representative in its odd uniqueness of all the oddly unique lives in this world." Updike's sense of odd uniqueness erupts in his painful, unpredictable self-image. This image is dominated by the scaly patches of psoriasis, an intermittent skin disease that helped determine his major choices in young manhood: a career as a writer where he could remain "closeted and unseen"; a brunette wife "with calm, smooth, deep-tanning skin"; and a place to live, Ipswich, Massachusetts, on whose great beach he could "bake and cure myself."

My mother tells me that up to the age of six I had no psoriasis; it came on strong after an attack of measles in February of 1938, when

I was in kindergarten. The disease—"disease" seems strong, for a condition that is not contagious, painful, or debilitating; yet psoriasis has the volatility of a disease, the sense of another presence coöccupying your body and singling you out from the happy herds of healthy, normal mankind—first attached itself to my memory while I was lying on the upstairs side porch of the Shillington house, amid the sickly, oleaginous smell of Siroil, on fuzzy sun-warmed towels, with my mother, sunbathing. We are both, in my mental picture, not quite naked. She would have been still a youngish woman at the time, and I remember being embarrassed by something, but whether by our being together this way or simply by my skin is not clear in this mottled recollection. She, too, had psoriasis; I had inherited it from her. Siroil and sunshine and not eating chocolate were our only weapons in our war against the red spots, ripening into silvery scabs, that invaded our skins in the winter. Siroil was the foremost medication available in the Thirties and Forties: a bottled preparation the consistency of pus, tar its effective ingredient and its drippy texture and bilious color and insinuating odor deeply involved with my embarrassment. Yet, as with our own private odors, those of sweat and earwax and even of excrement, there was also something satisfying about this scent, an intimate rankness that told me who I was.

One dabbed Siroil on; it softened the silvery scales but otherwise did very little good. Nor did abstaining from chocolate and "greasy" foods like potato chips and French fries do much visible good, though as with many palliations there was no knowing how much worse things would be otherwise. Only the sun, that living god, had real power over psoriasis; a few weeks of summer erased the spots from all of my responsive young skin that could be exposed—chest, legs, and face. Inspecting the many photographs taken of me as a child, including a set of me cavorting in a bathing suit in the back yard, I can see no trace of psoriasis. And I remember, when it rained, going out in a bathing suit with friends to play in the downpour and its warm puddles. Yet I didn't learn to swim, because of my appearance; I stayed away from "the Porgy," the dammed pond beyond the poorhouse, and from the public pool in West Reading, and the indoor pool at the Reading "Y," where my father in winter coached the high-school swimming team. To the travails of my freshman year at Harvard was added the humiliation of learning at last to swim, with my spots and my hydrophobia, in a class of quite naked boys. Recently the chunky, mild-spoken man who taught that class over thirty years ago came up to me at a party and pleasantly identified himself; I could scarcely manage politeness, his face so sharply brought back that old suppressed rich mix of chlorine and fear and brave gasping and naked, naked shame.

Psoriasis is a metabolic disorder that causes the epidermis, which

3

normally replaces itself at a gradual, unnoticeable rate, to speed up the process markedly and to produce excess skin cells. The tiny mechanisms gone awry are beyond the precise reach of internally taken medicine; a derivative of vitamin A, etretinate, and an anti-cancer drug, methotrexate, are effective but at the price of potential side-effects to the kidneys and liver more serious than the disease, which is, after all, superficial—too much, simply, of a good thing (skin). In the 1970s, dermatologists at Massachusetts General Hospital developed PUVA, a controlled light treatment: fluorescent tubes radiate long-wave ultraviolet (UV-A) onto skin sensitized by an internal dose of methoxsalen, a psoralen (the"P" of the acronym) derived from a weed, *Ammi majus,* which grows along the river Nile and whose sun-sensitizing qualities were known to the ancient Egyptians. So a curious primitivity, a savor of folk-medicine, clings to this new cure, a refinement of the old sun-cure. It is pleasant, once or twice a week, to stand nearly naked in a kind of glowing telephone booth. It was pleasant to lie on the upstairs porch, hidden behind the jigsawed wooden balusters, and to feel the slanting sun warm the fuzzy towel while an occasional car or pack of children crackled by on Shilling Alley. One became conscious, lying there trying to read, of birdsong, of distant shouts, of a whistle calling men back to work at the local textile factory, which was rather enchantingly called the Fairy Silk Mill.

My condition forged a hidden link with things elemental—with   4 the seasons, with the sun, and with my mother. A tendency to psoriasis is inherited—only through the maternal line, it used to be thought. My mother's mother had had it, I was told, though I never noticed anything wrong with my grandmother's skin—just her false teeth, which slipped down while she was napping in her rocking chair. Far in the future, I would marry a young brunette with calm, smooth, deep-tanning skin and was to imagine that thus I had put an end to at least my particular avenue of genetic error. Alas, our fourth child inherited my complexion and, lightly, in her late teens, psoriasis. The disease favors the fair, the dry-skinned, the pallid progeny of cloud-swaddled Holland and Ireland and Germany. Though my father was not red-haired, his brother Arch was, and when I grew a beard, as my contribution to the revolutionary Sixties, it came in reddish. And when I shaved it off, red spots had thrived underneath.

Psoriasis keeps you thinking. Strategies of concealment ramify,   5 and self-examination is endless. You are forced to the mirror, again and again; psoriasis compels narcissism, if we can suppose a Narcissus who did not like what he saw. In certain lights, your face looks passable; in slightly different other lights, not. Shaving mirrors and rear-view mirrors in automobiles are merciless, whereas the smoky mirrors in airplane bathrooms are especially flattering and soothing: one's face looks as tawny as a movie star's. Flying back from the Caribbean, I used to admire my improved looks; years went by before I noticed that I looked equally good, in the lavatory glow, on the flight down. I cannot pass a reflecting surface on the street without glancing in, in hopes that I have somehow changed. Nature and the self, the great moieties of earthly existence, are each cloven in two by a fascinated ambivalence. One hates one's abnormal, erupting skin but is led into a brooding, solicitous attention toward it. One hates the Nature that has imposed this affliction, but only this same Nature can be appealed to for erasure, for cure. Only Nature can forgive psoriasis; the sufferer in his self-contempt does not grant to other people this power. Perhaps the unease of my first memory has to do with my mother's presence; I wished to be alone with the sun, the air, the distant noises, the possibility of my hideousness eventually going away.

I recall remarkably few occasions when I was challenged, in the   6
brute world of childhood, about my skin. In the second grade, perhaps it was, the teacher, standing above our obedient rows, rummaged in my hair and said aloud, "Good heavens, child, what's this on your head?" I can hear these words breaking into the air above me and see my mother's face when, that afternoon, I recounted them to her, probably with tears; her eyes took on a fanatic glare and the next morning, like an arrow that had fixed her course, she went to the school to "have it out" with the teacher who had heightened her defective cub's embarrassment. Our doctor, Doc Rothermel in his big grit-and-stucco house, also, eerily, had psoriasis; far from offering a cure out of his magical expanding black bag, he offered us the melancholy confession that he had felt prevented, by his scaly wrists, from rolling back his sleeves and becoming—his true ambition—a surgeon. " 'Physician, heal thyself,' they'd say to me," he said. I don't, really, know how bad I looked, or how many conferences among adults secured a tactful silence from above. My peers (again, as I remember, which is a choosing to remember) either didn't notice anything terrible about my skin or else neglected to comment upon it. Children are frank, as we know from the taunts and nicknames they fling at one another; but also they all feel imperfect and vulnerable, which works for mutual forbearance. In high school, my gym class knew how I looked in the locker room and shower. Once, a boy from a higher class came up to me with an exclamation of cheerful disgust, touched my arm, and asked if I had syphilis. But my classmates held their tongues, and expressed no fear of contagion.

I participated, in gym shorts and tank top, in the annual gym   7
exhibitions. Indeed, as the tallest of the lighter boys, I stood shakily on top of "Fats" Sterner's shoulders to make the apex of our gym-

nastics pyramid. I braved it through, inwardly cringing, prisoner and victim of my skin. It was not really *me,* was the explanation I could not shout out. Like an obese person (like good-natured Fats so sturdy under me, a human rock, his hands gripping my ankles while I fought the sensation that I was about to lurch forward and fly out over the heads of our assembled audience of admiring parents), and unlike someone with a withered arm, say, or a port-wine stain splashed across his neck and cheek, I could change—every summer I *did* become normal and, as it were, beautiful. An overvaluation of the normal went with my ailment, a certain idealization of everyone who was not, as I felt myself to be, a monster.

Because it came and went, I never settled in with my psoriasis,   8
never adopted it as, inevitably, part of myself. It was temporary and in a way illusionary, like my being poor, and obscure, and (once we moved to the farm) lonely—a spell that had been put upon me, a test, as in a fairy story or one of those divinely imposed ordeals in the Bible. "Where's my public?" I used to ask my mother, coming back from the empty mailbox, by this joke conjuring a public out of the future.

My last public demonstration of my monstrosity, in a formal social   9
setting, occurred the day of my examination for the draft, in the summer of 1955. A year in England, with no sun, had left my skin in bad shape, and the examining doctor took one glance up from his plywood table and wrote on my form, "4-F: Psoriasis." At this point in my young life I had a job offer in New York, a wife, and an infant daughter, and was far from keen to devote two years to the national defense; I had never gone to summer camp, and pictured the Army as a big summer camp, with extra-rough bullies and extra-cold showers in the morning. My trepidation should be distinguished from political feelings; I had absolutely no doubts about my country's need, from time to time, to fight, and its right to call me to service. So suddenly and emphatically excused, I felt relieved, guilty, and above all ashamed at being singled out; the naked American men around me had looked at my skin with surprise and now were impressed by the exemption it had won me. I had not foreseen this result; psoriasis would handicap no killing skills and, had I reported in another season, might have been nearly invisible. My wife, when I got back to my parent's house with my news, was naturally delighted; but my mother, always independent in her moods, seemed saddened, as if she had laid an egg which, when candled by the government, had been pronounced rotten.

It pains me to write these pages. They are humiliating—"scab-   10
picking," to use a term sometimes levelled at modern autobiographical writers. I have written about psoriasis only twice before: I gave it to

Peter Caldwell in *The Centaur* and to an anonymous, bumptious cer-
amicist in the short story "From the Journal of a Leper." I expose it
this third time only in order to proclaim the consoling possibility that
whenever in my timid life I have shown some courage and originality
it has been because of my skin. Because of my skin, I counted myself
out of any of those jobs—salesman, teacher, financier, movie star—
that demand being presentable. What did that leave? Becoming a
craftsman of some sort, closeted and unseen—perhaps a cartoonist
or a writer, a worker in ink who can hide himself and send out a
surrogate presence, a signature that multiplies even while it conceals.
Why did I marry so young? Because, having once found a comely
female who forgave me my skin, I dared not risk losing her and trying
to find another. Why did I have children so young? Because I wanted
to surround myself with people who did not have psoriasis. Why, in
1957, did I leave New York and my nice employment there? Because
my skin was bad in the urban shadows, and nothing, not even screw-
ing a sunlamp bulb into the socket above my bathroom mirror, helped.
Why did I move, with my family, all the way to Ipswich, Massachusetts? Because this ancient Puritan town happened to have one of
the great beaches of the Northeast, in whose dunes I could, like a
sin-soaked anchorite of old repairing to the desert, bake and cure
myself.

RESPONDING TO READING

Key words: discovery   growing up   identity   medicine
memory   striving   writing

Rhetorical concepts: anecdote   autobiography   cause and effect
illustration

1.   Identify the effects of Updike's skin problems on his life, as he describes
them. How important has what he calls "my monstrosity" been to him? How
could such a condition, only skin deep, have such effects? Is his explanation
convincing?
2.   Compare Updike's attitude toward his skin with Nancy Mairs' attitude
toward her disease. Which of them has the more serious problem? Which of
them has the healthier attitude? Why do you say this?
3.   People often solve problems by outgrowing them, literally or figuratively,
as they mature. Did Updike ever experience this? Identify a problem, physical,
emotional, social, or other, which has disappeared or been resolved as you
have matured, and explain the process by which this has occurred. Did the
changes "just happen"? If not, what did you (or others) do to bring about
the change?

4. Many of us have imperfections, physical or otherwise, that may seem minor to other people but seem of overwhelming importance to us. If this is the case with you, describe the imperfection, and how it has led in some way to your definition of who you are. How is your self-definition related to what you think of yourself? Remember, what counts is how the person feels about the flaw, not how it might be seen from the outside.

Meditation: Now This Bell Tolling Softly for Another, Says to Me: Thou Must Die

JOHN DONNE

John Donne (1573–1631) was truly a Renaissance man, one who studied languages and the science of his day, graduated from Cambridge, read law, and served in Lord Essex's naval expeditions to Cadiz in 1596 and to the Azores in 1597. Despite a dazzling personality and brilliant early success as a poet, Donne's expectation of a career at court was thwarted both by his Jesuit background in a Protestant era and by his secret marriage to Ann More—"John Donne/Ann Donne/Undone"—whose irate father had him imprisoned and dismissed from his post as secretary to Thomas Egerton, England's Solicitor General and Keeper of the Great Seal. In order to succeed in either politics or the Church, Donne had to become Anglican, a decision so difficult for him to make that it took ten years. He was ordained as an Anglican clergyman in 1614, and appointed Dean of St. Paul's Cathedral in London in 1621, where he preached enormously popular sermons, dynamic and theatrical, until his death.

Donne's sermons are a dazzling mixture of the emotional and the intellectual, the sensual and the sacred. What critic Frank Kermode says of Donne's poetry applies equally well to his sermons: "Donne exhibits the play of an agile mind within the sensuous body [of his work], so that even his most passionate poems work by wit, abounding in argument and analogy; the poetry and the argument cannot be abstracted from each other."

Donne's meditation examines the interconnectedness of each of us to one another in birth, throughout life, and in death; Donne makes his point through a variety of complex and disparate images. The bell tolling for one and all, at morning and evening, mingles with the unifying consideration that "no man is an island, entire of itself; every man is a piece of the continent, a part of the main." "Another's danger" becomes our own, another's salvation and security becomes ours as well.

Perchance he for whom this bell tolls may be so ill, as that he 1
knows not it tolls for him; and perchance I may think myself so much
better than I am as that they who are about me, and see my state,
may have caused it to toll for me, and I know not that. The church
is Catholic, universal, so are all her actions; all that she does belongs
to all. When she baptizes a child, that action concerns me; for that

child is thereby connected to that body which is my head too, and ingrafted into that body whereof I am a member. And when she buries a man, that action concerns me: all mankind is of one author, and is one volume; when one man dies, one chapter is not torn out of the book, but translated into a better language; and every chapter must be so translated; God employs several translators; some pieces are translated by age, some by sickness, some by war, some by justice; but God's hand is in every translation, and his hand shall bind up all our scattered leaves again for that library where every book shall lie open to one another. As therefore the bell that rings to a sermon calls not upon the preacher only, but upon the congregation to come, so this bell calls us all; but how much more me, who am brought so near the door by this sickness. There was a contention as far as a suit (in which both poetry and dignity, religion and estimation, were mingled), which of the religious orders should ring to prayers first in the morning; and it was determined, that they should ring first that rose earliest. If we understand aright the dignity of this bell that tolls for our evening prayer, we would be glad to make it ours by rising early, in that application, that it might be ours as well as his, whose indeed it is. The bell doth toll for him that thinks it doth; and though it intermit again, yet from that minute that that occasion wrought upon him, he is united to God. Who casts not up his eye to the sun when it rises? but who takes off his eye from a comet when that breaks out? Who bends not his ear to any bell which upon any occasion rings? but who can remove it from that bell which is passing a piece of himself out of this world? No man is an island, entire of itself; every man is a piece of the continent, a part of the main. If a clod be washed away by the sea, Europe is the less, as well as if a promontory were, as well as if a manor of thy friend's or of thine own were: any man's death diminishes me, because I am involved in mankind, and therefore never send to know for whom the bell tolls; it tolls for thee. Neither can we call this a begging of misery, or a borrowing of misery, as though we were not miserable enough of ourselves, but must fetch in more from the next house, in taking upon us the misery of our neighbors. Truly it were an excusable convetousness if we did, for affliction is a treasure, and scarce any man hath enough of it. No man hath affliction enough that is not matured and ripened by it, and made fit for God by that affliction. If a man carry treasure in bullion, or in a wedge of gold, and have none coined into current money, his treasure will not defray him as he travels. Tribulation is treasure in the nature of it, but it is not current money in the use of it except we get nearer and nearer our home, heaven, by it. Another man may be sick too, and sick to death, and this affliction may lie in his bowels, as gold in a mine, and be of no use to him; but this bell, that tells me of his affliction, digs out and applies that gold to me: if by this consideration of another's danger I take mine own into contemplation, and so secure myself by making my recourse to my God, who is our only security.

RESPONDING TO WRITING

Key words: community   identity   symbols

Rhetorical concepts: analogy   meditation   metaphor

1.   What is a meditation? Why is this an appropriate form to consider the relations between life and death, the individual and society? Does one have to be formally or conventionally religious to meditate? Does it help? How?
2.   According to contemporary standards of rhetoric, pronouns and nouns that refer to people in general need either to be gender neutral or to refer to both men and women. What group does Donne mean when he says "man"? Does this seventeenth century terminology affect your understanding of the piece? Will you use contemporary terminology in your own writing? Why or why not?
3.   Notice the four rhetorical questions in the middle of this meditation. How would you answer them? How do they function as part of the argument leading to the assertion "No man is an island"?
4.   Donne's meditation, really a philosphical statement, proceeds by a series of assertions, some specfic, some general. Are these credible and convincing? How much of the work of the argument does Donne expect his readers to contribute?
5.   Identify Donne's metaphors of universal connectedness and show how he uses them to relate the individual to an enveloping social and religious context. Is it possible for any person ever to be "an island, entire of itself"? Why or why not? If you disagree with Donne, what metaphors of disconnectedness might you use?

Arriving at Moral Perfection
BENJAMIN FRANKLIN

In *Becoming Benjamin Franklin*, a comparison of Benjamin Franklin's *Autobiograhy* and his actual life, scholar Ormond Seavey comments on Franklin's catalogue of virtues that present a plan for "Arriving at Moral Perfection." The virtues for which Franklin strives, are not a plan for utter moral transformation but are more like "a suit of clothes worn over the natural self." Franklin's "natural self," says Seavey, is complicated and contradictory: "one who would live according to his highest ideal himself and another who jokes too much, argues rashly, sleeps late, and leaves his papers in disarray. These two Franklins serve as opposed and coordinated principles within the same self." Thus the list of virtues in Franklin's *Autobiography*— a work so popular that it has been continually in print from its publicaton three years after the author's death (1790)—itemizes the qualities necessary to succeed in business by working hard, or at least appearing to. Humility, acknowledges Franklin, was an afterthought.

Franklin, the prototype of the American self-made man, perpetrated many myths about himself in both his *Autobiography* and in *Poor Richard's Almanack*, which he wrote and published annually from 1732. Therein, he dispensed useful information and good advice that, if followed successfully, would enable readers to attain material prosperity, personal satisfaction, and public esteem. Indeed, Franklin's own life set the pace for generations to come. Born in 1706, he made enough money to retire from business at age 42, devoting the remainder of his life to science, public service, politics, and international diplomacy. Franklin the scientist made numerous discoveries in physics, navigation, and astronomy, and he applied his discoveries to practical inventions, such as the Franklin stove. Franklin the civil servant founded a public lending library, a municipal fire fighting company, the American Philosophical Society, and the University of Pennsylvania. Franklin the patriot served in the Continental Congress and as a Minister to France in the critical period during and after the Revolutionary War. Franklin, the composite of his several selves, was truly an American for all seasons.

It was about this time I conceived the bold and arduous project   1
of arriving at moral perfection. I wished to live without committing any fault at any time; I would conquer all that either natural inclination, custom, or company might lead me into. As I knew, or thought I knew, what was right and wrong, I did not see why I might not *always* do the one and avoid the other. But I soon found I had undertaken a task of more difficulty than I had imagined. While my attention was taken up and care employed in guarding against one fault, I was often surprized by another. Habit took the advantage of inattention. Inclination was sometimes too strong for reason. I concluded at length that the mere speculative conviction that it was our interest to be completely virtuous was not sufficient to prevent our slipping, and that the contrary habits must be broken and good ones acquired and established before we can have any dependence on a steady, uniform rectitude of conduct. For this purpose I therefore contrived the following method.

These names of virtues with their precepts were
1. Temperance
Eat not to dulness. Drink not to elevation.
2. Silence

Speak not but what may benefit others or yourself. Avoid trifling conversation.

3. Order

Let all your things have their places. Let each part of your business have its time.

4. Resolution

Resolve to perform what you ought. Perform without fail what you resolve.

5. Frugality

Make no expence but to do good to others or yourself; i.e., waste nothing.

6. Industry

Lose no time. Be always employed in something useful. Cut off all unnecessary actions.

7. Sincerity

Use no hurtful deceit. Think innocently and justly; and, if you speak, speak accordingly.

8. Justice

Wrong none by doing injuries or omitting the benefits that are your duty

9. Moderation

Avoid extremes. Forbear resenting injuries so much as you think they deserve.

10. Cleanliness

Tolerate no uncleanness in body, clothes or habitation.

11. Tranquillity

Be not disturbed at trifles or at accidents common or unavoidable.

12. Chastity

Rarely use venery but for health or offspring—never to dulness, weakness, or the injury of your own or another's peace or reputation.

13. Humility

Imitate Jesus and Socrates.

I made a little book in which I allotted a page for each of the virtues. I ruled each page with red ink so as to have seven columns, one for each day of the week, marking each column with a letter for the day. I crossed these columns with thirteen red lines, marking the beginning of each line with the first letter of one of the virtues, on which line and in its proper column I might mark by a little black spot every fault I found upon examination to have been committed respecting that virtue upon that day.

I determined to give a week's strict attention to each of the virtues successively. Thus in the first week my great guard was to avoid even the least offence against temperance, leaving the other virtues to their ordinary chance, only marking every evening the faults of the day. Thus if in the first week I could keep my first line marked "T." clear of spots, I supposed the habit of that virtue so much strengthened and its opposite weakened that I might venture extending my attention to include the next, and for the following week keep both lines clear of spots. Proceeding thus to the last, I could go thro' a course complete in thirteen weeks, and four courses in a year.

RESPONDING TO READING

Key words: community   education   identity   striving

Rhetorical concepts: autobiography   definition   process

1.   Franklin's definitions of the thirteen virtues are very brief. Should these be expanded? Why or why not? Would you change his list in any way?
2.   How does Franklin's list differ from modern books or articles giving good advice? How moral do you find his "virtues"?
4.   Franklin is responsible only to himself for sticking to his plan of self-improvement. Are people more likely to succeed in making changes for self-improvement if they do so with group support (e.g., Weight Watchers, Alcoholics Anonymous) than in isolation? What can a group provide that an individual cannot?
4.   Imagine you could follow Franklin's method for a full year. Would you then have achieved "moral perfection"? Why, or why not?

Resurrection

FREDERICK DOUGLASS

Frederick Douglass (1817–1885), born a slave in Talbot County, Maryland, devoted much of his life to interpreting and revising his public image, as revealed in the four very different versions of his autobiography that were published at intervals during his lifetime. Taken together, the various selves represent a black version of Benjamin Franklin's *Autobiography*, for they show the rise from slavery to freedom, from dependence to independence, from illiteracy to extraordinary command over the spoken and written word. As Douglass, too, fulfilled the American Dream, he became a national spokesperson for the abolitionist movement, serving as an advisor to Harriet Beecher Stowe, and to President Abraham Lincoln, among others. His post-bellum activities included campaigning for civil rights for blacks and women. Public acknowledgment of his stature culminated in his appointment as Minister to Haiti in 1890.
    The episode recounted in "Resurrection," which was taken from

the first version of *The Narrative of the Life of Frederick Douglass, An American Slave* (1845), explains the incident that was "the turning point in [his] career as a slave," for it enabled him to make the transformation from slave to human being. Douglass's autobiography, an abolitionist document like many other slave narratives, is exceptional in its forthright language and absence of stereotyping of either whites or blacks. His people are multidimensional, although the overseer, Mr. Covey, might have been the original of Harriet Beecher Stowe's arch villain, Simon Legree.

I have already intimated that my condition was much worse, dur-   1
ing the first six months of my stay at Mr. Covey's, than in the last six. The circumstances leading to the change in Mr. Covey's course toward me form an epoch in my humble history. You have seen how a man was made slave; you shall see how a slave was made a man. On one of the hottest days of the month of August, 1833, Bill Smith, William Hughes, a slave named Eli, and myself, were engaged in fanning wheat. Hughes was clearing the fanned wheat from before the fan. Eli was turning, Smith was feeding, and I was carrying wheat to the fan. The work was simple, requiring strength rather than intellect; yet, to one entirely unused to such work, it came very hard. About three o'clock of that day, I broke down; my strength failed me; I was seized with a violent aching of the head, attended with extreme dizziness; I trembled in every limb. Finding what was coming, I nerved myself up, feeling it would never do to stop work. I stood as long as I could stagger to the hopper with grain. When I could stand no longer, I fell, and felt as if held down by an immense weight. The fan of course stopped; every one had his own work to do; and no one could do the work of the other, and have his own go on at the same time.

Mr. Covey was at the house, about one hundred yards from the   2
treading-yard where we were fanning. On hearing the fan stop, he left immediately, and came to the spot where we were. He hastily inquired what the matter was. Bill answered that I was sick, and there was no one to bring wheat to the fan. I had by this time crawled away under the side of the post and rail-fence by which the yard was enclosed, hoping to find relief by getting out of the sun. He then asked where I was. He was told by one of the hands. He came to the spot, and, after looking at me awhile, asked me what was the matter. I told him as well as I could, for I scarce had strength to speak. He then gave me a savage kick in the side, and told me to get up. I tried to do so, but fell back in the attempt. He gave me another kick, and again told me to rise. I again tried, and succeeded in gaining my feet; but, stooping to get the tub with which I was feeding the fan, I again staggered and fell. While down in this situation, Mr. Covey took up

the hickory slat with which Hughes had been striking off the half-bushel measure, and with it gave me a heavy blow upon the head, making a large wound, and the blood ran freely; and with this again told me to get up. I made no effort to comply, having now made up my mind to let him do his worst. In a short time after receiving this blow, my head grew bigger. Mr. Covey had now left me to my fate. At this moment I resolved, for the first time, to go to my master, enter a complaint, and ask his protection. In order to do this, I must that afternoon walk seven miles; and this, under the circumstances, was truly a severe undertaking. I was exceedingly feeble; made so as much by the kicks and blows which I received, as by the severe fit of sickness to which I had been subjected. I, however, watched my chance, while Covey was looking in an opposite direction, and started for St. Michael's: I succeeded in getting a considerable distance on my way to the woods, when Covey discovered me, and called after me to come back, threatening what he would do if I did not come. I disregarded both his calls and his threats, and made my way to the woods as fast as my feeble state would allow; and thinking I might be overhauled by him if I kept to the road, I walked through the woods, keeping far enough from the road to avoid detection, and near enough to prevent losing my way. I had not gone far before my little strength again failed me. I could go no farther. I fell down, and lay for a considerable time. The blood was yet oozing from the wound on my head. For a time I thought I should bleed to death; and think now that I should have done so, but that the blood so matted my hair as to stop the wound. After lying there about three quarters of an hour, I nerved myself up again, and started on my way, through bogs and briers, barefooted and bareheaded, tearing my feet sometimes at nearly every step; and after a journey of about seven miles, occupying some five hours to perform it, I arrived at master's store. I then presented an appearance enough to affect any but a heart of iron. From the crown of my head to my feet, I was covered with blood. My hair was all clotted with dust and blood; my shirt was stiff with blood. My legs and feet were torn in sundry places with briers and thorns, and were also covered with blood. I suppose I looked like a man who had escaped a den of wild beasts, and barely escaped them. In this state I appeared before my master, humbly entreating him to interpose his authority for my protection. I told him all the circumstances as well as I could, and it seemed, as I spoke, at times to affect him. He would then walk the floor, and seek to justify Covey by saying he expected I deserved it. He asked me what I wanted. I told him, to let me get a new home; that as sure as I lived with Mr. Covey again, I should live with but to die with him; that Covey would surely kill me; he was in a fair way for it. Master Thomas ridiculed the idea that there was any danger of Mr. Covey's killing me, and said that he knew Mr. Covey, that he was a good man, and that he could not think of taking me from him; that, should he do so, he would lose the whole year's wages; that I belonged to Mr. Covey for one year, and that I must go back to him, come what might; and that I must not trouble him with any more stories, or that he would himself *get hold of me*. After threatening me thus, he gave me a very large dose of salts, telling me that I might remain in St. Michael's that night, (it being quite late,) but that I must be off back to Mr. Covey's early in the morning; and that if I did not, he would *get hold of me*, which meant that he would whip me. I remained all night, and, according to his orders, I started off to Covey's in the morning, (Saturday morning,) wearied in body and broken in spirit. I got no supper that night, or breakfast that morning. I reached Covey's about nine o'clock; and just as I was getting over the fence that divided Mrs. Kemp's fields from ours out ran Covey with his cowskin, to give me another whipping. Before he could reach me, I succeeded in getting to the cornfield; and as the corn was very high, it afforded me the means of hiding. He seemed very angry, and searched for me a long time. My behavior was altogether unaccountable. He finally gave up the chase, thinking, I suppose, that I must come home for something to eat; he would give himself no further trouble in looking for me. I spent that day mostly in the woods, having the alternative before me—to go home and be whipped to death, or stay in the woods and be starved to death. That night, I fell in with Sandy Jenkins, a slave with whom I was somewhat acquainted. Sandy had a free wife who lived about four miles from Mr. Covey's; and it being Saturday, he was on his way to see her. I told him my circumstances, and he very kindly invited me to go home with him. I went home with him, and talked this whole matter over, and got his advice as to what course it was best for me to pursue. I found Sandy an old adviser. He told me, with great solemnity, I must go back to Covey; but that before I went, I must go with him into another part of the woods, where there was a certain *root*, which, if I would take some of it with me, carrying it *always on my right side*, would render it impossible for Mr. Covey, or any other white man, to whip me. He said he had carried it for years; and since he had done so, he had never received a blow, and never expected to while he carried it. I at first rejected the idea, that the simple carrying of a root in my pocket would have any such effect as he had said, and was not disposed to take it; but Sandy impressed the necessity with much earnestness, telling me it could do no harm, if it did no good. To please him, I at length took the root, and, according to his direction, carried it upon my right side. This was Sunday morning. I immediately started for home; and upon entering the yard gate, out came Mr. Covey on his way to meeting. He spoke to me very kindly, bade me drive the pigs from a lot near by, and passed on towards the church. Now, this singular conduct of Mr. Covey really made me begin to think that there was something in the *root* which Sandy had given me; and had it been on any other day than Sunday, I could have attributed the conduct to no other cause than the influence of that root; and as it was, I was half inclined to think the *root* to be something more than I at first had taken it to be. All went well till Monday morning. On this morning, the virtue of the *root* was fully tested. Long before daylight, I was called to go and rub, curry, and feed, the horses. I obeyed, and was glad to obey. But whilst thus engaged, whilst in the act of throwing down some blades from the loft, Mr. Covey entered the stable with a long rope; and just as I was half out of the loft, he caught hold of my legs, and was about tying me. As soon as I found what he was up to, I gave a sudden spring, and as I did so, he holding to my legs, I was brought sprawling on the stable floor. Mr. Covey seemed now to think he had me, and could do what he pleased; but at this moment—from whence came the spirit I don't know—I resolved to fight; and, suiting my action to the resolution, I seized Covey hard by the throat; and as I did so, I rose. He held on to me, and I to him. My resistance was so entirely unexpected, that Covey seemed taken all aback. He trembled like a leaf. This gave me assurance, and I held him uneasy, causing the blood to run where I touched him with the ends of my fingers. Mr. Covey soon called out to Hughes for help. Hughes came, and while Covey held me, attempted to tie my right hand. While he was in the act of doing so, I watched my chance, and gave him a heavy kick close under the ribs. This kick fairly sickened Hughes, so that he left me in the hands of Mr. Covey. This kick had the effect of not only weakening Hughes, but Covey also. When he saw Hughes bending over with pain, his courage quailed. He asked me if I meant to persist in my resistance. I told him I did, come what might; that he had used me like a brute for six months, and that I was determined to be used so no longer. With that, he strove to drag me to a stick that was lying just out of the stable door. He meant to knock me down. But just as he was leaning over to get the stick, I seized him with both hands by his collar, and brought him by a sudden snatch to the ground. By this time, Bill came. Covey called upon him for assistance. Bill wanted to know what he could do. Covey said, "Take hold of him, take hold of him!" Bill said his master hired him out to work, and not to help whip me; so he left Covey and myself to fight our own battle out. We were at it for nearly two hours. Covey at length let me go, puffing and blowing at a great rate, saying that if I had not resisted, he would not have whipped me half so much. The truth was, that he had not whipped me at all. I considered him as getting entirely the worst end of the bargain; for he had drawn no blood from me, but I had from him. The whole six months afterwards, that I spent with Mr. Covey, he never laid the weight of his finger upon me in anger. He would occasionally say, he didn't want to get hold of me again. "No," thought I, "you need not; for you will come off worse than you did before."

This battle with Mr. Covey was the turning-point in my career as 3 a slave. It rekindled the few expiring embers of freedom, and revived within me a sense of my own manhood. It recalled the departed self-confidence, and inspired me again with a determination to be free. The gratification afforded by the triumph was a full compensation for whatever else might follow, even death itself. He only can understand the deep satisfaction which I experienced, who has himself repelled by force the bloody arm of slavery. I felt as I never felt before. It was a glorious resurrection, from the tomb of slavery, to the heaven of freedom. My long-crushed spirit rose, cowardice departed, bold defiance took its place; and I now resolved that, however long I might remain a slave in form, the day had passed forever when I could be a slave in fact. I did not hesitate to let it be known of me, that the white man who expected to succeed in whipping, must also succeed in killing me.

RESPONDING TO WRITING

Key words: community   discover   education   freedom
growing up   identity

Rhetorical concepts: autobiography   illustration   narrative/example

1.   Douglass's *Narrative*, from which this section is reprinted, is in whole and in part an example of "witnessing," as Elie Wiesel uses the term in "Why I Write," (pp.77–82). How does Douglass attempt to have his readers vicariously "witness" the experience?
2.   Who was Douglass's original audience for this section from his autobiography, first published in 1845? Would slave owners have been likely to read his autobiography? Blacks or whites, Northern or Southern, after the Civil War? Find passages that indicate the audiences Douglass had in mind.
3.   What, if anything, does Douglass expect members of any of the above audiences to do about slavery as a consequence of having read his narrative?
4.   Explain and justify Douglass's use of the following rhetorical strategies: a very long second paragraph and some long sentences; emphasizing some events and scarcely mentioning others that occur between the Friday afternoon and Monday morning of his narrative; using literary language to discuss an experience he had long before he become a writer and orator.

5. Douglass identifies his defiance of Mr. Covey as "the turning-point in my career as a slave," a watershed experience in establishing his self-identity. Write a narrative in which you recount and explain the significance of a comparable experience in which you attained an important change of self-image or status in others' eyes.

"I Just Wanna Be Average"

MIKE ROSE

In his award-winning *Lives on the Boundary* (1989), Mike Rose (born 1944) explains his understanding of the book's subtitle, *The Struggles and Achievements of America's Underprepared*. Growing up in Los Angeles, in a poor neighborhood near Watts, Rose remembers his early years as "a peculiar mix of physical warmth and barrenness." His father was ill and disabled, his mother worked nights as a waitress; his childhood days were "quiet, lazy, lonely." Only reading "opened up the world," but a mixup in high school placement tests, put Rose in the vocational track, a euphemism for the bottom level. There he was labeled "slow" and placed in a curriculum designed not to liberate the students but to occupy their time.

Prodded by a challenging teacher of sophomore biology, Rose switched to the college prep track and in 1966 graduated from Loyola University in Los Angeles. There he learned that learning meant more than mere memorizing. Ultimately he earned three more degrees, an M.S. in Education from the University of Southern California (1970), an M.A. in English (1970), and a Ph.D. in Educational Psychology (1981) from UCLA Rose has remained at UCLA as Associate Director of the UCLA Writing Programs. His experiences in tutoring veterans and Chicano, Asian, and black students provided firsthand research not only for *Lives on the Boundary* but also for his investigation of the writing processes of anxious writers, explained in *Writer's Block: The Cognitive Dimension* (1984).

My rhapsodic and prescientific astronomy carried me into my   1 teens, consumed me right up till high school, losing out finally, and only, to the siren call of pubescence—that endocrine hoodoo that transmogrifies nice boys into gawky flesh fiends. My mother used to bring home *Confidential* magazine, a peep-show rag specializing in the sins of the stars, and it beckoned me mercilessly: Jayne Mansfield's cleavage, Gina Lollobrigida's eyes, innuendos about deviant sexuality, ads for Frederick's of Hollywood—spiked heels, lacy brassieres, the epiphany of silk panties on a mannequin's hips. Along with Phil Everly, I was through with counting the stars above.

Budding manhood. Only adults talk about adolescence budding.   2 Kids have no choice but to talk in extremes; they're being wrenched and buffeted, rabbit-punched from inside by systemic thugs. Nothing sweet and pastoral here. Kids become ridiculous and touching at one and the same time: passionate about the trivial, fixed before the mirror, yet traversing one of the most important rites of passage in their lives—liminal people, silly and profoundly human. Given my own expertise, I fantasized about concocting the fail-safe aphrodisiac that would bring Marianne Bilpusch, the cloakroom monitor, rushing into my arms or about commanding a squadron of bosomy, linguistically mysterious astronauts like Zsa Zsa Gabor. My parents used to say that their son would have the best education they could afford. Maybe I would be a doctor. There was a public school in our neighborhood and several Catholic schools to the west. They had heard that quality schooling meant private, Catholic schooling, so they somehow got the money together to send me to Our Lady of Mercy, fifteen or so miles southwest of Ninety-first and Vermont. So much for my fantasies. Most Catholic secondary schools then were separated by gender.

I took two buses to get to Our Lady of Mercy. The first started   3 deep in South Los Angeles and caught me at midpoint. The second drifted through neighborhoods with trees, parks, big lawns, and lots of flowers. The rides were long but were livened up by a group of South L.A. veterans whose parents also thought that Hope had set up a shop in the west end of the county. There was Christy Biggars, who, at sixteen, was dealing and was, according to rumor, a pimp as well. There were Bill Cobb and Johnny Gonzales, grease-pencil artists extraordinaire, who left Nembutal-enhanced swirls of "Cobb" and "Johnny" on the corrugated walls of the bus. And then there was Tyrell Wilson. Tyrell was the coolest kid I knew. He ran the dozens like a metric halfback, laid down a rap that outrhymed and outpointed Cobb, whose rap was good but not great—the curse of a moderately soulful kid trapped in white skin. But it was Cobb who would sneak a radio onto the bus, and thus underwrote his patter with Little Richard, Fats Domino, Chuck Berry, the Coasters, and Ernie K. Doe's mother-in-law, an awful woman who was "sent from down below." And so it was that Christy and Cobb and Johnny G. and Tyrell and I and assorted others picked up along the way passed our days in the back of the bus, a funny mix brought together by geography and parental desire.

Entrance to school brings with it forms and releases and assess-   4 ments. Mercy relied on a series of tests, mostly the Stanford-Binet, for placement, and somehow the results of my tests got confused with those of another student named Rose. The other Rose apparently didn't do very well, for I was placed in the vocational track, a euphemism for the bottom level. Neither I nor my parents realized what this meant. We had no sense that Business Math, Typing, and English-

Level D were dead ends. The current spate of reports on the schools criticizes parents for not involving themselves in the education of their children. But how would someone like Tommy Rose, with his two years of Italian schooling, know what to ask? And what sort of pressure could an exhausted waitress apply? The error went undetected, and I remained in the vocational track for two years. What a place.

My homeroom was supervised by Brother Dill, a troubled and   5 unstable man who also taught freshman English. When his class drifted away from him, which was often, his voice would rise in paranoid accusations, and occasionally he would lose control and shake or smack us. I hadn't been there two months when one of his brisk, face-turning slaps had my glasses sliding down the aisle. Physical education was also pretty harsh. Our teacher was a stubby ex-lineman who had played old-time pro ball in the Midwest. He routinely had us grabbing our ankles to receive his stinging paddle across our butts. He did that, he said, to make men of us. "Rose," he bellowed on our first encounter; me standing geeky in line in my baggy shorts. " 'Rose'? What the hell kind of name is that?"

"Italian, sir," I squeaked.   6

"Italian! Ho. Rose, do you know the sound a bag of shit makes   7 when it hits the wall?"

"No, sir."   8

"Wop!"   9

Sophomore English was taught by Mr. Mitropetros. He was a 10 large, bejeweled man who managed the parking lot at the Shrine Auditorium. He would crow and preen and list for us the stars he'd brushed against. We'd ask questions and glance knowingly and snicker, and all that fueled the poor guy to brag some more. Parking cars was his night job. He had little training in English, so his lesson plan for his day work had us reading the district's required text, *Julius Caesar*, aloud for the semester. We'd finish the play way before the twenty weeks was up, so he'd have us switch parts again and again and start again: Dave Snyder, the fastest guy at Mercy, muscling through Caesar to the breathless squeals of Calpurnia, as interpreted by Steve Fusco, a surfer who owned the school's most envied paneled wagon. Week ten and Dave and Steve would take on new roles, as would we all, and render a water-logged Cassius and a Brutus that are beyond my powers of description.

Spanish I—taken in the second year—fell into the hands of a new 11 recruit. Mr. Montez was a tiny man, slight, five foot six at the most, soft-spoken and delicate. Spanish was a particularly rowdy class, and Mr. Montez was as prepared for it as a doily maker at a hammer throw. He would tap his pencil to a room in which Steve Fusco was propelling spitballs from his heavy lips, in which Mike Deetz was taunting Billy Hawk, a half-Indian, half-Spanish, reed-thin, quietly explosive boy. The vocational track at Our Lady of Mercy mixed kids traveling in from South L.A. with South Bay surfers and a few Slavs and Chicanos from the harbors of San Pedro. This was a dangerous miscellany: surfers and hodads and South-Central blacks all ablaze to the metronomic tapping of Hector Montez's pencil.

One day Billy lost it. Out of the corner of my eye I saw him strike 12 out with his right arm and catch Dweetz across the neck. Quick as a spasm, Dweetz was out of his seat, scattering desks, cracking Billy on the side of the head, right behind the eye. Snyder and Fusco and others broke it up, but the room felt hot and close and naked. Mr. Montez's tenuous authority was finally ripped to shreds, and I think everyone felt a little strange about that. The charade was over, and when it came down to it, I don't think any of the kids really wanted it to end this way. They had pushed and pushed and bullied their way into a freedom that both scared and embarrassed them.

Students will float to the mark you set. I and the others in the voca- 13 tional classes were bobbing in pretty shallow water. Vocational education has aimed at increasing the economic opportunities of students who do not do well in our schools. Some serious programs succeed in doing that, and through exceptional teachers—like Mr. Gross in *Horace's Compromise*—students learn to develop hypotheses and troubleshoot, reason through a problem, and communicate effectively—the true job skills. The vocational track, however, is most often a place for those who are just not making it, a dumping ground for the disaffected. There were a few teachers who worked hard at education; young Brother Slattery, for example, combined a stern voice with weekly quizzes to try to pass along to us a skeletal outline of world history. But mostly the teachers had no idea of how to engage the imaginations of us kids who were scuttling along at the bottom of the pond.

And the teachers would have needed some inventiveness, for 14 none of us was groomed for the classroom. It wasn't just that I didn't know things—didn't know how to simplify algebraic fractions, couldn't identify different kinds of clauses, bungled Spanish translations—but that I had developed various faulty and inadequate ways of doing algebra and making sense of Spanish. Worse yet, the years of defensive tuning out in elementary school had given me a way to escape quickly while seeming at least half alert. During my time in Voc. Ed., I developed further into a mediocre student and a somnambulant problem solver, and that affected the subjects I did have the wherewithal to handle: I detested Shakespeare; I got bored with history. My attention flitted here and there. I fooled around in class and read my books indifferently—the intellectual equivalent of playing with your food. I did what I had to do to get by, and I did it with half a mind.

But I did learn things about people and eventually came into my own socially. I liked the guys in Voc. Ed. Growing up where I did, I understood and admired physical prowess, and there was an abundance of muscle here. There was Dave Snyder, a sprinter and halfback of true quality. Dave's ability and his quick wit gave him a natural appeal, and he was welcome in any clique, though he always kept a little independent. He enjoyed acting the fool and could care less about studies, but he possessed a certain maturity and never caused the faculty much trouble. It was a testament to his independence that he included me among his friends—I eventually went out for track, but I was no jock. Owing to the Latin alphabet and a dearth of Rs and Ss., Snyder sat behind Rose, and we started exchanging one-liners and became friends.

There was Ted Richard, a much-touted Little League pitcher. He was chunky and had a baby face and came to Our Lady of Mercy as a seasoned street fighter. Ted was quick to laugh and he had a loud, jolly laugh, but when he got angry he'd smile a little smile, the kind that simply raises the corner of the mouth a quarter of an inch. For those who knew, it was an eerie signal. Those who didn't found themselves in big trouble, for Ted was very quick. He loved to carry on what we would come to call philosophical discussions: What is courage? Does God exist? He also loved words, enjoyed picking up big ones like *salubrious* and *equivocal* and using them in our conversations—laughing at himself as the word hit a chuckhole rolling off his tongue. Ted didn't do all that well in school—baseball and parties and testing the courage he'd speculated about took up his time. His textbooks were *Argosy* and *Field and Stream*, whatever newspapers he'd find on the bus stop—from *The Daily Worker* to pornography— conversations with uncles or hobos or businessmen he'd meet in a coffee shop, *The Old Man and the Sea*. With hindsight, I can see that Ted was developing into one of those rough-hewn intellectuals whose sources are a mix of the learned and the apocryphal, whose discussions are both assured and sad.

And then there was Ken Harvey. Ken was good-looking in a puffy way and had a full and oily ducktail and was a car enthusiast . . . a hodad. One day in religion class, he said the sentence that turned out to be one of the most memorable of the hundreds of thousands I heard in those Voc. Ed. years. We were talking about the the parable of the talents, about achievement, working hard, doing the best you can do, blah-blah-blah, when the teacher called on the restive Ken Harvey for an opinion. Ken thought about it, but just for a second, and said (with studied, minimal affect), "I just wanna be average." That woke me up. Average?! Who wants to be average? Then the athletes chimed in with the clichés that make you want to laryngec- tomize them, and the exchange became a platitudinous melee. At the time, I thought Ken's assertion was stupid, and I wrote him off. But his sentence has stayed with me all these years, and I think I am finally coming to understand it.

Ken Harvey was gasping for air. School can be a tremendously 18 disorienting place. No matter how bad the school, you're going to encounter notions that don't fit with the assumptions and beliefs that you grew up with—maybe you'll hear these dissonant notions from teachers, maybe from the other students, and maybe you'll read them. You'll also be thrown in with all kinds of kids from all kinds of back- grounds, and that can be unsettling—this is especially true in places of rich ethnic and linguistic mix, like the L.A. basin. You'll see a handful of students far excel you in courses that sound exotic and that are only in the curriculum of the elite: French, physics, trigo- nometry. And all this is happening while you're trying to shape an identity, your body is changing, and your emotions are running wild. If you're a working-class kid in the vocational track, the options you'll have to deal with this will be constrained in certain ways: You're defined by your school as "slow"; you're placed in a curriculum that isn't designed to liberate you but to occupy you, or, if you're lucky, train you, though the training is for work the society does not esteem; other students are picking up the cues from your school and your curriculum and interacting with you in particular ways. If you're a kid like Ted Richard, you turn your back on all this and let your mind roam where it may. But youngsters like Ted are rare. What Ken and so many others do is protect themselves from such suffocating mad- ness by taking on with a vengeance the identity implied in the vo- cational track. Reject the confusion and frustration by openly defining yourself as the Common Joe. Champion the average. Rely on your own good sense. Fuck this bullshit. Bullshit, of course, is everything you—and the others—fear is beyond you: books, essays, tests, aca- demic scrambling, complexity, scientific reasoning, philosophical in- quiry.

The tragedy is that you have to twist the knife in your own gray 19 matter to make this defense work. You'll have to shut down, have to reject intellectual stimuli or diffuse them with sarcasm, have to cul- tivate stupidity, have to convert boredom from a malady into a way of confronting the world. Keep your vocabulary simple, act stoned when you're not or act more stoned than you are, flaunt ignorance, materialize your dreams. It is a powerful and effective defense—it neutralizes the insult and the frustration of being a vocational kid and, when perfected, it drives teachers up the wall, a delightful secondary effect. But like all strong magic, it exacts a price.

My own deliverance from the Voc. Ed. world began with sophomore 20
biology. Every student, college prep to vocational, had to take biology, and unlike the other courses, the same person taught all sections. When teaching the vocational group, Brother Clint probably slowed down a bit or omitted a little of the fundamental biochemistry, but he used the same book and more or less the same syllabus across the board. If one class got tough, he could get tougher. He was young and powerful and very handsome, and looks and physical strength were high currency. No one gave him any trouble.

I was pretty bad at the dissecting table, but the lectures and the 21
textbook were interesting: plastic overlays that, with each turned page, peeled away skin, then veins and muscle, then organs, down to the very bones that Brother Clint, pointer in hand, would tap out on our hanging skeleton. Dave Snyder was in big trouble, for the study of life—versus the living of it—was sticking in his craw. We worked out a code for our multiple-choice exams. He'd poke me in the back: once for the answer under A, twice for B, and so on; and when he'd hit the right one, I'd look up to the ceiling as though I were lost in thought. Poke: cytoplasm. Poke, poke: methane. Poke, poke, poke: William Harvey. Poke, poke, poke, poke: islets of Langerhans. This didn't work out perfectly, but Dave passed the course, and I mastered the dreamy look of a guy on a record jacket. And something else happened. Brother Clint puzzled over this Voc. Ed. kid who was racking up 98s and 99s on his tests. He checked the school's records and discovered the error. He recommended that I begin my junior year in the College Prep program. According to all I've read since, such a shift, as one report put it, is virtually impossible. Kids at that level rarely cross tracks. The telling thing is how chancy both my placement into and exit from Voc. Ed. was; neither I nor my parents had anything to do with it. I lived in one world during spring semester, and when I came back to school in the fall, I was living in another.

Switching to College Prep was a mixed blessing. I was an erratic 22
student. I was undisciplined. And I hadn't caught onto the rules of the game: Why work hard in a class that didn't grab my fancy? I was also hopelessly behind in math. Chemistry was hard; toying with my chemistry set years before hadn't prepared me for the chemist's equations. Fortunately, the priest who taught both chemistry and second-year algebra was also the school's athletic director. Membership on the track team covered me; I knew I wouldn't get lower than a C.

U.S. history was taught pretty well, and I did okay. But civics was taken over by a football coach who had trouble reading the textook aloud—and reading aloud was the centerpiece of his pedagogy. College Prep at Mercy was certainly an improvement over the vocational program—at least it carried some status—but the social science curriculum was weak, and the mathematics and physical sciences were simply beyond me. I had a miserable quantitative background and ended up copying some assignments and finessing the rest as best I could. Let me try to explain how it feels to see again and again material you should once have learned but didn't.

You are given a problem. It requires you to simplify algebraic 23 fractions or to multiply expressions containing square roots. You know this is pretty basic material because you've seen it for years. Once a teacher took some time with you, and you learned how to carry out these operations. Simple versions, anyway. But that was a year or two or more in the past, and these are more complex versions, and now you're not sure. And this, you keep telling yourself, is ninth- or even eighth-grade stuff.

Next it's a word problem. This is also old hat. The basic elements 24 are as familiar as story characters: trains speeding so many miles per hour or shadows of buildings angling so many degrees. Maybe you know enough, have sat through enough explanations, to be able to begin setting up the problem: "If one train is going this fast . . ." or "This shadow is really one line of a triangle. . . ." Then: "Let's see . . ." "How did Jones do this?" "Hmmmm." "No." "No, that won't work." Your attention wavers. You wonder about other things: a football game, a dance, that cute new checker at the market. You try to focus on the problem again. You scribble on paper for a while, but the tension wins out and your attention flits elsewhere. You crumple the paper and begin daydreaming to ease the frustration.

The particulars will vary, but in essence this is what a number of 25 students go through, especially those in so-called remedial classes. They open their textbooks and see once again the familiar and impenetrable formulas and diagrams and terms that have stumped them for years. There is no excitement here. *No* excitement. Regardless of what the teacher says, this is not a new challenge. There is, rather, embarrassment and frustration and, not surprisingly, some anger in being reminded once again of long-standing inadequacies. No wonder so many students finally attribute their difficulties to something inborn, organic: "That part of my brain just doesn't work." Given the troubling histories many of these students have, it's miraculous that any of them can lift the shroud of hopelessness sufficiently to make deliverance from these classes possible.

RESPONDING TO READING

Key words: class community discovery education freedom
growing up identity minority power rights sociology
striving watershed

Rhetorical concepts: anecdote autobiography cause and effect
narrative/example

1.   Rose re-creates the ambience and context of a parochial California high
school in the 1960s. To what extent is Our Lady of Mercy in Los Angeles
representative of high school as you and your peers have experienced it?
What has remained constant over time? What has changed?

2.   Analyze the following passage to show how Rose creates a composite
character, "the Common Joe," to express a point of view and a range of
behavior that create more educational and personal and social problems that
they solve.

> "The tragedy is that you have to twist the knife in your own
> gray matter to make this defense work. You'll have to shut down,
> have to reject intellectual stimuli or diffuse them with sarcasm, have
> to cultivate stupidity, have to convert boredom from a malady into
> a way of confronting the world. . . . It is a powerful and effective
> defense—it neutralizes the insult and the frustration of being a vo-
> cational kid and, when perfected, it drives teachers up the wall. . . .
> But like all strong magic, it exacts a price."[paragraph 19]

How does this description differ from conventional explanations
of why students in the low track do not learn? What evidence does
Rose present to support his view? What is his attitude toward the
students he describes? How convincing do you find his explanation?

3.   Why would a student "just wanna be average," rather than to excel?
What aspects of the school itself—student placement, courses, attitudes of
teachers and students, for instance—contribute to the students' expectations
of themselves? What is the influence of the home? The outside culture? What
does it take for a student to move beyond the average?

4.   Describe your group in high school, with particular attention to their
expectations, and yours, and how these expectations developed.

Why I Write: Making No Become Yes

ELIE WIESEL

Elie Wiesel, a survivor of the Holocaust, explains that "For me, literature abolishes the gap between [childhood and death]. . . . Auschwitz marks the decisive, ultimate turning point . . . of the human adventure. Nothing will ever again be as it was. Thousands and thousands of deaths weigh upon every word. How speak of redemption after Treblinka? and how speak of anything else?" In May 1944, when Wiesel was 15, the German Gestapo, under Adolf Eichmann's orders to exterminate 600,000 Jews in six weeks, invaded Wiesel's peaceful Transylvanian village, Sighet, Romania, and deported the family, first to Birkenau concentration camp, then to Auschwitz and Buchenwald. Although six million Jews died, including Wiesel's father, mother, and sister, Wiesel survived. . . .to tell their story. After liberation in 1945, Wiesel studied philosophy in Paris, and then spent twenty years as a reporter for Jewish newspapers. In 1954 he was encouraged by novelist Francois Mauriac, to speak on behalf of the children in concentration camps, thereby setting in motion Wiesel's career shift to creative writing. In 1958 he moved to New York and published his first novel, *Night*, which opens, "In the beginning was faith, confidence, illusion." Since then he has written some twenty-five books of fiction, nonfiction, poetry, and drama, all of which witness man's inhumanity to man and profess the faith and fortitude needed to overcome the greatest adversity. In 1985 Wiesel was awarded the Congressional Gold medal; a year later he received the Nobel Peace Prize. In "Why I Write: Making No Become Yes," Wiesel says that he writes to give meaning to his experience of the Holocaust, to fulfill his vow, "If, by some miracle, I emerge alive, I will devote my life to testifying on behalf of those whose shadow will fall on mine forever and ever."

Why do I write? 1

Perhaps in order not to go mad. Or, on the contrary, to touch the 2 bottom of madness. Like Samuel Beckett, the survivor expresses himself "en désespoir de cause"—out of desperation.

Speaking of the solitude of the survivor, the great Yiddish and 3 Hebrew poet and thinker Aaron Zeitlin addresses those—his father, his brother, his friends—who have died and left him: "You have abandoned me," he says to them. "You are together, without me. I am here. Alone. And I make words."

So do I, just like him. I also say words, write words, reluctantly. 4

77

There are easier occupations, far more pleasant ones. But for the   5
survivor, writing is not a profession, but an occupation, a duty. Camus
calls it "an honor." As he puts it: "I entered literature through worship." Other writers have said they did so through anger, through
love. Speaking for myself, I would say—through silence.

It was by seeking, by probing silence that I began to discover the   6
perils and power of the word. I never intended to be a philosopher,
or a theologian. The only role I sought was that of witness. I believed
that, having survived by chance, I was duty-bound to give meaning
to my survival, to justify each moment of my life. I knew the story
had to be told. Not to transmit an experience is to betray it. This is
what Jewish tradition teaches us. But how to do this? "When Israel
is in exile, so is the word," says the Zohar. The word has deserted
the meaning it was intended to convey—impossible to make them
coincide. The displacement, the shift, is irrevocable.

This was never more true than right after the upheaval. We all   7
knew that we could never, never say what had to be said, that we
could never express in words, coherent, intelligible words, our experience of madness on an absolute scale. The walk through flaming
night, the silence before and after the selection, the monotonous
praying of the condemned, the Kaddish of the dying, the fear and
hunger of the sick, the shame and suffering, the haunted eyes, the
demented stares. I thought that I would never be able to speak of
them. All words seemed inadequate, worn, foolish, lifeless, whereas
I wanted them to be searing.

Where was I to discover a fresh vocabulary, a primeval language?   8
The language of night was not human, it was primitive, almost animal—hoarse shouting, screams, muffled moaning, savage howling,
the sound of beating. A brute strikes out wildly, a body falls. An
officer raises his arm and a whole community walks toward a common
grave. A soldier shrugs his shoulders, and a thousand families are
torn apart, to be reunited only by death. This was the concentration
camp language. It negated all other language and took its place. Rather
than a link, it became a wall. Could it be surmounted? Could the
reader be brought to the other side? I knew the answer was negative,
and yet I knew that "no" had to become "yes." It was the last wish
of the dead.

The fear of forgetting remains the main obsession of all those who   9
have passed through the universe of the damned. The enemy counted
on people's incredulity and forgetfulness. How could one foil this
plot? And if memory grew hollow, empty of substance, what would
happen to all we had accumulated along the way? Remember, said
the father to his son, and the son to his friend. Gather the names,
the faces, the tears. We had all taken an oath: "If, by some miracle,

I emerge alive, I will devote my life to testifying on behalf of those whose shadow will fall on mine forever and ever."

That is why I write certain things rather than others—to remain 10 faithful.

Of course, there are times of doubt for the survivor, times when 11 one gives in to weakness, or longs for comfort. I hear a voice within me telling me to stop mourning the past. I too want to sing of love and of its magic. I too want to celebrate the sun, and the dawn that heralds the sun. I would like to shout, and shout loudly: "Listen, listen well! I too am capable of victory, do you hear? I too am open to laughter and joy! I want to stride, head high, my face unguarded, without having to point to the ashes over there on the horizon, without having to tamper with facts to hide their tragic ugliness. For a man born blind, God himself is blind, but look, I see, I am not blind." One feels like shouting this, but the shout changes to a murmur. One must make a choice; one must remain faithful. A big word, I know. Nevertheless I use it, it suits me. Having written the things I have written, I feel I can afford no longer to play with words. If I say that the writer in me wants to remain loyal, it is because it is true. This sentiment moves all survivors; they owe nothing to anyone, but everything to the dead.

I owe them my roots and my memory. I am duty-bound to serve 12 as their emissary, transmitting the history of their disappearance, even if it disturbs, even if it brings pain. Not to do so would be to betray them, and thus myself. And since I am incapable of communicating their cry by shouting, I simply look at them. I see them and I write.

While writing, I question them as I question myself. I believe I 13 have said it before, elsewhere. I write to understand as much as to be understood. Will I succeed one day? Wherever one starts, one reaches darkness. God? He remains the God of darkness. Man? The source of darkness. The killers' derision, their victims' tears, the onlookers' indifference, their complicity and complacency—the divine role in all that I do not understand. A million children massacred— I shall never understand.

Jewish children—they haunt my writings. I see them again and 14 again. I shall always see them. Hounded, humiliated, bent like the old men who surround them as though to protect them, unable to do so. They are thirsty, the children, and there is no one to give them water. They are hungry, but there is no one to give them a crust of bread. They are afraid, and there is no one to reassure them.

They walk in the middle of the road, like vagabonds. They are 15 on the way to the station, and they will never return. In sealed cars, without air or food, they travel toward another world. They guess where they are going, they know it, and they keep silent. Tense, thoughtful, they listen to the the wind, the call of death in the distance.

All these children, these old people, I see them. I never stop seeing 16 them. I belong to them.

But they, to whom do they belong? 17

People tend to think that a murderer weakens when facing a child. 18 The child reawakens the killer's lost humanity. The killer can no longer kill the child before him, the child inside him.

But with us it happened differently. Our Jewish children had no 19 effect upon the killers. Nor upon the world. Nor upon God.

I think of them, I think of their childhood. Their childhood is a 20 small Jewish town, and this town is no more. They frighten me; they reflect an image of myself, one that I pursue and run from at the same time—the image of a Jewish adolescent who knew no fear, except the fear of God, whose faith was whole, comforting, and not marked by anxiety.

No, I do not understand. And if I write, it is to warn the reader 21 that he will not understand either. "You will not understand, you will never understand," were the words heard everywhere during the reign of night. I can only echo them. You, who never lived under a sky of blood, will never know what it was like. Even if you read all the books ever written, even if you listen to all the testimonies ever given, you will remain on this side of the wall, you will view the agony and death of a people from afar, through the screen of a memory that is not your own.

An admission of impotence and guilt? I do not know. All I know 22 is that Treblinka and Auschwitz cannot be told. And yet I have tried. God knows I have tried.

Have I attempted too much or not enough? Among some 25 23 volumes, only three or four penetrate the phantasmagoric realm of the dead. In my other books, through my other books, I have tried to follow other roads. For it is dangerous to linger among the dead, they hold on to you and you run the risk of speaking only to them. And so I have forced myself to turn away from them and study other periods, explore other destinies and teach other tales—the Bible and the Talmud, Hasidism and its fervor, the shtetl and its songs, Jerusalem and its echoes, the Russian Jews and their anguish, their awakening, their courage. At times, it has seemed to me that I was speaking of other things with the sole purpose of keeping the essential—the personal experience—unspoken. At times I have wondered: And what if I was wrong? Perhaps I should not have heeded my own advice and stayed in my own world with the dead.

But then, I have not forgotten the dead. They have their rightful 24 place even in the works about theHasidic capitals Ruzhany and Korets, and Jerusalem. Even in my biblical and Midrashic tales, I pursue their presence, mute and motionless. The presence of the dead then beckons in such tangible ways that it affects even the most removed characters. Thus they appear on Mount Moriah, where Abraham is about to sacrifice his son, a burnt offering to their common God. They appear on Mount Nebo, where Moses enters solitude and death. They appear in Hasidic and Talmudic legends in which victims forever need defending against forces that would crush them. Technically, so to speak, they are of course elsewhere, in time and space, but on a deeper, truer plane, the dead are part of every story, of every scene.

"But what is the connection?" you will ask. Believe me, there is 25 one. After Auschwitz everything brings us back to Auschwitz. When I speak of Abraham, Isaac and Jacob, when I invoke Rabbi Yohanan ben Zakkai and Rabbi Akiba, it is the better to understand them in the light of Auschwitz. As for the Maggid of Mezeritch and his disciples, it is in order to encounter the followers of their followers that I reconstruct their spellbound, spellbinding universe. I like to imagine them alive, exuberant, celebrating life and hope. Their happiness is as necessary to me as it was once to themselves.

And yet—how did they manage to keep their faith intact? How 26 did they manage to sing as they went to meet the Angel of Death? I know Hasidim who never vacillated—I respect their strength. I know others who chose rebellion, protest, rage—I respect their courage. For there comes a time when only those who do not believe in God will not cry out to him in wrath and anguish.

Do not judge either group. Even the heroes perished as martyrs, 27 even the martyrs died as heroes. Who would dare oppose knives to prayers? The faith of some matters as much as the strength of others. It is not ours to judge, it is only ours to tell the tale.

But where is one to begin? Whom is one to include? One meets 28 a Hasid in all my novels. And a child. And an old man. And a beggar. And a madman. They are all part of my inner landscape. The reason why? Pursued and persecuted by the killers, I offer them shelter. The enemy wanted to create a society purged of their presence, and I have brought some of them back. The world denied them, repudiated them, so I let them live at least within the feverish dreams of my characters.

It is for them that I write, and yet the survivor may experience 29 remorse. He has tried to bear witness; it was all in vain.

After the liberation, we had illusions. We were convinced that a 30 new world would be built upon the ruins of Europe. A new civilization would see the light. No more wars, no more hate, no more intolerance, no fanaticism. And all this because the witnesses would speak. And speak they did, to no avail.

They will continue, for they cannot do otherwise. When man, in 31 his grief, falls silent, Goethe says, then God gives him the strength to sing his sorrows. From that moment on, he may no longer choose not to sing, whether his song is heard or not. What matters is to struggle against silence with words, or through another form of silence. What matters is to gather a smile here and there, a tear here and there, a word here and there, and thus justify the faith placed in you, a long time ago, by so many victims.

Why do I write? To wrench those victims from oblivion. To help the dead vanquish death.   32

RESPONDING TO WRITING

Key words: community   freedom   identity   language   memory minority   power   race   writing

Rhetorical concepts: analysis   anecdote   autobiography   definition explanation   illustration   meditation   narration/example

1.   Wiesel says, "The only role I sought [as a writer] was that of witness (paragraph 6). What does he mean by "witness"? Illustrate your answer with examples throughout the essay.
2.   Wiesel says that "Not to transmit an experience is to betray it" (paragraph 6). Why does he cast his argument in terms of guilt and betrayal, survival, witnessing, and atonement?
3.   Wiesel makes his case through a number of ethical appeals. What are these? On what grounds does he expect that these will speak to readers who did not experience the Holocaust or concentration camps, and in many cases were not even alive during World War II?
4.   Why does Wiesel use so many rhetorical questions? When he answers them himself (as those who raise rhetorical questions often do), he assumes the roles of witness, preacher, teacher, rabbi, moralist—all of which combine to make him a very didactic writer. How does he expect his readers to respond—in attitudes and in actions?
5.   Does Wiesel succeed in "making no become yes" (paragraph 7)? Why or why not?

Literate Traditions

SHIRLEY BRICE HEATH

Shirley Brice Heath (born in 1941) has been a professor of anthropology and linguistics in the School of Education at Stanford University, having earned her Ph.D. in these subjects from Columbia in 1970. From 1969 to 1978, during the massive school desegregation in the South, Heath was a part-time instructor at, Winthrop College in the Appalachian Piedmont where she had grown up. Her job was to prepare prospective teachers to deal both theoretically and practically with an educational climate new to them all. The community members who took her classes, "black and white teachers, business leaders, ministers, and mill personnel," needed to learn "more about how others communicated: why students and teachers often could not understand each other, why questions were sometimes not answered, and why habitual ways of talking and listening did not always seem to work." From this concern for enabling integrated classrooms to become meaningful contexts for learning stemmed Heath's decade-long study in which she "lived, worked, and played with the children and their families and friends in Roadville and Trackton"—her names for the small neighboring Piedmont mill towns, white and black, at "the foot of the mountain."

The result is the remarkable, meticulously detailed *Ways with Words: Language, Life, and Work in Communities and Classrooms* (1983), of which "Literate Traditions" is a section. Heath's study, unique at the time, focused on the impact of community and cultural background on children's language learning and usage. She and her colleagues kept extensive records describing "the ways of living, eating, sleeping, worshiping, using space, and filling time which surrounded these language learners." Her analysis humanizes the townspeople, children and adults, black and white, as she interprets the story of their literacy. *Ways with Words* catapulted Heath into national prominence and an abundance of awards and honors, including a prestigious five-year MacArthur Fellowship.

Concepts of print

Newspapers, car brochures, advertisements, church materials, and homework and official information from school come into Trackton every day. In addition, there are numerous other rather more permanent reading materials in the community: boxes and cans of food products, house numbers, car names and license numbers, calendars and telephone dials, written messages on television, and name brands which are part of refrigerators, stoves, bicycles, and tools. There are few magazines, except those borrowed from the church, no books except school books, the Bible, and Sunday School lesson books, and a photograph album. Just as Trackton parents do not buy special toys for their young children, they do not buy books for them either; adults do not create reading and writing tasks for the young, nor do they consciously model or demonstrate reading and writing behaviors for them. In the home, on the plaza, and in the neighborhood, children are left to find their own reading and writing tasks: distinguishing one television channel from another, knowing the name brands of cars, motorcycles and bicycles, choosing one or another can of soup or cereal, reading price tags at Mr. Dogan's store to be sure they do not pay more than they would at the supermarket.

The receipt of mail in Trackton is a big event, and since several houses are residences for transients the postman does not know, the children sometimes take the mail and give it to the appropriate person. Reading names and addresses and return addresses becomes a game-like challenge among all the children, as the school-age try to show the preschoolers how they know "what dat says."

Preschool and school-age children alike frequently ask what something "says," or how it "goes," and adults respond to their queries, making their instructions fit the requirements of the tasks. Sometimes they help with especially hard or unexpected items, and they always correct errors of fact if they hear them. When Lem, Teegie, and other children in Trackton were about two years of age, I initiated the game of reading traffic signs when we were out in the car. Lillie Mae seemed to pay little attention to this game, until one of the children made an error. If Lem termed a "Yield" sign "Stop," she corrected him, saying, "Dat ain't no stop, dat say yield; you have to give the other fellow the right of way." Often the children would read names of fastfood chains as we drove by. Once when one had changed names, and Teegie read the old name, Tony corrected him: "It ain't Chicken Delight no more; it Famous Recipe now." When the children were preparing to go to school, they chose book bags, tee shirts, and stickers for their notebooks which carried messages. Almost all the older boys and girls in the community wore tee shirts with writings scrawled across the front, and the children talked about what these said and vied to have the most original and sometimes the most suggestive.

Reading was a public group affair for almost all members of 3 Trackton from the youngest to the oldest. Miss Lula sometimes read her Bible alone, and Annie Mae would sometimes quietly read magazines she brought home, but to read alone was frowned upon, and individuals who did so were accused of being antisocial. Aunt Berta had a son who as a child used to slip away from the cotton field and read under a tree. He is now a grown man with children, and he has obtained a college degree, but the community still tells tales about his peculiar boyhood habits of wanting to go off and read alone. In general, reading alone, unless one is very old and religious, marks an individual as someone who cannot make it socially.

Jointly or in group affairs, the children of Trackton *read to learn* 4 before they go to school to *learn to read*. The modification of old or broken toys and their incorporation with other items to create a new toy is a common event. One mastermind, usually Tony, announces the idea, and all the children help collect items and contribute ideas. On some of these occasions, such as when one of the boys wants to modify his bicylce for a unique effect, he has to read selectively portions of brochures on bicycles and instructions for tool sets. Reading is almost always set within a context of immediate action: one needs to read a letter's addresss to prove to the mailman that one should be given the envelope; one must read the price of a bag of coal at Mr. Dogan's store to make the decision to purchase or not. Trackton children are sent to the store almost as soon as they can walk, and since they are told to "watch out for Mr. Dogan's prices," they must learn to read price changes there from week to week for commonly purchased items and remember them for comparisons with prices in the supermarket. As early as age four, Teegie, Lem, Gary, and Gary B. could scan the price tag, which might contain several separate pieces of information, on familiar items and pick out the price. The decimal point and the predictability of the number of numerals which would be included in the price were clues which helped the children search each tag for only those portions meaningful to their decision-making.

Children remember and reassociate the contexts of print. When   5 they see a brand name, particular sets of numbers, or a particular logo, they often recall when and with whom they first saw it, or they call attention to how the occasion for this new appearance is not like the previous one. Slight shifts in print styles, and decorations of mascots used to advertise products, or alterations of written slogans are noticed by Trackton children. Once they have been in a supermarket to buy a loaf of bread, they remember on subsequent trips the location of the bread section and the placement of the kind of "light bread" their family eats. They seem to remember the scene and staging of print, so that upon recalling print they visualize the physical context in which it occurred and the reasons for reading it: that is, what it was they wanted to learn from reading a certain item or series of items. They are not tutored in these skills by adults of the community, but they are given numerous graded tasks from a very early age and are provided with older children who have learned to read to perform the tasks their daily life requires. Young children watch others read and write for a variety of purposes, and they have numerous opportunities for practice under the indirect supervision of older children, so that they come to use print independently and to be able to model appropriate behaviors for younger children coming up behind them.

The dependence on a strong sense of visual imagery often pre-   6 vented efficient transfer of skills learned in one context to another. All of the toddlers knew the name brands and names of cereals as they appeared on the boxes or in advertisements. Kellogg's was always written in script—the name of the cereal (raisin bran, etc) in all capital letters. On Nabisco products, Nabisco was written in small capitals and the cereal name in capital letters as well. I was curious to know whether or not the children "read" the names or whether they recognized the shapes of the boxes and the artwork on the boxes when they correctly identified the cereals. I cut out the name brands and cereal names and put them on plain cardboard of different sizes, and asked the children to read the names. After an initial period of hesitation, most of the children could read the newly placed names. All of the children could do so by age three. When they were between three and four, I cut out the printed letters from the cereal names to spell Kellogg's in small capitals and otherwise arranged the information on the plain cardboard as it appeared on the cereal boxes. The children volunteered the name of the cereal, but did not immediately read Kellogg's now that it was no longer in the familiar script. When I asked them to read it, they looked puzzled, said it look "funny," and they were not sure what it was. When I pointed out to them that the print small-capital K was another way of writing the script K, they watched with interest as I did the same for the rest of the letters. They were dubious about the script e and the print E being "the same," but they became willing to accept that what configured on the box also configured on the paper, though in some different ways.

Gradually we developed a game of "rewriting" the words they could read, shifting from script to all capitals, and from all capitals to initial capitals and subsequent small letters for individual words. It was always necessary to do this by moving from the known mental picture and "reading" of the terms (i.e. the script Kellogg's) to the unknown or unfamiliar (rendering of Kellogg's in small print capitals). Once shown they already "knew" the item, they accepted that they could "know" these items in new contexts and shapes. We continued this type of game with many of the items from their daily life they already knew how to read. When I first wrote house numbers just as they appeared on the house on a piece of notebook paper, the three- and four-year-olds said they could not read it; if I varied slightly the shape of the numerals on the notebook paper, they also did not read the numbers. Once comparisons and differences were pointed out, they recognized that they already "knew" how to read what had seemed like strange information to them on the notebook paper. Using the "real" print and my re-created print in a metaphorical way provided a bridge from the known to the unknown which allowed the children to use their familiar rules for recognition of print. They transferred their own daily operations as successful readers in an interactive way to pencil-and-paper tasks which were not immediately relevant in the community context.

Their strong tendency to visualize how print looked in its surrounding context was revealed when I asked the three- and four-year-old children to "draw" house doors, newspapers, soup cans, and a letter they would write to someone. Figure 1 illustrates how Gary's

Letter (Mel: 4 years)

Newspaper (Gary: 4 years, 6 months)

Soup can
(Mel: 4 years)

Figure 1. Preschool concepts of print

representation of a newspaper shows that he knew the letters of headlines were bigger than what came below, and that what was below was organized in straight lines. Moreover, the "headline" near the bottom of the page is smaller than that at the top. Mel writes a "letter" which includes the date, salutation, body, closing, and signature. His "letter" is somewhat atypical, but, since Mel's mother, a transient, wrote frequently to her family up-North, he had numerous opportunities to see letters. None of the other preschoolers provided any of the components of a letter other than body and signature. Mel, however, not only indicates several parts, but also scatters some alphabet letters through the body, and signs his name. Mel also "drew" a soup can, making its name brand biggest, and schematically representing the product information and even what I take to be the vertical pricing and inventory information for computerized checking at the bottom of the can. When asked to "read" what they had written, some giggled, others asked older brothers and sisters to do it and some "read" their writing, explaining its context. Mel's reading of his letter was prefaced by "Now I send you dis letter." Then he read "Dear Miz Hea, bring me a truck we go to Hardee's, Mel." Everyone giggled with Mel who enjoyed the joke of having written what he so often said orally to me. His rendering contained only the primary message, not the date or his letter's closing. It is doubtful that Mel knew what went in these slots, since when I asked him if he had read those parts to me, he shrugged his shoulders and said "I dunno." Trackton children had learned before school that they could read to learn, and they had developed expectancies of print. The graphic and everyday life contexts of writing were often critical to their interpretation of the meaning of print, for print to them was not isolated bits and pieces of lines and circles, but messages with varying internal structures, purposes, and uses. For most of these, oral communication surrounded the print.

"Talk is the thing"

In almost every situation in Trackton in which a piece of writing 9 is integral to the nature of the participants' interactions and their interpretations of meaning, talk is a necessary component. Knowing which box of cereal is Kellogg's raisin bran does little good without announcing that choice to older brothers and sisters helping pour the cereal. Knowing the kind of bicycle tire and tube on one's old bike is translated into action only at Mr. Green's bicycle shop or with a friend who has an old bike he is not using. Certain types of talk describe, repeat, reinforce, frame, expand, and even contradict written materials, and children in Trackton learn not only how to read print, but also when and how to surround the print in their lives with appropriate talk. For them there are far more occasions in the community which call for appropriate knowledge of forms and uses of talk around or about writing, then there are actual occasions for reading and writing extended connected discourse.

For Trackton adults, reading is a social activity; when something is read in Trackton, it almost always provokes narratives, jokes, side-tracking talk, and active negotiation of the meaning of written texts among the listeners. Authority in the written word does not rest in the words themselves, but in the meanings which are negotiated through the experiences of the group. The evening newspaper is read on the front porch for most months of the year. The obituaries on the back page are usually read first, followed by employment listings, advertisements for grocery and department store sales, and captions beneath pictures and headlines. An obituary is read for some trace of acquaintance with either the deceased, his relatives, place of birth, church, or school; active discussion follows about who the individual was and who he might have known. Circulars or letters to individuals regarding the neighborhood center and its recreational or medical services are read aloud and their meanings jointly negotiated by those who have had experience with such activities or know about the forms to be filled out to be eligible for such services. Neighbors share stories of what they did or what happened to them in similar circumstances. One day when Lillie Mae had received a letter about a daycare program, several neighbors were sitting on porches, working on cars nearby, or sweeping their front yards. Lillie Mae came out on her front porch, read the first paragraph of a letter, and announced:

TRACKTON TEXT X

Lillie Mae:	You hear this, it says Lem [then two years old] might can get into Ridgeway [a local neighborhood center daycare program], but I hafta have the papers ready and apply by next Friday.
Visiting friend:	You ever been to Kent to get his birth certificate? [friend is mother of three children already in school]
Mattie Crawford:	But what hours that program gonna be? You may not can get him there.
Lillie Mae:	They want the birth certificate? I got his vaccination papers.
Annie Mae:	Sometimes they take that, 'cause they can 'bout tell the age from those early shots.
Visiting friend:	But you better get it, 'cause you gotta have it when he go to school anyway.
Lillie Mae:	But it says here they don't know what hours yet. How am I gonna get over to Kent? How much does it cost? Lemme see if the program costs anything. (She reads aloud part of the letter.)

Conversation on various parts of the letter continued for nearly an hour, while neighbors and Lillie Mae pooled their knowledge of the pros and cons of such programs. They discussed ways of getting rides to Kent, the county seat thirty miles away, to which all mothers had to go to get their children's birth certificates to prove their age at school entrance. The question "What does this mean?" was answered not only from the information in print, but from the group's joint bringing of experience to the text. Lillie Mae, reading aloud, decoded the written text, but her friends and neighbors interpreted the text's meaning through their own experiences. The experience of any one individual had to become common to the group, however, and that was done through the recounting of members' experiences. Such recounting re-created scenes, embellished the truth, illustrated the character of the individuals involved, and to the greatest extent possible brought the audience into the experience itself. Beyond these recountings of episodes (such as one mother's efforts to get her doctor to give her "papers" to verify her son's age), there was a reintegration of these now commonly shared experiences with the text itself. After the reading episode, Lillie Mae had to relate the text's meaning to the experiences she had heard shared, and she checked out this final synthesis of meaning for her with some of the group. Some members did not care about this final synthesis and had wandered off, satisfied to have told their stories, but others commented that they thought her chosen course of action the right one, and her understanding of the letter to fit their interpretations.

About the only material not delivered for group negotiation is 11 that which involves private finances or information which members feel might somehow give them an opportunity their neighbors do not have. A postcard from a local mill announcing days on which the mill will be accepting new employment applications will not be shared aloud, but kept secret because of the competition for jobs. On the other hand, a newspaper story about the expansion of the mill will be read aloud, and all will pool information in general terms.

Tables 1 and 2 show that the uses of writing and reading in the 12

Table 1. Types of uses of reading in Trackton

INSTRUMENTAL:	Reading to accomplish practical goals of daily life (price tags, checks, bills, telephone dials, clocks, street signs, house numbers).
SOCIAL-INTERACTIONAL/ RECREATIONAL:	Reading to maintain social relationships, make plans, and introduce topics for discussion and story-telling (greeting cards, cartoons, letters, newspaper features, political flyers, announcements of community meetings).
NEWS-RELATED:	Reading to learn about third parties or distant events (local news items, circulars from the community center or school).
CONFIRMATIONAL:	Reading to gain support for attitudes or beliefs already held (Bible, brochures on cars, loan notes, bills).

Note. Listed in relative order of frequency of occasions when time on these types of tasks exceeded five minutes per day.

community are multiple, though there are few occasions for reading of extended connected discourse and almost no occasions for writing such material, except by those school children who diligently try to complete their homework assignments. Foremost among the types of uses of reading and writing are those which are *instrumental*. Adults and children read what they have to read to solve practical problems of daily life: price tags, traffic signs, house numbers, bills, checks. Other uses are perhaps not as critical to problem-solving, but *social-interactional* uses give information relevant to social relations and contacts with persons not in Trackton's primary group. Some write letters; many send greeting cards; almost all read bumper stickers, newspaper obituaries and features, and church news bulletins. Other types of reading and writing are *news-related*. From the local newspaper, political flyers, memos from the city offices, and circulars from the neighborhood center, Trackton residents learn information about local and distant events. They rarely read much more than headlines about distant events, since the evening news programs on television give them the same national or metropolitan news. Stories about the local towns are, however, read, because there is often no other source of information on happenings there. Some individuals in Trackton read for *confirmation*—to seek support for beliefs or ideas they already hold. Miss Lula reads the Bible. When the mayor maintains that one kind of car gets better mileage than another, and others disagree, he has to produce a brochure from a car dealer to prove his point. Children who become involved in boasts often called on written proof to confirm their lofty accounts of themselves or others. Every home has some permanent records—loan notes, tax forms, birth certificates—

Table 2. Types of uses of writing in Trackton

MEMORY AIDS: (primarily used by women)	Writing to serve as a reminder for the writer and, only occasionally, others (telephone numbers, notes on calendars).
SUBSTITUTES FOR ORAL MESSAGES: (primarily used by women)	Writing used when direct oral communication was not possible or would prove embarrassing (notes for tardiness or absence from school, greeting cards, letters).
FINANCIAL:	Writing to record numerals and to write out amounts and accompanying notes (signatures on checks and public forms, figures and notes for income tax preparation).
PUBLIC RECORDS: (church only)	Writing to announce the order of the church services and forthcoming events and to record financial and policy decisions (church bulletins, reports of the church building fund committee).

Note. Listed in relative order of frequency of occasions when time on these types of tasks exceeded five minutes per day.

which families keep, but can rarely find when they are needed. However, if they can be found and are read, they can confirm an oral statement.

The most frequent occasions for writing are those when Trackton 13
family members say they cannot trust their memory *(memory-supportive)*, or they have to write to *substitute for an oral message.* Beside the telephone, women write frequently called numbers and addresses; they tack calendars on the kitchen wall and add notes reminding them of dates for their children's vaccinations and the school holidays, etc. Some few women in the community write letters. Lillie Mae often writes relatives up-North to invite them to come home and to thank them for bringing presents. Women sometimes have to write notes to school about children's absences or tardiness or to request a local merchant to extend credit a few weeks longer. Men almost never write except to sign their paychecks, public forms, and to collect information for income tax preparation. One exception in Trackton is the mayor who meets once a month with a group of other church members to prepare Sunday church bulletins as well as to handle business related to the building fund or to plan for revival meetings. These written materials are negotiated cooperatively at the meetings; no individual takes sole responsibility.

Community literacy activities are public and social. Written in- 14
formation almost never stands alone in Trackton. It is reshaped and reworded into an oral mode by adults and children who incorporate chunks of the written text in their talk. They often reflect their own awareness that print imposes a different kind of organization on written materials than talk does. Literacy events in Trackton which bring the written word into a central focus in interactions and interpretations have their rules of occurrence and appropriateness, just as talking junk, fussing, or performing a playsong do. The group activities of reading the newspaper across porches, debating the power of a new car, or discussing the city's plans to bring in earthmoving equipment to clear lots behind the community, produce more speaking than reading, more group than individual effort. There are repeated metaphors, comparisons, and fast-paced, overlapping language as Trackton residents move from print to what it means in their lives. On some occasions, they attend to the text itself; on others, they use it only as a starting point for wide-ranging talk. On all occasions, they bring in knowledge related to the text and interpret beyond the text for their own context; in so doing, they achieve a new synthesis of information from the text and the joint experiences of community members.

RESPONDING TO READING

Key words: class community education family freedom
growing up language reading talking writing

Rhetorical concepts: analysis anecdote cause and effect
explanation illustration definition induction
narrative/example process research report

1. What is your own definition of "literacy"? What is Heath's? How does
your concept of the subject relate to Heath's definition of the term? Which
definition is more open, inclusive? What are the advantages and disadvantages of defining "literacy" as Heath does?
2. How are speaking, reading, and writing interrelated as a Trackton child
(or adult) becomes literate?
3. What sorts of evidence does Heath include to illustrate her discussion?
How does her involvement as a friend to the Trackton people enhance her
collection of information and her credibility as an interpreter of it?
4. In what ways did your own development as a literate person follow the
Trackton pattern? In what ways has it been different? If you are continuing
to develop your own literacy in ways not covered by Heath's focus—such as
the literacy demanded by using computers or doing college work in particular
disciplines, explain the process(es). How do you know when you have become
fluent?
5. If literacy is an ongoing process, what circumstances and conditions
impede, interrupt, or stop it (see Walker, Rose, Wiesel)? Can these, short of
death, be reversed? How? For examples, consult your own experiences and
any or all of these essays.

Aria: Memoir of a Bilingual Childhood

RICHARD RODRIGUEZ

Richard Rodriguez was born in San Francisco in 1944, the son of
Mexican immigrants. His writing often uses the example of his own
life to argue against bilingual education and to question affirmative
action. In "Aria: Memoir of a Bilingual Childhood," from his autobiography *Hunger of Memory: The Education of Richard Rodriguez* (1982),
Rodriguez focuses on the double burden of expulsion from the Eden
of his warm and loving Spanish-speaking family and integration into
the wider, harsher public world of English-speaking American life.
Although to speak English was to become remote from his parents
and estranged from their culture, it was not too high a price to pay,
he argues, for obtaining public identity in the mainstream culture—
an identity reinforced in Rodriguez's case by a Ph.D. in Renaissance
literature from the University of California at Berkeley.

Known to his family as "Mr. Secrets," Rodriguez, now an educational consultant and free-lance writer, comments on the self he presents in *Hunger of Memory:* "Autobiography is simply one version of a life. The woman who runs the cheese store on California Street used to say, 'I know all about you because I've read your autobiography.' But in fact, she *doesn't* know all about me. What is on those pages is a very selective and a very partial view of who I am. Many times readers of autobiography forget how much is missing. Writers withhold as much as they tell."

Supporters of bilingual education today imply that students like   1
me miss a great deal by not being taught in their family's language. What they seem not to recognize is that, as a socially disadvantaged child, I considered Spanish to be a private language. What I needed to learn in school was that I had the right—and the obligation—to speak the public language of *los gringos.* The odd truth is that my first-grade classmates could have become bilingual, in the conventional sense of that word, more easily than I. Had they been taught (as upper-middle-class children are often taught early) a second language like Spanish or French, they could have regarded it simply as that: another public language. In my case such bilingualism could not have been so quickly achieved. What I did not believe was that I could speak a single public language.

Without question, it would have pleased me to hear my teachers   2
address me in Spanish when I entered the classroom. I would have felt much less afraid. I would have trusted them and responded with ease. But I would have delayed—for how long postponed?—having to learn the language of public society. I would have evaded—and for how long could I have afforded to delay?—learning the great lesson of school, that I had a public identity.

Fortunately, my teachers were unsentimental about their respon-   3
sibility. What they understood was that I needed to speak a public language. So their voices would search me out, asking me questions. Each time I'd hear them, I'd look up in surprise to see a nun's face frowning at me. I'd mumble, not really meaning to answer. The nun would persist, 'Richard, stand up. Don't look at the floor. Speak up. Speak to the entire class, not just to me!' But I couldn't believe that the English language was mine to use. (In part, I did not want to believe it.) I continued to mumble. I resisted the teacher's demands. (Did I somehow suspect that once I learned public language my pleasing family life would be changed?) Silent, waiting for the bell to sound, I remained dazed, diffident, afraid.

Because I wrongly imagined that English was intrinsically a public   4
language and Spanish an intrinsically private one, I easily noted the difference between classroom language and the language of home.

At school, words were directed to a general audience of listeners. ('Boys and girls.') Words were meaningfully ordered. And the point was not self-expression alone but to make oneself understood by many others. The teacher quizzed: 'Boys and girls, why do we use that word in this sentence? Could we think of a better word to use there? Would the sentence change its meaning if the words were differently arranged? And wasn't there a better way of saying much the same thing?' (I couldn't say. I wouldn't try to say.)

Three months. Five. Half a year passed. Unsmiling, ever watchful, my teachers noted my silence. They began to connect my behavior with the difficult progress my older sister and brother were making. Until one Saturday morning three nuns arrived at the house to talk to our parents. Stiffly, they sat on the blue living room sofa. From the doorway of another room, spying the visitors, I noted the incongruity—the clash of two worlds, the faces and voices of school intruding upon the familiar setting of home. I overheard one voice gently wondering, 'Do your children speak only Spanish at home, Mrs. Rodriguez?' While another voice added, 'That Richard especially seems so timid and shy.'

That Rich-heard!

With great tact the visitors continued, 'Is it possible for you and your husband to encourage your children to practice their English when they are home?' Of course, my parents complied. What would they not do for their children's well-being? And how could they have questioned the Church's authority which those women represented? In an instant, they agreed to give up the language (the sounds) that had revealed and accentuated our family's closeness. The moment after the visitors left, the change was observed. '*Ahora,* speak to us *en inglés,*' my father and mother united to tell us.

At first, it seemed a kind of game. After dinner each night, the family gathered to practice 'our' English. (It was still then *inglés,* a language foreign to us, so we felt drawn as strangers to it.) Laughing, we would try to define words we could not pronounce. We played with strange English sounds, often overanglicizing our pronunciations. And we filled the smiling gaps of our sentences with familiar Spanish sounds. But that was cheating, somebody shouted. Everyone laughed. In school, meanwhile, like my brother and sister, I was required to attend a daily tutoring session. I needed a full year of special attention. I also needed my teachers to keep my attention from straying in class by calling out, *Rich-heard*—their English voices slowly prying loose my ties to my other name, its three notes, *Ri-car-do*. Most of all I needed to hear my mother and father speak to me in a moment of seriousness in broken—suddenly heartbreaking—English. The scene was inevitable: One Saturday morning I entered the kitchen where my parents were talking in Spanish. I did not realize that they were talking in Spanish however until, at the moment they saw me, I heard their voices change to speak English. Those *gringo* sounds they uttered startled me. Pushed me away. In that moment of trivial misunderstanding and profound insight, I felt my throat twisted by unsounded grief. I turned quickly and left the room. But I had no place to escape to with Spanish. (The spell was broken.) My brother and sisters were speaking English in another part of the house.

Again and again in the days following, increasingly angry, I was   9
obliged to hear my mother and father: 'Speak to us *en inglés.' (Speak.)* Only then did I determine to learn classroom English. Weeks after, it happened: One day in school I raised my hand to volunteer an answer. I spoke out in a loud voice. And I did not think it remarkable when the entire class understood. That day, I moved very far from the disadvantaged child I had been only days earlier. The belief, the calming assurance that I belonged in public, had at last taken hold.

Shortly after, I stopped hearing the high and loud sounds of *los*   10
gringos. A more and more confident speaker of English, I didn't trouble to listen to *how* strangers sounded, speaking to me. And there simply were too many English-speaking people in my day for me to hear American accents anymore. Conversations quickened. Listening to persons who sounded eccentrically pitched voices, I usually noted their sounds for an initial few seconds before I concentrated on *what* they were saying. Conversations became content-full. Transparent. Hearing someone's *tone* of voice—angry or questioning or sarcastic or happy or sad—I didn't distinguish it from the words it expressed. Sound and word were thus tightly wedded. At the end of a day, I was often bemused, always relieved, to realize how 'silent,' though crowded with words, my day in public had been. (This public silence measured and quickened the change in my life.)

At last, seven years old, I came to believe what had been tech-   11
nically true since my birth: I was an American citizen.

But the special feeling of closeness at home was diminished by   12
then. Gone was the desperate, urgent, intense feeling of being at home; rare was the experience of feeling myself individualized by family intimates. We remained a loving famly, but one greatly changed. No longer so close; no longer bound tight by the pleasing and troubling knowledge of our public separateness. Neither my older brother nor sister rushed home after school anymore. Nor did I. When I arrived home there would often be neighborhood kids in the house. Or the house would be empty of sounds.

Following the dramatic Americanization of their children, even   13
my parents grew more publicly confident. Especially my mother. She learned the names of all the people on our block. And she decided

we needed to have a telephone installed in the house. My father continued to use the word *gringo*. But it was no longer charged with the old bitterness or distrust. (Stripped of any emotional content, the word simply became a name for those Americans not of Hispanic descent.) Hearing him, sometimes, I wasn't sure if he was pronouncing the Spanish word *gringo* or saying gringo in English.

Matching the silence I started hearing in public was a new quiet 14 at home. The family's quiet was partly due to the fact that, as we children learned more and more English, we shared fewer and fewer words with our parents. Sentences needed to be spoken slowly when a child addressed his mother or father. (Often the parent wouldn't understand.) The child would need to repeat himself. (Still the parent misunderstood.) The young voice, frustrated, would end up saying, 'Never mind'—the subject was closed. Dinners would be noisy with the clinking of knives and forks against dishes. My mother would smile softly between her remarks; my father at the other end of the table would chew and chew at his food, while he stared over the heads of his children.

My mother! My father! After English became my primary language, 15 I no longer knew what words to use in addressing my parents. The old Spanish words (those tender accents of sound) I had used earlier— *mamá* and *papá*—I couldn't use anymore. They would have been too painful reminders of how much had changed in my life. On the other hand, the words I heard neighborhood kids call *their* parents seemed equally unsatisfactory. *Mother* and *Father; Ma, Papa, Pa, Dad, Pop* (how I hated the all-American sound of that last word especially)—all these terms I felt were unsuitable, not really terms of address for *my* parents. As a result, I never used them at home. Whenever I'd speak to my parents, I would try to get their attention with eye contact alone. In public conversations, I'd refer to 'my parents' or 'my mother and father.'

My mother and father, for their part, responded differently, as 16 their children spoke to them less. She grew restless, seemed troubled and anxious at the scarcity of words exchanged in the house. It was she who would question me about my day when I came home from school. She smiled at small talk. She pried at the edges of my sentences to get me to say something more. (What?) She'd join conversations she overheard, but her intrusions often stopped her children's talking. By contrast, my father seemed reconciled to the new quiet. Though his English improved somewhat, he retired into silence. At dinner he spoke very little. One night his children and even his wife helplessly giggled at his garbled English pronunciation of the Catholic Grace before Meals. Thereafter he made his wife recite the prayer at the start of each meal, even on formal occasions, when there were guests in the house. Hers became the public voice of the family. On official business, it was she, not my father, one would usually hear on the phone or in stores, talking to strangers. His children grew so accustomed to his silence that, years later, they would speak routinely of his shyness. (My mother would often try to explain: Both his parents died when he was eight. He was raised by an uncle who treated him like little more than a menial servant. He was never encouraged to speak. He grew up alone. A man of few words.) But my father was not shy, I realized, when I'd watch him speaking Spanish with relatives. Using Spanish, he was quickly effusive. Especially when talking with other men, his voice would spark, flicker, flare alive with sounds. In Spanish, he expressed ideas and feelings he rarely revealed in English. With firm Spanish sounds, he conveyed confidence and authority English would never allow him.

The silence at home, however, was finally more than a literal 17 silence. Fewer words passed between parent and child, but more profound was the silence that resulted from my inattention to sounds. At about the time I no longer bothered to listen with care to the sounds of English in public, I grew careless about listening to the sounds family members made when they spoke. Most of the time I heard someone speaking at home and didn't distinguish his sounds from the words people uttered in public. I didn't even pay much attention to my parents' accented and ungrammatical speech. At least not at home. Only when I was with them in public would I grow alert to their accents. Though, even then, their sounds caused me less and less concern. For I was increasingly confident of my own public identity.

I would have been happier about my public success had I not 18 sometimes recalled what it had been like earlier, when my family had conveyed its intimacy through a set of conveniently private sounds. Sometimes in public, hearing a stranger, I'd hark back to my past. A Mexican farmworker approached me downtown to ask directions to somewhere. '¿Hijito . . . ?' he said. And his voice summoned deep longing. Another time, standing beside my mother in the visiting room of a Carmelite convent, before the dense screen which rendered the nuns shadowy figures, I heard several Spanish-speaking nuns— their busy, singsong overlapping voices—assure us that yes, yes, we were remembered, all our family was remembered in their prayers. (Their voices echoed faraway family sounds.) Another day, a dark-faced old woman—her hand light on my shoulder—steadied herself against me as she boarded a bus. Her Spanish voice came near, like the face of a never-before-seen relative in the instant before I was kissed. Her voice, like so many of the Spanish voices I'd hear in public, recalled the golden age of my youth. Hearing Spanish then, I continued to be a careful, if sad, listener to sounds. Hearing a Spanish-speaking family walking behind me, I turned to look. I smiled for an instant, before my glance found the Hispanic-looking faces of strangers in the crowd going by.

RESPONDING TO READING

Key words: community discovery education family growing up
identity language loss memory minority race striving
talk transformation

Rhetorical concepts: anecdote autobiography comparison and contrast
illustration meditation narrative/example

1. What distinctions does Rodriguez make between private and public language? How do his quotations, in dialogue and dialect, reinforce his point?
2. Rodriguez says, "At last, seven years old, I came to believe what had been technically true since my birth: I was an American citizen." [paragraph 11] What does "citizenship" mean for Rodriguez? How is it related to bilingualism?
3. What is the effect of the bilingualism of the Rodriguez children on their home life? On their parents? What does Rodriguez think of the dilution or subduing of their Hispanic culture? How convincing is his interpretation?
4. In his outspoken opposition to bilingual education, Rodriguez has publicly and consistently advocated monolingualism in the schools. How does "Aria" reinforce his stance? Do you agree? Why or why not?
5. Rodriguez, like many other authors, uses himself and examples from his own life as evidence for an argument, here concerning the education that he would like applied to the entire bilingual student population. To what extent is Rodriguez, or any author, justified in using this technique? How convincing is it here? In other writings?
6. Like many authors writing about their childhoods, Rodriguez re-creates himself as a child character who changes over time in his narrative. To better understand this technique, try to make a point presenting your childhood self as a character in an incident that you narrate from your current perspective. How does language shape your identity?

The Need to Say It

PATRICIA HAMPL

Home for Patricia Hampl is St. Paul, Minnesota, where she was born in 1946. She earned a B.A. from the University of Minnesota in 1968, an M.F.A. from the University of Iowa in 1970, and has published two volumes of poetry, *Woman Before an Aquarium* (1978) and *Resort and Other Poems* (1983). She currently teaches English at her alma mater, though foreign travel, particularly in her ancestral homeland of Czechoslovakia, provides an international, often Old World, perspective. Conscious of her preoccupation with the past, she says, "I suppose I write about all the things I intended to leave behind, to grow out of, or deny: being a Midwesterner, a Catholic, a woman." The self she creates in her autobiography, *A Romantic Education* (1981), is the very embodiment of these characteristics.

In "The Need to Say It," first published in Janet Sternburg's *The Writer on Her Work* (Volume II, 1991), Hampl defends the writing of memoir as a way to present the truth of a life—not the literal truth, for memoir represents "the inevitable tango of memory and imagination," but a truth that incorporates a melding of the personal and public realms. Memoir, she says, "is not about the past, not a matter of nostalgia"; rather, it is rooted in despair and protest. Although we may despair that "all things die," whole civilizations as well as individuals, we can protest by translating what is vanishing into stories. When those stories are written from the choral voice of a nation, they become history; written from a personal voice, they become memoir. For Hampl, memoir combines traits of both fiction and the essay, and belongs to both the personal world and the public realm. Memoir transforms the self into history.

My Czech grandmother hated to see me with a book. She snatched 1 it away if I sat still too long (dead to her), absorbed in my reading. "Bad for you," she would say, holding the loathsome thing behind her back, furious at my enchantment.

She kept her distance from the printed word of English, but she 2 lavished attention on her lodge newspaper which came once a month, written in the quaint nineteenth-century Czech she and her generation had brought to America before the turn of the century. Like wedding cake saved from the feast, this language, over the years, had become a fossil, still recognizable but no longer something to be put in the mouth.

Did she read English? I'm not sure. I do know that she couldn't— 3 or didn't—write it. That's where I came in.

My first commissioned work was to write letters for her. "You 4 write for me, honey?" she would say, holding out a ballpoint she had been given at a grocery store promotion, clicking it like a castanet. My fee was cookies and milk, payable before, during, and after completion of the project.

I settled down at her kitchen table while she rooted around the 5 drawer where she kept coupons and playing cards and bank calendars. Eventually she located a piece of stationery and a mismatched envelope. She laid the small, pastel sheet before me, smoothing it out; a floral motif was clotted across the top of the page and bled down one side. The paper was so insubstantial even ballpoint ink seeped through to the other side. "That's okay," she would say. "We only need one side."

True. In life she was a gifted gossip, unfurling an extended riff 6 of chatter from a bare motif of rumor. But her writing style displayed a brevity that made Hemingway's prose look like nattering garrulity. She dictated her letters as if she were paying by the word.

"Dear Sister," she began, followed by a little time-buying cough 7 and throat-clearing. "We are all well here." Pause. "And hope you are well too." Longer pause, the steamy broth of inspiration heating up on her side of the table. Then, in a lurch, "Winter is hard so I don't get out much."

This was followed instantly by an unconquerable fit of envy: "Not 8 like you in California." Then she came to a complete halt, perhaps demoralized by this evidence that you can't put much on paper before you betray your secret self, try as you will to keep things civil.

She sat, she brooded, she stared out the window. She was locked 9 in the perverse reticence of composition. She gazed at me, but I understood she did not see me. She was looking for her next thought. "Read what I wrote," she would finally say, having lost not only what she was looking for but what she already had pinned down. I went over the little trail of sentences that led to her dead end.

More silence, then a sigh. She gave up the ghost. "Put 'God bless 10 you,'" she said. She reached across to see the lean rectangle of words on the paper. "Now leave some space," she said, "and put 'Love.'" I handed over the paper for her to sign.

She always asked if her signature looked nice. She wrote her one 11 word—Teresa—with a flourish. For her, writing was painting, a visual art, not declarative but sensuous.

She sent her lean documents regularly to her only remaining sister 12 who lived in Los Angeles, a place she had not visited. They had last seen each other as children in their village in Bohemia. But she never mentioned that or anything from that world. There was no taint of reminiscence in her prose.

Even at ten I was appalled by the minimalism of these letters. 13 They enraged me. "Is that all you have to say?" I would ask her, a nasty edge to my voice.

It wasn't long before I began padding the text. Without telling 14 her, I added an anecdote my father had told at dinner the night before, or I conducted this unknown reader through the heavy plot of my brother's attempt to make first string on the St. Thomas hockey team. I allowed myself a descriptive aria on the beauty of Minnesota winters (for the benefit of my California reader who might need some background material on the subject of ice hockey). A little of this, a little of that—there was always something I could toss into my grand-mother's meager soup to thicken it up.

Of course the protagonist of the hockey tale was not "my brother." 15 He was "my grandson." I departed from my own life without a regret and breezily inhabited my grandmother's.

I complained about my hip joint, I bemoaned the rising cost of 16 hamburger, I even touched on the loneliness of old age, and hinted at the inattention of my son's wife (that is, my own mother, who was next door, oblivious to treachery).

In time, my grandmother gave in to the inevitable. Without ever 17 discussing it, we understood that when she came looking for me, clicking her ballpoint, I was to write the letter, and her job was to keep the cookies coming. I abandoned her skimpy floral stationery, which badly cramped my style, and thumped down on the table a stack of ruled 8½ × 11.

"Just say something interesting," she would say. And I was off 18 to the races.

I took over her life in prose. Somewhere along the line, though, 19 she decided to take full possession of her sign-off. She asked me to show her how to write "Love" so she could add it to "Teresa" in her own hand. She practiced the new word many times on scratch paper before she allowed herself to commit it to the bottom of a letter.

But when she finally took the leap, I realized I had forgotten to 20 tell her about the comma. On a single slanting line she had written: *Love Teresa.* The words didn't look like a closure, but a command.

Write about what you know. This instruction from grade school was 21 the first bit of writing advice I was ever given. Terrific—that was just what I wanted to do. But privately, in a recess of my personality I could not gain access to by wish or by will, I was afraid this advice was a lie, concocted and disseminated nationwide by English teachers. The real, the secret, commandment was *Write about what matters.*

But they couldn't tell you that, I sensed, because nothing someone 22 like me had experienced in the environs of St. Luke's grade school in St. Paul, Minnesota, mattered to anybody, and such a commandment would bring the whole creaking apparatus of assignments and spell-ing tests crashing down. I was never able to convince myself that anyone wanted to know what I had done on my summer vacation. They were just counting on my being vain enough to be flattered into telling. And they were right. But I resented it; I resented having nothing—really—to write about.

Maybe I wouldn't have fretted over the standard composition 23 advice if I had valued my life in a simple way. Or rather, if I had valued the life around me. But literary types are born snobs, yearning for the social register of significance. And I was a literary kid from the get-go, falling into fairy tales and, later, enormous nineteenth-century novels as if into vats of imported heavy cream where I was perfectly content to drown.

I felt, I *believed*, my own life (and anything that touched it) was 24 just so much still water. You could drown there too, but to no purpose, anonymous as a gasp, flailing around without experiencing the luscious sinking that made life worthwhile—which was literature. I wrote about princesses and angels. I filled in the silences left in familiar Bible stories, making up a travelogue about the flight into Egypt, fleshing out the domestic arrangements of Martha and Mary with a little dialogue: "Don't you expect me to do those dishes, Martha," huffed Mary. "The Lord's on my side."

Later, I wrote about lesbians (though I wasn't one) and a de- 25 mented arsonist (though I was afraid to use my own fireplace at home). The beat went on: I was writing about things that mattered.

Later still, inevitably, I gave up, and wrote about my own life 26 after all, first in poems, and then in a memoir whose main figure was my Czech grandmother. She who commanded love.

What bedevils me about this brief history of my literary attempts 27 is that I ended up writing memoir (even the poems were routinely autobiographical), when that was the last thing I wanted to do. Wasn't it?

And as subplot to this conundum, how was it that I rattled on 28 with stories and descriptions of "what I knew" in those letters I wrote for my grandmother in her kitchen, and yet it never dawned on me that this was *writing*, that was *it*.

Put another way: how did I come to believe that *what I knew* was 29 also *what mattered?* And, more to the point for the future, *is* it what matters?

Maybe being oneself is always an acquired taste. For a writer it's 30 a big deal to bow—or kneel or get knocked down—to the fact that you are going to write your own books and not somebody else's. Not even those books of the somebody else you thought it was your express business to spruce yourself up to be.

The recognition of one's genuine material seems to involve a fall 31 from the phony grace of good intentions and elevated expectations. (I speak from experience, as memoirists are supposed to.)

A hush comes over the writing, an emotion akin to awe: so, 32 something just beyond my own intelligence seemed to whisper when I began writing about my grandmother's garden which I couldn't imagine anyone caring about, it isn't a matter of whether you *can* go home again. You just do. Language, that most ghostly kind of travel, hands out the tickets. It never occurred to me, once given my ticket, to refuse it.

Yet, it wasn't the ticket I wanted. I didn't want to go home, I 33 wanted to go—elsewhere. I wanted to write novels. Fat ones. Later, thinner ones—having moved from George Eliot to Virginia Woolf in my reading. But novels. About love and betrayal among grownup modern men and women who should have behaved better (I thought). An important subject (I believed). A subject not given its due by men writers (I attested).

Instead, I've written memoir. And, so far, precious little love and 34 betrayal of the sort I aspired to. Would that I could say that it's because I never experienced any betrayal along the way to or from love. But the equation between life and art hasn't proved to be so simple.

Still, I begin to see the elegance of a mathematical law in this 35 confusion of impulse and execution, of intention and finished product: the material I was determined to elude has claimed me, while the subjects I wished to enlist in my liberation have spurned me.

Shame seems to be an essential catalyst in the business. Item: 36 when I started college at the University in Minneapolis, I lost no time dumping the Catholic world my family had so carefully given me in St. Paul. In fact, that's why I went there: I understood many people had succeeded in losing their religion at the University. I didn't miss a beat turning down a scholarship at a Catholic college where I had been assured I would get more "individual attention." Who wanted individual attention? I wanted to be left alone to lose my soul.

For years, decades even, I considered it one solid accomplishment 37 that I had escaped the nuns. Result: I have spent the better part of five years writing a memoir about growing up Catholic, a book which has taken me for extended stays at several monasteries and Catholic shrines in Europe and America. The central character of the book: a contemplative nun, the very figure I was determined to dodge.

Item: I was ashamed (though I didn't know it, couldn't have called 38 it shame) that my Czech grandmother couldn't write English, that she was who she was at all. An immigrant is a quaint antecedent at a distance; mine was too close for the comfort of my literary ambition. The shame was real, disloyal, mean. Result: she came and got me, and became the heroine of my first memoir. She wrote it first: *Love Teresa*. And I did, finally.

RESPONDING TO READING

Key words: discovery education family growing up identity language memory transformation writing

Rhetorical concepts: anecdote   autobiography   definition   illustration
narrative/example

1.   Hampl says she has "written memoir." Examine what she has written
and notice the way she blends fact, analysis, and speculation about herself
and her writing; how would you define "memoir"? What other writing in
this book would also fit your definition?

2.   Does remembering invariably imply reinterpretation? Invention? How
does Hampl's writing (and gradually inventing) her grandmother's letters
address this issue?

3.   What kinds of successes does Hampl experience as she matures as a
human being and as a writer? What rebuffs and failures? Why does she have
"the need to say it"—and what determines her title?

4.   As Hampl does, use two or three incidents to tell the story of some aspect
of your development over time—as a writer, thinker, student, family member,
or whatever—like the stories of her early relationship with her grandmother.
Why should these stories matter to you? To your readers?

Being a Man

PAUL THEROUX

Paul Theroux presents himself in his numerous travel writings as a
man on the go but, paradoxically, at a leisurely pace for "the journey,
not the arrival, matters." Although he was born in Massachusetts
in 1941, earned a B.A. at the University of Massachusetts in 1961,
and still spends his summers on Cape Cod, he seems a citizen of
the world. After serving in the Peace Corps in Africa, he stayed
abroad as a lecturer in Malawi, Uganda, and Singapore from 1963
until 1970, and he has traveled worldwide ever since. In his numerous travel books, which range from *The Great Railway Bazaar: By
Train Through Asia* (1975), to *The Old Patagonian Express: By Train
Through the Americas* (1979), and *Riding the Iron Rooster: By Train
Through China* (1988), Theroux acknowledges playing the role of traveler with disguises and deceptions. He does so to give himself the
latitude to eavesdrop, spy, wheedle, and cajole revealing—often
damning—tidbits of information from the native populations.

The critical, artful self who narrates Theroux's travel writings also
appears in "Being a Man," which was first published in *Of Sunrise
and Sea Monsters* (1985). As usual, Theroux is critical of conventional
opinions, viewing the American quest for manliness as essentially
"puritanical, cowardly, neurotic and fueled largely by a fear of
women." Because stereotyped manliness is anti-intellectual, it is
particularly hard for an American man—especially one who doesn't
kill lions (like Ernest Hemingway), drink hard (like William Faulkner), or wrestle (like John Irving) to be a writer and be treated seriously.

There is a pathetic sentence in the chapter "Fetishism" in Dr. 1
Norman Cameron's book *Personality Development and Psychopathology*.
It goes, "Fetishists are nearly always men; and the commonest fetish
is a woman's shoe." I cannot read that sentence without thinking that
it is just one more awful thing about being a man—and perhaps it is
an important thing to know about us.

I have always disliked being a man. The whole idea of manhood 2
in America is pitiful, in my opinion. This version of masculinity is a
little like having to wear an ill-fitting coat for one's entire life (by
contrast, I imagine femininity to be an oppressive sense of nakedness).
Even the expression "Be a man!" strikes me as insulting and abusive.
It means: Be stupid, be unfeeling, obedient, soldierly and stop thinking. Man means "manly"—how can one think about men without
considering the terrible ambition of manliness? And yet it is part of
every man's life. It is a hideous and crippling lie; it not only insists
on difference and connives at superiority, it is also by its very nature
destructive—emotionally damaging and socially harmful.

The youth who is subverted, as most are, into believing in the 3
masculine ideal is effectively separated from women and he spends
the rest of his life finding women a riddle and a nuisance. Of course,
there is a female version of this male affliction. It begins with mothers
encouraging little girls to say (to other adults) "Do you like my new
dress?" In a sense, little girls are traditionally urged to please adults
with a kind of coquettishness, while boys are enjoined to behave like
monkeys towards each other. The nine-year-old coquette proceeds to
become womanish in a subtle power game in which she learns to be
sexually indispensable, socially decorative and always alert to a man's
sense of inadequacy.

Femininity—being lady-like—implies needing a man as witness and 4
seducer; but masculinity celebrates the exclusive company of men.
That is why it is so grotesque; and that is also why there is no manliness without inadequacy—because it denies men the natural friendship of women.

It is very hard to imagine any concept of manliness that does not 5
belittle women, and it begins very early. At an age when I wanted to
meet girls—let's say the treacherous years of thirteen to sixteen—I
was told to take up a sport, get more fresh air, join the Boy Scouts,
and I was urged not to read so much. It was the 1950s and if you
asked too many questions about sex you were sent to camp—boy's
camp, of course: the nightmare. Nothing is more unnatural or prison-
like than a boy's camp, but if it were not for them we would have no
Elks' Lodges, no pool rooms, no boxing matches, no Marines.

And perhaps no sports as we know them. Everyone is aware of 6
how few in number are the athletes who behave like gentlemen. Just

as high school basketball teaches you how to be a poor loser, the manly attitude towards sports seems to be little more than a recipe for creating bad marriages, social misfits, moral degenerates, sadists, latent rapists and just plain louts. I regard high school sports as a drug far worse than marijuana, and it is the reason that the average tennis champion, say, is a pathetic oaf.

Any objective study would find the quest for manliness essentially   7
right-wing, puritanical, cowardly, neurotic and fueled largely by a fear of women. It is also certainly philistine. There is no book-hater like a Little League coach. But indeed all the creative arts are obnoxious to the manly ideal, because at their best the arts are pursued by uncompetitive and essentially solitary people. It makes it very hard for a creative youngster, for any boy who expresses the desire to be alone seems to be saying that there is something wrong with him.

It ought to be clear by now that I have something of an objection   8
to the way we turn boys into men. It does not surprise me that when the President of the United States has his customary weekend off he dresses like a cowboy—it is both a measure of his insecurity and his willingness to please. In many ways, American culture does little more for a man than prepare him for modeling clothes in the L. L. Bean catalogue. I take this as a personal insult because for many years I found it impossible to admit to myself that I wanted to be a writer. It was my guilty secret, because being a writer was incompatible with being a man.

There are people who might deny this, but that is because the   9
American writer, typically, has been so at pains to prove his manliness that we have come to see literariness and manliness as mingled qualities. But first there was a fear that writing was not a manly profession—indeed, not a profession at all. (The paradox in American letters is that it has always been easier for a woman to write and for a man to be published.) Growing up, I had thought of sports as wasteful and humiliating, and the idea of manliness was a bore. My wanting to become a writer was not a flight from that oppressive role-playing, but I quickly saw that it was at odds with it. Everything in stereotyped manliness goes against the life of the mind. The Hemingway personality is too tedious to go into here, and in any case his exertions are well-known, but certainly it was not until this aberrant behavior was examined by feminists in the 1960s that any male writer dared question the pugnacity in Hemingway's fiction. All the bullfighting and arm wrestling and elephant shooting diminished Hemingway as a writer, but it is consistent with a prevailing attitude in American writing: one cannot be a male writer without first proving that one is a man.

It is normal in America for a man to be dismissive or even some   10 what apologetic about being a writer. Various factors make it easier. There is a heartiness about journalism that makes it acceptable—journalism is the manliest form of American writing and, therefore, the profession the most independent-minded women seek (yes, it is an illusion, but that is my point). Fiction-writing is equated with a kind of dispirited failure and is only manly when it produces wealth—money is masculinity. So is drinking. Being a drunkard is another assertion, if misplaced, of manliness. The American male writer is traditionally proud of his heavy drinking. But we are also a very literal-minded people. A man proves his manhood in America in old-fashioned ways. He kills lions, like Hemingway; or he hunts ducks, like Nathanael West; or he makes pronouncements like, "A man should carry enough knife to defend himself with," as James Jones once said to a *Life* interviewer. Or he says he can drink you under the table. But even tiny drunken William Faulkner loved to mount a horse and go fox hunting, and Jack Kerouac roistered up and down Manhattan in a lumberjack shirt (and spent every night of *The Subterraneans* with his mother in Queens). And we are familiar with the lengths to which Norman Mailer is prepared, in his endearing way, to prove that he is just as much a monster as the next man.

When the novelist John Irving was revealed as a wrestler, people 11 took him to be a very serious writer; and even a bubble reputation like Eric *(Love Story)* Segal's was enhanced by the news that he ran the marathon in a respectable time. How surprised we would be if Joyce Carol Oates were revealed as a sumo wrestler or Joan Didion active in pumping iron. "Lives in New York City with her three children" is the typical woman writer's biographical note, for just as the male writer must prove he has achieved a sort of muscular manhood, the woman writer—or rather her publicists—must prove her motherhood.

There would be no point in saying any of this if it were not 12 generally accepted that to be a man is somehow—even now in feminist-influenced America—a privilege. It is on the contrary an unmerciful and punishing burden. Being a man is bad enough; being manly is appalling (in this sense, women's lib has done much more for men than for women). It is the sinister silliness of men's fashions, and a clubby attitude in the arts. It is the subversion of good students. It is the so-called "Dress Code" of the Ritz-Carlton Hotel in Boston, and it is the institutionalized cheating in college sports. It is the most primitive insecurity.

And this is also why men often object to feminism but are afraid 13 to explain why: of course women have a justified grievance, but most men believe—and with reason—that their lives are just as bad.

RESPONDING TO READING

Key words: education   gender   growing up   identity   power
striving

Rhetorical concepts: comparison and contrast   definition   illustration
meditation   narrative/example

1.   Provide in your own words an extended definition of one of the gender-
related words Theroux discusses—masculine, male, man, manly, manliness,
female, femininity—identifying points of agreement or disagreement with
Theroux.
2.   What does it mean to you personally to be male or female?
3.   What connections does our culture make between sports and masculinity,
given the fact that many women also like sports and participate in them? To
what extent do sports provide a context for "male bonding"? What comparable contexts exist for "female bonding"?
4.   In America, is it really necessary to prove one's manhood, as Theroux
says? If so, how, in your opinion, should this be done? If not, why not? How
does one prove one's femininity?
5.   Write an essay on "coming of age" as either a human being, or as a man
or a woman. If you are writing about yourself, pick an incident crucial to
your maturation, explain it, and show why it was so important. Did you
recognize its importance beforehand, or only in retrospect? Was it meaningful
primarily to yourself, or did others (your family, your religious or social group)
recognize and acknowledge its significance as well? If so, in what ways?

QUESTIONS FOR REFLECTION AND WRITING

What Is My Physical Self?

1. In what ways do Kingston and Walker agree on what it means to be female? In what ways do they disagree?

2. Imagine a conversation about gender roles between Sanders and Walker. What points of agreement and disagreement would emerge? Where might they fail to understand each other? To what degree would their disagreements and misunderstandings be based on their sex? Their race? Their social class?

3. Imagine you have been transformed into someone of the opposite sex. What might it be like? How would it change who you are?

4. If you have had the experience of filling a role customarily played by someone of a different sex, age, cultural group, or social class, describe it and how it affected you. You might, for example, have been the only female in an all male class in engineering, or a middle-aged returning freshman in a class of eighteen-year-olds, or a college student working in construction.

5. We might see Ornstein and Thompson as arguing for the "self as brain," while both Mairs and Updike present the "self as body." Also notice the way the essays by Kingston, Walker, and Sanders present the self as largely determined by social constructions of class, sex, and race. Write an essay in which you define your own physical self, with reference to the approaches of these writers.

Who Am I in Relation to Others?

1. Compare the "virtues" in Franklin's list to the implied virtues in Donne's "Meditation." What do they have in common? Where do they differ? Whose list seems to you more virtuous? Why? What might Douglass say about Franklin's list?

2. Douglass and Rose both describe young men in deprived circumstances making decisions about their future. Why do the decisions turn out to be so different? Suppose Douglass were writing today: in what ways might his essay be different?

3. How does school affect a child's sense of who he or she is? Write an essay in which you evaluate the relationship between education and self-discovery.

4. Write an essay on who you are in relation to another person (such as a parent, grandparent, friend, lover, spouse, child, or boss), or in relation to a group (such as your family, living group, coworkers, or fellow citizens). To what extent does this relationship shape your personality, character, or development, either by enhancing or interfering with it? Are you "really" yourself in this context?

How Does My Writing Relate to My Self?

1. Most of us can "witness" important events in our own lives, occasions that either at the time seemed to be or in retrospect turn out to have been extraordinarily meaningful. As Wiesel does, tell the story of a significant experience—positive, negative, or a mixture— in a way that enables you to affirm who you are.

2. Try to remember how you learned to read and to write. What were the first words you read? Wrote? Compare your own experience to those Heath writes about in Trackton and show how your developing literacy related to your developing sense of self.

3. Compare Rodriguez's account of his growth through language, and the decline in family intimacy that occurred at the same time, with the essays by Heath and Hampl. To what degree is Rodriguez's experience special to second language learners, as opposed to the general experience of children educated beyond their parents' level?

4. Both Hampl and Theroux write about finding themselves as writers, defining who they are by their writing. Hampl's focus on the power of imagination may remind you of Walker, Douglass, Wiesel, and Rodriguez; Theroux's concern about sexual indentity may remind you of Kingston, Walker, and Sanders. Select two essays and write an essay showing how writers use words and their understanding of words as an important means of self-definition.

5. Recall how Hampl gradually embellished the letters she was writing for her grandmother, until she was finally inventing a great deal in order to tell a good story. Write about an experience you have had that reveals some important aspect of your personality, character, or values, for better or worse, to someone who does not know you. After you have finished, on the basis of what you have learned from this writing, discuss the following question as a supplement to your paper: In presenting themselves, to what extent can writers be trusted to tell the truth? The whole truth? What kind of truth: Literal? Psychological? Or some other kind entirely?

How Do I Know Who I Am?

1. Write an essay on some of the ways you have discovered who you are. Include at least one key aspect of your physical self, one important relationship to someone else, and your sense of who you are as a student and writer. What are the most essential elements of your personal image? What aspects do you see as permanent?

2. Tell about an important moment in your past that let you see clearly something about yourself that was, until that moment, obscure. Some writers call such a moment an "epiphany," an almost religious insight; others speak of the "aha!" experience, which reveals truth. Your writing will both capture the moment for yourself and help your audience see what you have seen.

2

How Do I Know
What I Know?

*A man woke up from a dream in which he dreamed he was
a cat, but could never be sure if he were a man who had
dreamt about being a cat or was actually a cat continuing
to dream of being a man. He drank some milk and went
about his business.*

PERSIAN FOLK TALE

Why Consider This Question?

If we are frank with ourselves, we are likely to admit that most
of our knowledge is a matter of believing as true what we have been
told to believe by those with more power or greater authority than
ourselves. As children, we tend to be content with such ways of
knowing. However, unless we look into how we have come to know
what we know, we forfeit our right to think independently and to
know things for ourselves.

What are the sources of our knowledge? While much of what we
know does indeed come from others—parents, books, teachers, and
so on—we also accumulate knowledge from other sources, such as
what Mary Belenky et al. call "just knowing," that is, an intuition
that we believe. We also trust the knowledge we derive from our own
observation and experience, which accumulate as we grow older. By
the time we enter college, most of us combine our own intuitions and
observation with what we have been taught. But sometimes what we
know conflicts directly with what someone else knows, or even with
other things that we know. Perhaps the science we learned in school
conflicts with the religion we absorbed at home, or the way we have
learned to treat the opposite sex turns out to be offensive to people

113

we admire. When conflicts occur, we need to question the adequacy of our sources of knowledge.

Where does intuition come from, and what do we do when our "just knowing" differs from the intuitions of someone else? We probably need to go beyond intuition to resolve the issues. Observation sometimes seems more reliable, since many of us like to believe that there is an objective reality "out there" that need only be recorded accurately in order to create knowledge. But not all observers wind up seeing the same things, and even those who see the same things sometimes interpret them differently. No authorities, intuitions, or observations are absolute or conclusive. We cannot really rest secure with what we know until we have thought about and assessed how we have come to know what we do and until we have come to terms with the problems that lie behind different ways of knowing.

We cannot, however, be forever waiting for final knowledge; we must live our lives. Perhaps the best we can do is to remain aware of the sources of our knowledge, whatever they may be, and to allow the possibility that new knowledge or new perspectives on old knowledge will arise. And then, like the dreamer in the Persian folk tale, we must still go about our business.

Our business, in this case, turns out to be reading and writing— our principal means of inquiry into problems. The readings that follow deal with the ways we come to know things. The first section presents some ways of thinking about thinking. The second section presents some ways of knowing specifically derived from the natural and social sciences. The third section asks us to understand the meaning of what we know of the past. Although we may not end the chapter with a conclusive answer to how we have come to know what we know, the variety of answers we discover through our reading and writing should enrich the question.

How Can I Think About Thinking?

The first set of readings focuses on the way we see and understand reality. The underlying issue here is not knowledge or learning about something so much as it is thinking about the ways in which we acquire and process any kind of knowledge. Such thinking about thinking has concerned many fields of study. Psychology, philosophy, linguistics, biology, and anthropology will look at the issue from substantially different angles. The psychologist may observe how children develop; the philosopher will ask about the relation of learning to truth; the linguist might argue that thinking is essentially a language function; the biologist could investigate the brain; and the anthropologist would inquire into the learning and language of our earliest ancestors. While there are many ways of thinking about thinking, the essays in this section raise some fundamental questions about the way our language and our perceptions lead to knowledge.

Susanne Langer, in "Signs and Symbols," sees the central distinction between the human race and "the animal mind" as our ability to use symbols. The human mind, she argues, does not merely mediate "between an event in the outer world and a creature's responsive action," but instead "transforms or, if you will, distorts the event into an image to be looked at, retained, and contemplated." For Langer, symbolic language is not merely essential for thinking; it is the defining characteristic of our species.

Plato's "Allegory of the Cave" questions our usual acceptance of what we see as "real." He is not concerned with the language of perception, as Langer is, but with our perception of reality itself: only the wisest of us, he says, can see what is real in "the region of the intelligible" or "the world of knowledge." What most people take to be real is not real, according to this allegory, despite the convictions and passions of those with limited vision.

The poem by Margaret Atwood teases us with its ambiguous reality. As we read "This Is a Photograph of Me," we try to make sense of the scene in the photograph, and we puzzle about the drowning. How can we understand the picture? How can we make sense of the poem? How can we figure out the reality that is all about us? How can we think about ways of thinking about such questions?

Finally, Frank Conroy, in "Think About it," shows the complexity of apparently ordinary ideas: "I thought about the words 'clear and present danger,' and the fact that if you looked at them closely they might not be as simple as they had first appeared." Through his accidental association with two judges, he learned that "documents alone do not keep democracy alive, nor maintain the state of law. . . . Living men and women, generation after generation, must continually remake democracy and the law." Referring to what we think we know, Conroy suggests we must continue to "think about it," using our own experiences, contexts, and understanding of the past. The meaning of even apparently simple and familiar concepts must be negotiated.

What Are Some Ways of Knowing?

Thomas S. Kuhn opens this section with "The Route to Normal Science," that is, the necessity for established norms and patterns (such as the right way to conduct a laboratory experiment) within which scientific (or other) discoveries can take place. He calls this pattern a "paradigm," the shared fundamentals under which scientists operate, the "rules and standards for scientific practice." But Kuhn does not take these paradigms to be truth; they are rather working agreements that change from time to time, a temporary "research consensus" that defines a field of study at a particular time. Without such a consensus, he argues, research and knowledge cannot go forward; but no paradigm can explain all observations. In fact, as new observations and theories appear, paradigms shift and new ones appear, neither more nor less true than the previous ones. Nevertheless, they are powerful lenses through which to view reality.

Stephen Jay Gould follows with "Evolution as Fact and Theory," an essay arguing for definitions and distinctions that allow us to think clearly about a controversial subject: "Well, evolution *is* a theory. It is also a fact. And facts and theories are different things, not rungs in a hierarchy of increasing certainty." His definitions are crucial to his argument; if we agree with his definitions, we are likely to agree with his conclusions. As a natural scientist and a writer, Gould delights in the intellectual game of creating possible explanations for observed phenomena, and he asks his readers to join in the play.

The third essay, from *Women's Ways of Knowing*, contrasts sharply with Gould's by emphasizing "the subjectivist position on knowing" as legitimate and important. Truth, for Mary Belenky and her colleagues, is not merely a rational process but is deeply involved with intuitions and emotions: "Truth, for subjective knowers, is an intuitive reaction—something experienced, not thought out, something felt rather than actively pursued or constructed." When we put the views of Belenky's "subjective knowers" next to Gould's, the two essays force us to question how we know what we know.

The differences between Gould and Belenky take on a new dimension when we encounter Jane van Lawick-Goodall's account of her many years observing the behavior of chimpanzees in their natural habitat. Her essay suggests that the apparently irreconcilable positions we have just encountered might, in fact, be put together by an intuitive and personal observer of natural phenomena. Her discoveries about chimpanzees have raised many questions about the distinctiveness of human beings. As we experience with her the touch of a female bushbuck or her fear of the leopard, we come to trust the observations she makes as a source of knowledge—and problems.

But the next essay, Evelyn Fox Keller's "A World of Difference," shows us the problems encountered by scientist Barbara McClintock, whose ways of knowing and proceeding conflict with the philosophical and sexual biases of her colleagues: "Despite the ungrudging respect and admiration of her colleagues, her most important work has, until recently, gone largely unappreciated, uncomprehended, and almost entirely unintegrated into the growing corpus of biological thought."

We are likely to argue with any one of the positions taken by these essays, and we might be unable to resolve the questions raised by the five of them taken together. But, as we test our own assumptions about ways of knowing by what these writers have to say, we are bound to deepen and complicate our own views. How, we would ask, does our way of knowing affect or determine what we know?

How Can I Understand What I Know?

The study of history might seem removed from the problems of how we come to know; the past appears to be finished, documented, resolved. But, although history begins with decisions about the collection of evidence, it moves quickly to questions about the meaning and use of the information that is accumulated. Is the purpose of history to inculcate patriotism, to teach lessons about behavior not to be repeated, to promote an understanding of cultural diversity, or to attain other goals by themselves or in combination? And even after the information has been gathered, how do we give meaning to what we know?

The first two essays in this section consider the ways in which history is taught and learned; they both point to the distinction between the names, dates, and other data to memorize and the meanings we give to that information. These meanings are also problematic and controversial: "slippery history," as Frances FitzGerald calls it in "America Revised," since history changes so rapidly through different interpretations. Linda Simon, in "The Naked Source," stresses "the role of imagination and intuition in the telling of histories." She points out that no source explains itself and that facts and answers are not what history is about: "Answers must generate questions, more questions, and still more subtle questions." It is through consideration of primary sources and the questions they raise that meaning starts to emerge. Only then can we begin to understand what we know.

Laurel Thatcher Ulrich's interpretation of an excerpt from the diary of Martha Ballard, an eighteenth-century midwife, shows an historian at work making meaning from the documents she has discovered. Like Conroy, Ulrich asks us to "think about it," using all we can learn from experience and history. "Before we can understand the full import" of a quotation, Ulrich tells us, "we need to know something about the legal position of unwed mothers in eighteenth-century New England." Historical documents are crucial to this task, but equally essential is the knowledge of law and social customs of men and women that historians bring to the documents. Historians seek to understand what they know by using their knowledge of the past to give meaning to documents from the past. We are not dealing with absolute truth, even when we read the best historians, but with the meaning that the writer creates, as well as with what we as readers bring to these meanings.

The final essay in the section is James Thurber's humorous reflection on his and others' failures at understanding during their "University Days." Here we see a fiasco in a science lab, bewilderment in economics class, and an ambiguous triumph at military drill. Thurber's conclusion seems to be the exact reverse of Conroy's: "I don't know. I don't think about it much anymore." But comedy sometimes works in reverse; Thurber's comic approach to university learning suggests a particular kind of understanding—the world is mysterious, so we had better be aware of our own ignorance and haplessness.

Rhetorical Issues: Writing as a Means of Learning: The Writing Processes

If we think of writing as *inquiry,* as an important and essential part of thinking and learning, we will value the time spent planning, drafting, revising, and editing our own work. This time is not to be given grudgingly to polishing a finished work; rather, it is creative thinking time to deepen and broaden our knowledge. Pages discarded (or recycled) from early drafts do not represent wasted time; the material is now rethought and incorporated into new and better ideas. A wholly new thesis statement, arrived at through rethinking and rewriting, does make us discard the old one, but we should feel no regret for the loss, which is really a gain.

When any one of us talks of "the writing process," we are likely to mean whatever we do to produce a particular paper—some sequence of thinking, writing, rethinking, rewriting, editing. But just as no two fingerprints are the same, neither are two writing processes; we might write a poem in a very different way from a lab report, or a memo, or a letter to the editor, or an essay. Likewise, different people have different styles of composing. Some compose writing the way Mozart composed music, thinking it through carefully in their minds—perhaps for a very long time—and then writing a fairly clean draft in a single sitting. As the prolific critic and fiction writer Joyce Carol Oates says, "If you are a writer, you can locate yourself behind a wall of silence and no matter what you are doing, driving a car or walking or doing housework . . . you can still be writing." This mental writing process works best with short pieces that can be easily kept in mind—a brief poem focused on a single metaphor, a short essay with a single major point, a narrative that proceeds chronologically, one point leading to the next in a direct time sequence. Writing in the head is difficult and exhausting for most of us. Mozart was exceptional; even as a young child, he was able to hear long and complex musical performances and write all the parts down perfectly when he got back home.

Other writers make many messy starts, using a first draft to explore the subject, to find connections among ideas, to discover a point of view and the right language. With persistence, every draft may bring them closer to the final product that continues to emerge. Most writers have to go through this painful process of revision after revision to produce their best work. Ernest Hemingway says casually that he wrote the last page of *Farewell to Arms* thirty-nine times, "getting the words right."

Computer word processing has made life a lot easier for writers who revise their work so much and for the tinkerers who are seldom satisfied. Computers make it easy to add, delete, and move words, sentences, or larger blocks of text under revision. Computers can save time and effort; you are always working with a clean screen or print-out, so you do not have to labor to decipher handwritten versions. And once you are done, you do not have to recopy the passages that were right the first time or retype the entire work.

Planning

Choosing a subject: Suppose you are writing an essay in response to question 4 at the end of this chapter: Write an essay, comic or serious, in which you explain the process of coming to know and understand something, such as learning to drive, cook, play a sport . . . learning the meaning of friendship, love, honor, duty, betrayal. . . .

Your first task will be to focus on a subject. What will you choose, and how will you decide? In keeping with the spirit of *Inquiry,* you will write a better paper if you pick a topic that interests you, that grows from what you have been reading and thinking about, or that comes from your own experience. The topic should be sufficiently complicated so you will be able to learn more about it from new perspectives. You will get bored if you simply rehash what you already know—and so will your readers.

Suppose that you have just been through a bad experience and found that several of your friends and family have stood by you in a way you never quite expected. You have come to understand friendship in a way that is different from how you have defined it in the past. The paper gives you a chance to explore that issue, and, right now, it is more important to you than the other possible topics. So you decide that your paper will be on how you have come to learn about the meaning of friendship.

Taking an inventory of your knowledge: Your second task, determining what you know about the subject and what you need to find out, will probably influence the direction the paper will take. What have you learned from your parents, from your siblings and other relations when you were young, from good and bad friends of yours and of other people? What have you read about friendship? You can examine some of the ways of knowing what you know; you might, for instance, examine what you were told or have read about friendship in the light of what you have experienced. As you think about your topic, you could jot down your answers in the form of key words, in clusters or lists. Or you can brainstorm with a classmate, taking notes as you talk. Or talk into a tape recorder. Or take notes— single key words or phrases—on your reading. Here are some areas you might explore:

What are the bases for my opinion?

1. Personal experience, such as
   a. Participating in an activity or event: My own friendships— some casual, some intimate, some new, some longstanding. Some outgrown.
   b. Knowing someone intimately (self, parent, friend): Parents' friendship deepened into romantic love (or, sadly, did not); my own first love.
   c. Living some place and getting to know the people and the territory: Neighbors in my hometown, my dorm, friendships at work.
   d. Experiencing a condition (needing help), the law (the effects of school desegregation), a circumstance (new roommate), a crisis (fight with best friend), a natural phenomenon (interests, attachments change as we grow older).
   e. Intuition (see Mary Belenky et al., "Just Knowing," (165)).

2. Others' views on the subject:
   a. Habit, custom, folk wisdom: The general belief that friendship is good. Friends should be loyal. Till death do us part.
   b. Rebellion against habit or custom: See Sharon Olds, "Sex Without Love" (336). Friends my parents did not approve.
   c. Reading, from:
      1. philosophy: Plato, platonic friendships.
      2. religion: The Bible—do unto others, if I have not charity I am nothing.

3. classics: Shakespeare—Mark Antony and Caesar, Hamlet and Laertes, King Lear and Kent.

4. literature and fine arts: fiction, poetry, sculpture, music, photographs.

5. *Inquiry,* other textbooks: Patricia Hampl, "The Need to Say It" (99), friendship with her grandmother; Richard Rodriguez, "Aria: Memoir of a Bilingual Childhood" (93), gradual distancing from Spanish-speaking parents as he went to school and learned English; Huck and Jim in "You Can't Pray a Lie" (236).

6. other disciplines, where relevant: such as business, economics, education, engineering, geography, history, psychology, sociology, each with a different perspective on friendship. Consider a variety of documents in addition to articles and books, such as interviews, speeches, policy statements, statistical tables and analyses, graphs, public records, surveys, institutional analyses, research reports, case studies, stock market reports, business forecasts.

7. mass media, including films, TV, newspapers, radio.

When you start to examine what you know, you'll probably be surprised to realize that you know a lot more than you thought you did. As you focus on a particular aspect of friendship, say, the friendship adult children can develop with their parents, or the possibility of a non-sexual friendship between young men and young women, you will start to find your reading, your observation, and your experience coming together to give you a topic worth pursuing.

Focusing

Clustering: Some people work well with charts, maps, and other spatial arrangements of thought. If you are comfortable with this mode of learning, you might plan your writing using some form of mapping by preparing a visual picture of the ideas for your paper. While there are many forms of mapping, the most popular is a procedure called clustering.

Use unlined paper and start with a topic that looks promising to you, writing it in the middle of the page. Suppose that you have written "adult friendships" as the topic that looks like a good focus for your paper. Put a circle around the phrase and let your mind search for words associated with it.

Writers use clustering to tap their unconscious knowledge and interests. Unlocking a mental treasure chest, they will put words anywhere on the page as they occur, not concerning themselves with connections or logic or anything except the discovery of ideas. This process is brainstorming by association. One might wind up with a dozen or more words or phrases on the page, perhaps going every which way: casual acquaintances, lovers, Uncle Charley, biblical David and Jonathan, loyalty, AIDS support, Twain's Huck and Jim, friendship over time, and so on. The idea here is to free one's mind from restrictions, even from the necessity of writing in straight lines, so that the fullest kind of creativity can take place.

The next stage is to connect and arrange the ideas on the page. In clustering, you draw large and winding circles around words that seem related to each other. Thus, you might connect one group of words that have to do with kinds of friends, another that have to do with levels of friendship, still another that deal with personal experience of friendship, and yet another listing famous friends.

If the assigned paper is relatively short, you cannot cover all the topics. Which one is likely to be the most interesting? What will you focus upon? And what will you say about the topic you will focus upon?

At this point, some writers will go back to a new clustering exercise, now restricted to the topic that seems most worth pursuing. Or, it may be time to get to the library to see if you can find more information that you need, before you start organizing your paper in too detailed a way. Or you might even want to start writing a discovery draft to see what the ideas look and sound like in sentences and paragraphs.

Outlining: For other writers a simple list will achieve the same purpose as clustering, or a formal outline will stimulate as well as organize ideas. If the latter approaches suit your learning style, how might you handle the same assignment?

A list of possible ideas is a good place to start. Begin noting down childhood experiences with friendship and how you learned about friendship. Next you might list some experiences with teenage friends. Perhaps you could write down some headings of what you have read or been taught about friendship. Maybe a section of the list could focus on friendships with the opposite sex, even leading into headings on differences (if any) from same-sex friendships. What do you gain and give in such relationships?

After some careful reading and note-taking, you will be ready to turn the list into a topic outline, one which arranges headings in a logical sequence and begins to focus the material. Perhaps you have decided that the best way to meet the assignment is to write about the way you have learned that you can be friends with people of the opposite sex, without attempting or needing a sexual relationship. Some of the material on the list you first wrote will have to be discarded to make room for the detail that will be needed to develop the new and more focused topic. Your topic outline might look something like this:

I. Childhood friends: some examples
II. Childhood learning about sex and friendship
III. Friendship requirements
    A. Common interests
    B. Common Values
    C. Acceptance
    D. Mutuality
    E. Time
IV. Sex requirements
    A. Power
    B. Self-definition
    C. Caring
    D. Sensuality, etc.
V. Can friendship with the opposite sex exist?
    A. Famous examples, pro and con
    B. My experience
VI. Adult definitions of friendship

As you begin to move from planning to drafting—and these stages frequently overlap—you may develop still other and more detailed outlines for your work. Perhaps topics I and II will blend into a single one; maybe you will need to abbreviate the material from childhood so you have enough room for your more mature learning. You will need to guard against mere repetition of experience for its own sake, so that you meet the demands of the assignment—which asked you to focus upon the *process* of coming to know and understand something—and renewed outlining will help keep you on track.

Other kinds of outlining will become more valuable as you start drafting. The sentence outline, for example, which we will look at shortly, is a particularly valuable way to help you see what needs to be changed in early drafts. But there is one danger in using outlining for planning: it is important not to be trapped by outlines into premature decisions about your topic; the outline exists to help you shape your inquiry, not to shut it down or close off possibilities you had not thought of at the time.

Other Planning and Focusing Activities: In addition to clustering and outlining, reading and notetaking, talking with others about the topic, writing notes or journal entries, imagining metaphors or analogies or stories—all of these and more can help you initiate and shape your ideas. For some people, the best planning emerges from sitting quietly and thinking; still others awake at night with brilliant ideas that must be written down on the spot, for they will be gone by morning.

Planning activities are a crucial part of the writing processes of most good writers. If you neglect to plan and just plunge into drafting, trusting to inspiration and luck, you are asking more of yourself than would most professionals. Most good writers never stop planning as long as the paper is in process, and some planning activities may go on even at the last minute; but, obviously, the earlier you plan the more efficiently you will work. Whatever planning techniques or approach you find suitable, you will save time and produce better work if you write out ideas, group them, and focus your thoughts before you start producing the drafts that lead to your finished work.

Drafting and Revising: Planning leads naturally to drafting, to the production of writing. But these stages are not wholly distinct. Writing out drafts and revising them is in one sense the next step in most writing processes, but in another sense the most powerful part of the planning stage. Planning does not stop when drafting begins; the creation of initial drafts (or "discovery drafts") tests the planning and often refines it.

How many drafts should you produce? Sometimes, as on a timed essay exam, you have no time to produce more than one. All you can do is plan carefully, write your response, and save a few moments at the end for editing. On the other hand, we have pointed out that professional writers often will put an important piece of writing through twenty or thirty drafts, an exhausting routine few students will want, or have the time, to emulate. Most students probably turn out one or two drafts for most of their college papers; another draft or two may make their writing much more satisfying and result in higher grades. Professional writers not only revise much more than less experienced writers do, but they revise differently, with a firmer understanding of writing processes. The professionals will throw away much of what they write in early drafts, as they revise, plan, and revise again. Many less experienced writers find it hard to throw away anything; they tend to edit for correctness rather than to revise and reshape. Thus, while it is impossible to say how many drafts you should produce, it is clear that you will write better if you use the professional approach to writing: early drafting is more likely to be a form of planning than a way to produce a finished product. The more revision you can do the better off you will be.

One reasonable way to combine revising and drafting is to use a sentence outline as a way to read and improve your initial draft. The sentence outline differs from the topic outline by containing complete sentences, rather than topic headings. Try abstracting your draft into one sentence for each paragraph, so that a twelve paragraph paper can be outlined in twelve numbered sentences on a single page. The sentence outline has two distinct advantages: (1) it helps you notice what each paragraph is saying and hence leads to revision of paragraphs, and (2) it helps you see the movement of your thought from paragraph to paragraph. You may find that the central idea of the paper is most clearly stated in paragraph ten, which suggests that it should be moved to the front of the paper. Or you may discover that you have said the same thing in paragraph seven that you say in paragraph two, which suggests that they should be combined or one of them should be eliminated. Most importantly, you can check to see that your focused topic has been set out clearly and that everything in the paper relates to it.

Many professional writers allot about half of the time available for writing a paper to revision. That is, if you can spend 20 hours on a paper, it should exist in draft form after 10 hours, so you can spend another 10 hours revising and reworking the draft. We have given more space in this introduction to *planning* than to *revising*, simply because we have no room to give examples of revision here. But do not be misled: careful revision (re-vision, a new seeing of the topic) is half of the writing process for most successful writers. When you are convinced that your paper is well focused on an interesting topic, that it is organized effectively, that you have convincing evidence for what you have to say, and that you have demonstrated as well as stated your ideas, you are ready for the final cleanup stage.

Editing: Do not confuse editing with revision. Sometimes it is easy to think that going through a paper with an eye to such matters as vocabulary, punctuation, and spelling is really revising. In fact sometimes a change in mechanics actually does develop into more substantial revision; for example, a badly constructed sentence will often reflect an idea that needs more thought to become clear. But careful editing of a discovery draft does not usually lead to a final draft, just to a clean discovery draft, that fools you into thinking it is finished because it looks so neat. But beware; the tidiness that premature editing can impose on your paper may make you reluctant to make necessary changes in the focus, organization, or development of ideas. If you keep in mind the general principle *revise before you edit*, you'll be less likely to spend time laboring over the spelling of words that you may delete later on, or tinkering with the style of paragraphs that will be dropped. Editing before revising is like eating dessert first; it gives you a false sense of completion when you may only have begun.

But the final stage every writer, no matter how experienced, must go through is to edit the writing. This means, for example, cleaning up the inevitable spelling errors and other mechanical slips, making sure that the subjects agree with the verbs and the sentences are complete, checking to be sure the quotations are accurate, and making sure that the paper presents you to a reader as a careful person who wants the writing to be taken seriously. We have cautioned against premature editing, a common problem, but now we must warn even more seriously about failing to edit at all. To ignore the editing stage of the writing process can be a serious mistake, for appearances count on a paper they way they do in person. A sloppy appearance makes it hard for others to respect what you have to say.

Finally, we must admit that some mystery still remains about writing. On some occasions, the most careful planning and endless revision still fail to produce a good essay. Some writers can work so efficiently in their heads that the writing process can be abbreviated, and every now and then someone turns out a superb first draft. But most of us, most of the time, find writing to be hard work and our early drafts usually need to be revised or even thrown away as we struggle to define and develop our best ideas while our work slowly improves. We often find ourselves coming to know much more about our topic as we go through the writing process, developing our thought as we develop our writing. So we might as well take advantage of what experienced writers have learned: develop our ideas through a writing process that allows time for multiple revisions and rethinking of the topic.

QUESTIONS FOR DISCOVERY AND DISCUSSION

1.   Choose a subject of any sort (it does not have to be a school subject: chess or baking will work as well as chemistry) about which you know more than many other people do. Identify the subject, and explain how you have come to know about it.

2.   Identify other possible ways of learning (from books, experience, a parent, and so on) about the subject you have just discussed. What might you know or not know about the subject if you had followed one of these other routes? Why?

3.   Imagine someone of a different sex, skin color, period of history, or educational level learning about the subject you have described. What is that person likely to know about it? Why?

4.   Explain how the *way* you have come to know your subject has affected *what* you know about it.

Signs and Symbols

SUSANNE K. LANGER

In Susanne Langer's view, the unique ability of humans to symbolize is what distinguishes our species from animals. This conviction led Langer (1895–1985), a philosopher, to a lifetime of research in which asking the right questions was more important than coming up with a right answer. Langer, who earned three degrees from Radcliffe (Ph.D., 1926), taught at Columbia University from 1945 to 1950 and thereafter at Connecticut College until her retirement in 1952.

Langer's focus on symbolic behavior integrates her research on topics as seemingly different as aesthetics (*Feeling and Form: A Theory of Art*, 1953); the nature of the human mind (*Mind: An Essay on Human Feelings*, 3 vols., 1967–1982); and symbolic logic (*Philosophy in a New Key: A Study in the Symbols of Reason, Rite, and Art*, 1942). Although the latter included "Signs and Symbols," that essay was also published in *Fortune* in 1944. It is a good example of how a specialist can convey abstractions and complicated concepts to a general audience. "Signs and Symbols" epitomizes the view that language is the "most amazing achievement of the symbolistic human mind," and the ability to use language distinguishes humans from other animals. Without language it is impossible to think or reason, contends Langer. Given the recent experiments in which chimpanzees and gorillas "talk" in American Sign Language or by pressing symbol or word keys on special typewriters, and even transmit their knowledge to others of their species, it will be interesting to see whether this animal behavior threatens the long-established definition of humankind as the exclusive user of symbols.

The trait that sets human mentality apart from every other is its 1 preoccupation with symbols, with images and names that *mean* things, rather than with things themselves. This trait may have been a mere sport of nature once upon a time. Certain creatures do develop tricks and interests that seem biologically unimportant. Pack rats, for instance, and some birds of the crow family take a capricious pleasure in bright objects and carry away such things for which they have, presumably, no earthly use. Perhaps man's tendency to see certain forms as *images*, to hear certain sounds not only as signals but as expressive tones, and to be excited by sunset colors or starlight, was originally just a peculiar sensitivity in a rather highly developed brain. But whatever its cause, the ultimate destiny of this trait was momentous; for all human activity is based on the appreciation and use of symbols. Language, religion, mathematics, all learning, all science and superstition, even right and wrong, are products of symbolic expression rather than direct experience. Our commonest words, such as "house" and "red" and "walking," are symbols; the pyramids of Egypt and the mysterious circles of Stonehenge are symbols; so are dominions and empires and astronomical universes. We live in a mind-made world, where the things of prime importance are images or words that embody ideas and feelings and attitudes.

The animal mind is like a telephone exchange; it receives stimuli 2
from outside through the sense organs and sends out appropriate responses through the nerves that govern muscles, glands, and other parts of the body. The organism is constantly interacting with its surroundings, receiving messages and acting on the new state of affairs that the messages signify.

But the human mind is not a simple transmitter like a telephone 3
exchange. It is more like a great projector; for instead of merely me-diating between an event in the outer world and a creature's respon-sive action, it transforms or, if you will, distorts the event into an image to be looked at, retained, and contemplated. For the images of things that we remember are not exact and faithful transcriptions even of our actual sense impressions. They are made as much by what we think as by what we see. It is a well-known fact that if you ask several people the size of the moon's disk as they look at it, their estimates will vary from the area of a dime to that of a barrel top. Like a magic lantern, the mind projects its ideas of things on the screen of what we call "memory"; but like all projections, these ideas are transfor-mations of actual things. They are, in fact, *symbols* of reality, not pieces of it.

A symbol is not the same thing as a sign; that is a fact that 4
psychologists and philosophers often overlook. All intelligent animals use signs; so do we. To them as well as to us sounds and smells and motions are signs of food, danger, the presence of other beings, or of rain or storm. Furthermore, some animals not only attend to signs but produce them for the benefit of others. Dogs bark at the door to be let in; rabbits thump to call each other; the cooing of doves and the growl of a wolf defending his kill are unequivocal signs of feelings and intentions to be reckoned with by other creatures.

We use signs just as animals do, though with considerably more 5
elaboration. We stop at red lights and go on green; we answer calls and bells, watch the sky for coming storms, read trouble or promise or anger in each other's eyes. That is animal intelligence raised to the human level. Those of us who are dog lovers can probably all tell wonderful stories of how high our dogs have sometimes risen in the scale of clever sign interpretation and sign using.

A sign is anything that announces the existence or the imminence 6 of some event, the presence of a thing or a person, or a change in a state of affairs. There are signs of the weather, signs of danger, signs of future good or evil, signs of what the past has been. In every case a sign is closely bound up with something to be noted or expected in experience. It is always a part of the situation to which it refers, though the reference may be remote in space and time. In so far as we are led to note or expect the signified event we are making correct use of a sign. This is the essence of rational behavior, which animals show in varying degrees. It is entirely realistic, being closely bound up with the actual objective course of history—learned by experience, and cashed in or voided by further experience.

If man had kept to the straight and narrow path of sign using, 7 he would be like the other animals, though perhaps a little brighter. He would not talk, but grunt and gesticulate and point. He would make his wishes known, give warnings, perhaps develop a social system like that of bees and ants, with such a wonderful efficiency of communal enterprise that all men would have plenty to eat, warm apartments—all exactly alike and perfectly convenient—to live in, and everybody could and would sit in the sun or by the fire, as the climate demanded, not talking but just basking, with every want satisfied, most of his life. The young would romp and make love, the old would sleep, the middle-aged would do the routine work almost unconsciously and eat a great deal. But that would be the life of a social, superintelligent, purely sign-using animal.

To us who are human, it does not sound very glorious. We want 8 to go places and do things, own all sorts of gadgets that we do not absolutely need, and when we sit down to take it easy we want to talk. Rights and property, social position, special talents and virtues, and above all our ideas, are what we live for. We have gone off on a tangent that takes us far away from the mere biological cycle that animal generations accomplish; and that is because we can use not only signs but symbols.

A symbol differs from a sign in that it does not announce the 9 presence of the object, the being, condition, or whatnot, which is its meaning, but merely *brings this thing to mind*. It is not a mere "substitute sign" to which we react as though it were the object itself. The fact is that our reaction to hearing a person's name is quite different from our reaction to the person himself. There are certain rare cases where a symbol stands directly for its meaning: in religious experience, for instance, the Host is not only a symbol but a Presence. But symbols in the ordinary sense are not mystic. They are the same sort of thing that ordinary signs are; only they do not call our attention to something necessarily present or to be physically dealt with—they call up merely a conception of the thing they "mean."

The difference between a sign and a symbol is, in brief, that a 10 sign causes us to think or act *in face of* the thing signified, whereas a symbol causes us to think *about* the thing symbolized. Therein lies the great importance of symbolism for human life, its power to make this life so different from any other animal biography that generations of men have found it incredible to suppose that they were of purely zoological origin. A sign is always embedded in reality, in a present that emerges from the actual past and stretches to the future; but a symbol may be divorced from reality altogether. It may refer to what is *not* the case, to a mere idea, a figment, a dream. It serves, therefore, to liberate thought from the immediate stimuli of a physically present world; and that liberation marks the essential difference between human and nonhuman mentality. Animals think, but they think *of* and *at* things; men think primarily *about* things. Words, pictures, and memory images are symbols that may be combined and varied in a thousand ways. The result is a symbolic structure whose meaning is a complex of all their respective meanings, and this kaleidoscope of *ideas* is the typical product of the human brain that we call the "stream of thought."

The process of transforming all direct experience into imagery or 11 into that supreme mode of symbolic expression, language, has so completely taken possession of the human mind that it is not only a special talent but a dominant, organic need. All our sense impressions leave their traces in our memory not only as signs disposing our practical reactions in the future but also as symbols, images representing our *ideas* of things; and the tendency to manipulate ideas, to combine and abstract, mix and extend them by playing with symbols, is man's outstanding characteristic. It seems to be what his brain most naturally and spontaneously does. Therefore his primitive mental function is not judging reality, but *dreaming his desires*.

Dreaming is apparently a basic function of human brains, for it 12 is free and unexhausting like our metabolism, heartbeat, and breath. It is easier to dream than not to dream, as it is easier to breathe than to refrain from breathing. The symbolic character of dreams is fairly well established. Symbol mongering, on this ineffectual, uncritical level, seems to be instinctive, the fulfillment of an elementary need rather than the purposeful exercise of a high and difficult talent.

The special power of man's mind rests on the evolution of this 13 special activity, not on any transcendently high development of animal intelligence. We are not immeasurably higher than other animals; we are different. We have a biological need and with it a biological gift that they do not share.

Because man has not only the ability but the constant need of 14 *conceiving* what has happened to him, what surrounds him, what is demanded of him—in short, of symbolizing nature, himself, and his hopes and fears—he has a constant and crying need of *expression*. What he cannot express, he cannot conceive; what he cannot conceive is chaos, and fills him with terror.

If we bear in mind this all-important craving for expression we 15 get a new picture of man's behavior; for from this trait spring his powers and his weaknesses. The process of symbolic transformation that all our experiences undergo is nothing more nor less than the process of *conception*, which underlies the human faculties of abstraction and imagination.

When we are faced with a strange or difficult situation, we cannot 16 react directly, as other creatures do, with flight, aggression, or any such simple instinctive pattern. Our whole reaction depends on how we manage to conceive the situation—whether we cast it in a definite dramatic form, whether we see it as a disaster, a challenge, a fulfillment of doom, or a fiat of the Divine Will. In words or dreamlike images, in artistic or religious or even in cynical form, we must *construe* the events of life. There is great virtue in the figure of speech, "I can *make* nothing of it," to express a failure to understand something. Thought and memory are processes of *making* the thought content and the memory image; the pattern of our ideas is given by the symbols through which we express them. And in the course of manipulating those symbols we inevitably distort the original experience, as we abstract certain features of it, embroider and reinforce those features with other ideas, until the conception we project on the screen of memory is quite different from anything in our real history.

Conception is a necessary and elementary process; what we do 17 with our conceptions is another story. That is the entire history of human culture—of intelligence and mortality, folly and superstition, ritual, language, and the arts—all the phenomena that set man apart from, and above, the rest of the animal kingdom. As the religious mind has to make all human history a drama of sin and salvation in order to define its own moral attitudes, so a scientist wrestles with the mere presentation of "the facts" before he can reason about them. The process of *envisaging* facts, values, hopes, and fears underlies our whole behavior pattern; and this process is reflected in the evolution of an extraordinary phenomenon found always, and only, in human societies—the phenomenon of language.

Language is the highest and most amazing achievement of the 18 symbolistic human mind. The power it bestows is almost inestimable, for without it anything properly called "thought" is impossible. The birth of language is the dawn of humanity. The line between man and beast—between the highest ape and the lowest savage—is the language line. Whether the primitive Neanderthal man was anthropoid or human depends less on his cranial capacity, his upright posture, or even his use of tools and fire, than on one issue we shall probably never be able to settle—whether or not he spoke.

In all physical traits and practical responses, such as skills and 19 visual judgments, we can find certain continuity between animal and human mentality. Sign using is an ever evolving, ever improving function throughout the whole animal kingdom, from the lowly worm that shrinks into his hole at the sound of an approaching foot, to the dog obeying his master's command, and even to the learned scientist who watches the movements of an index needle.

This continuity of the sign-using talent has led psychologists to 20 the belief that language is evolved from the vocal expressions, grunts and coos and cries, whereby animals vent their feelings or signal their fellows; that man has elaborated this sort of communication to the point where it makes a perfect exchange of ideas possible.

I do not believe that this doctrine of the origin of language is 21 correct. The essence of language is symbolic, not signific; we use it first and most vitally to formulate and hold ideas in our own minds. Conception, not social control, is its first and foremost benefit.

Watch a young child that is just learning to speak play with a toy; 22 he says the name of the object, e.g.: "Horsey! horsey! horsey!" over and over again, looks at the object, moves it, always saying the name to himself or to the world at large. It is quite a time before he talks to anyone in particular; he talks first of all to himself. This is his way of forming and fixing the *conception* of the object in his mind, and around this conception all his knowledge of it grows. *Names* are the essence of language; for the *name* is what abstracts the conception of the horse from the horse itself, and lets the mere idea recur at the speaking of the name. This permits the conception gathered from one horse experience to be exemplified again by another instance of a horse, so that the notion embodied in the name is a general notion.

To this end, the baby uses a word long before he *asks for* the object; 23 when he wants his horsey he is likely to cry and fret, because he is reacting to an actual environment, not forming ideas. He use the animal language of *signs* for his wants; talking is still a purely symbolic process—its practical value has not really impressed him yet.

Language need not be vocal; it may be purely visual, like written 24 language, or even tactual, like the deaf-mute system of speech; but it *must be denotative*. The sounds, intended or unintended, whereby animals communicate do not constitute a language, because they are signs, not names. They never fall into an organic pattern, a meaningful syntax of even the most rudimentary sort, as all language seems to do with a sort of driving necessity. That is because signs refer to actual situations, in which things have obvious reactions to each other that require only to be noted; but symbols refer to ideas, which are not physically there for inspection, so their connections and features have to be represented. This gives all true language a natural tendency toward growth and development, which seems almost like a life of its own. Languages are not invented; they grow with our need for expression.

In contrast, animal "speech" never has a structure. It is merely 25 an emotional response. Apes may greet their ration of yams with a shout of "Nga!" But they do not say "Nga" between meals. If they could *talk about* their yams instead of just saluting them, they would be the most primitive men instead of the most anthropoid of beasts. They would have ideas, and tell each other things true or false, rational or irrational; they would make plans and invent laws and sing their own praises, as men do.

RESPONDING TO READING

Key words: community discovery identity language symbols

Rhetorical concepts: cause and effect comparison and contrast
deduction definition illustration process speculation

1. How does Langer define signs? Symbols? Where does Langer, a philosopher, use evidence from anthropology and biology for her definitions? To what degree do you agree with Langer's way of distinguishing humans from animals?

2. How do you know when you are responding to signs? Give some examples of human behavior that reflects the use of *signs*, in Langer's sense. Is this, as Langer says, evidence of "animal intellignece raised to the human level" (paragraph 5)?

3. Analyze some of your sigificant *symbolic* behavior to show how you think about what you do. Are signs and symbols ever intermingled in your thinking? Explain.

4. Define, in discussion or in writing, an abstract term—a quality or concept that can be explained in terms of its causes, effects, or other non-physical aspects, such as love, peace, sphistication, beauty, maturity, or riskiness. How do you know what you know about the term you have chosen? Illustrate your definition with two or three specific examples from your own experience.

5. Does a particular term (such as "peace" or "love") have the same meaning for an historian as for a psychologist? A biologist? A novelist? A parent? A child? A teenager? Will this term have the same meaning for all people of a given group (historians, parents)? Why or why not? Explain. Write an essay defining the various meanings of the term you have chosen.

The Allegory of the Cave

PLATO

Plato (c. 427c.–347 B.C.), Greek educator, literary artist, and philosopher of ethics, politics, aesthetics, and rhetoric, perfected the Socratic dialogue, a verbal exchange of ideas that enables the participants to get at the essentials of the truth through its question and answer format. Socratic dialogues, as in "The Allegory of the Cave" that follows, involve a cast of characters, some more fully delineated than they are here, discussing, sometimes arguing, about an issue in an effort to reach the truth. The dominant character, Socrates (although he is not identified by name in the pages that follow), invariably has the broadest, deepest understanding of the issues under debate. His penetrating logic ultimately compels both understanding and consensus, leaving the other characters little choice but to agree with him. Thus Glaucon's brief responses in "The Allegory of the Cave," "I see," "Of course," "Necessarily," echo and reaffirm Socrates's main points but do not dispute them.

The Republic, in which "The Allegory of the Cave" appears, presents the first Utopia, an ideal state which according to Plato is a static, closed society whose major groups are the guardians, the military, and the workers. When all work in harmony, justice prevails. Despite their aristocratic status, the guardians must live in a state of Spartan communism, lest they succumb to the temptations of wealth and the exercise of military power. If the poverty-stricken masses revolt, democracy (undesirable) or even tyranny (even worse) could result. (But Plato's views were not static; ever self-critical, in a later dialogue, *The Laws*, he greatly modified the *Republic*'s political doctrines.)

Thus the education of guardians in *The Republic* is crucial. "The Allegory of the Cave" uses an extended analogy to show how the unphilosophical person is at the mercy of sense impressions, transient, finite, fickle. It is as if one sees flickering shadows of objects reflected on a cave wall, and hears echos, and mistakes these for reality. In contrast, the genuinely philosophical person attains true knowledge, apprehending universal forms as timeless and unchanging; these contain the essence of the subject.

Next, said I, here is a parable to illustrate the degrees in which   1
our nature may be enlightened or unenlightened. Imagine the condition of men living is a sort of cavernous chamber underground, with an entrance open to the light and a long passage all down the cave. Here they have been from childhood, chained by the leg and also by the neck, so that they cannot move and can see only what is in front of them, because the chains will not let them turn their heads. At some distance higher up is the light of a fire burning behind them; and between the prisoners and the fire is a track with a parapet built

along it, like the screen at a puppet-show, which hides the performers while they show their puppets over the top.

I see, said he.   2

Now behind this parapet imagine persons carrying along various   3
artificial objects, including figures of men and animals in wood or stone or other materials, which project above the parapet. Naturally, some of these persons will be talking, others silent.

It is a strange picture, he said, and a strange sort of prisoners.   4

Like ourselves, I replied; for in the first place prisoners so confined   5
would have seen nothing of themselves or of one another, except the shadows thrown by the fire-light on the wall of the Cave facing them, would they?

Not if all their lives they had been prevented from moving their   6
heads.

And they would have seen as little of the objects carried past.   7

Of course.   8

Now, if they could talk to one another, would they not suppose   9
that their words referred only to those passing shadows which they saw?

Necessarily.   10

And suppose their prison had an echo from the wall facing   11
them? When one of the people crossing behind them spoke, they could only suppose that the sound came from the shadow passing before their eyes.

No doubt.   12

In every way, then, such prisoners would recognize as reality   13
nothing but the shadows of those artificial objects.

Inevitably.   14

Now consider what would happen if their release from the chains   15
and the healing of their unwisdom should come about in this way. Suppose one of them were set free and forced suddenly to stand up, turn his head, and walk with eyes lifted to the light; all these movements would be painful, and he would be too dazzled to make out the objects whose shadows he had been used to see. What do you think he would say, if someone told him that what he had formerly seen was meaningless illusion, but now, being somewhat nearer to reality and turned towards more real objects, he was getting a truer view? Suppose further that he were shown the various objects being carried by and were made to say, in reply to questions, what each of them was. Would he not be perplexed and believe the objects now shown him to be not so real as what he formerly saw?

Yes, not nearly so real.   16

And if he were forced to look at the fire-light itself, would not   17 his eyes ache, so that he would try to escape and turn back to the things which he could see distinctly, convinced that they really were clearer than these other objects now being shown to him?

Yes.   18

And suppose someone were to drag him away forcibly up the 19
steep and rugged ascent and not let him go until he had hauled him out into the sunlight, would he not suffer pain and vexation at such treatment, and, when he had come out into the light, find his eyes so full of its radiance that he could not see a single one of the things that he was now told were real?

Certainly he would not see them all at once.   20

He would need, then, to grow accustomed before he could see 21
things in that upper world. At first it would be easiest to make out shadows, and then the images of men and things reflected in water, and later on the things themselves. After that, it would easier to watch the heavenly bodies and the sky itself by night, looking at the light of the moon and stars rather than the Sun and the Sun's light in the day-time.

Yes, surely.   22

Last of all, he would be able to look at the Sun and contemplate 23
its nature, not as it appears when reflected in water or any alien medium, but as it is in itself in its own domain.

No doubt.   24

And now he would begin to draw the conclusion that it is the 25
Sun that produces the seasons and the course of the year and controls everything in the visible world, and moreover is in a way the cause of all that he and his companions used to see.

Clearly he would come at last to that conclusion.   26

Then if he called to mind his fellow prisoners and what passed 27
for wisdom in his former dwelling-place, he would surely think himself happy in the change and be sorry for them. They may have had a practice of honouring and commending one another, with prizes for the man who had the keenest eye for the passing shadows and the best memory for the order in which they followed or accompanied one another, so that he could make a good guess as to which was going to come next. Would our released prisoner be likely to covet those prizes or to envy the men exalted to honour and power in the Cave? Would he not feel like Homer's Achilles, that he would far sooner 'be on earth as a hired servant in the house of a landless man' or endure anything rather than go back to his old beliefs and live in the old way?

Yes, he would prefer any fate to such a life.   28

Now imagine what would happen if he went down again to take 29
his former seat in the Cave. Coming suddenly out of the sunlight,

his eyes would be filled with darkness. He might be required once more to deliver his opinion on those shadows, in competition with the prisoners who had never been released, while his eyesight was still dim and unsteady; and it might take some time to become used to the darkness. They would laugh at him and say that he had gone up only to come back with his sight ruined; it was worth no one's while even to attempt the ascent. If they could lay hands on the man who was trying to set them free and lead them up, they would kill him.

Yes, they would.   30

Every feature in this parable, my dear Glaucon, is meant to fit 31 our earlier analysis. The prison dwelling corresponds to the region revealed to us through the sense of sight, and the fire-light within it to the power of the Sun. The ascent to see the things in the upper world you may take as standing for the upward journey of the soul into the region of the intelligible; then you will be in possession of what I surmise, since that is what you wish to be told. Heaven knows whether it is true; but this, at any rate, is how it appears to me. In the world of knowledge, the last thing to be perceived and only with great difficulty is the essential Form of Goodness. Once it is perceived, the conclusion must follow that, for all things, this is the cause of whatever is right and good; in the visible world it gives birth to light and to the lord of light, while it is itself sovereign in the intelligible world and the parent of intelligence and truth. Without having had a vision of this Form no one can act with wisdom, either in his own life or in matters of state.

RESPONDING TO READING

Key words: discovery   education   freedom   power   reality
symbol   transformation

Rhetorical concepts: analogy   cause and effect
comparison and contrast   deduction   explanation   illustration
metaphor   narrative/example

1.   Try drawing or describing in your own words Plato's picture of the men in the cave. Why do they not turn around to see the light? Why do they not notice that the figures they take for reality are only "puppets"? Why are the men "prisoners"? Why are they "like ourselves"?
2.   The next scene shows us one man set free, trying to cope with the new vision of reality freedom brings. What is the first reaction? The second?
3.   The third scene shows one of the men forcibly "hauled out into the sun." What is the sequence of his reactions? Why? What is his response now to

those left behind in the cave? What is the response of those in the cave to his new vision?

4. The last paragraph details Plato's explanation of the meaning of his parable. What does he mean by "the region of the intelligible," "the world of knowledge," and "the essential Form of Goodness"?

5. To what degree does your present vision of reality correspond to Plato's? Do you agree that there are "essential forms" of goodness and the like that exist in a reality beyond daily experience? Are you willing to accept that your day-to-day experiences are a world of shadows, distorted reflections of some other world? What would such a concept suggest about the way you should act in the world? Construct an allegory to explain your version of reality.

6. How did you learn about "reality"? How firmly convinced are you that your version of reality is the true one? How do you feel about Plato, or anyone else, disputing the reality of your reality? Plato says that "no one can act with wisdom, either in his own life or in matters of state" without a vision of essential forms. How would a different sense of reality affect the way you lead your life?

This Is a Photograph of Me

MARGARET ATWOOD

To say that Margaret Atwood is a feminist Canadian nationalist, although accurate, pigeonholes a writer whose work transcends categories. Atwood's schooling in Ottawa, where she was born in 1939, was punctuated by extended family trips to the bush country of northern Ontario and Quebec. While her father conducted entomological research, Atwood learned the survival skills that she later demonstrated to be essential for women and for Canadians (*Survival: A Thematic Guide to Canadian Literature*, 1972) and developed the keen attention to minute details that surfaces in her poetry. She published her first book of poetry, *Double Persephone*, the year she graduated from the University of Toronto, and she earned an M.A. from Radcliffe College in the following year, 1962.

Since then Atwood has published some twenty volumes of poetry and nine novels, as well as short stories, essays, and children's books, becoming in the process Canada's "national heroine of the arts" (*Contemporary Authors* V. 25, p. 19). Her novels, enormously popular with critics and readers on both sides of the border, include *The Edible Woman* (1962), *Surfacing* (1972), *Bodily Harm* (1982), and *Cat's Eye* (1989). The chilling, dystopian *Handmaid's Tale* (1985) depicts a feminist *Brave New World* in which women, reduced to chattel in a repressive male-dominated religious state, survive through their ability to subvert and sabotage the patriarchal system. Their secret motto is "Don't let the bastards get you down." "This Is a Photograph of Me," from Atwood's second volume, the prizewinning *The*

Circle Game (1964), deals, like her fiction, with the significance of an individual's life and death, and its impact on the fabric of society and nature. Where, indeed, does one fit into the picture?

It was taken some time ago.
At first it seems to be
a smeared
print: blurred lines and grey flecks
blended with the paper;

then, as you scan
it, you see in the left-hand corner
a thing that is like a branch: part of a tree
(balsam or spruce) emerging
and, to the right, halfway up
what ought to be a gentle
slope, a small frame house.

In the background there is a lake,
and beyond that, some low hills.

(The photograph was taken
the day after I drowned.

I am in the lake, in the center
of the picture, just under the surface.

It is difficult to say where
precisely, or to say
how large or small I am:
the effect of water
on light is a distortion

but if you look long enough,
eventually
you will be able to see me.)

RESPONDING TO READING

Key words: art discovery gender identity loss nature photography poetry power reality symbols

Rhetorical concepts: analogy metaphor poetry

1.   Sketch the scene described in the poem's first twelve lines. Try to capture the imprecision of the photograph, which "seems to be a smeared print." At the same time, try to reproduce the details: the part of a tree that is "balsam or spruce," the small frame house, a lake, low hills, and so on. The trickiest part of the sketch will be the hidden presence of the speaker under the water of the lake.

2.   You, as the observer of the photograph and the reader of the poem, have an important part to play in making sense of the scene and the poem. You appear in line six, scanning the photograph, and then again twice in the last stanza; at the end, you will be able to see the speaker under the water. Write an essay on the relationship between the "you" of the poem and its speaker.

3.   The poem conceals its central action, the death of the speaker. In this way, it forces the reader to speculate about the causes of death (murder? suicide? accident?) and the motives or stories behind each possible cause. By further placing two art forms (photography and poetry) between us and the "reality" of the scene, the poet makes us struggle to discern what is going on and wonder about how we can come to know anything at all about what happened. The very act of seeing is thrown into question: "the effect of water on light is a distortion." How do we know what we know?

Think About It

FRANK CONROY

Frank Conroy (born 1936) leads a life to which many writers aspire, alternating between Massachusetts and Washington, D.C. In 1981 he was appointed director of the literature program for the National Endowment for the Arts. His literary reputation began with the nomination of his first book, the autobiographical *Stop-time* (1967), for a National Book Award. His second book, *Midair* (1985), is a collection of short stories similar in form, technique, and subject to his autobiography. Conroy publishes widely in periodicals such as the *New Yorker* and *Harper's*, in which "Think About It" originally appeared. Since graduation from Haverford College in 1958, Conroy has also taught writing at the University of Iowa, M.I.T., and Brandeis.

"Think About It" has the same deceptively easy pace and casual anecdotal tone that pervades Conroy's other autobiographical writing. His wondering, awkward but curious, teenage self is the consciousness and semi-consciousness through which growing knowledge and understanding are filtered, patiently sought but not always understood at the time. Only later, does something else happen—a chance remark, a new experience—that triggers the dormant understanding and makes meaning from the fragments stored away. If we think about it, much thinking works that way.

When I was sixteen I worked selling hot dogs at a stand in the   1
Fourteenth Street subway station in New York City, one level above
the trains and one below the street, where the crowds continually
flowed back and forth. I worked with three Puerto Rican men who
could not speak English. I had no Spanish, and although we understood each other well with regard to the tasks at hand, sensing and
adjusting to each other's body movements in the extremely confined
space in which we operated, I felt isolated with no one to talk to. On
my break I came out from behind the counter and passed the time
with two old black men who ran a shoeshine stand in a dark corner
of the corridor. It was a poor location, half hidden by columns, and
they didn't have much business. I would sit with my back against the
wall while they stood or moved around their ancient elevated stand,
talking to each other or to me, but always staring into the distance
as they did so.

As the weeks went by I realized that they never looked at anything   2
in their immediate vicinity—not at me or their stand or anybody who
might come within ten or fifteen feet. They did not look at approaching customers once they were inside the perimeter. Save for the instant
it took to discern the color of the shoes, they did not even look at
what they were doing while they worked, but rubbed in polish,
brushed, and buffed by feel while looking over their shoulders, into
the distance, as if awaiting the arrival of an important person. Of
course there wasn't all that much distance in the underground station,
but their behavior was so focused and consistent they seemed somehow to transcend the physical. A powerful mood was created, and I
came almost to believe that these men could see through walls,
through girders, and around corners to whatever hyperspace it was
where whoever it was they were waiting and watching for would
finally emerge. Their scattered talk was hip, elliptical, and hinted at
mysteries beyond my white boy's ken, but it was the staring off, the
long, steady staring off, that had me hypnotized. I left for a better
job, with handshakes from both of them, without understanding what
I had seen.

Perhaps ten years later, after playing jazz with black musicians in   3
various Harlem clubs, hanging out uptown with a few young artists
and intellectuals, I began to learn from them something of the extraordinarily varied and complex riffs and rituals embraced by different people to help themselves get through life in the ghetto. Fantasy
of all kinds—from playful to dangerous—was in the very air of Harlem. It was the spice of uptown life.

Only then did I understand the two shoeshine men. They were   4
trapped in a demeaning situation in a dark corner in an underground

corridor in a filthy subway system. Their continuous staring off was a kind of statement, a kind of dance. Our bodies are here, went the statement, but our souls are receiving nourishment from distant sources only we can see. They were powerful magic dancers, sorcerers almost, and thirty-five years later I can still feel the pressure of their spell.

The light bulb may appear over your head, is what I'm saying, 5 but it may be a while before it actually goes on. Early in my attempts to learn jazz piano, I used to listen to recordings of a fine player named Red Garland, whose music I admired. I couldn't quite figure out what he was doing with his left hand, however; the chords eluded me. I went uptown to an obscure club where he was playing with his trio, caught him on his break, and simply asked him. "Sixths," he said cheerfully. And then he went away.

I didn't know what to make of it. The basic jazz chord is the 6 seventh, which comes in various configurations, but it is what it is. I was a self-taught pianist, pretty shaky on theory and harmony, and when he said sixths I kept trying to fit the information into what I already knew, and it didn't fit. But it stuck in my mind—a tantalizing mystery.

A couple of years later, when I began playing with a bass player, 7 I discovered more or less by accident that if the bass played the root and I played a sixth based on the fifth note of the scale, a very interesting chord involving both instruments emerged. Ordinarily, I suppose I would have skipped over the matter and not paid much attention, but I remembered Garland's remark and so I stopped and spent a week or two working out the voicings, and greatly strengthened my foundations as a player. I had remembered what I hadn't understood, you might say, until my life caught up with the information and the light bulb went on.

I remember another, more complicated example from my sopho- 8 more year at the small liberal-arts college outside Philadelphia. I seemed never to be able to get up in time for breakfast in the dining hall. I would get coffee and a doughnut in the Coop instead—a basement area with about a dozen small tables where students could get something to eat at odd hours. Several mornings in a row I noticed a strange man sitting by himself with a cup of coffee. He was in his sixties, perhaps, and sat straight in his chair with very little extraneous movement. I guessed he was some sort of distinguished visitor to the college who had decided to put in some time at a student hangout. But no one ever sat with him. One morning I approached his table and asked if I could join him.

"Certainly," he said. "Please do." He had perhaps the clearest 9 eyes I had ever seen, like blue ice, and to be held in their steady gaze was not, at first, an entirely comfortable experience. His eyes gave nothing away about himself while at the same time creating in me the eerie impression that he was looking directly into my soul. He asked a few quick questions, as if to put me at my ease, and we fell into conversation. He was William O. Douglas from the Supreme Court, and when he saw how startled I was he said, "Call me Bill. Now tell me what you're studying and why you get up so late in the morning." Thus began a series of talks that stretched over many weeks. The fact that I was an ignorant sophomore with literary pretensions who knew nothing about the law didn't seem to bother him. We talked about everything from Shakespeare to the possibility of life on other planets. One day I mentioned that I was going to have dinner with Judge Learned Hand. I explained that Hand was my girlfriend's grandfather. Douglas nodded, but I could tell he was surprised at the coincidence of my knowing the chief judge of the most important court in the country save the Supreme Court itself. After fifty years on the bench Judge Hand had become a famous man, both in and out of legal circles—a living legend, to his own dismay. "Tell him hello and give him my best regards," Douglas said.

Learned Hand, in his eighties, was a short, barrel-chested man 10 with a large, square head, huge, thick, bristling eyebrows, and soft brown eyes. He radiated energy and would sometimes bark out remarks or questions in the living room as if he were in court. His humor was sharp, but often leavened with a touch of self-mockery. When something caught his funny bone he would burst out with explosive laughter—the laughter of a man who enjoyed laughing. He had a large repertoire of dramatic expressions involving the use of his eyebrows—very useful, he told me conspiratorially, when looking down on things from behind the bench. (The court stenographer could not record the movement of his eyebrows.) When I told him I'd been talking to William O. Douglas, they first shot up in exaggerated surprise, and then lowered and moved forward in a glower.

"*Justice* William O. Douglas, young man," he admonished. "Jus- 11 tice Douglas, if you please." About the Supreme Court in general, Hand insisted on a tone of profound respect. Little did I know that in private correspondence he had referred to the Court as "The Blessed Saints, Cherubim and Seraphim," "The Jolly Boys," "The Nine Tin Jesuses," The Nine Blameless Ethiopians," and my particular favorite, "The Nine Blessed Chalices of the Sacred Effluvium."

Hand was badly stooped and had a lot of pain in his lower back. 12 Martinis helped, but his strict Yankee wife approved of only one before dinner. It was my job to make the second and somehow slip it to him. If the pain was particularly acute he would get out of his chair and lie flat on the rug, still talking, and finish his point without missing a beat. He flattered me by asking for my impression of Justice Douglas, instructed me to convey his warmest regards, and then began talking about the Dennis case, which he described as a particularly tricky and difficult case involving the prosecution of eleven leaders of the Communist party. He had just started in on the First Amendment and free speech when we were called in to dinner.

William O. Douglas loved the outdoors with a passion, and we 13 fell into the habit of having coffee in the Coop and then strolling under the trees down toward the duck pond. About the Dennis case, he said something to this effect: "Eleven Communists arrested by the government. Up to no good, said the government; dangerous people, violent overthrow, etc. First Amendment, said the defense, freedom of speech, etc." Douglas stopped walking. "Clear and present danger."

"What?" I asked. He often talked in a telegraphic manner, and 14 one was expected to keep up with him. It was sometimes like listening to a man thinking out loud.

"Clear and present danger," he said. "That was the issue. Did 15 they constitute a clear and present danger? I don't think so. I think everybody took the language pretty far in Dennis." He began walking, striding along quickly. Again, one was expected to keep up with him. "The FBI was all over them. Phones tapped, constant surveillance. How could it be clear and present danger with the FBI watching every move they made? That's a ginkgo," he said suddenly, pointing at a tree. "A beauty. You don't see those every day. Ask Hand about clear and present danger."

I was in fact reluctant to do so. Douglas's argument seemed to 16 me to be crushing—the last word, really—and I didn't want to embarrass Judge Hand. But back in the living room, on the second martini, the old man asked about Douglas. I sort of scratched my nose and recapitulated the conversation by the ginkgo tree.

"What?" Hand shouted. "Speak up, sir, for heaven's sake." 17

"He said the FBI was watching them all the time so there couldn't 18 be a clear and present danger," I blurted out, blushing as I said it.

A terrible silence filled the room. Hand's eyebrows writhed on 19 his face like two huge caterpillars. He learned forward in the wing chair, his face settling, finally, into a grim expression. "I am astonished," he said softly, his eyes holding mine, "at Justice Douglas's newfound faith in the Federal Bureau of Investigation." His big, granite head moved even closer to mine, until I could smell the martini. "I had understood him to consider it a politically corrupt, incompetent organization, directed by a power-crazed lunatic." I realized I had been holding my breath throughout all of this, and as I relaxed, I saw the faintest trace of a smile cross Hand's face. Things are sometimes more complicated than they first appear, his smile seemed to say. The old man leaned back. "The proximity of the danger is something to think about. Ask him about that. See what he says."

I chewed the matter over as I returned to campus. Hand had 20 pointed out some of Douglas's language about the FBI from other sources that seemed to bear out his point. I thought about the words "clear and present danger," and the fact that if you looked at them closely they might not be as simple as they had first appeared. What degree of danger? Did the word "present" allude to the proximity of the danger, or just the fact that the danger was there at all—that it wasn't an anticipated danger? Were there other hidden factors these great men were weighing of which I was unaware?

But Douglas was gone, back to Washington. (The writer in me is 21 tempted to create a scene here—to invent one for dramatic purposes— but of course I can't do that.) My brief time as a messenger boy was over, and I felt a certain frustration, as if, with a few more exchanges, the matter of *Dennis v. United States* might have been resolved to my satisfaction. They'd left me high and dry. But, of course, it is precisely because the matter did not resolve that has caused me to think about it, off and on, all these years. "The Constitution," Hand used to say to me flatly, "is a piece of paper. The Bill of Rights is a piece of paper." It was many years before I understood what he meant. Documents alone do not keep democracy alive, nor maintain the state of law. There is no particular safety in them. Living men and women, generation after generation, must continually remake democracy and the law, and that involves an ongoing state of tension between the past and the present which will never completely resolve.

Education doesn't end until life ends, because you never know 22 when you're going to understand something you hadn't understood before. For me, the magic dance of the shoeshine men was the kind of experience in which understanding came with a kind of click, a resolving kind of click. The same with the experience at the piano. What happened with Justice Douglas and Judge Hand was different, and makes the point that understanding does not always mean resolution. Indeed, in our intellectual lives, our creative lives, it is perhaps those problems that will never resolve that rightly claim the lion's share of our energies. The physical body exists in a constant state of tension as it maintains homeostasis, and so too does the active mind embrace the tension of never being certain, never being absolutely sure, never being done, as it engages the world. That is our special fate, our inexpressibly valuable condition.

RESPONDING TO READING

Key words: community discovery education growing up
memory power reality striving talk

Rhetorical concepts: anecdote explanation illustration meditation
narrative/example story

1.   Information comes quickly, Conroy says, but understanding only much
later: "The light bulb may appear over your head . . . but it may be a while
before it actually goes on." Explain this idea by describing how the jazz
musicians helped Conroy understand the shoeshine men.
2.   How did the experience of conveying messages between the two justices
help Conroy understand the role of "living men and women" in the making
of democracy? What did he come to know and how did he come to know it?
3.   Think about something you have come to understand a long time after
you experienced it. Describe what happened in the first place and what led
to your later knowledge.
4.   Knowledge, according to Conroy, "does not always mean resolution."
Indeed, this ability to know while "never being certain, never being absolutely
sure, never being done," is "our inexpressibly valuable condition." This high
value for uncertainty conflicts with what most people think about knowledge,
that it gives answers. Consider the degree of certainty in the other essays
and the poem in this section. How much uncertainty can you tolerate in your
knowledge?

The Route to Normal Science

THOMAS S. KUHN

Thomas S. Kuhn, who earned a doctorate in physics from Harvard University in 1949, has taught at Harvard (1948–56); the University of California, Berkeley (1958–64); Princeton (1964–79); and since 1979 the Massachusetts Institute of Technology. As a professor of philosophy and history of science, Kuhn has studied the ways scientists think and work from a philosophical and humanistic perspective. Although he is the author of works ranging from *The Copernican Revolution: Planetary Astronomy in the Development of Western Thought* (1957) to *The Essential Tension* (1977), Kuhn is best known to readers outside the sciences for *The Structure of Scientific Revolutions* (1962), which includes "The Route to Normal Science."

Kuhn begins "The Route to Normal Science" by defining paradigms—structures or patterns that allow scientists to share a common set of assumptions, theories, laws, or applications as they look at their fields. If their research is based on shared paradigms, and they "learned the bases of their field from the same concrete models," they are "committed to the same rules and standards for scientific practice" and do not disagree over the fundamentals. Kuhn devotes the rest of the essay to explaining how and why this is so. The concepts of "paradigm" and "paradigm shift" have become central, economical ways to conceptualize not only how scientists think and work (the focus of Kuhn's examples) but how knowledge is created and transmitted in a variety of fields.

In this essay, "normal science" means research firmly based upon one or more past scientific achievements, achievements that some particular scientific community acknowledges for a time as supplying the foundation for its further practice. Today such achievements are recounted, though seldom in their original form, by science textbooks, elementary and advanced. These textbooks expound the body of accepted theory, illustrate many or all of its successful applications, and compare these applications with exemplary observations and experiments. Before such books became popular early in the nineteenth century (and until even more recently in the newly matured sciences), many of the famous classics of science fulfilled a similar function. Aristotle's *Physica*, Ptolemy's *Almagest*, Newton's *Principia* and *Opticks*, Franklin's *Electricity*, Lavoisier's *Chemistry*, and Lyell's *Geology*— these and many other works served for a time implicitly to define the legitimate problems and methods of a research field for succeeding generations of practitioners. They were able to do so because they shared two essential characteristics. Their achievement was sufficiently unprecedented to attract an enduring group of adherents away from competing modes of scientific activity. Simultaneously, it was sufficiently open-ended to leave all sorts of problems for the redefined group of practitioners to resolve.

Achievements that share these two characteristics I shall hence- 2 forth refer to as "paradigms," a term that relates closely to "normal science." By choosing it, I mean to suggest that some accepted examples of actual scientific practice—examples which include law, theory, application, and instrumentation together—provide models from which spring particular coherent traditions of scientific research. These are the traditions which the historian describes under such rubrics as "Ptolemaic astronomy" (or "Copernican"), "Aristotelian dynamics" (or "Newtonian"), "corpuscular optics" (or "wave optics"), and so on. The study of paradigms, including many that are far more specialized than those named illustratively above, is what mainly pepares the student for membership in the particular scientific community with which he will later practice. Because he there joins men who learned the bases of their field from the same concrete models, his subsequent practice will seldom evoke overt disagreement over fundamentals. Men whose research is based on shared paradigms are committed to the same rules and standards for scientific practice. That commitment and the apparent consensus it produces are prerequisites for normal science, i.e., for the genesis and continuation of a particular research tradition.

Because in this essay the concept of a paradigm will often sub- 3 stitute for a variety of familiar notions, more will need to be said about the reasons for its introduction. Why is the concrete scientific achievement, as a locus of professional commitment, prior to the various concepts, laws, theories, and points of view that may be abstracted from it? In what sense is the shared paradigm a fundamental unit for the student of scientific development, a unit that cannot be fully reduced to logically atomic components which might functon in its stead? There can be a sort of scientific research without paradigms, or at least without any so unequivocal and so binding as the ones named above. Acquisition of a paradigm and of the more esoteric type of research it permits is a sign of maturity in the development of any given scientific field.

If the historian traces the scientific knowledge of any selected 4 group of related phenomena backward in time, he is likely to encounter some minor variant of a pattern here illustrated from the history of physical optics. Today's physics textbooks tell the student that light is photons, i.e., quantum-mechanical entities that exhibit some characteristics of waves and some of particles. Research proceeds accordingly, or rather according to the more elaborate and mathematical characterization from which this usual verbalization is derived. That characterization of light is, however, scarely half a century old. Before it was developed by Planck, Einstein, and others early in this century, physics texts taught that light was transverse wave motion, a conception rooted in a paradigm that derived ultimately from the optical writings of Young and Fresnel in the early nineteenth century. Nor was the wave theory the first to be embraced by almost all practitioners of optical science. During the eighteenth century the paradigm for this field was provided by Newton's *Opticks*, which taught that light was material corpuscles. At that time physicists sought evidence, as the early wave theorists had not, of the pressure exerted by light particles impinging on solid bodies.

These transformations of the paradigms of physical optics are   5 scientific revolutions, and the successive transition from one paradigm to another via revolution is the usual developmental pattern of mature science. It is not, however, the pattern characteristic of the period before Newton's work, and that is the contrast that concerns us here. No period between remote antiquity and the end of the seventeenth century exhibited a single generally accepted view about the nature of light. Instead there were a number of competing schools and subschools, most of them espousing one variant or another of Epicurean, Aristotelian, or Platonic theory. One group took light to be particles emanating from material bodies; for another it was a modification of the medium that intervened between the body and the eye; still another explained light in terms of an interaction of the medium with an emanation from the eye; and there were other combinations and modifications besides. Each of the corresponding schools derived strength from its relation to some particular metaphysic, and each emphasized, as paradigmatic observations, the particular cluster of optical phenomena that its own theory could do most to explain. Other observations were dealt with by *ad hoc* elaborations, or they remained as outstanding problems for further research.

At various times all these schools made significant contributions   6 to the body of concepts, phenomena, and techniques from which Newton drew the first nearly uniformly accepted paradigm for physical optics. Any definition of the scientist that excludes at least the more creative members of these various schools will exclude their modern successors as well. Those men were scientists. Yet anyone examining a survey of physical optics before Newton may well conclude that, though the field's practitioners were scientists, the net result of their activity was something less than science. Being able to take no common body of belief for granted, each writer on physical optics felt forced to build his field anew from its foundations. In doing so, his choice of supporting observation and experiment was relatively free, for there was no standard set of methods or of phenomena that every optical writer felt forced to employ and explain. Under these circumstances, the dialogue of the resulting books was often directed as much to the members of other schools as it was to nature. That pattern is not unfamiliar in a number of creative fields today, nor is it incompatible with significant discovery and invention. It is not, however, the pattern of development that physical optics acquired after Newton and that other natural sciences make familiar today.

The history of electrical research in the first half of the eighteenth   7
century provides a more concrete and better known example of the way a science develops before it acquires its first universally received paradigm. During that period there were almost as many views about the nature of electricity as there were important electrician experimenters, men like Haukshee, Gray, Desaguliers, Du Fay, Nollett, Watson, Franklin, and others. All their numerous concepts of electricity had something in common—they were partially derived from one or another version of the mechanico-corpuscular philosophy that guided all scientific research of the day. In addition, all were components of real scientific theories, of theories that had been drawn in part from experiment and observation that partially determined the choice and interpretation of additional problems undertaken in research. Yet though all the experiments were electrical and though most of the experimenters read each other's works, their theories had no more than a family resemblance.

One early group of theories, following seventeenth-century prac-   8
tice, regarded attraction and frictional generation as the fundamental electrical phenomena. This group tended to treat repulsion as a secondary effect due to some sort of mechanical rebounding and also to postpone for as long as possible both discussion and systematic research on Gray's newly discovered effect, electrical conduction. Other "electricians" (the term is their own) took attraction and repulsion to be equally elementary manifestations of electricity and modified their theories and research accordingly. (Actually, this group is remarkably small—even Franklin's theory never quite accounted for the mutual repulsion of two negatively charged bodies.) But they had as much difficulty as the first group in accounting simultaneously for any but the simplest conduction effects. Those effects, however, provided the starting point for still a third group, one which tended to speak of electricity as a "fluid" that could run through conductors rather than as an "effluvium" that emanated from non-conductors. This group, in its turn, had difficulty reconciling its theory with a number of

attractive and repulsive effects. Only through the work of Franklin and his immediate successors did a theory arise that could account with something like equal facility for very nearly all these effects and that therefore could and did provide a subsequent generation of "electricians" with a common paradigm for its research.

Excluding those fields, like mathematics and astronomy, in which 9 the first firm paradigms date from prehistory and also those, like biochemistry, that arose by division and recombination of specialties already matured, the situations outlined above are historically typical. Though it involves my continuing to employ the unfortunate simplification that tags an extended historical episode with a single and somewhat arbitrarily chosen name (e.g., Newton or Franklin), I suggest that similar fundamental disagreements characterized, for example, the study of motion before Aristotle and of statics before Archimedes, the study of heat before Black, of chemistry before Boyle and Boerhaave, and of historical geology before Hutton. In parts of biology—the study of heredity, for example—the first universally received paradigms are still more recent; and it remains an open question what parts of social science have yet acquired such paradigms at all. History suggests that the road to a firm research consensus is extraordinarily arduous.

History also suggests, however, some reasons for the difficulties 10 encountered on the road. In the absence of a paradigm or some candidate for paradigm, all of the facts that could possibly pertain to the development of a given science are likely to seem equally relevant. As a result, early fact-gathering is a far more nearly random activity than the one that subsequent scientific development makes familiar. Furthermore, in the absence of a reason for seeking some particular form of more recondite information, early fact-gathering is usually restricted to the wealth of data that lie ready to hand. The resulting pool of facts contains those accessible to casual observation and experiment together with some of the more esoteric data retrievable from established crafts like medicine, calendar making, and metallurgy. Because the crafts are one readily accessible source of facts that could not have been casually discovered, technology has often played a vital role in the emergence of new sciences.

But though this sort of fact-collecting has been essential to the 11 origin of many significant sciences, anyone who examines, for example, Pliny's encyclopedic writings or the Baconian natural histories of the seventeenth century will discover that it produces a morass. One somehow hesitates to call the literature that results scientific. The Baconian "histories" of heat, color, wind, mining, and so on, are filled with information, some of it recondite. But they juxtapose facts that will later prove revealing (e.g., heating by mixture) with others (e.g., the warmth of dung heaps) that will for some time remain too complex to be integrated with theory at all. In addition, since any description must be partial, the typical natural history often omits from its immensely circumstantial accounts just those details that later scientists will find sources of important illumination. Almost none of the early "histories" of electricity, for example, mention that chaff, attracted to a rubbed glass rod, bounces off again. That effect seemed mechanical, not electrical. Moreover, since the casual fact-gatherer seldom possesses the time or the tools to be critical, the natural histories often juxtapose descriptions like the above with others, say, heating by antiperistasis (or by cooling), that we are now quite unable to confirm.[1] Only very occasionally, as in the cases of ancient statics, dynamics, and geometrical optics, do facts collected with so little guidance from pre-established theory speak with sufficient clarity to permit the emergence of a first paradigm.

This is the situation that creates the schools characteristic of the   12 early stages of a science's development. No natural history can be interpreted in the absence of at least some implicit body of intertwined theoretical and methodological belief that permits selection, evaluation, and criticism. If that body of belief is not already implicit in the collection of facts—in which case more than "mere facts" are at hand—it must be externally supplied, perhaps by a current metaphysic, by another science, or by personal and historical accident. No wonder, then, that in the early stages of the development of any science different men confronting the same range of phenomena, but not usually all the same particular phenomena, describe and interpret them in different ways. What is surprising, and perhaps also unique in its degree to the fields we call science, is that such initial divergences should ever largely disappear.

For they do disappear to a very considerable extent and then   13 apparently once and for all. Furthermore, their disappearance is usually caused by the triumph of one of the pre-paradigm schools, which, because of its own characteristic beliefs and pre-conceptions, emphasized only some special part of the too sizable and inchoate pool of information. Those electricians who thought electricity a fluid and therefore gave particular emphasis to conduction provide an excellent case in point. Led by this belief, which could scarcely cope with the known multiplicity of attractive and repulsive effects, several of them conceived the idea of bottling the electrical fluid. The immediate fruit of their efforts was the Leyden jar, a device which might never have

---

[1]Bacon [in the *Novum Organum*] says, "Water slightly warm is more easily frozen than quite cold"; *antiperistasis:* means a reaction caused by an opposite action, in this case, heating by means of cooling. [Eds.]

been discovered by a man exploring nature casually or at random, but which was in fact independently developed by at least two investigators in the early 1740's. Almost from the start of his electrical researches, Franklin was particularly concerned to explain that strange and, in the event, particularly revealing piece of special apparatus. His success in doing so provided the most effective of the arguments that made his theory a paradigm, though one that was still unable to account for quite all the known cases of electrical repulsion.[2] To be accepted as a paradigm, a theory must seem better than its competitors, but it need not, and in fact never does, explain all the facts with which it can be confronted.

What the fluid theory of electricity did for the subgroup that held 14 it, the Franklinian paradigm later did for the entire group of electricians. It suggested which experiments would be worth performing and which, because directed to secondary or to overly complex manifestations of electricity, would not. Only the paradigm did the job far more effectively, partly because the end of interschool debate ended the constant reiteration of fundamentals and partly because the confidence that they were on the right track encouraged scientists to undertake more precise, esoteric, and consuming sorts of work.[3] Freed from the concern with any and all electrical phenomena, the united group of electricians could pursue slected phenomena in far more detail, designing much special equipment for the task and employing it more stubbornly and systematically than electricains had ever done before. Both fact collection and theory articulation became highly directed activities. The effectiveness and efficiency of electrical research increased accordingly, providing evidence for a societal version of Francis Bacon's acute methodological dictum: "Truth emerges more readily from error than from confusion."

We shall be examining the nature of this highly directed or 15 paradigm-based research in the next section, but must first note briefly how the emergence of a paradigm affects the structure of the group that practices the field. When, in the development of a natural science, an individual or group first produces a synthesis able to attract most of the next generation's practitioners, the older schools gradually disappear. In part their disappearance is caused by their members'

---

[2] The troublesome case was the mutual repulsion of negatively charged bodies.

[3] It should be noted that the acceptance of Franklin's theory did not end quite all debate. In 1759 Robert Symmer proposed a two-fluid version of that theory, and for many years thereafter electricians were divided about whether electricity was a single fluid or two. But the debates on this subject only confirm what has been said above about the manner in which a universally recognized achievement unites the profession. Electricians, though they continued divided on this point, rapidly concluded that no experimental tests could distinguish the two versions of the theory and that they were therefore equivalent. After that, both schools could and did exploit all the benefits that the Franklinian theory provided.

conversion to the new paradigm. But there are always some men who cling to one or another of the older views, and they are simply read out of the profession, which thereafter ignores their work. The new paradigm implies a new and more rigid definition of the field. Those unwilling or unable to accommodate their work to it must proceed in isolation or attach themselves to some other group.[4] Historically, they have often simply stayed in the departments of philosophy from which so many of the special sciences have been spawned. As these indications hint, it is sometimes just its reception of a paradigm that transforms a group previously interested merely in the study of nature into a profession or, at least, a discipline. In the sciences (though not in fields like medicine, technology, and law, of which the principal *raison d'être* is an external social need), the formation of specialized journals, the foundation of specialists' societies, and the claim for a special palce in the curriculum have usually been associated with a group's first reception of a single paradigm. At least this was the case between the time, a century and a half ago, when the institutional pattern of scientific specialization first developed and the very recent time when the paraphernalia of specialization acquired a prestige of their own.

The more rigid definition of the scientific group has other con- 16 sequences. When the individual scientist can take a paradigm for granted, he need no longer, in his major works, attempt to build his field anew, starting from first principles and justifying the use of each concept introduced. That can be left to the writer of textbooks. Given a textbook, however, the creative scientist can begin his research where it leaves off and thus concentrate exclusively upon the subtlest and most esoteric aspects of the natural phenomena that concern his group. And as he does this, his research communiqués will begin to change in ways whose evolution has been too little studied but whose modern end products are obvious to all and oppressive to many. No longer will his researchers usually be embodied in books addressed, like Franklin's *Experiments . . . on Electricity* or Darwin's *Origin of Species*, to anyone who might be interested in the subject matter of the field. Instead they will usually appear as brief articles addressed only to professional colleagues, the men whose knowledge of a shared

---

[4]The history of electricity provides an excellent example which could be duplicated from the careers of Priestley, Kelvin, and others. Franklin reports that Nollet, who at mid-century was the most influential of the Continental electricians, "lived to see himself the last of his Sect, except Mr. B.—his *Eleve* [pupil] and immediate Disciple." More interesting, however, is the endurance of whole schools in increasing isolation from professional science. Consider, for example, the case of astrology, which was once an integral part of astronomy. Or consider the continuation in the eighteenth, and early nineteenth centuries of a previously respected tradition of "romantic" chemistry. . . .

paradigm can be assumed and who prove to be the only ones able to read the papers addressed to them.

Today in the sciences, books are usually either texts or retrospec- 17 tive reflections upon one aspect or another of the scientific life. The scientist who writes one is more likely to find his professional reputation impaired than enhanced. Only in the earlier, pre-paradigm, stages of the development of the various sciences did the book ordinarily possess the same relation to professional achievement that it still retains in other creative fields. And only in those fields that still retain the book, with or without the article, as a vehicle for research communication are the lines of professionalization still so loosely drawn that the layman may hope to follow progress by reading the practitioners' original reports. Both in mathematics and astronomy, research reports had ceased already in antiquity to be intelligible to a generally educated audience. In dynamics, research became similarly esoteric in the latter Middle Ages, and it recaptured general intelligibility only briefly during the early seventeenth century when a new paradigm replaced the one that had guided medieval research. Electrical research began to require translation for the layman before the end of the eighteenth century, and most other fields of physical science ceased to be generally accessible in the nineteenth. During the same two centuries similar transitions can be isolated in the various parts of the biological sciences. In parts of the social sciences they may well be occurring today. Although it has become customary, and is surely proper, to deplore the widening gulf that separates the professional scientist from his colleagues in other fields, too little attention is paid to the essential relationship between that gulf and the mechanisms intrinsic to scientific advance.

Ever since prehistoric antiquity one field of study after another 18 has crossed the divide between what the historian might call its prehistory as a science and its history proper. These transitions to maturity have seldom been so sudden or so unequivocal as my necessarily schematic discussion may have implied. But neither have they been historically gradual, coextensive, that is to say, with the entire development of the fields within which they occurred. Writers on electricity during the first four decades of the eighteenth century possessed far more information about electrical phenomena than had their sixteenth-century predecessors. During the half-century after 1740, few new sorts of electrical phenomena were added to their lists. Nevertheless, in important respects, the electrical writings of Cavendish, Coulomb, and Volta in the last third of the eighteenth century seem further removed from those of Gray, Du Fay, and even Franklin than are the writings of these early eighteenth-century electrical discoverers from those of the sixteenth century.[5] Sometime between 1740 and 1780, electricians were for the first time enabled to take the foundations of their field for granted. From that point they pushed on to more concrete and recondite problems, and increasingly they then reported their results in articles addressed to other electricians rather than in books addressed to the learned world at large. As a group they achieved what had been gained by astronomers in antiquity and by students of motion in the Middle Ages, of physical optics in the late seventeenth century, and of historical geology in the early nineteenth. They had, that is, achieved a paradigm that proved able to guide the whole group's research. Except with the advantage of hindsight, it is hard to find another criterion that so clearly proclaims a field a science.

RESPONDING TO READING

Key words: community   education   reality   science

Rhetorical concepts: analysis   cause and effect   definition   explanation illustration   narrative/example   process

1.   What is "normal science" (paragraph 1 and elsewhere), or by analogy, any other "normal" academic discipline? What is the relation of "paradigm" to "normal science" (paragraph 2 and elsewhere)?
2.   Why don't textbooks make revolutionary breakthroughs in their presentation of the knowledge of the discipline they represent? Who reads textbooks? Who reads the cutting-edge articles or books? What use(s) do their respective readers make of the material they encounter?
3.   Every field is full of disagreements and conflicting ways of interpreting and configuring the knowledge of its subject. For instance, critics read literature from a variety of perspectives—Freudian, Marxian, historical, feminist, moral, and many more. How can you, as the reader of a textbook, identify the authors' prevailing interpretation of the subject matter?
4.   How can you decide which of a number of alternative, possibly conflicting, interpretations of a topic within a discipline is right? (For instance, some American historians see the white settlement of the West as fulfillment of America's "manifest destiny;" others interpret white settlement as exploitation of the Native American population. Who's right? See Frances Fitz-Gerald, "America Revised," pp. 192–200.)
5.   How do you (or students in general) know when you know enough to disagree with what you read?

---

[5]The post-Franklinian developments include an immense increase in the sensitivity of charge detectors, the first reliable and generally diffused techniques for measuring charge, the evolution of the concept of capacity and its relation to a newly refined notion of electric tension, and the quantification of electrostatic force. . . .

Evolution as Fact and Theory

STEPHEN JAY GOULD

Science, like any other body of knowledge, is ever-changing. Facts can be reassessed, reinterpreted; intellectual constructs can be reconfigured—suppose someone redrew the constellations to represent great works of art instead of great mythological stories? New contexts can provide new ways to understand familiar information, as Stephen Jay Gould (born 1941) shows in his discussion of "Evolution as Fact and Theory," originally published in *Discover*, a journal of popular science. The greatest fun of science, or any subject, according to Gould, is "when it plays with interesting ideas, examines their implications, and recognizes that old information may be explained in surprisingly new ways." Thus, in his refutation of Creationism, Gould deals not only with the facts and theory of evolution, but with the chilling wish "to mute the healthy debate about theory that has brought new life to evolutionary biology."

Since earning his Ph.D. from Columbia in 1967, Gould has been teaching paleontology, biology, and history of science at Harvard, and explaining his ideas in "surprisingly new ways" to students, peers, and general readers of his columns in *Natural History*. These columns have been collected in *Ever Since Darwin* (1977); *The Panda's Thumb* (1980); *Hen's Teeth and Horse's Toes* (1983); and *Bully for Brontosaurus* (1991).

Gould's reinterpretations of scientific history favor the underdogs, as is evident in *The Mismeasure of Man* (1981). There Gould reinterprets the research methods and philosophy behind nineteenth- and twentieth-century IQ testing and other quantitiatve methods of determining intelligence, showing how flawed measurement procedures and wrong interpretations of information invariably favored educated white Anglo–Saxon males and contributed to the oppression of everyone else. Gould's perceptive writing and critical thinking have been rewarded with the American Book Award in Science (1981) and numerous other academic prizes.

Kirtley Mather, who died last year at age 89, was a pillar of both 1 science and the Christian religion in America and one of my dearest friends. The difference of half a century in our ages evaporated before our common interests. The most curious thing we shared was a battle we each fought at the same age. For Kirtley had gone to Tennessee with Clarence Darrow to testify for evolution at the Scopes trial of 1925. When I think that we are enmeshed again in the same struggle for one of the best documented, most compelling and exciting concepts in all of science, I don't know whether to laugh or cry.

According to idealized principles of scientific discourse, the 2 arousal of dormant issues should reflect fresh data that give renewed life to abandoned notions. Those outside the current debate may therefore be excused for suspecting that creationists have come up with something new, or that evolutionists have generated some serious internal trouble. But nothing has changed; the creationists have not a single new fact or argument. Darrow and Bryan were at least more entertaining than we lesser antagonists today. The rise of creationism is politics, pure and simple; it represents one issue (and by no means the major concern) of the resurgent evangelical right. Arguments that seemed kooky just a decade ago have re-entered the mainstream.

Creationism Is Not Science

The basic attack of the creationists falls apart on two general counts before we even reach the supposed factual details of their complaints against evolution. First, they play upon a vernacular misunderstanding of the word "theory" to convey the false impression that we evolutionists are covering up the rotten core of our edifice. Second, they misuse a popular philosophy of science to argue that they are behaving scientifically in attacking evolution. Yet the same philosophy demonstrates that their own belief is not science, and that "scientific creationism" is therefore meaningless and self-contradictory, a superb example of what Orwell called "newspeak." 3

In the American vernacular, "theory" often means "imperfect fact"—part of a hierarchy of confidence running downhill from fact to theory to hypothesis to guess. Thus the power of the creationist argument: evolution is "only" a theory, and intense debate now rages about many aspects of the theory. If evolution is less than a fact, and scientists can't even make up their minds about the theory, then what confidence can we have in it? Indeed, President Reagan echoed this argument before an evangelical group in Dallas when he said (in what I devoutly hope was campaign rhetoric): "Well, it is a theory. It is a scientific theory only, and it has in recent years been challenged in the world of science—that is, not believed in the scientific community to be as infallible as it once was." 4

Well, evolution *is* a theory. It is also a fact. And facts and theories are different things, not rungs in a hierarchy of increasing certainty. Facts are the world's data. Theories are structures of ideas that explain and interpret facts. Facts do not go away when scientists debate rival theories to explain them. Einstein's theory of gravitation replaced Newton's, but apples did not suspend themselves in mid-air pending the outcome. And human beings evolved from apelike ancestors whether they did so by Darwin's proposed mechanism or by some other, yet to be discovered. 5

Moreover, "fact" does not mean "absolute certainty." The final proofs of logic and mathematics flow deductively from stated premises 6 and achieve certainty only because they are *not* about the empirical world. Evolutionists make no claim for perpetual truth, though creationists often do (and then attack us for a style of argument that they themselves favor). In science, "fact" can only mean "confirmed to such a degree that it would be perverse to withhold provisional assent." I suppose that apples might start to rise tomorrow, but the possibility does not merit equal time in physics classrooms.

Evolutionists have been clear about this distinction between fact   7
and theory from the very beginning, if only because we have always acknowledged how far we are from completely understanding the mechanisms (theory) by which evolution (fact) occurred. Darwin continually emphasized the difference between his two great and separate accomplishments: establishing the fact of evolution, and proposing a theory—natural selection—to explain the mechanism of evolution. He wrote in *The Descent of Man*: "I had two distinct objects in view; firstly, to show that species had not been separately created, and secondly, that natural selection had been the chief agent of change . . . Hence if I had erred in . . . having exaggerated its [natural selection's] power . . . I have at least, as I hope, done good service in aiding to overthrow the dogma of separate creations."

Thus Darwin acknowledged the provisional nature of natural se-   8
lection while affirming the act of evolution. The fruitful theoretical debate that Darwin initiated has never ceased. From the 1940s through the 1960s, Darwin's own theory of natural selection did achieve a temporary hegemony that it never enjoyed in his lifetime. But renewed debate characterizes our decade, and, while no biologist questions the importance of natural selection, many now doubt its ubiquity. In particular, many evolutionists argue that substantial amounts of genetic change may not be subject to natural selection and may spread through populations at random. Others are challenging Darwin's linking of natural selection with gradual, imperceptible change through all intermediary degrees; they are arguing that most evolutionary events may occur far more rapidly than Darwin envisioned.

Scientists regard debates on fundamental issues of theory as a   9
sign of intellectual health and a source of excitement. Science is— and how else can I say it?—most fun when it plays with interesting ideas, examines their implications, and recognizes that old information may be explained in surprising new ways. Evolutionary theory is now enjoying this uncommon vigor. Yet amidst all this turmoil no biologist has been led to doubt the fact that evolution occurred; we are debating *how* it happened. We are all trying to explain the same thing: the tree of evolutionary descent linking all organisms by ties of genealogy. Creationists pervert and caricature this debate by conveniently neglecting the common conviction that underlies it, and by

falsely suggesting that we now doubt the very phenomenon we are struggling to understand.

Using another invalid argument, creationists claim that "the 10 dogma of separate creations," as Darwin characterized it a century ago, is a scientific theory meriting equal time with evolution in high school biology curricula. But a prevailing viewpoint among philosophers of science belies this creationist argument. Philosopher Karl Popper has argued for decades that the primary criterion of science is the falsifiability of its theories. We can never prove absolutely, but we can falsify. A set of ideas that cannot, in principle, be falsified is not science.

The entire creationist argument involves little more than a rhe- 11 torical attempt to falsify evolution by presenting supposed contradictions among its supporters. Their brand of creationism, they claim, is "scientific" because it follows the Popperian model in trying to demolish evolution. Yet Popper's argument must apply in both directions. One does not become a scientist by the simple act of trying to falsify another scientific system; one has to present an alternative system that also meets Popper's criterion—it too must be falsifiable in principle.

"Scientific creationism" is a self-contradictory, nonsense phrase 12 precisely because it cannot be falsified. I can envision observations and experiments that would disprove any evolutionary theory I know, but I cannot imagine what potential data could lead creationists to abandon their beliefs. Unbeatable systems are dogma, not science. Lest I seem harsh or rhetorical, I quote creationism's leading intellectual, Duane Gish, Ph.D., from his recent (1978) book *Evolution? The Fossils Say No!* "By creation we mean the bringing into being by a supernatural Creator of the basic kinds of plants and animals by the process of sudden, or fiat, creation. We do not know how the Creator created, what processes He used, *for He used processes which are not now operating anywhere in the natural universe* [Gish's italics]. This is why we refer to creation as special creation. We cannot discover by scientific investigations anything about the creative processes used by the Creator." Pray tell, Dr. Gish, in the light of your last sentence, what then is "scientific" creationism?

The Fact of Evolution

Our confidence that evolution occurred centers upon three gen- 13 eral arguments. First, we have abundant, direct, observational evidence of evolution in action, from both the field and the laboratory. It ranges from countless experiments on change in nearly everything about fruit flies subjected to artificial selection in the laboratory to the famous British moths that turned black when industrial soot darkened the trees upon which they rest. (The moths gain protection from sharp-sighted bird predators by blending into the background.) Creationists do not deny these observations; how could they? Creationists have tightened their act. They now argue that God only created "basic kinds," and allowed for limited evolutionary meandering within them. Thus toy poodles and Great Danes come from the dog kind and moths can change color, but nature cannot convert a dog to a cat or a monkey to a man.

The second and third arguments for evolution—the case for ma- 14 jor changes—do not involve direct observation of evolution in action. They rest upon inference, but are no less secure for that reason. Major evolutionary change requires too much time for direct observation on the scale of recorded human history. All historical sciences rest upon inference, and evolution is no different from geology, cosmology, or human history in this respect. In principle, we cannot observe processes that operated in the past. We must infer them from results that still survive: living and fossil organisms for evolution, documents and artifacts for human history, strata and topography for geology.

The second argument—that the imperfection of nature reveals 15 evolution—strikes many people as ironic, for they feel that evolution should be most elegantly displayed in the nearly perfect adaptation expressed by some organisms—the chamber of a gull's wing, or butterflies that cannot be seen in ground litter because they mimic leaves so precisely. But perfection could be imposed by a wise creator or evolved by natural selection. Perfection covers the tracks of past history. And past history—the evidence of descent—is our mark of evolution.

Evolution lies exposed in the *imperfections* that record a history of 16 descent. Why should a rat run, a bat fly, a porpoise swim, and I type this essay with structures built of the same bones unless we all inherited them from a common ancestor? An engineer, starting from scratch, could design better limbs in each case. Why should all the large native mammals of Australia be marsupials, unless they descended from a common ancestor isolated on this island continent? Marsupials are not "better," or ideally suited for Australia; many have been wiped out by placental mammals imported by man from other continents. This principle of imperfection extends to all historical scienies. When we recognize the etymology of September, October, November, and December (seventh, eighth, ninth, and tenth, from the Latin), we know that two additional items (January and February) must have been added to an original calendar of ten months.

The third argument is more direct: transitions are often found in 17 the fossil record. Preserved transitions are not common—and should not be, according to our understanding of evolution (see next section)—but they are not entirely wanting, as creationists often claim. The lower jaw of reptiles contians several bones, that of mammals only one. The non-mammalian jawbones are reduced, step by step, in mammalian ancestors until they become tiny nubbins located at the back of the jaw. The "hammer" and "anvil" bones of the mammalian ear are descendants of these nubbins. How could such a transition be accomplished? the creationists ask. Surely a bone is either entirely in the jaw or in the ear. Yet paleontologists have discovered two transitional lineages or therapsids (the so-called mammal-like reptiles) with a double jaw joint—one composed of the old quadrate and articular bones (soon to become the hammer and anvil), the other of the squamosal and dentary bones (as in modern mammals). For that matter, what better transitional form could we desire than the oldest human, *Australopithecus afarensis*, with its apelike palate, its human upright stance, and a cranial capacity larger than any ape's of the same body size but a full 1,000 cubic centimeters below ours? If God made each of the half dozen human species discovered in ancient rocks, why did he create in an unbroken temporal sequence of progressively more modern features—increasing cranial capacity, reduced face and teeth, larger body size? Did he create to mimic evolution and test our faith thereby?

An Example of Creationist Argument

Faced with these facts of evolution and the philosophical bankruptcy of their own position, creationists rely upon distortion and innuendo to buttress their rhetorical claim. If I sound sharp or bitter, indeed I am—for I have become a major target of these practices. 18

I count myself among the evolutionists who argue for a jerky, or episodic, rather than a smoothly gradual, pace of change. In 1972 my colleague Niles Eldredge and I developed the theory of punctuated equilibrium [*Discover*, October]. We argued that two outstanding facts of the fossil record—geologically "sudden" origin of new species and failure to change thereafter (stasis)—reflect the predictions of evolutionary theory, not the imperfections of the fossil record. In most theories, small isolated populations are the source of new species, and the process of speciation takes thousands or tens of thousands of years. This amount of time, so long when measured against our lives, is a geological microsecond. It represents much less than 1 per cent of the average life span for a fossil invertebrate species—more than 10 million years. Large, widespread, and well-established species, on the other hand, are not expected to change very much. We 19 believe that the inertia of large populations explains the stasis of most fossil species over millions of years.

We proposed the theory of punctuated equilibrium largely to pro- 20 vide a different explanation for pervasive trends in the fossil record. Trends, we argued, cannot be attributed to gradual transformation within lineages, but must arise from the differential success of certain kinds of species. A trend, we argued, is more like climbing a flight of stairs (punctuations and stasis) than rolling up an inclined plane.

Since we proposed punctuated equilibria to explain trends, it is 21 infuriating to be quoted again and again by creationists—whether through design or stupidity, I do not know—as admitting that the fossil record includes no transitional forms. Transitional forms are generally lacking at the species level, but are abundant between larger groups. The evolution from reptiles to mammals, as mentioned earlier, is well documented. Yet a pamphlet entitled "Harvard Scientists Agree Evolution Is a Hoax" states: "The facts of punctuated equilibrium which Gould and Eldredge . . . are forcing Darwinists to swallow fit the picture that Bryan insisted on, and which God has revealed to us in the Bible."

Continuing the distortion, several creationists have equated the 22 theory of punctuated equilibrium with a caricature of the beliefs of Richard Goldschmidt, a great early geneticist. Goldschmidt argued, in a famous book published in 1940, that new groups can arise all at once through major mutations. He referred to these suddenly transformed creatures as "hopeful monsters." (I am attracted to some aspects of the non-caricatured version, but Goldschmidt's theory still has nothing to do with punctuated equilibrium.) Creationist Luther Sunderland talks of the "punctuated equilibrium hopeful monster theory" and tells his hopeful readers that "it amounts to tacit admission that anti-evolutionists are correct in asserting there is no fossil evidence supporting the theory that all life is connected to a common ancestor." Duane Gish writes, "According to Goldschmidt, and now apparently according to Gould, a reptile laid an egg from which the first bird, feathers and all, was produced." Any evolutionist who believed such nonsense would rightly be laughed off the intellectual stage; yet the only theory that could ever envision such a scenario for the evolution of birds is creationism—God acts in the egg.

Conclusion

I am both angry at and amused by the creationists; but mostly I 23 am deeply sad. Sad for many reasons. Sad because so many people who respond to creationist appeals are troubled for the right reason, but venting their anger at the wrong target. It is true that scientists have often been dogmatic and elitist. It is true that we have often allowed the white-coated, advertising image to represent us—"Scientists say that Brand X cures bunions ten times faster than . . ." We have not fought it adequately because we derive benefits from appearing as a new priesthood. It is also true that faceless bureaucratic state power intrudes more and more into our lives and removes choices that should belong to individuals and communities. I can understand that requiring that evolution be taught in the schools might be seen as one more insult on all these grounds. But the culprit is not, and cannot be, evolution or any other fact of the natural world. Identify and fight your legitimate enemies by all means, but we are not among them.

I am sad because the practical result of this brouhaha will not be expanded coverage to include creationism (that would also make me sad), but the reduction or excision of evolution from high school curricula. Evolution is one of the half dozen "great ideas" developed by science. It speaks to the profound issues of genealogy that fascinate all of us—the "roots" phenomenon writ large. Where did we come from? Where did life arise? How did it develop? How are organisms related? It forces us to think, ponder, and wonder. Shall we deprive millions of this knowledge and once again teach biology as a set of dull and unconnected facts, without the thread that weaves diverse material into a supple unity. 24

But most of all I am saddened by a trend I am just beginning to discern among my colleagues. I sense that some now wish to mute the healthy debate about theory that has brought new life to evolutionary biology. It provides grist for creationist mills, they say, even if only by distortion. Perhaps we should lie low and rally round the flag of strict Darwinism, at least for the moment—a kind of old-time religion on our part. 25

But we should borrow another metaphor and recognize that we too have to tread a straight and narrow path, surrounded by roads to perdition. For if we ever begin to suppress our search to understand nature, to quench our own intellectual excitement in a misguided effort to repesent a united front where it does not and should not exist, then we are truly lost. 26

RESPONDING TO READING

Key words: community   discovery   education   language   nature   reading   reality   science   transformation   writing

Rhetorical concepts: analysis   anecdote   cause and effect   definition   explanation   induction   narrative/example   process

1.   Give the two different definitions Gould cites of the word "theory"—the scientific one and the vernacular (everyday) one. Then define what he means by a "fact." Using these definitions, explain what he means when he says, "Well, evolution *is* a theory. It is also a fact." How does he differentiate between evolution as a fact and evolution as a theory?

2.   What is the subject of scientific debate over evolution, the "fun" and "play" Gould refers to? What is the misunderstanding of that debate that Gould seeks to refute? Does his own writing reveal the sense of "fun" (paragraph 9) he advocates?

3.   What does Gould mean by insisting that any set of scientific ideas must be able to be falsified? Name some "unbeatable systems" that cannot be falsified, besides Creationism, and decide what characterizes them. From this sequence of definitions, come up with the rules for scientific debate according to Gould. Does Gould himself follow these rules?

4.   Why have Gould's antagonists reacted to his theories with what he calls "distortion and innuendo"? Why would religious people do such things? Are the legitimate complaints about science that Gould lists in his "Conclusion" sufficient reason? Is this the kind of debate that Kuhn called "normal science"? How do you respond to Gould's assertion in his second paragraph that "the rise of creationism is politics, pure and simple"?

5.   Reflect upon how you have come to know about evolution and what it means. If Gould's perspective is new to you, discuss the source of his knowledge and the source of yours. Is this a matter of conflicting belief systems, of different definitions, of different paradigms of knowledge, or what?

"Just Knowing": The Inner Expert

MARY FIELD BELENKY, BLYTHE MCVICKER CLINCHY, NANCY RULE GOLDBERGER, and JILL MATTUCK TARULE

Mary Field Belenky is the co-principal investigator of Listening Partners, a project promoting intellectual development in rural women at the University of Vermont. Blythe McVicker Clinchy is Professor of Psychology at Wellesley College. Nancy Rule Goldberger is on the faculty of The Fielding Institute, Santa Barbara, California. Jill Mattuck Terule is Professor in the clinical psychology division of the Lesley College Graduate School in Boston.

" 'Just Knowing': The Inner Expert," is from *Women's Ways of Knowing: The Development of Self, Voice, and Mind* (Basic Books, 1986), a work that represents the culmination of a five-year research project investigating how women "view reality and draw conclusions about truth, knowledge, and authority." Believing, as many academic feminists do, that throughout history the "male-dominated majority culture" has set the standards and values that guide men and women alike, these psychologists decided to talk directly to a crosssection of American women to find out how and why they know what they know.

The researchers grouped their findings into five categories, which also constitute the book's major divisions. In *silence* women "experience themselves as mindless and voiceless and subject to the whims of external authority." In *received knowledge* women believe that they can receive, even reproduce, knowledge from the "all-knowing external authorities," but cannot create knowledge on their own. In *subjective knowledge* truth and knowledge are believed to be "personal, private, and subjectively known or intuited." In *procedural knowledge* women want to learn and apply objective procedures to obtain and communicate knowledge. In *constructed knowledge* women "experience themselves as creators of knowledge, and value both subjective and objective strategies for knowing." The process of women's intellectual development is captured in their common metaphor, "gaining a voice." "Just Knowing" focuses on the stage of subjective knowledge, listening to one's inner, expert voice.

Once the modest and often belated process of reliance on the self 1 is initiated and supported, women typically move full speed into the subjectivist position on knowing. Subjectivism is for women a position from which they redefine the nature of authority. It is the position at which their views of experts and expertise undergo radical change. The orientation to authority shifts from external to internal. Along with the discovery of personal authority arises a sense of voice—in its earliest form, a "still small voice" to which a woman begins to attend rather than the long-familiar external voices that have directed her life. This interior voice has become, for us, the hallmark of women's emergent sense of self and sense of agency and control.

Early in the tradition into subjectivism, women can have a difficult 2 time identifying the new source of knowing and articulating the process. One woman communicated a sense of inner conviction in the words "I just know," and described a process that bypasses awareness. "I try not to think about stuff because usually the decision is already made up inside you and then when the time comes, if you trust yourself, you just know the answer."

Subjective knowers may be shaky about their own judgment but 3 are proud if others affirm their conclusions and opinions. Some told us they were mystified that they could know something before others and had no idea where their own good ideas came from. One woman said she relied on her own experience and "prayed that she was right," an indication that she must still have feared that ultimately her subjective assessment would be evaluated against some external criterion.

Other women were better able to describe this newly recognized 4 power of subjective knowing. It was as if there were some oracle within that stood opposed to the voices and dictums of the outside world.

It's like a certain feeling that you have inside you. It's like someone could say something to you and you have a feeling. I don't know if it's like a jerk or something inside you. It's hard to explain.

> There's a part of me that I didn't even realize I had until re-
> cently—instinct, intuition, whatever. It helps me and protects me.
> It's perceptive and astute. I just listen to the inside of me and I know
> what to do.

Truth, for subjective knowers, is an intuitive reaction—something   5
experienced, not thought out, something felt rather than actively pursued or constructed. These women do not see themselves as part of
the process, as constructors of truth, but as conduits through which
truth emerges. The criterion for truth they most often refer to is
"satisfaction" or "what feels comfortable to me." They do not mention
that rational procedures play a part in the search for truth.

Occasionally women distinguish between truth as *feelings* that   6
come from within and *ideas* that come from without. This differentiation between thinking and feeling thus appears for the first time
during the period of subjective knowing. This split, for women, may
be a consequence of their belief that thinking is not womanly or that
thought will destroy the capacity for feeling. Thus they relegate ideas
to male authority and, as such, the ideas may or may not have relevance to their lives.

They view truth as unique to each individual, an accident of   7
personal history and experience.

> Every person has her own unique body of knowledge that's been
> given to them through their life's experiences. And realizing that
> mine is as valid as the next person's, whether or not that person has
> gone through six or seven years of college, I feel that my knowledge
> is as important and real and valuable as theirs is.

For women at the positions of silence and received knowledge,   8
there is absolute truth that is true for everyone; at the position of
subjective knowing, truth is absolute only for the individual. The
subjective knower takes a huge step: She sees truth as subjectified
and personal. The subjectivist discovers that each person's life experience gives a different view of reality from that of any other person.
What is more, truth is necessarily a private matter and, at least from
the point of view of these women, should not be imposed on others.

Two very different women—one black from an urban ghetto, the   9
other white from a rural backwater, both enrolled in a college program—had essentially the same way of expressing their perspective
on private subjective truth, a point of view held by other women as
well.

> I think what one person sees to be a fact is not necessarily a fact in
> the eyes of another. So I tend to weigh anything in light of how I
> feel about it. I am only searching for what is valid to me.

I don't try to suffocate people with my ideas or anything like that. I only know for myself. That is a truth for me. I believe in myself and my powers.

Truths can converge; however, in case of disagreement, subjec-   10
tivist women's own experience and inner voice are the final arbiters. Although so-called experts may have done more thinking on a subject, subjectivists feel that they don't have to accept what the experts say. Another person's opinion may be misguided or disagreeable; but they have a tolerance for differences, since others "must obviously believe in their opinion." Subjectivist women recognize that others may disagree with them but seem to be less concerned than men in persuading others to their point of view. For most, resolution of disagreement is impossible; attempts at resolution only lead to unpleasant battles and threaten to disrupt relationships.

When faced with controversy, subjectivist women become strictly   11
pragmatic—"what works best for me." They refer back to the centrality of their personal experience, whether they are talking about right choices for themselves or others. They insist that, since everyone's experience is unique, no one has the right to speak for others or to judge what others have to say. "You have to be in a situation to know what is right or wrong. You can't look at someone from a distance and say, 'Well, they should do this or that.' Maybe it wouldn't work for everybody."

In situations in which the inner voice is silent and personal ex-   12
perience is lacking, subjective knowers adopt a cafeteria approach to knowledge, an attitude of "let's try a little bit of everything until something comes up that works for me." There are no thought-out procedures in the search for lurking truths. The process is magical and mysterious: "It's like the truth hits you dead in the face, and it knocks you out. When you come to, that is it."

RESPONDING TO READING

Key words: community   discovery   gender   identity   power
reality   rights   striving

Rhetorical concepts: definition   explanation   induction
narrative/example   process

1.   Describe what Belenky et al. call "the new source of knowing" (paragraph 2) or "subjective knowing." Where does it come from? What is its difference from rational procedures or external authority?
2.   If "each person's life experience gives a different view of reality," then

it follows that "truth is subjectified and personal." How does this view of reality differ from Langer's symbolic view or Plato's concept of essential forms? How does this view of truth differ from the scientific perspectives of Kuhn or Gould?

3. What are the arguments for and against letting everyone rest content with his or her own sense of reality and truth? Why, for instance, should Gould feel "sad" about the views of creationists, particularly if their views are true for them? Are there political issues at stake for Belenky et al., just as Gould argued that there were for the creationists?

4. Recall and explain an experience that you have had of "just knowing," to someone who seems skeptical of intuition. Tell what happened and what you came to know or understand as a result. How did you know that you really understood? Are you as certain today of that understanding as you were at the time it occurred? If you have ever had doubts or second thoughts, what were these? What, if anything, did you do to accommodate this new perspective?

First Observations

JANE GOODALL

Although Jane Goodall was born (1934) and reared in London, she has lived in Africa since she was eighteen, when she served as an assistant to Dr. Louis Leakey, an anthropologist and paleontologist studying human origins in Kenya. Her research since 1960 has been conducted in Tanzania at the Gombe Stream Chimpanzee Reserve, a rugged area with steep mountains and dense jungles on the shore of Lake Tanganyika. Her careful observation of chimpanzees, not only only in groups but as individuals ("David Graybeard," "Goliath") in their native habitat over many years has made her a respected world expert. She is only the eighth person in the history of Cambridge University to have received a Ph.D. without first earning an undergraduate degree; her thesis, *Behavior of the Free-Ranging Chimpanzee*, consolidated five years' work at Gombe.

In "First Observations," from *In the Shadow of Man* (1971), Goodall describes how she watched chimpanzees at Gombe, with patience, perseverance, and unquenchable excitement. She also explains two of her numerous discoveries about animal behavior that have dramatically changed the knowledge of the field. One is her conclusive discovery that chimpanzees, previously believed to be vegetarian, eat meat. The other is that, in addition to using tools—in this case, blades of grass to "fish" for termites—chimpanzees make their own tools and stockpile them for future use. Such observations as these have forced anthropologists to redefine "man" in a more complex manner than simply as "a tool making and using animal."

For about a month I spent most of each day either on the Peak or   1
overlooking Mlinda Valley where the chimps, before or after stuffing
themselves with figs, ate large quantities of small purple fruits that
tasted, like so many of their foods, as bitter and astringent as sloes
or crab apples. Piece by piece, I began to form my first somewhat
crude picture of chimpanzee life.

The impression that I had gained when I watched the chimps at   2
the msulula tree of temporary, constantly changing associations of
individuals within the community was substantiated. Most often I
saw small groups of four to eight moving about together. Sometimes
I saw one or two chimpanzees leave such a group and wander off on
their own or join up with a different association. On other occasions
I watched two or three small groups joining to form a larger one.

Often, as one group crossed the grassy ridge separating the   3
Kasekela Valley from the fig trees on the home valley, the male
chimpanzee, or chimpanzees, of the party would break into a run,
sometimes moving in an upright position, sometimes dragging a
fallen branch, sometimes stamping or slapping the hard earth. These
charging displays were always accompanied by loud pant-hoots and
afterward the chimpanzee frequently would swing up into a tree overlooking the valley he was about to enter and sit quietly, peering down
and obviously listening for a response from below. If there were
chimps feeding in the fig trees they nearly always hooted back, as
though in answer. Then the new arrivals would hurry down the steep
slope and, with more calling and screaming, the two groups would
meet in the fig trees. When groups of females and youngsters with
no males present joined other feeding chimpanzees, usually there
was none of this excitement; the newcomers merely climbed up into
the trees, greeted some of those already there, and began to stuff
themselves with figs.

While many details of their social behavior were hidden from me   4
by the foliage, I did get occasional fascinating glimpses. I saw one
female, newly arrived in a group, hurry up to a big male and hold
her hand toward him. Almost regally he reached out, clasped her
hand in his, drew it toward him, and kissed it with his lips. I saw
two adult males embrace each other in greeting. I saw youngsters
having wild games through the treetops, chasing around after each
other or jumping again and again, one after the other, from a branch
to a springy bough below. I watched small infants dangling happily
by themselves for minutes on end, patting at their toes with one hand,
rotating gently from side to side. Once two tiny infants pulled on opposite ends of a twig in a gentle tug-of-war. Often, during the heat
of midday or after a long spell of feeding, I saw two or more adults

grooming each other, carefully looking through the hair of their companions.

At that time of year the chimps usually went to bed late, making   5
their nests when it was too dark to see properly through binoculars, but sometimes they nested earlier and I could watch them from the Peak. I found that every individual, except for infants who slept with their mothers, made his own nest each night. Generally this took about three minutes: the chimp chose a firm foundation such as an upright fork or crotch, or two horizontal branches. Then he reached out and bent over smaller branches onto this foundation, keeping each one in place with his feet. Finally he tucked in the small leafy twigs growing around the rim of his nest and lay down. Quite often a chimp sat up after a few minutes and picked a handful of leafy twigs, which he put under his head or some other part of his body before settling down again for the night. One young female I watched went on and on bending down branches until she had constructed a huge mound of greenery on which she finally curled up.

I climbed up into some of the nests after the chimpanzees had   6
left them. Most of them were built in trees that for me were almost impossible to climb. I found that there was quite complicated interweaving of the branches in some of them. I found, too, that the nests were fouled with dung; and later, when I was able to get closer to the chimps, I saw how they were always careful to defecate and urinate over the edge of their nests, even in the middle of the night.

During that month I really came to know the country well, for I   7
often went on expeditions from the Peak, sometimes to examine nests, more frequently to collect specimens of the chimpanzees' food plants, which Bernard Verdcourt had kindly offered to identify for me. Soon I could find my way around the sheer ravines and up and down the steep slopes of three valleys—the home valley, the Pocket, and Mlinda Valley—as well as a taxi driver finds his way about in the main streets and byways of London. It is a period I remember vividly, not only because I was beginning to accomplish something at last, but also because of the delight I felt in being completely by myself. For those who love to be alone with nature I need add nothing further; for those who do not, no words of mine could ever convey, even in part, the almost mystical awareness of beauty and eternity that accompanies certain treasured moments. And, though the beauty was always there, those moments came upon me unaware: when I was watching the pale flush preceding dawn; or looking up through the rustling leaves of some giant forest tree into the greens and browns and black shadows that occasionally ensnared a bright fleck of the blue sky; or when I stood, as darkness fell, with one hand on the still-warm trunk

of a tree and looked at the sparkling of an early moon on the never still, sighing water of the lake.

One day, when I was sitting by the trickle of water in Buffalo Wood, pausing for a moment in the coolness before returning from a scramble in Mlinda Valley, I saw a female bushbuck moving slowly along the nearly dry streambed. Occasionally she paused to pick off some plant and crunch it. I kept absolutely still, and she was not aware of my presence until she was little more than ten yards away. Suddenly she tensed and stood staring at me, one small forefoot raised. Because I did not move, she did not know what I was—only that my outline was somehow strange. I saw her velvet nostrils dilate as she sniffed the air, but I was downwind and her nose gave her no answer. Slowly she came closer, and closer—one step at a time, her neck craned forward—always poised for instant flight. I can still scarcely believe that her nose actually touched my knee; yet if I close my eyes I can feel again, in imagination, the warmth of her breath and the silken impact of her skin. Unexpectedly I blinked and she was gone in a flash, bounding away with loud barks of alarm until the vegetation hid her completely from my view.

It was rather different when, as I was sitting on the Peak, I saw a leopard coming toward me, his tail held up straight. He was at a slightly lower level than I, and obviously had no idea I was there. Ever since arrival in Africa I had had an ingrained, illogical fear of leopards. Already, while working at the Gombe, I had several times nearly turned back when, crawling through some thick undergrowth, I had suddenly smelled the rank smell of cat. I had forced myself on, telling myself that my fear was foolish, that only wounded leopards charged humans with savage ferocity.

On this occasion, though, the leopard went out of sight as it started to climb up the hill—the hill on the peak of which I sat. I quickly hastened to climb a tree, but halfway there I realized that leopards can climb trees. So I uttered a sort of halfhearted squawk. The leopard, my logical mind told me, would be just as frightened of me if he knew I was there. Sure enough, there was a thudding of startled feet and then silence. I returned to the Peak, but the feeling of unseen eyes watching me was too much. I decided to watch for the chimps in Mlinda Valley. And, when I returned to the Peak several hours later, there, on the very rock which had been my seat, was a neat pile of leopard dung. He must have watched me go and then, very carefully, examined the place where such a frightening creature had been and tried to exterminate my alien scent with his own.

As the weeks went by the chimpanzees became less and less afraid. Quite often when I was on one of my food-collecting expeditions I came across chimpanzees unexpectedly, and after a time I found that some of them would tolerate my presence provided they were in fairly thick forest and I sat still and did not try to move closer than sixty to eighty yards. And so, during my second month of watching from the peak, when I saw a group settle down to feed I sometimes moved closer and was thus able to make more detailed observations.

It was at this time that I began to recognize a number of different 12 individuals. As soon as I was sure of knowing a chimpanzee if I saw it again, I named it. Some scientists feel that animals should be labeled by numbers—that to name them is anthropomorphic—but I have always been interested in the *differences* between individuals, and a name is not only more individual than a number but also far easier to remember. Most names were simply those which, for some reason or other, seemed to suit the individuals to whom I attached them. A few chimps were named because some facial expression or mannerism reminded me of human acquaintances.

The easiest individual to recognize was old Mr. McGregor. The 13 crown of his head, his neck, and his shoulders were almost entirely devoid of hair, but a slight fill remained around his head rather like a monk's tonsure. He was an old male—perhaps between thirty and forty years of age (the longevity record of a captive chimp is forty-seven years). During the early months of my acquaintance with him, Mr. McGregor was somewhat belligerent. If I accidentally came across him at close quarters he would threaten me with an upward and backward jerk of his head and a shaking of branches before climbing down and vanishing from my sight. He reminded me, for some reason, of Beatrix Potter's old gardener in *The Tale of Peter Rabbit.*

Ancient Flo with her deformed, bulbous nose and ragged ears 14 was equally easy to recognize. Her youngest offspring at that time were two-year-old Fifi, who still rode everywhere on her mother's back, and her juvenile son, Figan, who was always to be seen wandering around with his mother and little sister. He was then about six years old; it was approximately a year before he would attain puberty. Flo often traveled with another old mother, Olly. Olly's long face was also distinctive; the fluff of hair on the back of her head—though no other feature—reminded me of my aunt, Olwen. Olly, like Flo, was accompanied by two children, a daughter younger than Fifi, and an adolescent son about a year older than Figan.

Then there was William, who, I am certain, must have been Olly's 15 blood brother. I never saw any special signs of friendship between them, but their faces were amazingly alike. They both had long upper lips that wobbled when they suddenly turned their heads. William had the added distinction of several thin, deeply etched scar marks running down his upper lip from his nose.

Two of the other chimpanzees I knew well by sight at that time 16 were David Graybeard and Goliath. Like David and Goliath in the Bible, these two individuals were closely associated in my mind because they were very often together. Goliath, even in those days of his prime, was not a giant, but he had a splendid physique and the springy movements of an athlete. He probably weighed about one hundred pounds. David Graybeard was less afraid of me from the start than were any of the other chimps. I was always pleased when I picked out his handsome face and well-marked silvery beard in a chimpanzee group, for with David to calm the others, I had a better chance of approaching to observe them more closely.

Before the end of my trial period in the field I made two really 17 exciting discoveries—discoveries that made the previous months of frustration well worth while. And for both of them I had David Graybeard to thank.

One day I arrived on the Peak and found a small group of chimps 18 just below me in the upper branches of a thick tree. As I watched I saw that one of them was holding a pink-looking object from which he was from time to time pulling pieces with his teeth. There was a female and a youngster and they were both reaching out toward the male, their hands actually touching his mouth. Presently the female picked up a piece of the pink thing and put it to her mouth: it was at this moment that I realized the chimps were eating meat.

After each bite of meat the male picked off some leaves with his 19 lips and chewed them with the flesh. Often, when he had chewed for several minutes on this leafy wad, he spat out the remains into the waiting hands of the female. Suddenly, he dropped a small piece of meat, and like a flash the youngster swung after it to the ground. Even as he reached to pick it up the undergrowth exploded and an adult bushpig charged toward him. Screaming, the juvenile leaped back into the tree. The pig remained in the open, snorting and moving backward and forward. Soon I made out the shapes of three small striped piglets. Obviously the chimps were eating a baby pig. The size was right and later, when I realized that the male was David Graybeard, I moved closer and saw that he was indeed eating piglet.

For three hours I watched the chimps feeding. David occasionally 20 let the female bite pieces from the carcass and once he actually detached a small piece of flesh and placed it in her outstretched hand. When he finally climbed down there was still meat left on the carcass; he carried it away in one hand, followed by the others.

Of course I was not sure, then, that David Graybeard had caught 21 the pig for himself, but even so, it was tremendously exciting to know that these chimpanzees actually ate meat. Previously scientists had believed that although these apes might occasionally supplement their diet with a few insects or small rodents and the like they were primarily vegetarians and fruit eaters. No one had suspected that they might hunt larger mammals.

It was within two weeks of this observation that I saw something 22 that excited me even more. By then it was October and the short rains had begun. The blackened slopes were softened by feathery new grass shoots and in some places the ground was carpeted by a variety of flowers. The Chimpanzees' Spring, I called it. I had had a frustrating morning, tramping up and down three valleys with never a sign or sound of a chimpanzee. Hauling myself up the steep slope of Mlinda Valley I headed for the Peak, not only weary but soaking wet from crawling through dense undergrowth. Suddenly I stopped, for I saw a slight movement in the long grass about sixty yards away. Quickly focusing my binoculars I saw that it was a single chimpanzee, and just then he turned in my direction. I recognized David Graybeard.

Cautiously I moved around so that I could see what he was doing. 23 He was squatting beside the red earth mound of a termite nest, and as I watched I saw him carefully push a long grass stem down into a hole in the mound. After a moment he withdrew it and picked something from the end with his mouth. I was too far away to make out what he was eating, but it was obvious that he was actually using a grass stem as a tool.

I knew that on two occasions casual observers in West Africa had 24 seen chimpanzees using objects as tools: one had broken open palm-nut kernels by using a rock as a hammer, and a group of chimps had been observed pushing sticks into an underground bees' nest and licking off the honey. Somehow I had never dreamed of seeing anything so exciting myself.

For an hour David feasted at the termite mound and then he 25 wandered slowly away. When I was sure he had gone I went over to examine the mound. I had found a few crushed insects strewn about, and a swarm of worker termites sealing the entrances of the nest passages into which David had obviously been poking his stems. I picked up one of his discarded tools and carefully pushed it into a hole myself. Immediately I felt the pull of several termites as they seized the grass, and when I pulled it out there were a number of workers termites and a few soldiers, with big red heads, clinging on with their mandibles. There they remained, sticking out at right angles to the stem with their legs waving in the air.

Before I left I trampled down some of the tall dry grass and 26 constructed a rough hide—just a few palm fronds leaned up against the low branch of a tree and tied together at the top. I planned to wait there the next day. But it was another week before I was able to watch a chimpanzee "fishing" for termites again. Twice chimps arrived, but each time they saw me and moved off immediately. Once a swarm of fertile winged termites—the princes and princesses, as they are called—flew off on their nuptial flight, their huge white wings fluttering frantically as they carried the insects higher and higher. Later I realized that it is at this time of year, during the short rains, when the worker termites extend the passages of the nest to the surface, preparing for these emigrations. Several such swarms emerge between October and January. It is principally during these months that the chimpanzees feed on termites.

On the eighth day of my watch David Graybeard arrived again, 27 together with Goliath, and the pair worked there for two hours. I could see much better: I observed how they scratched open the sealed-over passage entrances with a thumb or forefinger. I watched how they bit the end off their tools when they became bent, or used the other end, or discarded them in favor of new ones. Goliath once moved at least fifteen yards from the heap to select a firm-looking piece of vine, and both males often picked three or four stems while they were collecting tools, and put the spares beside them on the ground until they wanted them.

Most exciting of all, on several occasions they picked small leafy 28 twigs and prepared them for use by stripping off the leaves. This was the first recorded example of a wild animal not merely *using* an object as a tool, but actually modifying an object and thus showing the crude beginnings of tool*making*.

Previously man had been regarded as the only tool-making ani- 29 mal. Indeed, one of the clauses commonly accepted in the definition of man was that he was a creature who "made tools to a regular and set pattern." The chimpanzees, obviously, had not made tools to any set pattern. Nevertheless, my early observations of their primitive toolmaking abilities convinced a number of scientists that it was necessary to redefine man in a more complex manner than before. Or else, as Louis Leakey put it, we should by definition have to accept the chimpanzee as Man.

RESPONDING TO READING

Key words: animals   community   discovery   identity   nature
science

Rhetorical concepts: analogy   analysis   anecdote   explanation
illustration   induction   metaphor   narrative/example   research report

1.   Goodall uses metaphors from human life to help readers interpret her description of chimpanzee life. Find some of these metaphors and explain their effects. What do they tell you about Goodall's "way of knowing" the animals?

2.   Goodall's love of nature is connected with being "completely by myself." She describes "the almost mystical awareness of beauty and eternity that accompanies certain treasured moments." The scene with the female bush-buck is an example. Which of the various ways of knowing in this section seems closest to what Goodall exemplifies?

3.   Goodall describes two "exciting" discoveries about the chimpanzees. What are these discoveries and what do they have in common? Do these discoveries, and other aspects of her "first observations," suggest what kinds of things she was looking for?

4.   Describe a particularly exciting observation you have made about human nature, an animal, a plant, or another part of the country or world, to someone who is unfamiliar with your subject. How did you know what to look for, what procedures to use, what to expect? Or was your discovery entirely accidental or serendipitous? How did you know when you were on to something significant? Compare the completeness and reliability of the kind of knowledge gained from firsthand observation with the knowledge you have gained in other ways.

A World of Difference

EVELYN FOX KELLER

Since earning her Ph.D. from Harvard in 1963, Evelyn Fox Keller (born 1936) has held academic appointments in a diversity of fields: physics, mathematical biology, humanities, and mathematics; currently, she is Professor of Rhetoric, Women's Studies, and History of Science at the University of California, Berkeley. Her two major books reflect this confluence of interests. *A Feeling for the Organism* (1983) is a biography of Barbara McClintock, genetic researcher and Nobel Prize winner, who regards herself as "an outsider to the world of modern biology—not because she is a woman but because she is a philosophical and methodological deviant."

Keller's second book, *Reflections on Gender and Science* (1985), is a collection of nine essays that, from historical, psychoanalytic, and philosophical perspectives, explore the question, "How much of the nature of science is bound up with the idea of masculinity, and what would it mean for science if it were otherwise?" Examining science through a feminist lens, Keller finds its fundamental assumption in the "deeply rooted popular mythology" that defines "objectivity, reason, and mind as male, and subjectivity, feeling, and nature as female." Science has been produced almost exclusively by white, middle class men upholding, under the guise of "scientific neutral-ity," "the impersonal, the rational, and the general." Women, seen by men as "protectors of the personal, the emotional, the particular," have been shut out. In the chapter reprinted here, "A World of Difference," Keller analyzes the causes and consequences of these gender-related differences as manifested in Barbara McClintock's style of doing science.

O Lady! We receive but what we give,
And in our life alone does Nature live:
Ours is her wedding garment, ours her shroud!
SAMUEL TAYLOR COLERIDGE, "Dejection: An Ode"

If we want to think about the ways in which science might be 1
different, we could hardly find a more appropriate guide than Barbara
McClintock. Known to her colleagues as a maverick and a visionary,
McClintock occupies a place in the history of genetics at one and the
same time central and peripheral—a place that, for all its eminence,
is marked by difference at every turn.

Born in 1902, McClintock began in her twenties to make contribu- 2
tions to classical genetics and cytology that earned her a level of
recognition few women of her generation could imagine. Encouraged
and suported by many of the great men of classical genetics (including
T. H. Morgan, R. A Emerson, and Lewis Stadler), McClintock was
given the laboratory space and fellowship stipends she needed to
pursue what had quickly become the central goal of her life: understanding the secrets of plant genetics. She rejected the more conventional opportunities then available to women in science (such as a
research assistantship or a teaching post at a woman's college) and
devoted herself to the life of pure research. By the mid 1930s, she
had already made an indelible mark on the history of genetics. But
the fellowships inevitably ran out. With no job on the horizon,
McClintock thought she would have to leave science. Morgan and
Emerson, arguing that "it would be a scientific tragedy if her work
did not go forward" (quoted in Keller 1983, p. 74), prevailed upon
the Rockefeller Foundation to provide two years interim support. Morgan described her as "the best person in the world" in her field but
deplored her "personality difficulties": "She is sore at the world because of her conviction that she would have a much freer scientific
opportunity if she were a man" (p. 73). Not until 1942 was Mc-
Clintock's professional survival secured: at that time, a haven was
provided for her at the Carnegie Institution of Washington at Cold
Spring Harbor, where she has remained ever since. Two years later
she was elected to the National Academy of Science; in 1945 she
became president of the Genetics Society of America.

This dual theme of success and marginality that poignantly de- 3
scribes the first stage of McClintock's career continues as the leitmotif
of her entire professional life. Despite the ungrudging respect and
admiration of her colleagues, her most important work has, until
recently, gone largely unappreciated, uncomprehended, and almost
entirely unintegrated into the growing corpus of biological thought.
This was the work, begun in her forties, that led to her discovery that

genetic elements can move, in an apparently coordinated way, from one chromosomal site to another—in short, her discovery of genetic transposition. Even today, as a Nobel laureate and deluged with other awards and prizes for this same work, McClintock regards herself as, in crucial respects, an outsider to the world of modern biology—not because she is a woman but because she is a philosophical and methodological deviant.

Complexity and Difference

To McClintock, nature is characterized by an a priori complexity   4 that vastly exceeds the capacities of the human imagination. Her recurrent remark, "Anything you can think of you will find,"[2] is a statement about the capacities not of mind but of nature. It is meant not as a description of our own ingenuity as discoverers but as a comment on the resourcefulness of natural order; in the sense not so much of adaptability as of largesse and prodigality. Organisms have a life and an order of their own that scientists can only begin to fathom. "Misrepresented, not appreciated, . . . [they] are beyond our wildest expectations. . . . They do everything we [can think of], they do it better, more efficiently, more marvelously." In comparison with the ingenuity of nature, our scientific intelligence seems pallid. It follows as a matter of course that "trying to make everything fit into set dogma won't work. . . . There's no such thing as a central dogma into which everything will fit."

In the context of McClintock's views of nature, attitudes about - 5 research that would otherwise sound romantic fall into logical place. The need to "listen to the material" follows from her sense of the order of things. Precisely because the complexity of nature exceeds our own imaginative possibilities, it becomes essential to "let the experiment tell you what to do." Her major criticism of contemporary research is based on what she sees as inadequate humility. She feels that "much of the work done is done because one wants to impose an answer on it—they have the answer ready, and they [know what] they want the material to tell them, so anything it doesn't tell them, they don't really recognize as there, or they think it's a mistake and throw it out. . . . If you'd only just let the material tell you."

Respect for complexity thus demands from observers of nature   6 the same special attention to the exceptional case that McClintock's own example as a scientist demands from observers of science: "If the material tells you, 'It may be this,' allow that. Don't turn it aside

---

[1]All quotations from Barbara McClintock are taken from private interviews conducted between September 24, 1978, and February 25, 1979; most of them appear in Keller 1983.

and call it an exception, an aberration, a contaminant. . . . That's what's happened all the way along the line with so many good clues." Indeed, respect for individual difference lies at the very heart of McClintock's scientific passion. "The important thing is to develop the capacity to see one kernel [of maize] that is different, and make that understandable," she says. "If [something] doesn't fit, there's a reason, and you find out what it is." The prevailing focus on classes and numbers, McClintock believes, encourages researchers to over-look difference, to "call it an exception, an aberration, a contaminant." The consequences of this seem to her very costly. "Right and left," she says, they miss "what is going on."

She is, in fact, here describing the history of her own research. 7 Her work on transposition in fact began with the observation of an aberrant pattern of pigmentation on a few kernels of a single corn plant. And her commitment to the significance of this singular pattern sustained her through six years of solitary and arduous investiga-tion—all aimed at making the difference she saw understandable.

Making difference understandable does not mean making it dis- 8 appear. In McClintock's world view, an understanding of nature can come to rest with difference. "Exceptions" are not there to "prove the rule"; they have meaning in and of themselves. In this respect, difference constitutes a principle for ordering the world radically un-like the principle of division of dichotomization (subject–object, mind–matter, feeing–reason, disorder–law). Whereas these opposi-tions are directed toward a cosmic unity typically excluding or devour-ing one of the pair, toward a unified, all-encompassing law, respect for difference remains content with multiplicity as an end in itself.

And just as the terminus of knowledge implied by difference can 9 be distinguished from that implied by division, so the starting point of knowledge can also be distinguished. Above all, difference, in this world view, does not posit division as an epistemological prerequi-site—it does not imply the necessity of hard and fast divisions in nature, or in mind, or in the relation between mind and nature. Division severs connection and imposes distance; the recognition of difference provides a starting point for relatedness. It serves both as a clue to new modes of connectedness in nature, and as an invitation to engagement with nature. For McClintock, certainly, respect for difference serves both these functions. Seeing something that does not appear to fit is, to her, a challenge to find the larger multidimen-sional pattern into which it does fit. Anomalous kernels of corn were evidence not of disorder or lawlessness, but of a larger system of order, one that cannot be reduced to a single law.

Difference thus invites a form of engagement and understanding 10 that allows for the preservation of the indivdual. The integrity of each kernel (or chromosome or plant) survives all our own pattern-making attempts; the order of nature transcends our capacities for ordering. And this transcendence is manifested in the enduring uniqueness of each organism: "No two plants are exactly alike. They're all different, and as a consequence, you have to know that difference," she explains. "I start with the seedling, and I don't want to leave it. I don't feel I really know the story if I don't watch the plant all the way along. So I know every plant in the field. I know them intimately, and I find it a great pleasure to know them." From days, weeks, and years of patient observation comes what looks like privileged insight: "When I see things, I can interpret them right away." As one colleague described it, the result is an apparent ability to write the "autobiography" of every plant she works with.

McClintock is not here speaking of relations to other humans, but 11 the parallels are nonetheless compelling. In the relationship she describes with plants, as in human relations, respect for difference constitutes a claim not only on our interest but on our capacity for empathy—in short on the highest form of love: love that allows for intimacy without the annihilation of difference. I use the word *love* neither loosely nor sentimentally, but out of fidelity to the language McClintock herself uses to describe a form of attention, indeed a form of thought. Her vocabulary is consistently a vocabulary of affection, of kinship, of empathy. Even with puzzles, she explains, "The thing was dear to you for a period of time, you really had an affection for it. Then after a while, it disappears and it doesn't bother you. But for a short time you feel strongly attached to that little toy." The crucial point for us is that McClintock can risk the suspension of boundaries between subject and object without jeopardy to science precisely because, to her, science is not premised on that division. Indeed, the intimacy she experiences with the objects she studies—intimacy born of a lifetime of cultivated attentiveness—is a wellspring of her powers as a scientist.

The most vivid illustration of this process comes from her own 12 account of a breakthrough in one particularly recalcitrant piece of cytological analysis. She describes the state of mind accompanying the crucial shift in orientation that enabled her to identify chromosomes she had earlier not been able to distinguish: "I found that the more I worked with them, the bigger and bigger [the chromosomes] got, and when I was really working with them I wasn't outside, I was down there. I was part of the system. I was right down there with them, and everything got big. I even was able to see the internal parts of the chromosomes—actually everything was there. It surprised me because I actually felt as if I was right down there and these were my friends. . . . As you look at these things, they become part of you. And you forget yourself."

Cognition and Perception

In this world of difference, division is relinquished without gen- 13 erating chaos. Self and other, mind and nature survive not in mutual alienation, or in symbiotic fusion, but in structural integrity. The "feeling for the organism" that McClintock upholds as the sine qua non of good research need not be read as "partcipation mystique"; it is a mode of access—honored by time and human experience if not by prevailing conventions in science—to the reliable knowledge of the world around us that all scientists seek. It is a form of attention strongly reminiscent of the concept of "focal attention" developed by Ernest Schachtel to designate "man's [sic] capacity to center his attention on an object fully, so that he can perceive or understand it from many sides, as fully as possible" (p. 251). In Schachtel's language, "focal attention" is the principal tool that, in conjunction with our natural interest in objects per se, enables us to progress from mere wishing and wanting to thinking and knowing—that equips us for the fullest possible knowledge of reality in its own terms. Such "object-centered" perception presupposes "a temporary eclipse of all the perceiver's egocentric thoughts and strivings, of all preoccupation with self and self-esteem, and a full turning towards the object, . . . [which, in turn] leads not to a loss of self, but to a heightened feeling of aliveness" (p. 181). Object-centered perception, Schachtel goes on to argue, is in the service of a love "which wants to affirm others in their total and unique being . . . [which affirms objects as] "part of the same world of which man is a part" (p. 226). It requires

> an experiential realization of the kinship between oneself and the other . . . a realization [that] is made difficult by fear and by arrogance—by fear because then the need to protect oneself by flight, appeasement, or attack gets in the way; by arrogance because then the other is no longer experienced as akin, but as inferior to oneself. (p. 227)

The difference between Schachtel and McClintock is that what Schachtel grants to the poet's perceptual style in contrast to that of the scientist, McClintock claims equally for science. She enlists a "feeling for the organism"—not only for living organisms but for any object that fully claims our attention—in pursuit of the goal shared by all scientists: reliable (that is, shareable and reproducible) knowledge of natural order.

This difference is a direct reflection of the limitations of Schachtel's   14
picture of science. It is drawn not from observation of scientists like
McClintock but only from the more stereotypic scientist, who "looks
at the object with one or more hypotheses . . . in mind and thus 'uses'
the object to corroborate or disprove a hypothesis, but does not encounter the object as such, in its own fullness." For Schachtel,

> modern natural science has as its main goal prediction, i.e. the power
> to manipulate objects in such a way that certain predicted events
> will happen. . . . Hence, the scientist usually will tend to perceive
> the object merely from the perspective of [this] power. . . . That is
> to say that his view of the object will be determined by the ends
> which he pursues in his experimentation. . . . He may achieve a
> great deal in this way and add important data to our knowledge,
> but to the extent to which he remains within the framework of this
> perspective he will not perceive the object in its own right. (1959,
> p. 171)

To McClintock, science has a different goal: not prediction per se, but
understanding; not the power to manipulate, but empowerment—
the kind of power that results from an understanding of the world
around us, that simultaneously reflects and affirms our connection
to that world.

What Counts as Knowledge

At the root of this difference between McClintock and the ste-   15
reotypic scientist lies that unexamined starting point of science: the
naming of nature. Underlining every discussion, there exists a larger
assumption about the nature of the universe in which that discussion
takes place. The power of this unseen ground is to be found not in
its influence on any particular argument in science but in its framing
of the very terms of argument—in its definition of the tacit aims and
goals of science. As I noted in the introduction to this section, scientists may spend fruitful careers, building theories of nature that
are astonishingly successful in their predictive power, without ever
feeling the need to reflect on these fundamental philosophical issues.
Yet if we want to ask questions about that success, about the value
of alternative scientific descriptions of nature, even about the possibility of alternative criteria of success, we can do so only by examining
those most basic assumptions that are normally not addressed.

We have to remind ourselves that, although all scientists share a   16
common ambition for knowledge, it does not follow that what counts
as knowledge is commonly agreed upon. The history of science reveals a wide diversity of questions asked, explanations sought, and

methodologies employed in this common quest for knowledge of the natural world; this diversity is in turn reflected in the kinds of knowledge acquired, and indeed in what counts as knowledge. To a large degree, both the kinds of questions one asks and the explanations that one finds satisfying depend on one's a priori relation to the objects of study. In particular, I am suggesting that questions asked about objects with which one feels kinship are likely to differ from questions asked about objects one sees as unalterably alien. Similarly, explanations that satisfy us about a natural world that is seen as "blind, simple and dumb," ontologically inferior, may seem less self-evidently satisfying for a natural world seen as complex and, itself, resourceful. I suggest that individual and communal conceptions of nature need to be examined for their role in the history of science, not as causal determinants but as frameworks upon which all scientific programs are developed. More specifically, I am claiming that the difference between McClintock's conception of nature and that prevailing in the community around her is an essential key to our understanding of the history of her life and work.

It provides, for example, the context for examining the differences [17] between McClintock's interests *as a geneticist* and what has historically been the defining focus of both classical and molecular genetics—differences crucial to the particular route her research took. To most geneticists, the problem of inheritance is solved by knowing the mechanism and structure of genes. To McClintock, however, as to many other biologists, mechanism and structure have never been adequate answers to the question "How do genes work?" Her focus was elsewhere: on function and organization. To her, an adequate understanding would, by definition, have to include an account of how they function in relation to the rest of the cell, and of course, to the organism as a whole.

In her language, the cell itself is an organism. Indeed, "Every [18] component of the organism is as much an organism as every other part." When she says, therefore, that "one cannot consider the [gene] as such as being all important—more important is the overall organism," she means the genome as a whole, the cell, the ensemble of cells, the organism itself. Genes are neither "beads on a string" nor functionally disjoint pieces of DNA. They are organized functional units, whose very function is defined by their position in the organization as a whole. As she says, genes function "only with respect to the environment in which [they are] found.

Interests in function and in organization are historically and [19] conceptually related to each other. By tradition, both are primary preoccupations of developmental biology, and McClintock's own interests in development followed from and supported these interests.

By the same tradition, genetics and developmental biology have been two separate subjects. But for a geneticist for whom the answer to the question of how genes work must include function and organization, the problem of heredity becomes inseparable from the problem of development. The division that most geneticists felt they had to live with (happily or not) McClintock could not accept. To her, development, as the coordination of function, was an integral part of genetics.

McClintock's views today are clearly fed by her work on trans- 20 position. But her work on transposition was itself fed by these interests. Her own account (see Keller 1983, pp. 115–17) of how she came to this work and of how she followed the clues she saw vividly illustrates the ways in which her interests in function and organization— and in development—focused her attention on the patterns she saw and framed the questions she asked about the significance of these patterns. I suggest that they also defined the terms that a satisfying explanation had to meet.

Such an explanation had to account not so much for how trans- 21 position occurred, as for why it occurred. The patterns she saw indicated a programmatic disruption in normal developmental function. When she succeeded in linking this disruption to the location (and change in location) of particular genetic elements, that very link was what captured her interest. (She knew she was "on to something important.") The fact that transposition occurred—the fact that genetic sequences are not fixed—was of course interesting too, but only secondarily so. To her, the paramount interest lay in the meaning of its occurrence, in the clue that transposition provided for the relation between genetics and development. Necessarily, a satisfying account of this relation would have to take due note of the complexity of the regulation process.

Transposition and the Central Dogma

Just two years after McClintock's first public presentation of her 22 work on transposition came the culminating event in the long search for the mechanism of inheritance. Watson and Crick's discovery of the structure of DNA enabled them to provide a compelling account of the essential genetic functions of replication and instruction. According to their account, the vital information of the cell is encoded in the DNA. From there is it copied onto the RNA, which, in turn, is used as a blueprint for the production of the proteins responsible for genetic traits. In the picture that emerged—DNA to RNA to protein (which Crick himself dubbed the "cental dogma")—the DNA is posited as the central actor in the cell, the executive governor of cellular organization, itself remaining impervious to influence from the subordinate agents to which it dictates. Several years later, Watson and Crick's original model was emended by Jacques Monod and François Jacob to allow for environmental control of the rates of protein synthesis. But even with this modification, the essential autonomy of DNA remained unchallenged: information flowed one way, always from, and never to, the DNA.

Throughout the 1950s and 1960s, the successes of molecular genetics were dramatic. By the end of the 1960s, it was possible to say (as Jacques Monad did say), "The Secret of Life? But this is in large part known—in principle, if not in details" (quoted in Judson 1979, p. 216). A set of values and interests wholly different from McClintock's seemed to have been vindicated. The intricacies, and difficulties, of corn genetics held little fascination in comparison with the quick returns from research on the vastly simpler and seemingly more straightforward bacterium and bacteriophage. As a result, communication between McClintock and her colleagues grew steadily more difficult; fewer and fewer biologists had the expertise required even to begin to understand her results. 23

McClintock of course shared in the general excitement of this period, but she did not share in the general enthusiasm for the central dogma. The same model that seemed so immediately and overwhelmingly satisfying to so many of her colleagues did not satisfy her. Although duly impressed by its explanatory power, she remained at the same time acutely aware of what it did not explain. It neither addressed the questions that were of primary interest to her—bearing on the relation between genetics and development—nor began to take into account the complexity of genetic organization that she had always assumed, and that was now revealed to her by her work on transposition. 24

McClintock locates the critical flaw of the central dogma in its presumption: it claimed to explain too much. Baldly put, what was true of *E. coli* (the bacterium most commonly studied) was *not* true of the elephant, as Monod (and others) would have had it (Judson 1979, p. 613). Precisely because higher organisms are multicellular, she argued, they necessarily require a different kind of economy. The central dogma was without question inordinately successful as well as scientifically productive. Yet the fact that it ultimately proved inadequate even to the dynamics of *E. coli* suggests that its trouble lay deeper than just a too hasty generalization from the simple to the complex; its presumptuousness, I suggest, was built into its form of explanation. 25

McClintock has been abundantly vindicated: transposition is acknowledged, higher organisms and development have once again 26 captured the interest of biologists, and almost everyone agrees that genetic organization is manifestly more complex than had previously been thought. But not everyone shares her conviction that we are in the midst of a revolution that "will reorganize the way we look at things, the way we do research." Many researchers remain confident that the phenomenon of transposition can somehow be incorporated, even if they do not yet see how, into an improved version of the central dogma. Their attachment to this faith is telling. Behind the continuing skepticism about McClintock's interpretation of the role of transposition in development and evolution, there remains a major gap between her underlying interests and commitments and those of most of her colleagues.

The Issue of Gender

How much of this enduring difference reflects the fact that Mc- 27 Clintock is a woman in a field still dominated by men? To what extent are her views indicative of a vision of "what will happen to science," as Erik Erikson asked in 1964 (1965, p. 243), "if and when women are truly represented in it—not by a few glorious exceptions, but in the rank and file of the scientific elite?"

On the face of it, it would be tempting indeed to call McClintock's 28 vision of science "a feminist science." Its emphasis on intuition, on feeling, on connection and relatedness, all seem to confirm our most familiar stereotypes of women. And to the extent that they do, we might expect that the sheer presence of more women in science would shift the balance of community sentiment and lead to the endorsement of that vision. However, there are both general and particular reasons that argue strongly against this simple view.

The general argument is essentially the same as that which I made 29 against the notion of "a different science," in the introduction to part 3. To the extent that science is defined by its past and present practitioners, anyone who aspires to membership in that community must conform to its existing code. As a consequence, the inclusion of new members, even from a radically different culture, cannot induce immediate or direct change. To be a successful scientist, one must first be adequately socialized. For this reason, it is unreasonable to expect a sharp differentiation between women scientists and their male colleagues, and indeed, most women scientists would be appalled by such a suggestion.

McClintock is in this sense no exception. She would disclaim any 30 analysis of her work as a woman's work, as well as any suggestion that her views represent a woman's perspective. To her, science is not a matter of gender, either male or female; it is, on the contrary, a

place where (ideally at least) "the matter of gender drops away."
Furthermore, her very commitment to science is of a piece with her
lifelong wish to transcend gender altogether. Indeed, her adamant
rejection of female stereotypes seems to have been a prerequisite for
her becoming a scientist at all. (See Keller 1983, chaps. 2 and 3.) In
her own image of herself, she is a maverick in all respects—as a
woman, as a scientist, even as a woman scientist.

Finally, I want to reemphasize that it would be not only misleading 31
but actually contradictory to suggest that McClintock's views of science were shared by none of her colleagues. Had that been so, she
could not have had even marginal status as a scientist. It is essential
to understand that, in practice, the scientific tradition is far more
pluralistic than any particular description of it suggests, and certainly
more pluralistic than its dominant ideology. For McClintock to be
recognized as a scientist, the positions that she represents, however
unrepresentative, had to be, and were, identifiable as belonging somewhere within that tradition.

But although McClintock is not a total outsider to science, she is 32
equally clearly not an insider. And however atypical she is as a
woman, what she is *not* is a man. Between these two facts lies a crucial
connection—a connection signaled by the recognition that, as Mc-
Clintock herself admits, the matter of gender never does drop away.

I suggest that the radical core of McClintock's stance can be located 33
right here: Because she is not a man, in a world of men, her commitment to a gender-free science has been binding; because concepts
of gender have so deeply influenced the basic categories of science,
that commitment has been transformative. In short, the relevance of
McClintock's gender in this story is to be found not in its role in her
personal socialization but precisely in the role of gender in the construction of science.

Of course, not all scientists have embraced the conception of sci- 34
ence as one of "putting nature on the rack and torturing the answers
out of her." Nor have all men embraced a conception of masculinity
that demands cool detachment and domination. Nor even have all
scientists been men. But most have. And however variable the attitudes of individual male scientists toward science and toward masculinity, the metaphor of a marriage between mind and nature
necessarily does not look the same to them as it does to women. And
this is the point.

In a science constructed around the naming of object (nature) as 35
female and the parallel naming of subject (mind) as male, any scientist
who happens to be a woman is confronted with an a priori contradiction in terms. This poses a critical problem of identity: any scientist
who is not a man walks a path bounded on one side by inauthenticity

and on the other by subversion. Just as surely as inauthenticity is the cost a woman suffers by joining men in misogynist jokes, so it is, equally, the cost suffered by a woman who identifies with an image of the scientist modeled on the patriarchal husband. Only if she undergoes a radical disidentification from self can she share masculine pleasure in mastering a nature cast in the image of woman as passive, inert, and blind. Her alternative is to attempt a radical redefinition of terms. Nature must be renamed as not female, or, at least, as not an alienated object. By the same token, the mind, if the female scientist is to have one, must be renamed as not necessarily male, and accordingly recast with a more inclusive subjectivity. This is not to say that the male scientist cannot claim similar redefinition (certainly many have done so) but, by contrast to the woman scientist, his identity does not require it.

For McClintock, given her particular commitments to personal 36 integrity, to be a scientist, and not a man, with a nonetheless intact identity, meant that she had to insist on a different meaning of mind, of nature, and of the relation between them. Her need to define for herself the relation between subject and object, even the very terms themselves, came not from a feminist consciousness, or even from a female consciousness. It came from her insistence on her right to be a scientist—from her determination to claim science as a human rather than a male endeavor. For such a claim, difference makes sense of the world in ways that division cannot. It allows for the kinship that she feels with other scientists, without at the same time obligating her to share all their assumptions.

Looked at in this way, McClintock's stance is, finally, a far more 37 radical one than that implied in Erikson's question. It implies that what could happen to science "when women are truly represented in it" is not simply, or even, "the addition, to the male kind of creative vision, of women's vision" (p. 243), but I suggest, a thoroughgoing transformation of the very possibilities of creative vision, for everyone. It implies that the kind of change we might hope for is not a direct or readily apparent one but rather an indirect and subterranean one. A first step toward such a transformation would be the undermining of the commitment of scientists to the masculinity of their profession that would be an inevitable concomitant of the participation of large numbers of women.

However, we need to remember that, as long as success in science 38 does not require self-reflection, the undermining of masculinist or other ideological commitments is not a sufficient guarantee of change. But nature itself is an ally that can be relied upon to provide the impetus for real change: nature's responses recurrently invite reexamination of the terms in which our understanding of science is constructed. Paying attention to those responses—"listening to the material"—may help us to reconstruct our understanding of science in terms born out of the diverse spectrum of human experience rather than out of the narrow spectrum that our culture has labeled masculine.

Bibliography

Erikson, Erik H. 1965. Concluding Remarks. In *Women in the Scientific Professions,* ed. J. Mattfeld and C. van Aiken, Cambridge: MIT Press.

Judson, Horace 1979. *The Eighth Day of Creation: Makers of the Revolution in Biology.* New York: Simon & Schuster.

Keller, Evelyn Fox 1983. *A Feeling for the Organism: The Life and Work of Barbara McClintock.* New York: Freeman.

Schachtel, Ernest 1959. *Metamorphosis.* New York: Basic Books.

RESPONDING TO READING

Key words: community discovery gender identity nature power reality science

Rhetorical concepts: analysis biography cause and effect definition explanation illustration narrative/example process

1.   How can Keller reconcile her statements that McClintock had by her twenties "a level of recognition that few women of her generation could "imagine" (paragraph 2), and, in the next paragraph, that "her most important work had, until recently, gone largely unappreciated, uncomprehended, and almost entirely unintegrated into the growing corpus of biological thought"? Explain the apparent contradiction and the way Keller resolves it.

2.   Describe McClintock's concept of the relation between the researcher and nature. Account for such statements as "Anything you can think of you will find" (paragraph 4), "[Organisms] are beyond our wildest expectations" (paragraph 4), and "let the experiment tell you what to do" (paragraph 5). When Keller applies the term "intimacy" to this relation between McClintock and the objects she studies, does that seem excessive? How would you describe this method of gaining knowledge? How is it like and unlike other methods you have been reading about, say Goodall's, Belenky's, Conroy's, Langer's? How does the Coleridge fragment quoted at the beginning relate to McClintock's sense of the relation between the observer and nature? What is the connection between "the poet's conceptual style" and the scientist's?

3.   What does McClintock mean by "difference" (which "lies at the very heart of McClintock's scientific passion," paragraph 6)? Why does she disagree with prevailing views of difference and division (paragraph 9)? How is "difference" distinguishable from "division" and why do the two terms suggest separate approaches to knowledge? What is "the feeling for the organism"? How does this "form of engagement and understanding" lead to

the "preservation of the individual," whether a kernel of corn or a human being?

4.   To what degree is it appropriate to call McClintock's approach "feminist science"? What might be considered feminist in her view of the explanatory power of DNA for genetics (paragraphs 19–20), and for transposition (paragraphs 21–23)? Consider her positions in relation to Kuhn's (masculine?) explanation of "normal science." Keller disputes McClintock's opinion on the degree to which the scientists can "transcend gender altogether"; what do you think of Keller's argument on this subject?

5.   How significant are gender differences for your own work in or outside of school (or in the future)? As part of your planning for this topic, interview a few people who may see gender issues differently from the way you do now: a graduate student, or an older female professor, or a personnel manager. Then write an essay in which you try to convince your classmates that gender issues will or will not play a role in your, and their, future.

America Revised

FRANCES FITZGERALD

Frances FitzGerald's work as an investigative journalist provides a constant critique of establishment America on many dimensions: social, political, religious, and intellectual. That she favors the overlooked and the oppressed is in the tradition of her public spirited ancestors, many of them energetic, intelligent, activist women. These include Elizabeth Peabody, a notable nineteenth-century abolitionist and educator; Mary Parkman Peabody, FitzGerald's grandmother, active in community work and once jailed for civil rights activities; and Marietta Tree, FitzGerald's mother, appointed by President John F. Kennedy as the United States representative to the United Nations Human Rights Commission.

FitzGerald (born 1940) writes primarily for *The New Yorker*, where all three of her books were first published serially. *Fire in the Lake: The Vietnamese and Americans in Vietnam* (1973), winner of both a Pulitzer Prize and a National Book Award, made a strong antiwar protest that helped shape American opinion against military intervention in Vietnam. *Cities on a Hill: A Journey Through Contemporary American Cultures* (1986) critically examines several counterculture communities of the 1960s–80s, whose members sought to reinvent themselves, collectively and individually. In *America Revised: A History of Schoolbooks in the Twentieth Century* (1979), FitzGerald investigates how history books have been written and rewritten to promote what politicians and publishers believe is the national interest, irrespective of the facts, as the chapter reprinted here reveals. What schoolchildren learn about their heritage from these books is whatever version of the facts is popular or politically in fashion at the time.

Those of us who grew up in the fifties believed in the permanence   1
of our American-history textbooks. To us as children, those texts were
the truth of things: they were American history. It was not just that
we read them before we understood that not everything that is printed
is the truth, or the whole truth. It was that they, much more than
other books, had the demeanor and trappings of authority. They were
weighty volumes. They spoke in measured cadences: imperturbable,
humorless, and as distant as Chinese emperors. Our teachers treated
them with respect, and we paid them abject homage by memorizing

a chapter a week. But now the textbook histories have changed, some of them to such an extent that an adult would find them unrecognizable.

One current junior-high-school American history begins with a story about a Negro cowboy called George McJunkin. It appears that when McJunkin was riding down a lonely trail in New Mexico one cold spring morning in 1925 he discovered a mound containing bones and stone implements, which scientists later proved belonged to an Indian civilization ten thousand years old. The book goes on to say that scientists now believe there were people in the Americas at least twenty thousand years ago. It discusses the Aztec, Mayan, and Incan civilizations and the meaning of the word "culture" before introducing the European explorers.[1]

Another history text—this one for the fifth grade—begins with the story of how Henry B. Gonzalez, who is a member of Congress from Texas, learned about his own nationality. When he was ten years old, his teacher told him he was an American because he was born in the United States. His grandmother, however, said, "The cat was born in the oven. Does that make him bread?" After reporting that Mr. Gonzalez eventually went to college and law school, the book explains that "the melting pot idea hasn't worked out as some thought it would," and that now "some people say that the people of the United States are more like a salad bowl than a melting pot."[2]

Poor Columbus! He is a minor character now, a walk-on in the middle of American history. Even those books that have not replaced his picture with a Mayan temple or an Iroquois mask do not credit him with discovering America—even for the Europeans. The Vikings, they say, preceded him to the New World, and after that the Europeans, having lost or forgotten their maps, simply neglected to cross the ocean again for five hundred years. Columbus is far from being the only personage to have suffered from time and revision. Captain John Smith, Daniel Boone, and Wild Bill Hickok—the great self-promoters of American history—have all but disappeared, taking with them a good deal of the romance of the American frontier. General Custer has given way to Chief Crazy Horse; General Eisenhower no longer liberates Europe single-handed; and, indeed, most generals, even to Washington and Lee, have faded away, as old soldiers do, giving place to social reformers such as William Lloyd Garrison and Jacob Riis. A number of black Americans have risen to prominence: not only George Washington Carver but Frederick Douglass and Mar-

---

[1]Wood, Gabriel, and Biller, *America* (1975), p. 3.

[2]King and Anderson, *The United States* (sixth level), Houghton Mifflin Social Studies Program (1976), pp. 15–16.

tin Luther King, Jr. W. E. B. Du Bois now invariably accompanies Booker T. Washington. In addition, there is a mystery man called Crispus Attucks, a fugitive slave about whom nothing seems to be known for certain except that he was a victim of the Boston Massacre and thus became one of the first casualties of the American Revolution. Thaddeus Stevens has been reconstructed[3]—his character changed, as it were, from black to white, from cruel and vindictive to persistent and sincere. As for Teddy Roosevelt, he now champions the issue of conservation instead of charging up San Juan Hill. No single President really stands out as a hero, but all Presidents—except certain unmentionables in the second half of the nineteenth century— seem to have done as well as could be expected, given difficult circumstances.

Of course, when one thinks about it, it is hardly surprising that 5
modern scholarship and modern perspectives have found their way into children's books. Yet the changes remain shocking. Those who in the sixties complained of the bland optimism, the chauvinism, and the materialism of their old civics texts did so in the belief that, for all their protests, the texts would never change. The thought must have had something reassuring about it, for that generation never noticed when its complaints began to take effect and the songs about radioactive rainfall and houses made of ticky-tacky began to appear in the textbooks. But this is what happened.

The history texts now hint at a certain level of unpleasantness in 6
American history. Several books, for instance, tell the story of Ishi, the last "wild" Indian in the continental United States, who, captured in 1911 after the massacre of his tribe, spent the final four and a half years of his life in the University of California's museum of anthropology, in San Francisco. At least three books show the same stunning picture of the breaker boys, the child coal miners of Pennsylvania— ancient children with deformed bodies and blackened faces who stare stupidly out from the entrance to a mine. One book quotes a soldier on the use of torture in the American campaign to pacify the Philippines at the beginning of the century. A number of books say that during the American Revolution the patriots tarred and feathered those who did not support them, and drove many of the loyalists from the country. Almost all the present-day history books note that the United States interned Japanese-Americans in detention camps during the Second World War.

---

[3]Thaddeus Stevens (1792–1868): Republican congressman from Pennsylvania. A leader in the House during and after the Civil War, he was a determined abolitionist who hated the South and violently opposed Lincoln's moderate reconstruction plan. Stevens dominated the committee that impeached Andrew Johnson.

Ideologically speaking, the histories of the fifties were implacable, 7
seamless. Inside their covers, America was perfect: the greatest nation
in the world, and the embodiment of democracy, freedom, and technological progress. For them, the country never changed in any important way: its values and its political institutions remained constant
from the time of the American Revolution. To my generation—the
children of the fifties—these texts appeared permanent just because
they were so self-contained. Their orthodoxy, it seemed, left no hand-
holds for attack, no lodging for decay. Who, after all, would dispute
the wonders of technology or the superiority of the English colonists
over the Spanish? Who would find fault with the pastorale of the West
or the Old South? Who would question the anti-Communist crusade?
There was, it seemed, no point in comparing these visions with reality,
since they were the public truth and were thus quite irrelevant to
what existed and to what anyone privately believed. They were—or
so it seemed—the permanent expression of mass culture in America.

But now the texts have changed, and with them the country that 8
American children are growing up into. The society that was once
uniform is now a patchwork of rich and poor, old and young, men
and women, blacks, whites, Hispanics, and Indians. The system that
ran so smoothly by means of the Constitution under the guidance of
benevolent conductor Presidents is now a rattletrap affair. The past
is no highway to the present; it is a collection of issues and events
that do not fit together and that led in no single direction. The word
"progress" has been replaced by the word "change": children, the
modern texts insist, should learn history so that they can adapt to
the rapid changes taking place around them. History is proceeding
in spite of us. The present, which was once portrayed in the concluding chapters as a peaceful haven of scientific advances and Pres-
idential inaugurations, is now a tangle of problems: race problems,
urban problems, foreign-policy problems, problems of pollution, poverty, energy depletion, youthful rebellion, assassination, and drugs.
Some books illustrate these problems dramatically. One, for instance,
contains a picture of a doll half buried in a mass of untreated sewage;
the caption reads, "Are we in danger of being overwhelmed by the
products of our society and wastage created by their production?
Would you agree with this photographer's interpretation?"[4] Two
books show the same picture of an old black woman sitting in a
straight chair in a dingy room, her hands folded in graceful resignation;[5] the surrounding text discusses the problems faced by the

---

[4]Sellers et al., *As It Happened* (1975), p. 812.

[5]Graff, *The Free and the Brave*, 2nd ed. (1972), p. 696; and Graff and Krout, *The Adventure*, 2nd
ed. (1973), p. 784.

urban poor and by the aged who depend on Social Security. Other books present current problems less starkly. One of the texts concludes sagely:

> Problems are part of life. Nations face them, just as people face them, and try to solve them. And today's Americans have one great advantage over past generations. Never before have Americans been so well equipped to solve their problems. They have today the means to conquer poverty, disease, and ignorance. The technetronic age has put that power into their hands.[6]

Such passages have a familiar ring. Amid all the problems, the deus ex machina of science still dodders around in the gloaming of pious hope.

Even more surprising than the emergence of problems is the discovery that the great unity of the texts has broken. Whereas in the fifties all texts represented the same political view, current texts follow no pattern of orthodoxy. Some books, for instance, portray civil-rights legislation as a series of actions taken by a wise, paternal government; others convey some suggestion of the social upheaval involved and make mention of such people as Stokely Carmichael and Malcolm X. In some books, the Cold War has ended; in others, it continues, with Communism threatening the free nations of the earth.

The political diversity in the books is matched by a diversity of pedagogical approach. In addition to the traditional narrative histories, with their endless streams of facts, there are so-called "discovery," or "inquiry," texts, which deal with a limited number of specific issues in American history. These texts do not pretend to cover the past; they focus on particular topics, such as "stratification in Colonial society" or "slavery and the American Revolution," and illustrate them with documents from primary and secondary sources. The chapters in these books amount to something like case studies, in that they include testimony from people with different perspectives or conflicting views on a single subject. In addition, the chapters provide background information, explanatory notes, and a series of questions for the student. The questions are the heart of the matter, for when they are carefully selected they force students to think much as historians think: to define the point of view of the speaker, analyze the ideas presented, question the relationship between events, and so on. One text, for example, quotes Washington, Jefferson, and John Adams on the question of foreign alliances and then asks, "What did John Adams assume that the international situation would be after the American Revolution? What did Washington's attitude toward the

---

[6]Wood, Gabriel, and Biller, *America* (1975), p. 812.

French alliance seem to be? How do you account for his attitude?" Finally, it asks, "Should a nation adopt a policy toward alliances and cling to it consistently, or should it vary its policies toward other countries as circumstances change?"[7] In these books, history is clearly not a list of agreed-upon facts or a sermon on politics but a babble of voices and a welter of events which must be ordered by the historian.

In matters of pedagogy, as in matters of politics, there are not 11 two sharply differentiated categories of books; rather, there is a spectrum. Politically, the books run from moderate left to moderate right; pedagogically, they run from the traditional history sermons, through a middle ground of narrative texts with inquiry-style questions and of inquiry texts with long stretches of narrative, to the most rigorous of case-study books. What is common to the current texts—and makes all of them different from those of the fifties—is their engagement with the social sciences. In eighth-grade histories, the "concepts" of social science make fleeting appearances. But these "concepts" are the very foundation stones of various elementary-school social-studies series. The 1970 Harcourt Brace Jovanovich series, for example, boasts in its preface of "a horizontal base or ordering of conceptual schemes" to match its "vertical arm of behavioral themes."[8] What this means is not entirely clear, but the books do proceed from easy questions to hard ones, such as—in the sixth-grade book—"How was interaction between merchants and citizens different in the Athenian and Spartan social systems?" Virtually all the American-history texts for older children include discussions of "role," "status," and "culture." Some of them stage debates between eminent social scientists in roped-off sections of the text; some include essays on economics or sociology; some contain pictures and short biographies of social scientists of both sexes and diverse races. Many books seem to accord social scientists a higher status than American Presidents.

Quite as striking as these political and pedagogical alterations is 12 the change in the physical appearance of the texts. The schoolbooks of the fifties showed some effort in the matter of design: they had maps, charts, cartoons, photographs, and an occasional four-color picture to break up the columns of print. But beside the current texts they look as naïve as Soviet fashion magazines. The print in the fifties books is heavy and far too black, the colors muddy. The photographs are conventional news shots—portraits of Presidents in three-quarters profile, posed "action" shots of soldiers. The other illustrations tend

---

[7]Fenton, gen. ed., *A New History of the United States*, grade eleven (1969), p. 170.

[8]Brandwein et al., *The Social Sciences* (1975), introductions to all books.

to be Socialist-realist-style drawings (there are a lot of hefty farmers with hoes in the Colonial-period chapters) or incredibly vulgar made-for-children paintings of patriotic events. One painting shows Columbus standing in full court dress on a beach in the New World from a perspective that could have belonged only to the Arawaks. By contrast, the current texts are paragons of sophisticated modern design. They look not like *People* or *Family Circle* but, rather, like *Architectural Digest* or *Vogue*. One of them has an Abstract Expressionist design on its cover, another a Rauschenberg-style collage, a third a reproduction of an American primitive painting. Inside, almost all of them have a full-page reproduction of a painting of the New York school— a Jasper Johns flag, say, or "The Boston Massacre," by Larry Rivers. But these reproductions are separated only with difficulty from the over-all design, for the time charts are as punctilious as Albers' squares in their color gradings. The amount of space given to illustrations is far greater than it was in the fifties; in fact, in certain "slow-learner" books the pictures far outweigh the text in importance. However, the illustrations have a much greater historical value. Instead of made-up paintings or anachronistic sketches, there are cartoons, photographs, and paintings drawn form the periods being treated. The chapters on the Colonial period will show, for instance, a ship's carved prow, a Revere bowl, a Copley painting—a whole gallery of Early Americana. The nineteenth century is illustrated with nineteenth-century cartoons and photographs—and the photographs are all of high artistic quality. As for the twentieth-century chapters, they are adorned with the contents of a modern-art museum.

The use of all this art and high-quality design contains some irony. [13] The nineteenth-century photographs of child laborers or urban slum apartments are so beautiful that they transcend their subjects. To look at them, or at the Victor Gatto painting of the Triangle shirtwaist-factory fire, is to see not misery or ugliness but an art object. In the modern chapters, the contrast between style and content is just as great: the color photographs of junkyards or polluted rivers look as enticing as *Gourmet's* photographs of food. The book that is perhaps the most stark in its description of modern problems illustrates the horrors of nuclear testing with a pretty Ben Shahn picture of the Bikini explosion, and the potential for global ecological disaster with a color photograph of the planet swirling its mantle of white clouds.[9] Whereas in the nineteen-fifties the texts were childish in the sense that they were naïve and clumsy, they are now childish in the sense that

---

[9] Ver Steeg and Hofstadter, *A People* (1974), pp. 722–23.

they are polymorphous-perverse. American history is not dull any longer; it is a sensuous experience.

The surprise that adults feel in seeing the changes in history texts   14
must come from the lingering hope that there is, somewhere out there, an objective truth. The hope is, of course, foolish. All of us children of the twentieth century know, or should know, that there are no absolutes in human affairs, and thus there can be no such thing as perfect objectivity. We know that each historian in some degree creates the world anew and that all history is in some degree contemporary history. But beyond this knowledge there is still a hope for some reliable authority, for some fixed stars in the universe. We may know journalists cannot be wholly unbiased and that "balance" is an imaginary point between two extremes, and yet we hope that Walter Cronkite will tell us the truth of things. In the same way, we hope that our history will not change—that we learned the truth of things as children. The texts, with their impersonal voices, encourage this hope, and therefore it is particularly disturbing to see how they change, and how fast.

Slippery history! Not every generation but every few years the   15
content of American-history books for children changes appreciably. Schoolbooks are not, like trade books, written and left to their fate. To stay in step with the cycles of "adoption" in school districts across the country, the publishers revise most of their old texts or substitute new ones every three or four years. In the process of revision, they not only bring history up to date but make changes—often substantial changes—in the body of the work. History books for children are thus more contemporary than any other form of history. How should it be otherwise? Should students read histories written ten, fifteen, thirty years ago? In theory, the system is reasonable—except that each generation of children reads only one generation of schoolbooks. That transient history is those children's history forever—their particular version of America.

Bibliography

Brandwein, Paul Franz, et al. *The Social Sciences: Concepts and Values.* 6 Vols., seven levels, kindergarten through grade six. New York: Harcourt Brace Jovanovich, 1975. First edition, 1957.

Fenton, Edwin. *A New History of the United States: An Inquiry Approach.* By Irwin Bartlett, Edwin Fenton, David Fowler, and Seymour Mandlebaum. New York: Holt Rinehart & Winston, 1975. In the Holt Social Studies Curriculum for grades nine through twelve. First published 1966.

Graff, Henry F. 1972. *The Free and the Brave: The Story of the American People.* Chicago: Rand McNally. First edition 1967.

Graff, Henry F., and Krout, John A. 1973. *The Adventures of the American People.* Chicago: Rand McNally. Second edition, revised printing.

King, David C., and Anderson, Charlotte C. 1976. *The United States.* Boston: Houghton Mifflin. This is the sixth-level text in *Windows on Our World,* the Houghton Mifflin Social Studies Program, Lee F. Anderson, general editor.

Sellers, Charles G., et al. 1975. *As It Happened: A History of the United States.* New York: McGraw-Hill.

Van Steeg, Clarence L., and Hofstadter, Richard 1971. *A People and a Nation.* New York: Harper and Row. Edition used was printed in 1974.

Wood, Leonard C., Gabriel, Ralph H., and Biller, Edward L. *America: Its People and Values.* New York: Harcourt Brace Jovanovich, 1971, 1975.

RESPONDING TO WRITING

Key words: discovery education power reading reality writing

Rhetorical concepts: analysis anecdote illustration narrative/example

1.   How does "America Revised" illustrate FitzGerald's conclusion that history is "slippery" (paragraph 15)? In what ways, if any, are the history textbooks you have used different from the history books of the 1970s on which FitzGerald bases her claim?

2.   When you read a textbook in any subject do you hope to find "somewhere out there, an objective truth"? Has FitzGerald's analysis of history textbooks of the 1970s convinced you that "This hope is, of course, foolish"? If so, what do you recommend that teachers and students do differently?

3.   What does FitzGerald mean by "each historian in some degree creates the world anew and all history is in some degree contemporary history" (paragraph 14)? Try to make the same claim by substituting the names of other disciplines for history and see how compelling a case you can construct.

4.   Analyze an American history textbook with which you are familar, to see how it deals with a controversial topic, for example, the settlement of the West, slavery, the Vietnam War, women's suffrage, labor unions, Hispanic-American culture, the Civil Rights movement. What evidence, including primary sources and photographs, does the book use to support its interpretation? From whose point of view does the author present the information? What conclusions are you as a reader supposed to draw? Or, compare two textbooks on the same point to determine where they agree and disagree, and why.

The Naked Source

LINDA SIMON

Linda Simon (born 1946) earned a Ph.D. from Brandeis University in 1983. A freelance writer and currently Director of the Writing Center at Harvard, Simon is the author of *the Biography of Alice B. Toklas* (1977), *Thornton Wilder: His World* (1979), and *Margaret Beaufort:*

Matriarch of the House of Tudor (1982). As a biographer, Simon has had considerable opportunity to practice what she advocates in "The Naked Source," originally published in *The Michigan Quarterly Review*, 1988. *Alice B. Toklas*, for instance, is derived from a wealth of primary sources: letters, diaries, conversations, photographs and paintings, poetry and other creative writing, visits to the houses and locations that Toklas shared with Gertrude Stein, as well as others' published accounts of the pair and the period.

Students do not understand history, claims Simon, because they lack a "real sense of the past." The way that history is taught, with an emphasis on names and dates and others' interpretations (secondary sources) fails to give students "a sense of historical mindedness, a sense that lives were lived in a context." Instead of writing term papers derived from other peoples' research, students should be asked to write history the way real historians do it, by consulting a variety of "naked sources"—through archives, interviews, old newspapers, and magazines. Then they should learn to "make them speak" by the proper selection, arrangement, and emphasis required to write a historical narrative. For when they set out to be historians, students are writing literature, not taking a test; only then can they adequately convey a sense of the past.

It is true that my students do not know history. That annals of 1 the American past, as students tell it, are compressed into a compact chronicle: John Kennedy and Martin Luther King flourish just a breath away from FDR and Woodrow Wilson, who themselves come right on the heels of Jefferson and Lincoln. The far and distant past is more obscure still.

Some, because they are bright and inquisitive, have learned names, 2 dates, and the titles of major events. But even these masters of Trivial Pursuit often betray their ignorance of a real sense of the past. Teachers all have favorite oneliners that point to an abyss in historical knowledge. Mine is: Sputnik *who?*

There is no debate here. Students do not know history. Students 3 should learn history. There is less agreement about what they should know, why they should know it, and far less agreement about how they should pursue this study of the past.

When I ask my students why they need to know history, they 4 reply earnestly: We need to learn history because those who do not know history are doomed to repeat the mistakes of the past. They have heard this somewhere, although no one can attribute the remark. And if they are told that George Santayana said it, they know not who Santayana was, although if you care to inform them they will dutifully record his name, dates (1863–1952), and the title of the work (*The Life of Reason*) in which the remark was made.

Is that so? I ask. What will not be repeated? 5

Inevitably they respond emotionally with the example of the 6

Holocaust. Some have watched an episode of a PBS series. Some have seen the film *The Diary of Anne Frank*. Such genocide, they reply, will not be repeated because we know about it. Undaunted by examples of contemporary genocide, they remain firm in their conviction. Genocide, they maintain. And the Great Depression.

The Great Depression has made a big impact on the adolescent   7 imagination. Given any work of literature written at any time during the 1930s, some students will explain it as a direct response to the Great Depression. Wasn't everyone depressed, after all? And aren't most serious works of literature grim, glum, dark, and deep. There you have it.

But now we know about the Great Depression. And so it will not,   8 cannot, happen again.

I am not persuaded that requiring students to read Tacitus or   9 Thucydides, Carl Becker or Francis Parkman, Samuel Eliot Morison or Arnold Toynbee will remedy this situation, although I believe that students, and we, might well benefit from these writers' illumination. What students lack, after all, is a sense of historical-mindedness, a sense that lives were lived in a context, a sense that events (the Battle of Barnet, for example) had consequences (if men were slain on the battlefield, they could not return to the farm), a sense that answers must generate questions, more questions, and still more subtle questions.

As it is, students learning history, especially in the early grades,   10 are asked prescribed questions and are given little opportunity to pursue their own inquiry or satisfy their own curiosity. The following questions are from current high school texts:

> Has the role of the present United Nations proved that the hopes and dreams of Woodrow Wilson were achievable? If so, how? If not, why?

> What were the advantages of an isolationist policy for the United States in the nineteenth century? Were there disadvantages?

Questions such as these perpetuate the idea that history is a body   11 of knowledge on which students will be tested. The first question, in other words, asks students: Did you read the section in the text on the role of the United Nations? Did you read the section on Wilson's aims in proposing the League of Nations? Can you put these two sections together?

The second question asks students: Did you understand the term   12 *isolationist?* Did you read the section on U.S. foreign relations in the nineteenth century? Can you summarize the debate that the authors of the textbook recount?

Questions such as these perpetuate the idea that history can un- 13
cover "facts" and "truth," that history is objective, and that students,
if only they are diligent, can recover "right answers" about the past.
Questions such as these ignore the role of historians. Even those
bright students who can recall dates and events rarely can recall the
name of a historian, much less any feeling about who this particular
man or woman was. For many students, historical facts are things
out there, like sea shells or autumn leaves, and it hardly matters who
fetches them. The sea shell will look the same whether it is gathered
in Charles Beard's pocket or Henri Pirenne's.

What students really need to learn, more than "history," is a 14
sense of the historical method of inquiry. They need to know what
it is that historians do and how they do it. They need to understand
the role of imagination and intuition in the telling of histories, they
need to practice, themselves, confronting sources, making judgments,
and defending conclusions.

When I ask my freshmen what they think historians do, they 15
usually offer me some lofty phrases about "influencing the course of
future events." But what I mean is: what do historians do after breakfast? That is a question few of my students can answer. And they are
surprised when I read them the following passage by British historian
A. L. Rowse from his book *The Use of History*.

> You might think that in order to learn history you need a library of
> books to begin with. Not at all: that only comes at the end. What
> you need at the beginning is a pair of stout walking shoes, a pencil
> and a notebook; perhaps I should add a good county guide covering
> the area you mean to explore . . . and a map of the country . . . that
> gives you field footpaths and a wealth of things of interest, marks
> churches and historic buildings and ruins, wayside crosses and holy
> wells, prehistoric camps and dykes, the sites of battles. When you
> can't go for a walk, it is a quite good thing to study the map and
> plan where you would like to go. I am all in favour of the open-air
> approach to history; the most delightful and enjoyable, the most
> imaginative and informative, and—what not everybody under-
> stands—the best training.

It is the best training because it gives the would-be historian an 16
encounter with the things that all historians look at and puzzle over:
primary sources about the past. Historians look at battlefields and
old buildings, read letters and diaries and documents, interview
eyewitnesses or participants in events. And they ask questions of
these sources. Gradually, after asking increasingly sophisticated questions, they make some sense, for themselves, of what once happened.

What professional historians do, however, is not what most stu- 17
dents do when they set out to learn history within the confines of a

course. Instead of putting students face to face with primary sources, instructors are more likely to send them to read what other people say about the past. Students begin with a library of books of secondary sources, or they may begin with a text. But that, cautions Rowse, should come "at the end." Instead of allowing students to gain experience in weighing evidence and making inferences, the structures of many courses encourage them to amass information. "I found it!" exclaim enthusiastic students. They need to ask, "But what does it mean?"

They need to ask that question of the kinds of sources that his- 18
torians actually use. Instead of reading Morison's rendering of Columbus's voyages, for example, students might read Columbus himself: his journal, his letters to the Spanish monarchs. Then they can begin to decide for themselves what sort of man this was and what sort of experience he had. Morison—as excellent a historian as he is—comes later. With some sense of the sources that Morison used, students can begin to evaluate his contribution to history, to understand how he drew conclusions from the material available to him, to see how "facts" are augmented by historical intuition. They can begin to understand, too, that the reconstruction of the past is slow and painstaking work.

Courses that cover several decades or even millennia may give 19
students a false impression of historical inquiry. Historians, like archaeologists or epidemiologists, move slowly through bumpy and perilous terrain. They are used to travelling for miles only to find themselves stranded at a dead end. Once, in the archives of Westminster Abbey, I eagerly awaited reading a fragment of a letter from King Henry VI (after all, that is how it was described in the card catalog), only to lift out of an envelope the corner of a page, about an inch across, with the faintest ink-mark the only evidence that it had, five hundred years before, been a letter at all.

Slowly the historian assembles pieces of the past. A household 20
expense record might be the only artifact proving that a certain medieval woman existed. How much can be known about her? How much can be known by examining someone's checkbook today? Yet historians must make do with just such odd legacies: wills and land deeds, maps and drawings, family portraits or photographs. Can you imagine the excitement over the discovery of a diary or a cache of letters? At last, a text. But the diary may prove a disappointment, a frustration. William James recorded the title of a book he may have been reading or the name of a visitor. Didn't he understand that a historian or biographer would need the deep, reflective ruminations of which we know he was more than capable?

Students have not had these experiences. When they are asked

21

to write, they write *about* history. The research paper or the term
paper seems to many of them another form of test—this time a take-
home drawn out over weeks. Even if they have learned that "voice"
and "audience" are important for a writer, they see history papers
as different. They must be objective; they must learn proper foot-
noting and documentation. They must compile an impressive bibliography. Most important, they must find something out. The research
paper produces nothing so much as anxiety, and the student often
feels overwhelmed by the project.

They might, instead, be asked to write history as historians do
it. They might be introduced to archives—in their college, in their
community, in their state capital. They might be encouraged to interview people, and to interview them again and again until they
begin to get the kind of information that will enlighten them about a
particular time or event. They might be encouraged to read newspapers on microfilm or the bound volumes of old magazines that
are yellowing in the basement of their local library. And then they
might be asked to write in that most challenging form: the historical
narrative.

22

"I can recall experiencing upon the completing of my first work
of history," George Kennan wrote once, ". . . a moment of panic
when the question suddenly presented itself to me: What is it that I
have done here? Perhaps what I have written is not really history but
rather some sort of novel, the product of my own imagination,—an
imagination stimulated, inspired and informed, let us hope, by the
documents I have been reading, but imagination nevertheless." Most
historians share Kennan's reaction.

23

Students, of course, can never discover the boundary between
"fact" and imaginative construction unless they have contact with
primary sources. They cannot know where the historian has intervened to analyze the information he or she has discovered. "Most of
the facts that you excavate," Morison wrote in "History as A Literary
Art," "are dumb things; it is for you to make them speak by proper
selection, arrangement, and emphasis." Morison suggested that beginning historians look to such writers as Sherwood Anderson and
Henry James for examples of the kind of palpable description and
intense characterization that can make literature—historical or fictional—come alive.

24

Students need to be persuaded that they are writing literature,
not taking a test, when they set out to be historians. Their writing
needs to be read and evaluated not only for the facts that they have
managed to compile, but for the sense of the past that they have
conveyed. They need to discover that the past was not only battles
and elections, Major Forces and Charismatic Leaders, but ordinary

25

people, growing up, courting, dancing to a different beat, camping by a river that has long since dried up, lighting out for a territory that no longer exists. Except in the imagination of historians, as they confront the naked source, unaided.

RESPONDING TO READING

Key words: discovery education power reading reality writing

Rhetorical concepts: analysis definition explanation illustration narrative/example process

1.   Simon distinguishes between students who "have learned names, dates, and the titles of major events" and those who "know history." What is that distinction and how does it compare with the "slippery history" concept of FitzGerald? What does Simon mean by "historical-mindedness?"
2.   What is the problem for Simon with saying that "those who do not know history are doomed to repeat the mistakes of the past"? By mocking that famous saying, she outrages a kind of proverbial wisdom. Do you agree with her objections?
3.   What does Simon mean when she says that "answers must generate questions, more questions, and still more subtle questions"? If history is a matter of questions rather than merely answers, how does that change the way in which we come to know history?
4.   Select an historical "fact" in dispute (such as young George Washington's chopping down the cherry tree or his later wooden teeth) and find out how it became a "fact." What is the historical method of inquiry and how does it relate to historical fact?
5.   Describe the kind of history course that Simon would prefer and compare it to the history courses you have taken.
6.   Obtain a "naked source"—an old diary, letter (or collection of letters), a birth, marriage, or death certificate, a deed or property record, the memories of your oldest relative, newspapers from the distant past, or the like. If nothing old is available, use a more recent source—photographs, home movies or videos, student newspaper archives, etc. Now turn that source into history by making sense of it in context. After you have written that paper, write another about the experience you have gone through: how did you come to know what you (finally) knew about your subject?

Understanding Paternity

LAUREL THATCHER ULRICH

Laurel Thatcher Ulrich's life as a wife and mother of five children has strongly influenced the focus and method of her work as a historian. Valedictorian of her graduating class at the University of

Utah in 1960, she soon married and began her family. In the late 1960s, she says, "I discovered the women's movement and began redefining myself and my work," which eventually led to a Ph.D. in history and a professorship at the University of New Hampshire. "Women's history," she says, "brought together my personal activities and thinking about myself, and my scholarship. I feel very fortunate to have been part of a transitional generation of women, who started out their lives very traditionally. I come to women's history with a sympathy and appreciation of things that some other historians might dismiss as mundane."

For her first book, *Good Wives: Image and Reality in the Lives of Women in Northern New England 1650–1750* (1982), Ulrich examined "court records, gravestones, letters, and diaries, discovering women who were not just good wives, but traders, negotiators in Indian wars— even murderers and thieves." She uses comparable materials in *A Midwife's Tale: The Life of Martha Ballard, Based on Her Diary, 1795– 1812*, recipient of numerous awards including the Pulitzer Prize. The section reprinted here, "Understanding Paternity: Separating Romance from Reality," is characteristic of Ulrich's materials and method of interpreting ten terse segments of the diary of Martha Ballard. Ulrich uses court records, statutes governing legal proceedings, marriage lists, other people's diaries and letters, inventories of household goods, fiction, other scholars' research, and her own knowledge of the customs of the time to offer a new, feminist interpretation to out-of-wedlock births.

It snowed on October 23, 1791, the day Martha was summoned 1
to Sally Pierce. Because this was going to be an illegitimate birth, she knew what she had to ask. She also knew what Sally would say.

> Shee was safe delivered at 1 hour pm of a fine son, her illness very severe, but I left her cleverly & returnd . . . about sun sett. Sally declard that my son Jonathan was the father of her child.

In the margin Martha wrote simply, "Sally Pierce's son. Birth 27th."

Before we can understand the full import of that entry, we need 2
to know something about the legal position of unwed mothers in eighteenth-century New England. Massachusetts law had always defined sexual intercourse between unmarried persons as a crime. In the seventeenth and early eighteenth centuries, courts had punished men who fathered children out of wedlock as rigorously as the women concerned, often relying on testimony taken from mothers during delivery to establish the fathers' identity, but by the middle of the eighteenth century, most historians argue, fornication had become a woman's crime.

William Nelson has shown that while fornication prosecutions 3
still accounted for more than a third of criminal actions in Massachusetts between 1760 and 1774, in only one case was the *father* of an illegitimate child prosecuted—a black man suspected of cohabiting

**Table I. Lincoln County Court of General Sessions
Fornication and Paternity Actions, 1761–1799**

Date	Women	Men: "Unknown"	Presented	Convicted
1761–1765	9	2	1	1
1766–1770	20	3	3	2
1771–1775	11	2	0	0
1776–1780	12	1	2	1
1781–1785	21	0	4	4
1786–1790	0	0	3	2
1791–1795	0	0	6	6
1796–1799	0	0	0	0

NOTE: Kennebec County was separated from Lincoln in 1799. There are no fornication or maintenance cases in the first General Sessions Record Books for the new county. Unfortunately, court papers for the early nineteenth century have not survived.

with a white woman. By the end of the century, actions against women had also disappeared from court dockets. Prosecutions dropped from seventy-two per year in the years 1760–1774 to fifty-eight during the revolutionary years and finally to fewer than five after 1786. Nelson found only four prosecutions after 1790 in the entire Commonwealth. Lincoln County records show the same decline. Between 1761 and 1785, seventy-three women but only ten men were presented for fornication or related crimes. No women were presented after 1785.[1]

Historians are still debating the significance of such changes. 4 Some stress liberalization, arguing that as courts became more concerned with mediating property disputes than enforcing Puritan standards of moral behavior, sex became a private affair. Others perceive the decline in fornication prosecutions as reflecting generational tensions in a society that had given up the legalism of the Puritans but had not yet developed the repressive individualism of the Victorians. More recent studies have emphasized gender issues, arguing that changes in fornication proceedings reflected a larger argument over female sexuality, an argument vividly displayed in eighteenth-century novels of seduction, some of which openly challenged the prevailing double standard.[2]

Against such evidence, Sally Pierce's declaration appears a quaint 5

[1]Diary of Martha Moore Ballard, I (1785–1799), Maine State Library, Augusta, August 25, 1793. Hereafter abbr. MMB

[2]William E. Nelson, *Americanization of the Common Law: The Impact of Legal Change on Massachusetts Society, 1760–1830* (Cambridge, Mass.: Harvard University Press, 1975), pp. 110–111; Lincoln County Court of General Sessions of the Peace, Records and Files, Lincoln County Court House, Wiscasset, Maine, Books 1–2.

and inexplicable throwback to an earlier era. It was not. Evidence from Martha's diary and from supporting legal documents casts doubt on the notion that sexual behavior had in fact become a private concern. The diary suggests that even in a newly settled lumbering town like Hallowell, sexual norms (though neither Puritan nor Victorian) were clearly defined and communally enforced, that courts seldom prosecuted sexual deviance because informal mechanisms of control were so powerful. It also casts doubt on the use of General Sessions records or elite literature to define the double standard. There were certainly inequities in the way male and female culpability was defined in this period, yet there is no evidence that in rural communities women who bore children out of wedlock were either ruined or abandoned as early novels would suggest.

The prosecutorial double standard originated in a 1668 Massachusetts law that introduced the English practice of asking unwed mothers to name the father of their child during delivery. At first glance, questioning a woman in labor seems a form of harassment. In practice, it was a formality allowing the woman, her relatives, or in some cases the selectmen of her town to claim child support. The man she accused could not be convicted of fornication (confession or witnesses were needed for that), but unless there was overwhelming evidence to the contrary, he would be judged the "reputed father" of her child and required to pay for its support. The assumption was that a woman asked to testify at the height of travail would not lie. 6

In fact, early courts showed a remarkable reluctance to question such testimony. Although Alice Metherell of Kittery, Maine, had been convicted of a false oath in an earlier case of bastardy (she had delivered a black child after accusing a white man), she was able in 1695 to get maintenance from John Thompson and even to defend herself against a slander suit from him. As late as 1724 Bathsheba Lyston's accusation of Daniel Paul stood, even though a witness testified that the summer before, "she was a telling what a great Liberty a Young woman has to what a young man hath for, said She, I will Let any Young man get me with child and then, Said She, I can lay it to who I please because a woman has that Liberty granted to them."[3] Courts were obviously less concerned about the possibility of a false accusation than about the problem of having to provide public support 7

---

[3]The three points of view are exemplified by Nelson, *Americanization of the Common Law,* pp. 110, 251–253; Daniel Scott Smith and Michael Hindus, "Premarital Pregnancy in America, 1640–1971; An Overview and an Interpretation," *Journal of Interdisciplinary History* 5 (1975): 537–570; and Cathy N. Davidson, *Revolution and the Word: The Rise of the Novel in America* (New York: Oxford University Press, 1986), pp. 106–109. For an excellent summary of the literature on eighteenth-century sexuality, see John D'Emilio and Estelle B. Freedman, *Intimate Matters: A History of Sexuality in America* (New York: Harper & Row, 1988), pp. 42–52.

for fatherless children. Yet one need not interpret the law cynically. It formalized a common assumption in English society, evident in the Chesapeake as well as in New England, that women were guardians of the sexual values of the community. In this regard, the witnesses in the procedure were as important as the mother herself.[4]

Other than Nelson's general overview, there has been little scholarship on changes in fornication procedures in Massachusetts in the middle decades of the eighteenth century.[5] We know that courts gradually abandoned the practice of fining married couples whose first child was born too soon, but we know almost nothing about the single women whose cases began to dominate the dockets by midcentury. Unfortunately, earlier studies have made it difficult to trace the direction of change by failing to relate paternity suits to fornication procedures. They have also given too little attention to the documentary impact of changes in legal procedures.

A 1786 "Act for the Punishment of Fornication, and for the Maintenance of Bastard Children" confirmed the old laws, but made one important change. A new clause made it possible for women to avoid appearing at the Court of General Sessions to answer a fornication charge by voluntarily confessing to the crime before a single justice of the peace and paying a fine (six shillings for the first offense and twelve shillings for any later ones). William Nelson has assumed this was a first step in the decriminalization of sexual behavior. Possibly— though he fails to notice that the procedure made it easier for a woman to initiate a paternity action. If a woman named a man at the time of her initial confession, and then "being put upon the discovery of the truth respecting the same accusation in the time of her travail, shall thereupon accuse the same person," *he* would be tried before the Sessions and, if convicted, be required to provide for the child.[6] In fact, the two actions were typically combined on one form, suggesting that confessing to fornication was simply a preliminary step to suing for the maintenance of one's child.

This was the procedure Sally Pierce followed. On July 19, 1791,

8

9

---

[4]*Province and Court Records of Maine*, IV, ed. Neal W. Allen, Jr. (Portland: Maine Historical Society, 1958), pp. 47–50; VI (1975), pp. 150–153. Metherell was whipped rather than fined because of the unusual circumstances of her case.

[5]Mary Beth Norton, "Gender and Defamation in Seventeenth-century Maryland," *William and Mary Quarterly*, Third Series 44 (1987): 3–39, and "Gender, Crime, and Community in Seventeenth-Century Maryland," revision of a paper prepared for the Conference in Honor of Bernard Bailyn, Harvard University, October 30–31, 1987, pp. 28–36.

[6]Cornelia Hughes Dayton, *Women Before the Bar: Gender, Law, and Society in Connecticut, 1710–1790*, Ph.D. dissertation, Princeton University, 1986, is a model of what needs to be done. There are differences in law and procedure in New Haven, but the general trends are similar to those in Massachusetts. Also useful for understanding the history of the courts themselves is Hendrik Hartog, "The Public Law of a County Court: Judicial Government in Eighteenth-century Massachusetts," *The American Journal of Legal History* 20 (1976): 282–329.

Martha wrote that Mrs. Savage had come to the house to inform her "that Sally Pierce swore a Child on my son Jonathan & he was taken with a warrent. Mr Abisha Cowen is his Bondsman for appearance at Coart." In October, just as the law required, Sally confirmed her accusation before Martha Ballard. She was not the only unwed mother to do so. For thirteen of the twenty out-of-wedlock births in the diary, Martha recorded the name of the father, using stylized language that suggests she had indeed "taken testimony" as the law instructed. Lucy Shaw, for example, "declared that David Edwards was the True Father of the Child."[7] In five of the cases in which Martha made no record of the father's name, there were unusual circumstances. Two babies were stillborn, one of the mothers being in convulsions at delivery. In another case, Martha wrote, "Called at the riseing of the sun to Sarah White, she being in travil with her forth Child, & is yet unmarried."[8]

The remaining two were to a free black woman, Mehitable Slo- 11 cum, whom Martha always referred to in the diary as "Black Hitty." In the first of Hitty's deliveries, Martha mentioned no father. In the other, she identified him in the margin but not in the main entry as "Nicholas," adding, "This man is a Portugues who was Brot here by Mrs Hussey from Nantucket." The form of the entry suggests she was conveying casual information rather than the solemn testimony assumed in the other cases. If Hitty held an anomalous place in her midwife's diary, she nevertheless succeeded in contracting a marriage. Six months after the baby's birth, the town clerk recorded the marriage of "Nicholas Hilson to Hitty Slocum (Negroes)."[9]

All of this argues that the mothers, rather than Martha, initiated 12 the confession at delivery, and that it was part of a process of suing for maintenance. A black servant or the mother of several bastards was unlikely to sue. A stillbirth rendered the question moot. In the two remaining cases in which Martha failed to record the name of the father, there is no obvious explanation. Perhaps these two young women simply chose not to confront the father. Significantly, Sarah White, the mother of four, is the only one of Martha's patients to appear in the quarterly court records for Lincoln County, and she appeared only once, in 1782, when she was fined four shillings after a presentation by the grand jury.

There were surely differences in attitudes toward sexuality in 13

---

[7]*The Perpetual Laws, of the Commonwealth of Massachusetts, from the Establishment of its Constitution to the First Session of the General Court A.D. 1788* (Worcester: 1788), pp. 245–247.

[8]MMB, July 19, 1791.

[9]MMB, March 1804. In thirteen of the fourteen entries the verb is "declared"; in the one exception she wrote, "She *says* William Sands is the father."

**Table II. Martha Moore Ballard Diary, 1785–1812
Paternity Record**

Total Number of Deliveries	814	
Deliveries to single women	20	(2.4%)
Women giving father's name	13	
Women not giving father's name	7	
Stillborn child	2	
"Black Hitty"	2	
Sarah White's fourth child	1	
Unexplained	2	
Total First Births (1785–1797)	106	
Conceived out of wedlock	40	(38%)
Premarital pregnancy	31	(29%)
Illegitimacy	9	(8%)

Hallowell just as there were differences over politics or theology. Some families probably condoned premarital sex. Others encouraged formal and decorous behavior. Yet nearly everyone in the town agreed with certain fundamental propositions. One was that marriage should certainly follow, if it did not always precede, conception. Another was that fathers as well as mothers were responsible for children born out of wedlock. In courtship, sexual activity was connected with a comprehensive transition to adulthood, to good citizenship and economic productivity. The communal rituals of birth marked women as well as men as sexual beings, and affirmed the obligations as well as rights of fatherhood.

All of this contrasts sharply with the seduction literature of 14 the eighteenth century, which describes innocent young women strangely disconnected from their communities by the machinations of unprincipled lovers who abandon them in foreign countries, imprison them in mysterious villas, or leave them to die in strange taverns.[10] As Susan Staves has argued, such a construction of seduction belongs to a particular historical moment. Some young women in all periods of history have engaged in illicit intercourse, she writes, yet "such girls need not be seen as sweetly pathetic. Instead, they may be seen as loathsome temptresses, damned sinners, sordid criminals, pioneers of sexual freedom, boring fools, or simply as normal." Readers in the eighteenth century shed tears over such maidens not simply because they were powerless but because "those qualities that made them vulnerable to seducers—beauty, simplicity, and the ca-

---

[10]Reverend Eliphalet Gillet marriages, September 20, 1794: Hallowell [ME] Town and Vital Records I, n.p.

pacity for affection—were precisely those qualities the culture found desirable in women."[11]

Such values had been heard of in the Kennebec. In 1795 a Lincoln 15 County woman sued a man in county court claiming that for three years he had begged her to marry him. Finally, "by his assiduity, assertion, protestations, and assurances of his feeling" (one suspects the presence of a lawyer here), he "so endeared himself to her" that she agreed. "Wanting craftily, subtilly and cruelly to deceive, seduce and despoil her of her innocence and happy virgin situation," he "obtained his cruel purpose." Pregnant and abandoned by her seducer, she was "rendered Miserable and her good Name Forever lost."[12] What is remarkable about the case is that the woman avoided the old system of justice by initiating a civil suit before the Court of Common Pleas rather than an action of paternity before the local justice of the peace. Perhaps she found it impossible to simultaneously defend her "innocence" and pay a voluntary fine for fornication. The seducer was acquitted.

This story might have come from the pages of a novel. In senti- 16 mental literature, of course, the heroine would never have attempted any sort of suit at all, yet the language of her plea echoes the argument of contemporary fiction, most of which turns on a belief in female innocence and to a large extent female passivity. In contrast, the old system of justice asked young women to cooperate with old women in witnessing to male culpability. It also required an acceptance of female sexuality and an acknowledgment of fleshly sin. Such a system had difficulty comprehending rape, let alone seduction; its working assumption was that if a woman became pregnant, she had somehow acquiesced. Still, on its own terms it did hold men responsible for their behavior. It is difficult to imagine a sentimental heroine naming her seducer at the height of travail or describing the day and place of

---

[11]Franklin P. Rice, *Vital Records of Oxford, Massachusetts, to the End of the Year 1849* (Worcester, Mass.: 1905), pp. 14–15, 112–113; George F. Daniels, *History of the Town of Oxford, Massachusetts* (Oxford [MA]: 1892), pp. 379–380, 618–619; Charles Frederic Farlow, comp., Charles Henry Pope, ed., *Ballard Genealogy* (Boston, 1911), pp. 82–83; Porter-Barton Notes copied by J. J. Haskell and Notes on Barton Genealogy by Edith Riccius King, Mosher and Barton Family Records, MeSL. It is difficult to know how Stephen and Dorothy Barton construed Richardson's novels. Clarissa's character was apparently more impressive than her unhappy history; by the early nineteenth century there were at least four Clarissa Harlowes among Dorothy and Stephen's descendants. The most famous of Clarissa's namesakes may have had an intimate relation with a married man during the Civil War: Elizabeth Brown Pryor, *Clara Barton: Professional Angel* (Philadelphia: University of Pennsylvania Press, 1987), pp. 112–115.

[12]Susan Staves, "British Seduced Maidens," *Eighteenth Century Studies*, 14 (1980–1981), 109, 120. American novels of seduction include [Sally S. B. K. Wood], *Julia and the Illuminated Baron* (Portsmouth, N.H., 1800); Susanna Rowson, *Charlotte Temple*, ed. Cathy N. Davidson (New York: Oxford University Press, 1986 [1794]); and Hannah Foster, *The Coquette: or, The History of Eliza Wharton*, Intro. Herbert Ross Brown (New York: Columbia University Press, 1939 [1797]).

conception for the local J.P. Sentimental heroines died rather than confront their betrayers.

In Hallowell, betrayed women collected cash payments, then went   17
on to marry other men. For a sentimental heroine, a forced marriage to her seducer could never have been an acceptable solution as it was for Sally Pierce.

If one did not know about Sally's confession to Martha in October,   18
it would be easy to miss the suppressed anxiety, the suspense, the tension of the entries regarding Jonathan through the early winter of 1792. "Jonathan stayed from home last night," Martha wrote on December 29, and on January 6, "Jonathan has not been at home since yesterday." The same entry reappeared on January 11, January 29, and in slightly different form on February 20: "Jonathan has not been here this day till morning." He was missing again on February 26, but three days later his mother wrote, "My son Jonathan Brot his wife & little son here."

Henry Sewall's records show that Jonathan and Sally had been   19
published on February 11, which means they could have been legally married on February 24 or sometime thereafter. Like the Pollards, the Ballards were not present at their son's wedding, though Martha made the new bride welcome as soon as she could.[13] "Helpt Sally nurs her Babe," she wrote on March 2. Soon she was referring to the "Babe" as "Jack." Jonathan and Sally stayed alternately at the Ballards' and at the Pierces' for the next four weeks, and on April 4, 1792, "went to housekeeping."

For Jonathan, only one wedding ritual remained. At the Hallowell   20
town meeting in June he, along with six other newly married men, was elected a "hog reeve," a humorous acknowledgment by the town fathers that another roving stag had been yoked.

RESPONDING TO READING

Key words: community   class   family   gender   identity   rights writing

Rhetorical concepts: analysis   anecdote   biography   explanation illustration   narrative/example   research report

---

[13]Mary Gillpatrick, Sheepscott Great Pond, single woman v. Elisha Parkhurst, New Milford, *Brick maker:* LCCCP Records, 8:216.

1. Reread the first paragraph of this excerpt from *A Midwife's Tale*. How did you interpret it the first time you read it? How has Ulrich's interpretation changed its meaning for you? What sources of information does this professional historian have access to that a general reader would not know about? Explain your understanding of the first paragraph in relation to Linda Simon's argument about "the imagination of historians" in the previous essay ("The Naked Source").

2. In many eighteenth and nineteenth century novels of seduction, the double standard of morality prevailed. The woman who succumbed to sexual temptation was doomed to a life of social ostracism, or to death; the man got off without penalty. How does Ulrich's interpretation of the passage in paragraph 1 present a social reality that contradicts the fiction?

3. Why does Ballard's 39-word diary entry require such a long explanation? Is it what Linda Simon called "a naked source"? Why?

4. Pick a "fact" or phenomenon of contemporary history—for example, the high percentage of teenage pregnancies in the 1980s; one consequence of the Persian Gulf War; the presence on the Supreme Court of Justice Sandra Day O'Connor or Thurgood Marshall (or any other justice). Identify it briefly; then explain it for readers who might come across this bit of the past two centuries from now. Use whatever sources you need: newspaper clippings, histories, interviews, biographies and autobiographies, photographs, site visits, maps, letters, and your own common sense. Explain and interpret your sources as Ulrich did with Ballard's diary.

University Days

JAMES THURBER

James Thurber's (1894–1961) sublime sense of the ridiculous is paramount throughout the articles, stories, fables, and quirky line drawings he contributed to *The New Yorker* for forty years. To polish his stories Thurber told them at parties—and, he explained in *The Paris Review*, "I write them there too. I never quite know when I'm not writing. Sometimes my wife comes up to me at a party and says, 'Dammit, Thurber, stop writing.' She usually catches me in the middle of a paragraph. Or my daughter will look up from the dinner table and ask, 'Is he sick?' 'No,' my wife says, 'he's writing something.' " Thurber actually spent most of his effort on rewriting, "to make the finished version smooth, to make it seem effortless," spending up to two thousand hours on as many as fifteen revisions, discarding 90 percent of his words to distill the final short piece.

The results are well worth the effort. Thurber explores the bizarre commonplaces of ordinary people in ordinary life in such books as *Is Sex Necessary?* (1929), with E. B. White, and the autobiographical *My Life and Hard Times* (1933), from which "University Days" is taken. Among his other twenty volumes are a play, *The Male Animal* (1939), with Elliott Nugent; a cartoon book, *Men, Women, and Dogs* (1943); and *The Years with Ross* (1959), an account of the magical, symbiotic relationship between the *New Yorker* and its crusty, perfectionist editor, Harold Ross.

Much of our understanding—of anything—comes from the context in which we learn it. "University Days" extracts humor from the numerous ways college students misunderstand what they are supposed to be learning in the various formal and informal contexts college provides. Thurber asks us to notice and smile at his own inability, as a botany student, to see cells "despite every adjustment of the microscope known to man," and at a hapless cub reporter's inability to understand what made writing lively.

I passed all the other courses that I took at my University, but I could never pass botany. This was because all botany students had to spend several hours a week in a laboratory looking through a microscope at plant cells, and I could never see through a microscope. I never once saw a cell through a microscope. This used to enrage my instructor. He would wander around the laboratory pleased with the progress all the students were making in drawing the involved and, so I am told, interesting structure of flower cells, until he came to me. I would just be standing there. "I can't see anything," I would say. He would begin patiently enough, explaining how anybody can see through a microscope, but he would always end up in a fury; claiming that I could *too* see through a microscope but just pretended that I couldn't. "It takes away from the beauty of flowers anyway," I used to tell him. "We are not concerned with beauty in this course," he would say. "We are concerned solely with what I may call the *mechanics* of flars." "Well," I'd say. "I can't see anything." "Try it just once again," he'd say, and I would put my eye to the microscope and see nothing at all, except now and again a nebulous milky substance—a phenomenon of maladjustment. You were supposed to see a vivid, restless clockwork of sharply defined plant cells. "I see what looks like a lot of milk," I would tell him. This, he claimed, was the result of my not having adjusted the microscope properly, so he would readjust it for me, or rather, for himself. And I would look again and see milk.

I finally took a deferred pass, as they called it, and waited a year and tried again. (You had to pass one of the biological sciences or you couldn't graduate.) The professor had come back from vacation brown as a berry, bright-eyed, and eager to explain cell-structure again to his classes. "Well," he said to me, cheerily, when we met in the first laboratory hour of the semester, "we're going to see cells this time, aren't we?" "Yes, sir," I said. Students to the right of me and left of me and in front of me were seeing cells; what's more, they were quietly drawing pictures of them in their notebooks. Of course, I didn't see anything.

"We'll try it," the professor said to me, grimly, "with every ad- 3 justment of the microscope known to man. As God is my witness, I'll arrange this glass so that you see cells through it or I'll give up teaching. In twenty-two years of botany, I—" He cut off abruptly for he was beginning to quiver all over, like Lionel Barrymore, and he genuinely wished to hold onto his temper; his scenes with me had taken a great deal out of him.

So we tried it with every adjustment of the microscope known to 4 man. With only one of them did I see anything but blackness or the familiar lacteal opacity, and that time I saw, to my pleasure and amazement, a variegated constellation of flecks, specks, and dots. These I hastily drew. The instructor, noting my activity, came from an adjoining desk, a smile on his lips and his eyebrows high in hope. He looked at my cell drawing. "What's that?" he demanded, with a hint of squeal in his voice. "That's what I saw," I said. "You didn't, you didn't, you *did*n't!" he screamed, losing control of his temper instantly, and he bent over and squinted into the microscope. His head snapped up. "That's your eye!" he shouted. "You've fixed the lens so that it reflects! You've drawn your eye!"

Another course that I didn't like, but somehow managed to pass, 5 was economics. I went to that class straight from the botany class, which didn't help me any in understanding either subject. I used to get them mixed up. But not as mixed up as another student in my economics class who came there direct from a physics laboratory. He was a tackle on the football team, named Bolenciecwcz. At that time Ohio State University had one of the best football teams in the country, and Bolenciecwcz was one of its outstanding stars. In order to be eligible to play it was necessary for him to keep up in his studies, a very difficult matter, for while he was not dumber than an ox he was not any smarter. Most of his professors were lenient and helped him along. None gave him more hints, in answering questions, or asked him simpler ones than the economics professor, a thin, timid man named Bassum. One day when we were on the subject of transportation and distribution, it came Bolenciecwcz's turn to answer a question. "Name one means of transportation," the professor said to him. No light came into the big tackle's eyes. "Just any means of transportation," said the professor. Bolenciecwcz sat staring at him. "That is," pursued the professor, "any medium, agency, or method of going from one place to another." Bolenciecwcz had the look of a man who is being led into a trap. "You may choose among steam, horse-drawn, or electrically propelled vehicles" said the instructor. "I might suggest the one which we commonly take in making long journeys across land." There was a profound silence in which everybody stirred uneasily, including Bolenciecwcz and Mr. Bassum. Mr. Bassum abruptly broke this silence in an amazing manner. "Choo-choo-choo," he said, in a low voice, and turned instantly scarlet. He glanced appealingly around the room. All of us, of course, shared Mr. Bassum's desire that Bolenciecwcz should stay abreast of the class in economics, for the Illinois game, one of the hardest and most important of the season, was only a week off. "Toot, toot, too-tooooooot!" some student with a deep voice moaned, and we all looked encouragingly at Bolenciecwcz. Somebody else gave a fine imitation of a locomotive letting off steam. Mr. Bassum himself rounded off the little show, "Ding, dong, ding, dong," he said, hopefully. Bolenciecwcz was staring at the floor now, trying to think, his great brow furrowed, his huge hands rubbing together, his face red.

"How did you come to college this year, Mr. Bolenciecwcz?" asked 6 the professor. "*Chuffa* chuffa, *chuffa* chuffa."

"M'father sent me," said the football player. 7

"What on?" asked Bassum. 8

"I git an 'lowance," said the tackle, in a low, husky voice, ob- 9 viously embarrassed.

"No, no," said Bassum. "Name a means of transportation. What 10 did you *ride* here on?"

"Train," said Bolenciecwcz. 11

"Quite right," said the professor. "Now, Mr. Nugent, will you 12 tell us—"

If I went through anguish in botany and economics—for different 13 reasons—gymnasium work was even worse. I don't even like to think about it. They wouldn't let you play games or join in the exercises with your glasses on and I couldn't see with mine off. I bumped into professors, horizontal bars, agricultural students, and swinging iron rings. Not being able to see, I could take it but I couldn't dish it out. Also, in order to pass gymnasium (and you had to pass it to graduate) you had to learn to swim if you didn't know how. I didn't like the swimming pool, I didn't like swimming, and I didn't like the swimming instructor, and after all these years I still don't. I never swam but I passed my gym work anyway, by having another student give my gymnasium number (978) and swim across the pool in my place. He was a quiet, amiable blonde youth, number 473, and he would have seen through a microscope for me if we could have got away with it, but we couldn't get away with it. Another thing I didn't like about gymnasium work was that they made you strip the day you registered. It is impossible for me to be happy when I am stripped and being asked a lot of questions. Still, I did better than a lanky agricultural student who was cross-examined just before I was. They asked each student what college he was in—that is, whether Arts, Engineering, Commerce, or Agriculture. "What college are you in?" the instructor snapped at the youth in front of me. "Ohio State University," he said promptly.

It wasn't that agricultural student but it was another a whole lot 14 like him who decided to take up journalism, possibly on the ground that when farming went to hell he could fall back on newspaper work. He didn't realize, of course, that that would be very much like falling back full-length on a kit of carpenter's tools. Haskins didn't seem cut out for journalism, being too embarrassed to talk to anybody and unable to use a typewriter, but the editor of the college paper assigned him to the cow barns, the sheep house, the horse pavilion, and the animal husbandry department generally. This was a genuinely big "beat," for it took up five times as much ground and got ten times as great a legislative appropriation as the College of Liberal Arts. The agricultural student knew animals, but nevertheless his stories were dull and colorlessly written. He took all afternoon on each one of them, on account of having to hunt for each letter on the typewriter. Once in a while he had to ask somebody to help him hunt. "C" and "L," in particular, were hard letters for him to find. His editor finally got pretty much annoyed at the farmer-journalist because his pieces were so uninteresting. "See here, Haskins," he snapped at him one day, "why is it we never have anything hot from you on the horse pavilion? Here we have two hundred head of horses on this campus— more than any other university in the Western Conference except Purdue—and yet you never get any real low down on them. Now shoot over to the horse barns and dig up something lively." Haskins shambled out and came back in about an hour; he said he had something. "Well, start it off snappily," said the editor. "Something people will read." Haskins set to work and in a couple of hours brought a sheet of typewritten paper to the desk; it was a two-hundred word story about some disease that had broken out among the horses. Its opening sentence was simple but arresting. It read: "Who has noticed the sores on the tops of the horses in the animal husbandry building?"

Ohio State was a land grant university and therefore two years 15 of military drill was compulsory. We drilled with old Springfield rifles and studied the tactics of the Civil War even though the World War was going on at the time. At 11 o'clock each morning thousands of freshmen and sophomores used to deploy over the campus, moodily creeping up on the old chemistry building. It was good training for the kind of warfare that was waged at Shiloh but it had no connection with what was going on in Europe. Some people used to think there was German money behind it, but they didn't dare say so or they would have been thrown in jail as German spies. It was a period of muddy thought and marked, I believe, the decline of higher education in the Middle West.

As a soldier I was never any good at all. Most of the cadets were 16 glumly indifferent soldiers, but I was no good at all. Once General Littlefield, who was commandant of the cadet corps, popped up in front of me during regimental drill and snapped, "You are the main trouble with this university!" I think he meant that my type was the main trouble with the university but he may have meant me individually. I was mediocre at drill, certainly—that is, until my senior year. By that time I had drilled longer than anybody else in the Western Conference, having failed at military at the end of each preceding year so that I had to do it all again. I was the only senior still in uniform. The uniform which, when new, had made me look like an interurban railway conductor, now that it had become faded and too tight made me look like Bert Williams in his bellboy act. This had a definitely bad effect on my morale. Even so, I had become by sheer practice little short of wonderful at squad manoeuvres.

One day General Littlefield picked our company out of the whole 17 regiment and tried to get it mixed up by putting it through one movement after another as fast as we could execute them: squads right, squads left, squads on the right into line, squads right about, squads left front into line etc. In about three minutes one hundred and nine men were marching in one direction and I was marching away from them at an angle of forty degrees, all alone. "Company, halt!" shouted General Littlefield, "That man is the only man who has it right!" I was made a corporal for my achievement.

The next day General Littlefield summoned me to his office. He 18 was swatting flies when I went in. I was silent and he was silent too, for a long time. I don't think he remembered me or why he had sent for me, but he didn't want to admit it. He swatted some more flies, keeping his eyes on them narrowly before he let go with the swatter. "Button up your coat!" he snapped. Looking back on it now I can see that he meant me although he was looking at a fly, but I just stood there. Another fly came to rest on a paper in front of the general and began rubbing its hind legs together. The general lifted the swatter cautiously. I moved restlessly and the fly flew away. "You startled him!" barked General Littlefield, looking at me severely. I said I was sorry. "That won't help the situation!" snapped the General, with cold military logic. I didn't see what I could do except offer to chase some more flies toward his desk, but I didn't say anything. He stared out the window at the faraway figures of co-eds crossing the campus toward the library. Finally, he told me I could go. So I went. He either didn't know which cadet I was or else he forgot what he wanted to see me about. It may have been that he wished to apologize for having called me the main trouble with the university; or maybe he had decided to compliment me on my brilliant drilling of the day before and then at the last minute decided not to. I don't know. I don't think about it much anymore.

RESPONDING TO READING

Key words: discovery   education   growing up   humor
story   striving   writing

Rhetorical concepts: anecdote   autobiography   humor   illustration
narrative/example   process   story.

1.   Are today's students conspicuously different from those in Thurber's World War I era? Identify their similarities and differences.
2.   Humorists have fun at the expense of readily identifiable stereotypes: the nerd, the dumb jock, the country bumpkin, egghead professors, and others. In brief, humor isn't fair. Should it be? Why, or why not?
3.   The process of learning is often problematic and painful. Why? At what point can the learner gain sufficient perspective on the process to see it in a humorous light? Give an example from your own experience.
4.   Write an essay, comic or serious, in which you explain the process of coming to know and understand something, such as learning to drive, cook, play a sport or game, operate a particular machine; learning the meaning of friendship, love, honor, duty, betrayal, and so on.

QUESTIONS FOR REFLECTION AND WRITING

How Can I Think About Thinking?

1. Write an essay on a characteristic or capability that you understand to be uniquely human. How have you come to know what you know on the subject? In the course of your essay, compare and contrast the ways Langer and Plato answer this question, and relate their responses to your own.

2. Can you convey in imaginative writing what you take to be "reality"? Try writing your own allegory of the cave, or of the beach, or of the lab, or of whatever scene allows you to clarify your thinking. What kinds of people mistake reality for something else? What distinguishes these people from those who see reality clearly?

3. Why do you think Margaret Atwood left the "me" out of the "photograph of me"? What does Conroy mean when he says that knowledge "does not always mean resolution"? Using the Atwood and Conroy writings as points of reference, and a personal experience as an example, write an essay on how you can come to know things that are not clear.

4. Using writing you have done in relation to the previous chapter as exploratory notes, write a poem or autobiographical sketch called "a photograph of me" that conveys your own notion of reality symbolically, without including yourself in the photograph.

What Are Some Ways of Knowing?

1. Apply Kuhn's concept of the "paradigm" to the assumptions about knowledge made by the other writers in this section. Which authors share the same paradigm? Do any work from a sharply different paradigm than others? Remember, the paradigm is a commonly accepted pattern of assumptions about the way knowledge is generated, which kinds of questions are appropriate to ask, what kind of evidence may be used, and so on. Write an essay on the agreements and disagreement about such assumptions that you see in any two of the following: Gould, Belenky et al., Goodall, and Keller.

2. Since Barbara McClintock (in Keller's piece) appears to have accepted the paradigm (to use Kuhn's term) of the sciences, why was she not accepted by other scientists? What was not "normal" about her science? Goodall also had trouble being taken seriously by other scientists. What do these scientists have in common? What do these cases suggest might be added to Kuhn's model of the paradigm?

3.   To what degree, if at all, do Goodall and McClintock exemplify the subjectivist position in Belenky et al. "Just Knowing"? Write an essay on "just knowing," using Goodall, McClintock, and your own experience as evidence for what you say.

How Can I Understand What I Know?

1.   Describe what Laurel Thatcher Ulrich does as an historian to give meaning to the diary of Martha Ballard. Since the diary is what Linda Simon calls a "naked source," imagine what a different historian, perhaps in some other time period, might have done differently.

2.   Reinterpretations of history are always going on. For instance, in recent years, some scholars have proposed that Sigmund Freud's discovery of the power of the subconscious was not (as commonly believed) a great psychological innovation; it was rather, they argue, Freud's own defense against believing the tales of childhood sexual abuse his patients were revealing. Again, some historians have asked us to change our opinion of England's Prime Minister Chamberlain, long believed to have mistakenly appeased Hitler at Munich and thus making World War II inevitable. These revisionist historians argue that Chamberlain fooled Hitler, and gained time for England to arm itself for the inevitable war. Choose a historical controversy, and review the arguments for both traditional and revisionist interpretations. Do not overlook the possibilities of using local issues (the founding of your college or your town, for example) or family issues (why did your great-grandfather come to America?) Then write a paper on the ways of interpreting the past that your research has turned up.

How Do I Know What I Know?

1.   Write an essay on how you have come to know something. Select a focused topic in history (the underground railway in the Civil War, oil and the Persian Gulf War, for example), in science (the uses of aspirin, the meaning of a black hole), or in some area about which you have special knowledge. Consider the normal knowledge of the field you have chosen, describing its paradigm (following Kuhn's

definition). Then consider the relation of the paradigm to what you
have learned and the way you learned it. To what degree is what you
know exactly the same as what everyone else in the field knows? Is
there something special about your way of knowing and (hence) what
you know?

3

WHAT IS REALLY IMPORTANT?

*The bare vastness of the Hopi landscape emphasizes the
visual impact of every plant, every rock, every arroyo.
Nothing is overlooked or taken for granted. Each ant, each
lizard, each lark is imbued with great value simply because
the creature is there, simply because the creature is alive in
a place where any life at all is precious.*

LESLIE MARMON SILKO

Why Consider This Question?

We might say, with Silko, that everything is really important, since
it is *there*. Every living thing is precious, each in its own way: the
lizard is not worth more than the ant. But put a child in the picture,
and a hungry mountain lion, say, and our neutrality is likely to shift;
most of us would find ourselves willing to sacrifice the puma if necessary to save the child. Change the picture again, now adding a
human family in need of food and water. How much of the landscape,
if any, should we sacrifice to provide a family with necessities and
comforts? Now our values conflict, with our humanity appealing for
the family but our knowledge of the fragility of the landscape asking
us to leave it as it is. And so we seek ways to live in harmony with
our world, as a still greater good, when we can, if we can. But the
need to choose, to value one thing over another, is never far away
from us. Our choices demonstrate our values and what we think is
really important.

What is really important depends on who asks the question, on
who answers it, and under what circumstances it occurs. When we
ask it of ourselves, and answer it ourselves, the question looks very
much like "What should I do now?" In this sense, values are actions,

since we show that we value something by acting to support or defend it. That people are willing to die for freedom, for instance, as rebels, soldiers, authors of incendiary books or champions of unsettling ideas (think of Gandhi or Martin Luther King, Jr.), demonstrates that they hold this principle in the highest regard. On the other hand, we may say that we value something (democracy, for example) but show by our actions (neglecting to vote) that we do not, in fact, value it very much. Our actions surely speak louder than our words.

But the question is not only a personal one. We look at our friends, our family, our political representatives, and also ask, *What is really important?* How do we respond to a friend who is cheating on tests to get a good grade? A relative asks our opinion on whether it is better to stay in school or to make some good money at an unskilled job. As voters, we must choose between politicians promising low taxes or those promoting good schools and other government services. Is the competition of international free trade better than the protection of jobs at home by imposing high tariffs on foreign goods? On what basis can we choose which is most important?

When we find ourselves puzzled about such conflicts in values, or when we find others disputing what we have simply assumed to be important, we need to look at and beyond our values to find out their sources. *Inquiry* has asked this kind of question before: Chapter 1 asked *how* we come to know who we are; Chapter 2 asked *how* we know what we know. Here we are asking *how* we have come to value what we value. Like the other questions, this one asks us to think about our own thinking and to examine just how we have arrived at our current stand.

One way to think about our own values is to divide them into those we have accepted from our society and those we have chosen to guide our personal lives. Of course, some values work perfectly well at both levels; we internalize and live by many of our social values. Thus the Ten Commandments forbid us to lie and steal, a set of values most of us accept personally—though little white lies sometimes seem necessary. Traffic laws demand that we stop at red lights, as we normally do with no pain. Such codes, rules, and regulations embody the values that let societies function. But the Ten Commandments also speak about honoring our fathers and mothers, a problem for us if they have been irresponsible or abusive. And we may be selective about which traffic laws we choose to obey; only a minority always respect the 55 mile an hour speed limit. And sometimes, agonizingly, our personal values may conflict directly with society's values, as Rosa Parks tested when she refused to ride in the back of an Alabama bus, or as Huck Finn (in the first reading in this chapter) experiences when he decides not to turn in his friend Jim, a runaway slave.

But it would be a mistake to think that there are only two kinds of values. Religion, philosophy, psychology, ecology, history, and many other fields of inquiry present us with many statements about what is most important. And we must survive. People without basic necessities will place food, clothing, and shelter above any theoretical statements of value. John Stuart Mill argued that it is better to be "Socrates dissatisfied than a pig satisfied," but it is a sure thing that a starving Socrates would have placed a high value on a slice of ham. Nevertheless, Socrates valued his intellectual freedom enough to die for it. We are particularly likely to consider questions of value when something we cherish is absent, threatened, or taken away. The sick value good health; the hungry, food; the unemployed or underemployed, jobs; the oppressed, liberty. We are not free agents with regard to values; our conditions of life have as much to do with what we find most important as our abstract beliefs.

The readings in this chapter focus on developing values, applying values to nature, and resolving conflicts of value. Since such decisions determine how we think and how we act, it is hard to imagine a more important question than "What Is Really Important?"

How Do We Develop a Sense of Values?

We are what we value. Although we may consider ourselves free agents in our choice of what is really important, what we value is to a large extent determined by others whose opinions, choices, lifestyles we admire. As our points of reference change over time, so may our values. As young children, we are inevitably influenced by our parents and by our older siblings. We are also influenced by what we like and dislike about our physical environment, our religious upbringing, our schools. As adolescents and teenagers we become acutely sensitive to the values of our peers; physical appearance, the "right" clothing, and popularity often seem more important than academic achievement, technical skill, or service to others. What values prevail into adulthood depend to an extent on what our society values, who we choose as role models, and what rewards or other reinforcement we receive for our own behavior. Conflicting values are the source of numerous disagreements between their respective advocates: children versus parents, students versus teachers, one set of social or community standards versus another.

That values are not static is clear from our continuing need to define and redefine what we mean, for instance, by "honesty" or "nature," two of the topics of this chapter. As Socrates says, "The unexamined life is not worth living"; if we take education seriously, that is, if we examine the meaning of what we believe and do, we develop our values by testing them in situations. Mark Twain's "You Can't Pray a Lie" may be interpreted on a social level as the conflict between Huck Finn's loyalty to his friend Jim, a slave whose escape he is abetting, and his belief that he ought to respect the community standards promoted by Miss Watson, who had convinced Huck that Hell awaits those who do not follow these standards. On a moral level Huck's "natural goodness" enables him to understand the Golden Rule intuitively and therefore to make the right choice, for he "can't pray a lie." This decision exposes the immorality of what passes for religion in the community, the moral standard Huck must replace despite the (to him) terrible price to be paid.

In "Lies for the Public Good," philosopher Sissela Bok explores the ethical implications of whether public officials are ever justified in lying to the citizenry from a variety of allegedly noble motives, such as to conduct sensitive negotiations for some important public end. She concludes, reaffirming her hierarchy of values, that the access of the people to accurate information in a democracy is more important in the long run than secrecy is in the short run. When governments assert the right to lie, they take power from the people (who would not have given it up voluntarily) and thereby undermine the very society they claim to preserve.

The ability to make—and pay the price for making—morally correct decisions that are personally or politically difficult is one aspect of *character* as Joan Didion defines the term in "On Self Respect." For Didion, self-respect is the fundamental value, arrived at through the practice and development of other values—discipline, honesty, commitment to principle, willingness to accept responsibility for one's actions, good and bad.

The primary and basic values discussed in the writings of Twain, Bok, and Didion, honesty and self-respect, encompass a host of other values. It is such a composite of values that Paul Fussell finds so admirable in *The Boy Scout Handbook*. The *Handbook* contains "invaluable" advice of various sorts: practical (know first aid), civic/moral ("get involved"), and intellectual ("don't read trash"). But Fussell claims that its best advice is ethical and is concerned with learning to think, to take the initiative, to respect the rights of others, to be honest. Adherence to these values, he says, would prevent the very problems that Bok addresses in "Lies for the Public Good," for "A scout does not bomb and invade a neutral county, and then lie about it."

What Does Nature Mean?

It could be argued that nature, like beauty, is in the eye of the beholder. The concept of Mother Nature implies a nurturing environment, offering its bounty to the inhabitants of the Peaceable Kingdom it sustains, animals and humans alike. In contrast is the concept of "Nature red in tooth and claw" used in nineteenth-century arguments. At various times poets, philosophers, and politicians have seen the natural world as operating according to immutable—or unchanging—laws. Other contradictory interpretations regard the natural world as indifferent or inspiring to human nature; and as the source of freedom, or as a major impediment to the progress of civilization. What the nineteenth century took for granted in its vastness and abundance the twentieth century plundered. How the next century will treat the contaminated, ravaged natural world that extends from the depths of the seas to outer space remains to be seen, and is discussed in the writings of Carl Sagan, Rachel Carson, and William Warner in Chapters 5 and 6 in this book.

The writings in this chapter by Stephen Hawking, Italo Calvino, Leslie Silko, and Sue Hubbell offer views of nature ranging from the entire universe, to the landscape (Western, Eastern, and cosmic), to a narrower focus on the poison snakes of the Ozarks. The views of a physicist, a fabulist, an author and cultural interpreter, a philosopher, and a naturalist, are essentially complementary, rather than contradictory. They offer readers numerous avenues to understand and appreciate the subject. Even when it is beautiful, and it is, the natural world is not just a pretty picture, and these writers do not present postcard snapshots. They ask us to see nature as a location of important knowledge and values.

In "Our Picture of the Universe," the first chapter of *A Brief History of Time*, Stephen Hawking provides an overview of the major ways Western scientists and philosophers have conceived of the universe—whether round (Aristotle), stationary (Ptolemy), in motion (Galileo), subject to gravitational forces (Newton), expanding (Hubble)—all ways of satisfying a natural human understanding of the "underlying order of the world." Italo Calvino's story "All at One Point" uses the scientific knowledge that Hawking summarizes, but compresses it in a fantastic fiction: the Big Bang as a warm and wonderful cosmic joke. Leslie Marmon Silko's "Landscape, History, and the Pueblo Imagination" explains the Pueblo Indians' world view, a way of understanding nature not through theories, mathematics, and physics but through a belief that endows everything in the universe with "spirit and being," which remain linked in the universe even after death. Just as nothing in nature goes to waste, so the knowledge of nature and respect for its spirit are recycled in the Indian tales that affirm the powerful, loving connection between human beings and the earth.

In "Poison Snakes" Sue Hubbell defends a species she can count on to strike fear and loathing in her readers' hearts. From working as a farmer and beekeeper in the same Ozark territory as copperheads and cottonmouths, Hubbell has learned to know, respect, and appreciate these reptiles. To the naturalist, all creatures great and small, poison snakes included, are significant members of the cosmic community.

How Do We Resolve Conflicts in Values?

Each person's values, determined as they are by race, class, gender, culture, and life experiences, can never wholly conform to the values of another because no two lives are identical. Society works— when it does—by blending these different interpretations of values into a general consensus, with the most important values enforced by law. Nor are the interests of families, states, and nations the same, even those governed by the same principles. Life, liberty and the pursuit of happiness have a host of different translations at different times in different contexts—as testified by diverse philosophies of childrearing and politics—permissive, regimented, or middle-of-the-road, but always for one's own good. To realize that these varying interpretations are bound to produce disagreement, we have only to scan the contradictory baby books, or records of innumerable wars, coups, elections that threw the rascals out, perhaps to install another set of rascals—or tyrants or even monsters—more powerful than the first.

If there were a single, uniformly successful way to resolve conflicts in values, either on a personal or an international level, we might expect after all these years to know what it was. What we decide is right for us as individuals may or may not be in tune with what society wants, but if, like Huck Finn, "you can't pray a lie," then at least we have our personal standards to guide us. For Rita Levi-Montalcini, "Doing Science in Secret" was the only way to conduct her research on chicken embryos during the bombing of Italy throughout the World War II. As a Jew she was persecuted by the Nazis; as an Italian she was subject to the Allied bombing raids on industrial Turin. To continue her scientific research was as important as life itself; indeed, it was a way of sustaining that life. For Levi-Montalcini to risk her life for scientific research was not for her a conflict of values, but a necessary way to give priority to her highest value, whether or not other people would have taken the same risks. By embodying her values in her life, and doing so at considerable risk, she demonstrated what Didion called "character"—a willingness to pay the price for self-respect.

In "The Ignored Lesson of Anne Frank," psychoanalyst Bruno Bettelheim (a survivor of Nazi concentration camps) criticizes the value system that Anne Frank and her family adopted when hiding from the Nazis in Holland. Even in wartime, the Franks wanted to continue living as a gentle, cultivated family. This, says Bettelheim, was the most dangerous possible choice they could have made, for they ignored the tactics that might have helped them survive and indeed refused to acknowledge "the seriousness of the threat of death." Had they given survival priority over family togetherness, they might have survived, and Bettelheim thinks they should have changed their values to do so.

Critics always assume that they know best, that their understanding of a situation and their values are superior to those they judge. They see conflict where the objects of their critique do not. From the critic's inevitable stance, Jonathan Kozol and Sharon Olds offer critical interpretations of the value hierarchies in different social contexts. Kozol's values are revealed in his title, "Distancing the Homeless"; by keeping the homeless out of sight, an otherwise affluent society keeps them out of mind. Kozol's writing functions as a conscience, probing and prodding his readers to take their moral blinders off and act according to his values of social responsibility, instead of their own. In "Sex Without Love" Sharon Olds's controlling metaphor equates the athletic perfectionism of "the ones who make love without love" with the isolation and self-focus of the great runner. She counts on her readers to share her values, though she runs the risk that athletes who value the purity of their sport will miss the irony and read the poem as a celebration of their value hierarchy rather than hers. Poetry does not insist on its values the way essays do, and through her metaphors Olds asks readers to bring their own sexual values into the poem.

Rhetorical Issues: Definition

Definition is central to reasoned discussions and analyses of almost any topic: literary criticism, presentations of scientific or historical information, philosophical arguments, economic interpretations, and answers to examination questions. Extended definitions may themselves be entire essays. It is appropriate to discuss definitions in a chapter on values because it is hard, perhaps impossible, to talk about values without defining the terms used to name and explain the values. A value or any other abstraction (truth, beauty, justice, love, freedom, nature) is general yet has a multitude of connotations. There are occasions when we will avoid definition, precisely because we want readers to apply individual perceptions and values to what we say—a risky plan, used mainly by poets. Although the Trojan war was fought, claims Homer, over the beautiful Helen of Troy, possessor of "the face that launched a thousand ships," nowhere does the poet describe what she looked like. He says nothing about her height, weight, face, figure, or coloring; he can count on all who encounter Helen in his poem to endow her with their own ideals of the ultimate of female beauty, with whatever attributes they value.

But the vagueness of definition the poet finds useful can destroy an essay. When we're writing about an abstraction or using any other term central to our argument or analysis, we need to stake out a claim to our point of view by defining it—our way instead of someone else's. The definition of "character," as Joan Didion discusses in "On Self-Respect" and Paul Fussell examines in "The Boy Scout Handbook," is crucial in determining the right way to live, with oneself and in society. One's integrity or self-worth does not come easily or all at once, but in small increments, built through decisions and actions that cumulatively form the essential self. When you use the term "character," can you be sure that your readers will understand without explanation what you mean by it? If not, and the term is essential to your discussion, then you will need to define it.

A good definition, whatever perspectives and values may be embedded in it, can forestall pages and pages of explanation and misunderstanding; definition is the writer's ounce of prevention. Definition answers the fundamental question, What is X? Or, What is X not? Some of the more common types of definitions are explained below.

Definition According to Purpose. A definition according to purpose identifies the qualities a behavior or phenomenon (a role, principle or policy, activity, or literary or artistic work) has or should have in order to fulfill its potential. Thus such a definition might answer such questions as, What is the purpose of X? ("A lie is an untruth intended to deceive.") What is X for? ("Nature exists to serve humankind" or "for its own sake.") What does X do? ("A scientist does empirical research.") What is the role of X? ("Self-respect maintains a person's integrity.") Definitions such as these are often loaded with values, whether or not the definers acknowledge their biases.

Descriptive Definitions. A descriptive definition identifies the distinctive characteristics of an abstraction, individual, or group that set it apart from others. Thus a descriptive definition might begin by *naming* something, answering the question "What is X called?" A possible answer might be Leslie Silko (unique among all other women); a copperhead (as opposed to all other species of snakes); or *Huckleberry Finn* (and no other novel by Mark Twain). A descriptive definition may also *specify the relationship among the parts of a unit or group,* addressing the questions: What is the structure of X? (the universe, for instance). How is X organized or put together? (a social system). Or it may *identify the features of something:* What does X look like? ("Kozol's homeless shelters display infected and untreated sores, scabies, diarrhea, poorly set limbs, protruding elbows. . . .") What is X's personality? ("Anne Frank's genteel, otherworldly father was unprepared for survival.") What is the essence, the fundamental nature of X? such as truth, beauty, the natural world.

Process Definitions. A process definition classifies its subject according to various processes that either cause or produce it, or in which it participates. How is X produced? (Joan Didion's "On Self-Respect" shows what the term means by illustrating how she developed that quality.) How does it work? (In "Doing Science in Secret," Rita Levi-Montalcini explains how a cell biologist did her work.)

Logical Definitions. A logical definition, often used in scientific and philosophical writing, answers two related questions: Into what general category does X fit? and How does it differ from all other members of that category? For example, Sissela Bok considers "Lies for the Public Good" as a subcategory of lies in general (whose intent is to deceive); they consist of what the liars identify as "noble lies" and "white lies." The five key principles for writing logical definitions are also useful in evaluating definitions in other people's writing.

1. For economy's sake, *use the most specific category, or class, to which the defined item belongs.* If you're talking about lies, you can exclude other forms of deception from your discussion.

2. *Any division of a class must include all members of that class.* "Noble lies" must consider all types of lies told from ostensibly noble motives. *Negative definitions* explain what is excluded from a given classification, and what is not. If all lies involve deliberate deception, then a piece of misinformation is not a lie unless it is deliberate.

3. *Subdivisions must be smaller than the class divided.* In *Lying* Bok discusses "lies in a crisis," "lies in the public interest," "lies protecting peers and clients" among others.

4. *Categories should be mutually exclusive;* they should not overlap. Although a physician might lie by not telling a patient that death was imminent, Bok discusses such "lies to clients" in one chapter on the subject and does not intermingle this with "lies in a crisis" or "noble lies."

5. *The basis for subdividing categories must be consistent throughout each stage of subdivision.* Bok's division of lies depends on their purpose, not on their substance.

In brief, when you are using definitions in your writing, you need to be aware of the following concerns:

- What am I defining, and why? To explain a concept, argue a point, clear up a misconception, present a new perspective?

- What do my intended readers know about the term(s) I am defining? Enough so I can be fairly technical? Or must I stick to the fundamentals? Will my readers have a pre-existing definition in mind against which I can play off mine? Can I let my own biases show, or should I aim for neutrality? Do I need to use outside authorities to reinforce my own definitions?

- Where in my essay do I need definitions (every time I introduce new terms or concepts?), and how many will I need? How simple or elaborate must they be?

- How comprehensive or restrictive should my definitions be?

- What techniques of definition will I use? labeling and categorization, description, illustration, analysis, comparison and contrast, considerations of cause and effect, argument, analogy? Or some combination?

QUESTIONS FOR DISCOVERY AND DISCUSSION

1.   Look up the word "sophistication" in a collegiate or unabridged dictionary. Notice the Greek root and its meaning. Then notice that the dictionary gives a series of definitions, some of which are positive and some of which are negative. Why do you suppose that this word means such different things under different circumstances?

2.   Give your own definition of sophistication in a particular area (for example, clothing, wine, sports, food). Indicate whether you see the particular kind of sophistication you have chosen as positive or negative. Be explicit about the values that are important to you as you define the term.

3.   Find some other words that seem to have both positive and negative meanings; another example would be "sophomore," which combines two roots expressing wisdom and foolishness. Check the dictionary for their roots and notice the various definitions recorded there. You might even want to consult the Oxford English Dictionary, which will give you the meanings of the word at different periods of history (for instance, the word "awful" was positive around 1600: it meant "awe-inspiring"). Be prepared to discuss the reasons for the different definitions or for the changes in a word's meaning over time; what values does the word express in its various meanings.

4.   What is really important to you: Winning? Loving? Succeeding? Escaping notice? Or what? Why? Can you find ways to persuade

others that it should be important to them also? If you can, describe how; if you can't, what might make you more convincing? How sure are you that what you value is indeed important?

5.   The sarcastic bumper sticker reads, "Whoever has the most when he dies, wins." Define the meanings of "most" and "wins," and explain the values the saying endorses.

You Can't Pray a Lie

MARK TWAIN

Mark Twain's (1835–1910) quintessentially American values shine most brightly in his most enduring contribution to American literature, *The Adventures of Huckleberry Finn* (1885), from which "You Can't Pray a Lie" is a pivotal section. Samuel Clemens, who took the pen name of Mark Twain, grew up in Hannibal, Missouri, on the banks of the Mississippi river that flows not only through *Huck Finn* but *The Adventures of Tom Sawyer* (1876). The mighty river also forms the context for *Old Times on the Mississippi* (1875), a spirited account of Twain's apprenticeship and experiences as a steamboat pilot, and *Life on the Mississippi* (1883). As a consequence of bankruptcy from unwise investments and the deaths of his wife and daughter, Twain's attacks on American culture and human nature became progressively caustic, in such works as "The Man That Corrupted Hadleyburg" (1900) and *The Mysterious Stranger*, published posthumously in 1916.

In "You Can't Pray a Lie," Jim and Huck are floating on a raft down the Mississippi, both escaping—Huck from an abusive father and the restrictions of town life; Jim from the society in which he is a slave. Huck is caught between conflicting values; if he tells Jim's owner where Jim is—as he believes he should—because "she tried to be good to you every way she knowed how," he will be betraying an honorable man who loved and protected him, the man who considered him "the best friend old Jim ever had in the world, and the *only* one he's got now."

When breakfast was ready, we lolled on the grass and eat it smoking hot. Jim laid it in with all his might, for he was most about starved. Then when we had got pretty well stuffed, we laid off and lazied. 1

By-and-by Jim says: 2

"But looky here, Huck, who wuz it dat 'uz killed in dat shanty, ef it warn't you?" 3

Then I told him the whole thing, and he said it was smart. He said Tom Sawyer couldn't get up no better plan than what I had. Then I says: 4

"How do you come to be here, Jim, and how'd you get here?" 5

He looked pretty uneasy, and didn't say nothing for a minute. Then he says: 6

"Maybe I better not tell." 7

"Why, Jim?"   8

"Well, dey's reasons. But you wouldn' tell on me ef I 'uz to tell   9
you, would you, Huck?"

"Blamed if I would, Jim."   10

"Well, I b'lieve you, Huck. I—I *run off*."   11

"Jim!"   12

"But mind, you said you wouldn't tell—you know you said you   13
wouldn't tell, Huck."

"Well, I did. I said I wouldn't, and I'll stick to it. Honest *injun* I   14
will. People would call me a low down Ablitionist and despise me for
keeping mum—but that don't make no difference. I ain't agoing to tell,
and I ain't agoing back there anyways. Sonow, le's know all about it."

"Well, you see, it 'uz dis way. Ole Missus—dat's Miss Watson—   15
she pecks on me all de time, en treats me pooty rough, but she awluz
said she wouldn' sell me down to Orleans. But I noticed dey wuz a
nigger trader roun' de place considable, lately, en I begin to git oneasy.
Well, one night I creeps to de do', pooty late, en de do' warn't quite
shet, en I hear ole missus tell de widder she gwyne to sell me down
to Orleans, but she didn' want to, but she could git eight hund'd
dollars for me, en it 'uz sich a big stack o' money she couldn' resis'.
De widder she try to git her to say she wouldn' do it, but I never
waited to hear de res'. I lit out mighty quick, I tell you . . . .

We slept most all day, and started out at night, a little ways be-   16
hind a monstrous long raft that was as long going by as a procession.
She had four long sweeps at each end, so we judged she carried as
many as thirty men, likely. She had five big wigwams aboard, wide
apart, and an open camp fire in the middle, and a tall flag-pole at
each end. There was a power of style about her. It *amounted* to something being a raftsman on such a craft as that.

We went drifting down into a big bend, and the night clouded   17
up and got hot. The river was very wide, and was walled with solid
timber on both sides; you couldn't see a break in it hardly ever, or a
light. We talked about Cairo, and wondered whether we would know
it when we got to it. I said likely we wouldn't, because I had heard
say there warn't but about a dozen houses there, and if they didn't
happen to have them lit up, how was we going to know we was
passing a town? Jim said if the two big rivers joined together there,
that would show. But I said maybe we might think we was passing
the foot of an island and coming into the same old river again. That
disturbed Jim—and me too. So the question was, what to do? I said,
paddle ashore the first time a light showed, and tell them pap was
behind, coming along with a trading-scow, and was a green hand at
the business, and wanted to know how far it was to Cairo. Jim thought
it was a good idea, so we took a smoke on it and waited.

There warn't nothing to do, now, but to look out sharp for the 18
town, and not pass it without seeing it. He said he'd be mighty sure
to see it, because he'd be a free man the minute he seen it, but if he
missed it he'd be in the slave country again and no more show for
freedom. Every little while he jumps up and says:

"Dah she is!"   19

But it warn't. It was Jack-o-lanterns, or lightning-bugs; so he set 20
down again, and went to watching, same as before. Jim said it made
him all over trembly and feverish to be so close to freedom. Well, I
can tell you it made me all over trembly and feverish, too, to hear
him, because I begun to get it through my head that he *was* most
free—and who was to blame for it? Why, *me*. I couldn't get that out
of my conscience, no how nor no way. It got to troubling me so I
couldn't rest; I couldn't stay still in one place. It hadn't ever come
home to me before, what this thing was that I was doing. But now it
did; and it staid with me, and scorched me more and more. I tried
to make out to myself that *I* warn't to blame, because *I* didn't run Jim
off from his rightful owner; but it warn't no use, conscience up and
says, every time, "But you knowed he was running for his freedom,
and you could a paddled ashore and told somebody." That was so—
I couldn't get around that, noway. That was where it pinched. Conscience says to me, "What had poor Miss Watson done to you, that
you could see her nigger go off right under your eyes and never say
one single word? What did that poor old woman do to you, that you
could treat her so mean? Why, she tried to learn you your book, she
tried to learn you your manners, she tried to be good to you every
way she knowed how. *That's* what she done."

I got to feeling so mean and so miserable I most wished I was 21
dead. I fidgeted up and down the raft, abusing myself to myself, and
Jim was fidgeting up and down past me. We neither of us could keep
still. Every time he danced around and says, "Dah's Cairo!" it went
through me like a shot, and I thought if it *was* Cairo I reckoned I
would die of miserableness.

Jim talked out loud all the time while I was talking to myself. He 22
was saying how the first thing he would do when he got to a free
State he would go to saving up money and never spend a single cent,
and when he got enough he would buy his wife, which was owned
on a farm close to where Miss Watson lived; and then they would
both work to buy the two children, and if there master wouldn't sell
them, they'd get an Ab'litionist to go and steal them.

It most froze me to hear such talk. He wouldn't ever dared to talk 23
such talk in his life before. Just see what a difference it made in him
the minute he judged he was about free. It was according to the old

saying, "give a nigger an inch and he'll take an ell." Thinks I, this is what comes of my not thinking. Here was this nigger which I had as good as helped to run away, coming right out flat-footed and saying he would steal his children—children that belonged to a man I didn't even know; a man that hadn't ever done me no harm.

I was sorry to hear Jim say that, it was such a lowering of him. 24 My conscience got to stirring me up hotter than ever, until at last I says to it, "Let up on me—it ain't too late, yet—I'll paddle ashore at the first light, and tell." I felt easy, and happy, and light as a feather, right off. All my troubles was gone. I went to looking out sharp for a light, and sort of singing to myself. By-and-by one showed. Jim sings out:

"We's safe, Huck, we's safe! Jump up and crack yo' heels, dat's 25 de good ole Cairo at las', I jis knows it!"

I says: 26

"I'll take the canoe and go see, Jim. It mightn't be, you know." 27

He jumped and got the canoe ready, and put his old coat in the 28 bottom for me to set on, and give me the paddle; and as I shoved off, he says:

"Pooty soon I'll be a-shout'n for joy, en I'll say, it's all on accounts 29 o' Huck; I's a free man, en I couldn't ever ben free ef it hadn' been for Huck; Huck done it. Jim won't ever forgit you, Huck; you's de bes' fren' Jim's ever had; en you's de *only* fren' ole Jim's got now."

I was paddling off, all in a sweat to tell on him; but when he says 30 this, it seemed to kind of take the tuck all out of me. I went along slow then, and I warn't right down certain whether I was glad I started or whether I warn't. When I was fifty yards off, Jim says:

"Dah you goes, de ole true Huck; de on'y white genlman dat ever 31 kep' his promise to ole Jim."

Well, I just felt sick. But I says, I *got* to do it—I can't get *out* of 32 it. Right then, along comes a skiff with two men in it, with guns, and they stopped and I stopped. One of them says:

"What's that, yonder?" 33

"A piece of a raft," I says. 34

"Do you belong on it?" 35

"Yes, sir." 36

"Any men on it?" 37

"Only one, sir." 38

"Well, there's five niggers run off to-night, up yonder above the 39 head of the bend. Is your man white or black?"

I didn't answer up prompt. I tried to, but the words wouldn't 40 come. I tried, for a second or two, to brace up and out with it, but I warn't man enough—hadn't the spunk of a rabbit. I see I was weakening; so I just give up trying, and up and says—

"He's white."   41

"I reckon we'll go and see for ourselves."   42

"I wish you would," says I, "because it's pap that's there, and   43
maybe you'd help me tow the raft ashore where the light is. He's
sick—and so is mam and Mary Ann."

"Oh, the devil! we're in a hurry, boy. But I s'pose we've got to.   44
Come—buckle to your paddle, and let's get along."

I buckled to my paddle and they laid to their oars. When we had   45
made a stroke or two, I says:

"Pap'll be mighty much obleeged to you, I can tell you. Everybody   46
goes away when I want them to help me tow the raft ashore, and I
can't do it by myself."

"Well, that's infernal mean. Odd, too. Say, boy, what's the matter   47
with your father?"

"It's the—a—the—well, it ain't anything, much."   48

They stopped pulling. It warn't but a mighty little ways to the   49
raft, now. One says:

"Boy, that's a lie. What *is* the matter with your pap? Answer up   50
square, now, and it'll be the better for you."

"I will, sir, I will, honest—but don't leave us, please. It's the—   51
the—gentlemen, if you'll only pull ahead, and let me heave you the
head-line, you won't have to come a-near the raft—please do."

"Set her back, John, set her back!" says one. They backed water.   52
"Keep away, boy—keep to looard. Confound it, I just expect the wind
has blowed it to us. Your pap's got the small-pox, and you know it
precious well. Why didn't you come out and say so? Do you want to
spread it all over?"

"Well," says I, a-blubbering, "I've told everybody before, and   53
then they just went away and left us."

"Poor devil, there's something in that. We are right down sorry   54
for you, but we—well, hang it, we don't want the small-pox, you see.
Look here, I'll tell you what to do. Don't you try to land by yourself,
or you'll smash everything to pieces. You float along down about
twenty miles and you'll come to a town on the left-hand side of the
river. It will be long after sun-up, then, and when you ask for help,
you tell them your folks are all down with chills and fever. Don't be
a fool again, and let people guess what is the matter. Now we're
trying to do you a kindness; so you just put twenty miles between
us, that's a good boy. It wouldn't do any good to land yonder where
the light is—it's only a wood-yard. Say—I reckon you father's poor,
and I'm bound to say he's in pretty hard luck. Here—I'll put a twenty
dollar gold piece on this board, and you get it when it floats by. I feel

mighty mean to leave you, but my kingdom! it won't do to fool with small-pox, don't you see?"

"Hold on, Parker," says the other man, "here's a twenty to put 55 on the board for me. Good-bye, boy, you do as Mr. Parker told you, and you'll be all right."

"That's so, my boy—good-bye, good-bye. If you see any runaway 56 niggers, you get help and nab them, and you can make some money by it."

"Good-bye, sir," says I, "I won't let no runaway niggers get by 57 me if I can help it."

They went off, and I got aboard the raft, feeling bad and low, 58 because I knowed very well I had done wrong, and I see it warn't no use for me to try to learn to do right; a body that don't get *started* right when he's little, ain't got no show—when the pinch comes there ain't nothing to back him up and keep him to his work, and so he gets beat. Then I thought a minute, and says to myself, hold on,— s'pose you'd a done right and give Jim up; would you felt better than what you do now? No, says I, I'd feel bad—I'd feel just the same way I do now. Well, then, says I, what's the use you learning to do right, when it's troublesome to do right and ain't no trouble to do wrong, and the wages is just the same? I was stuck. I couldn't answer that. So I reckoned I wouldn't bother no more about it, but after this always do whichever come handiest at the time.

I went into the wigwam; Jim warn't there. I looked all around; he 59 warn't anywhere. I says:

"Jim!"   60

"Here I is, Huck. Is dey out o' sight yit? Don't talk loud."   61

He was in the river, under the stern oar, with just his nose out. 62 I told him they was out of sight, so he come aboard. He says:

"I was a-listenin' to all de talk, en I slips into de river en was 63 gwyne to shove for sho' if dey came aboard. Den I was gwyne to swim to de raf' agin when dey was gone. But lawsy, how you did fool 'em, Huck! Dat *wuz* de smartes' dodge! I tell you, chile, I 'speck it save' ole Jim—ole Jim ain't gwyne to forgit you for dat, honey."

Then we talked about the money. It was a pretty good raise, 64 twenty dollars apiece. Jim said we could take deck passage on a steamboat now, and the money would last us as far as we wanted to go in the free States. He said twenty mile more warn't far for the raft to go, but he wished we was already there.

Towards daybreak we tied up, and Jim was mighty particular about 65 hiding the raft good. Then he worked all day fixing things in bundles, and getting all ready to quit rafting. . . .

[Jim is later captured and Huck must again decide what to do.]

Once I said to myself it would be a thousand times better for Jim 66
to be a slave at home where his family was, as long as he'd *got* to be
a slave, and so I'd better write a letter to Tom Sawyer and tell him to
tell Miss Watson where he was. But I soon give up that notion, for
two things: she'd be mad and disgusted at his rascality and ungrate-
fulness for leaving her, and so she'd sell him straight down the river
again; and if she didn't, everybody naturally despises an ungrateful
nigger, and they'd make Jim feel it all the time, and so he'd feel ornery
and disgraced. And then think of *me!* It would get all around, that
Huck Finn helped a nigger to get his freedom; and if I was to ever
see anybody from that town again, I'd be ready to get down and lick
his boots for shame. That's just the way: a person does a low-down
thing, and then he don't want to take no consequences of it. Thinks
as long as he can hide it, it ain't no disgrace. That was my fix exactly.
The more I studied about this, the more my conscience went to grinding me, and the more wicked and low-down and ornery I got to
feeling. And at last, when it hit me all of a sudden that here was the
plain hand of Providence slapping me in the face and letting me know
my wickedness was being watched all the time from up there in
heaven, whilst I was stealing a poor old woman's nigger that hadn't
ever done me no harm, and now was showing me there's One that's
always on the lookout, and ain't agoing to allow no such miserable
doings to go only just so fur and no further, I most dropped in my
tracks I was so scared. Well, I tried the best I could to kinder soften
it up somehow for myself, by saying I was brung up wicked, and so
I warn't so much to blame; but something inside of me kept saying,
"There was the Sunday school, you could a gone to it; and if you'd
a done it they'd a learnt you, there, that people that acts as I'd been
acting about that nigger goes to everlasting fire."

It made me shiver. And I about made up my mind to pray; and 67
see if I couldn't try to quit being the kind of a boy I was, and be
better. So I kneeled down. But the words wouldn't come. Why
wouldn't they? It warn't no use to try and hide it from Him. Nor
from *me*, neither. I knowed very well why they wouldn't come. It was
because my heart warn't right; it was because I warn't square; it was
because I was playing double. I was letting *on* to give up sin, but away
inside of me I was holding on to the biggest one of all. I was trying
to make my mouth *say* I would do the right thing and the clean thing,
and go and write to that nigger's owner and tell where he was; but
deep down in me I knowed it was a lie—and He knowed it. You can't
pray a lie—I found that out.

So I was full of trouble, full as I could be; and didn't know what 68 to do. At last I had an idea; and I says, I'll go and write the letter—and *then* see if I can pray. Why, it was astonishing, the way I felt as light as a feather, right straight off, and my troubles all gone. So I got a piece of paper and a pencil, all glad and excited, and set down and wrote:

> Miss Watson your runaway nigger Jim is down here two mile below Pikesville and Mr. Phelps has got him and he will give him up for the reward if you send.   HUCK FINN.

I felt good and all washed clean of sin for the first time I had ever   69
felt so in my life, and I knowed I could pray now. But I didn't do it straight off, but laid the paper down and set there thinking—thinking how good it was all this happened so, and how near I come to being lost and going to hell. And went on thinking. And got to thinking over our trip down the river; and I see Jim before me, all the time, in the day, and in the night-time, sometimes moonlight, sometimes storms, and we a floating along, talking, and singing, and laughing. But somehow I couldn't seem to strike no places to harden me against him, but only the other kind. I'd see him standing my watch on top of his'n, stead of calling me, so I could go on sleeping; and see him how glad he was when I come back out of the fog; and when I come to him again in the swamp, up there where the feud was; and such-like times; and would always call me honey, and pet me, and do everything he could think of for me, and how good he always was; and at last I struck the time I saved him by telling the men we had small-pox aboard, and he was so grateful, and said I was the best friend old Jim ever had in the world, and the *only* one he's got now; and then I happened to look around, and see that paper.

It was a close place. I took it up, and held it in my hand. I was   70
a trembling, because I'd got to decide, forever, betwixt two things, and I knowed it. I studied a minute, sort of holding my breath, and then says to myself:

"All right, then, I'll *go* to hell"—and tore it up.   71

It was awful thoughts, and awful words, but they was said. And   72
I let them stay said; and never thought no more about reforming. I shoved the whole thing out of my head; and said I would take up wickedness again, which was in my line, being brung up to it, and the other warn't. And for a starter, I would go to work and steal Jim out of slavery again; and if I could think up anything worse, I would do that, too; because as long as I was in, and in for good, I might as well go the whole hog.

RESPONDING TO READING

Key words: community discovery education family freedom
growing up identity minority rights striving story
watershed

Rhetorical concepts: analogy analysis fiction humor story

1.   This excerpt from Twain's novel poses a basic conflict between an individual's conscience and the rules of society. Look first at Huck's developing
conscience. What establishes his personal sense of values? Why is it so hard
for him to believe his own conscience? What leads him to do what society
tells him is wrong? What does Huck actually mean when he decides that he
will go to hell? Why is it an "awful" thought?
2.   Examine the society Huck and Jim live in and its rules, as established in
the passage. How does this society view slaves? What other values does this
society express? Why does Huck accept as right these values, despite the fact
that we as readers see so much wrong? What does it mean to reject the values
of one's society?
3.   How do you respond to Huck's lies to the men on the river? Ought we
to question our right to break the rules when conscience says we should?
Explain and justify your answer.
4.   Write about a situation from your experience in which personal values
and social values conflict. Could you, for example, turn in a friend for shop-
lifting or cheating on a test? Have you, or a close friend, ever driven under
the influence of alcohol? Read ahead to the next selection, Sissela Bok's "Lies
for the Public Good" and to Thoreau's "Civil Disobedience" in Chapter 5 for
additional views on the subject. Use enough descriptive detail and dialogue
in your own writing so that your reader can visualize the situation, as we
can with the passage from *Huckleberry Finn*. What decision about values
emerged from the situation you describe? What is the meaning of the decision
in the short term (for the situation you describe) and in the long term (for
establishing a meaningful set of values)?

Lies for the Public Good
SISSELA BOK

Sissela Bok, professor of moral philosophy at Brandeis University,
was born in Stockholm, Sweden, in 1934, the daughter of Gunnar
Myrdal (winner of the Nobel Prize in economics) and Alva Myrdal
(winner of the Nobel Peace Prize). That Bok admired her mother
enormously is clear from her most recent book, *Alva Myrdal: A Daughter's Memoir* (1991), a biography that focuses on the intellectual and
moral development of the woman known as "the conscience of the
disarmament movement," and on her struggle to achieve for herself

"the freedom and opportunity she won for millions of other women."
Bok's *A Strategy for Peace* (1989) is a natural companion to the biography, examining how governments and individuals operating on
moral principles can reduce threats to human survival from nuclear
warfare and environmental negligence.

Bok has also written two highly acclaimed studies of ethics: *Lying:
Moral Choices in Public and Private Life* (1978) and *Secrets: On the Ethics
of Concealment and Revelation* (1983). Secrecy, she says, both confers
power and imposes a burden, raising complicated moral questions
such as "How far should one go in protecting one's secrets? Should
one conceal all that friends and colleagues decide? Are there times
when secrecy *must* be breached?" Lying and secrecy, says Bok, "in-
tertwine and overlap. Lies are part of the arsenal used to guard and
to invade secrecy; and secrecy allows lies to go undiscovered and to
build up." They differ, however, in one important respect. In most
instances lying, even telling white lies, is wrong, but secrecy need
not be. Whereas every lie needs to be justified, not all secrets do,
for "secrecy is needed for human survival, yet it enhances every
form of abuse." In "Lies for the Public Good," from *Lying*, Bok
examines various types of "noble lies"—lies intended to benefit the
public and to avoid long-range harm, though neither benefit may in
fact occur.

But the most characteristic defense for these [noble] lies is a sep- 1
arate one, based on the benefits they may confer and the long-range
harm they can avoid. The intention may be broadly paternalistic, as
when citizens are deceived "for their own good," or only a few may
be lied to for the benefit of the community at large. Error and self-
deception mingle with these altruistic purposes and blur them; the
filters through which we must try to peer at lying are thicker and
more distorting than ever in these practices. But I shall try to single
out, among these lies, the elements that are consciously and purposely
intended to benefit society.

A long tradition in political philosophy endorses some lies for the 2
sake of the public. Plato . . . first used the expression "noble lie" for
the fanciful story that might be told to people in order to persuade
them to accept class distinctions and thereby safeguard social harmony. According to this story, God Himself mingled gold, silver, iron,
and brass in fashioning rulers, auxiliaries, farmers, and craftsmen,
intending these groups for separate tasks in a harmonious hierarchy.

The Greek adjective which Plato used to characterize this false- 3
hood expresses a most important fact about lies by those in power:
this adjective is *"gennaion,"* which means "noble" in the sense of both
"high-minded" and "well-bred." The same assumption of nobility,
good breeding, and superiority to those deceived is also present in
Disraeli's statement that a gentleman is one who knows when to tell
the truth and when not to. In other words, lying is excusable when

undertaken for "noble" ends by those trained to discern these purposes.

Rulers, both temporal and spiritual, have seen their deceits in the   4
benign light of such social purposes. They have propagated and maintained myths played on the gullibility of the ignorant, and sought stability in shared beliefs. They have seen themselves as high-minded and well-bred—whether by birth or by training—and as superior to those they deceive. Some have gone so far as to claim that those who govern have a *right* to lie.[1] The powerful tell lies believing that they have greater than ordinary understanding of what is at stake; very often, they regard their dupes as having inadequate judgment, or as likely to respond in the wrong way to truthful information.

At times, those who govern also regard particular circumstances   5
as too uncomfortable, too painful, for most people to be able to cope with rationally. They may believe, for instance, that their country must prepare for long-term challenges of great importance, such as a war, an epidemic, or a belt-tightening in the face of future shortages. Yet they may fear that citizens will be able to respond only to short-range dangers. Deception at such times may seem to the government leaders as the only means of attaining the necessary results.

The perspective of the liar is paramount in all such decisions to   6
tell "noble" lies. If the liar considers the responses of the deceived at all, he assumes that they will, once the deceit comes to light and its benefits are understood, be uncomplaining if not positively grateful. The lies are often seen as necessary merely at one *stage* in the education of the public. . . .

Some experienced public officials are impatient with any effort to   7
question the ethics of such deceptive practices (except actions obviously taken for private ends). They argue that vital objectives in the national interest require a measure of deception to succeed in the face of powerful obstacles. Negotiations must be carried on that are best left hidden from public view; bargains must be struck that simply cannot be comprehended by a politically unsophisticated electorate. A certain amount of illusion is needed in order for public servants to be effective. Every government, therefore, has to deceive people to some extent in order to lead them.

These officials view the public's concern for ethics as understand-   8
able but hardly realistic. Such "moralistic" concerns, put forth without any understanding of practical exigencies, may lead to the setting of impossible standards; these could seriously hamper work without actually changing the underlying practices. Government officials could then feel so beleaguered that some of them might quit their

---

[1]Arthur Sylvester, "The Government Has the Right to Lie," *Saturday Evening Post*, 18 November 1967, p. 10.

jobs; inefficiency and incompetence would then increasingly afflict the work of the rest.

If we assume the perspective of the deceived—those who experience the consequences of government deception—such arguments are not persuasive. We cannot take for granted either the altruism or the good judgment of those who lie to us, no matter how much they intend to benefit us. We have learned that much deceit for private gain masquerades as being in the public interest. We know how deception, even for the most unselfish motive, corrupts and spreads. And we have lived through the consequences of lies told for what were believed to be noble purposes.   9

Equally unpersuasive is the argument that there always has been government deception, and always will be, and that efforts to draw lines and set standards are therefore useless annoyances. It is certainly true that deception can never be completely absent from most human practices. But there are great differences among societies in the kinds of deceit that exist and the extent to which they are practiced, differences also among individuals in the same government and among successive governments within the same society. This strongly suggests that it is worthwhile trying to discover why such differences exist and to seek ways of raising the standards of truthfulness.   10

The argument that those who raise moral concerns are ignorant of political realities, finally, ought to lead, not to a dismissal of such inquiries, but to a more articulate description of what these realities are, so that a more careful and informed debate could begin. We have every reason to regard government as more profoundly injured by a dismissal of criticism and a failure to consider standards than by efforts to discuss them openly. If duplicity is to be allowed in exceptional cases, the criteria for these exceptions should themselves be openly debated and publicly chosen. Otherwise government leaders will have free rein to manipulate and distort the facts and thus escape accountability to the public.   11

The effort to question political deception cannot be ruled out so summarily. The disparagement of inquiries into such practices has to be seen as the defense of unwarranted power—power bypassing the consent of the governed. In the pages to come I shall take up just a few cases to illustrate both the clear breaches of trust that no group of citizens could desire, and circumstances where it is more difficult to render a judgment.   12

Examples of Political Deception

In September 1964, a State Department official, reflecting a growing administration consensus, wrote a memorandum advocating a   13 momentous deceit of the American public.[2] He outlined possible courses of action to cope with the deteriorating military situation in South Vietnam. These included a stepping up of American participation in the "pacification" in South Vietnam and a "crescendo" of military action against North Vietnam, involving heavy bombing by the United States. But an election campaign was going on; the President's Republican opponent, Senator Goldwater, was suspected by the electorate of favoring escalation of the war in Vietnam and of brandishing nuclear threats to the communist world. In keeping with President Johnson's efforts to portray Senator Goldwater as an irresponsible war hawk, the memorandum ended with a paragraph entitled "Special considerations during the next two months," holding that:

> During the next two months, because of the lack of "rebuttal time" before election to justify particular actions which may be distorted to the U.S. public, we must act with special care—signaling to . . . [the South Vietnamese] that we are behaving energetically despite the restraints of our political season, and to the U.S. public that we are behaving with good purpose and restraint.

As the campaign wore on, President Johnson increasingly professed to be the candidate of peace. He gave no indication of the growing pressure for escalation from high administrative officials who would remain in office should he win; no hint of the hard choice he knew he would face if elected.[3] Rather he repeated over and over again that: 14

> [T]he first responsibility, the only real issue in this campaign, the only thing you ought to be concerned about at all, is: Who can best keep the peace?[4]

The stratagem succeeded; the election was won; the war escalated. 15 Under the name of Operation Rolling Thunder, the United States launched massive bombing raids over North Vietnam early in 1965. In suppressing genuine debate about these plans during the election campaign and masquerading as the party of peace, government members privy to the maneuver believed that they knew what was best for the country and that history would vindicate them. They meant

---

[2]The Senator Gravel Edition, *The Pentagon Papers* (Boston: Beacon Press, 1971), 3:556–59.

[3]As early as March 1964, Lyndon Johnson knew that such a hard choice might have to be made. See telephone transcript cited by Doris Kearns in *Lyndon Johnson and the American Dream* (New York: Harper & Row, 1976), p. 197.

[4]Theodore H. White, *The Making of the President 1964* (New York: Atheneum, 1965), p. 373.

to benefit the nation and the world by keeping the danger of a communist victory at bay. If a sense of *crisis* was needed for added justification, the Domino Theory strained for it: one regime after another was seen as toppling should the first domino be pushed over.

But why the deceit, if the purposes were so altruistic? Why not 16 espouse these purposes openly before the election? The reason must have been that the government could not count on popular support for the scheme. In the first place, the sense of crisis and threat from North Vietnam would have been far from universally shared. To be forthright about the likelihood of escalation might lose many votes; it certainly could not fit with the campaign to portray President Johnson as the candidate most likely to keep the peace. Second, the government feared that its explanations might be "distorted" in the election campaign, so that the voters would not have the correct information before them. Third, time was lacking for the government to make an effort at educating the people about all that was at issue. Finally, the plans were not definitive; changes were possible, and the Vietnamese situation itself very unstable. For all these reasons, it seemed best to campaign for negotiation and restraint and let the Republican opponent be the target for the fear of United States belligerence.

President Johnson thus denied the electorate any chance to give 17 or to refuse consent to the escalation of the war in Vietnam. Believing they had voted for the candidate of peace, American citizens were, within months, deeply embroiled in one of the cruelest wars in their history. Deception of this kind strikes at the very essence of democratic government. It allows those in power to override or nullify the right vested in the people to cast an informed vote in critical elections. Deceiving the people for the sake of the people is a self-contradictory notion in a democracy, unless it can be shown that there has been genuine consent to deceit. The actions of President Johnson were therefore inconsistent with the most basic principle of our political system.

What if all government officials felt similarly free to deceive pro- 18 vided they believed the deception genuinely necessary to achieve some important public end? The trouble is that those who make such calculations are always susceptible to bias. They overestimate the likelihood that the benefit will occur and that the harm will be averted; they underestimate the chances that the deceit will be discovered and ignore the effects of such a discovery on trust; they underrate the comprehension of the deceived citizens, as well as their ability and their right to make a reasoned choice. And, most important, such a benevolent self-righteousness disguises the many motives for political lying which could *not* serve as moral excuses: the need to cover up past mistakes; the vindictiveness; the desire to stay in power. These self-serving ends provide the impetus for countless lies that are rationalized as "necessary" for the public good.

As political leaders become accustomed to making such excuses, they grow insensitive to fairness and to veracity. Some come to believe that any lie can be told so long as they can convince themselves that people will be better off in the long run. From there, it is a short step to the conclusion that, even if people will not be better off from a particular lie, they will benefit by all maneuvers to keep the right people in office. Once public servants lose their bearings in this way, all the shabby deceits of Watergate—the fake telegrams, the erased tapes, the elaborate cover-ups, the bribing of witnesses to make them lie, the televised pleas for trust—become possible.

While Watergate may be unusual in its scope, most observers would agree that deception is part and parcel of many everyday decisions in government. Statistics may be presented in such a way as to diminish the gravity of embarrassing problems. Civil servants may lie to members of Congress in order to protect programs they judge important, or to guard secrets they have been ordered not to divulge. If asked, members of Congress who make deals with one another to vote for measures they would otherwise oppose deny having made such deals. False rumors may be leaked by subordinates who believe that unwise executive action is about to be taken. Or the leak may be correct, but falsely attributed in order to protect the source. . . .

These common lies are now so widely suspected that voters are at a loss to know when they can and cannot believe what a candidate says in campaigning. The damage to trust has been immense. I have already referred to the poll which found 69 percent of Americans agreeing, both in 1975 and 1976, that the country's leaders had consistently lied to the American people over the past ten years. Over 40 percent of the respondents also agreed that:

> Most politicians are so similar that it doesn't really make much difference who gets elected.[5]

Many refuse to vote under such circumstances. Others look to appearance or to personality factors for clues as to which candidate might be more honest than the others. Voters and candidates alike are the losers when a political system has reached such a low level of trust. Once elected, officials find that their warnings and their calls to common sacrifice meet with disbelief and apathy, even when co-

---

[5]*Cambridge Survey Research*, 1975, 1976.

operation is most urgently needed. Law suits and investigations multiply. And the fact that candidates, should they win, are not expected to have meant what they said while campaigning, nor held accountable for discrepancies, only reinforces the incentives for them to bend the truth the next time, thus adding further to the distrust of the voters.

Political lies, so often assumed to be trivial by those who tell them, 23 rarely are. They cannot be trivial when they affect so many people and when they are so peculiarly likely to be imitated, used to retaliate, and spread from a few to many. When political representatives or entire governments arrogate to themselves the right to lie, they take power from the public that would not have been given up voluntarily.

Deception and Consent

Can there be exceptions to the well-founded distrust of deception 24 in public life? Are there times when the public itself might truly not care about possible lies, or might even prefer to be deceived: Are some white lies so trivial or so transparent that they can be ignored? And can we envisage public discussion of more seriously misleading government statements such that reasonable persons could consent to them in advance?

White lies, first of all, are as common to political and diplomatic 25 affairs as they are to the private lives of most people. Feigning enjoyment of an embassy gathering or a political rally, toasting the longevity of a dubious regime or an unimpressive candidate for office—these are forms of politeness that mislead few. It is difficult to regard them as threats to either individuals or communities. As with all white lies, however, the problem is that they spread so easily, and that lines are very hard to draw. Is it still a white lie for a secretary of state to announce that he is going to one country when in reality he travels to another? Or for a president to issue a "cover story" to the effect that a cold is forcing him to return to the White House, when in reality an international crisis made him cancel the rest of his campaign trip? Is it a white lie to issue a letter of praise for a public servant one has just fired? Given the vulnerability of public trust, it is never more important than in public life to keep the deceptive element of white lies to an absolute minimum, and to hold down the danger of their turning into more widespread deceitful practices.

Certain additional forms of deception may be debated and au- 26 thorized in advance by elected representatives of the public. The use of unmarked police cars to discourage speeding by drivers is an example of such a practice. Various forms of unannounced, sometimes covert, auditing of business and government operations are others.

Whenever these practices are publicly regulated, they can be limited so that abuses are avoided. But they must be *openly* debated and agreed to in advance, with every precaution against abuses of privacy and the rights of individuals, and against the spread of such covert activities. It is not enough that a public official assumes that consent would be given to such practices. . . .

Another form of deception takes place when the government re- 27 gards the public as frightened, or hostile, and highly volatile. In order not to create a panic, information about early signs of an epidemic may be suppressed or distorted. And the lie to a mob seeking its victim is like lying to the murderer asking where the person he is pursuing has gone. It can be acknowledged and defended as soon as the threat is over. In such cases, one may at times be justified in withholding information; perhaps on rare occasions, even in lying. But such cases are so rare that they hardly exist for practical purposes.

The fact that rare circumstances exist where the justification for 28 government lying seems powerful creates a difficulty—these same excuses will often be made to serve a great many more purposes. For some governments or public officials, the information they wish to conceal is almost never of the requisite certainty, the time never the right one, and the public never sufficiently dispassionate. For these reasons, it is hard to see how a practice of lying to the public about devaluation or changes in taxation or epidemics could be consented to in advance, and therefore justified.

Are there any exceptionally dangerous circumstances where the 29 state of crisis is such as to justify lies to the public for its own protection? We have already discussed lying to enemies in an acute crisis. Sometimes the domestic public is then also deceived, at least temporarily, as in the case of the U-2 incident. Wherever there is a threat—from a future enemy, as before World War II, or from a shortage of energy—the temptation to draw upon the excuses for deceiving citizens is very strong. The government may sincerely doubt that the electorate is capable of making the immediate sacrifices needed to confront the growing danger. (Or one branch of the government may lack confidence in another, for similar reasons, as when the administration mistrusts Congress.) The public may seem too emotional, the time not yet ripe for disclosure. Are there crises so exceptional that deceptive strategies are justifiable? . . .

Do we want to live in a society where public officials can resort 30 to deceit and manipulation whenever they decide that an exceptional crisis has arisen? Would we not, on balance, prefer to run the risk of failing to rise to a crisis honestly explained to us, from which the government might have saved us through manipulation? And what protection from abuse do we foresee should we surrender this choice?

In considering answers to these questions, we must take into 31
account more than the short-run effects of government manipulation.
President Roosevelt's manner of bringing the American people to
accept first the possibility, then the likelihood, of war [World War II]
was used as an example by those who wanted to justify President
Johnson's acts of dissimulation. And these acts in turn were pointed
to by those who resorted to so many forms of duplicity in the Nixon
administration. Secrecy and deceit grew at least in part because of
existing precedents.[6]

The consequences of spreading deception, alienation, and lack of 32
trust could not have been documented for us more concretely than
they have in the past decades. We have had a very vivid illustration
of how lies undermine our political system. While deception under
the circumstances confronting President Roosevelt may in hindsight
be more excusable than much that followed, we could no more consent
to it in advance than to all that come later.

Wherever lies to the public have become routine, then, very spe- 33
cial safeguards should be required. The test of public justification of
deceptive practices is more needed than ever. It will be a hard test to
satisfy, the more so the more trust is invested in those who lie and
the more power they wield. Those in government and other positions
of trust should be held to the highest standards. Their lies are not
ennobled by their positions; quite the contrary. Some lies—notably
minor white lies and emergency lies rapidly acknowledged—may be
more *excusable* than others, but only those deceptive practices which
can be openly debated and consented to in advance are *justifiable* in
a democracy.

RESPONDING TO READING

Key words: community   discovery   language   power
reading   rights   writing

Rhetorical concepts: analysis   cause and effect   deduction
definition   explanation   illustration   meditation

1. In Bok's view "noble lie," "white lie," and "lies for the public good" are
all oxymorons, and all are wrong. Explain, using Bok's definitions as the
basis of your discussion. Why are definitions crucial to her argument?
2. Bok is a moral philosopher. Using "Lies for the Public Good" as a charac-

---

[6]See Arthur M. Schlesinger, Jr., *The Imperial Presidency* (Boston: Houghton Mifflin, 1973,
p. 356: "The power to withhold and the power to leak led on inexorably to the power to
lie . . . uncontrolled secrecy made it easy for lying to become routine." See also David Wise, *The
Politics of Lying* (New York: Random House, 1973).

teristic illustration of her work, identify some of the central concerns, values, and ways of thinking of a moral philosopher.

3.   What sort of impact does Bok expect her work to have on the rest of society? For what audience(s) is Bok writing? How would she expect public officials, for instance, to react to her argument?

4.   In your opinion, is lying or other deception "for the public good" ever justified? If not, explain why not. If so, explain the circumstances in which you believe lying to the public is justified. Must any safeguards be employed in the situation(s) you envision? What are they? Be sure to take Bok's definitions and argument into account.

5.   Have you ever lied with good intentions? If so, narrate the circumstances and what happened. Was your lie justifiable? On what grounds? To what degree does Bok's essay help you see more clearly the values behind your action? If you have never lied with good intentions, tell about an occasion on which you resisted the temptation to lie.

On Self-Respect

JOAN DIDION

"People with self-respect," says Joan Didion in the following essay, "exhibit a certain toughness, a kind of moral nerve; they display what was once called *character* . . . the willingness to accept responsibility for one's own life." In one way or another, Didion's collections of essays, *Slouching Towards Bethlehem* (1968) and *The White Album* (1979), and her novels focus on people who lack character, struggle with self-respect, and, too often, lose the struggle. Many of the major characters in the novels *Run River* (1963), *Play It As It Lays* (1971), *A Book of Common Prayer* (1977), and *Democracy* (1984) and in the essays in *After Henry* (1992), are estranged from the traditional values of religion, family, and society. They do not know what to do or where to turn to find the stability, peace, and certainty they seek.

Didion was born in Sacramento, California, in 1934, and educated at the University of California, Berkeley. In 1964 she married writer John Gregory Dunne, and the couple moved to Los Angeles to collaborate on screenplays (*Panic in Needle Park* [1971], *A Star is Born* [1976]) and to try to forge a family and community "in the face of what many people believe to be a moral vacuum." In response to an interviewer's suggestion that "You seem to live your life on the edge, or, at least, on the literary idea of the edge," Didion replied, "Again, it's a literary idea, and it derives from what engaged me imaginatively as a child. I can recall disapproving of the golden mean, always thinking there was more to be learned from the dark journey. The dark journey engaged me more." The dark journey is what passionate writers take, and life on the edge is where they live; to do so demands the character and self-respect required to compel readers to, as Didion says, *"listen to me, see it my way, change your mind."*

Once, in a dry season, I wrote in large letters across two pages 1
of a notebook that innocence ends when one is stripped of the delusion that one likes oneself. Although now, some years later, I marvel
that a mind on the outs with itself should have nonetheless made
painstaking record of its every tremor, I recall with embarrassing
clarity the flavor of those particular ashes. It was a matter of misplaced
self-respect.

I had not been elected to Phi Beta Kappa. This failure could 2
scarcely have been more predictable or less ambiguous (I simply
did not have the grades), but I was unnerved by it; I had somehow
thought myself a kind of academic Raskolnikov, curiously exempt
from the cause-effect relationships which hampered others. Although
even the humorless nineteen-year-old that I was must have recognized
that the situation lacked real tragic stature, the day that I did not make
Phi Beta Kappa nonetheless marked the end of something, and innocence may well be the word for it. I lost the conviction that lights
would always turn green for me, the pleasant certainty that those
rather passive virtues which had won me approval as a child automatically guaranteed me not only Phi Beta Kappa keys but happiness,
honor, and the love of a good man; lost a certain touching faith in
the totem power of good manners, clean hair, and proven competence
on the Stanford-Binet scale. To such doubtful amulets had my self-
respect been pinned, and I faced myself that day with the nonplused
apprehension of someone who has come across a vampire and has
no crucifix at hand.

Although to be driven back upon oneself is an uneasy affair at 3
best, rather like trying to cross a border with borrowed credentials,
it seems to me now the one condition necessary to the beginnings of
real self-respect. Most of our platitudes notwithstanding, self-decep-
tion remains the most difficult deception. The tricks that work on
others count for nothing in that very well-lit back alley where one
keeps assignations with oneself: no winning smiles will do here, no
prettily drawn lists of good intentions. One shuffles flashily but in
vain through one's marked cards—the kindness done for the wrong
reason, the apparent triumph which involved no real effort, the seemingly heroic act into which one had been shamed. The dismal fact is
that self-respect has nothing to do with the approval of others—who
are, after all, deceived easily enough; has nothing to do with reputation, which, as Rhett Butler told Scarlett O'Hara, is something people with courage can do without.

To do without self-respect, on the other hand, is to be an unwilling 4
audience of one to an interminable documentary that details one's fail-
ings, both real and imagined, with fresh footage spliced in for every
screening. *There's the glass you broke in anger, there's the hurt on X's face;*

watch now, this next scene, the night Y came back from Houston, see how you muff this one. To live without self-respect is to lie awake some night, beyond the reach of warm milk, phenobarbital, and the sleeping hand on the coverlet, counting up the sins of commission and omission, the trusts betrayed, the promises subtly broken, the gifts irrevocably wasted through sloth or cowardice or carelessness. However long we postpone it, we eventually lie down alone in that notoriously uncomfortable bed, the one we make ourselves. Whether or not we sleep in it depends, of course, on whether or not we respect ourselves.

To protest that some fairly improbable people, some people who   5
could not possibly respect themselves, seem to sleep easily enough is to miss the point entirely, as surely as those people miss it who think that self-respect has necessarily to do with not having safety pins in one's underwear. There is a common superstition that "self-respect" is a kind of charm against snakes, something that keeps those who have it locked in some unblighted Eden, out of strange beds, ambivalent conversations, and trouble in general. It does not at all. It has nothing to do with the face of things, but concerns instead a separate peace, a private reconciliation. Although the careless, suicidal Julian English in *Appointment in Samarra* and the careless, incurably dishonest Jordan Baker in *The Great Gatsby* seem equally improbable candidates for self-respect, Jordan Baker had it, Julian English did not. With that genius for accommodation more often seen in women than in men, Jordan took her own measure, made her own peace, avoided threats to that peace: "I hate careless people," she told Nick Carraway. "It takes two to make an accident."

Like Jordan Baker, people with self-respect have the courage of   6
their mistakes. They know the price of things. If they choose to commit adultery, they do not then go running, in an access of bad conscience, to receive absolution from the wronged parties; nor do they complain unduly of the unfairness, the undeserved embarrassment, of being named co-respondent. In brief, people with self-respect exhibit a certain toughness, a kind of moral nerve; they display what was once called *character*, a quality which, although approved in the abstract, sometimes loses ground to other, more instantly negotiable virtues. The measure of its slipping prestige is that one tends to think of it only in connection with homely children and United States senators who have been defeated, preferably in the primary, for reelection. Nonetheless, character—the willingness to accept responsibility for one's own life—is the source from which self-respect springs.

Self-respect is something that our grandparents, whether or not   7
they had it, knew all about. They had instilled in them, young, a certain discipline, the sense that one lives by doing things one does

not particularly want to do, by putting fears and doubts to one side, by weighing immediate comforts against the possibility of larger, even intangible, comforts. It seemed to the nineteenth century admirable, but not remarkable, that Chinese Gordon put on a clean white suit and held Khartoum against the Mahdi; it did not seem unjust that the way to free land in California involved death and difficulty and dirt. In a diary kept during the winter of 1846, an emigrating twelve-year-old named Narcissa Cornwall noted coolly: "Father was busy reading and did not notice that the house was being filled with strange Indians until Mother spoke about it." Even lacking any clue as to what Mother said, one can scarcely fail to be impressed by the entire incident: the father reading, the Indians filing in, the mother choosing the words that would not alarm, the child duly recording the event and noting further that those particular Indians were not, "fortunately for us," hostile. Indians were simply part of the *donnée*.

In one guise or another, Indians always are. Again, it is a question   8 of recognizing that anything worth having has its price. People who respect themselves are willing to accept the risk that the Indians will be hostile, that the venture will go bankrupt, that the liaison may not turn out to be one in which *every day is a holiday because you're married to me*. They are willing to invest something of themselves; they may not play at all, but when they do play, they know the odds.

That kind of self-respect is a discipline, a habit of mind that can   9 never be faked but can be developed, trained, coaxed forth. It was once suggested to me that, as an antidote to crying, I put my head in a paper bag. As it happens, there is a sound physiological reason, something to do with oxygen, for doing exactly that, but the psychological effect alone is incalculable: it is difficult in the extreme to continue fancying oneself Cathy in *Wuthering Heights* with one's head in a Food Fair bag. There is a similar case for all the small disciplines, unimportant in themselves; imagine maintaining any kind of swoon, commiserative or carnal, in a cold shower.

But those small disciplines are valuable only insofar as they rep-   10 resent larger ones. To say that Waterloo was won on the playing fields of Eton is not to say that Napoleon might have been saved by a crash program in cricket; to give formal dinners in the rain forest would be pointless did not the candlelight flickering on the liana call forth deeper, stronger disciplines, values instilled long before. It is a kind of ritual, helping us to remember who and what we are. In order to remember it, one must have known it.

To have that sense of one's intrinsic worth which constitutes self-   11 respect is potentially to have everything: the ability to discriminate, to love and to remain indifferent. To lack it is to be locked within oneself, paradoxically incapable of either love or indifference. If we do not respect ourselves, we are on the one hand forced to despise those who have so few resources as to consort with us, so little perception as to remain blind to our fatal weaknesses. On the other, we are peculiarly in thrall to everyone we see, curiously determined to live out—since our self-image is untenable—their false notions of us. We flatter ourselves by thinking this compulsion to please others an attractive trait: a gist for imaginative empathy, evidence of our willingness to give. *Of course* I will play Francesca to your Paolo, Helen Keller to anyone's Annie Sullivan: no expectation is too misplaced, no role too ludicrous. At the mercy of those we cannot but hold in contempt, we play roles doomed to failure before they are begun, each defeat generating fresh despair at the urgency of divining and meeting the next demand made upon us.

It is the phenomenon sometimes called "alienation from self." In   12
its advanced stages, we no longer answer the telephone, because someone might want something; that we could say *no* without drowning in self-reproach is an idea alien to this game. Every encounter demands too much, tears the nerves, drains the will, and the specter of something as small as an unanswered letter arouses such disproportionate guilt that answering it becomes out of the question. To assign unanswered letters their proper weight, to free us from the expectations of others, to give us back to ourselves—there lies the great, the singular power of self-respect. Without it, one eventually discovers the final turn of the screw: one runs away to find oneself, and finds no one at home.

RESPONDING TO READING

Key words: community discovery education growing up
identity power striving watershed writing

Rhetorical concepts: analysis autobiography cause and effect
deduction definition explanation illustration meditation

1.   What, in Didion's view, differentiates self-respect from reputation? Do you agree with Didion that self-respect is far more important than reputation? Why or why not?
2.   Explain Didion's observation "people with self-respect have the courage of their mistakes. They know the price of things." (paragraph 6).
3.   What is the relation of risk-taking to self-respect (*see* paragraphs 7–8)? Illustrate your answer with reference to your own experience, or that of someone you know or have read about. The risk might be physical (in war, in sports, or in using dangerous machines), intellectual (experimenting with new, daring, shocking, or otherwise radical ideas in any discipline), economic (quitting or changing jobs, investing in an impossible dream or scheme), or some other sort. What "price," if any, was paid?

4.   How are self-discipline and self-respect interrelated? How can a person develop either, or both? Why, in Didion's view, are they worth the effort? Do you agree? To illustrate your answer, interpret an experience or life pattern of your own or someone you know well—for instance, the discipline and practice required to become a champion athlete, or a successful musician or writer, or to overcome or accommodate to a physical, mental, or emotional disability (*see*, for instance, Nancy Mairs, "On Being a Cripple," 38). Does fighting discrimination, as explained by Frederick Douglass (62), Sojourner Truth (360), and Martin Luther King, Jr. (541), require comparable self-discipline? In what ways does such effort enhance self-respect?

The Boy Scout Handbook

PAUL FUSSELL

The writings of Paul Fussell (born 1924), a professor of English at the University of Pennsylvania, are distinguished by an elegant, eminently readable style and by his pervasive concern with "intellect, discrimination, honesty, individuality, complexity, irony"—and wit. He explains, "I am persuaded by the performance of George Orwell that literary, cultural, social, ethical, and political commentary can be virtually the same thing." From this consistent perspective he has written about such diverse subjects as *Poetic Meter and Poetic Form* (1965), *War Time: Understanding and Behavior in the Second World War* (1989), and *Bad: Or, the Dumbing of America* (1991)—a denunciation of everything in American culture that is "phony, clumsy, witless, untalented, vacant, or boring" but which many believe to be "genuine, graceful, bright, or fascinating." *The Great War and Modern Memory* (1975), a study of the British literary experience of World War I, won both the National Book Critics Circle Award and the National Book Award. Before beginning his graduate education at Harvard (Ph.D., 1954), Fussell was twice wounded during infantry service in World War II, which he regards as the formative experience of his life. His works are deeply concerned with values. In his books on World Wars I and II, he analyzes the myths wars generate, attempting to cut through the "rationalizations and euphemisms people needed to deal with an unacceptable actuality."

Fussell's concern with values led also to his essay of appreciation of the virtues promoted in the 1979 edition of the classic *Boy Scout Handbook*; it was published in 1982 in a collection of essays of the same name. Fussell's essay "*The Boy Scout Handbook*" is also an exemplary model of a book review—comprehensive, self-contained, graceful—its opinion in this case sustained throughout by a firm approval of the values the *Handbook* promotes.

It's amazing how many interesting books humanistic criticism 1
manages not to notice. Staring fixedly at its handful of teachable masterpieces, it seems content not to recognize that a vigorous literary-moral life constantly takes place just below (sometimes above)

its vision. What a pity Lionel Trilling or Kenneth Burke never paused to examine the intersection of rhetoric and social motive among, say, the Knights of Columbus or the Elks. That these are their fellow citizens is less important than that the desires and rituals of these groups are desires and rituals, and thus of permanent social and psychological consequence. The culture of the Boy Scouts deserves this sort of look-in, especially since the right sort of people don't know much about it.

The right sort consists, of course, of liberal intellectuals. They 2 have often gazed uneasily at the Boy Scout movement. After all, a general, the scourge of the Boers, invented it; Kipling admired it; the Hitlerjugend (and the Soviet Pioneers) aped it. If its insistence that there is a God has not sufficed to alienate the enlightened, its khaki uniforms, lanyards, salutes, badges, and flag-worship have seemed to argue incipient militarism, if not outright fascism. The movement has often seemed its own worst enemy. Its appropriation of Normal Rockwell as its official Apelles has not endeared it to those of exquisite taste. Nor has its cause been promoted by events like the TV appearance a couple of years ago of the Chief Pardoner, Gerald Ford, rigged out in scout neckerchief, assuring us from the teleprompter that a Scout is Reverent. Then there are the leers and giggles triggered by the very word "scoutmaster," which in knowing circles is alone sufficient to promise comic pederastic narrative. "*All* scoutmasters are homosexuals," asserted George Orwell, who also insisted that "*All* tobacconists are Fascists."

But anyone who imagines that the scouting movement is either 3 sinister or stupid or funny should spend a few hours with the latest edition of *The Official Boy Scout Handbook* (1979). Social, cultural, and literary historians could attend to it profitably as well, for after *The Red Cross First Aid Manual, The World Almanac,* and the Gideon Bible, it is probably the best-known book in this country. Since the first edition in 1910, twenty-nine million copies have been read in bed by flashlight. The first printing of this ninth edition is 600,000. We needn't take too seriously the ascription of authorship to William ("Green Bar Bill") Hillcourt, depicted on the title page as an elderly gentleman bare-kneed in scout uniform and identified as Author, Naturalist, and World Scouter. He is clearly the Ann Page or Reddy Kilowatt of the movement, and although he's doubtless contributed to this handbook (by the same author is *Baden-Powell: The Two Lives of a Hero* [1965]), it bears all the marks of composition by committee, or "task force," as it's called here. But for all that, it's admirably written. And although a complex sentence is as rare as a reference to girls, the rhetoric of this new edition has made no compromise with what we are told is the new illiteracy of the young. The book assumes an audience prepared by a very good high-school education, undaunted by terms like *biosphere, ideology,* and *ecosystem.*

The pliability and adaptability of the scout movement explains its 4 remarkable longevity, its capacity to flourish in a world dramatically different from its founder's. Like the Roman Catholic Church, the scout movement knows the difference between cosmetic and real change, and it happily embraces the one to avoid any truck with the other. Witness the new American flag patch, now worn at the top of the right sleeve. It betokens no access of jingoism or threat to a civilized internationalism. It simply conduces to dignity by imitating a similar affectation of police and fire departments in anarchic towns like New York City. The message of the flag patch is not "I am a fascist, straining to become old enough to purchase and wield guns." It is, rather, "I can be put to quasi-official use, and like a fireman or policeman I am trained in first aid and ready to help."

There are other innovations, none of them essential. The breeches 5 of thirty years ago have yielded to trousers, although shorts are still in. The wide-brimmed army field hat of the First World War is a fixture still occasionally seen, but it is now augmented by headwear deriving from succeeding mass patriotic exercises: overseas caps and berets from World War II, and visor caps of the sort worn by General Westmoreland and sunbelt retirees. The scout handclasp has been changed, perhaps because it was discovered in the context of the new internationalism that the former one, which the little finger was separated from the other three on the right hand, transmitted inappropriate suggestions in the Third World. The handclasp is now the normal civilian one, but given with the left hand. There's now much less emphasis on knots than formerly; as if to signal this change, the neckerchief is no longer religiously knotted at the tips. What used to be known as artificial respiration ("Out goes the bad air, in comes the good") has given way to "rescue breathing." The young are now being familiarized with the metric system. Some bright empiric has discovered that a paste made of meat tenderizer is the best remedy for painful insect stings. Constipation is not the bugbear it was a generation ago. And throughout there is a striking new lyricism. "Feel the wind blowing through your hair," the scout is adjured, just as he is exhorted to perceive that Being Prepared for life means learning "to live happy" and—equally important—"to die happy." There's more emphasis now on fun and less on duty; or rather, duty is validated because, properly viewed, it is a pleasure. (If that sounds like advice useful to grownups as well as to sprouts, you're beginning to get the point.)

There are only two possible causes of complaint. The term "free 6 world" surfaces too often, although the phrase is mercifully uncapitalized. And the Deism is a bit insistent. The United States is defined as a country "whose people believe in a supreme being." The words "In God We Trust" on the coinage and currency are taken almost as a constitutional injunction. The camper is told to carry along the "Bible, Testament, or prayer book of your faith," even though, for light backpacking, he is advised to leave behind air mattress, knife and fork, and pancake turner. When the scout finds himself lost in the woods, he is to "stay put and have faith that someone will find you." In aid of this end, "Prayer will help." But the religiosity is so broad that it's harmless. The words "your church" are followed always by the phrase "or synagogue." The writers have done as well as they can considering that they're saddled with the immutable twelve points of Baden-Powell's Scout Law, stating unambiguously that "A Scout is Reverent" and "faithful to his religious duties." But if "You have the right to worship God in your own way," you must see to it that "others retain their right to worship God in their way." Likewise, if "you have the right to speak your mind without fear of prison or punishment," you must "ensure that right for others, even when you do not agree with them." If the book adheres to any politics, they can hardly be described as conservative; they are better described as slightly archaic liberal. It is broadly hinted that industrial corporations are prime threats to clean air and conservation. In every illustration depicting more than three boys, one is black. The section introducing the reader to some Great Americans pays respects not only to Franklin and Edison and John D. Rockefeller and Einstein; it also makes much of Walter Reuther and Samuel Gompers, as well as Harriet Tubman, Martin Luther King, and Whitney Young. There is a post-Watergate awareness that public officials must be watched closely. One's civic duties include the obligation to "keep up on what is going on around you" in order to "get involved" and "help change things that are not good."

Few books these days could be called compendia of good sense. 7 This is one such, and its good sense is not merely about swimming safely and putting campfires "cold out." The good sense is psychological and ethical as well. Indeed, this handbook is among the very few remaining popular repositories of something like classical ethics, deriving from Aristotle and Cicero. Except for the handbooks' adhesions to the motif of scenic beauty, it reads as if the Romantic movement had never taken place. The constant moral theme is the inestimable benefits of looking objectively outward and losing consciousness of self in the work to be done. To its young audience vulnerable to invitations to "trips" and trances and anxious self-absorption, the book calmly says: "Forget yourself." What a shame the psychobabblers of Marin County will never read it.

There is other invaluable advice, applicable to adults as well as to 8 scouts. Some is practical, like "Never use flammable fluids to start a charcoal fire. They burn off fast, lighting only a little of the charcoal." Some is civil-moral: "Take a 2-hour walk where you live. Make a list of things that please you, another of things that should be improved." And then the kicker: "Set out to improve them." Some advice is even intellectual, and pleasantly uncompromising: "Reading trash all the time makes it impossible for anyone to be anything but a second-rate person." But the best advice is ethical: "Learn to think." "Gather knowledge." "Have initiative." "Respect the rights of others." Actually, there's hardly a better gauge for measuring the gross official misbehavior of the seventies than the ethics enshrined in this handbook. From its explicit ethics you can infer such propositions as "A scout does not tap his acquaintances' telephones," or "A scout does not bomb and invade a neutral country, and then lie about it," or "A scout does not prosecute war unless, as the Constitution provides, it has been declared by the Congress." Not to mention that because a scout is clean in thought, word, and deed, he does not, like Richard Nixon, designate his fellow citizens "shits" and then both record his filth and lie about the recordings ("A Scout tells the truth").

Responding to Orwell's satiric analysis of "Boys' Weeklies" forty years ago, the boys' author Frank Richards, stigmatized by Orwell as a manufacturer of excessively optimistic and falsely wholesome stories, observed that "The writer for young people should . . . endeavor to give his young readers a sense of stability and solid security, because it is good for them, and makes for happiness and peace of mind." Even if it is true, as Orwell objects, that the happiness of youth is a cruel delusion, then, says Richards, "Let youth be happy, or as happy as possible. Happiness is the best preparation for misery, if misery must come. At least the poor kid will have had something." In the current world of Making It and Getting Away with It, there are not many books devoted to associating happiness with virtue. The shelves of the CIA and the State Department must be bare of them. "Horror swells around us like an oil spill," Terrence Des Pres said recently. "Not a day passes without more savagery and harm." He was commenting on Philip Hallie's *Lest Innocent Blood Be Shed*, an account of a whole French village's trustworthiness, loyalty, helpfulness, friendliness, courtesy, kindness, cheerfulness, and bravery in hiding scores of Jews during the Occupation. Des Pres concludes: "*Goodness.* When was the last time anyone used that word in earnest, without irony, as anything more than a doubtful cliché?" *The Official Boy Scout Handbook*, for all its focus on Axmanship, Backpacking, Cooking, First Aid, Flowers, Hiking, Map and Compass, Semaphore, Trees, and Weather, is another book about goodness. No home, and certainly no government office, should be without a copy. The generously low price of $3.50 is enticing, and so is the place on the back cover where you're invited to inscribe your name.

RESPONDING TO READING

Key words: community   education   family   growing up
identity   reading

Rhetorical concepts: analysis   deduction   explanation   illustration

1.   What values does *The Boy Scout Handbook* promote? What worldview do these values incorporate? What values are most important in the world represented in the *Handbook?*
2.   Which of the values promoted in *The Boy Scout Handbook* do you share? Why are these important to you? Are there any promoted in the *Handbook* that you consider of little or no importance? How do you account for differences, if any, between your values and those of the *Handbook?*
3.   To what extent can people learn values from reading a book, such as *The Bible* or *The Boy Scout Handbook?* To enhance the learning is an interpreter, such as a member of the clergy or a scoutmaster, necessary? Desirable? Or is the interpreter likely to get in the way, distorting the message?
4.   Suppose that your values differ markedly from those of your friends, your family, or your society—or another's. Who is right? How can you tell?
5.   Imagine Huck Finn reading and evaluating *The Boy Scout Handbook.* Would he agree with Fussell? Where would he differ? Why?

Our Picture of the Universe

STEPHEN HAWKING

"We find ourselves in a bewildering world," writes theoretical physicist Stephen Hawking (born 1942) in his best-selling *A Brief History of Time: From the Big Bang to Black Holes* (1988). "What do we know about the universe?" he asks, in a series of fundamental questions that his work attempts to answer: "How do we know it? Where did the universe come from and where is it going? Did the universe have a beginning, and if so, what happened *before* then? What is the nature of time? Will it ever come to an end?" And, perhaps most significantly, "What is our place in the universe and where did . . . we come from?"

Hawking is a professor at Cambridge University, from which he earned a Ph.D. in 1966, after receiving a B.A. from Oxford in 1962. Despite the physical hardship of Lou Gehrig's disease, he has consistently excelled in his chosen profession. He approaches the status of the great theoretical physicists who preceded him, holding the same position at Cambridge that Isaac Newton once had; and he is often compared with Albert Einstein. Hawking seeks a "unified theory" of the universe that will explain the behavior of everything from subatomic particles to stars and planets. In his dazzling conclusion to *A Brief History of Time*, Hawking blends Einstein's theories, atomic physics, and his own geometrical models to present a scheme that allows "the universe to begin in an explosion and end in a contraction, without ever causing time itself or the laws of physics to cease to apply." Hawking has been praised for having a "natural teacher's gifts," the rare ability to explain in plain, non-mathematical English a host of mathematically formidable ideas about the origin and fate of the universe.

A well-known scientist (some say it was Bertrand Russell) once 1 gave a public lecture on astronomy. He described how the earth orbits around the sun and how the sun, in turn, orbits around the center of a vast collection of stars called our galaxy. At the end of the lecture, a little old lady at the back of the room got up and said: "What you have told us is rubbish. The world is really a flat plate supported on the back of a giant tortoise." The scientist gave a superior smile before replying, "What is the tortoise standing on?" "You're very clever, young man, very clever," said the old lady. "But it's turtles all the way down!"

Most people would find the picture of our universe as an infinite   2
tower of tortoises rather ridiculous, but why do we think we know
better? What do we know about the universe, and how do we know
it? Where did the universe come from, and where is it going? Did the
universe have a beginning, and if so, what happened *before* then?
What is the nature of time? Will it ever come to an end? Recent
breakthroughs in physics, made possible in part by fantastic new
technologies, suggest answers to some of these longstanding questions. Someday these answers may seem as obvious to us as the earth
orbiting the sun—or perhaps as ridiculous as a tower of tortoises.
Only time (whatever that may be) will tell.

As long ago as 340 B.C. the Greek philosopher Aristotle, in his   3
book *On the Heavens*, was able to put forward two good arguments
for believing that the earth was a round sphere rather than a flat plate.
First, he realized that eclipses of the moon were caused by the earth
coming between the sun and the moon. The earth's shadow on the
moon was always round, which would be true only if the earth was
spherical. If the earth had been a flat disk, the shadow would have
been elongated and elliptical, unless the eclipse always occurred at a
time when the sun was directly under the center of the disk. Second,
the Greeks knew from their travels that the North Star appeared lower
in the sky when viewed in the south than it did in more northerly
regions. (Since the North Star lies over the North Pole, it appears to
be directly above an observer at the North Pole, but to someone
looking from the equator, it appears to lie just at the horizon.) From
the difference in the apparent position of the North Star in Egypt and
Greece, Aristotle even quoted an estimate that the distance around
the earth was 400,000 stadia. It is not known exactly what length a
stadium was, but it may have been about 200 yards, which would
make Aristotle's estimate about twice the currently accepted figure.
The Greeks even had a third argument that the earth must be round,
for why else does one first see the sails of a ship coming over the
horizon, and only later see the hull?

Aristotle thought that the earth was stationary and that the sun,   4
the moon, the planets, and the stars moved in circular orbits about
the earth. He believed this because he felt, for mystical reasons, that
the earth was the center of the universe, and that circular motion was
the most perfect. This idea was elaborated by Ptolemy in the second
century A.D. into a complete cosmological model. The earth stood at
the center, surrounded by eight spheres that carried the moon, the
sun, the stars, and the five planets known at the time, Mercury, Venus,
Mars, Jupiter, and Saturn (Fig. 1). The planets themselves moved on
smaller circles attached to their respective spheres in order to account

for their rather complicated observed paths in the sky. The outermost sphere carried the so-called fixed stars, which always stay in the same positions relative to each other but which rotate together across the sky. What lay beyond the last sphere was never made very clear, but it certainly was not part of mankind's observable universe.

Ptolemy's model provided a reasonably accurate system for pre- 5 dicting the positions of heavenly bodies in the sky. But in order to predict these positions correctly, Ptolemy had to make an assumption that the moon followed a path that sometimes brought it twice as close to the earth as at other times. And that meant that the moon ought sometimes to appear twice as big as at other times! Ptolemy recognized this flaw, but nevertheless his model was generally, although not universally, accepted. It was adopted by the Christian church as the picture of the universe that was in accordance with Scripture, for it had the great advantage that it left lots of room outside the sphere of fixed stars for heaven and hell.

A simpler model, however, was proposed in 1514 by a Polish 6 priest, Nicholas Copernicus. (At first, perhaps for fear of being branded a heretic by his church, Copernicus circulated his model anonymously.) His idea was that the sun was stationary at the center and that the earth and the planets moved in circular orbits around

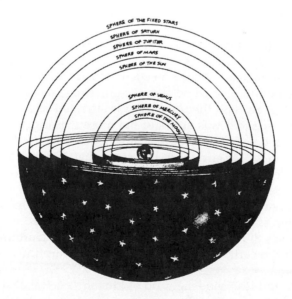

Figure 1

the sun. Nearly a century passed before this idea was taken seriously. Then two astronomers—the German, Johannes Kepler, and the Italian, Galileo Galilei—started publicly to support the Copernican theory, despite the fact that the orbits it predicted did not quite match the ones observed. The death blow to the Aristotelian/Ptolemaic theory came in 1609. In that year, Galileo started observing the night sky with a telescope, which had just been invented. When he looked at the planet Jupiter, Galileo found that it was accompanied by several small satellites or moons that orbited around it. This implied that everything did *not* have to orbit directly around the earth, as Aristotle and Ptolemy had thought. (It was, of course, still possible to believe that the earth was stationary at the center of the universe and that the moons of Jupiter moved on extremely complicated paths around the earth, giving the *appearance* that they orbited Jupiter. However, Copernicus's theory was much simpler.) At the same time, Johannes Kepler had modified Copernicus's theory, suggesting that the planets moved not in circles but in ellipses (an ellipse is an elongated circle). The predictions now finally matched the observations.

As far as Kepler was concerned, elliptical orbits were merely an   7
ad hoc hypothesis, and a rather repugnant one at that, because ellipses were clearly less perfect than circles. Having discovered almost by accident that elliptical orbits fit the observations well, he could not reconcile them with his idea that the planets were made to orbit the sun by magnetic forces. An explanation was provided only much later, in 1687, when Sir Isaac Newton published his *Philosophiae Naturalis Principia Mathematica*, probably the most important single work ever published in the physical sciences. In it Newton not only put forward a theory of how bodies move in space and time, but he also developed the complicated mathematics needed to analyze those motions. In addition, Newton postulated a law of universal gravitation according to which each body in the universe was attracted toward every other body by a force that was stronger the more massive the bodies and the closer they were to each other. It was this same force that caused objects to fall to the ground. (The story that Newton was inspired by an apple hitting his head is almost certainly apocryphal. All Newton himself ever said was that the idea of gravity came to him as he sat "in a contemplative mood" and "was occasioned by the fall of an apple.") Newton went on to show that, according to his law, gravity causes the moon to move in an elliptical orbit around the earth and causes the earth and the planets to follow elliptical paths around the sun.

The Copernican model got rid of Ptolemy's celestial spheres, and   8
with them, the idea that the universe had a natural boundary. Since "fixed stars" did not appear to change their positions apart from a

rotation across the sky caused by the earth spinning on its axis, it became natural to suppose that the fixed stars were objects like our sun but very much farther away.

Newton realized that, according to his theory of gravity, the stars   9 should attract each other, so it seemed they could not remain essentially motionless. Would they not all fall together at some point? In a letter in 1691 to Richard Bentley, another leading thinker of his day, Newton argued that this would indeed happen if there were only a finite number of stars distributed over a finite region of space. But he reasoned that if, on the other hand, there were an infinite number of stars, distributed more or less uniformly over infinite space, this would not happen, because there would not be any central point for them to fall to.

This argument is an instance of the pitfalls that you can encounter   10 in talking about infinity. In an infinite universe, every point can be regarded as the center, because every point has an infinite number of stars on each side of it. The correct approach, it was realized only much later, is to consider the finite situation, in which the stars all fall in on each other, and then to ask how things change if one adds more stars roughly uniformly distributed outside this region. According to Newton's law, the extra stars would make no difference at all to the original ones on average, so the stars would fall in just as fast. We can add as many stars as we like, but they will still always collapse in on themselves. We now know it is impossible to have an infinite static model of the universe in which gravity is always attractive.

It is an interesting reflection on the general climate of thought   11 before the twentieth century that no one had suggested that the universe was expanding or contracting. It was generally accepted that either the universe had existed forever in an unchanging state, or that it had been created at a finite time in the past more or less as we observe it today. In part this may have been due to people's tendency to believe in eternal truths, as well as the comfort they found in the thought that even though they may grow old and die, the universe is eternal and unchanging.

Even those who realized that Newton's theory of gravity showed   12 that the universe could not be static did not think to suggest that it might be expanding. Instead, they attempted to modify the theory by making the gravitational force repulsive at very large distances. This did not significantly affect their predictions of the motions of the planets, but it allowed an infinite distribution of stars to remain in equilibrium—with the attractive forces between nearby stars balanced by the repulsive forces from those that were farther away. However, we now believe such an equilibrium would be unstable: if the stars in some region got only slightly nearer each other, the attractive forces between them would become stronger and dominate over the repulsive forces so that the stars would continue to fall toward each other. On the other hand, if the stars got a bit farther away from each other, the repulsive forces would dominate and drive them farther apart.

Another objection to an infinite static universe is normally ascribed to the German philosopher Heinrich Olbers, who wrote about this theory in 1823. In fact, various contemporaries of Newton had raised the problem, and the Olbers article was not even the first to contain plausible arguments against it. It was, however, the first to be widely noted. The difficulty is that in an infinite static universe nearly every line of sight would end on the surface of a star. Thus one would expect that the whole sky would be as bright as the sun, even at night. Olbers's counterargument was that the light from distant stars would be dimmed by absorption by intervening matter. However, if that happened the intervening matter would eventually heat up until it glowed as brightly as the stars. The only way of avoiding the conclusion that the whole of the night sky should be as bright as the surface of the sun would be to assume that the stars had not been shining forever but had turned on at some finite time in the past. In that case the absorbing matter might not have heated up yet or the light from distant stars might not yet have reached us. And that brings us to the question of what could have caused the stars to have turned on in the first place.

The beginning of the universe had, of course, been discussed long before this. According to a number of early cosmologies and the Jewish/Christian/Muslim tradition, the universe started at a finite, and not very distant, time in the past. One argument for such a beginning was the feeling that it was necessary to have "First Cause" to explain the existence of the universe. (Within the universe, you always explained one event as being caused by some earlier event, but the existence of the universe itself could be explained in this way only if it had some beginning.) Another argument was put forward by St. Augustine in his book *The City of God*. He pointed out that civilization is progressing and we remember who performed this deed or developed that technique. Thus man, and so also perhaps the universe, could not have been around all that long. St. Augustine accepted a date of about 5000 B.C. for the Creation of the universe according to the book of Genesis. (It is interesting that this is not so far from the end of the last Ice Age, about 10,000 B.C., which is when archaeologists tell us that civilization really began.)

Aristotle, and most of the other Greek philosophers, on the other hand, did not like the idea of a creation because it smacked too much of divine intervention. They believed, therefore, that the human race and the world around it had existed, and would exist, forever. The ancients had already considered the argument about progress described above, and answered it by saying that there had been periodic floods or other disasters that repeatedly set the human race right back to the beginning of civilization.

The questions of whether the universe had a beginning in time 16 and whether it is limited in space were later extensively examined by the philosopher Immanuel Kant in his monumental (and very obscure) work, *Critique of Pure Reason,* published in 1781. He called these questions antinomies (that is, contradictions) of pure reason because he felt that there were equally compelling arguments for believing the thesis, that the universe had a beginning, and the antithesis, that it had existed forever. His argument for the thesis was that if the universe did not have a beginning, there would be an infinite period of time before any event, which he considered absurd. The argument for the antithesis was that if the universe had a beginning, there would be an infinite period of time before it, so why should the universe begin at any one particular time? In fact, his cases for both the thesis and the antithesis are really the same argument. They are both based on his unspoken assumption that time continues back forever, whether or not the universe had existed forever. As we shall see, the concept of time has no meaning before the beginning of the universe. This was first pointed out by St. Augustine. When asked: What did God do before he created the universe? Augustine didn't reply: He was preparing Hell for people who asked such questions. Instead, he said that time was a property of the universe that God created, and that time did not exist before the beginning of the universe.

When most people believed in an essentially static and unchang- 17 ing universe, the question of whether or not it had a beginning was really one of metaphysics or theology. One could account for what was observed equally well on the theory that the universe had existed forever or on the theory that it was set in motion at some finite time in such a manner as to look as though it had existed forever. But in 1929, Edwin Hubble made the landmark observation that wherever you look, distant galaxies are moving rapidly away from us. In other words, the universe is expanding. This means that at earlier times objects would have been closer together. In fact, it seemed that there was a time, about ten or twenty thousand million years ago, when they were all at exactly the same place and when, therefore, the density of the universe was infinite. This discovery finally brought the question of the beginning of the universe into the realm of science.

Hubble's observations suggested that there was a time, called the 18 big bang, when the universe was infinitesimally small and infinitely dense. Under such conditions all the laws of science, and therefore all ability to predict the future, would break down. If there were events earlier than this time, then they could not affect what happens at the present time. Their existence can be ignored because it would have no observational consequences. One may say that time had a beginning at the big bang, in the sense that earlier times simply would not be defined. It should be emphasized that this beginning in time is very different from those that had been considered previously. In an unchanging universe a beginning in time is something that has to be imposed by some being outside the universe; there is no physical necessity for a beginning. One can imagine that God created the universe at literally any time in the past. On the other hand, if the universe is expanding, there may be physical reasons why there had to be a beginning. One could still imagine that God created the universe at the instant of the big bang, or even afterwards in just such a way as to make it look as though there had been a big bang, but it would be meaningless to suppose that it was created *before* the big bang. An expanding universe does not preclude a creator, but it does place limits on when he might have carried out his job!

In order to talk about the nature of the universe and to discuss 19 questions such as whether it has a beginning or an end, you have to be clear about what a scientific theory is. I shall take the simple-minded view that a theory is just a model of the universe, or a restricted part of it, and a set of rules that relate quantities in the model to observations that we make. It exists only in our minds and does not have any other reality (whatever that might mean). A theory is a good theory if it satisfies two requirements: It must accurately describe a large class of observations on the basis of a model that contains only a few arbitrary elements, and it must make definite predictions about the results of future observations. For example, Aristotle's theory that everything was made out of four elements, earth, air, fire, and water, was simple enough to qualify, but it did not make any definite predictions. On the other hand, Newton's theory of gravity was based on an even simpler model, in which bodies attracted each other with a force that was proportional to a quantity called their mass and inversely proportional to the square of the distance beween them. Yet it predicts the motions of the sun, the moon, and the planets to a high degree of accuracy.

Any physical theory is always provisional, in the sense that it is 20 only a hypothesis: you can never prove it. No matter how many times the results of experiments agree with some theory, you can never be sure that the next time the result will not contradict the theory. On the other hand, you can disprove a theory by finding even a single observation that disagrees with the predictions of the theory. As philosopher of science Karl Popper has emphasized, a good theory is characterized by the fact that it makes a number of predictions that could in principle be disproved or falsified by observation. Each time new experiments are observed to agree with the predictions the theory survives, and our confidence in it is increased; but if ever a new observation is found to disagree, we have to abandon or modify the theory. At least that is what is supposed to happen, but you can always question the competence of the person who carried out the observation.

In practice, what often happens is that a new theory is devised 21 that is really an extension of the previous theory. For example, very accurate observations of the planet Mercury revealed a small difference between its motion and the predictions of Newton's theory of gravity. Einstein's general theory of relativity predicted a slightly different motion from Newton's theory. The fact that Einstein's predictions matched what was seen, while Newton's did not, was one of the crucial confirmations of the new theory. However, we still use Newton's theory for all practical purposes because the difference between its predictions and those of general relativity is very small in the situations that we normally deal with. (Newton's theory also has the great advantage that it is much simpler to work with than Einstein's!)

The eventual goal of science is to provide a single theory that 22 describes the whole universe. However, the approach most scientists actually follow is to separate the problem into two parts. First, there are the laws that tell us how the universe changes with time. (If we know what the universe is like at any one time, these physical laws tell us how it will look at any later time.) Second, there is the question of the initial state of the universe. Some people feel that science should be concerned with only the first part; they regard the question of the initial situation as a matter for metaphysics or religion. They would say that God, being omnipotent, could have started the universe off any way he wanted. That may be so, but in that case he also could have made it develop in a completely arbitrary way. Yet it appears that he chose to make it evolve in a very regular way according to certain laws. It therefore seems equally reasonable to suppose that there are also laws governing the initial state.

It turns out to be very difficult to devise a theory to describe the 23 universe all in one go. Instead, we break the problem up into bits and invent a number of partial theories. Each of these partial theories describes and predicts a certain limited class of observations, neglecting the effects of other quantities, or representing them by simple sets of numbers. It may be that this approach is completely wrong. If everything in the universe depends on everything else in a fundamental way, it might be impossible to get close to a full solution by investigating parts of the problem in isolation. Nevertheless, it is certainly the way that we have made progress in the past. The classic example again is the Newtonian theory of gravity, which tells us that the gravitational force between two bodies depends only on one number associated with each body, its mass, but is otherwise independent of what the bodies are made of. Thus one does not need to have a theory of the structure and constitution of the sun and the planets in order to calculate their orbits.

Today scientists describe the universe in terms of two basic partial theories—the general theory of relativity and quantum mechanics. They are the great intellectual achievements of the first half of this century. The general theory of relativity describes the force of gravity and the large-scale structure of the universe, that is, the structure on scales from only a few miles to as large as a million million million million (1 with twenty-four zeros after it) miles, the size of the observable universe. Quantum mechanics, on the other hand, deals with phenomena on extremely small scales, such as a millionth of a millionth of an inch. Unfortunately, however, these two theories are known to be inconsistent with each other—they cannot both be correct. One of the major endeavors in physics today, and the major theme of this book, is the search for a new theory that will incorporate them both—a quantum theory of gravity. We do not yet have such a theory, and we may still be a long way from having one, but we do already know many of the properties that it must have. And we shall see, in later chapters, that we already know a fair amount about the predictions a quantum theory of gravity must make.

Now, if you believe that the universe is not arbitrary, but is governed by definite laws, you ultimately have to combine the partial theories into a complete unified theory that will describe everything in the universe. But there is a fundamental paradox in the search for such a complete unified theory. The ideas about scientific theories outlined above assume we are rational beings who are free to observe the universe as we want and to draw logical deductions from what we see. In such a scheme it is reasonable to suppose that we might progress ever closer toward the laws that govern our universe. Yet if there really is a complete unified theory, it would also presumably determine our actions. And so the theory itself would determine the outcome of our search for it! And why should it determine that we come to the right conclusions from the evidence? Might it not equally well determine that we draw the wrong conclusion? Or no conclusion at all?

The only answer that I can give to this problem is based on Darwin's principle of natural selection. The idea is that in any population of self-reproducing organisms, there will be variations in the genetic material and upbringing that different individuals have. These differences will mean that some individuals are better able than others to draw the right conclusions about the world around them and to act accordingly. These individuals will be more likely to survive and reproduce and so their pattern of behavior and thought will come to dominate. It has certainly been true in the past that what we call intelligence and scientific discovery has conveyed a survival advantage. It is not so clear that this is still the case: our scientific discoveries may well destroy us all, and even if they don't, a complete unified theory may not make much difference to our chances of survival. However, provided the universe has evolved in a regular way, we might expect that the reasoning abilities that natural selection has given us would be valid also in our search for a complete unified theory, and so would not lead us to the wrong conclusions.

Because the partial theories that we already have are sufficient to 27 make accurate predictions in all but the most extreme situations, the search for the ultimate theory of the universe seems difficult to justify on practical grounds. (It is worth noting, though, that similar arguments could have been used against both relativity and quantum mechanics, and these theories have given us both nuclear energy and the microelectronics revolution!) The discovery of a complete unified theory, therefore, may not aid the survival of our species. It may not even affect our life-style. But ever since the dawn of civilization, people have not been content to see events as unconnected and inexplicable. They have craved an understanding of the underlying order in the world. Today we still yearn to know why we are here and where we came from. Humanity's deepest desire for knowledge is justification enough for our continuing quest. And our goal is nothing less than a complete description of the universe we live in.

RESPONDING TO READING

Key words: discovery   education   nature   power   reality science

Rhetorical concepts: analysis   cause and effect   definition explanation   induction   narrative/example   process research report

1.   Hawking's narrative of how we have come to know about the structure of the universe assumes that observation and theories ideally should work together to create knowledge. But, as he points out, certain beliefs have interfered with acceptance of observation (as with Aristotle and Kepler). Identify some of the ways in which belief and observation may fail to work

together; include Hawking's examples and add others from your own reading
or experience.

2.   Describe the way Hawking goes about answering the question, when did
the universe begin? How does he get from that question to the concept of
time and then to his assertion that "the concept of time has no meaning
before the beginning of the universe." Are you surprised that he cites St.
Augustine in support of his very modern idea? Why? When Hawking speaks
of bringing the question of the beginning of the universe "into the realm of
science," what does he mean?

3.   Compare Hawking's definition of "what a scientific theory is" to Gould's
in Chapter 2. How are the two definitions alike and how are they different?
To what do you attribute the differences? To what degree does Kuhn's explanation (also in Chapter 2) of "normal science" help us understand the
different approaches of scientists to the "good ideas" (see the next chapter)
they come up with? Why does Hawking argue for the value of "partial theories"?

4.   Hawking ends the chapter by considering the "continuing quest" for a
unified theory, "the ultimate theory of the universe." Explain his views and
the evidence he uses. To what degree do you think that continuing this quest
is really important? What answer would Hawking give to the question, "What
does nature mean?" What answer would you give?

All at One Point

ITALO CALVINO

Italian novelist and short story writer Italo Calvino (1923–1985) is
world renowned for his nineteen volumes of novels and short stories
and for his collection of *Italian Folktales* (1980). For Calvino, to write
any narrative was to write a fable, whose "irreplaceable scheme" he
explained as "the child abandoned in the woods or the knight who
must survive encounters with beasts and enchantments." In Calvino's fables, as in the traditional ones, the central character is either
young or appears youthfully enchanted with nature, possessing "a
sense of tranquility and discovery of the mysteries of life." *Cosmicomics* (1968), like *Invisible Cities* (1972) and *If on a winter's night a
traveler* (1979), fuses reality and fantasy in a manner resembling that
of two other master storytellers, Jorge Luis Borges and Gabriel García
Márquez. *Cosmicomics*, says critic Theresa de Lauretis, is a "highly
imaginative, scientifically informed, funny and inspired meditation
on one insistent question: What does it mean to be human, to live
and die, to reproduce and to create, to desire and to be?" This
question is explored through the adventures of Qfwfq, "a strange,
chameleon-like creature present at the beginning of the universe,
the formation of the stars, and the disappearance of the dinosaurs."

"All at One Point" takes place at the moment—though there are
no moments yet—before the Big Bang begins space and time. All
future matter, including potential life forms, is jammed together at

one point without dimension, poised to explode and create the universe. Naturally, in Calvino's imagination, that situation was terribly crowded, particularly so when the immigrant family (from where?) Z'Zu "wanted to hang lines across our point to dry their washing." Happily, one generous woman offers to make some noodles to share, an act of love with the most earth-shattering consequences. Though Calvino echoes the knowledge that Hawking presents, he has a different view of what is really important.

Through the calculations begun by Edwin P. Hubble on the galaxies' velocity of recession, we can establish the moment when all the universe's matter was concentrated in a single point, before it began to expand in space.

Naturally, we were all there,—*old Qfwfq said,*—where else could   1 we have been? Nobody knew then that there could be space. Or time either: what use did we have for time, packed in there like sardines?

I say "packed like sardines," using a literary image: in reality   2 there wasn't even space to pack us into. Every point of each of us coincided with every point of each of the others in a single point, which was where we all were. In fact, we didn't even bother one another, except for personality differences, because when space doesn't exist, having somebody unpleasant like Mr. Pber^t Pber^d underfoot all the time is the most irritating thing.

How many of us were there? Oh, I was never able to figure that   3 out, not even approximately. To make a count, we would have had to move apart, at least a little, and instead we all occupied that same point. Contrary to what you might think, it wasn't the sort of situation that encourages sociability; I know, for example, that in other periods neighbors called on one another; but there, because of the fact that we were all neighbors, nobody even said good morning or good evening to anybody else.

In the end each of us associated only with a limited number of   4 acquaintances. The ones I remember most are Mrs. Ph(i)Nk$_o$, her friend De XuaeauX, a family of immigrants by the name of Z'zu, and Mr. Pber^t Pber^d, whom I just mentioned. There was also a cleaning woman—"maintenance staff" she was called—only one, for the whole universe, since there was so little room. To tell the truth, she had nothing to do all day long, not even dusting—inside one point not even a grain of dust can enter—so she spent all her time gossiping and complaining.

Just with the people I've already named we would have been   5 overcrowded; but you have to add all the stuff we had to keep piled up in there: all the material that was to serve afterwards to form the universe, now dismantled and concentrated in such a way that you weren't able to tell what was later to become part of astronomy (like the nebula of Andromeda) from what was assigned to geography (the Vosges, for example) or to chemistry (like certain beryllium isotopes). And on top of that, we were always bumping against the Z'zu family's household goods: camp beds, mattresses, baskets; these Z'zus, if you weren't careful, with the excuse that they were a large family, would begin to act as if they were the only ones in the world: they even wanted to hang lines across our point to dry their washing.

But the others also had wronged the Z'zus, to begin with, by   6
calling them "immigrants," on the pretext that, since the others had been there first, the Z'zus had come later. This was mere unfounded prejudice—that seems obvious to me—because neither before nor after existed, nor any place to immigrate from, but there were those who insisted that the concept of "immigrant" could be understood in the abstract, outside of space and time.

It was what you might call a narrow-minded attitude, our outlook   7
at that time, very petty. The fault of the environment in which we had been reared. An attitude that, basically, has remained in all of us, mind you: it keeps cropping up even today, if two of us happen to meet—at the bus stop, in a movie house, at an international dentists' convention—and start reminiscing about the old days. We say hello—at times somebody recognizes me, at other times I recognize somebody—and we promptly start asking about this one and that one (even if each remembers only a few of those remembered by the others), and so we start in again on the old disputes, the slanders, the denigrations. Until somebody mentions Mrs. Ph(i)Nk$_o$—every conversation finally gets around to her—and then, all of a sudden, the pettiness is put aside, and we feel uplifted, filled with a blissful, generous emotion. Mrs. Ph(i)Nk$_o$, the only one that none of us has forgotten and that we all regret. Where has she ended up? I have long since stopped looking for her: Mrs. Ph(i)Nk$_o$, her bosom, her thighs, her orange dressing gown—we'll never meet her again, in this system of galaxies or in any other.

Let me make one thing clear: this theory that the universe, after   8
having reached an extremity of rarefactions, will be condensed again has never convinced me. And yet many of us are counting only on that, continually making plans for the time when we'll all be back there again. Last month, I went into the bar here on the corner and whom did I see? Mr. Pber^t Pber^d. "What's new with you? How do you happen to be in this neighborhood?" I learned that he's the agent for a plastic firm, in Pavia. He's the same as ever, with his silver tooth, his loud suspenders. "When we go back there," he said to me, in a whisper, "the thing we have to make sure of is, this time, certain people remain out . . . You know who I mean: those Z'zus . . ."

I would have liked to answer him by saying that I've heard a 9
number of people make the same remark, concluding: "You know
who I mean . . . Mr. Pber^t Pber^d . . ."

To avoid the subject, I hastened to say: "What about Mrs.
Ph(i)Nk$_o$? Do you think we'll find her back there again?"

"Ah, yes . . . She, by all means . . . " he said, turning purple. 11

For all of us the hope of returning to that point means, above all, 12
the hope of being once more with Mrs. Ph(i)Nk$_o$. (This applies even
to me, though I don't believe in it.) And in that bar, as always happens,
we fell to talking about her, and were moved; even Mr. Pber^t Pber^d's
unpleasantness faded, in the face of that memory.

Mrs. Ph(i)Nk$_o$'s great secret is that she never aroused any jealousy 13
among us. Or any gossip, either. The fact that she went to bed with
her friend, Mr. De XuaeauX, was well known. But in a point, if there's
a bed, it takes up the whole point, so it isn't a question of *going* to
bed, but of *being* there, because anybody in the point is also in the
bed. Consequently, it was inevitable that she should be in bed also
with each of us. If she had been another person, there's no telling
all the things that would have been said about her. It was the cleaning
woman who always started the slander, and the others didn't have
to be coaxed to imitate her. On the subject of the Z'zu family—for a
change!—the horrible things we had to hear: father, daughters, brothers, sisters, mother, aunts: nobody showed any hesitation even before
the most sinister insinuation. But with her it was different: the happiness I derived from her was the joy of being concealed, punctiform,
in her, and of protecting her, punctiform, in me; it was at the same
time vicious contemplation (thanks to the promiscuity of the punctiform convergence of us all in her) and also chastity (given her punctiform impenetrability). In short: what more could I ask?

And all of this, which was true of me, was true also for each of 14
the others. And for her: she contained and was contained with equal
happiness, and she welcomed us and loved and inhabited all equally.

We got along so well all together, so well that something extraor- 15
dinary was bound to happen. It was enough for her to say, at a certain
moment: "Oh, if I only had some room, how I'd like to make some
noodles for you boys!" And in that moment we all thought of the
space that her round arms would occupy, moving backward and forward with the rolling pin over the dough, her bosom leaning over the
great mound of flour and eggs which cluttered the wide board while
her arms kneaded and kneaded, white and shiny with oil up to the
elbows; we thought of the space that the flour would occupy, and the
wheat for the flour, and the fields to raise the wheat, and the mountains from which the water would flow to irrigate the fields, and the
grazing lands for the herds of calves that would give their meat for

the sauce; of the space it would take for the Sun to arrive with its rays, to ripen the wheat; of the space for the Sun to condense from the clouds of stellar gases and burn; of the quantities of stars and galaxies and galactic masses in flight through space which would be needed to hold suspended every galaxy, every nebula, every sun, every planet, and at the same time we thought of it, this space was inevitably being formed, at the same time that Mrs. Ph(i)Nk$_o$ was uttering those words: " . . . ah, what noodles, boys!" the point that contained her and all of us was expanding in a halo of distance in light-years and light-centuries and billions of light-millennia, and we were being hurled to the four corners of the universe (Mr. Pber^t Pber^d all the way to Pavia), and she, dissolved into I don't know what kind of energy-light-heat, she, Mrs. Ph(i)Nk$_o$, she who in the midst of our closed, petty world had been capable of a generous impulse, "Boys, the noodles I would make for you!," a true outburst of general love, initiating at the same moment the concept of space and, properly speaking, space itself, and time, and universal gravitation, and the gravitating universe, making possible billions and billions of suns, and of planets, and fields of wheat, and Mrs. Ph(i)Nk$_o$s, scattered through the continents of the planets, kneading with floury, oil-shiny, generous arms, and she lost at that very moment, and we, mourning her loss.

RESPONDING TO READING

Key words: community   discovery   family   loss   nature reality   science   story   transformation

Rhetorical concepts: analogy   cause and effect   fiction humor   process

1.   Calvino is clearly having fun with the concepts Hawking has presented. Look closely at his description of the point on which the story takes place: how fully does he understand the concepts? Show where Calvino's scientific knowledge is expressed and evaluate its adequacy as science and as a basis for fiction.
2.   The story proceeds through a series of logical impossibilities, connecting the almost incomprehensible moment before space and time begin with everyday human life. Describe a few of those connections and explain why they are logically impossible. Why is Calvino doing such fantastic things in his story?
3.   No one knows why the universe began, though most religions propose reasons. What does Calvino suggest as the cause of the Big Bang? What do you think of his suggestion?
4.   Do you find this kind of humor engaging? Annoying? Boring? Or what?

Explain, with quotations from the text, just why you react to the story as you do.

5. Write your own cosmicomic, inventing an explanation for a scientific phenomenon. What is important in your story?

Landscape, History, and the Pueblo Imagination

LESLIE MARMON SILKO

Leslie Marmon Silko opens her acclaimed novel *Ceremony* (1977) with the observation, "You don't have anything if you don't have the stories." Stories, she says, "aren't just entertainment," they are all that Native Americans have "to fight off illness and death." Silko, of Native American, Mexican, and Caucasian descent, was born in 1948 and reared on the Laguna Pueblo, New Mexico. She attended the Bureau of Indian Affairs schools at Laguna before earning a B.A. from the University of New Mexico. Although she has taught at her alma mater and at the University of Arizona, a MacArthur fellowship in 1983 provided five years' support for her writing. *Storyteller*, a collection of poems, stories, and legends was published in 1981; her second novel, *Almanac of the Dead*, which took ten years to write, was published in 1991. *Ceremony*, which depicts the struggle of Tayo, a half-breed veteran of World War II, for sanity and wholeness after returning from military service to a New Mexico Indian reservation, asserts that "the only cure . . . is a good ceremony." Tayo overcomes the ravages of alcoholism, racism, and violence through learning that ceremony is not merely a formal ritual, but a way of conducting one's life to attain the harmony that comes from an integration of human life and the cosmos.

In "Landscape, History, and the Pueblo Imagination" (1986) Silko reinforces this integrated world view. Storytelling, she says, is a communal act with everyone in the pueblo, from the youngest child to the oldest person expected to listen, remember, and tell part of the story. If even a key figure in the tribe were to die unexpectedly, the system would remain intact, the stories transcending the individual. Truth thus becomes communal, as well, living "somewhere within the web of differing versions" and outright contradictions. The narratives the Pueblos tell are linked with prominent features of the landscape; they delineate the complex relationship humans must maintain with the natural world if they are to survive in the high desert plateau.

From a High Arid Plateau in New Mexico

You see that after a thing is dead, it dries up. It might take weeks   1
or years, but eventually if you touch the thing, it crumbles under your
fingers. It goes back to dust. The soul of the thing has long since

departed. With the plants and wild game the soul may have already been borne back into bones and blood or thick green stalk and leaves. Nothing is wasted. What cannot be eaten by people or in some way used must then be left where other living creatures may benefit. What domestic animals or wild scavengers can't eat will be fed to the plants. The plants feed on the dust of these few remains.

The ancient Pueblo people buried the dead in vacant rooms or   2 partially collapsed rooms adjacent to the main living quarters. Sand and clay used to construct the roof make layers many inches deep once the roof has collapsed. The layers of sand and clay make for easy gravedigging. The vacant room fills with cast-off objects and debris. When a vacant room has filled deep enough, a shallow but adequate grave can be scooped in a far corner. Archaeologists have remarked over formal burials complete with elaborate funerary objects excavated in trash middens of abandoned rooms. But the rocks and adobe mortar of collapsed walls were valued by the ancient people. Because each rock has been carefully selected for size and shape, then chiseled to an even face. Even the pink clay adobe melting with each rainstorm had to be prayed over, then dug and carried some distance. Corn cobs and husks, the rinds and stalks and animals bones were not regarded by the ancient people as filth or garbage. The remains were merely resting at a midpoint in their journey back to dust. Human remains are not so different. They should rest with the bones and rinds where they all may benefit living creatures—small rodents and insects— until their return is completed. The remains of things—animals and plants, the clay and the stones—were treated with respect. Because for the ancient people all these things had spirit and being.

The antelope merely consents to return home with the hunter.   3 All phases of the hunt are conducted with love. The love the hunter and the people have for the Antelope People. And the love of the antelope who agree to give up their meat and blood so that human beings will not starve. Waste of meat or even the thoughtless handling of bones cooked bare will offend the antelope spirits. Next year the hunters will vainly search the dry plains for antelope. Thus it is necessary to return carefully the bones and hair, and the stalks and leaves to the earth who first created them. The spirits remain close by. They do not leave us.

The dead become dust, and in this becoming they are once more   4 joined with the Mother. The ancient Pueblo people called the earth the Mother Creator of all things in this world. Her sister, the Corn Mother, occasionally merges with her because all succulent green liferises out of the depths of the earth.

Rocks and clay are part of the Mother. They emerge in various 5
forms, but at some time before, they were smaller particles or great
boulders. At a later time they may again become what they once
were. Dust.

A rock shares this fate with us and with animals and plants as 6
well. A rock has being or spirit, although we may not understand it.
The spirit may differ from the spirit we know in animals or plants or
in ourselves. In the end we all originate from the depths of the earth.
Perhaps this is how all beings share in the spirit of the Creator. We
do not know.

From the Emergence Place

Pueblo potters, the creators of petroglyphs and oral narratives, 7
never conceived of removing themselves from the earth and sky. So
long as the human consciousness remains *within* the hills, canyons,
cliffs, and the plants, clouds, and sky, the term *landscape*, as it has
entered the English language, is misleading. "A portion of territory
the eye can comprehend in a single view" does not correctly describe
the relationship between the human being and his or her surroundings. This assumes the viewer is somehow *outside* or *separate from* the
territory he or she surveys. Viewers are as much a part of the landscape as the boulders they stand on. There is no high mesa edge or
mountain peak where one can stand and not immediately be part of
all that surrounds. Human identity is linked with all the elements of
Creation through the clan: you might belong to the Sun Clan or the
Lizard Clan or the Corn Clan or the Clay Clan. Standing deep within
the natural world, the ancient Pueblo understood the thing as it was—
the squash blossom, grasshopper, or rabbit itself could never be created by the human hand. Ancient Pueblos took the modest view that
the thing itself (the landscape) could not be improved upon. The
ancients did not presume to tamper with what had already been
created. Thus *realism*, as we now recognize it in painting and sculpture, did not catch the imaginations of Pueblo people until recently.

The squash blossom itself is *one thing*: itself. So the ancient Pueblo 8
potter abstracted what she saw to be the key elements of the squash
blossom—the four symmetrical petals, with four symmetrical sta-
mens in the center. These key elements, while suggesting the squash
flower, also link it with the four cardinal directions. By representing
only its intrinsic form, the squash flower is released from a limited
meaning or restricted identity. Even in the most sophisticated abstract
form, a squash flower or a cloud or a lightning bolt became intricately
connected with a complex system of relationships which the ancient

Pueblo people maintained with each other, and with the populous natural world they lived within. A bolt of lightning is itself, but at the same time it may mean much more. It may be a messenger of good fortune when summer rains are needed. It may deliver death, perhaps the result of manipulations by the Gunnadeyahs, destructive necromancers. Lightning may strike down an evil-doer. Or lightning may strike a person of good will. If the person survives, lightning endows him or her with heightened power.

Pictographs and petroglyphs of constellations or elk or antelope   9 draw their magic in part from the process wherein the focus of all prayer and concentration is upon the thing itself, which, in its turn, guides the hunter's hand. Connection with the spirit dimensions requires a figure or form which is all-inclusive. A "lifelike" rendering of an elk is too restrictive. Only the elk *is* itself. A *realistic* rendering of an elk would be only one particular elk anyway. The purpose of the hunt rituals and magic is to make contact with *all* the spirits of the Elk.

The land, the sky, and all that is within them—the landscape—   10 includes human beings. Interrelationships in the Pueblo landscape are complex and fragile. The unpredictability of the weather, the aridity and harshness of much of the terrain in the high plateau country explain in large part the relentless attention the ancient Pueblo people gave the sky and the earth around them. Survival depended upon harmony and cooperation not only among human beings, but among all things—the animate and the less animate, since rocks and mountains were known to move, to travel occasionally.

The ancient Pueblos believed the Earth and the Sky were sisters   11 (or sister and brother in the post-Christian version). As long as good family relations are maintained, then the Sky will continue to bless her sister, the Earth, with rain, and the Earth's children will continue to survive. But the old stories recall incidents in which troublesome spirits or beings threaten the earth. In one story, a malicious ka'tsina, called the Gambler, seizes the Shiwana, or Rainclouds, the Sun's beloved children. The Shiwana are snared in magical power late one afternoon on a high mountain top. The Gambler takes the Rainclouds to his mountain stronghold where he locks them in the north room of his house. What was his idea? The Shiwana were beyond value. They brought life to all things on earth. The Gambler wanted a big stake to wager in his games of chance. But such greed, even on the part of only one being, had the effect of threatening the survival of all life on earth. Sun Youth, aided by old Grandmother Spider, outsmarts the Gambler and the rigged game, and the Rainclouds are set free. The drought ends, and once more life thrives on earth.

Through the Stories We Hear Who We Are

All summer the people watch the west horizon, scanning the sky 12
from south to north for rain clouds. Corn must have moisture at the
time the tassels form. Otherwise pollination will be incomplete, and
the ears will be stunted and shriveled. An inadequate harvest may
bring disaster. Stories told at Hopi, Zuni, and at Acoma and Laguna
describe drought and starvation as recently as 1900. Precipitation in
west-central New Mexico averages fourteen inches annually. The
western pueblos are located at altitudes over 5,600 feet above sea level,
where winter temperatures at night fall below freezing. Yet evidence
of their presence in the high desert plateau country goes back ten
thousand years. The ancient Pueblo people not only survived in this
environment, but many years they thrived. In A.D. 1100 the people
at Chaco Canyon had built cities with apartment buildings of stone
five stories high. Their sophistication as sky-watchers was surpassed
only by Mayan and Inca astronomers. Yet this vast complex of knowledge and belief, amassed for thousands of years, was never recorded
in writing.

Instead, the ancient Pueblo people depended upon collective 13
memory through successive generations to maintain and transmit an
entire culture, a world view complete with proven strategies for survival. The oral narrative, or "story," became the medium in which
the complex of Pueblo knowledge and belief was maintained. Whatever the event or the subject, the ancient people perceived the world
and themselves within that world as part of an ancient continuous
story composed of innumerable bundles of other stories.

The ancient Pueblo vision of the world was inclusive. The impulse 14
was to leave nothing out. Pueblo oral tradition necessarily embraced
all levels of human experience. Otherwise, the collective knowledge
and beliefs comprising ancient Pueblo culture would have been incomplete. Thus stories about the Creation and Emergence of human
beings and animals into this World continue to be retold each year
for four days and four nights during the winter solstice. The "humma-
hah" stories related events from the time long ago when human
beings were still able to communicate with animals and other living
things. But, beyond these two preceding categories, the Pueblo oral
tradition knew no boundaries. Accounts of the appearance of the first
Europeans in Pueblo country or of the tragic encounters between
Pueblo people and Apache raiders were no more and no less important than stories about the biggest mule deer ever taken or adulterous
couples surprised in cornfields and chicken coops. Whatever happened, the ancient people instinctively sorted events and details into
a loose narrative structure. Everything became a story.

Traditionally everyone, from the youngest child to the oldest per- 15
son, was expected to listen and to be able to recall or tell a portion,
if only a small detail, from a narrative account or story. Thus the
remembering and retelling were a communal process. Even if a key
figure, an elder who knew much more than others, were to die unexpectedly, the system would remain intact. Through the efforts of a
great many people, the community was able to piece together valuable
accounts and crucial information that might otherwise have died with
an individual.

Communal storytelling was a self-correcting process in which 16
listeners were encouraged to speak up if they noted an important fact
or detail omitted. The people were happy to listen to two or three
different versions of the same event or the same humma-hah story.
Even conflicting versions of an incident were welcomed for the entertainment they provided. Defenders of each version might joke and
tease one another, but seldom were there any direct confrontations.
Implicit in the Pueblo oral tradition was the awareness that loyalties,
grudges, and kinship must always influence the narrator's choices as
she emphasizes to listeners this is the way *she* has always heard the
story told. The ancient Pueblo people sought a communal truth, not
an absolute. For them this truth lived somewhere within the web of
differing versions, disputes over minor points, outright contradictions
tangling with old feuds and village rivalries.

A dinner-table conversation, recalling a deer hunt forty years ago 17
when the largest mule deer ever was taken, inevitably stimulates
similar memories in listeners. But hunting stories were not merely
after-dinner entertainment. These accounts contained information of
critical importance about behavior and migration patterns of mule
deer. Hunting stories carefully described key landmarks and locations
of fresh water. Thus a deer-hunt story might also serve as a "map."
Lost travelers, and lost piñon-nut gatherers, have been saved by sight-
ing a rock formation they recognize only because they once heard a
hunting story describing this rock formation.

The importance of cliff formations and water holes does not end 18
with hunting stories. As offspring of the Mother Earth, the ancient
Pueblo people could not conceive of themselves within a specific landscape. Location, or "place," nearly always plays a central role in the
Pueblo oral narratives. Indeed, stories are most frequently recalled as
people are passing by a specific geographical feature or the exact place
where a story takes place. The precise date of the incident often is
less important than the place or location of the happening. "Long,
long ago," "a long time ago," "not too long ago," and "recently" are
usually how stories are classified in terms of time. But the places

where the stories occur are precisely located, and prominent geographical details recalled, even if the landscape is well-known to listeners. Often because the turning point in the narrative involved a peculiarity or special quality of a rock or tree or plant found only at that place. Thus, in the case of many of the Pueblo narratives, it is impossible to determine which come first: the incident or the geographical feature which begs to be brought alive in a story that features some unusual aspect of this location.

There is a giant sandstone boulder about a mile north of Old 19 Laguna, on the road to Paguate. It is ten feet tall and twenty feet in circumference. When I was a child, and we would pass this boulder driving to Paguate village, someone usually made reference to the story about Kochininako, Yellow Woman, and the Estrucuyo, a monstrous giant who nearly ate her. The Twin Hero Brothers saved Kochininako, who had been out hunting rabbits to take home to feed her mother and sisters. The Hero Brothers had heard her cries just in time. The Estrucuyo had cornered her in a cave too small to fit its monstrous head. Kochininako had already thrown to the Estrucuyo all her rabbits, as well as her moccasins and most of her clothing. Still the creature had not been satisfied. After killing the Estrucuyo with their bows and arrows, the Twin Hero Brothers slit open the Estrucuyo and cut out its heart. They threw the heart as far as they could. The monster's heart landed there, beside the old trail to Paguate village, where the sandstone boulder rests now.

It may be argued that the existence of the boulder precipitated 20 the creation of a story to explain it. But sandstone boulders and sandstone formations of strange shapes abound in the Laguna Pueblo area. Yet most of them do not have stories. Often the crucial element in a narrative is the terrain—some specific detail of the setting.

A high dark mesa rises dramatically from a grassy plain fifteen 21 miles southeast of Laguna, in an area known as Swanee. On the grassy plain one hundred and forty years ago, my great-grandmother's uncle and his brother-in-law were grazing their herd of sheep. Because visibility on the plain extends for over twenty miles, it wasn't until the two sheepherders came near the high dark mesa that the Apaches were able to stalk them. Using the mesa to obscure their approach, the raiders swept around from both ends of the mesa. My great-grandmother's relatives were killed, and the herd lost. The high dark mesa played a critical role: the mesa had compromised the safety which the openness of the plains had seemed to assure. Pueblo and Apache alike relied upon the terrain, the very earth herself, to give them protection and aid. Human activities or needs were maneuvered to fit the existing surroundings and conditions. I imagine the last afternoon of my distant ancestors as warm and sunny for late September. They might have been traveling slowly, bringing the sheep closer to Laguna in preparation for the approach of colder weather. The grass was tall and only beginning to change from green to a yellow which matched the late-afternoon sun shining off it. There might have been comfort in the warmth and the sight of the sheep fattening on good pasture which lulled my ancestors into their fatal inattention. They might have had a rifle whereas the Apaches had only bows and arrows. But there would have been four or five Apache raiders, and the surprise attack would have canceled any advantage the rifles gave them.

Survival in any landscape comes down to making the best use of all available resources. On that particular September afternoon, the raiders made better use of the Swanee terrain than my poor ancestors did. Thus the high dark mesa and the story of the two lost Laguna herders became inextricably linked. The memory of them and their story resides in part with the high black mesa. For as long as the mesa stands, people within the family and clan will be reminded of the story of that afternoon long ago. Thus the continuity and accuracy of the oral narratives are reinforced by the landscape—and the Pueblo interpretation of that landscape is *maintained*. 22

The Migration Story: An Interior Journey

The Laguna Pueblo migration stories refer to specific places— mesas, springs, or cottonwood trees—not only locations which can be visited still, but also locations which lie directly on the state highway route linking Paguate village with Laguna village. In traveling this road as a child with older Laguna people I first heard a few of the stories from that much larger body of stories linked with the Emergence and Migration. It may be coincidental that Laguna people continue to follow the same route which, according to the Migration story, the ancestors followed south from the Emergence Place. It may be that the route is merely the shortest and best route for car, horse, or foot traffic between Laguna and Paguate villages. But if the stories about boulders, springs, and hills are actually remnants from a ritual that retraces the creation and emergence of the Laguna Pueblo people as a culture, as the people they became, then continued use of that route creates a unique relationship between the ritual-mythic world and the actual, everyday world. A journey from Paguate to Laguna down the long incline of Paguate Hill retraces the original journey from the Emergence Place, which is located slightly north of the Paguate village. Thus the landscape between Paguate and Laguna takes on a deeper significance: the landscape resonates the spiritual or mythic dimension of the Pueblo world even today. 23

Although each Pueblo culture designates a specific Emergence 24
Place—usually a small natural spring edged with mossy sandstone
and full of cattails and wild watercress—it is clear that they do not
agree on any single location or natural spring as the one and only
true Emergence Place. Each Pueblo group recounts its own stories
about Creation, Emergence, and Migration, although they all believe
that all human beings, with all the animals and plants, emerged at
the same place and at the same time.

Natural springs are crucial sources of water for all life in the high 25
desert plateau country. So the small spring near Paguate village is
literally the source and continuance of life for the people in the area.
The spring also functions on a spiritual level, recalling the original
Emergence Place and linking the people and the spring water to all
other people and to that moment when the Pueblo people became
aware of themselves as they are even now. The Emergence was an
emergence into a precise cultural identity. Thus the Pueblo stories
about the Emergence and Migration are not to be taken as literally as
the anthropologists might wish. Prominent geographical features and
landmarks which are mentioned in the narratives exist for ritual purposes, not because the Laguna people actually journeyed south for
hundreds of years from Chaco Canyon or Mesa Verde, as the archaeologists say, or eight miles from the site of the natural springs at
Paguate to the sandstone hilltop at Laguna.

The eight miles, marked with boulders, mesas, springs, and river 26
crossings, are actually a ritual circuit or path which marks the interior
journey the Laguna people made: a journey of awareness and imagination in which they emerged from being within the earth and from
everything included in earth to the culture and people they became,
differentiating themselves for the first time from all that had surrounded them, always aware that interior distances cannot be reckoned in physical miles or in calendar years.

The narratives linked with prominent features of the landscape 27
between Paguate and Laguna delineate the complexities of the relationship which human beings must maintain with the surrounding
natural world if they hope to survive in this place. Thus the journey
was an interior process of the imagination, a growing awareness that
being human is somehow different from all other life—animal, plant,
and inanimate. Yet we are all from the same source: the awareness
never deteriorated into Cartesian duality, cutting off the human from
the natural world.

The people found the opening into the Fifth World too small to 28
allow them or any of the animals to escape. They had sent a fly out
through the small hole to tell them if it was the world which the
Mother Creator had promised. It was, but there was the problem of

getting out. The antelope tried to butt the opening to enlarge it, but the antelope enlarged it only a little. It was necessary for the badger with her long claws to assist the antelope, and at last the opening was enlarged enough so that all the people and animals were able to emerge up into the Fifth World. The human beings could not have emerged without the aid of antelope and badger. The human beings depended upon the aid and charity of the animals. Only through interdependence could the human beings survive. Families belonged to clans, and it was by clan that the human being joined with the animal and plant world. Life on the high arid plateau became viable when the human beings were able to imagine themselves as sisters and brothers to the badger, antelope, clay, yucca, and sun. Not until they could find a viable relationship to the terrain, the landscape they found themselves in, could they *emerge*. Only at the moment the requisite balance between human and *other* was realized could the Pueblo people become a culture, a distinct group whose population and survival remained stable despite the vicissitudes of climate and terrain.

Landscape thus has similarities with dreams. Both have the power 29 to seize terrifying feelings and deep instincts and translate them into images—visual, aural, tactile—into the concrete where human beings may more readily confront and channel the terrifying instincts or powerful emotions into rituals and narratives which reassure the individual while reaffirming cherished values of the group. The identity of the individual as a part of the group and the greater Whole is strengthened, and the terror of facing the world alone is extinguished.

Even now, the people at Laguna Pueblo spend the greater portion 30 of social occasions recounting recent incidents or events which have occurred in the Laguna area. Nearly always, the discussion will precipitate the retelling of older stories about similar incidents or other stories connected with a specific place. The stories often contain disturbing or provocative material, but are nonetheless told in the presence of children and women. The effect of these inter-family or interclan exchanges is the reassurance for each person that she or he will never be separated or apart from the clan, no matter what might happen. Neither the worst blunders or disasters nor the greatest financial prosperity and joy will ever be permitted to isolate anyone from the rest of the group. In the ancient times, cohesiveness was all that stood between extinction and survival, and, while the individual certainly was recognized, it was always as an individual simultaneously bonded to family and clan by a complex bundle of custom and ritual. You are never the first to suffer a grave loss or profound humiliation. You are never the first, and you understand that you will probably not be the last to commit or be victimized by a repugnant act. Your family and clan are able to go on at length about others now passed on, others older or more experienced than you who suffered similar losses.

The wide deep arroyo near the Kings Bar (located across the 31 reservation borderline) has over the years claimed many vehicles. A few years ago, when a Viet Nam veteran's new red Volkswagen rolled backwards into the arroyo while he was inside buying a six-pack of beer, the story of his loss joined the lively and large collection of stories already connected with that big arroyo. I do not know whether the Viet Nam veteran was consoled when he was told the stories about the other cars claimed by the ravenous arroyo. All his savings of combat pay had gone for the red Volkswagen. But this man could not have felt any worse than the man who, some years before, had left his children and mother-in-law in his station wagon with the engine running. When he came out of the liquor store his station wagon was gone. He found it and its passengers upside down in the big arroyo. Broken bones, cuts and bruises, and a total wreck of the car. The big arroyo has a wide mouth. Its existence needs no explanation. People in the area regard the arroyo much as they might regard a living being, which has a certain character and personality. I seldom drive past that wide deep arroyo without feeling a familiarity with and even a strange affection for this arroyo. Because as treacherous as it may be, the arroyo maintains a strong connection between human beings and the earth. The arroyo demands from us the caution and attention that constitute respect. It is this sort of respect the old believers have in mind when they tell us we must respect and love the earth.

Hopi Pueblo elders have said that the austere and, to some eyes, 32 barren plains and hills surrounding their mesa-top villages actually help to nurture the spirituality of the Hopi *way*. The Hopi elders say the Hopi people might have settled in locations far more lush where daily life would not have been so grueling. But there on the high silent sandstone mesas that overlook the sandy arid expanses stretching to all horizons, the Hopi elders say the Hopi people must "live by their prayers" if they are to survive. The Hopi way cherishes the intangible: the riches realized from interaction and interrelationships with all beings above all else. Great abundances of material things, even food, the Hopi elders believe, tend to lure human attention away from what is most valuable and important. The views of the Hopi elders are not much different from those elders in all the Pueblos.

The bare vastness of the Hopi landscape emphasizes the visual 33 impact of every plant, every rock, every arroyo. Nothing is overlooked or taken for granted. Each ant, each lizard, each lark is imbued with great value simply because the creature is there, simply because the creature is alive in a place where any life at all is precious. Stand on the mesa edge at Walpai and look west over the bare distances toward the pale blue outlines of the San Francisco peaks where the ka'tsina spirits reside. So little lies between you and the sky. So little lies between you and the earth. One look and you know that simply to survive is a great triumph, that every possible resource is needed, every possible ally—even the most humble insect or reptile. You realize you will be speaking with all of them if you intend to last out the year. Thus it is that the Hopi elders are grateful to the landscape for aiding them in their quest as spiritual people.

Out Under the Sky

My earliest memories are of being outside, under the sky. I re- 34 member climbing the fence when I was three years old, and heading for the plaza in the center of Laguna village because other children passing by had told me there were ka'tsinas there dancing with pieces of wood in their mouths. A neighbor woman retrieved me before I ever saw the wood-swallowing ka'tsinas, but from an early age I knew that I wanted to be outside. Outside walls and fences.

My father had wandered all the hills and mesas around Laguna 35 when he was a child. Because the Indian School and the taunts of the other children did not set well with him. It had been difficult in those days to be part Laguna and part white, or *amedicana*. It was still difficult when I attended the Indian School at Laguna. Our full-blooded relatives and clanspeople assured us we were theirs and that we belonged there because we had been born and reared there. But the racism of the wider world we call America had begun to make itself felt years before. My father's response was to head for the mesas and hills with his older brother, their dog, and .22 rifles. They retreated to the sandstone cliffs and juniper forests. Out in the hills they were not lonely because they had all the living creatures of the hills around them, and, whatever the ambiguities of racial heritage, my father and my uncle understood what the old folks had taught them: the earth loves all of us regardlessly, because we are her children.

I started roaming those same mesas and hills when I was nine 36 years old. At eleven I rode away on my horse, and explored places my father and uncle could not have reached on foot. I was never afraid or lonely, although I was high in the hills, many miles from home. Because I carried with me the feeling I'd acquired from listening to the old stories, that the land all around me was teeming with creatures that were related to human beings and to me. The stories had also left me with a feeling of familiarity and warmth for the mesas and hills and boulders where the incidents or action in the stories had taken place. I felt as if I had actually been to those places, although I had only heard stories about them. Somehow the stories had given a kind of being to the mesas and hills, just as the stories had left me with the sense of having spent time with the people in the stories, although they had long since passed on.

It is unremarkable to sense the presence of those long passed at 37 the locations where their adventures took place. Spirits range without boundaries of any sort. Spirits may be called back in any number of ways. The method used in the calling also determines how the spirit manifests itself. I think a spirit may or may not choose to remain at the site of its passing or death. I think they might be in a number of places at the same time. Storytelling can procure fleeting moments to experience who they were and how life felt long ago. What I enjoyed most as a child was standing at the site of an incident recounted in one of the ancient stories Aunt Susie had told us as girls. What excited me was listening to old Aunt Susie tell us an old-time story and then for me to realize that I was familiar with a certain mesa or cave that figured as the central location of the story she was telling. That was when the stories worked best. Because then I could sit there listening and be able to visualize myself as being located *within* the story being told, within the landscape. Because the storytellers did not just tell the stories, they would in their way act them out. The storyteller would imitate voices for vast dialogues between the various figures in the story. So we sometimes say the moment is alive again within us, within our imaginations and our memory, as we listen.

Aunt Susie once told me how it had been when she was a child 38 and her grandmother agreed to tell the children stories. The old woman would always ask the youngest child in the room to go open the door. "Go open the door," her grandmother would say. "Go open the door so our esteemed ancestors may bring us the precious gift of their stories." Two points seem clear: the spirits could be present and the stories were valuable because they taught us how we were the people we believed we were. The myth, the web of memories and ideas that create an identity, a part of oneself. This sense of identity was intimately linked with the surrounding terrain, to the landscape which has often played a significant role in a story or in the outcome of a conflict.

The landscape sits in the center of Pueblo belief and identity. Any 39 narratives about the Pueblo people necessarily give a great deal of attention and detail to all aspects of a landscape. For this reason, the Pueblo people have always been extremely reluctant to relinquish their land for dams or highways. For this reason, Taos Pueblo fought from 1906 until 1973 to win back their sacred Blue Lake, which was illegally taken from them by the creation of Taos National Forest. For this reason, the decision in the early 1950s to begin open-pit mining of the huge uranium deposits north of Laguna, near Paguate village, has had a powerful psychological impact upon the Laguna people. Already a large body of stories has grown up around the subject of what happens to people who disturb or destroy the earth. I was a child when the mining began and the apocalyptic warning stories were being told. And I have lived long enough to begin hearing the stories which verify the earlier warnings.

All that remains of the gardens and orchards that used to grow 40 in the sandy flats southeast of Paguate village are the stories of the lovely big peaches and apricots the people used to grow. The Jackpile Mine is an open pit that has been blasted out of the many hundreds of acres where the orchards and melon patches once grew. The Laguna people have not witnessed changes to the land without strong reactions. Descriptions of the landscape *before* the mine are as vivid as any description of the present-day destruction by the open-pit mining. By its very ugliness and by the violence it does to the land, the Jackpile Mine insures that from now on it, too, will be included in the vast body of narratives which make up the history of the Laguna people and the Pueblo landscape. And the description of what that landscape looked like *before* the uranium mining began will always carry considerable impact.

Landscape as a Character in Fiction

Drought or the disappearance of game animals may signal dis- 41 harmony or even witchcraft. When the rain clouds fail to appear in time to help the corn plants, or the deer are suddenly scarce, then we know the very sky and earth are telling human beings that all is not well. A deep arroyo continues to claim victims.

When I began writing I found that the plots of my short stories 42 very often featured the presence of elements out of the landscape, elements which directly influenced the outcome of events. Nowhere is landscape more crucial to the outcome than in my short story, "Storyteller." The site is southwest Alaska, near the village of Bethel, on the Kuskokwim River. Tundra country. Here the winter landscape can suddenly metamorphize into a seamless blank white so solid that pilots in aircraft without electronic instruments lose their bearings and crash their planes straight into the frozen tundra, believing down to be up. Here on the Alaska tundra, in mid-February, not all the space-age fabrics, electronics, or engines can ransom human beings from the restless shifting forces of the winter sky and winter earth.

The young Yupik Eskimo woman works out an elaborate yet sub- 43 conscious plan to avenge the deaths of her parents. After months of baiting the trap, she lures the murderer onto the river ice where he falls through to his death. The murderer is a white man who operates the village trading post. For years the murderer has existed like a parasite, exploiting not only the fur-bearing animals and the fish, but the Yupik people themselves. When the Yupik woman kills him, the white trader has just finished cashing in on the influx of workers for the petroleum exploration and pipeline who have suddenly come to the tiny village. For the Yupik people, souls deserving punishment spend varying lengths of time in a place of freezing. The Yupik see the world's end coming with ice, not fire. Although the white trader possesses every possible garment, insulation, heating fuel, and gadget ever devised to protect him from the frozen tundra environment, he still dies, drowning under the freezing river ice. Because the white man had not reckoned with the true power of that landscape, especially not the power which the Yupik woman understood instinctively and which she used so swiftly and efficiently. The white man had reckoned with the young woman and determined he could overpower her. But the white man failed to account for the conjunction of the landscape with the woman. The Yupik woman had never seen herself as anything but a part of that sky, that frozen river, that tundra. The river ice and the blinding white are her accomplices, and yet the Yupik woman never for a moment misunderstands her own relationship with that landscape. After the white trader has crashed through the river ice, the young woman finds herself a great distance from either shore of the treacherous frozen river. She can see nothing but the whiteness of the sky swallowing the earth. But far away in the distance, on the side of her log and tundra sod cabin, she is able to see the spot of bright red. A bright red marker she had nailed up weeks earlier because she was intrigued by the contrast between all that white and the spot of brilliant red. The Yupik woman knows the appetite of the frozen river. She realizes that the ice and the fog, the tundra and the snow seek constantly to be reunited with the living beings which skitter across it. The Yupik woman knows that inevitably she and all things will one day lie in those depths. But the woman is young and her instinct is to live. The Yupik woman knows how to do this.

Inside the small cabin of logs and tundra sod, the old Storyteller 44 is mumbling the last story he will ever tell. It is the story of the hunter stalking a giant polar bear the color of the blue glacier ice. It is a story which the old Storyteller has been telling since the young Yupik woman began to arrange the white trader's death. But a sudden storm develops. The hunter finds himself on an ice floe off shore. Visibility is zero, and the scream of the wind blots out all sound. Quickly the hunter realizes he is being stalked. Hunted by all the forces, by all the elements of the sky and earth around him. When at last the hunter's own muscles spasm and cause the jade knife to fall and shatter the ice, the hunter's death in the embrace of the giant ice blue bear is the foretelling of the world's end. When humans have blasted and burned the last bit of life from the earth, an immeasurable freezing will descend with a darkness that obliterates the sun.

RESPONDING TO READING

Keywords: community   family   freedom   identity   language
memory   minority   nature   power   race   reality
rights   story   symbols   talk

Rhetorical concepts: analogy   anecdote   explanation   myth
narrative/example

1.   Contrast Silko's approach to understanding nature to Hawking's. What makes their writing so different? What assumptions about nature, human interaction with nature, and ways of understanding nature inform Silko's essay?
2.   Silko values "magic" and "the spirit dimensions" (paragraph 9) as part of the interaction of land with people; the "collective memory" transmits culture and storytelling conveys knowledge. Define what Silko finds important and why.
3.   The tale of Estrucuyo (paragraph 19) explains the giant sandstone boulder. Examine that tale and show how it exemplifies the Pueblo way of knowing and understanding what is important.
4.   The Yupik story at the end seems to deny the point Silko makes about the uniqueness of the Pueblo way of life. Does it? What are the similarities and differences between the two cultures, as shown in their stories?
5.   Silko's explanation of the relation of humans to nature suggests much about the Pueblos, Apaches, and Hopi. In what ways does this view of how people should live in time and landscape relate to issues in current America? "Survival in any landscape," Silko says, "comes down to making the best use of all available resources." What does that statement mean to you, in your particular environment? What are its implications for your survival? Your grandchildren's?
6.   Tell your readers (or listeners) a story that is told in your family, and explain what it means or let the meaning emerge through the characters and actions. Assume that your audience does not know you or your family well, if at all; they may be able to respond to the story's common human elements, but you will need to supply the individualizing specific details. In what ways does this story help you "hear who [you] are" (see paragraphs 12–21)?

Poison Snakes

SUE HUBBELL

Sue Hubbell (born in 1935) made a dramatic career shift at age thirty-eight, leaving her work as a librarian in Rhode Island to move to ninety acres of wilderness in the southern Missouri Ozarks. Living alone for a decade after her marriage ended and earning a "shaky, marginal" income from beekeeping (eighteen million honeybees at last estimate) gave her the closeness to the environment she loved best, and the freedom and perspective to write about it with distinction. She has published her observations in magazines (regularly in *The New Yorker*), newspapers, and in *A Country Year* (1986), of which "Poison Snakes" is a chapter. The book's subtitle, *Living the Questions* is taken from Rilke's *Letters to a Young Poet*:

> Be patient toward all that is unsolved in your heart and try to love the questions themselves . . . Do not . . . seek the answers, which cannot be given you because you would not be able to live them. And the point is to live everything. Live the questions now. Perhaps you will . . . gradually, without noticing it, live along some distant day into the answer.

Hubbell, like many other naturalists, is confident that patient, careful observation of the natural world will lead to the right questions, which are rewarding to explore whether or not the answers are forthcoming. Thus, she finds beauty in what the uninitiated might see as ugly—copperheads, for instance. Moreover, she has learned that to understand something is to dispel fear of it. Thus she sympathizes with copperheads, so mild mannered and timid that their "dearest wish when discovered is to escape." With such acceptance comes respect, love, and protectiveness of the total environment, bees, snakes, and all.

I've been out in back today checking beehives. When I leaned 1 over one of them to direct a puff of smoke from my bee smoker into the entrance to quiet the bees, a copperhead came wriggling out from under the hive. He had been frightened from his protected spot by the smoke and the commotion I was making, and when he found himself in the open, he panicked and slithered for the nearest hole he could find which was the entrance to the next beehive. I don't know what went on inside, but he came out immediately, wearing a surprised look on his face. I hadn't known that a snake could look surprised, but this one did. Then, after pausing to study the matter more carefully, he glided off to the safety of the woods.

He was a young snake, not even two feet long. Like the other 2 poisonous snakes found in the Ozarks, the cottonmouths, copperheads belong to the genus *Agkistrodon*, which means fish-hook toothed. The copperheads in my part of the Ozarks are the southern variety, *Agkistrodon contortrix contortrix*, which makes them sound very twisty indeed. They are a pinkish coppery color with darker hourglass-patterned markings. They have wide jaws, which give their heads a triangular shape. Like the cottonmouths, they are pit vipers, which means that between eye and nostril they have a sensory organ that helps them aim in striking at warm-blooded prey. They eat other small snakes, mice, lizards and frogs.

The surprising thing about copperheads are their mild manners, timidity and fearfulness. They have, after all, a potent defensive weapon in their venom, and yet their dearest wish when they are discovered is to escape. This rocky upland peninsula of land between the river and creek is a lovely habitat for copperheads. I often find them under the beehives, and they are common in the open field. Twice I have had them in the cabin. Every time I come upon copperheads they simply try to get away from me and never offer to strike.   3

Once I had an old and heavy Irish setter who was badly bitten when he clumsily stepped on a copperhead. To the snake, being walked on by eighty-five pounds of dog represented a direct attack, and so he struck. The dog's leg swelled and he was in obvious pain. Within a few hours his heartbeat was rapid, his breath shallow, and I took him to the vet. Afterwards he watched where he put his feet. I do, too, and wear leather boots when I walk through the field or in the woods, and in the warm months I give decent warning when I turn over a stack of old boards. I have enormous respect for a small animal with venom so potent that it can make a large dog very sick. I weigh more than the dog, and so I might not have such a severe reaction; there is no record of a human death caused by a copperhead bite in Missouri, but I don't want to risk the pain.   4

I respect copperheads, but I also have another set of feelings toward them, a combination of amazement and sympathy that an animal should be so frightened by me, so eager to escape, so little inclined to use the powerful means that he has to defend himself.   5

Copperheads contrast oddly with the eastern hognose snakes, sometimes called puff adders, that I also see here sometimes. These are harmless, but put on a tremendous show of ferocity. I came upon a hognose one day in the field, and he raised up the first third of his body and spread his neck wide, hissing horribly, trying to convince me that he was a cobra. I was fooled hardly at all and stood quietly watching him; after some more half-hearted hissing and spreading he gave up the attempt to frighten me, remembered urgent business he had elsewhere and slithered away into the tall grasses.   6

Apart from copperheads, there are few dangerous snakes here. There are supposed to be rattlers, but in the twelve years I have been   7 walking the woods and river banks I have never met one. Most of the snakes around are harmless or, like the black rat snakes, which eat rodents, beneficial, and I have no sympathy with the local habit of killing every snake in sight. It is an Ozark custom to pack a pistol along with the beer on a float trip. The pistol is for shooting the cottonmouths that are supposed to fill the river and be thick upon its banks.

In point of fact the river is too cold and swift for cottonmouths, and since I have lived here I have seen only one. He was idling in a warm, shallow pool at the side of the creek that runs along my southern property line. I stopped to look at him from a safe distance. Heavy-bodied and dark, confident and self-assured, he watched me in his turn and did not retreat as a copperhead would have. Instead, he coiled and raised his head, in a defensive posture, ready to strike if I were to advance. He opened his mouth wide, and I could see the white, cottony-looking interior that gives the snake his common name. After he was sure I was not going to come closer, he dropped into the water slowly and with dignity and swam away from me to the bank, where he disappeared under the safe cover of the branches hanging over the pool.   8

This species of cottonmouth are called *Agkistrodon piscivorus leu-*   9 *costoma,* or white-mouthed *agkistrodon* who eats fish. They are often found in warmish water, and are primarily fish-eaters, but they also feed on other snakes, rodents, frogs and lizards.

The cottonmouth I saw was evidently an old one, for he was big,   10 probably nearly four feet in length; only a slight hint of his cross-banding was visible. Young cottonmouths are lighter, more patterned, and newborn cottonmouths, like copperheads, have yellow-tipped tails. Both cottonmouths and copperheads belong to the evolutionarily advanced group of snakes that do not lay eggs. The young are retained within the mother's body, protected by a saclike membrane, until they are born. Like other snakes, they shed their skins as they grow.

A treasured possession of mine is one of those snakeskins, fragile   11 but perfect, with even the eye scales intact. It is always startling to me to notice people shudder when they see it. There is enough psy-chomythology about humankind's aversion to snakes to reach from here to Muncie, Indiana, some of it entertaining, much of it contra-dictory. Whatever the reason, many people are irrationally afraid of snakes, and this makes for poor observation. It is hard to tell what a snake is up to if you are running away from it or killing it. This may account for the preponderance of folklore over natural history in con-versations about snakes. It may be why Ozarkers have told me that the hognose snake is poisonous, that snakes go blind in August, that the hills are full of the dread hoop snake who holds his tail in his mouth and comes roaring down hillsides after folks to attack them with the horn on his tail—a horn so deadly that if it gets stuck in a tree, the tree will die within a few days.

My favorite folk story about snakes is the one about copperheads, 12 who are said to spit out their venom on a flat rock before taking a drink of water and then, having drunk, suck it back up into their fangs. I always liked it because I thought it was a grand Ozark stretcher. But then I found the exact same story in a Physiologus, a medieval bestiary. It is a snake story at least eight hundred years old, perhaps more. So it turns out that the yarn is a piece of natural history after all. It is just that it has to do with the nature of the human mind, not nature of the snakish kind.

RESPONDING TO READING

Key words: animals   discovery   identity   nature
reality   science

Rhetorical concepts: anecdote   definition   explanation   humor
meditation   narrative/example

1.   Hubbell says that she has "enormous respect" for the copperhead, meaning that she does not want to risk the pain of a snakebite. What other signs of "respect" does she show for the snake in this essay? Would you consider her attitude toward snakes common? Do you share it? What does her attitude toward snakes say about her attitude toward nature?
2.   How would you describe what the writer does when (paragraph 1) she describes the copperhead as looking "surprised?" Find other places where she uses this same technique to describe snakes, and consider the effect of that way of describing nature. How, for instance, does she distinguish the copperheads, the puff adders, and the cottonmouths from each other? How appropriate is it to reduce the distance between humans and nature this way?
3.   Why does Hubbell present so much knowledge about various snakes in this essay? For what purposes? Would her attitude and information convince readers to dispel their fears of snakes?
4.   Would you place Hubbell closer to Goodall (Chapter 2) or to Silko as an observer of nature? What is important to Hubbell as a naturalist?
5.   Write an essay on some aspect of nature about which people have fears: snakes, spiders, mice, thunder, darkness, etc. What may be the source of such fear and what are the results of it? Does this fear affect observation in the way that Hubbell describes? How does this fear affect relationships to nature in general?

Doing Science in Secret

RITA LEVI-MONTALCINI

Rita Levi-Montalcini, born in Turin, Italy, in 1909, was co-recipient of the Nobel Prize in medicine in 1986 for her discovery of and research on the Nerve Growth Factor (NGF). The work for which she received the prize began during World War II with her independent, makeshift, underground research at home in Italy. This work is described in "Doing Science in Secret," a chapter from her autobiography, *In Praise of Imperfection* (1988), and continued for thirty years postwar with a team of researchers at Washington University in St. Louis. The NGF molecule is unusual in its ability to stimulate the growth of nerve cells in the central nervous system, in the immune system, and in organs—sometimes tenfold within a few days' treatment.

Levi-Montalcini's experience of doing world-class science contradicts the conventional wisdom that to follow a carefully designed plan of research steadily and surely will lead to the desired results. Although her research team discovered the NGF molecule in 1959, they spent another twenty-five years of repeated experiments on related problems before they eventually understood its profound potential for medical research and treatment of neurological disorders. Levi-Montalcini explains that in scientific research "It is a well-known though often neglected rule that many apparently unsolvable problems, at one point or another unexpectedly find their solution."

Levi-Montalcini's research during World War II was accomplished under the most unpromising circumstances imaginable—as a persecuted Jew in Italy under bombardment by the Allies. Her account of the way she managed to do research at that time is quiet testimony to what can be done when one decides what is really important.

Since I could no longer attend any university institutes, I decided   1
at the end of December 1939 to practice medicine—in clandestine fashion, since this, too, was forbidden. I would look after those patients I had had in my care in past years when they were hospitalized in the university's Medical Clinic. These poor people, who lived in the attics of houses in old Turin, did not care about the laws and were glad of my visits and the help I could offer within the limits of my scarce finances. The constraint of having to turn to Aryan doctors to have prescriptions signed, however, forced me in spite of myself to reduce and then abandon this activity. I took refuge in reading and

cultivated relationships with the many friends who scorned the danger of being accused of pietism.

On 10 June 1940, a dear friend and I were hard at work writing   2
her doctoral thesis when, alarmed by the unusual activity in the streets, we opened the windows. It was six o'clock in the evening. From the loudspeakers set up in the piazzas and main thoroughfares came the loud voice of the Duce: "Fighting men of the army, of the sea and of the air. Blackshirts of the revolution and of the legions. . . . Attention! A fateful hour is striking in the sky of our Fatherland. The hour of irrevocable decisions. A declaration of war has already been presented to the ambassadors." From the Piazza Venezia, where an immense crowd had been assembled, the listeners still ignorant of the ambassadors in question roared their enthusiastic approval. Once the patriotic fervor orchestrated by the Fascist leaders had died down, he continued, stressing each word: ". . . to the ambassadors of Great Britain and France."

Italy's ignoble attack on France, by then already in extremis,   3
started the next day. The "Battle of the Alps" cost the French an exiguous number of casualties, the Italians about two thousand, and many cases of frostbite because the summer equipment of the latter proved inadequate to a sudden onslaught of winter cold. In the months that followed, Italy's lack of military preparation was revealed in all its tragedy on the Greek and East African fronts, while Naples and Sicily were bombed intensively by the British air force.

A few months after the beginning of the war, in the fall of 1940,   4
Rodolfo Amprino, recently returned from the States, came to visit me. I was surprised when he asked me, in a brusque, "Piedmontese" manner, about my projects, it not having occurred to me, in that wartime climate, that my personal problems would be anything but irrelevant to others. My surprise was even greater in that my relations with Rodolfo, since our meeting eight years before at the Anatomy Institute, had been limited to laconic exchanges of information on histological techniques. Or rather, to be more precise, on the basis of his mastery in the field he would tell me things and I would clumsily follow his instructions.

My silence in response to his question provoked a sudden and   5
somewhat irritated reaction: "One doesn't lose heart in the face of the first difficulties. Set up a small laboratory and take up your interrupted research. Remember Ramón y Cajal who in a poorly equipped institute, in the sleepy city that Valencia must have been in the middle of the last century, did the fundamental work that established the basis of all we know about the nervous system of vertebrates." Rodolfo could not have sown his suggestion on more fertile ground. At that moment he seemed to me Ulysses as Dante immor-

talizes him in the twenty-sixth canto of the *Inferno*, when the Greek hero encourages his fellow voyagers not to lose heart but to continue on their course toward the unknown: "My companions I made so eager for the road with these brief words that then I could hardly have held them back."

Rodolfo had, in fact, touched a chord that had been vibrating in   6
me since earliest childhood: the desire to undertake a voyage of adventure to unknown lands. Even more appealing than virgin forest was the jungle lying before me at that moment: the nervous system, with its billions of cells gathered in populations each different from the other and all locked into the apparently inextricable nets of the nervous circuits which intersect in all directions along the cerebro-spinal axis. The pleasure I was already savoring in anticipation was enhanced by the prospect of carrying out the project under the conditions contingent on the prohibitive racial laws. If Ramón y Cajal, with his giant's step and exceptional intuition, had dared foray into that jungle, why should I not venture along the path he had opened for me? My first experience with Visintini had been encouraging. Though unable to continue the same line of research, lacking both space (I only had my small bedroom to work in) and competence in electrophysiology, I could nonetheless analyze other aspects of the developing nervous system by relying on my expertise in the selective coloring of nervous tissues with the silver-impregnation technique and on my ability in microsurgery. Ramón y Cajal's success—as well as the much more modest one of Visintini and myself in studying the function and structure of the nervous system of chick embryos—was the result of the tactic of studying the system in its *statu nascendi*, when it is made up of only some thousand cells interconnected by a still moderate number of neuronal circuits. Chick embryos were ideal material also because they could be easily procured and incubated at home.

I submitted my intention to Mother, Gino, and Paola and received   7
their approval. Mother, in fact, would have been willing to accept any sacrifice rather than face another separation. Gino and Paola, who had been against our moving to the United States because they were both strongly bound to Italy and confident that Nazi-Fascism would be defeated, understood my need to resume the work so suddenly interrupted by my return from Belgium.

The instruments necessary for the realization of this project were   8
few. The need for an incubator was met by a small thermostat which worked very well for the purpose. Another, high-temperature one served to seal the embryos in paraffin. The embryos were then silver-stained and cut into series using a microtomer. The most expensive items were a stereomicroscope, needed for operating on the embryos,

and a binocular Zeiss microscope with all the eyepieces and photographic apparatus. The equipment was completed by a series of watchmaker's forceps, ophthalmic microscissors and surgical instruments consisting of common sewing needles which, with a very fine-grained grindstone, I transformed into extremely sharp microscalpels and spatulae. The collection of instruments, glassware, and chemical reagents was like what one of my nineteenth-century predecessors would have found necessary. Gino built me a glass thermoregulated box with two circular openings on the front. Through these I could insert my arms and operate on the embryos under the microscope in an environment of 38°C., protected against possible infection: a point of caution that revealed itself to be entirely unnecessary but had the advantage of surrounding me with a religious sort of respect. My mother also saw to the maintaining of the latter by forbidding my room to curious visitors, telling them that I was operating and could not be disturbed. The "tour de force" of fitting so much apparatus in the small space available to me added to the pleasure of managing to work under prohibitive conditions. The most cumbersome piece was undoubtedly dear old Levi himself who, with his great corporeal mass and meager agility, threatened to destroy all the carefully laid out histological sections with a mere swinging of his large hands each time he moved. "Excuse me, I'll be more careful" he would mutter, without, however, giving too much weight to these accidents on the job.

I spent the winter and spring of 1941 busy with preparations and the first experiments, which turned out well. The worsening of the military situation and the defeat of the Italians in northern Africa, with the English occupation of Ethiopia in April and the loss of eastern Africa, caused the campaign against the Jews to become even more bitter: they were now enemies to be fought on the home front to make up for losses suffered beyond the country's borders. Articles in the newspapers were matched by anti-Semitic graffiti and posters pasted on walls all over the city. On 16 October, Gino came home proud of an honor paid to him. "They've put me in Einstein's company," he told us. On the poster whose contents the partisan Emanuele Artom reproduced in his diary, Gino's name is listed immediately in front of Einstein's, along with other eminent persons belonging to the "Jewish race," such as Franklin Delano Roosevelt, La Pasionaria, Haile Selassie, and Lenin. After listing the horrible crimes committed by these "Jews," the manifesto urged their punishment: "Are we going to put an end to it once and for all, then? Not to the concentration camps, but up against the wall and then at them with a flame thrower! Long live the Duce! Long live Hitler!" The following day, vaguely aware of the fact that they had included in their list the names of persons who did not belong to the Jewish race, the authors urged the citizenry to fire upon Jews at the slightest suspicion, entrusting the Creator with the posthumous task of discriminating any errors. Artom comments in his diary: "To read posters in which one is threatened with death, accused of many crimes, is an experience it is not given to everybody to endure." He was to endure it to the last drop. Revealed early in 1944 as the political commissar of the Action Party, a Jew, and a partisan, he was subjected to horrible tortures at the hands of the SS and killed without his torturers being able to get a single name or complaint out of him. All this his mother learned from Oscar, another partisan who witnessed Emanuele's death.

In 1941, and up to the time of the Nazi invasion of the country, 10 insults and threats were not followed by acts of actual persecution. Thus, from the spring of 1941, I was able to carry on, in the calm of a minuscule laboratory not unlike a convent cell, a research problem that absorbed all of my time from then until the invasion. My aim was to analyze how excision of still non-innervated tissues in the peripheral territories, or limbs, affects the differentiation and subsequent development both of motor cells in the spinal cord and of sensory cells in the dorsal root ganglia at a very early stage of embryonic life. Previously, this problem, one of the first to be tackled experimentally by researchers into the development of the nervous system in the first two decades of the century, had scarcely interested me. Amphibian tadpoles had been the subject of these experiments, but the results obtained seemed to me too vague to lend themselves to satisfactory interpretation. These findings suddenly appeared in a different light one summer day of 1940, shortly after Italy had entered the war on Germany's side.

My conversion, if such it can be called, occurred while I was riding 11 on a train used before the war for the transportation of livestock. After war had been declared, civilian trains were taken over for troop transportation, and these livestock trains, or cattle cars, were used for civilians, for short journeys in the provinces. The wagons, which lacked seats, doors, and windows, offered great panoramic views through the windowless open sides. I was traveling on one, along with my friend Guido, the formidable whistler of classical arias, on our way to a small mountain village. I sat down in what was considered to be one of the best places—the floor of the wagon—with my legs dangling over the side in the open air. The slow progress of the train, the vertical bars that offered firm support and, in my case, Guido's vigilant hand, ensured against possible falls and allowed me to see the fields in their full summer's growth. While enjoying the view and the air which smelled of hay, I was distractedly reading an article Levi had given to me two years before. Published in 1934 in an American periodical, it was the work of a pupil of Hans Spemann, the German biologist who was awarded the Nobel Prize in 1935 for his discovery of a factor (or of factors, which even today have not been precisely identified) called the "organizer" because of its property of inducing the differentiation of organs and of whole embryos that come into direct contact with the tissues releasing it. The author of the article, Viktor Hamburger, had not analyzed this phenomenon, but his interpretation of the effect he described was clearly influenced by the same concept of an inductive reaction of certain tissues on others during the early stages of embryonic development. Hamburger had studied how the ablation of chick embryo limb buds affected the sensory and motor neurons responsible for their innervation. The author observed that, one week after such an operation, the motor column and the sensory spinal ganglia responsible for the innervation of the limbs were greatly reduced in volume. Hamburger interpreted these findings as pointing to the absence of an inductive factor, otherwise normally released by the innervated tissues and necessary for the differentiation of motor and sensory nerve cells; without the factor, these cells could not undergo differentiation. For me, Hamburger's limpid style and the rigor of his analysis—in sharp contrast with those of previous authors who had described the same phenomenon in amphibian larvae—cast new light on the problem. I don't know how far the idyllic circumstances in which I read the article contributed to my desire to delve into this phenomenon, but in memory my decision is indissolubly bound up with that summer afternoon and the smell of hay wafting into the wagon. I did not imagine at the time, however, that this interest and my subsequent research would determine my future.

The summer of 1941 was overshadowed by the anguish caused 12 by the news of the triumphant advance of Hitler's troops into Russia and of their successes on all fronts. We were, furthermore, deprived of all news of Levi whom we feared had fallen into Nazi hands since his refusal to leave Belgium after the German occupation. It was with immense joy that, at summer's end, we welcomed him back—shockingly thin and pale after a dangerous trip across Germany. It turned out that, after a year in Nazi-controlled Liège, meeting his friends secretly in a little café outside of town, he had been unable to endure any longer the hunger, loneliness, and boredom, and had set out for home. I was especially happy to see him, and asked him to join me in my new research. He accepted with great pleasure, and thus it was that from that autumn till a year later when we were both forced to leave the city, his imperious voice resounded in my bedroom-laboratory from morning to night. Work would be interrupted when his loyal pupils arrived, and the topic of conversation would shift from chick embryos to the madmen and criminals who were running our country.

In the winter and spring of 1942, our research yielded unhoped- 13
for successes. The examination of embryos whose budding limbs had been excised in three-day specimens, and impregnated using the silver technique, revealed with extraordinary clarity the nerve cells and the fibers that sprang both out of the motor neurons of the spinal column and out of the sensory ganglia in embryos sacrificed at brief intervals from the time of the excision to the end of the twenty-day incubation period. These findings suggested a different explanation from the one advanced by Hamburger to explain the almost complete disappearance of the motor cells in the spinal ganglia that innervated the limbs in embryos not subjected to such destructive treatment. It was a question of the absence not of an inductive factor necessary to their differentiation, but of a trophic factor that is released by innervated tissues and that, under normal conditions, the nerve fibers convey toward the cellular bodies. In fact, in embryos with excised limbs, the differentiation of nerve cells proceeds normally, but a degenerative process followed by the death of the cells begins to occur as soon as the fibers springing out of the cord and from the ganglia reach the stump of the amputated limb. Their death appeared to be caused by the absence of a trophic factor and not, as Hamburger had hypothesized, by an inductive one belonging to the category of those known as "organizers."

Many years later, I often asked myself how we could have dedi- 14
cated ourselves with such enthusiasm to solving this small neuroembryological problem while German armies were advancing throughout Europe, spreading destruction and death wherever they went and threatening the very survival of Western civilization. The answer lies in the desperate and partially unconscious desire of human beings to ignore what is happening in situations where full awareness might lead one to self-destruction.

In the second half of 1942, with the Allies' systematic bombing 15
of the cities in northern Italy and of Turin in particular, a favorite target because of its great industries, life in the city became every day more dangerous. Almost every night, the lugubrious whine of sirens, warning of British planes overhead, forced us to go down into the basement in spite of the risk—which became tragic reality for hundreds of people—of being buried under the ruins of bombed buildings. Every time the alarm sounded, I would carry down to the precarious safety of the cellars the Zeiss binocular microscope and my most precious silver-stained embryonic sections. These vigils usually dragged on for hours, amid the murmurs of women praying, until the sirens announced that the danger had, for the time being,

come to an end. Very often, however, a squeal announcing a new series of planes forced us to rush down again.

When autumn was well under way, we decided, like the majority 16 of the people of Turin, to move out of town. Thus, in a small house in the hilly Astigiano highlands, an hour away from Turin, I set up my laboratory on a small table in the corner of a room that served also as dining area and family sitting room. Since eggs had become extremely scarce, I cycled from one hill to another begging farmers to sell me some "for my babies." Casually I inquired whether there were roosters in the chicken coop because, as I explained, "fertilized eggs are more nutritious." An unforeseen difficulty arose when my activities in the common room fell under Gino's eyes. He noticed how I used spatulae and ophthalmic scissors to extract from the eggs five-day-old embryos that had been operated on, and how then, instead of throwing the eggs away, I carried them into the kitchen and used them to fix our meals. From that day on, he categorically refused to eat the scrambled eggs and omelets, which up until then he had thought excellent.

Levi lived in a different locality outside of Turin but returned 17 every day. On alternate days, and always after heavy bombings, which my family and I would witness in dismay from the top of the hill, gazing at the sky lit by the glare of fires, I also returned to Turin to meet him. With other friends, we warmed ourselves by a stove in the kitchen of my home, the only warm room in the freezing apartment, and ate the steaming cornmeal that an old housekeeper poured us from the pot while recounting the night's events. With a smiling, rubicund face, he expressed the pride he took in his work, saying, "I do everything on my own"—though doing nothing but stir the cornmeal. These were the most serene moments of those wintry days in the city devastated by night bombing raids. The ruins of bombed building, broken pipelines, damaged electrical and telephone plants were swept aside and repaired with unbelievable speed, but hopelessness and despair were written on everybody's face. At dusk began the assault on the overcrowded trains carrying people back to the shelters scattered about in the hills.

In spite of the almost prohibitive conditions—the difficulty of 18 procuring fertilized eggs, and the repeated failure of the power supply upon which depended the functioning of my incubator and the development of the embryos—I completed some projects which I was to carry further a few years later in the United States. Their central theme was the study of the interaction of genetic and environmental factors in the regulation of the differentiation processes of the nervous system during the early stages of its development. At the beginning of spring, from the window of my small room in our cottage, I con-

templated the ducklings following their mother in single file, diving
from time to time as she did into the ditches that, after rain, flowed
down the sides of the little road I used to cycle along every day. In
specific areas of the embryonic nervous system, cells in the first stages
of differentiation detach themselves from cellular clusters of cephalic
nuclei and move singularly, one after the other like the little ducklings,
toward distant locations along rigidly programmed routes, as is demonstrated by the fact that the spatial and temporal modalities of these
migrations are identical in different embryos. In other sectors of the
developing nervous system, thousands of cells move about like colonies of migrating birds or insects—like the Biblical locusts that I was
to see many years later in Ecuador. The fact that I was for the first
time observing natural phenomena unknown to those who live in
cities, such as the springtime awakening of nature, cheered me and
stimulated my interest in studying the developing nervous system.
Now the nervous system appeared to me in a different light from
its description in textbooks of neuroanatomy, where its structure
is described as rigid and unchangeable. Only by following, from hour
to hour in different specimens, as in a cinematographic sequence,
the development of nerve centers and circuits, did I come to realize
how dynamic these processes are; how individual cells behave in a
way similar to that of living beings; how plastic and malleable is
the entire nervous system. This system, which more than any other
must adapt its structure and functions to environmental requirements, was to remain the main object of my research in the years
that followed. Its analysis came into focus and grew in that country
milieu probably much better than it would have in an academic
institution.

In the summer of 1943 occurred the event marking the end of an [19]
era for Italy and the beginning of a most dramatic period. On the
evening of 25 July, at 10:45 P.M., while we were listening to the radio,
the program was interrupted by an announcer reading out the following news:

> Attention, Attention! His Majesty the King Emperor has accepted
> the resignation from the offices of Head of the Government presented
> by the Prime Minister and Secretary of State His Excellency Cavalier
> Benito Mussolini, and has nominated Head of the Government,
> Prime Minister and Secretary of State, His Excellency, the Marshal
> of Italy, Pietro Badoglio.

The news was received in my home, as throughout the entire peninsula, with immense jubilation. The demonstrations of enthusiasm
were profoundly genuine yet, at the same time, indicative of a collective irresponsibility—or, to describe it in less severe terms, a lack

of awareness of the danger looming over us, with German troops stationed in Italy and more massing on its frontiers.

The following morning, I went into Turin as usual. On the train, 20 people were hugging each other, crying and laughing. At the station, from trains that until the previous day had spilled onto the platforms a gloomy and silent crowd, now descended passengers who behaved as if they were intoxicated. They began to cast off Fascist insignia— until the previous day, the precious symbols of support for the regime, and now objects of derision and shame. Leading fascists stayed shut up in their houses that day and the following ones; less important party members mixed in with the crowd who accepted them good-naturedly. Everybody, for that matter, felt somewhat guilty.

If optimism among the "Aryans" was to some extent justified, as 21 they were not directly in the Nazis' gunsights, it was, on the contrary, completely absurd in the small Jewish population, ourselves included. Even though we were only partly aware of what had happened and was still happening in the European countries invaded by the Germans, it was folly not to have taken immediate precautions to save ourselves after 25 July. Faith in the Italians who welcomed us back among them, a common hatred for Nazism, and the absurd conviction that what happened in other countries could not happen in Italy were the source of this irresponsible attitude, an attitude which was to cause thousands of people untold suffering and death.

RESPONDING TO READING

Key words: community discovery family freedom minority
power race rights science striving

Rhetorical concepts: anecdote autobiography explanation
illustration induction narrative/example process
research report

1. Levi-Montalcini, a Jew, was persecuted by the Nazis during World War II, yet continued to do scientific research even though she could have been killed at any moment. Why did she work so hard, when her effort might have been terminated at any moment?
2. Although Levi-Montalcini was the victim of persecution, nowhere in either "Doing Science in Secret" or anywhere else in her autobiography does she exhibit any trace of self-pity. What qualities emerge in this writer that convey the essence of her personal integrity and values that enable her to triumph over persecution?
3. What does Levi-Montalcini's discussion reveal about the way scientists think about their work? Do their work?

4. Levi-Montalcini's choice of values helps to define the meaning of civilization. Explain.

5. Have you ever done or can you imagine doing any work for which you would be willing to risk your life? Explain what this work is and why it is worth living—and dying—for.

The Ignored Lesson of Anne Frank
BRUNO BETTELHEIM

Two striking influences on Bruno Bettelheim's career were his psychoanalytic education in Vienna (he was born there in 1903), where he earned a Ph.D. from the University of Vienna in 1938, and his imprisonment for a year in Nazi concentration camps in Dachau and Buchenwald. After his release in 1939 he emigrated to the United States, where as a child psychologist at the University of Chicago he developed an international reputation as a specialist in the emotional disorders of childhood, especially autism and juvenile psychosis. In the Orthogenic School, which Bettelheim directed for thirty years, he created a therapeutic environment in which each detail of everyday life was intended to be the exact opposite of the death camps' systematic dehumanization. He discusses this treatment of emotionally disturbed children in *Love Is Not Enough* (1950), *Truants from Life* (1955), and *The Empty Fortress* (1967).

Bettelheim has said that his effort to interpret his experiences in the Nazi camps was the central focus of his career, motivating his research and writing as well as his child therapy; he was the first scholar to detail the Nazis' methods in "Individual and Mass Behavior in Extreme Situations," (1943). Two of his books focus specifically on the lessons of the Holocaust, *The Informed Heart: Autonomy in a Mass Age* (1960) and *Surviving and Other Essays* (1979), which includes "The Ignored Lesson of Anne Frank" (originally published in *Harper's* in 1960). In his view, both psychotic children and the death camp victims are damaged by their tragic adaptations to the "extreme situations" of their existence; they would be better off to resist. Bettelheim was "acclaimed throughout the world," wrote critic William McPherson, because he himself was a survivor who bore witness, "not only to the disintegration of the personality but to the resurgence and resilience of the human spirit." But survival has its price. Bettelheim committed suicide in 1990, shortly after moving from his elegant California mansion to a Maryland retirement home, plagued by ill health and pessimism about the future.

When the world first learned about the Nazi concentration and 1
death camps, most civilized people felt the horrors committed in them to be so uncanny as to be unbelievable. It came as a severe shock that supposedly civilized nations could stoop to such inhuman acts. The implication that modern man has such inadequate control over his

cruel and destructive proclivities was felt as a threat to our views of ourselves and our humanity. Three different psychological mechanisms were most frequently used for dealing with the appalling revelation of what had gone on in the camps:

(1) its applicability to man in general was denied by asserting—contrary to evidence—that the acts of torture and mass murder were committed by a small group of insane or perverted persons;

(2) the truth of the reports was denied by declaring them vastly exaggerated and ascribing them to propaganda (this originated with the German government, which called all reports on terror in the camps "horror propaganda"—*Greuelpropaganda*);

(3) the reports were believed, but the knowledge of the horror repressed as soon as possible.

All three mechanisms could be seen at work after liberation of   2
those prisoners remaining. At first, after the discovery of the camps and their death-dealing, a wave of extreme outrage swept the Allied nations. It was soon followed by a general repression of the discovery in people's minds. Possibly this reaction was due to something more than the blow dealt to modern man's narcissism by the realization that cruelty is still rampant among men. Also present may have been the dim but extremely threatening realization that the modern state now has available the means for changing personality, and for destroying millions it deems undesirable. The ideas that in our day a people's personalities might be changed against their will by the state, and that other populations might be wholly or partially exterminated, are so fearful that one tries to free oneself of them and their impact by defensive denial, or by repression.

The extraordinary world-wide success of the book, play, and   3
movie *The Diary of Anne Frank* suggests the power of the desire to counteract the realization of the personality-destroying and murderous nature of the camps by concentrating all attention on what is experienced as a demonstration that private and intimate life can continue to flourish even under the direct persecution by the most ruthless totalitarian system. And this although Anne Frank's fate demonstrates how efforts at disregarding in private life what goes on around one in society can hasten one's own destruction.

What concerns me here is not what actually happened to the Frank   4
family, how they tried—and failed—to survive their terrible ordeal. It would be very wrong to take apart so humane and moving a story, which aroused so much well-merited compassion for gentle Anne Frank and her tragic fate. What is at issue is the universal and uncritical response to her diary and to the play and movie based on it, and

what this reaction tells about our attempts to cope with the feelings her fate—used by us to serve as a symbol of a most human reaction to Nazi terror—arouses in us. I believe that the world-wide acclaim given her story cannot be explained unless we recognize in it our wish to forget the gas chambers, and our effort to do so by glorifying the ability to retreat into an extremely private, gentle, sensitive world, and there to cling as much as possible to what have been one's usual daily attitudes and activities, although surrounded by a maelstrom apt to engulf one at any moment.

The Frank family's attitude that life could be carried on as before   5
may well have been what led to their destruction. By eulogizing how they lived in their hiding place while neglecting to examine first whether it was a reasonable or an effective choice, we are able to ignore the crucial lesson of their story—that such an attitude can be fatal in extreme circumstances.

While the Franks were making their preparations for going pas-   6
sively into hiding, thousands of other Jews in Holland (as elsewhere in Europe) were trying to escape to the free world, in order to survive and/or fight. Others who could not escape went underground—into hiding—each family member with, for example, a different gentile family. We gather from the diary, however, that the chief desire of the Frank family was to continue living as nearly as possible in the same fashion to which they had been accustomed in happier times.

Little Anne, too, wanted only to go on with life as usual, and   7
what else could she have done but fall in with the pattern her parents created for her existence? But hers was not a necessary fate, much less a heroic one; it was a terrible but also a senseless fate. Anne had a good chance to survive, as did many Jewish children in Holland. But she would have had to leave her parents and go live with a gentile Dutch family, posing as their own child, something her parents would have had to arrange for her.

Everyone who recognized the obvious knew that the hardest way   8
to go underground was to do it as a family; to hide out together made detection by the SS most likely; and when detected, everybody was doomed. By hiding singly, even when one got caught, the others had a chance to survive. The Franks, with their excellent connections among gentile Dutch families, might well have been able to hide out singly, each with a different family. But instead, the main principle of their planning was continuing their beloved family life—an understandable desire, but highly unrealistic in those times. Choosing any other course would have meant not merely giving up living together, but also realizing the full measure of the danger to their lives.

The Franks were unable to accept that going on living as a family   9
as they had done before the Nazi invasion of Holland was no longer

a desirable way of life, much as they loved each other; in fact, for them and others like them, it was most dangerous behavior. But even given their wish not to separate, they failed to make appropriate preparations for what was likely to happen.

There is little doubt that the Franks, who were able to provide 10 themselves with so much while arranging for going into hiding, and even while hiding, could have provided themselves with some weapons had they wished. Had they had a gun, Mr. Frank could have shot down at least one or two of the "green police" who came for them. There was no surplus of such police, and the loss of an SS with every Jew arrested would have noticeably hindered the functioning of the police state. Even a butcher knife, which they certainly could have taken with them into hiding, could have been used by them in self-defense. The fate of the Franks wouldn't have been very different, because they all died anyway except for Anne's father. But they could have sold their lives for a high price, instead of walking to their death. Still, although one must assume that Mr. Frank would have fought courageously, as we know he did when a soldier in the first World War, it is not everybody who can plan to kill those who are bent on killing him, although many who would not be ready to contemplate doing so would be willing to kill those who are bent on murdering not only them but also their wives and little daughters.

An entirely different matter would have been planning for escape 11 in case of discovery. The Franks' hiding place had only one entrance; it did not have any other exit. Despite the fact, during their many months of hiding, they did not try to devise one. Nor did they make other plans for escape, such as that one of the family members—as likely as not Mr. Frank—would try to detain the police in the narrow entrance way—maybe even fight them, as suggested above—thus giving other members of the family a chance to escape, either by reaching the roofs of adjacent houses, or down a ladder into the alley behind the house in which they were living.

Any of this would have required recognizing and accepting the 12 desperate straits in which they found themselves, and concentrating on how best to cope with them. This was quite possible to do, even under the terrible conditions in which the Jews found themselves after the Nazi occupation of Holland. It can be seen from many other accounts, for example from the story of Marga Minco, a girl of about Anne Frank's age who lived to tell about it. Her parents had planned that when the police should come for them, the father would try to detain them by arguing and fighting with them, to give the wife and daughter a chance to escape through a rear door. Unfortunately it did not quite work out this way, and both parents got killed. But their short-lived resistance permitted their daughter to make her escape as planned and to reach a Dutch family who saved her.[1]

This is not mentioned as a criticism that the Frank family did not 13 plan or behave along similar lines. A family has every right to arrange their life as they wish or think best, and to take the risks they want to take. My point is not to criticize what the Franks did, but only the universal admiration of their way of coping, or rather of not coping. The story of little Marga who survived, every bit as touching, remains totally neglected by comparison.

Many Jews—unlike the Franks, who through listening to British 14 radio news were better informed than most—had no detailed knowledge of the extermination camps. Thus is was easier for them to make themselves believe that complete compliance with even the most outrageously debilitating and degrading Nazi orders might offer a chance for survival. But neither tremendous anxiety that inhibits clear thinking and with it well-planned and determined action, nor ignorance about what happened to those who responded with passive waiting for being rounded up for their extermination, can explain the reaction of audiences to the play and movie retelling Anne's story, which are all about such waiting that results finally in destruction.

I think it is the fictitious ending that explains the enormous suc- 15 cess of this play and movie. At the conclusion we hear Anne's voice from the beyond, saying, "In spite of everything, I still believe that people are really good at heart." This improbable sentiment is supposedly from a girl who had been starved to death, had watched her sister meet the same fate before she did, knew that her mother had been murdered, and had watched untold thousands of adults and children being killed. This statement is not justified by anything Anne actually told her diary.

Going on with intimate family living, no matter how dangerous 16 it might be to survival, was fatal to all too many during the Nazi regime. And if all men are good, then indeed we can all go on with living our lives as we have been accustomed to in times of undisturbed safety and can afford to forget about Auschwitz. But Anne, her sister, her mother, may well have died because her parents could not get themselves to believe in Auschwitz.

While play and movie are ostensibly about Nazi persecution and 17 destruction, in actuality what we watch is the way that, despite this terror, lovable people manage to continue living their satisfying intimate lives with each other. The heroine grows from a child into a young adult as normally as any other girl would, despite the most

---

[1]Marga Minco, *Bitter Herbs* (New York: Oxford University Press), 1960.

abnormal conditions of all other aspects of her existence, and that of her family. Thus the play reassures us that despite the destructiveness of Nazi racism and tyranny in general, it is possible to disregard it in one's private life much of the time, even if one is Jewish.

True, the ending happens just as the Franks and their friends had 18 feared all along: their hiding place is discovered, and they are carried away to their doom. But the fictitious declaration of faith in the goodness of all men which concludes the play falsely reassures us since it impresses on us that in the combat between Nazi terror and continuance of intimate family living the latter wins out, since Anne has the last word. This is simply contrary to fact, because it was she who got killed. Her seeming survival through her moving statement about the goodness of men releases us effectively of the need to cope with the problems Auschwitz presents. That is why we are so relieved by her statement. It explains why millions loved play and movie, because while it confronts us with the fact that Auschwitz existed it encourages us at the same time to ignore any of its implications. If all men are good at heart, there never really was an Auschwitz; nor is there any possibility that it may recur.

The desire of Anne Frank's parents not to interrupt their intimate 19 family living, and their inability to plan more effectively for their survival, reflect the failure of all too many others faced with the threat of Nazi terror. It is a failure that deserves close examination because of the inherent warnings it contains for us, the living.

Submission to the threatening power of the Nazi state often led 20 both to the disintegration of what had once seemed well-integrated personalities and to a return to an immature disregard for the dangers of reality. Those Jews who submitted passively to Nazi persecution came to depend on primitive and infantile thought processes: wishful thinking and disregard for the possibility of death. Many persuaded themselves that they, out of all the others, would be spared. Many more simply disbelieved in the possibility of their own death. Not believing in it, they did not take what seemed to them desperate precautions, such as giving up everything to hide out singly; or trying to escape even if it meant risking their lives in doing so; or preparing to fight for their lives when no escape was possible and death had become an immediate possibility. It is true that defending their lives in active combat before they were rounded up to be transported into the camps might have hastened their deaths, and so, up to a point, they were protecting themselves by "rolling with the punches" of the enemy.

But the longer one rolls with the punches dealt not by the normal 21 vagaries of life, but by one's eventual executioner, the more likely it

becomes that one will no longer have the strength to resist when
death becomes imminent. This is particularly true if yielding to the
enemy is accompanied not by a commensurate strengthening of the
personality, but by an inner disintegration. We can observe such a
process among the Franks, who bickered with each other over trifles,
instead of supporting each other's ability to resist the demoralizing
impact of their living conditions.

Those who faced up to the announced intentions of the Nazis   22
prepared for the worst as a real and imminent possibility. It meant
risking one's life for a self-chosen purpose, but in doing so, creating
at least a small chance for saving one's own life or those of others,
or both. When Jews in Germany were restricted to their homes, those
who did not succumb to inertia took the new restrictions as a warning
that it was high time to go underground, join the resistance movement, provide themselves with forged papers, and so on; if they had
not done so long ago. Many of them survived.

Some distant relatives of mine may furnish an example. Early in   23
the war, a young man living in a small Hungarian town banded together with a number of other Jews to prepare against a German
invasion. As soon as the Nazis imposed curfews on the Jews, his
group left for Budapest—because the bigger capital city with its
greater anonymity offered chances for escaping detection. Similar
groups from other towns converged in Budapest and joined forces.
From among themselves they selected typically "Aryan" looking men
who equipped themselves with false papers and immediately joined
the Hungarian SS. These spies were then able to warn of impending
persecution and raids.

Many of these groups survived intact. Furthermore, they had also   24
equipped themselves with small arms, so that if they were detected,
they could put up enough of a fight for the majority to escape while
a few would die fighting to make the escape possible. A few of
the Jews who had joined the SS were discovered and immediately
shot, probably a death preferable to one in the gas chambers. But
most of even these Jews survived, hiding within the SS until liberation.

Compare these arrangements not just to the Franks' selection of   25
a hiding place that was basically a trap without an outlet but with
Mr. Frank's teaching typically academic high-school subjects to his
children rather than how to make a getaway: a token of his inability
to face the seriousness of the threat of death. Teaching high-school
subjects had, of course, its constructive aspects. It relieved the ever-
present anxiety about their fate to some degree by concentrating on
different matters, and by implication it encouraged hope for a future

in which such knowledge would be useful. In this sense such teaching was purposeful, but it was erroneous in that it took the place of much more pertinent teaching and planning: how best to try to escape when detected.

Unfortunately the Franks were by no means the only ones who, 26 out of anxiety, became unable to contemplate their true situation and with it to plan accordingly. Anxiety, and the wish to counteract it by clinging to each other, and to reduce its sting by continuing as much as possible with their usual way of life incapacitated many, particularly when survival plans required changing radically old ways of living that they cherished, and which had become their only source of satisfaction.

My young relative, for example, was unable to persuade other 27 members of his family to go with him when he left the small town where he had lived with them. Three times, at tremendous risk to himself, he returned to plead with his relatives, pointing out first the growing persecution of the Jews, and later the fact that transport to the gas chambers had already begun. He could not convince these Jews to leave their homes and break up their families to go singly into hiding.

As their desperation mounted, they clung more determinedly to 28 their old living arrangements and to each other, became less able to consider giving up the possessions they had accumulated through hard work over a lifetime. The more severely their freedom to act was reduced, and what little they were still permitted to do restricted by insensible and degrading regulations imposed by the Nazis, the more did they become unable to contemplate independent action. Their life energies drained out of them, sapped by their ever-greater anxiety. The less they found strength in themselves, the more they held on to the little that was left of what had given them security in the past—their old surroundings, their customary way of life, their possessions—all these seemed to give their lives some permanency, offer some symbols of security. Only what had once been symbols of security now endangered life, since they were excuses for avoiding change. On each successive visit the young man found his relatives more incapacitated, less willing or able to take his advice, more frozen into inactivity, and with it further along the way to the crematoria where, in fact, they all died.

Levin renders a detailed account of the desperate but fruitless 29 efforts made by small Jewish groups determined to survive to try to save the rest. She tells how messengers were "sent into the provinces to warn Jews that deportation meant death, but their warnings were ignored because most Jews refused to contemplate their own annihilation."[2] I believe the reason for such refusal has to be found in their inability to take action. If we are certain that we are helpless to protect ourselves against the danger of destruction, we cannot contemplate it. We can consider the danger only as long as we believe there are ways to protect ourselves, to fight back, to escape. If we are convinced none of this is possible for us, then there is no point in thinking about the danger; on the contrary, it is best to refuse to do so.

As a prisoner in Buchenwald, I talked to hundreds of German 30 Jewish prisoners who were brought there as part of the huge pogrom in the wake of the murder of vom Rath in the fall of 1938. I asked them why they had not left Germany, given the utterly degrading conditions they had been subjected to. Their answer was: How could we leave? It would have meant giving up our homes, our work, our sources of income. Having been deprived by Nazi persecution and degradation of much of their self-respect, they had become unable to give up what still gave them a semblance of it: their earthly belongings. But instead of using possessions, they became captivated by them, and this possession by earthly goods became the fatal mask for their possession by anxiety, fear, and denial.

How the investment of personal property with one's life energy 31 could make people die bit by bit was illustrated throughout the Nazi persecution of the Jews. At the time of the first boycott of Jewish stores, the chief external goal of the Nazis was to acquire the possessions of the Jews. They even let Jews take some things out of the country at that time if they would leave the bulk of their property behind. For a long time the intention of the Nazis, and the goal of their first discriminatory laws, was to force undesirable minorities, including Jews, into emigration.

Although the extermination policy was in line with the inner logic 32 of Nazi racial ideology, one may wonder whether the idea that millions of Jews (and other foreign nationals) could be submitted to extermination did not partially result from seeing the degree of degradation Jews accepted without fighting back. When no violent resistance occurred, persecution of the Jews worsened, slow step by slow step.

Many Jews who on the invasion of Poland were able to survey 33 their situation and draw the right conclusions survived the Second World War. As the Germans approached, they left everything behind and fled to Russia, much as they distrusted and disliked the Soviet system. But there, while badly treated, they could at least survive. Those who stayed on in Poland believing they could go on with life-

[2]Nora Levin, *The Holocaust* (New York: Thomas Y. Crowell, 1968).

as-before sealed their fate. Thus in the deepest sense the walk to the gas chamber was only the last consequence of these Jews' inability to comprehend what was in store; it was the final step of surrender to the death instinct, which might also be called the principle of inertia. The first step was taken long before arrival at the death camp.

We can find a dramatic demonstration of how far the surrender 34 to inertia can be carried, and the wish not to know because knowing would create unbearable anxiety, in an experience of Olga Lengyel.[3] She reports that although she and her fellow prisoners lived just a few hundred yards from the crematoria and the gas chambers and knew what they were for, most prisoners denied knowledge of them for months. If they had grasped their true situation, it might have helped them save either the lives they themselves were fated to lose, or the lives of others.

When Mrs. Lengyel's fellow prisoners were selected to be sent to 35 the gas chambers, they did not try to break away from the group, as she successfully did. Worse, the first time she tried to escape the gas chambers, some of the other selected prisoners told the supervisors that she was trying to get away. Mrs. Lengyel desperately asks the question: How was it possible that people denied the existence of the gas chambers when all day long they saw the crematoria burning and smelled the odor of burning flesh? Why did they prefer ignoring the exterminations to fighting for their very own lives? She can offer no explanation, only the observation that they resented anyone who tried to save himself from the common fate, because they lacked enough courage to risk action themselves. I believe they did it because they had given up their will to live and permitted their death tendencies to engulf them. As a result, such prisoners were in the thrall of the murdering SS not only physically but also psychologically, while this was not true for those prisoners who still had a grip on life.

Some prisoners even began to serve their executioners, to help 36 speed the death of their own kind. Then things had progressed beyond simple inertia to the death instinct running rampant. Those who tried to serve their executioners in what were once their civilian capacities were merely continuing life as usual and thereby opening the door to their death.

For example, Mrs. Lengyel speaks of Dr. Mengele, SS physician 37 at Auschwitz, as a typical example of the "business as usual" attitude that enabled some prisoners, and certainly the SS, to retain whatever

---

[3]Olga Lengyel, *Five Chimneys: The Story of Auschwitz* (Chicago: Ziff-Davis, 1947).

balance they could despite what they were doing. She described how Dr. Mengele took all correct medical precautions during childbirth, rigorously observing all aseptic principles, cutting the umbilical cord with greatest care, etc. But only half an hour later he sent mother and infant to be burned in the crematorium.

Having made his choice, Dr. Mengele and others like him had to   38 delude themselves to be able to live with themselves and their experience. Only one personal document on the subject has come to my attention, that of Dr. Nyiszli, a prisoner serving as "research physician" at Auschwitz.[4] How Dr. Nyiszli deluded himself can be seen, for example, in the way he repeatedly refers to himself as working in Auschwitz as a physician, although he worked as the assistant of a criminal murderer. He speaks of the Institute for Race, Biological, and Anthropological Investigation as "one of the most qualified medical centers of the Third Reich," although it was devoted to proving falsehoods. That Nyiszli was a doctor didn't alter the fact that he—like any of the prisoner foremen who served the SS better than some SS were willing to serve it—was a participant in the crimes of the SS. How could he do it and live with himself?

The answer is: by taking pride in his professional skills, irre-   39 spective of the purpose they served. Dr. Nyiszli and Dr. Mengele were only two among hundreds of other—and far more prominent— physicians who participated in the Nazis' murderous pseudo-scientific human experiments. It was the peculiar pride of these men in their professional skill and knowledge, without regard for moral implications, that made them so dangerous. Although the concentration camps and crematoria are no longer here, this kind of pride still remains with us; it is characteristic of a modern society in which fascination with technical competence has dulled concern for human feelings. Auschwitz is gone, but so long as this attitude persists, we shall not be safe from cruel indifference to life at the core.

I have met many Jews as well as gentile anti-Nazis, similar to the   40 activist group in Hungary described earlier, who survived in Nazi Germany and in the occupied countries. These people realized that when a world goes to pieces and inhumanity reigns supreme, man cannot go on living his private life as he was wont to do, and would like to do; he cannot, as the loving head of a family, keep the family living together peacefully, undisturbed by the surrounding world; nor can he continue to take pride in his profession or possessions,

---

[4]Miklos Nyiszli, *Auschwitz: A Doctor's Eyewitness Account* (New York: Frederick Fell, 1960).

when either will deprive him of his humanity, if not also of his life. In such times, one must radically reevaluate all of what one has done, believed in, and stood for in order to know how to act. In short, one has to take a stand on the new reality—a firm stand, not one of retirement into an even more private world.

If today, Negroes of Africa march against the guns of a police that   41 defends *apartheid*—even if hundreds of dissenters are shot down and tens of thousands rounded up in camps—their fight will sooner or later assure them of a chance for liberty and equality. Millions of the Jews of Europe who did not or could not escape in time or go underground as many thousands did, could at least have died fighting as some did in the Warsaw ghetto at the end, instead of passively waiting to be rounded up for their own extermination.

RESPONDING TO READING

Key words: community family freedom growing up
loss minority power race reality rights story

Rhetorical concepts: analysis anecdote biography
cause and effect illustration induction narrative/example

1.   Bettelheim opens his essay by listing three "psychological mechanisms" for dealing with the horror of the Nazi regime. Do you see any signs of those mechanisms in the previous essay by Rita Levi-Montalcini? Do you see signs of them in yourself as you read Bettelheim's analysis of what the Frank family might have done differently? What are the implications of the "inhuman acts" of the Nazis for "our views of ourselves and our humanity"? How do you cope with these implications?
2.   What does Bettelheim say about the relation between the private world (symbolized by the Franks' hiding place) and the public world, and what does he see as the advantages and disadvantages of separating the two? Is your own private life separated from your public life? Is that healthy? Write an essay in which you seek to convince the others in your class of what you see as the appropriate relationship of the private and the public world.
3.   Do you agree that the Franks ought not to have chosen the maintenance of "their beloved family life" as the highest value? How do you respond to Bettelheim's rejection of "the universal admiration of their way of coping, or rather of not coping"? Do you agree that the optimistic last words of Anne Frank in the play "falsely reassure us"?
4.   Select either a personal experience, a fictional world, or a historical one (aside from the holocaust Bettelheim and Levi-Montalcini write about) in which "a world goes to pieces." To what degree did people attempt to maintain normal experience under abnormal circumstances and what was the result?

Distancing the Homeless

JONATHAN KOZOL

Jonathan Kozol brings the methods of an investigative reporter, the zeal of a social reformer, and the compassion of a moralist to his analysis of our nation's social ills. During the course of his career as a critic of American schools and, by extension, society in general, Kozol (born 1936) has retained a lifelong anger with inadequate public policy, indifferent bureaucracy, insufficient humaneness. But anger is not enough. Typical of Kozol's method and approach to his subject is *Rachel and Her Children: Homeless Families in America* (1988), from which he adapted "Distancing the Homeless" for the *Yale Review* (Winter 1988). Kozol writes to arouse his readers, comfortable, educated, well-fed, to action by putting them where the subject is in order to demonstrate what it is like to be illiterate, undereducated, or poor. Through interviews and visits to scenes of misery and deprivation, Kozol gives statistics a human face, quotations a human voice.

Kozol's first critique of American education, *Death at an Early Age: The Destruction of the Hearts and Minds of Negro Children in the Boston Public Schools* (1967) won the National Book Award. Written during the civil rights and school desegregation movements of the 1960s, this book documents the repressive teaching methods designed, Kozol claimed, to keep the children separate but unequal. Kozol, himself a Harvard graduate (1958), Rhodes Scholar, and recipient of numerous prestigious fellowships, transcends his elitist background in focusing on minorities and the poor. Even his book on middle-class education, *The Night Is Dark and I Am Far from Home* (1975), claims that schools mirror larger social inequities, educating the more affluent at the expense of the poor. *Illiterate America* (1985) analyzes the nature, causes, and effects of illiteracy that denies sixty million people meaningful participation in American society. Kozol's most recent book, *Savage Inequalities: Children in America's Schools* (1991), reinforces his humanitarian concerns.

It is commonly believed by many journalists and politicians that the homeless of America are, in large part, former patients of large mental hospitals who were deinstitutionalized in the 1970s—the consequence, it is sometimes said, of misguided liberal opinion, which favored the treatment of such persons in community-based centers. It is argued that this policy, and the subsequent failure of society to build such centers or to provide them in sufficient number, is the primary cause of homelessness in the United States.

Those who work among the homeless do not find that explanation satisfactory. While conceding that a certain number of the homeless are, or have been, mentally unwell, they believe that, in the case of most unsheltered people, the primary reason is economic rather than clinical. The cause of homelessness, they say with disarming logic, is the lack of homes and of income with which to rent or acquire them.

They point to the loss of traditional jobs in industry (two million 3 every year since 1980) and to the fact that half of those who are laid off end up in work that pays a poverty-level wage. They point to the parallel growth of poverty in families with children, noting that children, who represent one quarter of our population, make up forty percent of the poor: since 1968, the number of children in poverty has grown by three million, while welfare benefits to families with children have declined by thirty-five percent.

And they note, too, that these developments have coincided with 4 a time in which the shortage of low-income housing has intensified as the gentrification of our major cities has accelerated. Half a million units of low-income housing have been lost each year to condominium conversion as well as to arson, demolition, or abandonment. Between 1978 and 1980, median rents climbed thirty percent for people in the lowest income sector, driving many of these families into the streets. After 1980, rents rose at even faster rates. In Boston, between 1982 and 1984, over eighty percent of the housing units renting below three hundred dollars disappeared, while the number of units renting above six hundred dollars nearly tripled.

Hard numbers, in this instance, would appear to be of greater 5 help than psychiatric labels in telling us why so many people become homeless. Eight million American families now pay half or more of their income for rent or a mortgage. Six million more, unable to pay rent at all, live doubled up with others. At the same time, federal support for low-income housing dropped from $30 billion (1980) to $9 billion (1986). Under Presidents Ford and Carter, five hundred thousand subsidized private housing units were constructed. By President Reagan's second term, the number had dropped to twenty-five thousand. "We're getting out of the housing business, period," said a deputy assistant secretary of the Department of Housing and Urban Development in 1985.

One year later, the *Washington Post* reported that the number of 6 homeless families in Washington, D.C., had grown by five hundred percent over the previous twelve months. In New York City, the waiting list for public housing now contains two hundred thousand names. The waiting is eighteen years.

Why, in the face of these statistics, are we impelled to find a 7 psychiatric explanation for the growth of homelessness in the United States?

A misconception, once it is implanted in the popular imagination, 8 is not easy to uproot, particularly when it serves a useful social role. The notion that the homeless are largely psychotics who belong in institutions, rather than victims of displacement at the hands of enterprising realtors, spares us from the need to offer realistic solutions to the fact of deep and widening extremes of wealth and poverty in the United States. It also enables us to tell ourselves that the despair of homeless people bears no intimate connection to the privileged existence we enjoy—when, for example, we rent or purchase one of those restored townhouses that once provided shelter for people now huddled in the street.

But there may be another reason to assign labels to the destitute.   9
Terming economic victims "psychotic" or "disordered" helps to place them at a distance. It says that they aren't quite like us—and, more important, that we could not be like them. The plight of homeless families is a nightmare. It may not seem natural to try to banish human beings from our midst, but it *is* natural to try to banish nightmares from our minds.

So the rituals of clinical contamination proceed uninterrupted by   10
the economic facts described above. Research that addresses homelessness as an *injustice* rather than as a medical *misfortune* does not win the funding of foundations. And the research which *is* funded, defining the narrowed borders of permissible debate, diverts our attention from the antecedent to the secondary cause of homelessness. Thus it is that perfectly ordinary women whom I know in New York City—people whose depression or anxiety is a realistic consequence of months and even years in crowded shelters or the streets—are interrogated by invasive research scholars in an effort to decode their poverty, to find clinical categories for their despair and terror, to identify the secret failing that lies hidden in their psyche.

Many pregnant women without homes are denied prenatal care   11
because they constantly travel from one shelter to another. Many are anemic. Many are denied essential dietary supplements by recent federal cuts. As a consequence, some of their children do not live to see their second year of life. Do these mothers sometimes show signs of stress? Do they appear disorganized, depressed, disordered? Frequently. They are immobilized by pain, traumatized by fear. So it is no surprise that when researchers enter the scene to ask them how they "feel," the resulting reports tell us that the homeless are emotionally unwell. The reports do not tell us we have *made* these people ill. They do not tell us that illness is a natural response to intolerable conditions. Nor do they tell us of the strength and the resilience that so many of these people still retain despite the miseries they must endure. They set these men and women apart in capsules labeled "personality disorder" or "psychotic," where they no longer threaten our complacence.

I visited Haiti not many years ago, when the Duvalier family was   12 still in power. If an American scholar were to have made a psychological study of the homeless families living in the streets of Port-au-Prince—sleeping amidst rotten garbage, bathing in open sewers—and if he were to return to the United States to tell us that the reasons for their destitution were "behavioral problems" or "a lack of mental health," we would be properly suspicious. Knowledgeable Haitians would not merely be suspicious. They would be enraged. Even to initiate such research when economic and political explanations present themselves so starkly would appear grotesque. It is no less so in the United States.

One of the more influential studies of this nature was carried out 13
in 1985 by Ellen Bassuk, a psychiatrist at Harvard University. Drawing upon interviews with eight homeless parents, Dr. Bassuk contends, according to the *Boston Globe*, that "90 percent [of these people] have problems other than housing and poverty that are so acute they would be unable to live successfully on their own." She also precludes the possibility that illness, where it does exist, may be provoked by destitution. "Our data," she writes, "suggest that mental illness tends to precede homelessness." She concedes that living in the streets can make a homeless person's mental illness worse; but she insists upon the fact of prior illness.

The Executive Director of the Massachusetts Commission on Chil- 14
dren and Youth believes that Dr. Bassuk's estimate is far too high. The staff of Massachusetts Human Services Secretary Phillip Johnston believes the appropriate number is closer to ten percent.

In defending her research, Bassuk challenges such critics by claim- 15
ing that they do not have data to refute her. This may be true. Advocates for the homeless do not receive funds to defend the sanity of the people they represent. In placing the burden of proof upon them, Dr. Bassuk has created an extraordinary dialectic: how does one prove that people aren't unwell? What homeless mother would consent to enter a procedure that might "prove" her mental health? What overburdened shelter operator would divert scarce funds to such an exercise? It is an unnatural, offensive, and dehumanizing challenge.

Dr. Bassuk's work, however, isn't the issue I want to raise here; 16
the issue is the use or misuse of that work by critics of the poor. For example, in a widely syndicated essay published in 1986, the newspaper columnist Charles Krauthammer argued that the homeless are essentially a deranged segment of the population and that we must find the "political will" to isolate them from society. We must do this, he said, "whether they like it or not." Arguing even against the marginal benefits of homeless shelters, Krauthammer wrote: "There is a

better alternative, however, though no one dares speak its name."
Krauthammer dares: that better alternative, he said, is "asylum."

One of Mr. Krauthammer's colleagues at the *Washington Post*, the 17
columnist George Will, perceives the homeless as a threat to public
cleanliness and argues that they ought to be consigned to places where
we need not see them. "It is," he says, "simply a matter of public
hygiene" to put them out of sight. Another journalist, Charles Murray,
writing from the vantage point of a social Darwinist, recommends
the restoration of the almshouses of the 1800s. "Granted Dickensian
horror stories about almshouses"; he begins, there were nonetheless
"good almshouses"; he proposes "a good correctional 'halfway
house' " as a proper shelter for a mother and child with no means
of self-support.

In the face of such declarations, the voices of those who work 18
with and know the poor are harder to hear.

Manhattan Borough President David Dinkins made the following 19
observation on the basis of a study commissioned in 1986: "No facts
support the belief that addiction or behavioral problems occur with
more frequency in the homeless family population than in a similar
socioeconomic population. Homeless families are not demographi-
cally different from other public assistance families when they enter
the shelter system. . . . Family homelessness is typically a housing
and income problem: the unavailability of affordable housing and the
inadequacy of public assistance income."

In a "hypothetical world," write James Wright and Julie Lam of 20
the University of Massachusetts, "where there were no alcoholics, no
drug addicts, no mentally ill, no deinstitutionalization, . . . indeed,
no personal social pathologies at all, there would still be a formidable homelessness problem, simply because at this stage in American
history, there is not enough low-income housing" to accomodate
the poor.

New York State's respected Commissioner of Social Services, 21
Cesar Perales, makes the point in fewer words: "Homelessness is less
and less a result of personal failure, and more and more is caused by
larger forces. There is no longer affordable housing in New York City
for people of poor and modest means."

Even the words of medical practitioners who care for homeless 22
people have been curiously ignored. A study published by the Massachusetts Medical Society, for instance, has noted that the most frequent illnesses among a sample of the homeless population, after
alcohol and drug use, are trauma (31 percent), upper respiratory
disorders (28 percent), limb disorders (19 percent), mental illness (16
percent), skin diseases (15 percent), hypertension (14 percent), and

neurological illnesses (12 percent). (Excluded from this tabulation are lead poisoning, malnutrition, acute diarrhea, and other illnesses especially common among homeless infants and small children.) Why, we may ask, of all these calamities, does mental illness command so much political and press attention? The answer may be that the label of mental illness places the destitute outside the sphere of ordinary life. It personalizes an anguish that is public in its genesis; it individualizes a misery that is both general in cause and general in application.

The rate of tuberculosis among the homeless is believed to be ten 23 times that of the general population. Asthma, I have learned in countless interviews, is one of the most common causes of discomfort in the shelters. Compulsive smoking, exacerbated by the crowding and the tension, is more common in the shelters than in any place that I have visited except prison. Infected and untreated sores, scabies, diarrhea, poorly set limbs, protruding elbows, awkwardly distorted wrists, bleeding gums, impacted teeth, and other untreated dental problems are so common among children in the shelters that one rapidly forgets their presence. Hunger and emaciation are everywhere. Children as well as adults can bring to mind the photographs of people found in camps for refugees of war in 1945. But these miseries bear no stigma, and mental illness does. It conveys a stigma in the Soviet Union. It conveys a stigma in the United States. In both nations the label is used, whether as a matter of deliberate policy or not, to isolate and treat as special cases those who, by deed or word or by sheer presence, represent a threat to national complacence. The two situations are obviously not identical, but they are enough alike to give Americans reason for concern.

Last summer, some twenty-eight thousand homeless people were 24 afforded shelter by the city of New York. Of this number, twelve thousand were children and six thousand were parents living together in families. The average child was six years old, the average parent twenty-seven. A typical homeless family included a mother with two or three children, but in about one-fifth of these families two parents were present. Roughly ten thousand single persons, then, made up the remainder of the population of the city's shelters.

These proportions vary somewhat from one area of the nation to 25 another. In all areas, however, families are the fastest-growing sector of the homeless population, and in the Northeast they are by far the largest sector already. In Massachusetts, three-fourths of the homeless now are families with children; in certain parts of Massachusetts— Attleboro and Northhampton, for example—the proportion reaches ninety percent. Two-thirds of the homeless children studied recently in Boston were less than five years old.

Of an estimated two or three million homeless people nationwide, 26 about 500,000 are dependent children, according to Robert Hayes, counsel to the National Coalition for the Homeless. Including their parents, at least 750,000 homeless people in America are family members.

What is to be made, then, of the supposition that the homeless 27 are primarily the former residents of mental hospitals, persons who were carelessly released during the 1970s? Many of them are, to be sure. Among the older men and women in the streets and shelters, as many as one-third (some believe as many as one-half) may be chronically disturbed, and a number of these people were deinstitutionalized during the 1970s. But in a city like New York, where nearly half the homeless are small children with an average age of six, to operate on the basis of such a supposition makes no sense. Their parents, with an average age of twenty-seven, are not likely to have been hospitalized in the 1970s, either.

Nor is it easy to assume, as was once the case, that single men— 28 those who come closer to fitting the stereotype of the homeless vagrant, the drifting alcoholic of an earlier age—are the former residents of mental hospitals. The age of homeless men has dropped in recent years; many of them are only twenty-one to twenty-eight years old. Fifty percent of homeless men in New York City shelters in 1984 were there for the first time. Most had previously had homes and jobs. Many had never before needed public aid.

A frequently cited set of figures tells us that in 1955, the average 29 daily census of nonfederal psychiatric institutions was 677,000, and that by 1984, the number had dropped to 151,000. Subtract the second number from the first, conventional logic tells us, and we have an explanation for the homelessness of half a million people. A closer look at the same number offers us a different lesson.

The sharpest decline in the average daily census of these insti- 30 tutions occurred prior to 1978, and the largest part of that decline, in fact, appeared at least a decade earlier. From 677,000 in 1955, the census dropped to 378,000 in 1972. The 1974 census was 307,000. In 1976 it was 230,000; in 1977 it was 211,000; and in 1978 it was 190,000. In no year since 1978 has the average daily census dropped by more than 9,000 persons, and in the six-year period from 1978 to 1984, the total decline was 39,000 persons. Compared with a decline of 300,000 from 1955 to 1972, and of nearly 200,000 more from 1972 to 1978, the number is small. But the years since 1980 are the period in which the present homeless crisis surfaced. Only since 1983 have homeless individuals overflowed the shelters.

If the large numbers of the homeless lived in hospitals before they 31
reappeared in subway stations and in public shelters, we need to ask
where they were and what they had been doing from 1972 to 1980.
Were they living under bridges? Were they waiting out the decade in
the basements of deserted buildings?

No. The bulk of those who had been psychiatric patients and 32
were released from hospitals during the 1960s and early 1970s had
been living in the meantime in low-income housing, many in skid-
row hotels or boarding houses. Such housing—commonly known as
SRO (single-room occupancy) units—was drastically diminished by
the gentrification of our cities that began in 1970. Almost fifty percent
of SRO housing was replaced by luxury apartments or by office buildings between 1970 and 1980, and the remaining units have been dis-
appearing at even faster rates. As recently as 1986, after New York
City had issued a prohibition against conversion of such housing, a
well-known developer hired a demolition team to destroy a building
in Times Square that had previously been home to indigent people.
The demolition took place in the middle of the night. In order to avoid
imprisonment, the developer was allowed to make a philanthropic
gift to homeless people as a token of atonement. This incident, bizarre
as it appears, reminds us that the profit motive for displacement of
the poor is very great in every major city. It also indicates a more
realistic explanation for the growth of homelessness during the 1980s.

Even for those persons who are ill and were deinstitutionalized 33
during the decades before 1980, the precipitating cause of homelessness in 1987 is not illness but loss of housing. SRO housing, unattractive as it may have been, offered low-cost sanctuaries for the
homeless, providing a degree of safety and mutual support for those
who lived within them. They were a demeaning version of the community health centers that society had promised; they were the de
facto "halfway houses" of the 1970s. For these people too, then—at
most half of the homeless single persons in America—the cause of
homelessness is lack of housing.

A writer in the *New York Times* describes a homeless woman 34
standing on a traffic island in Manhattan. "She was evicted from her
small room in the hotel just across the street," and she is determined
to get revenge. Until she does, "nothing will move her from that
spot. . . . Her argumentativeness and her angry fixation on revenge,
along with the apparent absence of hallucinations, mark her as a
paranoid." Most physicians, I imagine, would be more reserved in
passing judgment with so little evidence, but this author makes his
diagnosis without hesitation. "The paranoids of the street," he says,
"are among the most difficult to help."

Perhaps so. But does it depend on who is offering the help? Is 35 anyone offering to help this woman get back her home? Is it crazy to seek vengeance for being thrown into the street? The absence of anger, some psychiatrists believe, might indicate much greater illness.

The same observer sees additional symptoms of pathology ("neg- 36 ative symptoms," he calls them) in the fact that many homeless persons demonstrate a "gross deterioration in their personal hygiene" and grooming, leading to "indifference" and "apathy." Having just identifed one woman as unhealthy because she is so far from being "indifferent" as to seek revenge, he now sees apathy as evidence of illness; so consistency is not what we are looking for in this account. But how much less indifferent might the homeless be if those who decide their fate were less indifferent themselves? How might their grooming and hygiene be improved if they were permitted access to a public toilet?

In New York City, as in many cities, homeless people are denied 37 the right to wash in public bathrooms, to store their few belongings in a public locker, or, in certain cases, to make use of public toilets altogether. Shaving, cleaning of clothes, and other forms of hygiene are prohibited in the men's room of Grand Central Station. The terminal's three hundred lockers, used in former times by homeless people to secure their goods, were removed in 1986 as "a threat to public safety," according to a study made by the New York City Council.

At one-thirty every morning, homeless people are ejected from 38 the station. Many once attempted to take refuge on the ramp that leads to Forty-second Street because it was protected from the street by wooden doors and thus provided some degree of warmth. But the station management responded to this challenge in two ways. The ramp was mopped with a strong mixture of ammonia to produce a noxious smell, and when the people sleeping there brought cardboard boxes and newspapers to protect them from the fumes, the entrance doors were chained wide open. Temperatures dropped some nights to ten degrees. Having driven these people to the streets, city officials subsequently determined that their willingness to risk exposure to cold weather could be taken as further evidence of mental illness.

At Pennsylvania Station in New York, homeless women are denied 39 the use of toilets. Amtrak police come by and herd them off each hour on the hour. In June 1985, Amtrak officials issued this directive to police: "It is the policy of Amtrak to not allow the homeless and undesirables to remain. . . . Officers are encouraged to eject all undesirables. . . . Now is the time to train and educate them that their presence will not be tolerated as cold weather sets in." In an internal memo, according to CBS, an Amtrak official asked flatly: "Can't we get rid of this trash?"

I have spent many nights in conversation with the women who 40
are huddled in the corridors and near the doorway of the public toilets
in Penn Station. Many are young. Most are cogent. Few are dressed
in the familiar rags suggested by the term *bag ladies*. Unable to bathe
or use the toilets in the station, almost all are in conditions of intolerable physical distress. The sight of clusters of police officers, mostly
male, guarding a toilet from use by homeless women speaks volumes
about the public conscience of New York.

Where do these women defecate? How do they bathe? What will 41
we do when, in her physical distress, a woman finally disrobes in
public and begins to urinate right on the floor? "Gross deterioration,"
someone will call it, evidence of mental illness. In the course of an
impromptu survey in the streets last September, Mayor Koch observed
a homeless woman who had soiled her own clothes. Not only was
the woman crazy, said the mayor, but those who differed with him
on his diagnosis must be crazy, too. "I am the Number One social
worker in this town—with sanity," said he.

It may be that this woman was psychotic, but the mayor's com- 42
ment says a great deal more about his sense of revulsion and the
moral climate of a decade in which words like these may be applauded
than about her mental state.

A young man who had lost his job, then his family, then his 43
home, all in the summer of 1986, spoke with me for several hours in
Grand Central Station on the weekend following Thanksgiving. "A
year ago," he said, "I never thought that somebody like me would end
up in a shelter. Nothing you've ever undergone prepares you. You
walk into the place [a shelter on the Bowery]—the smell of sweat and
urine hits you like a wall. Unwashed bodies and the look of absolute
despair on many, many faces there would make you think you were
in Dante's Hell. . . . What you fear is that you will be here forever.
You do not know if it is ever going to end. You think to yourself: it
is a dream and I will awake. Sometimes I think: it's an experiment.
They are watching you to find out how much you can take. . . . I was
a pretty stable man. Now I tremble when I meet somebody in the
ordinary world. I'm trembling right now. . . . For me, the loss of work
and loss of wife had left me rocking. Then the welfare regulations hit
me. I began to feel that I would be reduced to trash. . . . Half the
people that I know are suffering from chest infections and sleep deprivation. The lack of sleep leaves you debilitated, shaky. You exaggerate your fears. If a psychiatrist came along he'd say that I was
crazy. But I was an ordinary man. There was nothing wrong with
me. I lost my kids. I lost my home. Now would you say that I was
crazy if I told you I was feeling sad?"

If the plight of homeless adults is the shame of America," writes 44
Fred Hechinger in the *New York Times*, "the lives of homeless children
are the nation's crime."

In November 1984, a fact already known to advocates for the 45
homeless was given brief attention by the press. Homeless families,
the *New York Times* reported, "mostly mothers and young children,
have been sleeping on chairs, counters, and floors of the city's emergency welfare offices." Reacting to such reports, the mayor declared:
"The woman is sitting on a chair or on a floor. It is not because we
didn't offer her a bed. We provide a shelter for every single person
who knocks on our door." On the same day, however, the city reported that in the previous eleven weeks it had been unable to give
shelter to 153 families, and in the subsequent year, 1985, the city later
reported that about two thousand children slept in welfare offices
because of lack of shelter space.

Some eight hundred homeless infants in New York City, reported 46
the National Coalition for the Homeless, "routinely go without sufficient food, cribs, health care, and diapers." The lives of these children "are put at risk," while "high-risk pregnant women" are
repeatedly forced to sleep in unsafe "barracks shelters" or welfare
offices called Emergency Assistance Units (EAUs) . "Coalition monitors, making sporadic random checks, found eight women in their
ninth month of pregnancy sleeping in EAUs. . . . Two women denied
shelter began having labor contractions at the EAU." In one instance,
the Legal Aid Society was forced to go to court after a woman lost
her child by miscarriage while lying on the floor of a communal
bathroom in a shelter which the courts had already declared unfit to
house pregnant women.

The coalition also reported numerous cases in which homeless 47
mothers were obliged to choose between purchasing food or diapers
for their infants. Federal guidelines issued in 1986 deepened the nutrition crisis faced by mothers in the welfare shelters by counting the
high rent paid to the owners of the buildings as a part of family
income, rendering their residents ineligible for food stamps. Families
I interviewed who had received as much as $150 in food stamps
monthly in June 1986 were cut back to $33 before Christmas.

"Now you're hearing all kinds of horror stories," said President 48
Reagan, "about the people that are going to be thrown out in the
snow to hunger and [to] die of cold and so forth. . . . We haven't cut
a single budget." But in the four years leading up to 1985, according
to the *New Republic*, Aid to Families with Dependent Children had

been cut by $4.8 billion, child nutrition programs by $5.2 billion, food stamps by $6.8 billion. The federal government's authority to help low-income families with housing assistance was cut from $30 billion to $11 billion in Reagan's first term. In his fiscal 1986 budget, the president proposed to cut that by an additional ninety-five percent.

"If even one American child is forced to go to bed hungry at 49 night," the president said on another occasion, "that is a national tragedy. We are too generous a people to allow this." But in the years since the president spoke these words, thousands of poor children in New York alone have gone to bed too sick to sleep and far too weak to rise the next morning to attend a public school. Thousands more have been unable to attend school at all because their homeless status compels them to move repeatedly from one temporary shelter to another. Even in the affluent suburbs outside New York City, hundreds of homeless children are obliged to ride as far as sixty miles twice a day in order to obtain an education in the public schools to which they were originally assigned before their families were displaced. Many of these children get to school too late to eat their breakfast; others are denied lunch at school because of federal cuts in feeding programs.

Many homeless children die—and others suffer brain damage— 50 as a direct consequence of federal cutbacks in prenatal programs, maternal nutrition, and other feeding programs. The parents of one such child shared with me the story of the year in which their child was delivered, lived, and died. The child, weighing just over four pounds at birth, grew deaf and blind soon after, and for these reasons had to stay in the hospital for several months. When he was released on Christmas Eve of 1984, his mother and father had no home. He lived with his parents in the shelters, subways, streets, and welfare offices of New York City for four winter months, and was readmitted to the hospital in time to die in May 1985.

When we met and spoke the following year, the father told me 51 that his wife had contemplated and even attempted suicide after the child's death while he had entertained the thought of blowing up the welfare offices of New York City. I would tell him that to do so would be illegal and unwise. I would never tell him it was crazy.

"No one will be turned away," says the mayor of New York City, 52 as hundreds of young mothers with their infants are turned from the doors of shelters season after season. That may sound to some like denial of reality. "Now you're hearing all these stories," says the President of the United States as he denies that anyone is cold or hungry or unhoused. On another occasion he says that the unsheltered "are homeless, you might say, by choice." That sounds every bit as self-deceiving.

The woman standing on the traffic island screaming for revenge 53
until her room has been restored to her sounds relatively healthy by
comparison. If three million homeless people did the same, and all
at the same time, we might finally be forced to listen.

RESPONDING TO READING

Key words: class   community   family   freedom   identity
loss   minority   power   reality   rights   striving   talk

Rhetorical concepts: analogy   analysis   anecdote
cause and effect   explanation   illustration   narrative/example   process
research report

1.   What are the causes of homelessness, in Kozol's view?
2.   Why, in Kozol's view, is homelessness a matter of public policy rather
than individual failure, both in its causes and its solutions?
3.   What techniques does Kozol use to make the homeless less "distant," to
humanize the homeless and give statistics and abstractions a human face?
Since his intended readers are, presumably, neither poor nor homeless, on
what grounds does he expect them to identify with the subject? What do
Kozol's readers have in common with the homeless?
4.   What effects does Kozol intend "Distancing the Homeless" to have on
his readers? What does he expect them to do to relieve the plight of individuals? To change social policy?
5.   Write an essay in which you identify a social problem; humanize it
through interviews, portraits, illustrations of its context; and propose a solution that will engage your readers.

Sex Without Love
SHARON OLDS

Rarely is a poet in today's culture able to devote her life primarily
to her art, but Sharon Olds (born 1946) has been able to do so. She
earned a B.A. from Stanford in 1964, and a Ph.D. from Columbia in
1972. Her widely published poetry has been collected in three books,
Satan Says (1980); *The Dead and the Living* (1984); and *The Gold Cell*
(1990). She teaches poetry workshops at New York and Columbia
universities and at Goldwater Hospital.

Olds's poetry transcends the autobiographical by transforming
what appear to be private revelations into universal truths about sex,
death, terror, and love. Many of her earlier poems focused with
grimness, or, as in "Sex Without Love," with grim humor, on the
phenomenon of "the single body alone in/the universe against its
own best time." More recently her poetry has moved from the per-

spective of a child growing up in a troubled family, plagued by
alcoholism, spousal and child abuse, divorce, incest, to the perspective of a wife and mother, to commenting on growing up and
growing old.

How do they do it, the ones who make love
Without love? Beautiful as dancers,
gliding over each other like ice-skaters
over the ice, fingers hooked
inside each other's bodies, faces   5
red as steak, wine, wet as the
children at birth whose mothers are going to
give them away. How do they come to the
come to the come to the God come to the
still waters, and not love   10
the ones who came there with them, light
rising slowly as steam off their joined
skin? These are the true religious,
the purists, the pros, the ones who will not
accept a false Messiah, love the   15
priest instead of the God. They do not
mistake the lover for their own pleasure,
they are like great runners: they know they are alone
with the road surface, the cold, the wind,
the fit of their shoes, their over-all cardio-   20
vascular health—just factors, like the partner
in the bed, and not the truth, which is the single body alone in
the universe against its own best time.

RESPONDING TO READING

Key words: discovery   freedom   gender   identity   loss
reality   striving

Rhetorical concepts: analogy   definition   illustration   metaphor
poetry

1. In the first three lines, the persons in the poem are described first as
dancers, then as ice skaters. List the different metaphors Olds uses for "the
ones who make love without love." What do these metaphors have in common?
2. List the religious references in the poem. Does it bother you to see these
loveless lovers called "the true religious" (what does that mean?) or to hear
that they "will not . . . love the priest instead of the God"? What is the
attitude of the poet towards these self-obsessed individuals, each of whom
is a "single body alone in the universe"? Write an essay showing both the

advantages and disadvantages of "sex without love" as the poem sees it. Do you agree?

3.   What do you owe to yourself and what do you owe to others? In one sense, this poem looks at this complex issue and evaluates those who have come down firmly on their own account. Examine this issue by recounting an incident you have experienced in which this conflict in values was difficult to resolve.

QUESTIONS FOR REFLECTION AND WRITING

How Do We Develop a Sense of Values?

1.   People's values often change as they mature or in other ways gain a different perspective on the world. Identify and define a value (such as friendship, heroism, or self-respect) that you see differently now than you did some years ago. Explain it in an essay that shows its evolution, as does Didion's "On Self-Respect." Or narrate an incident, as in "You Can't Pray a Lie," that shows the value changing in action.

2.   Pick a book influential in your life, such as *The Bible, The Girl Scout Handbook, Zen and the Art of Motorcycle Maintenance, Baby and Child Care*, or any other volume of inspiration or advice. If no such book influenced you, than choose a form of popular art that did: *Nancy Drew*, perhaps, or Heinlein's early science fiction, or even *Mechanics Illustrated*. Analyze some of its salient features, as Paul Fussell does in "The Boy Scout Handbook," to show why it was or remains so influential.

3.   For a term paper, do a formal or informal survey to determine the five most important values of your peer group. Refer to the essays by Bok (for a model of how to define values) and by Didion (for help in assessing their role in human development) as you write your own essay evaluating these values. How sound is the value system that your peer group has developed?

4.   Do you have a value powerful enough to die for, or to live for? Or to "go to hell" for, as Huck Finn did? If you do, define that value, as part of an essay showing how you developed it and why it is so important to you. If you do not have such a value, write an essay explaining why you do not.

What Does Nature Mean?

1.   What does nature mean to you? Is it a specific environment (like Yosemite or the White Mountains) at the present time, or a more general concept? Pick a place (as Silko did), a phenomenon (as Hawking did), a people (Silko), or a species (Hubbell) to focus on and analyze. Include some description of what nature is *not* as part of your definition.

2.   Look ahead to the essays by Rachel Carson, and William Warner in Chapter 5. Each of them is speaking of nature, now a nature threatened and under attack. Compare Silko's and Hubbell's view of nature

with theirs, showing similarities and differences. To what degree have we lost the concept of nature that Hubbell articulates?

3. We use many ways to close nature out of our lives, from the doors and windows of our houses to the TV sets in Winnebago campers. We do this for many good reasons, including health and safety. Write an essay on nature as a threat, showing what you think the relation of people today should be to nature.

How Do We Resolve Conflicts in Values?

1. Identify a value conflict in our contemporary society: shrinking public funding versus expanding social needs for the helpless and homeless, the taxpayers' revolt versus spending for public schools and colleges, a fetus's right to life versus a woman's right to choice, freedom of speech versus freedom from public insult, or the like. Define and explain the conflict, and offer a solution, as Bettelheim and Kozol do.

2. Identify a value conflict in your own life. Perhaps it is between social demands and private ones, as it was for Huck Finn, or between family goals and personal ones (see Bettelheim), or between your desire to help others and the difficulty of doing so (Kozol), or between your own needs and those of others, or whatever. Write an essay setting out the problem, posing alternative ways of behaving, and coming to some sort of conclusion.

What is Really Important?

1. Write an essay on what is most important for your own self-respect. Look back to the essays by Douglass, Walker, Rose, and Rodriguez in Chapter 1, and forward to the essays by Murray and King in Chapter 5, to enrich your sense of the dimensions of self-respect. Have you an earned sense of self-respect, as Didion defines it?

2. How have you come to know what is really important, and how does that knowledge relate to who you are? Using materials from the first three chapters of this book, focus an essay upon what matters most to you and why.

4
═

WHAT IS A GOOD IDEA?

"It was the very best butter."
THE DORMOUSE, shaking
his stopped watch in *Alice in Wonderland*

Why Consider This Question?

The question "What is a good idea?" is enduring and important; it affects all aspects of our lives, from daily decisions about routine matters to large philosophical and cultural issues. Many of the "good ideas" that we act upon in our day-to-day lives emerge from received opinions we have not thought much about, and they sometimes work out in practice as badly as the Dormouse's attempt to repair his watch with "the *very* best butter." On the other hand, many of our happiest times and most successful endeavors are the result of good ideas about what to study, where to live, whom to marry, how to spend our lives. We are always on the lookout for good ideas: we want to elect politicians with good ideas for the future, we want scientists to provide good ideas about how to understand the world, and we look to the arts for good ideas about values and meaning. But what is a good idea?

One way to estimate the value of ideas is by looking at what happens when they are acted upon. All ideas do not, or do not have to, lead to action; but most ideas have consequences, and we tend to judge their value by their results. Some confirmed socialists argue that the ideas of Karl Marx were essentially good, even though they have worked out badly in the former Soviet Union and Eastern Europe; but most observers see the economic devastation of the former Soviet empire as proof that Communism was a bad idea to begin with. Surely one test of the value of an idea is to examine what happens when it is applied in practice.

Some philosophers and scientists, however, maintain that the practical effects of ideas are irrelevant; discovery of new knowledge is always a good idea, whether or not the knowledge is put into action. Still other thinkers see new knowledge as inherently dangerous, precisely because it is likely to lead to actions or thoughts that may be destructive. Was the development of atomic energy, and atomic weapons, a good idea? Some will argue that the discovery of nuclear energy was inherently a good idea, whatever its use or misuse may be, but the argument rages on. Atomic bombs dropped on Japan in 1945 were, some will say, an unnecessary and racist expression of mindless vengeance; others claim that they saved many more lives than they cost by bringing the war to a speedy end. The present use of nuclear energy leads to as much dispute: advocates point to a limitless energy source that is relatively clean, while opponents claim that nuclear waste is dangerous and almost undisposable and that nuclear accidents are inevitable.

Even when good ideas seem to be working out fine, we often find ourselves in trouble. Some of our best ideas seem to conflict with others of our best ideas. It is a wonderful idea to prolong life with good nutrition, healthful habits, and medical interventions, but it is also a good idea to conserve the resources of the planet, to open opportunities for the next generation, and to die with dignity. We should protect our forests and open spaces for future generations, but we should also develop our resources to create jobs and economic expansion. How can we tell which good idea to put into action when such conflicts occur, and why?

Certainly the perception about what is a good idea shifts over time, and what made perfect sense in past times seems quaint and curious now. When we speak of "an idea whose time has come," we refer to the way a new idea can overturn old habits of thought. For example, a new conception of the importance of the individual in the eighteenth century led to such changes as the end of slavery and the development of psychology. We can see such shifts in our own time, as environmentalism moves from a fringe movement to mainstream thinking and as the concept of culture moves from a European to a global context. Historians of ideas have attempted to understand just why such changes in the way people think about things take place. But no one knows exactly why ideas that appear strange to one generation seem simple good sense to another.

If we are willing to say that no idea is good in itself, but is good only for particular times, places, and peoples, we may have a method to think systematically about what makes ideas good. That is, we may need to examine the particular situation and consequences of an idea to situate it concretely in order to examine its worth. We will understand that under other circumstances or times or places we might need to come to a quite different judgment. Such relativism, however, conflicts with still another idea, that certain enduring principles such as truth, goodness, beauty, and justice, are eternal, applicable under all circumstances.

The readings that follow consider three aspects of the question "What is a good idea?" The first section looks at democracy from a variety of perspectives as a way of examining an idea according to how well it works out. The next section explores several scientific ideas that have had a revolutionary impact on modern thought as a way of examining how a particular research community expresses and evaluates its ideas. The third section speaks to aspects of human creativity, the basic source of all good ideas. This chapter assumes that we will bring other ideas, knowledge, and experiences into play in order to test the "good ideas" we encounter.

What Is a Good Political Idea?

Of all political ideas, that of democracy seems to have best stood the test of time. Starting with the ancient Greeks and continuing around the world with increasing power through the 1990s, the concept that political legitimacy must derive from the consent of the governed seems almost beyond dispute. Thomas Jefferson's "Declaration of Independence" is one of the clearest statements of this idea, and its sentences have become so familiar to most American that we tend not to notice its argument. Jefferson bases his argument on "the Laws of Nature and of Nature's God" and on "truths" held to be "self-evident." A careful reading of the document must inquire into what such statements mean and where they came from. Further, as the other readings in the section suggest, we must ask how well these ideas have worked out in practice.

Abraham Lincoln's speech at Gettysburg is also part of the common heritage of Americans. And once again, the familiar phrases of the "Address" do not explain themselves. The "liberty" of the opening paragraph and the "new birth of freedom" of the last paragraph, for instance—are they the same, or different in some ways? Are Lincoln's assumptions about government, in his last sentence ("of the people, by the people, for the people") the same as Jefferson's? Are they the same as those we hold today?

When we look closely at these democratic political ideas, many questions emerge. Who, exactly, are the "people" whose consent democracy requires and in whose name battles are fought? The democratic tradition does not provide comfortable answers to this question. For the Greeks, the people turned out to be a very limited group, with no women or slaves, for instance, as part of the electoral process.

Even for the founders of American democracy, the definition of those giving consent excluded many peoples, and women did not vote until well into the twentieth century. How can we reconcile these limitations with the powerful statements of Jefferson and Lincoln?

Those who have been excluded from the political process have sought to be heard and to challenge this democracy in practice. Sojourner Truth's "Ain't I a Woman?" and Elizabeth Cady Stanton's "Declaration of Sentiments" responded to the ideas of Jefferson and Lincoln by protesting the obvious failure of nineteenth-century American democracy to include women. "Then that little man in black there, he says women can't have as much rights as men, 'cause Christ wasn't a woman!" Sojourner Truth states, with biting sarcasm; and Stanton echoes Jefferson's "Declaration" with one of her own, now specifically including women. Alice Walker is a veteran of modern efforts to expand the benefits of democracy. Despite her clear awareness of still unfulfilled goals, in "The Civil Rights Movement: What Good Was It?" she offers hope and vision to those disappointed at the slowness of progress: the Civil Rights movement "gave us hope for tomorrow. It called us into life."

What Is a Good Scientific Idea?

In recent years, some thinkers have begun to question the belief that scientific and technological advances are always good. The environmental and anti-nuclear movements, in particular, have asked us to look carefully at the harm as well as the benefits of such ideas as nuclear energy, rural electrification, and the widespread use of fossil fuels. Are our scientific ideas leading us to technological destruction? Nonetheless, it is beyond question that scientific ideas and their practical results in technology have added greatly to our knowledge, health, and comfort. How can we distinguish a good scientific idea from a bad one?

Isaac Asimov opens this section with "Those Crazy Ideas," which first examines his own scientific creativity, then analyzes Darwin's discovery of "a new and revolutionary scientific principle," and finally presents a series of criteria for scientific creativity in genral. The next essay, "Understanding Natural Selection," is a portion of Darwin's landmark work. We need to test Asimov's interpretation of Darwin against our own experience of reading Darwin. The next essay, Barbara Culliton's "Science's Restive Public," looks at the role of the non-scientist in understanding and setting policy for scientific research. Culliton reminds scientists, and all of us, that "the application of new knowledge is not always to the good." The public, she argues, has some role in deciding what is and is not a good scientific idea.

The next essay, "A Structure for Deoxyribose Nucleic Acid," describes another landmark in scientific creativity, one which has been compared to Darwin's: the discovery of the basis of human genetics (DNA) by a team of scientists led by James Watson and Francis Crick. It also provides a case study of scientific creativity, which asks us to test Asimov's criteria.

Yet another test of what goes into a good scientific idea emerges from Arthur Koestler's essay, "The Cosmic Mystery," which examines a creative scientist's commitment to an idea that turned out to be "completely false." Here we see Kepler's "pseudo-discovery," which nonetheless led to the birth of modern cosmology. If a bad idea, such as Kepler's "complete answer" to the structure of the solar system, can eventually lead to such important knowledge, does that mean that it really was a good idea? What, then, is a good scientific idea? And if the scientific idea is discovered by a woman, such as Caroline Herschel in the poem by Siv Cedering, why is that idea not attended to as it would be if discovered by a man?

How Can We Recognize and Encourage Creativity?

The questions about scientific ideas lead directly to the underlying question of the third section, about the nature of creativity in general. Linda Hogan opens the section with "Hearing Voices," speaking as an Indian woman with an affinity for scientist Barbara McClintock (*see* Keller's essay about her in Chapter 2): "It is important to me that McClintock listened to the voices of corn. It is important to the continuance of life that she told the truth of her method and that it reminded us all of where our strength, our knowing, and our sustenance come from." As a poet, Hogan is concerned with "the living, breathing power of the word," which she sees as the voice of the earth itself. When we compare Hogan's view of creativity with Asimov's, we see the ways in which ideas about creativity emerge from particular people writing from particular cultural contexts.

In "The Reach of Imagination," Jacob Bronowski reminds us of Susanne Langer's essay "Signs and Symbols" (Chapter 2) when he argues that the imagination is "a specifically *human* gift." Imagination for Bronowski requires symbols and language, and this gift is available to all humans. Those who choose to apply their imagination to science are not, he argues, essentially different from those who use it in the arts: "All great scientists have used their imagination freely." He argues that scientific creativity and literary creativity have the same roots and tend to flower during the same historical periods.

Gretel Ehrlich, in "Life At Close Range," also sees imagination and activity as linked, but she does so as a writer on a ranch: "Sometimes when strangers ask what I do, I say I write, but around here, they think I said 'ride.' I do both of course . . . but I couldn't write if I didn't ride." Finally Alexander Calandra, in "Angels on a Pin," presents a case for creativity as mocking academic patterns of learning.

Surely, creativity is a good idea. But each of these writers sees it as a powerful yet mysterious force rooted in the physical but transcending the physical, rooted in traditional learning but going beyond it. There are no obvious formulas for creativity; only questions and responses. How can we encourage creativity, and how can we find it in ourselves?

Rhetorical Issues: Argument and Evidence

Many of the papers that you are asked to write have to do with examining ideas—and coming to conclusions about them. The papers may be described in various ways, such as "position paper," "persuasion essay," "interpretation," or "argument," but all of them will ask you to define a topic, take a position on it, and defend that position with evidence. Our concern here is with the ways in which you can develop different kinds of evidence to support the positions you may take in such papers.

We use the term "argument" the way rhetoricians do, not as a quarrel but as a piece of writing whose aim is both *inquiry* and *persuasion*. Most of the papers you are assigned ask you to construct an argument: "Show how . . . ," "Demonstrate that . . . ," "To what degree do you agree with . . . ," "What is the principal reason for . . . ," and so on. Note that an argument asks for more than a description, a summary, or a review of what other people have said, though all of these may take place as part of the argument. The inquiry of the writing takes place during the writing process as you work through possible answers to the questions posed by the topic; the final draft presents the results of that inquiry in as convincing a way as possible.

In most cases, you can think of your argument in terms of *claims* that you make about your topic and *evidence* that you bring in support of those claims. Different kinds of claims call for different kinds of evidence, and you always need to show how the evidence supports your claims. There is a long tradition, going back to Aristotle, of describing ways of making and supporting arguments. We will summarize a few of the most useful of these.

In recent years, some new approaches to the making of arguments have become more and more acceptable both in and out of school, and these approaches are also represented in this book. The usual way of speaking about argument, with claims and evidence, serves well for traditional essays that make a logical case, such as the readings in this chapter by Jefferson, Asimov, or Bronowski. But arguments can also be made in untraditional ways through personal stories or folk lore, for example, as do Sojourner Truth and Linda Hogan. The discussion of argument that follows is suggestive of ways to inquire into topics and to present that inquiry, rather than a blueprint to follow.

Claims. There are many kinds of claims, each of which calls for a different kind of inquiry. Here are some of the most common:

- Claims of fact: Did this happen? Are the numbers right?
- Claims of value: What is this worth? Is it good or bad?
- Claims of interpretation: What does this mean? What kind of thing is this?
- Claims of policy: What should be done?
- Claims of cause: What brought this about?
- Claims of judgment: What is my position on this problem?

Most essays will make more than one of these (or other) claims; you need not restrict yourself to only one kind of claim. But most essays will *focus* on one kind of claim as the principal one, and the mode of inquiry is likely to follow from that principal claim. Thus Jefferson, in the "Declaration of Independence," makes all of the claims listed above, but his central idea is the policy claim: "That these United Colonies are, and of Right ought to be Free and Independent States." The long list of grievances against the king are presented as claims of cause and of fact: "To prove this, let Facts be submitted to a candid world." The claim of interpretation precedes the presentation of facts: "The history of the present King of Great Britain is a history of repeated injuries and usurpations, all having in direct object the establishment of an absolute Tyranny over these States." The claim of value in the second paragraph begins "We hold these truths to be self-evident . . . ."

The claims that you make in your essays need to be *arguable,* that is, worthy of debate; the claims Jefferson articulated were arguable enough to lead to war. In most cases facts are not arguable, since we need only verify them: the speed of sound, or the number of days in John F. Kennedy's presidency. But, as Jefferson's list of what he called "Facts" demonstrates, even if facts are not usually arguable, the interpretation of them almost always is. Sometimes facts become arguable when the context changes: a line is not necessarily the shortest distance between two points, and the weight of a liter of water changes on the moon. Again, what everybody knows (the sun rises in the east, dogs bark) is not arguable—unless what everyone knows happens to be wrong (Shakespeare is hard to read, mathematics is for males). Personal feelings are not arguable (I like chocolate ice cream better than vanilla) but personal opinions are if you claim they are generally true (frozen yogurt is better than ice cream because it contains less animal fat). As you work through your planning and revising process, a principal goal should be to develop an arguable claim that can serve as the focus of your writing.

Claims ought to be particular, appropriate, and interesting. For example, Alice Walker does not claim that the civil rights movement is generally good, but that it "gave us hope for tomorrow." Arthur Koestler does not claim that Kepler was stupid, but rather mistaken. Jacob Bronowski does not merely praise science but claims that scientific creativity has the same roots as artistic creativity. And Siv Cedering does not have Caroline Hershel say that men and women both can think and that prejudice is petty compared to the universe; her speaker says

> . . . And however important man becomes,
> he is nothing compared to the stars.
> There are secrets, dear sister, and it is
> for us to reveal them.

Evidence. Aristotle spoke of three kinds of appeals that support arguments: *logos, pathos,* and *ethos.* While these appeals are interconnected and often occur in the same argument, each of them asks for a different response from the reader. *Logos* is the most rational of the three; it is the logical, sequential presentation of data and argument and asks for intellectual agreement. *Pathos* has to do with feeling, a method of arguing that relies on emotion more than on logic. You might notice in the first section of this chapter that Jefferson's *logos* is responded to by Sojourner Truth's *pathos. Ethos* means the ethical character of the speaker or author, as perceived by the reader or audience, to support an argument. For example, politicians depend upon *ethos* to win approval for themselves and their programs, an appeal made easier by the media assistants who help present a winning picture on television; when *ethos* fails, the politician is bound to fail (President Nixon's resignation was foreshadowed by his inept attempt to reclaim his lost character: "I am not a crook!"). *Ethos* has considerable force in Hogan's essay in this chapter.

While most college papers ask you to attend principally to *logos,* there are occasions on which the other kinds of appeals can be appropriate. If your learning style is relatively intuitive, you may find that evidence from your own experience or emotions is the most powerful you can use. It might be prudent, however, to be sure that the faculty member who will be responding to the paper is open to such appeals before you pursue them.

The evidence you use ought to be appropriate to the kinds of claims you make. For example, a claim of fact needs to be supported by facts, with some further evidence that the facts are, in fact, true. Notice Jefferson's list of facts in support of the "Declaration of Independence," for example, that King George "has kept among us, in time of peace, Standing Armies without the Consent of our Legislature." At the time, that fact was obvious to all and hence required no additional support; today, however, if you were using that statement, you might provide evidence of the size and extent of those British forces. Your facts are likely to come from the research section of the library: almanacs, encyclopedias, biographical dictionaries, and the like. You will also find facts, with sources documented, in articles in professional journals or books. Research studies will sometimes yield statistics, which are like facts in the sense that they can be instantly convincing if the source is credible. Some facts come out of personal experience ("Ain't I a Woman?"). Facts and statistics are not, however, simple proofs, for they can be interpreted in various ways. When you give factual or statistical evidence, be alert to the cautions that Linda Simon gave in "The Naked Source (pp. 200–206): the interpretation of the data determines what the facts really mean. The British government did not accept Jefferson's interpretation of the facts he cited, and that difference of interpretation led to war.

Claims of value, interpretation, or judgment will often call for a different kind of evidence. You may want to cite the opinions of authorities (*see* Chapter 5 on use of sources) as well as factual material. For example, Isaac Asimov supports his claim (in "Those Crazy Ideas") that mathematical breakthroughs are made by youngsters by citing three facts: "Evariste Galois evolved group theory at twenty-one. Isaac Newton worked out calculus at twenty-three. Albert Einstein presented the theory of relativity at twenty-six." If you wanted to make the same point, you could cite Asimov as an authority, as well as the facts he accumulates. You may also use quotation and discussion of quotation as evidence for your claims, particularly if you are analyzing a text. (Notice how the quotation from Asimov supports the claim that facts are powerful evidence.) Your personal experience is likely to be relevant, and you might be able to bring in an appropriate anecdote, if you can connect it to the claim you are making. A personal narrative can be powerful evidence; certainly many of the writers in *Inquiry* use such stories as compelling examples of what they seek to show. The arguments of Margaret Walker, Nancy Mairs, John Updike, Frederick Douglass, Mike Rose, Elie Wiesel, Richard Rodriguez, and Patricia Hampl (just to cite writers from the first chapter) are compelling because their claims are supported by their lives; *ethos* and *pathos* are combined.

Claims of cause look to the past and hence ask for historical evidence; claims of policy look to the future and so call for evidence that a proposed change might work—perhaps because it has worked in the past. Jefferson makes both claims in "The Declaration of Independence"; the list of abuses by the British government supports the claims of cause, and the call for independence claims the new policy will remedy those abuses. Stanton's response, in the "Declaration of Sentiments," in turn questions the policy claim with new evidence and suggests a new policy—equal treatment of women—to remedy the abuses she cites.

As you read the selections in *Inquiry*, you will find many kinds of evidence that do not fit into neat categories. The poems by Margaret Atwood in Chapter 2 and by Sharon Olds in Chapter 3 use metaphor and analogy as ways to support the claims made by the speaker. Shirley Brice Heath, in Chapter 1, uses interviews and what anthropologists call a "thick description" (a full and detailed rendering of a society) as evidence for her claims about the nature of literacy. The comic writing of James Thurber (Chapter 2) uses exaggeration and a naive speaker to make witty arguments. Similarly, in your own writing, you will find a wide range of possibilities for supplying evidence for your claims. What is most important is that you remain aware of the need to supply evidence, that you know claims are not convincing unless they are supported.

How can you tell if you have given the right kind of evidence, or enough evidence, for your claim? There is no formula to answer that question. In one sense, whether or not your evidence is satisfactory is a matter to be negotiated with your audience. Try out your drafts with a fellow student, or a peer group, or a reading circle. Discuss the issue with your instructor. Keep in mind that you, as writer, are more likely to find your argument convincing than will any audience; you have already made up your mind. Your readers will not be quite so willing to credit the unstated evidence or the many sources you have read but not quoted; the audience needs to understand your claims and to see how your evidence supports those claims.

Connections. The missing link between the claim and the evidence is the connection between them, sometimes called the *warrant* by logicians. You may be tempted to omit this link, since you already are convinced that your evidence supports your claims; the connection between them seems self-evident. Thus you are likely to assert your claim of value ("Bronowski's explanation of Newton's discovery is brilliantly clear") and follow it with a quotation from the essay giving Bronowski's explanation. But the evidence does not in itself prove your claim; it lies there, dead on the page, until you show how it relates to the claim. You need to discuss the quoted material, showing where and why it is brilliant.

The same requirement for connection applies to any evidence you use. If you cite a chart or statistics or an authority, you need to show how what you have cited relates to your claims. Personal anecdotes are in some ways the most convincing kind of evidence because the connection of stories to claims is usually direct and emotional; but you need to be convincing enough to show how something that is true for you is not merely personal, but representative. Mike Rose, for example, is careful to point out that his experience "on the boundary" (see Chapter 1) can stand for the experience of most people with his kind of background—except that he achieved success.

Just as with evidence, the amount of detail in the connection between evidence and claim is a matter of negotiation between you and your audience. If you are using logical appeals, you will need to be careful that you have made the connection clear and that you have been explicit about how the evidence is to be interpreted to support your claim; remember, facts and quotations do not explain themselves. Less logical or more personal appeals allow more latitude; some stories are so compelling that too much explanation might be superfluous. But if you want to convince your readers that your claims are sound and you really do have a "good idea," you will pay attention to the nature of your claims, the kind of evidence that the claim demands you provide, and the connections that you need to make between the claims and the evidence.

QUESTIONS FOR DISCOVERY AND DISCUSSION

1. Explain a good idea you have had and tell what happened as a result of that idea.

2. In light of the results, was the idea as good as it seemed originally? Why, or why not?

3. Excluding the political and scientific ideas this introduction has already discussed, pick out a good idea you have encountered in your reading or in your classes. What makes you think that idea was good? What are the arguments in its favor? What can be said in opposition? Under what circumstances might that idea not be good?

4. Try to come up with a good idea that no one has yet tried out. Focus upon some area that you already know about and let your imagination work. Then put together some reasons to convince other people that your idea is a good one.

5. Consider the kind of claims you would have to make to convince an audience that your idea was sound. What kinds of evidence would support those claims? How much evidence would be appropriate? What explicit connections would you make between the evidence and the claims?

Declaration of Independence

THOMAS JEFFERSON

Just two weeks before his death, which occurred on July 4, 1826—fifty years to the day after the signing of the *Declaration of Independence*—Thomas Jefferson wrote his final judgment of his "expression of the American mind":

> The Declaration will be . . . the signal of arousing men to burst the chains under which monkish ignorance and superstition had persuaded them to bind themselves, and to assume the blessings and security of self-government. That form which we have substituted, restores the free right to the unbounded exercise of reason and freedom of opinion. All eyes were opened, or opening, to the rights of man. The general spread of the light of science has already laid open to view the palpable truth, that the mass of mankind has not been born with saddles on their back, nor a few booted and spurred, ready to ride them legitimately, by the Grace of God.

Although Benjamin Franklin and John Adams collaborated in drafting this document, its language and thought are quintessential Jefferson. He was the architect of the framework of American democracy, refusing to sign the Constitution until the Bill of Rights was added. The *Declaration* is principled and far-sighted, retaining the idealistic vision of the ultimate perfectibility of society, in which all citizens are expected to recognize the "rights of man" and act on them to secure the "unalienable rights" of "Life, Liberty, and the pursuit of Happiness."

Politician, philosopher, architect, inventor, and writer, Jefferson was born in 1743 near Charlottesville, Virginia, and was educated at the College of William and Mary. He served as a delegate to the Continental Congress in 1775, as Governor of the Commonwealth of Virginia, and as third President of the United States. His instructions for his epitaph specified only three of his many accomplishments for inclusion on his tombstone: founding of the University of Virginia, and authorship of the Declaration of Independence and the Statute of Virginia for Religious Freedom.

When in the course of human events, it becomes necessary for 1 one people to dissolve the political bands which have connected them with another, and to assume among the Powers of the earth, the separate and equal station to which the Laws of Nature and of Nature's God entitle them, a decent respect to the opinions of mankind requires that they should declare the causes which impel them to the separation.

We hold these truths to be self-evident, that all men are created   2
equal, that they are endowed by their Creator with certain unalienable
Rights, that among these are Life, Liberty and the pursuit of Happiness. That to secure these rights, Governments are instituted among
Men deriving their just powers from the consent of the governed.
That whenever any Form of Government becomes destructive of these
ends, it is the Right of the People to alter or to abolish it, and to
institute new Government, laying its foundation on such principles
and organizing its powers in such form, as to them shall seem most
likely to effect their Safety and Happiness. Prudence, indeed, will
dictate that Governments long established should not be changed
for light and transient causes; and accordingly all experience hath
shown, that mankind are more disposed to suffer, while evils are sufferable, than to right themselves by abolishing the forms to which
they are accustomed. But when a long train of abuses and usurpations pursuing invariably the same Object evinces a design to reduce
them under absolute Despotism, it is their right, it is their duty, to
throw off such government, and to provide new Guards for their
future security. Such has been the patient sufferance of these Colonies; and such is now the necessity which constrains them to alter
their former Systems of Government. The history of the present
King of Great Britain is a history of repeated injuries and usurpations, all having in direct object the establishment of an absolute
Tyranny over these States. To prove this, let Facts be submitted to a
candid world.

He has refused his Assent to Laws, the most wholesome and   3
necessary for the public good.

He has forbidden his Governors to pass Laws of immediate and   4
pressing importance, unless suspended in their operation till his Assent should be obtained; and when so suspended, he has utterly
neglected to attend them.

He has refused to pass other Laws for the accommodation of large   5
districts of people, unless those people would relinquish the right of
Representation in the Legislature, a right inestimable to them and
formidable to tyrants only.

He has called together legislative bodies at places unusual, un-   6
comfortable, and distant from the depository of their Public Records,
for the sole purpose of fatiguing them into compliance with his
measures.

He has dissolved Representative Houses repeatedly, for opposing   7
with manly firmness his invasions on the rights of the people.

He has refused for a long time, after such dissolutions, to cause   8
others to be elected; whereby the Legislative Powers, incapable of
Annihilation, have returned to the People at large for their exercise;

the State remaining in the mean time exposed to all the dangers of invasion from without, and convulsions within.

He has endeavoured to prevent the population of these States; 9 for that purpose obstructing the Laws of Naturalization of Foreigners; refusing to pass others to encourage their migration hither, and raising the conditions of new Appropriations of Lands.

He has obstructed the Administration of Justice, by refusing his 10 Assent to Laws for establishing Judiciary Powers.

He has made Judges dependent on his Will alone, for the tenure 11 of their offices, and the amount and payment of their salaries.

He has erected a multitude of New Offices, and sent hither 12 swarms of Officers to harass our People, and eat out their substance.

He has kept among us, in time of peace, Standing Armies without 13 the Consent of our Legislature.

He has affected to render the Military independent of and su- 14 perior to the Civil Power.

He has combined with others to subject us to jurisdictions foreign 15 to our constitution, and unacknowledged by our laws; giving his Assent to their acts of pretended Legislation:

For quartering large bodies of armed troops among us: 16

For protecting them, by a mock Trial, from Punishment for any 17 Murders which they should commit on the Inhabitants of these States:

For cutting off our Trade with all parts of the world: 18

For imposing Taxes on us without our Consent: 19

For depriving us in many cases, of the benefits of Trial by Jury: 20

For transporting us beyond Seas to be tried for pretended offenses: 21

For abolishing the free System of English Laws in a Neighbouring 22 Province, establishing therein an Arbitrary government, and enlarging its boundaries so as to render it at once an example and fit instrument for introducing the same absolute rule into these Colonies:

For taking away our Charters, abolishing our most valuable Laws, 23 and altering fundamentally the Forms of our Governments:

For suspending our own Legislatures, and declaring themselves 24 invested with Power to legislate for us in all cases whatsoever.

He has abdicated Government here, by declaring us out of his 25 Protection and waging War against us.

He has plundered our seas, ravaged our Coasts, burnt our towns 26 and destroyed the Lives of our people.

He is at this time transporting large Armies of foreign Mercenaries 27 to compleat works of death, desolation and tyranny, already begun with circumstances of Cruelty & perfidy scarcely paralleled in the most barbarous ages, and totally unworthy the Head of a civilized nation.

He has constrained our fellow Citizens taken Captive on the high 28

Seas to bear Arms against their Country, to become the executioners of their friends and Brethren, or to fall themselves by their Hands.

He has excited domestic insurrections amongst us, and has en-   29 deavoured to bring on the inhabitants of our frontiers, the merciless Indian Savages, whose known rule of warfare, is an undistinguished destruction of all ages, sexes and conditions.

In every stage of these Oppressions We Have Petitioned for Re-   30 dress in the most humble terms: Our repeated petitions have been answered only by repeated injury. A Prince, whose character is thus marked by every act which may define a Tyrant, is unfit to be the ruler of a free People.

Not have We been wanting in attention to our British brethren.   31 We have warned them from time to time of attempts by their legislature to extend an unwarrantable jurisdiction over us. We have reminded them of the circumstances of our emigration and settlement here. We have appealed to their native justice and magnanimity and we have conjured them by the ties of our common kindred to disavow these usurpations, which would inevitably interrupt our connections and correspondence. They too have been deaf to the voice of justice and of consanguinity. We must, therefore acquiesce in the necessity, which denounces our Separation, and hold them, as we hold the rest of mankind, Enemies in War, in Peace Friends.

We, therefore, the Representatives of the United States of Amer-   32 ica, in General Congress, Assembled, appealing to the Supreme Judge of the world for the rectitude of our intentions, do, in the Name, and by Authority of the good People of these Colonies, solemnly publish and declare, That these United Colonies are, and of Right ought to be Free and Independent States; that they are Absolved from all Allegiance to the British Crown, and that all political connection between them and the State of Great Britain, is and ought to be totally dissolved; and that as Free and Independent States, they have full power to levy War, conclude Peace, contract Alliances, establish Commerce, and to do all other Acts and Things which Independent States may of right do. And for the support of this Declaration, with a firm reliance on the protection of Divine Providence, we mutually pledge to each other our lives, our Fortunes and our sacred Honor.

RESPONDING TO READING

Key words: community   freedom   nature   power
rights   striving

Rhetorical concepts: cause and effect   deduction   explanation
illustration   narrative/example   proclamation

1. What, according to the *Declaration of Independence*, are the colonists' most significant grievances? How does the organization of the document reflect these?

2. How can revolutionaries know when the time is right to stage their coup and overthrow their government? Is the justice of one's cause measured only by the success of the coup?

3. Jefferson distrusted organized religion and believed that religion should be "subject to the laws of nature and probability, and discernible by reason" (Harold Hellenbrand, *The Unfinished Revolution*, 1990, 53). Do you see evidence for such beliefs in the *Declaration of Independence*?

4. What American values are embodied in the *Declaration of Independence*? Which of these remain important to Americans today? To you individually?

5. Define one of the values in the *Declaration of Independence*; show its significance to some aspect of American life—such as culture, politics, economic opportunities, or education.

6. Write your own "declaration of independence," possibly in collaboration with another person, as Jefferson did, in which you justify your opposition to an oppressor or oppressive situation. Is a simple declaration of freedom sufficient? What will you have to do to enforce your claim?

Declaration of Sentiments

ELIZABETH CADY STANTON

When Elizabeth Cady (1815–1902) was ten, her brother died, and she vowed that she would fulfill the ambitions of her father, an influential lawyer and judge in Johnstown, New York. Although she studied Greek and became a top student at Emma Willard's Troy Female Seminary, her father forbade her to go to college. However, through her marriage to abolitionist agitator Henry Stanton, she was able—despite her responsibility for running a household that included the couple's seven children—to engage in social activity far more radical than attendance at college. In a public career that spanned more than fifty years, she was a militant feminist who, in collaboration with her friend, Susan B. Anthony, never stopped agitating for women's rights. These goals included the right to vote—promoted through various Woman Suffrage Associations which she helped to found—and the rights for married women to own property, to be entitled to the wages they earned, and to have equal guardianship of their children. As president of a Women's Temperance society, 1852–1853, she scandalized even her ardent supporters by recommending that drunkenness be a sufficient ground for divorce. In arguing that to be truly equal with men, women have to fight for their sexual self-determination, she was a century ahead of her time.

"Declaration of Sentiments," composed in 1848, was Stanton's first theoretical political document, written for the Women's Rights Convention that she and four other feminists organized to assert that "all men and women are created equal." As political analyst Bruce Miroff has noted, through following the *Declaration of Independence* point-by-point and in parallel language, "Stanton took a classic American idiom and infused it with a radical message not contemplated by its authors," taking "the most democratic and egalitarian American values and turning them against a dominant culture that claimed to uphold them."

When, in the course of human events, it becomes necessary for   1
one portion of the family of man to assume among the people of the earth a position different from that which they have hitherto occupied, but one to which the laws of nature and of nature's God entitle them, a decent respect to the opinions of mankind requires that they should declare the causes that impel them to such a course.

We hold these truths to be self-evident: that all men and women   2
are created equal; that they are endowed by their Creator with certain inalienable rights; that among these are life, liberty, and the pursuit of happiness; that to secure these rights governments are instituted, deriving their just powers from the consent of the governed. Whenever any form of government becomes destructive of these ends, it is the right of those who suffer from it to refuse allegiance to it, and to insist upon the institution of a new government, laying its foundation on such principles, and organizing its powers in such form, as to them shall seem most likely to effect their safety and happiness. Prudence, indeed, will dictate that governments long established should not be changed for light and transient causes; and accordingly all experience hath shown that mankind are more disposed to suffer, while evils are sufferable, than to right themselves by abolishing the forms to which they were accustomed. But when a long train of abuses and usurpations, pursuing invariably the same object evinces a design to reduce them under absolute despotism, it is their duty to throw off such government, and to provide new guards for their future security. Such has been the patient sufferance of the women under this government, and such is now the necessity which constrains them to demand the equal station to which they are entitled.

The history of mankind is a history of repeated injuries and usur-   3
pations on the part of man toward woman, having in direct object the establishment of an absolute tyranny over her. To prove this, let facts be submitted to a candid world.

He has never permitted her to exercise her inalienable right to   4
the elective franchise.

He has compelled her to submit to laws, in the formation of which   5
she had no voice.

He has withheld from her rights which are given to the most   6
ignorant and degraded men—both natives and foreigners.

Having deprived her of this first right of a citizen, the elective 7
franchise, thereby leaving her without representation in the halls of
legislation, he has oppressed her on all sides.

He has made her, if married, in the eye of the law, civilly dead.   8

He has taken from her all right in property, even to the wages 9
she earns.

He has made her, morally, an irresponsible being, as she can 10
commit many crimes with impunity, provided they be done in the
presence of her husband. In the covenant of marriage, she is compelled to promise obedience to her husband, he becoming, to all
intents and purposes, her master—the law giving him power to deprive her of her liberty, and to administer chastisement.

He has so framed the laws of divorce, as to what shall be the 11
proper causes, and in case of separation, to whom the guardianship
of the children shall be given, as to be wholly regardless of the happiness of women—the law, in all cases, going upon a false supposition
of the supremacy of man, and giving all power into his hands.

After depriving her of all rights as a married woman, if single, 12
and the owner of property, he has taxed her to support a government
which recognizes her only when her property can be made profitable to it.

He has monopolized nearly all the profitable employments, and 13
from those she is permitted to follow, she receives but a scanty re-
muneration. He closes against her all the avenues to wealth and distinction which he considers most honorable to himself. As a teacher
of theology, medicine, or law, she is not known.

He has denied her the facilities for obtaining a thorough educa- 14
tion, all colleges being closed against her.

He allows her in Church, as well as State, but a subordinate 15
position, claiming Apostolic authority for her exclusion from the ministry, and, with some exceptions from any public participation in the
affairs of the Church.

He has created a false public sentiment by giving to the world a 16
different code of morals for men and women, by which moral delin-
quencies which exclude women from society, are not only tolerated,
but deemed of little account in man.

He has usurped the prerogative of Jehovah himself, claiming it as 17
his right to assign for her a sphere of action, when that belongs to
her conscience and to her God.

He has endeavored, in every way that he could, to destroy her 18
confidence in her own powers, to lessen her self-respect, and to make
her willing to lead a dependent and abject life.

Now, in view of this entire disenfranchisement of one-half the 19
people of this country, their social and religious degradation—in view

of the unjust laws above mentioned, and because women do feel themselves aggrieved, oppressed, and fraudulently deprived of their most sacred rights, we insist that they have immediate admission to all the rights and privileges which belong to them as citizens of the United States.

In entering upon the great work before us, we anticipate no small   20 amount of misconception, misrepresentation, and ridicule; but we shall use every instrumentality within our power to effect our object. We shall employ agents, circulate tracts, petition the State and National legislatures, and endeavor to enlist the pulpit and the press in our behalf. We hope this Convention will be followed by a series of Conventions embracing every part of the country.

1898

RESPONDING TO READING

Key words: community freedom gender nature power rights striving

Rhetorical concepts: cause and effect deduction explanation illustration imitation narrative/example proclamation

1. What, according to Stanton, are women's most significant grievances? How does the imitation of the *Declaration of Independence* make the *Declaration of Sentiments* more powerful than a mere statement of grievances?
2. What did Jefferson mean by "the laws of Nature and Nature's God"? How do these terms shift in meaning in Stanton's document?
3. How much has changed since Stanton wrote? To what degree have the underlying grievances been addressed? Can women still "anticipate no small amount of misconception, misrepresentation, and ridicule" when asserting the rights and privileges of citizens?

The Gettysburg Address

ABRAHAM LINCOLN

To understand the meaning of a speech, it is important to understand the context in which it was given. Abraham Lincoln's "Gettysburg Address" is considered "one of the greatest speeches in all history. Greatness is like granite: it is molded in fire, and lasts for centuries," says critic Gilbert Highet in "The Gettysburg Address," masterfully evoking its context:

> The dedication of the graveyard at Gettysburg was one of the supreme moments of American history. The battle itself had been a turning point of the war. Losses were heavy on both sides. Thousands of dead were left

on the field, and thousands of wounded died in the hot days following the battle. At first, their burial was more or less haphazard; but thoughtful men gradually came to feel that an adequate burying place and memorial were required.

At first, Lincoln, though President, was not invited to deliver the address on November 19, 1863. But when the invitation came, Lincoln was grateful for the opportunity to show that he could say something worthy of a solemn occasion. In the days when public officials still prepared their own speeches, Lincoln took great care in writing this address, which he began in the White House and completed at the Gettysburg hotel the night before the ceremony.

Although the contemporary press undervalued the speech, in part because it was so short, poet Carl Sandburg, a biographer of Lincoln, claims that this magnificent document portends the Emancipation Proclamation, which Lincoln in fact delivered on the following New Year's Day. In reiterating the proposition of the Declaration of Independence that "all men are created equal," Lincoln implied that the slaves were people embraced by this Declaration.

1 Four score and seven years ago our fathers brought forth on this continent, a new nation, conceived in liberty, and dedicated to the proposition that all men are created equal.

2 Now we are engaged in a great civil war, testing whether that nation, or any nation so conceived and so dedicated, can long endure. We are met on a great battlefield of that war. We have come to dedicate a portion of that field, as a final resting place for those who here gave their lives that that nation might live. It is altogether fitting and proper that we should do this.

3 But, in a larger sense, we cannot dedicate—we cannot consecrate—we cannot hallow—this ground. The brave men, living and dead, who struggled here, have consecrated it, far above our poor power to add or detract. The world will little note, nor long remember what we say here, but it can never forget what they did here. It is for us the living, rather, to be dedicated here to the unfinished work which they who fought here have thus so far nobly advanced. It is rather for us to be here dedicated to the great task remaining before us—that from these honored dead we take increased devotion—that we here highly resolve that these dead shall not have died in vain—that this nation, under God, shall have a new birth of freedom—and that government of the people, by the people, for the people, shall not perish from the earth.

RESPONDING TO READING

Key words: community   freedom   loss   memory   power
rights   striving

Rhetorical concepts: meditation   proclamation   speech

1. What, for Lincoln, is the most significant reason for waging the Civil War? For ending it?

2. Lincoln's speech, though short, embodies a number of values both of the American culture and the Christian religion. What are these? If Lincoln had lived to act on these values, how might these have been the basis for postwar reconciliation between the North and the South?

3. Compare and contrast Lincoln's speech with Thomas Jefferson's *Declaration of Independence*.

4. What can you learn about the art of speechwriting from studying Lincoln's "Gettysburg Address"?

5. Under what circumstances is war justified? According to what principles should those contemplating war make their decision? How have these principles worked out in practice, as wars have gone on? Use the American Civil War, or some other war, as your reference.

Ain't I a Woman?

SOJOURNER TRUTH

Sojourner Truth, originally named Isabella, was born into slavery (c. 1797) in Ulster County, New York, and fled to freedom in 1827. One of her first acts as a free woman was to sue for the return of one of her four children, who had been sold illegally to an Alabama slaveowner. For the next sixteen years she lived and worked as a domestic servant in New York City, becoming an active evangelist in association with a clergyman, who encouraged her efforts to convert prostitutes.

In 1843, the mystical visions and voices that had governed her life told her to adopt a new name, "Sojourner Truth," and to take to the road as an itinerant preacher. Early in her sojourn, in Northampton, Massachusetts, she encountered and became a popular champion of abolition, often sharing the platform with Frederick Douglass, whose eloquence she rivaled even though she remained illiterate throughout her life. Her speeches employed the vitality and cadences of a great Blues singer to hold the audience spellbound: "Children, I talk to God and God talks to me!" Until her death in 1883, supported by her bestselling ghostwritten *Narrative of Sojourner Truth* (1850), she promoted causes spiritual and separatist, but got nowhere with her call for a "Negro State." After the Civil War, under the influence of Elizabeth Cady Stanton, Sojourner Truth also promoted feminist causes, as "Ain't I a Woman?" reveals, reminding her audiences that half the freed slaves were women.

Well, children, where there is so much racket there must be something out of kilter. I think that 'twixt the negroes of the South and the women at the North, all talking about rights, the white men will be in a fix pretty soon. But what's all this here talking about? 1

That man over there says women need to be helped into carriages, 2
and lifted over ditches, and to have the best place everywhere. Nobody ever helps me into carriages, or over mud-puddles, or gives me
any best place! And ain't I a woman? Look at me! Look at my arm! I
have ploughed and planted, and gathered into barns, and no man
could head me! And ain't I a woman? I could work as much and eat
as much as a man—when I could get it—and bear the lash as well!
And ain't I a woman? I have borne thirteen children, and seen them
most all sold off to slavery, and when I cried out with my mother's
grief, none but Jesus heard me! And ain't I a woman?

Then they talk about this thing in the head; what's this they call 3
it? [Intellect, someone whispers.] That's it, honey. What's that got to
do with women's rights or negro's rights? If my cup won't hold but
a pint, and yours holds a quart, wouldn't you be mean not to let me
have my little half-measure full?

Then that little man in black there, he says women can't have as 4
much rights as men, 'cause Christ wasn't a woman! Where did your
Christ come from? Where did your Christ come from? From God and
a woman! Man had nothing to do with Him.

If the first woman God ever made was strong enough to turn the 5
world upside down all alone, these women together ought to be able
to turn it back, and get it right side up again! And now they is asking
to do it, the men better let them.

Obliged to you for hearing me, and now old Sojourner ain't got 6
nothing more to say.

RESPONDING TO READING

Key words: community family freedom gender identity
power race rights talk

Rhetorical concepts: comparison and contrast deduction definition
illustration proclamation speech

1. Identify the setting of this speech. Who are "that man over there" and
"that little man in black"? What kind of talk ("all this here talking") is Sojourner Truth responding to? How does she establish her credentials as someone with authority?

2. Sojourner Truth's speech is about the same length as Lincoln's "Gettysburg Address," and the two have much else in common. The questions in
this book about Lincoln's speech ask you to deduce the value system from
it; do the same analysis here. Then compare the values expressed in both
speeches. Could the values in this speech also serve as the basis for reconciliation, here between black and white, men and women?

3. To what degree are the grievances set out in this speech now resolved?

Refer to the Margaret Walker essay ("On Being Female, Black, and Free"), and other selections you find pertinent, as well as to your own experience as you prepare your response.

The Civil Rights Movement: What Good Was It?

ALICE WALKER

Alice Walker (born 1944) was the youngest of her Georgia share-cropper parents' eight children. Growing up in a rigidly segregated hometown, and in a three room house filled to bursting, Walker escaped through walking in the fields, writing detailed notebooks, and reading: "Books became my world because the world I was in was very hard." Her formal education, two years at Spelman College followed by two at Sarah Lawrence (B.A. 1965) launched her in a career as a writer. "The Civil Rights Movement: What Good Was It?" was Walker's first published essay, written when she was 23. She chose to reprint it in 1983 in her collection of essays, *In Search of Our Mothers' Gardens*. This indicates that although it is an eye-witness commentary on living in the South during the Civil Rights movement of the 1960s, the issues, the experiences of Walker and other blacks, the significance of Dr. King's activities (see "Letter from Birmingham Jail," pp. 541–557), and the social and political causes on which it focuses are still very much alive.

As Walker told an interviewer, "Writing to me is not about audience. It's about living. It's about expanding myself as much as I can and seeing myself in as many roles and situations as possible," particularly those depicting poor and working class blacks. Her first novel, *Meridian* (1976), has been called the best novel of the civil rights movement. Her most recent book is her fifth volume of poetry, *Her Blue Body Everything We Know: Earthling Poems (1965–90)* (1991). Walker is best known for *The Color Purple* (1983), winner of the Pulitzer Prize and the National Book Award, inspiring in its portrayal of Celie, who overcomes sexual and racial harrassment, poverty, and illiteracy to fulfill Everywoman's dream, "I got love, I got work, I got money, friends and time."

Someone said recently to an old black lady from Mississippi, whose legs had been badly damaged by local police who arrested her for "disturbing the peace," that the Civil Rights Movement was dead, and asked, since it was dead, what she thought about it. The old lady replied, hobbling out of his presence on her cane, that the Civil Rights Movement was like herself, "if it's dead, it shore ain't ready to lay down!" 1

This old lady is a legendary freedom fighter in her small town in the Delta. She has been severely mistreated for insisting on her rights 2 as an American citizen. She has been beaten for singing Movement songs, placed in solitary confinement in prisons for talking about freedom, and placed on bread and water for praying aloud to God for her jailers' deliverance. For such a woman the Civil Rights Movement will never be over as long as her skin is black. It also will never be over for over twenty million others with the same "affliction," for whom the Movement can never "lay down," no matter how it is killed by the press and made dead and buried by the white American public. As long as one black American survives, the struggle for equality with other Americans must also survive. This is a debt we owe to those blameless hostages we leave to the future, our children.

Still, white liberals and deserting Civil Rights sponsors are quick 3
to justify their disaffection from the Movement by claiming that it is all over. "And since it is over," they will ask, "would someone kindly tell me what has been gained by it?" They then list statistics supposedly showing how much more advanced segregation is now than ten years ago—in schools, housing, jobs. They point to a gain in conservative politicians during the last few years. They speak of ghetto riots and of the survey that shows that most policemen are admittedly too anti-Negro to do their jobs in ghetto areas fairly and effectively. They speak of every area that has been touched by the Civil Rights Movement as somehow or other going to pieces.

They rarely talk, however, about human attitudes among Negroes 4
that have undergone terrific changes just during the past seven to ten years (not to mention all those years when there was a Movement and only the Negroes knew about it). They seldom speak of changes in personal lives because of the influence of people in the Movement. They see general failure and few, if any, individual gains.

They do not understand what it is that keeps the Movement from 5
"laying down" and Negroes from reverting to their former *silent* second-class status. They have apparently never stopped to wonder why it is always the white man—on his radio and in his newspaper and on his television—who says that the Movement is dead. If a Negro were audacious enough to make such a claim, his fellows might hanker to see him shot. The Movement is dead to the white man because it no longer interests him. And it no longer interests him because he can afford to be uninterested: he does not have to live by it, with it, or for it, as Negroes must. He can take a rest from the news of beatings, killings, and arrests that reach him from North and South—if his skin is white. Negroes cannot now and will never be able to take a rest from the injustices that plague them, for they—not the white man— are the target.

Perhaps it is naive to be thankful that the Movement "saved" a 6
large number of individuals and gave them something to live for, even

if it did not provide them with everything they wanted. (Materially, it provided them with precious little that they wanted.) When a movement awakens people to the possibilities of life, it seems unfair to frustrate them by then denying what they had thought was offered. But what was offered? What was promised? What was it all about? What good did it do? Would it have been better, as some have suggested, to leave the Negro people as they were, unawakened, unallied with one another, unhopeful about what to expect for their children in some future world?

I do not think so. If knowledge of my condition is all the freedom   7
I get from a "freedom movement," it is better than unawareness, forgottenness, and hopelessness, the existence that is like the existence of a beast. Man only truly lives by knowing; otherwise he simply performs, copying the daily habits of others, but conceiving nothing of his creative possibilities as a man, and accepting someone else's superiority and his own misery.

When we are children, growing up in our parents' care, we await   8
the spark from the outside world. Sometimes our parents provide it—if we are lucky—sometimes it comes from another source far from home. We sit, paralyzed, surrounded by our anxiety and dread, hoping we will not have to grow up into the narrow world and ways we see about us. We are hungry for a life that turns us on; we yearn for a knowledge of living that will save us from our innocuous lives that resemble death. We look for signs in every strange event; we search for heroes in every unknown face.

It was just six years ago that I began to be alive. I had, of course,   9
been living before—for I am now twenty-three—but I did not really know it. And I did not know it because nobody told me that I—a pensive, yearning, typical high-school senior, but Negro—existed in the minds of others as I existed in my own. Until that time my mind was locked apart from the outer contours and complexion of my body as if it and the body were strangers. The mind possessed both thought and spirit—I wanted to be an author or a scientist—which the color of the body denied. I had never seen myself and existed as a statistic exists, or as a phantom. In the white world I walked, less real to them than a shadow; and being young and well hidden among the slums, among people who also did not exist—either in books or in films or in the government of their own lives—I waited to be called to life. And, by a miracle, I was called.

There was a commotion in our house that night in 1960. We had   10
managed to buy our first television set. It was battered and overpriced, but my mother had gotten used to watching the afternoon soap operas at the house where she worked as a maid, and nothing could satisfy

her on days when she did not work but a continuation of her "stories."
So she pinched pennies and bought a set.

I remained listless throughout her "stories," tales of pregnancy, 11
abortion, hypocrisy, infidelity, and alcoholism. All these men and
women were white and lived in houses with servants, long staircases
that they floated down, patios where liquor was served four times a
day to "relax" them. But my mother, with her swollen feet eased out
of her shoes, her heavy body relaxed in our only comfortable chair,
watched each movement of the smartly coiffed women, heard each
word, pounced upon each innuendo and inflection, and for the du-
ration of these "stories" she saw herself as one of them. She placed
herself in every scene she saw, with her braided hair turned blond,
her two hundred pounds compressed into a sleek size-seven dress,
her rough dark skin smooth and *white*. Her husband became "dark
and handsome," talented, witty, urbane, charming. And when she
turned to look at my father sitting near her in his sweatshirt with his
smelly feet raised on the bed to "air," there was always a tragic look
of surprise on her face. Then she would sigh and go out to the kitchen
looking lost and unsure of herself. My mother, a truly great woman
who raised eight children of her own and half a dozen of the neighbors' without a single complaint, was convinced that she did not exist
compared to "them." She subordinated her soul to theirs and became
a faithful and timid supporter of the "Beautiful White People." Once
she asked me, in a moment of vicarious pride and despair, if I didn't
think that "they" were "jest naturally smarter, prettier, better." My
mother asked this: a woman who never got rid of any of her children,
never cheated on my father, was never a hypocrite if she could help
it, and never even tasted liquor. She could not even bring herself to
blame "them" for making her believe what they wanted her to believe:
that if she did not look like them, think like them, be sophisticated
and corrupt-for-comfort's-sake like them, she was a nobody. Black
was not a color on my mother; it was a shield that made her invisible.

Of course, the people who wrote the soap-opera scripts always 12
made the Negro maids in them steadfast, trusty, and wise in a home-
remedial sort of way; but my mother, a maid for nearly forty years,
never once identified herself with the scarcely glimpsed black servant's face beneath the ruffled cap. Like everyone else, in her daydreams at least, she thought she was free.

Six years ago, after half-heartedly watching my mother's soap 13
operas and wondering whether there wasn't something more to be
asked of life, the Civil Rights Movement came into my life. Like a
good omen for the future, the face of Dr. Martin Luther King, Jr.,
was the first black face I saw on our new television screen. And, as

in a fairy tale, my soul was stirred by the meaning for me of his mission—at the time he was being rather ignominiously dumped into a police van for having led a protest march in Alabama—and I fell in love with the sober and determined face of the Movement. The singing of "We Shall Overcome"—that song betrayed by nonbelievers in it— rang for the first time in my ears. The influence that my mother's soap operas might have had on me became impossible. The life of Dr. King, seeming bigger and more miraculous than the man himself, because of all he had done and suffered, offered a pattern of strength and sincerity I felt I could trust. He had suffered much because of his simple belief in nonviolence, love, and brotherhood. Perhaps the majority of men could not be reached through these beliefs, but because Dr. King kept trying to reach them in spite of danger to himself and his family, I saw in him the hero for whom I had waited so long.

What Dr. King promised was not a ranch-style house and an acre 14 of manicured lawn for every black man, but jail and finally freedom. He did not promise two cars for every family, but the courage one day for all families everywhere to walk without shame and unafraid on their own feet. He did not say that one day it will be us chasing prospective buyers out of our prosperous well-kept neighborhoods, or in other ways exhibiting our snobbery and ignorance as all other ethnic groups before us have done; what he said was that we had a right to live anywhere in this country we chose, and a right to a meaningful well-paying job to provide us with the upkeep of our homes. He did not say we had to become carbon copies of the white American middle class; but he did say we had the right to become whatever we wanted to become.

Because of the Movement, because of an awakened faith in the 15 newness and imagination of the human spirit, because of "black and white together"—for the first time in our history in some human relationship on and off TV—because of the beatings, the arrests, the hell of battle during the past years, I have fought harder for my life and for a chance to be myself, to be something more than a shadow or a number, than I had ever done before in my life. Before, there had seemed to be no real reason for struggling beyond the effort for daily bread. Now there was a chance at that other that Jesus meant when He said we could not live by bread alone.

I have fought and kicked and fasted and prayed and cursed and 16 cried myself to the point of existing. It has been like being born again, literally. Just "knowing" has meant everything to me. Knowing has pushed me out into the world, into college, into places, into people.

Part of what existence means to me is knowing the difference 17 between what I am now and what I was then. It is being capable of looking after myself intellectually as well as financially. It is being able to tell when I am being wronged and by whom. It means being awake to protect myself and the ones I love. It means being a part of the world community, and being *alert* to which part it is that I have joined, and knowing how to change to another part if that part does not suit me. To know is to exist: to exist is to be involved, to move about, to see the world with my own eyes. This, at least, the Movement has given me.

The hippies and other nihilists would have me believe that it is 18 all the same whether the people in Mississippi have a movement behind them or not. Once they have their rights, they say, they will run all over themselves trying to be just like everybody else. They will be well fed, complacent about things of the spirit, emotionless, and without the marvelous humanity and "soul" that the Movement has seen them practice time and time again. "What has the Movement done," they ask, "with the few people it has supposedly helped?" "Got them white-collar jobs, moved them into standardized ranch houses in white neighborhoods, given them nondescript gray flannel suits?" "What are these people now?" they ask. And then they answer themselves, "Nothings!"

I would find this reasoning—which I have heard many, many 19 times from hippies and nonhippies alike—amusing if I did not also consider it serious. For I think it is a delusion, a cop-out, an excuse to disassociate themselves from a world in which they feel too little has been changed or gained. The real question, however, it appears to me, is not whether poor people will adopt the middle-class mentality once they are well fed; rather, it is whether they will ever be well fed enough to be able to choose whatever mentality they think will suit them. The lack of a movement did not keep my mother from *wishing* herself bourgeois in her daydreams.

There is widespread starvation in Mississippi. In my own state of 20 Georgia there are more hungry families than Lester Maddox[1] would like to admit—or even see fed. I went to school with children who ate red dirt. The Movement has prodded and pushed some liberal senators into pressuring the government for food so that the hungry may eat. Food stamps that were two dollars and out of the reach of many families not long ago have been reduced to fifty cents. The price is still out of the reach of some families, and the government, it seems to a lot of people, could spare enough free food to feed its own people. It angers people in the Movement that it does not; they point to the billions in wheat we send free each year to countries abroad. Their government's slowness while people are hungry, its unwillingness to

---

[1]Governor of Georgia, 1967–71.

believe that there are Americans starving, its stingy cutting of the price of food stamps, make many Civil Rights workers throw up their hands in disgust. But they do not give up. They do not withdraw into the world of psychedelia. They apply what pressure they can to make the government give away food to hungry people. They do not plan so far ahead in their disillusionment with society that they can see these starving families buying identical ranch-style houses and sending their snobbish children to Bryn Mawr and Yale. They take first things first and try to get them fed.

They do not consider it their business, in any case, to say what 21 kind of life the people they help must lead. How one lives is, after all, one of the rights left to the individual—when and if he has opportunity to choose. It is not the prerogative of the middle class to determine what is worthy of aspiration. There is also every possibility that the middle-calss people of tomorrow will turn out ever so much better than those of today. I even know some middle-class people of today who are not *all* bad.

I think there are so few Negro hippies because middle-class Ne- 22 groes, although well fed, are not careless. They are required by the treacherous world they live in to be clearly aware of whoever or whatever might be trying to do them in. They are middle class in money and position, but they cannot afford to be middle class in complacency. They distrust the hippie movement because they know that it can do nothing for Negroes as a group but "love" them, which is what all paternalists claim to do. And since the only way Negroes can survive (which they cannot do, unfortunately, on love alone) is with the support of the group, they are wisely wary and stay away.

A white writer tried recently to explain that the reason for the 23 relatively few Negro hippies is that Negroes have built up a "super cool" that cracks under LSD and makes them have a "bad trip." What this writer doesn't guess is that Negroes are needing drugs less than ever these days for any kind of trip. While the hippies are "tripping," Negroes are going after power, which is so much more important to their survival and their children's survival than LSD and pot.

Everyone would be surprised if the Israelis ignored the Arabs and 24 took up "tripping" and pot smoking. In this country we are the Israelis. Everybody who can do so would like to forget this, of course. But for us to forget it for a minute would be fatal. "We Shall Overcome" is just a song to most Americans, *but we must do it.* Or die.

What good was the Civil Rights Movement? If it had just given 25 this country Dr. King, a leader of conscience, for once in our lifetime, it would have been enough. If it had just taken black eyes off white television stories, it would have been enough. If it had fed one starving child, it would have been enough.

If the Civil Rights Movement is "dead," and if it gave us nothing 26
else, it gave us each other forever. It gave some of us bread, some of
us shelter, some of us knowledge and pride, all of us comfort. It gave
us our children, our husbands, our brothers, our fathers, as men
reborn and with a purpose for living. It broke the pattern of black
servitude in this country. It shattered the phony "promise" of white
soap operas that sucked away so many pitiful lives. It gave us history
and men far greater than Presidents. It gave us heroes, selfless men
of courage and strength, for our little boys and girls to follow. It gave
us hope for tomorrow. It called us to life.

Because we live, it can never die.   27

RESPONDING TO READING

Key words: class community discovery education family
freedom growing up identity minority power
race rights striving transformation

Rhetorical concepts: analysis autobiography cause and effect
illustration narrative/example process

1.   To what degree does your own experience confirm or deny Walker's
statement that the Civil Rights "Movement is dead to the white man because
it no longer interests him"?
2.   Examine Walker's argument that "Man only truly lives by knowing." This
echoes Socrates's statement that "the unexamined life is not worth living."
Do you agree with Walker that it is always a good idea to "yearn for a
knowledge of living," to be "called to life" through reflection? Does Walker's
mother, "a truly great woman" dreaming reality through the soap operas,
exemplify a person "called to life" as the writer defines it? Why or why not?
3.   Describe the two visions of life presented to the writer by the soap operas
and by Dr. Martin Luther King, Jr. Why does Walker not feel it wrong that
some people choose a vision of life she disagrees with? What, finally, does
she find life-giving about the Movement?
4.   What gives meaning to your own life? What good ideas dominate your
goals and knowledge of yourself? Do you have a figure (such as King was
for Walker) who models this meaning for you? Do you relate your life in any
way to political ideas? Develop an argument about the place of goals, ideals,
and models, in your life or anyone's life.

What Is a Good Scientific Idea?

Those Crazy Ideas

ISAAC ASIMOV

Isaac Asimov (1920–1992) was an astonishingly prolific writer of nearly five hundred volumes, notably of science and science fiction. He wrote seven days a week, from 7:30 A.M. until 10:00 P.M.; his demanding schedule allowed two—and only two—drafts of everything. The first on a typewriter and, in recent years, the second on a computer. Over the course of fifty years he averaged a book every six weeks. "Nightfall" was chosen by the Science Fiction Writers of America as "the best science fiction work of all time."

Called by astronomer Carl Sagan "the greatest explainer of the age," Asimov earned a Ph.D. in chemistry from Columbia in 1948 and won numerous awards for his science writing as well as for his science fiction. He said, "I'm on fire to explain, and happiest when it's something reasonably intricate which I can make clear step by step." Three things, he claims, are essential in explaining technical subjects for general readers. "One is an understanding of what it is you're trying to explain." Another is "an understanding of the position of those to whom you're trying to explain it." Many scientists, Asimov observes, cannot remember what it is like to be a newcomer to a field, and their writing is too technical, too complicated for lay readers to understand. The third quality science writers need is self assurance, so they can write simply without worrying about sounding ignorant. "In my case," said Asimov, "since I'm an extraordinarily self-assured person, I'm not afraid."

Asimov's writing is considered by reviewers such as Ray Sokolov and Alfred Bester as "encyclopedic, witty, with a gift for colorful and illuminating examples and explanations"—qualities apparent in "Those Crazy Ideas." There he explains the creative processes by which two scientists, Charles Darwin and Alfred Russel Wallace, arrived independently at the theory of evolution. He then analyzes how they worked to illustrate the common characteristics of the creative process, a combination of education, intelligence, intuition, courage, and luck.

Time and time again I have been asked (and I'm sure others who 1 have, in their time, written science fiction have been asked too): "Where do you get your crazy ideas?"

Over the years, my answers have sunk from flattered confusion 2 to a shrug and a feeble smile. Actually, I don't really know, and the lack of knowledge doesn't really worry me, either, as long as the ideas keep coming.

370

But then some time ago, a consultant firm in Boston, engaged in 3
a sophisticated space-age project for the government, got in touch
with me.

What they needed, it seemed, to bring their project to a successful 4
conclusion were novel suggestions, startling new principles, conceptual breakthroughs. To put it into the nutshell of a well-turned phrase,
they needed "crazy ideas."

Unfortunately, they didn't know how to go about getting crazy 5
ideas, but some among them had read my science fiction, so they
looked me up in the phone book and called me to ask (in essence),
"Dr. Asimov, where do you get your crazy ideas?"

Alas, I still didn't know, but as speculation is my profession, I 6
am perfectly willing to think about the matter and share my thoughts
with you.

The question before the house, then, is: How does one go about 7
creating or inventing or dreaming up or stumbling over a new and
revolutionary scientific principle?

For instance—to take a deliberately chosen example—how did 8
Darwin come to think of evolution?

To begin with, in 1831, when Charles Darwin was twenty-two, 9
he joined the crew of a ship called the *Beagle*. This ship was making
a five-year voyage about the world to explore various coast lines and
to increase man's geographical knowledge. Darwin went along as
ship's naturalist, to study the forms of life in far-off places.

This he did extensively and well, and upon the return of the *Beagle* 10
Darwin wrote a book about his experiences (published in 1840) which
made him famous. In the course of this voyage, numerous observations led him to the conclusion that species of living creatures changed
and developed slowly with time; that new species descended from
old. This, in itself was not a new idea. Ancient Greeks had had
glimmerings of evolutionary notions. Many scientists before Darwin,
including Darwin's own grandfather, had theories of evolution.

The trouble, however, was that no scientist could evolve an ex- 11
planation for the *why* of evolution. A French naturalist, Jean Baptiste
de Lamarck, had suggested in the early 1800s that it came about by
a kind of conscious effort or inner drive. A tree-grazing animal, attempting to reach leaves, stretched its neck over the years and transmitted a longer neck to its descendants. The process was repeated
with each generation until a giraffe in full glory was formed.

The only trouble was that acquired characteristics are not inher- 12
ited and this was easily proved. The Lamarckian explanation did not
carry conviction.

Charles Darwin, however, had nothing better to suggest after 13
several years of thinking about the problem.

But in 1798, eleven years before Darwin's birth, an English clergy- 14
man named Thomas Robert Malthus had written a book entitled *An
Essay on the Principle of Population*. In this book Malthus suggested that
the human population always increased faster than the food supply
and that the population had to be cut down by either starvation,
disease, or war; that these evils were therefore unavoidable.

In 1838 Darwin, still puzzling over the problem of the develop- 15
ment of species, read Malthus's book. It is hackneyed to say "in a
flash" but that, apparently, is how it happened. In a flash, it was clear
to Darwin. Not only human beings increased faster than the food
supply; all species of living things did. In every case, the surplus
population had to be cut down by starvation, by predators, or by
disease. Now no two members of any species are exactly alike; each
has slight individual variations from the norm. Accepting this fact,
which part of the population was cut down?

Why—and this was Darwin's breakthrough—those members of 16
the species who were less efficient in the race for food, less adept at
fighting off or escaping from predators, less equipped to resist disease,
went down.

The survivors, generation after generation, were better adapted, 17
on the average, to their environment. The slow changes toward a
better fit with the environment accumulated until a new (and more
adapted) species had replaced the old. Darwin thus postulated the
reason for evolution as being the action of *natural selection*. In fact,
the full title of his book is *On the Origin of Species by Means of Natural
Selection, or the Preservation of Favoured Races in the Struggle for Life*. We
just call it *The Origin of Species* and miss the full flavor of what it was
he did.

It was in 1838 that Darwin received this flash and in 1844 that he 18
began writing his book, but he worked on for fourteen years gathering
evidence to back his thesis. He was a methodical perfectionist and
no amount of evidence seemed to satisfy him. He always wanted
more. His friends read his preliminary manuscripts and urged him
to publish. In particular, Charles Lyell (whose book *Principles of Geology*, published in 1830–1833, first convinced scientists of the great
age of the earth and thus first showed there was *time* for the slow
progress of evolution to take place) warned Darwin that someone
would beat him to the punch.

While Darwin was working, another and younger English natu- 19
ralist, Alfred Russel Wallace, was traveling in distant lands. He too
found copious evidence to show that evolution took place and he too
wanted to find a reason. He did not know that Darwin had already
solved the problem.

He spent three years puzzling, and then in 1858, he too came 20 across Malthus's book and read it. I am embarrassed to have to become hackneyed again, but in a flash he saw the answer. Unlike Darwin, however, he did not settle down to fourteen years of gathering and arranging evidence.

Instead, he grabbed pen and paper and at once wrote up his 21 theory. He finished this in two days.

Naturally, he didn't want to rush into print without having his 22 notions checked by competent colleagues, so he decided to send it to some well-known naturalist. To whom? Why, to Charles Darwin. To whom else?

I have often tried to picture Darwin's feeling as he read Wallace's 23 essay which, he afterward stated, expressed matters in almost his own words. He wrote to Lyell that he had been forestalled "with a vengeance."

Darwin might easily have retained full credit. He was well known 24 and there were many witnesses to the fact that he had been working on his project for a decade and a half. Darwin, however, was a man of the highest integrity. He made no attempt to suppress Wallace. On the contrary, he passed on the essay to others and arranged to have it published along with a similar essay of his own. The year after, Darwin published his book.

Now the reason I chose this case was that here we have two men 25 making one of the greatest discoveries in the history of science independently and simultaneously and under precisely the same stimulus. Does that mean *anyone* could have worked out the theory of natural selection if they had but made a sea voyage and combined that with reading Malthus?

Well, let's see. Here's where the speculation starts. 26

To begin with, both Darwin and Wallace were thoroughly grounded 27 in natural history. Each had accumulated a vast collection of facts in the field in which they were to make their breakthrough. Surely this is significant.

Now every man in his lifetime collects facts, individual pieces of 28 data, items of information. Let's call these "bits" (as they do, I think, in information theory). The "bits" can be of all varieties: personal memories, girls' phone numbers, baseball players' batting averages, yesterday's weather, the atomic weights of the chemical elements.

Naturally, different men gather different numbers of different 29 varieties of "bits." A person who has collected a larger number than usual of those varieties that are held to be particularly difficult to obtain—say, those involving the sciences and the liberal arts—is considered "educated."

There are two broad ways in which the "bits" can be accumulated. 30 The more common way, nowadays, is to find people who already possess many "bits" and have them transfer those "bits" to your mind in good order and in predigested fashion. Our schools specialize in this transfer of "bits" and those of us who take advantage of them receive a "formal education."

The less common way is to collect "bits" with a minimum amount 31 of live help. They can be obtained from books or out of personal experience. In that case you are "self-educated." (It often happens that "self-educated" is confused with "uneducated." This is an error to be avoided.)

In actual practice, scientific breakthroughs have been initiated by 32 those who were formally educated, as for instance by Nicolaus Copernicus, and by those who were self-educated, as for instance by Michael Faraday.

To be sure, the structure of science has grown more complex over 33 the years and the absorption of the necessary number of "bits" has become more and more difficult without the guidance of someone who has already absorbed them. The self-educated genius is therefore becoming rarer, though he has still not vanished.

However, without drawing any distinction according to the man- 34 ner in which "bits" have been accumulated, let's set up the first criterion for scientific creativity:

1) The creative person must possess as many "bits" of information 35 as possible; i.e., he must be educated.

Of course, the accumulation of "bits" is not enough in itself. We 36 have probably all met people who are intensely educated, but who manage to be abysmally stupid, nevertheless. They have the "bits," but the "bits" just lie there.

But what is there one can do with "bits"?   37

Well, one can combine them into groups of two or more. Everyone 38 does that; it is the principle of the string on the finger. You tell yourself to remember *a* (to buy bread) when you observe *b* (the string). You enforce a combination that will not let you forget *a* because *b* is so noticeable.

That, of course, is a conscious and artificial combination of "bits." 39 It is my feeling that every mind is, more or less unconsciously, continually making all sorts of combinations and permutations of "bits," probably at random.

Some minds do this with greater facility than others; some minds 40 have greater capacity for dredging the combinations out of the unconscious and becoming consciously aware of them. This results in "new ideas," in "novel outlooks."

The ability to combine "bits" with facility and to grow consciously 41 aware of the new combinations is, I would like to suggest, the measure of what we call "intelligence." In this view, it is quite possible to be educated and yet not intelligent.

Obviously, the creative scientist must not only have his "bits" on 42 hand but he must be able to combine them readily and more or less consciously. Darwin not only observed data, he also made deductions—clever and far-reaching deductions—from what he observed. That is, he combined the "bits" in interesting ways and drew important conclusions.

So the second criterion of creativity is: 43

2) The creative person must be able to combine "bits" with facility 44 and recognize the combinations he has formed; i.e., he must be intelligent.

Even forming and recognizing new combinations is insufficient 45 in itself. Some combinations are important and some are trivial. How do you tell which are which? There is no question but that a person who cannot tell them apart must labor under a terrible disadvantage. As he plods after each possible new idea, he loses time and his life passes uselessly.

There is also no question but that there are people who somehow 46 have the gift of seeing the consequences "in a flash" as Darwin and Wallace did; of feeling what the end must be without consciously going through every step of the reasoning. This, I suggest, is the measure of what we call "intuition."

Intuition plays more of a role in some branches of scientific knowl- 47 edge than others. Mathematics, for instance, is a deductive science in which, once certain basic principles are learned, a large number of items of information become "obvious" as merely consequences of those principles. Most of us, to be sure, lack the intuitive powers to see the "obvious."

To the truly intuitive mind, however, the combination of the few 48 necessary "bits" is at once extraordinarily rich in consequences. Without too much trouble they see them all, including some that have not been seen by their predecessors.[1]

It is perhaps for this reason that mathematics and mathematical 49 physics have seen repeated cases of first-rank breakthroughs by youngsters. Evariste Galois evolved group theory at twenty-one. Isaac Newton worked out calculus at twenty-three. Albert Einstein presented the theory of relativity at twenty-six, and so on.

In those branches of science which are more inductive and require 50 larger numbers of "bits" to begin with, the average age of the scientists

---

[1]The Swiss mathematician, Leonhard Euler, said that to the true mathematician, it is at once obvious that $e^{\pi i} = -1$.

at the time of the breakthrough is greater. Darwin was twenty-nine at the time of his flash, Wallace was thirty-five.

But in any science, however inductive, intuition is necessary for 51 creativity. So:

3) The creative person must be able to see, with as little delay as 52 possible, the consequences of the new combinations of "bits" which he has formed; i.e., he must be intuitive.

But now let's look at this business of combining "bits" in a little 53 more detail. "Bits" are at varying distances from each other. The more closely related two "bits" are, the more apt one is to be reminded of one by the other and to make the combination. Consequently, a new idea that arises from such a combination is made quickly. It is a "natural consequence" of an older idea, a "corollary." It "obviously follows."

The combination of less related "bits" results in a more startling 54 idea; if for no other reason than that it takes longer for such a combination to be made, so that the new idea is therefore less "obvious." For a scientific breakthrough of the first rank, there must be a combination of "bits" so widely spaced that the random chance of the combination being made is small indeed. (Otherwise, it will be made quickly and be considered but a corollary of some previous idea which will then be considered the "breakthrough.")

But then, it can easily happen that two "bits" sufficiently widely 55 spaced to make a breakthrough by their combination are not present in the same mind. Neither Darwin nor Wallace, for all their education, intelligence, and intuition, possessed the key "bits" necessary to work out the theory of evolution by natural selection. Those "bits" were lying in Malthus's book, and both Darwin and Wallace had to find them there.

To do this, however, they had to read, understand, and apprec- 56 iate the book. In short, they had to be ready to incorporate other people's "bits" and treat them with all the ease with which they treated their own.

It would hamper creativity, in other words, to emphasize intensity 57 of education at the expense of broadness. It is bad enough to limit the nature of the "bits" to the point where the necessary two would not be in the same mind. It would be fatal to mold a mind to the point where it was incapable of accepting "foreign bits."

I think we ought to revise the first criterion of creativity, then, to 58 read:

1) The creative person must possess as many "bits" as possible, 59 falling into as wide a variety of types as possible; i.e., he must be broadly educated.

As the total amount of "bits" to be accumulated increases with 60 the advance of science, it is becoming more and more difficult to gather enough "bits" in a wide enough area. Therefore, the practice of "brain-busting" is coming into popularity; the notion of collecting thinkers into groups and hoping that they will cross-fertilize one another into startling new breakthroughs.

Under what circumstances could this conceivably work? (After 61 all, anything that will stimulate creativity is of first importance to humanity.)

Well, to begin with, a group of people will have more "bits" on 62 hand than any member of the group singly since each man is likely to have some "bits" the others do not possess.

However, the increase in "bits" is not in direct proportion to the 63 number of men, because there is bound to be considerable overlapping. As the group increases, the smaller and smaller addition of completely new "bits" introduced by each additional member is quickly outweighed by the added tensions involved in greater numbers; the longer wait to speak, the great likelihood of being interrupted, and so on. It is my (intuitive) guess that five is as large a number as one can stand in such a conference.

Now of the three criteria mentioned so far, I feel (intuitively) that 64 intuition is the least common. It is more likely that none of the group will be intuitive than that none will be intelligent or none educated. If no individual in the group is intuitive, the group as a whole will not be intuitive. You cannot add non-intuition and form intuition.

If one of the group is intuitive, he is almost certain to be intelligent 65 and educated as well, or he would not have been asked to join the group in the first place. In short, for a brain-busting group to be creative, it must be quite small and it must possess at least one creative individual. But in that case, does that one individual need the group? Well, I'll get back to that later.

Why did Darwin work fourteen years gathering evidence for a 66 theory he himself must have been convinced was correct from the beginning? Why did Wallace send his manuscript to Darwin first instead of offering it for publication at once?

To me it seems that they must have realized that any new idea is 67 met by resistance from the general population who, after all, are not creative. The more radical the new idea, the greater the dislike and distrust it arouses. The dislike and distrust aroused by a first-class breakthrough are so great that the author must be prepared for unpleasant consequences (sometimes for expulsion from the respect of the scientific community; sometimes, in some societies, for death).

Darwin was trying to gather enough evidence to protect himself 68 by convincing others through a sheer flood of reasoning. Wallace wanted to have Darwin on his side before proceeding.

It takes courage to announce the results of your creativity. The 69 greater the creativity, the greater the necessary courage in much more than direct proportion. After all, consider that the more profound the breakthrough, the more solidified the previous opinions; the more "against reason" the new discovery seems, the more against cherished authority.

Usually a man who possesses enough courage to be a scientific 70 genius seems odd. After all, a man who has sufficient courage or irreverence to fly in the face of reason or authority *must* be odd, if you define "odd" as "being not like most people." And if he is courageous and irreverent in such a colossally big thing, he will certainly be courageous and irreverent in many small things so that being odd in one way, he is apt to be odd in others. In short, he will seem to the noncreative, conforming people about him to be a "crackpot."

So we have the fourth criterion: 71

4) The creative person must possess courage (and to the general 72 public may, in consequence, seem a crackpot).

As it happens, it is the crackpottery that is most often most no- 73 ticeable about the creative individual. The eccentric and absent-minded professor is a stock character in fiction; and the phrase "mad scientist" is almost a cliché.

(And be it noted that I am never asked where I get my interesting 74 or effective or clever or fascinating ideas. I am invariably asked where I get my *crazy* ideas.)

Of course, it does not follow that because the creative individual 75 is usually a crackpot, that any crackpot is automatically an unrecognized genius. The chances are low indeed, and failure to recognize that the proposition cannot be so reversed is the cause of a great deal of trouble.

Then, since I believe that combinations of "bits" take place quite 76 at random in the unconscious mind, it follows that it is quite possible that a person may possess all four of the criteria I have mentioned in superabundance and yet may never happen to make the necessary combination. After all, suppose Darwin had never read Malthus. Would he ever have thought of natural selection? What made him pick up the copy? What if someone had come in at the crucial time and interrupted him?

So there is a fifth criterion which I am at a loss to phrase in any 77 other way than this:

5) A creative person must be lucky.   78

To summarize: 79

A creative person must be 1) broadly educated, 2) intelligent, 80 3) intuitive, 4) courageous, and 5) lucky.

How, then, does one go about encouraging scientific creativity? 81
For now, more than ever before in man's history, we must; and the
need will grow constantly in the future.

Only, it seems to me, by increasing the incidence of the various 82
criteria among the general population.

Of the five criteria, number 5 (luck) is out of our hands. We can 83
only hope; although we must also remember Louis Pasteur's famous
statement that "Luck favors the prepared mind." Presumably, if we
have enough of the four other criteria, we shall find enough of number
five as well.

Criterion 1 (broad education) is in the hands of our school system. 84
Many educators are working hard to find ways of increasing the quality of education among the public. They should be encouraged to
continue doing so.

Criterion 2 (intelligence) and 3 (intuition) are inborn and their 85
incidence cannot be increased in the ordinary way. However, they
can be more efficiently recognized and utilized. I would like to see
methods devised for spotting the intelligent and intuitive (particularly
the latter) early in life and treating them with special care. This, too,
educators are concerned with.

To me, though, it seems that it is criterion 4 (courage) that receives 86
the least concern, and it is just the one we may most easily be able
to handle. Perhaps it is difficult to make a person more courageous
than he is, but that is not necessary. It would be equally effective to
make it sufficient to be less courageous; to adopt an attitude that
creativity is a permissible activity.

Does this mean changing society or changing human nature? I 87
don't think so. I think there are ways of achieving the end that do
not involve massive change of anything, and it is here that brain-
busting has its greatest chance of significance.

Suppose we have a group of five that includes one creative in- 88
dividual. Let's ask again what that individual can receive from the
non-creative four.

The answer to me, seems to be just this: Permission!   89

They must permit him to create. They must tell him to go ahead 90
and be a crackpot.[2]

How is this permission to be granted? Can four essentially non- 91
creative people find it within themselves to grant such permission?
Can the one creative person find it within himself to accept it?

---

[2]Always with the provision, of course, that the crackpot creation that results survives the test
of hard inspection. Though many of the products of genius seem crackpot at first, very few of the
creations that seem crackpot turn out, after all, to be products of genius.

I don't know. Here, it seems to me, is where we need experi-   92
mentation and perhaps a kind of creative breakthrough about creativity. Once we learn enough about the whole matter, who knows—
I may even find out where I get those crazy ideas.

RESPONDING TO READING

Key words: community   discovery   education   reality   science
striving

Rhetorical concepts: cause and effect   comparison and contrast
definition   explanation   illustration   narrative/example
process

1.   When is a "crazy idea" a good idea (i.e. a "new and revolutionary scientific principle") and not simply the crackpot notion of a mad scientist?
2.   What five qualities does Asimov say are necessary for creativity? In what
ways do these operate in people with different "styles" of creativity, such as
Charles Darwin and Alfred Russel Wallace?
3.   To what extent must a good idea find a receptive climate? What happens
to "crazy ideas" that are ahead of the times?
4.   What is your style of creativity? Is it the same under all circumstances,
or do you exercise different types of creativity in different areas that call for
different skills, understanding, and performance (such as writing, cooking,
playing the piano, playing tennis, or being a good friend)?
5.   How do you know when you have a good idea? How can you decide
whether one idea—of your own or someone else—is better than another?
When does creativity involve risk-taking? What is the relation of risk-taking
to what Asimov calls "courage"?

Understanding Natural Selection
CHARLES DARWIN

During his lukewarm study of medicine at Edinburgh University
from 1825 to 1828, and equally desultory preparation for the clergy
at Cambridge (B.A. 1831), Charles Darwin (1809–1882) was most
alert when studying natural phenomena, particularly beetles. He
was even known to pop a rare specimen into his mouth to preserve
it when his hands were full of other newly-collected insects. Ultimately this naturalist and biologist was to have over a hundred species of animals and plants named after him, ranging from a water
beetle to a giant tortoise, as well as sea channels and bays, mountains, towns, a volcano, and Darwin College at his alma mater.
    In 1859 Darwin published his major work, *On the Origin of Species*

by Means of Natural Selection, or the Preservation of Favoured Races in the Struggle for Life. This book was based on his painstaking observations of animals and plants that were begun during his voyage to South America aboard the Beagle, 1831–1836. The scientific world has not been the same since. "Understanding Natural Selection," a small portion of this work, contains the essence of Darwin's best known and most revolutionary principles, that in natural selection those variations, "infinitesimally small inherited modifications," endure if they aid in survival. The claim that these modifications occur gradually, rather than being produced at a single stroke by a Divine Creator, is the basis for Darwin's theory of evolution, which antagonized Victorian clergy and continues to challenge contemporary creationists.

Darwin's work prevailed, in part, because of his clear and elegant literary style. Using the techniques of popular literature to explain sophisticated scientific concepts and to present mountains of detailed information, Darwin is a highly engaging writer, making extensive use of the first person, metaphors, anecdotes, and illustrations. "I never study style," he said, "all that I do is to try to get the subject as clear as I can in my own head, and express it in the commonest language which occurs to me. But I generally have to think a good deal before the simplest arrangement and words occur to me."

It may be said that natural selection is daily and hourly scrutinizing, throughout the world, every variation, even the slightest; rejecting that which is bad, preserving and adding up all that is good; silently and insensibly working, whenever and wherever opportunity offers, at the improvement of each organic being in relation to its organic and inorganic conditions of life. We see nothing of these slow changes in progress, until the hand of time has marked the long lapses of ages, and then so imperfect is our view into long past geological ages, that we only see that the forms of life are now different from what they formerly were.   1

Although natural selection can act only through and for the good of each being, yet characters and structures, which we are apt to consider as of very trifling importance, may thus be acted on. When we see leaf-eating insects green, and bark-feeders mottled-grey; the alpine ptarmigan white in winter, the red-grouse the color of heather, and the black-grouse that of peaty earth, we must believe that these tints are of service to these birds and insects in preserving them from danger. Grouse, if not destroyed at some period of their lives, would increase in countless numbers; they are known to suffer largely from birds of prey; and hawks are guided by eyesight to their prey—so much so, that on parts of the Continent persons are warned not to keep white pigeons, as being the most liable to destruction. Hence I can see no reason to doubt that natural selection might be most effective in giving the proper color to each kind of grouse, and in keeping   2 that color, when once acquired, true and constant. Nor ought we to think that the occasional destruction of an animal of any particular color would produce little effect: we should remember how essential it is in a flock of white sheep to destroy every lamb with the faintest trace of black. In plants the down on the fruit and the color of the flesh are considered by botanists as characters of the most trifling importance: yet we hear from an excellent horticulturist, Downing, that in the United States smooth-skinned fruits suffer far more from a beetle, a curculio, than those with down; that purple plums suffer far more from a certain disease than yellow plums; whereas another disease attacks yellow-fleshed peaches far more than those with other colored flesh. If, with all the aids of art, these slight differences make a great difference in cultivating the several varieties, assuredly, in a state of nature, where the trees would have to struggle with other trees and with a host of enemies, such differences would effectually settle which variety, whether a smooth or downy, a yellow or purple fleshed fruit, should succeed.

In looking at many small points of difference between species, 3 which, as far as our ignorance permits us to judge, seem to be quite unimportant, we must not forget that climate, food, and so on probably produce some slight and direct effect. It is, however, far more necessary to bear in mind that there are many unknown laws of correlation to growth, which, when one part of the organization is modified through variation, and the modifications are accumulated by natural selection for the good of the being, will cause other modifications, often of the most unexpected nature.

As we see that those variations which under domestication appear 4 at any particular period of life, tend to reappear in the offspring of the same period; for instance, in the seeds of the many varieties of our culinary and agricultural plants; in the caterpillar and cocoon stages of the varieties of the silkworm; in the eggs of poultry, and in the color of the down of their chickens; in the horns of our sheep and cattle when nearly adult; so in a state of nature, natural selection will be enabled to act on and modify organic beings at any age, by the accumulation of profitable variations at that age, and by their inheritance at a corresponding age. If it profit a plant to have its seeds more and more widely disseminated by the wind, I can see no greater difficulty in this being effected through natural selection, than in the cotton-planter increasing and improving by selection the down in the pods on his cotton-trees. Natural selection may modify and adapt the larva of an insect to a score of contingencies, wholly different from those which concern the mature insect. These modifications will no doubt affect, through the laws of correlation, the structure of the adult; and probably in the case of those insects which live only for a few hours, and which never feed, a large part of their structure is merely the correlated result of successive changes in the structure of their larvae. So, conversely, modifications in the adult will probably often affect the structure of the larva; but in all cases natural selection will ensure that modifications consequent on other modifications at a different period of life, shall not be in the least degree injurious: for if they became so, they would cause the extinction of the species.

Natural selection will modify the structure of the young in relation   5
to the parent, and of the parent in relation to the young. In social animals it will adapt the structure of each individual for the benefit of the community; if each in consequence profits by the selected change. What natural selection cannot do, is to modify the structure of one species, without giving it any advantage, for the good of another species; and though statements to this effect may be found in works of natural history, I cannot find one case which will bear investigation. A structure used only once in an animal's whole life, if of high importance to it, might be modified to any extent by natural selection; for instance, the great jaws possessed by certain insects, and used exclusively for opening the cocoon—or the hard tip to the beak of nestling birds, used for breaking the egg. It has been asserted, that of the best short-beaked tumbler-pigeons more perish in the egg than are able to get out of it; so that fanciers assist in the act of hatching. Now, if nature had to make the beak of a full-grown pigeon very short for the bird's own advantage, the process of modification would be very slow, and there would be simultaneously the most rigorous selection of the young birds within the egg, which had the most powerful and hardest beaks, for all with weak beaks would inevitably perish: or, more delicate and more easily broken shells might be selected, the thickness of the shell being known to vary like every other structure.

Sexual Selection

Inasmuch as peculiarities often appear under domestication in   6
one sex and become hereditarily attached to that sex, the same fact probably occurs under nature, and if so, natural selection will be able to modify one sex in its functional relations to the other sex, or in relation to wholly different habits of life in the two sexes, as is sometimes the case with insects. And this leads me to say a few words on what I call sexual selection. This depends, not on a struggle for existence, but on a struggle between the males for possession of the females; the result is not death to the unsuccessful competitor, but few or no offspring. Sexual selection is, therefore, less rigorous than natural selection. Geneally, the most vigorous males, those which are

best fitted for their places in nature, will leave most progeny. But in many cases, victory will depend not on general vigor, but on having special weapons, confined to the male sex. A hornless stag or spurless cock would have a poor chance of leaving offspring. Sexual selection by always allowing the victor to breed might surely give indomitable courage, length to the spur, and strength to the wing to strike in the spurred leg, as well as the brutal cock-fighter, who knows well that he can improve his breed by careful selection of the best cocks. How low in the scale of nature this law of battle descends, I know not; male alligators have been described as fighting, bellowing, and whirling round, like Indians in a war dance, for the possession of the females; male salmons have been seen fighting all day long; male stag-beetles often bear wounds from the huge mandibles of other males. The war is, perhaps, severest between the males of polygamous animals, and these seem oftenest provided with special weapons. The males of carnivorous animals are already well armed; though to them and to others, special means of defence may be given through means of sexual selection, as the mane to the lion, the shoulder-pad to the boar, and the hooked jaw to the male salmon; for the shield may be as important for victory, as the sword or spear.

Amongst birds, the contest is often of a more peaceful character.   7 All those who have attended to the subject, believe that there is the severest rivalry between the males of many species to attract by singing the females. The rock-thrush of Guiana, birds of Paradise, and some others, congregate; and successive males display their gorgeous plumage and perform strange antics before the females, which standing by as spectators, at last choose the most attractive partner. Those who have closely attended to birds in confinement well know that they often take individual preferences and dislikes: thus Sir R. Heron has described how one pied peacock was eminently attractive to all his hen birds. It may appear childish to attribute any effect to such apparently weak means: I cannot here enter on the details necessary to support this view; but if man can in a short time give elegant carriage and beauty to his bantams, according to his standard of beauty, I can see no good reason to doubt that female birds, by selecting, during thousands of generations, the most melodious or beautiful males, according to their standard of beauty, might produce a marked effect. I strongly suspect that some well-known laws with respect to the plumage of male and female birds, in comparison with the plumage of the young, can be explained on the view of plumage having been chiefly modified by sexual selection, acting when the birds have come to the breeding age or during the breeding season; the modifications thus produced being inherited at corresponding ages or seasons, either by the males alone, or by the males and females; but I have not space here to enter on this subject.

Thus it is, as I believe, that when the males and females of any animal have the same general habits of life, but differ in structure, color, or ornament, such differences have been mainly caused by sexual selection; that is, individual males have had, in successive generations, some slight advantage over other males, in their weapons, means of defence, or charms; and have transmitted these advantages to their male offspring. Yet, I would not wish to attribute all such sexual differences to this agency: for we see peculiarities arising and becoming attached to the male sex in our domestic animals (as the wattle in male carriers, horn-like protuberances in the cocks of certain fowls, and so on), which we cannot believe to be either useful to the males in battle, or attractive to the females. We see analogous cases under nature, for instance, the tuft of hair on the breast of the turkey-cock, which can hardly be either useful or ornamental to this bird; indeed, had the tuft appeared under domestication, it would have been called a monstrosity. 8

Illustration of the Action of Natural Selection

. . . Let us take the case of a wolf, which preys on various animals, securing some by craft, some by strength, and some by fleetness; and let us suppose that the fleetest prey, a deer for instance, had from any change in the country increased in numbers, or that other prey had decreased in numbers, during that season of the year when the wolf is hardest pressed for food. I can under such circumstances see no reason to doubt that the swiftest and slimmest wolves would have the best chance of surviving, and so be preserved or selected—provided always that they retained strength to master their prey at this or at some other period of the year, when they might be compelled to prey on other animals. I can see no more reason to doubt this, than that man can improve the fleetness of his greyhounds by careful and methodical selection, or by that unconscious selection which results from each man trying to keep the best dogs without any thought of modifying the breed. 9

Even without any change in the proportional numbers of the animals on which our wolf preyed, a cub might be born with an innate tendency to pursue certain kinds of prey. Nor can this be thought very improbable; for we often observe great differences in the natural tendencies of our domestic animals; one cat, for instance, taking to catch rats, another mice; one cat . . . bringing home winged game, another hares or rabbits, and another hunting on marshy ground and 10 almost nightly catching woodcocks or snipes. The tendency to catch rats rather than mice is known to be inherited. Now, if any slight innate change of habit or of structure benefited an individual wolf, it would have the best chance of surviving and of leaving offspring. Some of its young would probably inherit the same habits or structure, and by the repetition of this process, a new variety might be formed which would either supplant or coexist with the parent-form of wolf. Or, again, the wolves inhabiting a mountainous district, and those frequenting the lowlands, would naturally be forced to hunt different prey; and from the continued preservation of the individuals best fitted for the two sites, two varieties might slowly be formed. These varieties would cross and blend where they met; but to this subject of intercrossing we shall soon have to return. I may add, that . . . there are two varieties of the wolf inhabiting the Catskill Mountains in the United States, one with a light greyhound-like form, which pursues deer, and the other more bulky, with shorter legs, which more frequently attacks the shepherd's flocks.

RESPONDING TO READING

Key words: animals   discovery   identity   nature   reality
science   transformation

Rhetorical concepts: analysis   cause and effect   definition
explanation   illustration   induction   process   research report.

1.   Notice that Darwin does not use the term "evolution" nor does he speak of the origin of the human race. What does he mean by "natural selection," and how did that concept lead into the controversy about evolution of humans?
2.   Refer to Stephen Jay Gould's "Evolution as Fact and Theory" in Chapter 2. Is Darwin speaking about what Gould calls evolution as fact? As theory? Or both, or neither?
3.   Compare the way Darwin proceeds in his argument with the way Gould does. Notice the differences in style, kinds of evidence, force of conclusions, and personal involvement. Which differences do you attribute to stylistic and rhetorical changes over the century that separates the two writers and which are essential differences in approach?
4.   Darwin later dropped much of his interest in what he here calls "sexual selection." Compare the strength of that argument with that of the argument for natural selection. Which has better supporting evidence? Which is the better idea? Why?
5.   Is it a good idea for scientists to look closely at the origin of humanity and of the earth, or should they leave such matters to philosophers and theologians? Do you see science and religion as fundamentally incompatible, or

as partners in a quest for knowledge and understanding, or as related in some other way? In your discussion of these matters, refer to some of the other selections in this book, such as those by Gould, Goodall, and Keller in Chapter 2; and those by Hawking and Levi-Montalcini in Chapter 3.

Science's Restive Public

BARBARA J. CULLITON

Barbara J. Culliton (born 1943) has been a science writer since graduating from Vassar College in 1965. Throughout her professional life she has worked in Washington, D.C., as a reporter for *Science News*, *Medical World News*, and *Science*, where she is currently a news editor. Since 1988, she has also been a commentator on the weekly PBS radio program, *Science Journal*.

In "Science's Restive Public," Culliton addresses an audience of scientists about the implications of public participation in issues that many of her readers consider to be the domain of specialists in science, most particularly, "the conduct and application of research." Although some of the references in the essay date from the time it was written (the mid 1970s), none of the issues have gone away. DNA research and gene splicing remain in the news, and issues of public health are even more public than before, given the advent of AIDS. Public concern for scientific issues continues to grow: the possible loss of earth's protective ozone layer threatens our descendants with radiation, droughts threaten our water supply while floods damage homes, demonstrations at family planning clinics focus on when life may be said to begin, and those protesting research using animals invade and destroy some laboratories.

As Culliton points out, science has many different publics, and not all of them are supportive. Many scientists look back at a history of public interference in scientific research as a dark age, typified by the forced recantation of Galileo of his findings about the structure of the universe. If scientific research and funding are in the hands of nonscientists, will that result in limitations on what scientists can do, what questions they can pursue, what experiments they can conduct? Or, on the other hand, will science be more responsible to the public good and less isolated, less arrogant?

This is the era of "public participation" in science. The once wide-   1
spread feeling that scientists alone should have domain over the scientific enterprise is being replaced by a philosophy that calls for public involvement in science, irrespective of the fact that many of the elders of science find the idea abhorrent. The public has demanded a voice in decisions about the conduct and application of research and, to some moderate extent, that voice is being heard. In some instances,

public involvement in science has more value in form than in substance. But in important ways, public influences are affecting the course of research itself. Certainly the advent of public participation has changed the social climate in which the scientific community works. There are things happening in the sciences now, in the mid-1970s, that were barely imaginable a decade ago.

At hospitals throughout the United States, nonphysicians now sit   2
on the committees that review all protocols for human experimentation. The National Institutes of Health, in September, 1977, held a public meeting to evaluate and set policy for mammography, inviting laymen as well as professionals to present their views about the use of X-rays to screen women for breast cancer. A month later, the relatively unknown but congressionally mandated National Commission on Digestive Diseases began a series of hearings, to be held in nine states, "to hear from the people who pay the price [of digestive disease] in pain—the patients and their families." The National Science Foundation is struggling with a congressional directive to establish a "science for citizens" program to provide scientific expertise to citizens' groups that wish to challenge government policy on environmental issues, energy matters, or whatever. In at least three western states, decisions about the use of nuclear power have been decided by referenda.

And there is recombinant DNA—at present one of the more com-   3
pelling issues. Questions about how, or even whether, to proceed with recombinant DNA experimentation have been asked in public for four years. In the early summer of 1976, the flamboyant mayor of Cambridge, Massachusetts, effectively and dramatically put recombinant DNA at the very center of debate about public participation in science when he threatened to prohibit that kind of research at Harvard and the Massachusetts Institute of Technology. Research with recombinant DNA has been on the agenda of official bodies in at least seven states in addition to Massachusetts. And at the top of the political hierarchy, bills that would govern recombinant DNA research are being considered by Congress.

If there is no mistaking that the era of public participation in   4
science is upon us, neither can there be much doubt that the majority of scientists are still quite uncomfortable with the idea that anyone other than an investigator and his or her peers should have any voice in decisions about research. The scientists' spectrum of opinion runs from a grudging acceptance of public participation as a cumbersome annoyance to an alarmed view of the public participation movement as a menace to their right of free inquiry. As Massachusetts Senator Edward M. Kennedy said, ". . . academia has been on the defensive. It has chosen to view public scrutiny as a threat to scientific inde-

pendence. It has chosen to view public involvement in particular research areas as inappropriate and representative of a trend toward
anti-intellectualism."[1]

Is the idea of public participation in science really a manifestation   5
of anti-intellectualism? Does the public really want to limit scientific
inquiry? What are the origins of the public participation movement
and who is science's "public"? Just what does "public participation"
mean? These are among the questions that require consideration in
any attempt to understand the present social and political climate and
its effects on the scientific community. Furthermore, they are pertinent to addressing a problem that was simply stated by Senator Kennedy and Senator Jacob K. Javits when they wrote in 1975: "Perhaps
as the relationship between science and the public has evolved and
changed in recent years, all parties have failed to understand both
what is happening and what, ideally, ought to happen in the future."[2]

The idea that the public should somehow monitor and possibly   6
curb science is a logical extension of the activist attitudes that became
so powerful during the 1960s, coupled with a general realization that
the application of new knowledge is not always to the good and with
a deepening mistrust of the ability of established institutions to make
good decisions. Large numbers of academics rallied in public protest
over domestic social issues and, then, over the war in Vietnam. The
environmental and consumer movements were growing. Welfare
agencies were confronted by clients who demanded a say in the way
programs for their benefit were developed. University students demanded, and in many cases won, what was said to be their right to
sit on curriculum committees and to evaluate their teachers. It is not
surprising that science too became an object of activist attention. People who feel left out of decisions that affect their lives have demanded
that the establishment let them in.

University of Chicago philosopher Stephen Toulmin describes the   7
present social environment with a striking metaphor: ". . . a lot of
the difficulties that arise about the relations between the scientific
community and the rest of society at the present time have important
and significant parallels with the medieval problems of relations between church and state. . . . What we're faced with . . . is the Protestant Reformation. What we're faced with is a demand from the rest
of society to be let in on the whole system of the ecclesiastical

---

[1]Edward M. Kennedy, in an address at the Harvard School of Public Health, May 1975.

[2]Edward M. Kennedy and Jacob K. Javits, in a letter to Willard Gaylin, president of the Institute
of Society, Ethics and the Life Sciences, October 19, 1975.

courts. . . . I think that [the public] suspect that the closure of the mechanisms of discussion is, in effect, a way of keeping them from debate about things that are really their business."[3]

But who is it that wants to be let in? The "public"? I think not; 8 certainly not the proverbial man in the street. What evidence there is about him indicates that he has not lost faith in science, even though he realizes that the indiscriminate application of technology can be harmful. But there are no convincing data that the general public is antiscience or that it wishes to undermine the scientific tradition. What is happening is something else; the scientists themselves are challenging the way the research enterprise is run. Many of the voices calling for some change in ways of doing business are the voices of men and women who have made a serious, essentially full-time career representing what they describe as the public interest. Workers in environmental and consumer organizations thus constitute one of science's many publics. Some of those workers have training in science; most have some special interest in research or technology. All of them have invested a good deal of their professional lives and identities in being public representatives, but they surely cannot be equated with the man on the street.

Another important public is composed of practicing scientists. To 9 a great extent, dissent against the traditional methods and presumptions of the scientific community is coming from within science itself. The difference is that the dissenters are taking their case to public forums. They appear in newspapers, on television, and before government bodies. Thus, when Harvard scientists who opposed certain kinds of recombinant DNA experiments failed to persuade the majority of their peers to take their side, they proceeded to take their fight, not to the university's board of overseers, but to the city mayor. One group of scientists has become, in effect, the public of another.

Science, of courses, has other publics too, most of them falling 10 into the category of special interest groups. In biomedical science, the American Cancer Society and the American Heart Association are a kind of public. Occasionally, the general public itself spontaneously makes its views about some scientific decision known. It did so in the spring and summer of 1977 when the Food and Drug Administration moved to take saccharin out of diet foods and colas. But this was a rare event, made possible by the occurrence of two circumstances. First, the issue directly touches the lives of millions of citizens who have no particular connection with science. Second, the public did not understand or fully accept the scientific data that convinced

---

[3] Stephen Toulmin, in remarks made at a conference on "Biomedical Research and the Public," Airlie House, April 1–3, 1976.

the FDA saccharin might be hazardous. And so when Congress voted to postpone the FDA's proposed ban, it did so in response to real public feeling. No discussion of public participation in science can ignore the pivotal role of Congress in making decisions that affect the course of science. Besides, it is the Congress that is so often the focal point of activities of all of science's other publics, for sooner or later each special interest public takes its case to Capitol Hill.

To acknowledge that for the most part the general public has little 11 to do with science policy is in no way to diminish the role played by science's various publics. In this decade, two important series of events have occurred that will affect indelibly the course of biomedical research. One is the creation of the National Commission for the Protection of Human Subjects of Biomedical and Behavioral Research, which grew out of a very public debate about experimentation on the human fetus. The other is the debate over research on recombinant DNA, an episode that has not yet concluded, but which is parallel in many aspects to the story of the National Commission, though the latter has to do with clinical research and the former a more "fundamental" science.

A comparison of the legislative origins of the National Commis- 12 sion and of proposed legislation governing recombinant DNA reveals the nature of the many publics of science and the manner in which they influence either specific research or the social and intellectual climate in which it takes place. It is often an adversarial process. In the case of recombinant DNA, public involvement depended totally upon the openness of the scientists who brought the issue before the world, and upon the opinions of scientific experts on both sides. In each case, public involvement and subsequent regulation occurred in areas that assumed public importance because of scientific progress. In neither case is there strong evidence that large numbers of citizens or legislators wished to limit free inquiry. Rather, they proceeded from a desire to protect individuals and society at large from harm. The intent is to control action, not thought. But it can be argued that the new sense of public awareness and the climate it engenders have put an end to the myth of the scientist-scholar free to follow his experimental life wherever it may lead.

Recombinant DNA research marks a maturing of biology. In the 13 early summer of 1973, scientists attending the Gordon Conference on nucleic acids first fully realized that techniques for combining genes from one species with those of another—recombinant DNA techniques—were well developed. It meant that scientists could create in the laboratory brand new organisms that had never existed in nature. It was very heady stuff. But the scientists present at that conference were not so swept away with excitement that they failed to take clear notice of the fact that careless use or misuse of the new technology could be hazardous. They decided to go public with their concerns. Conference leaders Maxine Singer of the National Institutes of Health and Dieter Soll of Yale, acting on behalf of the conference, wrote to the presidents of the National Academy of Sciences and the Institute of Medicine. They called attention to the theoretical hazards of the experimentation and urged that the issue be carefully considered; they published their letter in *Science*.[4] The Academy convened a committee chaired by Paul Berg, a Stanford biologist who was a leader in the recombinant DNA field and a man convinced of the need to proceed with caution. Within a year, the Berg committee had met and come to the conclusions that an international conference should be held to assess the safety issues and, most startlingly, that in the interim, scientists should observe a voluntary moratorium on certain types of potentially troublesome recombinant DNA experiments. Again, the issue was put before the public. Berg and his colleagues called for a moratorium at a press conference held at the Academy in July 1974, and formally made their appeal in a letter published that month in *Science* and *Nature*.[5]

These were extraordinary events, and in some quarters, Singer, 14 Soll, Berg, and the others were roundly criticized for voicing their concerns in the first place and endorsing the idea of a moratorium in the second. But they took the steps they did out of a great sense of responsibility to the public, and not unmindful of the fact that the present revolution in biology might be analogous to the revolution in physics that gave scientists the knowledge to make an atomic bomb. The biologists chose not to remain silent. But they were hardly prepared for the public reaction that was to come. Their international conference, held at Asilomar in Pacific Grove, California, in February 1975, drew wide and nearly universally laudatory press coverage. However, shortly thereafter, the voices of dissent were heard. The conference produced two pertinent recommendations, that the National Institutes of Health develop guidelines on recombinant DNA experimentation (the conferees produced a suggested draft), and that the moratorium on certain types of experiments continue until those guidelines could be developed.

At this point, the critics stepped in. Among their charges was 15 that what was being proposed amounted to scientists asking the public to allow them to regulate themselves (which is precisely what they

[4]*Science*, 181 (September 21, 1973): 113.

[5]*Science*, 181 (July 26, 1974): 303; and *Nature* 250 (July 19, 1974): 175.

were asking) and that the public had been wrongly left out of the decision-making. This position was argued at a special congressional hearing in the spring of 1975 called by Senator Kennedy. It was arranged in the form of a debate with two scientists arguing on one side that the public needed to be brought into the act and two who had been active at Asilomar arguing on the other side—that only scientists could set effective policy because only they could understand the complexities of the science itself.[6] In addition, they testified against the possibility of federal regulation of recombinant DNA research on grounds that it would stifle freedom of inquiry. The circumstances of that hearing were typical of what was to come. It was a public hearing but there was no public participation (except for Kennedy). Scientists were talking to each other in public, competing for public approval, but the public itself did not have much to say.

As interest in the recombinant DNA debate began to grow, alle- 16 gations that the public had been left out of the discussion were supplemented with claims that the research itself was an imminent hazard to the public health, not to mention a violation of the laws of God and evolution. And, as before, the dissenting voices were those of scientists (though not recombinant DNA researchers). The rhetoric escalated. Nobel laureate George Wald took the floor at a public hearing and likened an imaginary outbreak of recombinant DNA organisms to Legion fever—"unidentifiable and impossible to trace to its source." In a magazine piece entitled "New Strains of Life—or Death," Lieb Cavalieri of New York's Memorial Sloan Kettering Institute called forth images of a "new" Andromeda strain, neglecting to note that the old Andromeda strain is entirely fictional, and imagined a situation in which "cancer, normally not infectious, is spread in epidemic proportions by normally harmless bacteria."[7] Erwin Chargaff of Columbia University, in a letter to *Science*, referred to the "awesome irreversibility of what is being contemplated" by recombinant DNA experimentation, and said, "You can stop splitting the atom. You can stop visiting the moon; you can stop using aerosols; you may even decide not to kill entire populations by the use of a few bombs. But you cannot recall a new form of life. . . . An irreversible attack on the biosphere is something so unheard-of, so unthinkable to previous generations, that I could only wish that mine had not been guilty of it."[8]

On the other side, scientists talk about using recombinant DNA 17

---

[6]Hearing before the Senate Subcommittee on Health, April 22, 1975. For a report, see Barbara J. Culliton, *Science*, 188 (June 20, 1975): 1187–1189.

[7]Lieb Cavalieri, *The New York Times Magazine*, August 22, 1976.

[8]*Science*, 192 (June 4, 1976): 138–139.

research to grow new types of plants to provide food enough for all the world's peoples and speculate that recombinant DNA studies may hold the cure for cancer. As to the matter of risks, Nobel laureate James Watson, at a New York State hearing on legislation, called recombinant DNA "the most overblown thing since . . . the fall-out shelter debacle."[9]

Recombinant DNA is an example of an issue in which the public 18 and its elected representatives must depend upon scientists and their "expert" opinion in order to come to any sensible opinion about matters such as the relative risks as against benefits of the research. Indeed, as Cambridge mayor Alfred Vellucci noted in calling for city council hearings, he never would have taken on the issue had it not been for the fact that he had a group of illustrious scientists on his side. But sorting out the views of the two opposing sides is no easy matter. Faced with hyperbole about a subject that is difficult to understand in its scientific complexity, and confused by the spectacle of Nobel laureates and other leaders of the scientific establishment slugging it out in open meetings, legislators are turning to state and federal regulation—an imperfect solution to an insoluble problem—as might be expected. But legislators are, quite naturally, prone to legislate.

Recombinant DNA is an unfinished story. Persuaded that the 19 public has been left out of decision-making and that the risks are real, Senator Kennedy introduced a bill that would have created a national commission to regulate recombinant DNA research from Washington. For many months, it looked as if that bill would win full Senate approval. However, forceful lobbying by the scientific establishment (which is still learning how to deal with Capitol Hill) at least temporarily forestalled the creation of such a regulatory commission and switched attention to a less restrictive measure pending before the House of Representatives. In this discussion, the final outcome is not important. What is pertinent is that the entire recombinant DNA episode has contributed to the emergence of the traditional scientific community as a "public" in its own right, a public now engaged in what psychiatrist Gerald Klerman describes as renegotiating a contract: ". . . there is underway a renegotiation of the implicit contract between the larger society and the biomedical research community. Indeed, there is a renegotiation of the contract between our society and all the professions—medicine, law, the military and education. In this renegotiation, there are new alliances and new communication patterns."[10]

---

[9]Hearing before New York State Attorney General, New York City, October 21, 1976.

[10]Gerald Klerman, in remarks made at a conference on "Biomedical Research and the Public," Airlie House, April 1–3, 1976.

Among the new alliances or institutions to emerge from this re- 20
negotiation, the National Commission for the Protection of Human
Subjects of Biomedical and Behavioral Research is a unique manifestation of the idea that the public should participate in science, that
researchers should not be left to regulate themselves. Although it is
not a regulatory body per se, the National Commission—mandated
by Congress and appointed by the Secretary of Health, Education,
and Welfare—is in a position to make recommendations that in a
general sense amount to regulations. In an important sense, its authority and power derive from the public it represents. All of its
business is conducted in public. All of its recommendations about
what can be allowed in human experimentation are public. And the
HEW secretary is obliged to accept them or explain in public, in
writing, why not. The National Commission is for clinical research
analogous to what such a commission might be to basic research in
recombinant DNA and, by extension, other areas of biology. It is an
idea that was resolutely resisted at first as an inappropriate intrusion
into an investigator's right to inquiry.

The origins of the National Commission can be traced back to 21
1967 when South African surgeon Christian Barnard transplanted a
human heart into a grocer named Louis Washkansky. For eighteen
days, Washkansky lived on borrowed time, with a borrowed heart.
His name was on the front page of newspapers throughout the world.
Heart transplants captured the public imagination. Surgically, they
were a real tour de force. Emotionally, they were compelling. But they
also brought to public attention questions about the definition of
death, about surgeons playing God, about the appropriate uses of
medical technology. Furthermore, they raised ethical questions about
the fair distribution of a scarce resource, for fresh cadaver hearts were
in short supply.

In 1969, Senator Walter F. Mondale proposed establishing a na- 22
tional commission to contemplate these perplexing new ethical issues,
with an eye to federal intervention of some kind. However, there were
strenuous objections on grounds that the medical research community
should be free to regulate itself. It was also said that the government
should not try to institutionalize anything as personal (some said
irrelevant) as ethics. Mondale's proposal did not get very far at the
time, but it became part of the public record, ready to be taken up
again at a later time.

There were other circumstances in the late 1960s and early 1970s 23
that led Congress inexorably toward the idea of overseeing research
from Washington. A string of horror stories about scientists who
apparently lacked ethical standards was unearthed by the press and

investigated at congressional hearings. There was the Willowbrook scandal involving the exposure of young institutionalized children to hepatitis virus. There was the case of the cancer researcher who injected cancer cells into elderly patients dying of the disease. There was the Tuskegee syphilis experiment in which affected men were left untreated as controls even after penicillin became available. And these were startling, if somewhat overdramatized, reports of scientists perfusing the decapitated heads of fetuses in studies of blood flow. These were isolated incidents, to be sure, not representative of the vast majority of human experimentation. But they certainly seemed to be outrageous. A climate for congressional action was being created.

Another very important element in this brief history is the 1973 24 Supreme Court ruling legalizing abortion. During the preceding few years, a number of scientific advances, ranging from the perfection of techniques for amniocentesis to progress in the chromosomal and biochemical analysis of cells, had made fetal research attractive. Investigators were anxious to study the living fetus in the womb as well as fetal tissues. The abortion ruling, they believed, would make a variety of new studies possible. What was not anticipated, however, was the strength and political effectiveness of "right-to-life" groups whose opposition to abortion spilled over into opposition to all fetal research as well.

By early 1974 bills had been introduced in several state legislatures 25 and in Congress that would have banned fetal research. It was an unprecedented case of legislative intervention in biomedical science that was directed not so much against research as it was against abortion. Two groups of public fought against the proposed bans. One was made up of scientists who wanted to do fetal research. Another consisted of organizations especially interested in certain diseases; they wanted fetal research to go forward because they believed it would lead to desired medical progress. Parents of children with genetic diseases, for example, can make a very persuasive case for fetal research.

The fetal research controversy—every bit as emotional as that over 26 recombinant DNA—posed a substantial threat to scientific inquiry, but it also forged new alliances between legislators and scientists that might otherwise never have come about. In Massachusetts, for example, a state legislator who knew next to nothing about scientific research introduced a bill, at the behest of antiabortion constituents, that would have banned research on all fetuses, living or dead. As a result of that bill, scientists—many of them fetal researchers—who had never dealt with anyone in the statehouse, came out of their laboratories into the political arena. Months of intensive negotiations followed, with two valuable results. First, the objectionable bill was substantially modified. Second, the experience forged an alliance between legislators and scientists that led to the creation of a new committee, comprising scientists and laymen, to advise the legislature on proposed bills that would affect research.[11] The fetal research controversy and related issues about mass screening programs to detect genetic disease led to similar confrontations and, then, new alliances between legislators and scientists in other states as well. Maryland, for example, now has a public commission with authority over all of the state's genetic screening programs, its function being to protect the interests of the public and of science.

The battles that were being waged before state legislatures were   27 also being pressed on Capitol Hill where the stakes seemed even higher. Amendments to ban all fetal research were before both the House and Senate which were also engaged in a debate over the wisdom of creating what became the National Commission for the Protection of Human Subjects of Biomedical and Behavioral Research—fetuses included. The Senate, Senator Kennedy in particular, was for it, the House against; the outcome was apparent. In the Senate, it was conservative James L. Buckley who introduced an anti-fetal-research amendment, tacking it on to Kennedy's bill to establish a federal ethics commission. Then, in a compromise move, Kennedy introduced a "perfecting amendment" that called for a moratorium on fetal research instead of a permanent ban. The proposed commission would be instructed to study the issue and the ban would become permanent when the two houses of Congress met in conference to resolve differences in their respective versions of the National Research Act of 1974. The bill was signed though virtually no one thought it was very good legislation. For the first time, Congress placed a moratorium on a certain kind of research, temporarily limiting inquiry.

The National Commission, whose members are meant to repre-   28 sent the public, was appointed through the most political of processes but emerged as a body that does, in fact, represent a wide range of views. Its eleven members include only five scientists, one of whom was known for his prolife position. It has women, white and black, lawyers, and ethicists, both conservative and liberal. If ever there were a body in a position to limit inquiry, this one is, for it is empowered to ask not just how specific types of research might proceed but whether it should be allowed at all. Thus, it could have recommended against fetal research altogether. Instead, out of a process of give and

[11]Barbara J. Culliton, *Science*, 187 (January 24, 1975) 237–241.

take, of people of divergent beliefs trying hard to understand one another's point of view, there came a compromise which permits fetal research to be conducted as long as carefully spelled out ethical guidelines are followed. It has taken, and will most likely continue to take, compromise positions on research on prisoners, on children, on psychosurgery and on other groups and issues. In its painstakingly achieved compromise, it is probably most effectively representing a very heterogeneous public.

There is every reason to believe that the current trend toward 29 more public participation in science is going to continue. There is little reason to think that it will limit scientific inquiry, as has been feared. What experience there is to judge by indicates that the public can understand complex scientific and ethical problems and that it can arrive at reasoned opinions. The public committee of citizens appointed to review the recombinant DNA issue for the Cambridge City Council did not satisfy those who predicted it would try to stop the research; rather, it accepted by and large the recommendations of scientists who want the work to go on. Nonphysicians who are members of institutional review boards have not brought a halt to human experimentation. Neither has the National Commission.

Public participation is not dangerous for the scientific enterprise. 30 It is time-consuming, there is no doubt about that, as those who have defended clinical and basic research can well attest. And it is likely to lead to restraints that previously were not imposed. Nevertheless, the restraints that come from ethical considerations and recognition of the need for public accountability cannot be dismissed as inappropriate. To the contrary, they may lead in the end to greater public understanding of and appreciation for science. In any case, they are part of the social cost of democracy.

RESPONDING TO READING

Key words: community   discovery   education   nature   power
reality   rights   science

Rhetorical concepts: analysis   cause and effect
deduction   explanation   illustration   process

1.   Culliton announces a series of questions about public participation in science policy, including one asking if such public concern is "really a manifestation of anti-intellectualism." Define anti-intellectualism and give some examples from your experience and reading of American anti-intellectualism.

How is it manifested in relation to science? Then give some examples of public participation in science policy that are not anti-intellectualism.

2.   Do you agree with the "general realization that the application of new knowledge is not always to the good"? Give some examples to support your view. How can we tell if such application is a good idea or not? Who should make decisions on the matter?

3.   The two principal examples in this article are recombinant DNA research and fetal research, both of which have continued to cause public concern during the twenty years since the article was first published. Use these examples or other scientific issues you know about (AIDS research, space exploration, or nutrition, for example) to write an essay on science and the public. Do you agree, from today's perspective, with Culliton's conclusion twenty or so years ago that "public participation is not dangerous for the scientific enterprise"?

4.   Many universities have "oversight" committees on such matters as animal experimentation, nuclear waste, or research on human subjects. Does your campus have such committees? If not, why not? If so, do students and non-scientists sit on the committees and how often do they meet? How effective are they? Write an essay in which you describe and evaluate the degree of public participation in scientific research on your campus.

A Structure for Deoxyribose Nucleic Acid

JAMES D. WATSON and FRANCIS H. C. CRICK

Francis Crick (born in Northampton, England in 1916) earned a B.Sc. from University College, London, in 1937, but he did not receive a doctorate until 1954, from Cambridge University. There he worked as a research scientist for the British Admiralty throughout World War II, and from 1949 to 1977 in the Cavendish laboratories at the Medical Research Council Laboratory at Cambridge, one of the world's most prestigious biological research centers.

James Watson (born in Chicago in 1928) as a child read the *World Almanac* and starred for a time on the Quiz Kids radio show. He earned a Ph.D. in zoology from Indiana University in 1950 when he was twenty-two, and has been a professor at Harvard since 1956. As he candidly admitted in his gossipy and, therefore, controversial bestseller, *The Double Helix: A Personal Account of the Discovery of the Structure of DNA* (1968), he wanted to go to Cavendish, where the action was, and to work on what at the time was the most challenging problem in biochemistry, the attempt to unlock the master code to heredity in all living organisms. In *The Double Helix* Watson confesses to attaching himself to the research team most likely to make this discovery, and thereby to win the race for the Nobel Prize.

Indeed, Watson, Crick, and colleague Maurice Wilkins were awarded the 1962 Nobel Prize in Medicine for discovering the structure of the deoxyribose nucleic acid (DNA) molecule, considered as the greatest single breakthrough in twentieth century biology because it revealed how genetic material is reproduced. To discover "The Molecular Structure of Nucleic Acids," the researchers used a "Tinker-Toy approach," building models until they discovered the spiral staircase-like double helix—"a structure this pretty just had to exist," exulted Watson in *The Double Helix*. They reported their findings in the essay reprinted here from *Nature* (April 1953). As S. Michael Halloran notes in "The Birth of Molecular Biology" (*Rhetoric Review*, 1986), this essay is very different from the typical scientific article, in its brevity (900 words), its absence of research methodology and technical data, and its understated, genteel, personal and proprietary tone. The single sentence of paragraph 12 ("It has not escaped our notice . . .") stakes the authors' claim to the Nobel Prize.

We wish to suggest a structure for the salt of deoxyribose nucleic   1
acid (D.N.A.). This structure has novel features which are of considerable biological interest.

A structure for nucleic acid has already been proposed by Pauling   2
and Corey.[1] They kindly made their manuscript available to us in advance of publication. Their model consists of three intertwined chains, with the phosphates near the fibre axis, and the bases on the outside. In our opinion, this structure is unsatisfactory for two reasons: (1) We believe that the material which gives the X-ray diagrams is the salt, not the free acid. Without the acidic hydrogen atoms it is not clear what forces would hold the structure together, especially as the negatively charged phosphates near the axis will repel each other. (2) Some of the van der Waals distances appear to be too small.

Another three-chain structure has also been suggested by Fraser. . . .   3
In his model the phosphates are on the outside and the bases on the inside, linked together by hydrogen bonds. This structure as described is rather ill-defined, and for this reason we shall not comment on it.

We wish to put forward a radically different structure for the salt   4
of deoxyribose nucleic acid. This structure has two helical chains each coiled round the same axis [see Figure 1]. We have made the usual chemical assumptions, namely, that each chain consists of phosphate diester groups joining β-D-deoxyribofuranose residues with 3′,5′ linkages. The two chains (but not their bases) are related by a dyad perpendicular to the fibre axis. Both chains follow right-handed helices, but owing to the dyad the sequences of the atoms in the two chains run in opposite directions. Each chain loosely resembles Furberg's[2] model No. 1; that is, the bases are on the inside of the helix

[1]Pauling, L., and Corey, R. B., *Nature*, 171, 346 (1953); *Proc. U.S. Nat. Acad. Sci.*, 39, 84 (1953).

[2]Furberg, S., *Acta Chem. Scand.*, 6, 634 (1952).

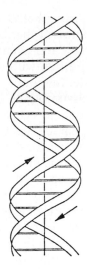

FIGURE 1. The Double Helix. This figure is purely diagrammatic. The two ribbons symbolize the two phosphate–sugar chains, and the horizontal rods the pairs of bases holding the chains together. The vertical line marks the fibre axis.

and the phosphates on the outside. The configuration of the sugar and the atoms near it is close to Furberg's "standard configuration," the sugar being roughly perpendicular to the attached base. There is a residue on each chain every 3·4 A, in the z-direction. We have assumed an angle of 36° between adjacent residues in the same chain, so that the structure repeats after 10 residues on each chain, that is, after 34 A. The distance of a phosphorus atom from the fibre axis is 10 A. As the phosphates are on the outside, cations have easy access to them.

The structure is an open one, and its water content is rather high. At lower water contents we would expect the bases to tilt so that the structure could become more compact.   5

The novel feature of the structure is the manner in which the two chains are held together by the purine and pyrimidine bases. The planes of the bases are perpendicular to the fibre axis. They are joined together in pairs, a single base from one chain being hydrogen-bonded to a single base from the other chain, so that the two lie side by side with identical z-co-ordinates. One of the pair must be a purine and the other a pyrimidine for bonding to occur. The hydrogen bonds are made as follows: purine position 1 to pyrimidine position 1; purine position 6 to pyrimidine position 6.   6

If it is assumed that the bases only occur in the structure in the   7 most plausible tautomeric forms (that is, with the keto rather than the enol configurations) it is found that only specific pairs of bases can bond together. These pairs are: adenine (purine) with thymine (pyrimidine), and guanine (purine) with cytosine (pyrimidine).

In other words, if an adenine forms one member of a pair, on 8 either chain, then on these assumptions the other member must be thymine; similarly for guanine and cytosine. The sequence of bases on a single chain does not appear to be restricted in any way. However, if only specific pairs of bases can be formed, it follows that if the sequence of bases on one chain is given, then the sequence on the other chain is automatically determined.

It has been found experimentally[3,4] that the ratio of the amounts 9 of adenine to thymine, and the ratio of guanine to cytosine, are always very close to unity for deoxyribose nucleic acid.

It is probably impossible to build this structure with a ribose sugar 10 in place of the deoxyribose, as the extra oxygen atom would make too close a van der Waals contact.

The previously published X-ray data[5,6] on deoxyribose nucleic acid 11 are insufficient for a rigorous test of our structure. So far as we can tell, it is roughly compatible with the experimental data, but it must be regarded as unproved until it has been checked against more exact results. Some of these are given in the following communications. We were not aware of the details of the results presented there when we devised our structure, which rests mainly though not entirely on published experimental data and stereo-chemical arguments.

It has not escaped our notice that the specific pairing we have 12 postulated immediately suggests a possible copying mechanism for the genetic material.

Full details of the structure, including the conditions assumed in 13 building it, together with a set of co-ordinates for the atoms, will be published elsewhere.

We are much indebted to Dr. Jerry Donohue for constant advice 14 and criticism, especially on interatomic distances. We have also been stimulated by a knowledge of the general nature of the unpublished experimental results and ideas of Dr. M. H. F. Wilkins, Dr. R. E. Franklin and their co-workers at King's College, London. One of us (J.D.W.) has been aided by a fellowship from the National Foundation for Infantile Paralysis.

---

[3]Chargaff, E., for references see Zamenhof, S., Brawerman, G., and Chargaff, E., *Biochim. et Biophys. Acta*, 9, 402 (1952).

[4]Wyatt, G. R., *J. Gen. Physiol.*, 36, 201 (1952).

[5]Astbury, W. T., Symp. Soc. Exp. Biol. 1, Nucleic Acid, 66 (Camb. Univ. Press, 1947).

[6]Wilkins, M. H. F., and Randall, J. T., *Biochim. et Biophys. Acta*, 10, 192 (1953).

RESPONDING TO READING

Key words: discovery   nature   science

Rhetorical concepts: analysis   cause and effect   definition
induction   process   research report

1.   Describe the features of this scientific report. To what degree does it
depend on previous research? On laboratory results? On theoretical speculation? To what audience is it addressed? Why?

2.   Does it seem strange to you that a major creative discovery in science (or
in anything) should be announced in the style of this article, addressed to
its particular audience? Examine paragraph 12, which describes the astonishing discovery of DNA replication. How might a newspaper headline or a
press agent trumpet such a finding? Compare that language to the sentence
beginning "It has not escaped our notice . . ." (paragraph 12).

3.   Compare this article with other announcements of revolutionary discoveries, such as atomic energy, or the theory of relativity, or the telephone, or
the transistor. You might also compare the article with announcements of
discoveries that turned out not to be as they were claimed, such as cold fusion
or extra-terrestial life forms. What conclusions can you come up with on
appropriate ways to reveal momentous discoveries in science?

The "Cosmic Mystery"

ARTHUR KOESTLER

Arthur Koestler, a prolific journalist, novelist, and popular philosopher, was born in Budapest in 1905 and educated at the University
of Vienna (1922–1926). As a journalist he worked in Egypt, Paris,
flew to the Arctic aboard the Graf Zeppelin, traveled through Central
Asia, and spent a year in the Soviet Union after becoming a member
of the Communist Party in 1931. As a war correspondent in Spain
in 1936, he was sentenced to death by the Fascists and released
through British intervention, only to spend 1939 in a series of alien
detention camps in France after war broke out there. In 1940 he
escaped to England, where he worked for the Ministry of Information
and became a British citizen after World War II. His internationally
acclaimed novel, *Darkness at Noon* (1940), is a powerful psychological
study of an aged Bolshevik victim of the Soviet purge trials of the
1930s. Disillusioned with the Soviet Union and Communism as a
consequence of these trials, he left the party in 1938.

After a quarter century of political writing, Koestler made a conscious decision to stop publishing anti-Communist works, and
turned to science and philosophy, examining such topics as evolution, psychology, the history of science, capital punishment, and the
nature of the creative process, in *The Act of Creation* (1964). *The Wa-*

tershed: A Biography of Johannes Kepler (1960), of which "The 'Cosmic Mystery' " is an early chapter, is adapted from *The Sleepwalkers: A History of Man's Changing Vision of the Universe* (1959). Kepler (1571–1630), the genius who discovered the "laws of dynamics and gravitation," founded modern astronomy and paved the way for Newtonian physics. Koestler's experiences among the persecuted and displaced of the world enabled him to understand and appreciate this strange, tormented genius who "stood astride the historical crest," the watershed (hence the book's title), "the intellectual divide that separated ancient and medieval thought from modern observational science." As Jacob Bronowski observes, among seventeenth century scientists Kepler alone "understood that gravity has no boundary, and put a law to it—which happened to be the wrong law."

From the frustrations of his first year in Gratz, Kepler escaped 1 into the cosmological speculations he had playfully pursued in his Tuebingen days. But now these speculations were becoming both more intense, and more mathematical in character. A year after his arrival—more precisely, on July 9, 1595, for he has carefully recorded the date—he was drawing a figure on the blackboard for his class, when an idea suddenly struck him with such force that he felt he was holding the key to the secret of creation in his hand. "The delight that I took in my discovery," he wrote later, "I shall never be able to describe in words."[1] It determined the course of his life, and remained his main inspiration throughout it.

The idea, centuries old in its essence, was that the universe is 2 built around certain symmetrical figures—triangle, square, pentagon, etc.—which form its invisible skeleton, as it were. Before going into detail, it will be better to explain at once that the idea itself was completely false; yet it led eventually to Kepler's Laws, the demolition of the antique universe on wheels, and the birth of modern cosmology. The pseudo-discovery which started it all is expounded in Kepler's first book, the *Mysterium Cosmographicum*,* which he published at the age of twenty-five.

In the preface to the work, Kepler explained how he came to make 3 his "discovery." While still a student in Tuebingen, he had heard from his teacher in astronomy, Maestlin, about Copernicus, and agreed that the sun must be in the center of the universe—"for physical, or if you prefer, for metaphysical reasons." He then began to wonder why there existed just six planets "instead of twenty or a

---

[1]O.O., Vol. VIII, p. 670 *seq.*, henceforth referred to as "Horoscope."

*The full title reads: *A Forerunner (Prodromus) to Cosmographical Treatises, containing the Cosmic Mystery of the admirable proportions between the Heavenly Orbits and the true and proper reasons for their Numbers, Magnitudes, and Periodic Motions,* by Johannes Kepler, Mathematicus of the Illustrious Estates of Styria, Tuebingen, *anno* 1596.

hundred," and why the distances and velocities of the planets were what they were. Thus started his quest for the laws of planetary motion.

At first he tried to find whether one orbit might perchance be   4
twice, three or four times as large as another. "I lost much time on this task, on this play with numbers; but I could find no order either in the numerical proportions or in the deviations from such proportions." He warns the reader that the tale of his various futile efforts "will anxiously rock thee hither and thither like the waves of the sea." Since he got nowhere, he tried "a startlingly bold solution": he inserted an auxiliary planet between Mercury and Venus, and another between Jupiter and Mars, both supposedly too small to be seen, hoping that now he would get some sensible sequence of ratios. But this did not work either; nor did various other devices which he tried.

> "I lost almost the whole of the summer with this heavy work. Finally I came close to the true facts on a quite unimportant occasion. I believe Divine Providence arranged matters in such a way that what I could not obtain with all my efforts was given to me through chance; I believe all the more that this is so as I have always prayed to God that he should make my plan succeed, if what Copernicus had said was the truth."[2]

The occasion of this decisive event was the aforementioned lecture   5
to his class, in which he had drawn, for quite different purposes, a geometrical figure on the blackboard. The figure showed (I must describe it in a simplified manner) a triangle fitted between two circles; in other words, the outer circle was circumscribed around the triangle, the inner circle inscribed into it.

As he looked at the two circles, it suddenly struck him that their   6
ratios were the same as those of the orbits of Saturn and Jupiter. The rest of the inspiration came in a flash. Saturn and Jupiter are the "first" (i.e., the two outermost) planets, and "the triangle is the first figure in geometry. Immediately I tried to inscribe into the next interval between Jupiter and Mars a square, between Mars and Earth a pentagon, between Earth and Venus a hexagon. . . ."

It did not work—not yet, but he felt that he was quite close to   7
the secret. "And now I pressed forward again. Why look for two-dimensional forms to fit orbits in space? One has to look for three-dimensional forms—and, behold, dear reader, now you have my discovery in your hands!"

---

[2]In 1945, a French unit was advancing on the town and started shelling it in the mistaken belief that the retreating German army had left a rear guard between its walls. At the critical moment a French officer—whose name was given to me as Colonel de Chastigny—arrived at the scene, identified it as Kepler's birthplace, stopped the firing, and saved Weil from destruction.

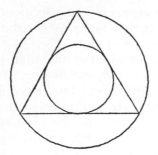

FIGURE 1.

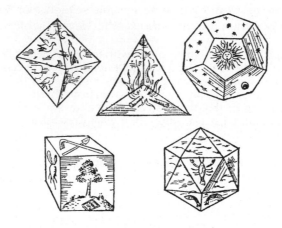

FIGURE 2. The five regular solids. From *Harmonices Mundi*, Liber II (1619).

The point is this. One can construct any number of regular pol-   8
ygons in a two-dimensional plane; but one can construct only a limited
number of regular solids in three-dimensional space. These "perfect
solids," of which all faces are identical, are: (1) the tetrahedron (pyramid) bounded by four equilateral triangles; (2) the cube; (3) the octahedron (eight equilateral triangles); (4) the dodecahedron (twelve
pentagons); and (5) the icosahedron (twenty equilateral triangles).

They were also called the "Pythagorean" or "Platonic" solids,   9
because early Greek thinkers ascribed mystical properties to them.
Being perfectly symmetrical, each can be *inscribed* into a sphere, so
that all its vertices (corners) lie on the surface of the sphere. Similarly,
each can be *circumscribed* around a sphere, so that the sphere touches
every face in its center. It is an odd fact, inherent in the nature of
three-dimensional space, that (as Euclid proved) the number of regular
solids is limited to these five forms. Whatever shape you choose as a

face, no other perfectly symmeterical solid can be constructed except these five. Other combinations just cannot be fitted together.

So there existed only five perfect solids—and five intervals be- 10 tween the planets! It was impossible to believe that this should be by chance, and not by divine arrangement. It provided the complete answer to the question why there were just six planets "and not twenty or a hundred." And it also answered the question why the distances between the orbits were as they were. They had to be spaced in such a manner that the five solids could be exactly fitted into the intervals, as an invisible skeleton or frame. And, lo, they fitted! Or at least they seemed to fit, more or less. Into the orbit, or sphere, of Saturn he inscribed a cube; and into the cube another sphere, which was that of Jupiter. Inscribed in that was the tetrahedron, and inscribed in it the sphere of Mars. Between the spheres of Mars and Earth came the dodecahedron; between Earth and Venus the icosahedron; between Venus and Mercury the octahedron. Eureka! The mystery of the universe was solved by young Kepler, teacher at the Protestant school in Gratz.

> "It is amazing!" Kepler informs his readers. "Although I had as yet no clear idea of the order in which the perfect solids had to be arranged, I nevertheless succeeded . . . in arranging them so happily that later on, when I checked the matter over, I had nothing to alter. Now I no longer regretted the lost time; I no longer tired of my work; I shied from no computation, however difficult. Day and night I spent with calculations to see whether the proposition that I had formulated fitted the Copernican orbits or whether my joy would be carried away by the winds. . . .Within a few days everything fell into its place. I saw one symmetrical solid after the other fit in so precisely between the appropriate orbits that if a peasant were to ask you on what kind of hook the heavens are fastened so that they don't fall down, it will be easy for thee to answer him. Farewell!"[3]

We had the privilege of witnessing one of the rare recorded in- 11 stances of a false inspiration, a supreme hoax of the Socratic *daimon*, the inner voice that speaks with such infallible, intuitive certainty to the deluded mind. That unforgettable moment before the figure on the blackboard carried the same inner conviction as Archimedes' "Eureka" or Newton's flash of insight about the falling apple. But there are few instances where a delusion led to momentous and true sci-

---

[3] "One of my ancestors, Heinrich, and his brother, Friedrich, were knighted . . . in 1430, by the Emperor [Sigismond] on the bridge over the Tiber in Rome." (Letter from Kepler to Vincento Bianchi, February 17, 1619; G.W., Vol. XVII, p. 321). The Patent of Nobility is still extant, but the two Keplers knighted in 1430 were called Friedrich and Konrad, not Friedrich and Heinrich.

entific discoveries and yielded new laws of nature. This is the ultimate fascination of Kepler—both as an individual and as a case history. For Kepler's misguided belief in the five perfect bodies was not a passing fancy, but remained with him, in a modified version, to the end of his life, showing all the symptoms of a paranoid delusion; and yet it functioned as the *vigor motrix*, the spur of his immortal achievements. He wrote the *Mysterium Cosmographicum* when he was twenty-five, but he published a second edition of it a quarter-century later, toward the end, when he had done his lifework, discovered his three Laws, destroyed the Ptolemaic universe, and laid the foundations of modern cosmology. The dedication to this second edition, written at the age of fifty, betrays the persistence of the *idée fixe*.

> "Nearly twenty-five years have passed since I published the present little book. . . . Although I was then still quite young and this publication my first work on astronomy, nevertheless its success in the following years proclaims with a loud voice that never before has anybody published a more significant, happier, and, in view of its subject, worthier first book. It would be mistaken to regard it as a pure invention of my mind (far be any presumption from my intent, and any exaggerated admiration from the reader's, when we touch the seven-stringed harp of the Creator's wisdom). For as if a heavenly oracle had dictated it to me, the published booklet was in all its parts immediately recognized as excellent and true throughout (as it is the rule with obvious acts of God)."

Now Kepler's style is often exuberant and sometimes bombastic, 12 but rarely to this extent. The apparent presumption is in fact the radiance of the *idée fixe*, an emanation of the immense emotive charge which such ideas carry. When the patient in a mental home declares that he is the mouthpiece of the Holy Ghost, he means it not as a boast but as a flat statement of fact.

Here we have, then, a young man of twenty-four, an aspirant of 13 theology, with only a sketchy knowledge of astronomy, who hits upon a crank idea, convinced that he has solved the "cosmic mystery." "There is no great ingenuity," to quote Seneca, "without an admixture of dementedness," but as a rule the dementedness devours the ingenuity. Kepler's history will show how exceptions to this rule may occur.

RESPONDING TO READING

Key words: discovery reality science striving watershed

Rhetorical concepts: analogy analysis anecdote biography cause and effect explanation illustration induction narrative/example process research report

1.   Consider Kepler's "false" discovery in comparison to the major "true" discoveries of Darwin and of Watson and Crick (in this chapter). Refer to the essays on scientific creativity by Asimov and by Kuhn (in Chapter 2) to help you examine the kind of creativity Kepler's mistaken idea represents. Despite its fundamental error, how does Kepler's work resemble other types of scientific creativity?

2.   Kepler's inspiration about orbit ratios "suddenly struck him" as a kind of inner truth, as Belenky (in Chapter 2) would describe it. Is the problem that inner truth does not work in science? Or that it works better for females than for males? What does Kepler's false discovery tell us about "just knowing"? What went wrong with Kepler's way of discovering truth? What went right?

3.   Consider the relation of observer to the thing observed. Kepler thought he was discovering laws of nature while he was actually (as we see now) imposing his assumptions upon nature. To what degree is it possible to be a neutral observer of anything? Use examples from your reading or experience.

4.   Consider the ways in which false ideas can lead (as with Kepler's) to good ideas. Many such examples exist. For example, chemistry developed out of the alchemists' belief that lead could be changed to gold, and erroneous notions of geography misled explorers into important new lands. Select a false notion that was (or is) widely held, such as astrology, or some fad diets, and examine the possibilities for positive results from it.

Letters from the Astronomers

SIV CEDERING

Siv Cedering, born in Sweden in 1939, came to the United States in 1953 and became an American citizen five years later. She has received awards for photography as well as poetry. Cedering's volumes of poetry include *Letters from the Island* (1973), *Mother Is* (1975), *The Blue Horse and Other Night Poems* (1979), and *Letters from the Floating World* (1984). The epigraphs of *Letters from the Floating World* have particular relevance to "Letter from Caroline Herschel (1750–1848)," the fourth of five "Letters from the Astronomers" in this volume:

The earth is the cradle of the mind,
but one cannot live in a cradle forever.
    Konstantin Tsiolkovsky (1837–1935)

Can you fasten the harness of the Pleiades,
    or untie Orion's bands?
Can you guide the morning star season by season
    and show the Bear and its cubs which way to go?
Have you grasped the celestial laws?
    Could you make their writ run on the earth?
                    —Job 38: 31–33

The other astronomers whose "letters" Cedering writes are Copernicus, Kepler, Galileo, and Einstein. That Caroline Herschel, a relatively obscure woman, belongs in the world class company of these men is part of Cedering's emphatic feminist message.

Letters from the Astronomers
IV. Caroline Herschel (1750–1848)

William is away, and I am minding
the heavens. I have discovered
eight new comets and three nebulae
never before seen by man,
and I am preparing an Index to   5
Flamsteed's observations, together with
a catalogue of 560 stars omitted from
the British Catalogue, plus a list of errata
in that publication. William says

I have a way with numbers, so I handle   10
all the necessary reductions and
calculations. I also plan
every night's observation
schedule, for he says my intuition
helps me turn the telescope to discover   15
star cluster after star cluster.

I have helped him polish the mirrors
and lenses of our new telescope. It is
the largest in existence. Can you imagine
the thrill of turning it to some new   20
corner of the heavens to see
something never before seen
from earth? I actually like

that he is busy with the Royal Society
and his club, for when I finish my other work   25
I can spend all night sweeping
the heavens.

Sometimes when I am alone
in the dark, and the universe reveals
yet another secret, I say the names   30

of my long lost sisters, forgotten
in the books that record
our science—

   Aglaonice of Thessaly,
   Hyptia,   35
   Hildegard,
   Catherina Hevelius,
   Maria Agnesi

—as if the stars themselves could

remember. Did you know that Hildegard   40
proposed a heliocentric universe
300 years before Copernicus? that she
wrote of universal gravitation 500 years
before Newton? But who would listen
to her? She was just a nun, a woman.   45
What is our age, if that age was dark?

As for my name, it will also be
forgotten, but I am not accused
of being a sorceress, like Aglaonice,
and the Christians do not threaten to   50
drag me to church, to murder me, like they did
Hyptia of Alexandria, the eloquent, young
woman who devised the instruments
used to accurately measure the position
and motion of   55

heavenly bodies.
However long we live, life is short, so I
work. And however important man becomes,
he is nothing compared to the stars.
There are secrets, dear sister, and it is   60
for us to reveal them. Your name, like mine,
is a song. Write soon,
                       Caroline

RESPONDING TO READING

Key words: discovery education family freedom gender identity
nature power reality rights science striving

Rhetorical concepts: analogy biography metaphor narrative/example
poetry

1. In this supposed letter from a well-known astronomer, sister of a world-famous astronomer, the poet contrasts the female and male worlds. For example, when she observes stars, the speaker says "when I finish my other work/ I can spend all night sweeping/ the heavens." Why does the poet break the line after the word "sweeping"? Find other metaphors and expressions in the poem that emphasize the sex role of the speaker. Do you see any veiled ironies or other forms of wit? What is the cumulative effect?

2. The poem speaks to the scientific talent of the speaker and to the history of female scientists. These, the poem says, "are secrets." Why were they secrets in the past? Do they remain secrets today? What does the poem suggest about the repression of scientific opportunity and recognition for women?

3. The poem also speaks to the "thrill" of scientific creativity and the "intuition" of the speaker. Compare the creativity of the speaker in this poem to that of Kepler, in passages quoted from his writings in the previous selection. What does the poem add to the notion of scientific creativity, as Kuhn (Chapter 2), for example, describes it?

How Can We Recognize

and Encourage Creativity?

Hearing Voices

LINDA HOGAN

In the process of becoming a poet and novelist, Linda Hogan, a Chickasaw born in Denver in 1947, worked as a nurse's aide, dental assistant, waitress, homemaker, secretary, administrator, teacher's aide, and library clerk. She earned an M.A. at the University of Colorado, Boulder, in 1978, and was a professor of American and American Indian Studies at the University of Minnesota before joining the faculty of the University of Colorado. Her most recent book of poetry is *Savings* (1988); her fourth poetry collection, *Seeing Through the Sun* (1985), received an American Book Award.

Hogan says of her work, "My writing comes from and goes back to . . . both the human and the global community. I am interested in the deepest questions, those of spirit, of shelter, of growth and movement toward peace and liberation, inner and outer." She is also an ardent conservationist, studying the relationship between humans and other species, and working as a volunteer in the conservation and rehabilitation of birds of prey. In "Hearing Voices" she amplifies these views, emphasizing how important it is to listen to the literal "language of this continent," the stories of this earth, "the stones giving guidance, the trees singing, the corn telling of inner earth, the dragonfly offering up a tongue."

When Barbara McClintock was awarded a Nobel Prize for her 1 work on gene transposition in corn plants, the most striking thing about her was that she made her discoveries by listening to what the corn spoke to her, by respecting the life of the corn and "letting it come."

McClintock says she learned "the stories" of the plants. She 2 "heard" them. She watched the daily green journeys of growth from earth toward sky and sun. She knew her plants in the way a healer or mystic would have known them, from the inside, the inner voices of corn and woman speaking to one another.

As an Indian woman, I come from a long history of people who 3 have listened to the language of this continent, people who have known that corn grows with the songs and prayers of the people, that it has a story to tell, that the world is alive. Both in oral traditions

413

and in mythology—the true language of inner life—account after account tells of the stones giving guidance, the trees singing, the corn telling of inner earth, the dragonfly offering up a tongue. This is true in the European traditions as well: Psyche received direction from the reeds and the ants, Orpheus knew the languages of earth, animals, and birds.

This intuitive and common language is what I seek for my writing,   4
work in touch with the mystery and force of life, work that speaks a few of the many voices around us, and it is important to me that McClintock listened to the voices of the corn. It is important to the continuance of life that she told the truth of her method and that it reminded us all of where our strength, our knowing, and our sustenance come from.

It is also poetry, this science, and I note how often scientific   5
theories lead to the world of poetry and vision, theories telling us how atoms that were stars have been transformed into our living, breathing bodies. And in those theories, or maybe they should be called stories, we begin to understand how we are each many people, including the stars we once were, and how we are in essence the earth and the universe, how what we do travels clear around the earth and returns. In a single moment of our living, there is our ancestral and personal history, our future, even our deaths planted in us and already growing toward their fulfillment. The corn plants are there, and like all the rest we are forever merging our borders with theirs in the world collective.

Our very lives might depend on this listening. In the Chernobyl   6
nuclear accident, the wind told the story that was being suppressed by the people. It gave away the truth. It carried the story of danger to other countries. It was a poet, a prophet, a scientist.

Sometimes, like the wind, poetry has its own laws speaking for   7
the life of the planet. It is a language that wants to bring back together what the other words have torn apart. It is the language of life speaking through us about the sacredness of life.

This life speaking life is what I find so compelling about the work   8
of poets such as Ernesto Cardenal, who is also a priest and was the Nicaraguan Minister of Culture. He writes: "The armadilloes are very happy with this government. . . . Not only humans desired liberation/the whole ecology wanted it." Cardenal has also written "The Parrots," a poem about caged birds who were being sent to the United States as pets for the wealthy, how the cages were opened, the parrots allowed back into the mountains and jungles, freed like the people, "and sent back to the land we were pulled from."

How we have been pulled from the land! And how poetry has   9
worked hard to set us free, uncage us, keep us from split tongues

that mimic the voices of our captors. It returns us to our land. Poetry is a string of words that parades without a permit. It is a lockbox of words to put an ear to as we try to crack the safe of language, listening for the right combination, the treasure inside. It is life resonating. It is sometimes called Prayer, Soothsaying, Complaint, Invocation, Proclamation, Testimony, Witness. Writing is and does all these things. And like that parade, it is illegitimately insistent on going its own way, on being part of the miracle of life, telling the story about what happened when we were cosmic dust, what it means to be stars listening to our human atoms.

But don't misunderstand me. I am not just a dreamer. I am also   10
the practical type. A friend's father, watching the United States stage another revolution in another Third World country, said, "Why doesn't the government just feed people and then let the political chips fall where they may?" He was right. It was easy, obvious, even financially more reasonable to do that, to let democracy be chosen because it feeds hunger. I want my writing to be that simple, that clear and direct. Likewise, I feel it is not enough for me just to write, but I need to live it, to be informed by it. I have found over the years that my work has more courage than I do. It has more wisdom. It teaches me, leads me places I never knew I was heading. And it is about a new way of living, of being in the world.

I was on a panel recently where the question was raised whether   11
we thought literature could save lives. The audience, book people, smiled expectantly with the thought. I wanted to say, Yes, it saves lives. But I couldn't speak those words. It saves spirits maybe, hearts. It changes minds, but for me writing is an incredible privilege. When I sit down at the desk, there are other women who are hungry, homeless. I don't want to forget that, that the world of matter is still there to be reckoned with. This writing is a form of freedom most other people do not have. So, when I write, I feel a responsibility, a commitment to other humans and to the animal and plant communities as well.

Still, writing has changed me. And there is the powerful need   12
we all have to tell a story, each of us with a piece of the whole pattern to complete. As Alice Walker says, We are all telling part of the same story, and as Sharon Olds has said, Every writer is a cell on the body politic of America.

Another Nobel Prize laureate is Betty William, a Northern Ireland   13
co-winner of the 1977 Peace Prize. I heard her speak about how, after witnessing the death of children, she stepped outside in the middle of the night and began knocking on doors and yelling, behaviors that would have earned her a diagnosis of hysteria in our own medical circles. She knocked on doors that might have opened with weapons

pointing in her face, and she cried out, "What kind of people have we become that we would allow children to be killed on our streets?" Within four hours the city was awake, and there were sixteen thousand names on petitions for peace. Now, that woman's work is a lesson to those of us who deal with language, and to those of us who are dealt into silence. She used language to begin the process of peace. This is the living, breathing power of the word. It is poetry. So are the names of those who signed the petitions. Maybe it is this kind of language that saves lives.

Writing begins for me with survival, with life and with freeing 14 life, saving life, speaking life. It is work that speaks what can't be easily said. It originates from a compelling desire to live and be alive. For me, it is sometimes the need to speak for other forms of life, to take the side of human life, even our sometimes frivolous living, and our grief-filled living, our joyous living, our violent living, busy living, our peaceful living. It is about possibility. It is based in the world of matter. I am interested in how something small turns into an image that is large and strong with resonance, where the ordinary becomes beautiful. I believe the divine, the magic, is here in the weeds at our feet, unacknowledged. What a world this is. Where else could water rise up to the sky, turn into snow crystals, magnificently brought together, fall from the sky all around us, pile up billions deep, and catch the small sparks of sunlight as they return again to water?

These acts of magic happen all the time; in Chaco Canyon, my 15 sister has seen a kiva, a ceremonial room in the earth, that is in the center of the canyon. This place has been uninhabited for what seems like forever. It has been without water. In fact, there are theories that the ancient people disappeared when they journeyed after water. In the center of it a corn plant was growing. It was all alone and it had been there since the ancient ones, the old ones who came before us all, those people who wove dog hair into belts, who witnessed the painting of flute players on the seeping canyon walls, who knew the stories of corn. And there was one corn plant growing out of the holy place. It planted itself yearly. With no water, no person to care for it, no overturning of the soil, this corn plant rises up to tell its story, and that's what this poetry is.

RESPONDING TO READING

Key words: community   discovery   freedom   identity   language memory   minority   nature   poetry   power   science   symbols

Rhetorical concepts: anecdote   cause and effect   deduction illustration   metaphor   narrative/example   process

1. Hogan argues that poetry and science come together in important ways ("It is also poetry, this science . . ." paragraph 5). Explain what she means.
2. As a Native American, "people who have listened to the language of this continent, people who have known . . . that the world is alive," Hogan speaks of the messages of the earth and its creatures to us. But she also cites the scientist Barbara McClintock (*see* Chapter 2) and European myths, and she provides other arguments as well. Are you convinced by her argument that we need to listen to the "world collective" and that the source of creativity is "hearing voices"? Why, or why not?
3. Hogan sees creativity as a form of saving "spirits, maybe hearts." Explain what she means and relate her vision to that of two or three other writers in this book.
4. Write about an experience you have had, or have read about, in which some non-human creature or object "spoke" to a person. What is the nature of such a message? How does it arrive? What preparation is necessary? What was the result? Or, if you are skeptical about such experiences, write about the problems they cause.

The Reach of Imagination

JACOB BRONOWSKI

In "The Reach of the Imagination," first published in *The American Scholar* (1967), Jacob Bronowski defines the imagination with his characteristically lyrical combination of science and the arts. Imagination chimes with nature, he says, and makes a harmony that characterizes "all great acts of the imagination," whether artistic or scientific.

Bronowski himself is that rare person whose life and works, temperament and training, combine science and art in creative ways. Born in Poland in 1908, Bronowski earned a Ph.D. in mathematics from Cambridge University in 1933, and worked for the British government during World War II as a statistician interpreting the effects of bombings. As a consequence of seeing the atomic devastation at Nagasaki—"we had dehumanized the enemy and ourselves in one blow"—Bronowski realized that he had to "bear witness . . . for the foundations of human decency," and vowed to make science accessible to people in general, rather than just to specialists. He spent thirty years doing just that, the last decade (he died in 1974) as a senior fellow of the Salk Institute for Biological Studies in San Diego.

"Superbly wise" in mathematics, physical science, biology, and literature, Bronowski wrote essays and books on all these subjects, as well as radio dramas, an opera, and television documentaries. The most highly acclaimed of his works is *Science and Human Values* (1965), a soul-searching work in which he explained the connection between creativity in the sciences and the arts. The progress of science, for instance, was not "an orderly sequence of logical innovations but a shifting pattern which could be appreciated only by recognising the interwoven strands of history, art, literature and philosophy." *The Ascent of Man* (1973), a collection of essays based on a BBC-TV series, was Bronowski's last, optimistic celebration of the attempts of humans to understand and control nature, from prehistoric times to the present.

For three thousand years, poets have been enchanted and moved   1
and perplexed by the power of their own imagination. In a short and summary essay I can hope at most to lift one small corner of that mystery; and yet it is a critical corner. I shall ask, What goes on in the mind when we imagine? You will hear from me that one answer to this question is fairly specific: which is to say, that we can describe the working of the imagination. And when we describe it as I shall do, it becomes plain that imagination is a specifically *human* gift. To imagine is the characteristic act, not of the poet's mind, or the painter's, or the scientist's, but of the mind of man.

My stress here on the word *human* implies that there is a clear   2
difference in this between the actions of men and those of other animals. Let me then start with a classical experiment with animals and children which Walter Hunter thought out in Chicago about 1910. That was the time when scientists were agog with the success of Ivan Pavlov in forming and changing the reflex actions of dogs, which Pavlov had first announced in 1903. Pavlov had been given a Nobel prize the next year, in 1904; although in fairness I should say that the award did not cite his work on the conditioned reflex, but on the digestive glands.

Hunter duly trained some dogs and other animals on Pavlov's   3
lines. They were taught that when a light came on over one of three tunnels out of their cage, that tunnel would be open; they could escape down it, and were rewarded with food if they did. But once he had fixed that conditioned reflex, Hunter added to it a deeper idea: he gave the mechanical experiment a new dimension, literally—the dimension of time. Now he no longer let the dog go to the lighted tunnel at once; instead, he put out the light, and then kept the dog waiting a little while before he let him go. In this way Hunter timed how long an animal can remember where he has last seen the signal light to his escape route.

The results were and are staggering. A dog or a rat forgets which   4
one of three tunnels has been lit up within a matter of seconds—in Hunter's experiment, ten seconds at most. If you want such an animal to do much better than this, you must make the task much simpler: you must face him with only two tunnels to choose from. Even so, the best that Hunter could do was to have a dog remember for five minutes which one of two tunnels had been lit up.

I am not quoting these times as if they were exact and universal: 5 they surely are not. Hunter's experiment, more than fifty years old now, had many faults of detail. For example, there were too few animals, they were oddly picked, and they did not all behave consistently. It may be unfair to test a dog for what he *saw,* when he commonly follows his nose rather than his eyes. It may be unfair to test any animal in the unnatural setting of a laboratory cage. And there are higher animals, such as chimpanzees and other primates, which certainly have longer memories than the animals that Hunter tried.

Yet when all these provisos have been made (and met, by more 6
modern experiments) the facts are still startling and characteristic. An animal cannot recall a signal from the past for even a short fraction of the time that a man can—for even a short fraction of the time that a child can. Hunter made comparable tests with six-year-old children and found, of course, that they were incomparably better than the best of the animals. There is a striking and basic difference between a man's ability to imagine something that he saw or experienced and an animal's failure.

Animals make up for this by other and extraordinary gifts. The 7
salmon and the carrier pigeon can find their way home as we cannot; they have, as it were, a practical memory that man cannot match. But their actions always depend on some form of habit: on instinct or on learning, which reproduce by rote a train of known responses. They do not depend, as human memory does, on calling to mind the recollection of absent things.

Where is it that the animal falls short? We get a clue to the answer, 8
I think, when Hunter tells us how the animals in his experiment tried to fix their recollection. They most often pointed themselves at the light before it went out, as some gun dogs point rigidly at the game they scent—and get the name *pointer* from the posture. The animal makes ready to act by building the signal into its action. There is a primitive imagery in its stance, it seems to me; it is as if the animal were trying to fix the light in its mind by fixing it in its body. And indeed, how else can a dog mark and (as it were) name one of three tunnels, when he has no such words as *left* and *right,* and no such numbers as *one, two, three?* The directed gesture of attention and readiness is perhaps the only symbolic device that the dog commands to hold on to the past, and thereby to guide himself into the future.

I used the verb *to imagine* a moment ago, and now I have some 9
ground for giving it a meaning. To *imagine* means to make images and to move them about inside one's head in new arrangements. When you and I recall the past, we imagine it in this direct and homely sense. The tool that puts the human mind ahead of the animal is imagery. For us, memory does not demand the preoccupation that it

demands in animals, and it lasts immensely longer, because we fix it in images or other substitute symbols. With the same symbolic vocabulary we spell out the future—not one but many futures, which we weigh one against another.

I am using the word *image* in a wide meaning, which does not 10 restrict it to the mind's eye as a visual organ. An image in my usage is what Charles Peirce called a *sign*, without regard for its sensory quality. Peirce distinguished between different forms of signs, but there is no reason to make his distinction here, for the imagination works equally with them all, and that is why we call them all images.

Indeed, the most important images for human beings are simply 11 words, which are abstract symbols. Animals do not have words, in our sense: there is no specific center for language, in the brain of any animal, as there is in the human brain. In this respect at least we know that the human imagination depends on a configuration in the brain that has only evolved in the last one or two million years. In the same period, evolution has greatly enlarged the front lobes in the human brain, which govern the sense of the past and the future; and it is a fair guess that they are probably the seat of our other images. (Part of the evidence for this guess is that damage to the front lobes in primates reduces them to the state of Hunter's animals.) If the guess turns out to be right, we shall know why man has come to look like a highbrow or an egghead: because otherwise there would not be room in his head for his imagination.

The images play out for us events which are not present to our 12 senses, and thereby guard the past and create the future—a future that does not yet exist, and may never come to exist in that form. By contrast, the lack of symbolic ideas, or their rudimentary poverty, cuts off an animal from the past and the future alike, and imprisons him in the present. Of all the distinctions between man and animal, the characteristic gift which makes us human is the power to work with symbolic images: the gift of imagination.

This is really a remarkable finding. When Philip Sidney in 1580 13 defended poets (and all unconventional thinkers) from the Puritan charge that they were liars, he said that a maker must imagine things that are not. Halfway between Sidney and us, William Blake said, "What is now proved was once only imagin'd." About the same time, in 1796, Samuel Taylor Coleridge for the first time distinguished between the passive fancy and the active imagination, "the living Power and prime Agent of all human Perception." Now we see that they were right, and precisely right: the human gift is the gift of imagination—and that is not just a literary phrase.

Nor is it just a literary gift; it is, I repeat, characteristically human. 14 Almost everything that we do that is worth doing is done in the first place in the mind's eye. The richness of human life is that we have many lives; we live the events that do not happen (and some that cannot) as vividly as those that do; and if thereby we die a thousand deaths, that is the price we pay for living a thousand lives. (A cat, of course, has only nine.) Literature is alive to us because we live its images, but so is any play of the mind—so is chess: the lines of play that we foresee and try in our heads and dismiss are as much a part of the game as the moves that we make. John Keats said that the unheard melodies are sweeter, and all chess players sadly recall that the combinations that they planned and which never came to be played were the best.

I make this point to remind you, insistently, that imagination is 15 the manipulation of images in one's head; and that the rational manipulation belongs to that, as well as the literary and artistic manipulation. When a child begins to play games with things that stand for other things, with chairs or chessmen, he enters the gateway to reason and imagination together. For the human reason discovers new relations between things not by deduction, but by that unpredictable blend of speculation and insight that scientists call induction, which— like other forms of imagination—cannot be formalized. We see it at work when Walter Hunter inquires into a child's memory, as much as when Blake and Coleridge do. Only a restless and original mind would have asked Hunter's questions and could have conceived his experiments, in a science that was dominated by Pavlov's reflex arcs and was heading toward the behaviorism of John Watson.

Let me find a spectacular example for you from history. What is 16 the most famous experiment that you had described to you as a child? I will hazard that it is the experiment that Galileo is said to have made in Sidney's age, in Pisa about 1590, by dropping two unequal balls from the Leaning Tower. There, we say, is a man in the modern mold, a man after our own hearts: he insisted on questioning the authority of Aristotle and St. Thomas Aquinas, and seeing with his own eyes whether (as they said) the heavy ball would reach the ground before the light one. Seeing is believing.

Yet seeing is also imagining. Galileo did challenge the authority 17 of Aristotle, and he did look hard at his mechanics. But the eye that Galileo used was the mind's eye. He did not drop balls from the Leaning Tower of Pisa—and if he had, he would have got a very doubtful answer. Instead, Galileo made an imaginary experiment in his head, which I will describe as he did years later in the book he wrote after the Holy Office silenced him: the *Discorsi . . . intorno à due nuove scienze* (Discourses Concerning Two New Sciences), which was smuggled out to be printed in the Netherlands in 1638.

Suppose, said Galileo, that you drop two unequal balls from the 18 tower at the same time. And suppose that Aristotle is right—suppose that the heavy ball falls faster, so that it steadily gains on the light ball, and hits the ground first. Very well. Now imagine the same experiment done again, with only one difference: this time the two unequal balls are joined by a string between them. The heavy ball will again move ahead, but now the light ball holds it back and acts as a drag or brake. So the light ball will be speeded up and the heavy ball will be slowed down; they must reach the ground together because they are tied together, but they cannot reach the ground as quickly as the heavy ball alone. Yet the string between them has turned the two balls into a single mass which is heavier than either ball—and surely (according to Aristotle) this mass should therefore move faster than either ball? Galileo's imaginary experiment has uncovered a contradiction; he says trenchantly, "You see how, from your assumption that a heavier body falls more rapidly than a lighter one, I infer that a (still) heavier body falls more slowly." There is only one way out of the contradiction: the heavy ball and the light ball must fall at the same rate, so that they go on falling at the same rate when they are tied together.

This argument is not conclusive, for nature might be more subtle 19 (when the two balls are joined) than Galileo has allowed. And yet it is something more important: it is suggestive, it is stimulating, it opens a new view—in a word, it is imaginative. It cannot be settled without an actual experiment, because nothing that we imagine can become knowledge until we have translated it into, and backed it by, real experience. The test of imagination is experience. But then, that is as true of literature and the arts as it is of science. In science, the imaginary experiment is tested by confronting it with physical experience; and in literature, the imaginative conception is tested by confronting it with human experience. The superficial speculation in science is dismissed because it is found to falsify nature; and the shallow work of art is discarded because it is found to be untrue to our own nature. So when Ella Wheeler Wilcox died in 1919, more people were reading her verses than Shakespeare's; yet in a few years her work was dead. It had been buried by its poverty of emotion and its trivialness of thought: which is to say that it had been proved to be as false to the nature of man as, say, Jean Baptiste Lamarck and Trofim Lysenko were false to the nature of inheritance. The strength of the imagination, its enriching power and excitement, lies in its interplay with reality—physical and emotional.

I doubt if there is much to choose here between science and the 20 arts: the imagination is not much more free, and not much less free, in one than in the other. All great scientists have used their imagination freely, and let it ride them to outrageous conclusions without crying "Halt!" Albert Einstein fiddled with imaginary experiments from boyhood, and was wonderfully ignorant of the facts that they were supposed to bear on. When he wrote the first of his beautiful papers on the random movement of atoms, he did not know that the Brownian motion which it predicted could be seen in any laboratory. He was sixteen when he invented the paradox that he resolved ten years later, in 1905, in the theory of relativity, and it bulked much larger in his mind than the experiment of Albert Michelson and Edward Morley which had upset every other physicist since 1881. All his life Einstein loved to make up teasing puzzles like Galileo's, about falling lifts and the detection of gravity; and they carry the nub of the problems of general relativity on which he was working.

Indeed, it could not be otherwise. The power that man has over 21 nature and himself, and that a dog lacks, lies in his command of imaginary experience. He alone has the symbols which fix the past and play with the future, possible and impossible. In the Renaissance, the symbolism of memory was thought to be mystical, and devices that were invented as mnemonics (by Giordano Bruno, for example, and by Robert Fludd) were interpreted as magic signs. The symbol is the tool which gives man his power, and it is the same tool whether the symbols are images or words, mathematical signs or mesons. And the symbols have a reach and a roundness that goes beyond their literal and practical meaning. They are the rich concepts under which the mind gathers many particulars into one name, and many instances into one general induction. When a man says *left* and *right*, he is outdistancing the dog not only in looking for a light; he is setting in train all the shifts of meaning, the overtones and the ambiguities, between *gauche* and *adroit* and *dexterous*, between *sinister* and the sense of right. When a man counts *one, two, three,* he is not only doing mathematics; he is on the path to the mysticism of numbers in Pythagoras and Vitruvius and Kepler, to the Trinity and the signs of the Zodiac.

I have described imagination as the ability to make images and 22 to move them about inside one's head in new arrangements. This is the faculty that is specifically human, and it is the common root from which science and literature both spring and grow and flourish together. For they do flourish (and languish) together; the great ages of science are the great ages of all the arts, because in them powerful minds have taken fire from one another, breathless and higgledy-piggledy, without asking too nicely whether they ought to tie their imagination to falling balls or a haunted island. Galileo and Shakespeare, who were born in the same year, grew into greatness in the same age; when Galileo was looking through his telescope at the moon, Shakespeare was writing *The Tempest;* and all Europe was in ferment, from Johannes Kepler to Peter Paul Rubens, and from the first table of logarithms by John Napier to the authorized version of the Bible.

Let me end with a last and spirited example of the common 23 inspiration of literature and science, because it is as much alive today as it was three hundred years ago. What I have in mind is man's ageless fantasy, to fly to the moon. I do not display this to you as a high scientific enterprise; on the contrary, I think we have more important discoveries to make here on earth than wait for us, beckoning, at the horned surface of the moon. Yet I cannot belittle the fascination which that ice-blue journey has had for the imagination of men, long before it drew us to our television screens to watch the tumbling of astronauts. Plutarch and Lucian, Ariosto and Ben Jonson wrote about it, before the days of Jules Verne and H. G. Wells and science fiction. The seventeenth century was heady with new dreams and fables about voyages to the moon. Kepler wrote one full of deep scientific ideas, which (alas) simply got his mother accused of witchcraft. In England, Francis Godwin wrote a wild and splendid work, *The Man in the Moone*, and the astronomer John Wilkins wrote a wild and learned one, *The Discovery of a New World*. They did not draw a line between science and fancy; for example, they all tried to guess just where in the journey the earth's gravity would stop. Only Kepler understood that gravity has no boundary, and put a law to it—which happened to be the wrong law.

All this was a few years before Isaac Newton was born, and it 24 was all in his head that day in 1666 when he sat in his mother's garden, a young man of twenty-three, and thought about the reach of gravity. This was how he came to conceive his brilliant image, that the moon is like a ball which has been thrown so hard that it falls exactly as fast as the horizon, all the way round the earth. The image will do for any satellite, and Newton modestly calculated how long therefore an astronaut would take to fall round the earth once. He made it ninety minutes, and we have all seen now that he was right; but Newton had no way to check that. Instead he went on to calculate how long in that case the distant moon would take to round the earth, if indeed it behaves like a thrown ball that falls in the earth's gravity, and if gravity obeyed a law of inverse squares. He found that the answer would be twenty-eight days.

In that telling figure, the imagination that day chimed with nature, 25 and made a harmony. We shall hear an echo of that harmony on the day when we land on the moon, because it will be not a technical but an imaginative triumph, that reaches back to the beginning of modern science and literature both. All great acts of imagination are like this, in the arts and in science, and convince us because they fill out reality with a deeper sense of rightness. We start with the simplest vocabulary of images, with *left* and *right* and *one, two, three,* and before we know how it happened the words and the numbers have conspired to make a match with nature: we catch in them the pattern of mind and matter as one.

RESPONDING TO READING

Key words: animals art discovery identity language
memory poetry reality science symbols writing

Rhetorical concepts: analogy analysis anecdote cause and effect
definition illustration meditation metaphor narrative/example
process

1. Bronowski is careful to define some problematic terms. Give his definitions for the following: image, imagination, fancy, sign, words. Compare these definitions to those used by Suzanne Langer (in Chapter 2).
2. "Almost everything that we do that is worth doing is done in the first place in the mind's eye." "Nothing that we imagine can become knowledge until we have translated it into, and backed it by, real experience." Explain what Bronowski means by this. Then test its truth by examples drawn from your reading and personal experience.
3. Bronowski argues that imagination in science and in the arts turns out to be much the same. Examine the evidence he gives for this assertion. How does his evidence compare with, say, Linda Hogan's, Siv Cedering's, or Isaac Asimov's earlier in this chapter? And how do such statements make sense in an age when many people talk about the opposition between the "two cultures" of science and humanities?
4. Consider the relationship between imagination and experience. Select an experience you have had, or that you have read about, which took place only after it had been fully imagined: some long-awaited adventure, trip, or evening that you perhaps lived out in your mind many times before it occurred. Did the experience do for you, or for your subject, what Newton's calculations did for him: "the imagination that day chimed with nature, and made a harmony"? Or were imagination and experience at odds? Describe what happened and reflect upon the way "the reach of imagination" affected what happened.

Life at Close Range

GRETEL EHRLICH

Gretel Ehrlich (born 1946) grew up in southern California, graduated from Bennington College, and began a career as a filmmaker. In 1976 she left an Eastern city (she does not say which one) confused and disoriented and, true to the American tradition, headed back out

West. Her move to Wyoming's open range was a dramatic change in geography and culture. Initially, she worked as a sheepherder, for as an outsider she wanted to be outside, literally and metaphorically. But instead of making her numb, as she expected, the arid country-side provided "the solace of open spaces, the constantly unrolling scroll of nature," and life on the sheep ranch woke her up: "The vitality of the people I was working with flushed out what had become a hallucinatory rawness inside me." The country was a clean slate, its absolute indifference a steadying influence that enabled Ehrlich to come to bedrock terms with herself, with no alibis, no self-promoting schemes. Again in the American tradition of self-discovery, she threw away her old clothes and bought new ones; she cut her hair. In becoming a new person she became her own person, transferring her filmmaker's keen vision to writing.

Within three years she became a full-time writer and rancher; she describes these experiences in her first book, *The Solace of Open Spaces* (1985): "The truest art I would strive for in any work would be to give the page the same quality as earth: weather would land on it harshly; light would elucidate the most difficult truths; wind would sweep away obtuse padding . . ." Both this book and "Life at Close Range," an essay written for Janet Sternburg's collection *The Writer and Her Work* (v. II, 1991), explain how the range and the open spaces influence her writing. Ehrlich, who could not write if she did not ride, sees the two activities as reinforcing one another.

It's June and soon we'll be moving cattle to the high mountain   1
pastures. Already the first slanting rains have come—black arrows that come back up as green grass. At this time of year it can still snow, but ducks and shorebirds stop over on our little lake to rest before going on to the Arctic or Canada. As soon as the mountain meltwater comes down, I go to work irrigating 125 acres of hay meadows and on the way, because I always carry binoculars, I keep track of what's on the pond: godwits, terns, mallards, teal, sora rails, snipes, and phalaropes. Coyotes come to drink early in the morning, vying with bald and golden eagles for a prairie dog on the way. It's not only what I do see as I set irrigation water, but what I don't see in the way of animals and birds that counts—those hidden ones like bears, mountain lions, badgers, ermine, and snakes who I know are here too, but I can't always see.

A writer's imagination must be like that: filled not just with literal   2
truths, but with the unseen, the unknown whose shy presence is felt. What's underneath the lake water, the sod-bound fields, the lid of my skull, I wonder?

Yesterday lightning ignited a ridge above our ranch and, as   3
quickly, a boisterous rain squall put it out. Then the hail came, dancing, blanching the land. The isolated ranch my husband and I inhabit often seems otherworldly: mist spills on us sweeping everything from sight, then on rising, the green-breasted earth steams. Last night the

moon was so bright a moth inside the house beat against the window, trying to get out, and in the morning, at almost the same place, I found a blue luna moth, big as my hand, trying to get in. A writer's life must be like those moths, beating down obstructions to get at truths.

Sometimes when strangers ask what I do, I say I write, but around 4 here, they think I said "ride." I do both of course, because most ranchwork is done on horseback. Writing is thought of as being cerebral work, while ranching, which takes up a good deal of my time, is mostly physical. But I couldn't write if I didn't ride and I'd find fourteen-hour days in the saddle quite tedious if I didn't have writing to come home to. In fact, I often write—notepad balanced on saddlehorn—gathering cattle, and when I'm in my writing room, a separate building on a hill with a view of the sorting corrals, I often get up mid-sentence to fix a panel of fence or change an irrigation dam, or put a stray horse away. This whole business of dividing body and mind is ludicrous. After all, the breath that starts the song of a poem, or the symphony of a novel—the same breath that lifts me into the saddle—starts in the body, and at the same time, enlivens the mind.

Our ranch is thirty miles from the nearest grocery store, eighty 5 miles from a movie theater, a hundred and fifty miles from an airport, yet I feel as if I were at the center of things, "in media res." Our ranch, and the entire ecosystem in which it lies, is my laboratory. Wherever I am on it, whatever I'm doing, I'm always thinking, remembering, feeling, observing, absorbing, and listening—to wasps eating ants, to the eddies of wind above oceans of pines, to the pond ducks fighting at breeding time, to the whir of nighthawks driving down. But it's a curious laboratory, one in which I don't do experiments on nature, but nature experiments with me. I'm a land steward, but it's the land that tells me what's right and what's wrong, and I have to learn to listen.

If you live in a place—any place, city or country—long enough 6 and deeply enough you can learn anything, the dynamics and interconnections that exist in every community, be it plant, human, or animal—you can learn what a writer needs to know. Here, as anywhere, the search for ways of knowing is a great discipline, an ultimate freedom in which you will find the entire world opens to you. When I began writing full time, I asked a well-known essayist his advice and he said, "Write from the heart," which was another way of saying, you must see through to the heart of things.

These days I do that by getting down on my hands and knees— 7 literally and figuratively—and inspecting life at close range. From monitoring grass plants, soil quality, insects, and animals, as well as the health of entire watersheds, I've learned to scrutinize and savor the constructs of language, the points at which ideas, ethics, and sensations meet or collide, the way the tone of a piece of writing— like muscle tone, or the ecotone of a landscape—moves smoothly or drops out from under my pen. From diving into the midst of other lives, in nature and in the human realm, working as nurturer, student, midwife, I've stumbled on the liberating sense of equality that exists everywhere and have been able to dismiss with great conviction the idiotic idea of human dominance over nature, and know it to be physically and intellectually absurd. With equality comes a sense of the holiness—sacred or secular—of every animate and inanimate thing.

Writing, like being a good hand with a horse, requires wakeful- 8 ness and a willingness to surrender. I try to burn away preconception and let what is actually here come in. Any act of writing is a meditation on existence. It implies stopping, breathing in and out. "Do not write more clearly than you can think," the physicist Niels Bohr said. The truth is hard; no false décor allowed.

Riding out across a six-thousand-acre mountain pasture becomes 9 an ambulation of mind. The body of the horse carries me into imagery, and memory, and, like the wind, I try to hone what has registered in me as a precision, making every word count, every word a tiny truth in itself. Roping a calf, I have to think ahead as the coil spins out, but at the same time, stay agile, flexible, alive in the present so that I can take my dallies with speed and care and not lose a thumb. Both jobs—writing and cowboying—take up the whole mind and heart. Weather pushes me the way I push at internal barriers and, after a decade or so, both jobs work together like mortar and pestle, the one pulverizing the other into clarity.

There is no knowing what makes a writer, what ingredients have 10 contributed. Was it the stories my very urban (and urbane) grand-father told me over and over? Was it the frustration of being almost silent during my young life which fed the need to communicate, albeit on my own terms? Was it my inordinate love of animals and books— the one love growing alongside the other that led me to this isolated, animal-rich place where the play of the mind and heart could take a far reach? It seems that any list of ingredients will do except deadness, frivolity, the refusal to enter silence and loneliness and listen to what is inside. A writer makes a pact with loneliness. It is her, or his, beach on which waves of desire, wild mind, speculation break. In my work, in my life, I am always moving toward and away from aloneness. To write is to refuse to cover up the rawness of being alive, of facing death.

Early in my life, maybe from reading D. H. Lawrence, I dedicated 11 myself to "living fully," which included reading, keeping my stan-dards high. To write and not read the best that has been written (and only the best; there's not time for anything less) is foolish. It's like a gardener putting in seeds where there is no ground. It is in the context of our ordinary, everyday lives that seeds germinate. In the larger sense, place ultimately becomes a mirror of mind.

In his notebooks, Henry James wrote: "The law of the artist is 12 the terrible law of fructification, of fertilization, the law of acceptance of all experience, of all suffering, of all life, all suggestion and sensation and illumination." Looking out the windows of my writing room at this moment, I see an elk carrying mist on his shoulders, drifting out of a canyon; a duck diving for food; a meadowlark alighting on a fence post, tilting his head back and singing after a June rain.

A good hand on a ranch requires vigilance, acute powers of ob- 13 servation, readiness to anticipate what might go wrong or what's coming next, a taste for recklessness, intuitive skills, patience, and what cowboys look for when they buy a horse: a lot of heart. Aspiring to those qualities as a rancher, I can only hope my writing will benefit as well.

RESPONDING TO READING

Key words: discovery   freedom   identity   nature   power
reading   reality   striving   writing

Rhetorical concepts: analogy   autobiography   comparison and contrast
definition   explanation   illustration   narrative/example

1.   "Writing, like being a good hand with a horse, requires wakefulness and a willingness to surrender" (paragraph 7), says Ehrlich. To what must the writer be awake? What must the writer be willing to surrender?
2.   What other connections does Ehrlich make between being a writer and being a rancher? Why do these endeavors have a natural affinity?
3.   Most writers are not ranchers; indeed, many live in large cities. How might a person, anywhere, develop "vigilance, acute powers of observation . . . a taste for recklessness, intuitive skills . . . heart," and other qualities necessary to write well?

Angels on a Pin

ALEXANDER CALANDRA

Alexander Calandra (born 1911) is professor emeritus of physics at Washington University in St. Louis. He has also taught at Brooklyn College, Webster College, and the University of Chicago, and has been guest lecturer at many campuses around the country.

In "Angels on a Pin," originally published in the *Saturday Review* (December 1968), Calandra uses a literary device common to social critics and satirists from Plato onward, a dialogue between a supposedly sophisticated questioner and an apparently naive respondent whose astute replies invariably outwit the questioner. In this case, the physics professor expects a prescribed, conventional answer to an exam question and the clever student offers a variety of creative alternative answers—all correct but so unanticipated that the professor has to call in a colleague to judge their merit. The comic possibilities of the situation were exploited in a skit presented (without Calandra's permission) on *Saturday Night Live,* an ironic violation of convention which led to an out-of-court settlement.

Is it possible for truly imaginative students to surpass their professors and not only get away with their insouciance but to be rewarded for intellectual creativity?

Some time ago, I received a call from a colleague who asked if I 1 would be the referee on the grading of an examination question. He was about to give a student a zero for his answer to a physics question, while the student claimed he should receive a perfect score and would if the system were not set up against the student. The instructor and the student agreed to submit this to an impartial arbiter, and I was selected.

I went to my colleague's office and read the examination question: 2 "Show how it is possible to determine the height of a tall building with the aid of a barometer."

The student had answered: "Take the barometer to the top of the 3 building, attach a long rope to it, lower the barometer to the street, and then bring it up, measuring the length of the rope. The length of the rope is the height of the building."

I pointed out that the student really had a strong case for full 4 credit, since he had answered the question completely and correctly. On the other hand, if full credit were given, it could well contribute to a high grade for the student in his physics course. A high grade is supposed to certify competence in physics, but the answer did not confirm this. I suggested that the student have another try at answering the question. I was not surprised that my colleague agreed, but I was surprised that the student did.

I gave the student six minutes to answer the question, with the 5 warning that his answer should show some knowledge of physics. At the end of five minutes, he had not written anything. I asked if he wished to give up, but he said no. He had many answers to this problem; he was just thinking of the best one. I excused myself for interrupting him, and asked him to please go on. In the next minute, he dashed off his answer, which read:

"Take the barometer to the top of the building and lean over the edge   6 of the roof. Drop the barometer, timing its fall with a stopwatch. Then, using the formula $S = \frac{1}{2} at^2$, calculate the height of the building."

At this point, I asked my colleague if *he* would give up. He con-   7 ceded, and I gave the student almost full credit.

In leaving my colleague's office, I recalled that the student had   8 said he had other answers to the problem, so I asked him what they were. "Oh, yes," said the student. "There are many ways of getting the height of a tall building with the aid of a barometer. For example, you could take the barometer out on a sunny day and measure the height of the barometer, the length of its shadow, and the length of the shadow of the building, and by the use of a simple proportion, determine the height of the building."

"Fine," I said. "And the others?"   9

"Yes," said the student. "There is a very basic measurement   10 method that you will like. In this method, you take the barometer and begin to walk up the stairs. As you climb the stairs, you mark off the length of the barometer along the wall. You then count the number of marks, and this will give you the height of the building in barometer units. A very direct method.

"Of course, if you want a more sophisticated method, you can   11 tie the barometer to the end of a string, swing it as a pendulum, and determine the value of 'g' at the street level and at the top of the building. From the difference between the two values of 'g,' the height of the building can, in principle, be calculated."

Finally, he concluded, there are many other ways of solving the   12 problem. "Probably the best," he said, "is to take the barometer to the basement and knock on the superintendent's door. When the superintendent answers, you speak to him as follows: 'Mr. Super-intendent, here I have a fine barometer. If you will tell me the height of this building, I will give you this barometer.' "

At this point, I asked the student if he really did not know the   13 conventional answer to this question. He admitted that he did, but said that he was fed up with high school and college instructors trying to teach him how to think, to use the "scientific method," and to explore the deep inner logic of the subject in a pedantic way, as is often done in the new mathematics, rather than teaching him the structure of the subject. With this in mind, he decided to revive scho-lasticism as an academic lark to challenge the Sputnik-panicked class-rooms of America.

RESPONDING TO READING

Key words: community   discovery   education   power   reality
rights   science

Rhetorical concepts: analogy   anecdote   humor   illustration
narrative/example   process   story

1.   The title refers to a criticism of school learning that had no relation to experience, exemplified by a medieval argument about how many angels could stand on the head of a pin. At the end of the essay, the rebellious student claims to be reviving such scholasticism to challenge the teaching of "the scientific method." How would you characterize the conflict between the student and his physics teacher? Explain.
2.   Relate the conflict between the student and the physics teacher to Thomas Kuhn's description of "The Route to Normal Science" (p. 147). Is the student being creative according to Kuhn's definition? Or is the student having "crazy ideas" as Isaac Asimov explains them (p. 370)? Is it a good idea to flout the expected and customary procedures of an institution? Consider the benefits as well as the difficulties.
3.   Relate and comment upon an experience you have had in which you knew what you were supposed to do but would have preferred to (or actually did do) something else. Did you play by the rules when you wanted to break them? Or did you break the rules, at some risk? What happened? What might have happened? As you look back now from an older and wiser stance, was the action right and creative? Duty-bound? Correct but cowardly? Arrogant but heroic?

QUESTIONS FOR REFLECTION AND WRITING

What Is a Good Political Idea?

1. Create a dialogue between Jefferson and Stanton. Focus on their agreement and disagreement over key terms, such as "laws of nature" or "self-evident truths" or "inalienable rights." Show both figures justifying their definitions as the basis for their political ideas. At some point, add a modern figure (such as yourself) into the conversation. The modern figure will know more about the results of these ideas than either Stanton or Jefferson could know, but will also be limited by being located in a particular time and place.

2. Create a similar dialogue between Lincoln and Sojourner Truth.

3. To what degree does Alice Walker, in her evaluation of the civil rights movement, draw upon the ideas stated by Jefferson and Lincoln? Where do these ideas appear in her essay and in what ways has she changed them?

4. Much has happened to the ideas behind democracy since Walker wrote her essay in the late 1960s. Writing from your own location in time and space, with consideration of the concepts and problems expressed by the writers in this section, examine democracy: is it still a good idea?

5. To what degree do we now, or did we ever, uphold in practice the principles set forth by Jefferson and Lincoln? What would Douglass (p. 62) or the homeless described by Kozol (p. 323) say about "inalienable rights" or "life, liberty, and the pursuit of happiness"? Write an essay about the relation of one of these principles to practice in democracy.

What Is a Good Scientific Idea?

1. Review the five criteria Asimov sets out for scientific creativity (p. 378). To what degree do those criteria work for Darwin? For Watson and Crick? For Kepler? (You may need to look up some information on these scientists to supplement what the essays supply.) If the criteria do not fit exactly, add or subtract some, or change them, so they apply to the scientists and their work.

2. Review Keller's "A World of Difference" (p. 177), her biographical essay on Barbara McClintock. To what degree is McClintock's experience with her colleagues similar to that of Caroline Herschel in the

Cedering poem? Interview a female scientist on your campus to compare her experiences with fellow scientists to the ones you have read about. What gender-related problems continue to exist for women scientists? Are there some additions you might make to the Asimov criteria for scientific creativity for women?

3.   What is a good scientific idea? Using an example from your reading or general knowledge, write an essay answering that question. Be sure to examine why you happen to think the way you do. In what way is your opinion a reflection of your sex, social class, nationality, race, or modernity?

How Can We Recognize and Encourage Creativity?

1.   Both Hogan and Ehrlich experience creativity in relation to the land. In what ways are they alike and in what ways are they different? What is significant about these similarities and differences?

2.   Bronowski argues that artistic and scientific creativity draw upon the same sources and origins. Test his idea by seeing if it helps you understand two or three of the writers you have read in this chapter: Asimov (p. 370), Koestler (p. 403), Hogan (p. 413), and Ehrlich (p. 425). To what degree do his ideas work out for the writers and scientists you have read?

3.   Write an essay on ways of recognizing and encouraging creativity. Can you distinguish creativity from simple egotism or blind nonconformity? Use examples from this section and from your own experience. Is it always a good idea to encourage creativity?

What Is a Good Idea?

1.   How can we recognize a good idea? Write an essay in which you present the conditions that allow good ideas to emerge and the circumstances that allow good ideas to develop. Be sure to use examples from your reading and experience; also show what happens when good ideas work badly or change over time.

2.   Using the readings in this chapter, identify one good idea and one bad idea. Compare and contrast them, and see if some general principles emerge from your discussion about ways to tell good ideas from bad ones.

5

What Can We Learn from the Past?

What's past is prologue.
SHAKESPEARE, *The Tempest*

Why Consider This Question?

We come to the past through the present; there is no other route. As Shakespeare knew, every yesterday promises a today and a tomorrow. So it is impossible to think of the past in the abstract, or even as a static time gone by, for the past contains the dynamics of our present and our future. As Arthur M. Schlesinger, Jr., observes in "The Challenge of Change" (*New York Times Magazine*, July 27, 1986), "Science and technology revolutionize our lives, but memory, tradition, and myth frame our response." Even when rapid changes in the present erase our sense of the past, we still cling consciously or unwittingly, to our familiar habits, values, expectations, and dreams. Not even Americans, who are fond of creating themselves anew in a brave new, brand new world, can escape the powerful influence of the past on the future.

We consider the question "What can I learn from the past?" because we must. There is no way to escape, even if we might want to. This chapter of *Inquiry* focuses on three perennial concerns—family history, environmental problems, and the evolution of ideas—all of which have implications for the future.

What Does Family History Mean?

"Happy families are all alike," begins Tolstoy's *Anna Karenina*, "Every unhappy family is unhappy in its own way." Tolstoy's arbitrary dismissal of happy families was a quick way to cut to the heart of his novel. Yet when we examine real life families, our own included, we find that every family, like every person, is both unique and has much in common with other families, happy, unhappy, or otherwise. To understand our family history is to know better who we are and who we will become.

For a nation populated largely by immigrants, understanding family history is particularly important. Most Americans can take very little, if anything, for granted about their family's long-term past, for coming to a new country often involves losing touch with one's ancestors. Often as a result of moves, wars, fires and natural disasters, or slavery, records (of births, marriages, citizenship, military service) are altered, lost, destroyed, or never kept. A few letters and artifacts (the family Bible, tintypes and crumbling photographs, an item or two of furniture or clothing) survive; most do not. Only those lucky enough to be part of such longstanding cultures as the Amish or the Mormons can feel sure that family histories are secure.

Then, too, new immigrants are often working so hard to survive and trying so hard to assimilate into the mainstream culture that they suppress or deny their roots in the process. Yet their children and grandchildren want to know about their ancestors and to pass along their discoveries to succeeding generations. To ask "Where did I come from?" is a way of finding out "Who am I?" As we come to know our role models, for better and for worse, we also ask "Where am I going?" To understand our ancestral past helps, as the essays in this section reveal, to predict our future as individuals and as members of the families we will create.

Among the things we want to know about our ancestors, whether individuals or members of families, tribes, or nations, are such matters as: What did they look like? Where did they live? How did they survive? What was their culture like? What did they do, and why? What were their values? How did they get along with one another? The authors of the essays in this section approach these questions from three perspectives, as a naturalist–anthropologist (Lopez), as a family historian (Murray), and as autobiographers (Welty and Sanders).

Barry Lopez's "Searching for Ancestors" describes the quest that he and two archaeologists undertook in northern Arizona to unearth, literally and figuratively, the prehistoric Southwest Indian culture, the "Anasazi." He takes pains to dispel the stereotype that equates primitive with simple and uncomplicated, showing through the evidence of their artifacts that these people were astronomers, skilled weavers, expert potters, clever farmers. Although it is relatively easy to see *what* the Anasazi did, it is less obvious to know why they did these things. What were their values? Lopez concludes that we can only understand so much from the objects we find, mostly about their economic and material culture, and that it is particularly hard to reconstruct their spiritual and aesthetic life.

In *Proud Shoes*, Pauli Murray interprets her extended, multi-racial family—including Cherokee Indians and prominent slave owners—in Chapel Hill, North Carolina, before and after the Civil War. In the chapter included in *Inquiry*, "The Inheritance of Values," she illustrates the character traits expected in her family: "stern devotion to duty, capacity for hard work, industry and thrift, and above all honor and courage in all things."

Eudora Welty examines her turn-of-the-century family in Jackson, Mississippi, for their influence on "one writer's beginnings." What made her a reader helped her become a novelist. Scott Russell Sanders, a writer of nonfiction, interprets the four-generation "inheritance of tools" in his family. Yet the heritage for both Welty and Sanders, like the heritage of Murray and the Anasazi, represents an embodiment of values, the transmission not only of how to read or to use tools, but of the reasons why these things are important, a taste for particular books or tools, and a style of using them. Family stories are legends of human potential and limitations, precepts for survival, stories with morals and codes of conduct. As we play out our heritage, we become who we are.

What Have We Done to the Earth?

"Those who cannot remember the past are condemned to repeat it," said philosopher George Santayana. As Linda Simon points out (Chapter 2), however, the reverse is not necessarily true: simply remembering the past is no assurance we will avoid repetition of it. Indeed, most learning is cumulative, for through instruction and practice we learn to correct our mistakes and, with vigilance and luck, not to make them again. Yet our nation's 50 percent divorce rate implies the truth of Samuel Johnson's assertion, that a "second marriage is a triumph of hope over experience." On a global scale, nations never seem to learn the art of peace from practicing the art of war, despite the collective wisdom of such deliberative bodies as the United Nations. To cite but a single example, the peace settlement for World War I, "the war to end all wars," prepared for the outbreak of World War II less than twenty years later.

Other problems seem perennial, their solutions partial, temporary, or causing more problems than they solve. We have yet to eliminate poverty and its accompanying features, including malnutrition, disease, illiteracy, homelessness, unemployment, drug abuse, and child and spousal abuse. The readings in this section focus on a major problem that our society has created and has yet to solve: the destruction of the natural environment. Yet the fact that thoughtful writers from a variety of disciplines offer solutions to this problem implies that change and improvement are possible. Just because we have made mistakes does not mean we have to go on making them. The authors write, in fact, not just to point out problems, but to point to their solutions.

In "The Obligation to Endure," from *Silent Spring*, biologist Rachel Carson argues that "The most alarming of all man's assaults upon the environment is the contamination," universal and irreversible, "of air, earth, rivers, and sea with dangerous and even lethal materials." Although Carson's warning had some effect, engendering legislation in the 1960s and 1970s to protect the environment and endangered species, the problems have continued, as William Warner's analysis of the pollution in "The Islands of Chesapeake Bay" demonstrates. Warner shows how the inhabitants, history, and economy of the main crabbing islands in the Chesapeake Bay are intertwined with the health of the crustacean population, which in turn is affected by state fishing regulations, industry, and the generation of power in the area. Our attempts to solve one set of problems can create problems as enduring as those they replace.

When John McPhee looks at the relation of people to nature, he sees a battle—one that nature is likely to win. After reading Carson and Warner, we might think that a victory of nature over the well-intentioned interference of humans would be worth cheering. But in "Los Angeles Against the Mountains" it is not easy to know who to root for. McPhee describes the attempts by residents of the Los Angeles area to build homes in the path of historic "debris flows," the thousands of tons of rock, mud, and brush that crash through mountain canyons during heavy rains. Is this deliberate attempt to control nature, this refusal to learn from the past, heroic, or just plain stupid?

It sometimes seems as if the obvious response to human attempts to control or change nature is to argue that we should just leave it alone. But obvious answers may not be the best ones. As Margaret Knox points out in "Africa Daze Montana Knights," what is obvious to one group seems clearly wrong to another. She deplores the fact that "those fighting on the side of the earth are increasingly vicious with one another." Like McPhee, she sees the battle between humans and nature, but she also notices that human interests are themselves in conflict; a starving family is less likely to appreciate the need to preserve a rare animal than to anticipate a good meal. The warfare is not just people attacking the earth "and nature fights back," but "people fighting people on behalf of nature." Whether in Africa or

Montana, what she calls "a rational solution" is hard to find. Everyone can agree that we should respond to "the level of crisis into which we have plunged our earth." But how?

How Does an Idea Evolve?

Cartoons show ideas as popping into one's head, and sometimes it feels that way. Aha! We know a good idea when we have one, and sometimes we even know what to do with it. If not, some creative thinking will usually provide us with a number of options, as well as the language in which to express our understanding. But ideas seldom spring from thin air; they favor the prepared mind, and flourish in a congenial environment.

Good ideas often wither if they emerge in a hostile or unreceptive environment, only to flourish when the climate is right. Although the drafters of the Declaration of Independence asserted, for example, that "all men are created equal," they actually meant free white men, not free white women, or slaves, or the original Native American settlers. That this definition has broadened over the two succeeding centuries is more the result of social and political movements and pressures than the consequence of individual enlightenment; a desire for justice for all has come to mean something new as social conditions have changed.

The notion of civil disobedience, for instance, is embedded in a number of related concepts. There has to be a civil state or other governing authority for the dissident to disobey. There has to be the opportunity for dissension; "off with his head" does not meet with argument in a totalitarian state. There has to be the belief that might does not necessarily mean right, according to centuries of dissidents, from Socrates to Thoreau to Gandhi to Martin Luther King, Jr. There has to be a willingness to act on that belief, to question authority, to test the law, and if necessary, to suffer the consequences of one's assaults on the status quo—fines, imprisonment, even death.

Harriet Tubman, a Maryland slave, and Henry David Thoreau, a New England intellectual, were contemporaries and were motivated in their civil disobedience by a common concern, opposition to slavery. Tubman, whose character, career, and principles Susan Griffin celebrates in "I Like to Think of Harriet Tubman," violated two laws, one repeatedly. In 1846, on hearing rumors that she was about to be sold, she escaped to freedom in Philadelphia. For the next dozen years, she became the "Moses of her people," conducting over 300 fugitive slaves along the "Underground Railroad" to Canada. Exercising the extraordinary courage, ingenuity, discipline, and persistence that characterize other notable civil dissidents, Tubman, "who defied the law," "was never caught, and/had no use for the law/when the law was wrong." Thoreau's form of civil disobedience, refusing to pay the Massachusetts poll tax because of its implications for supporting the Mexican War and the existence of slavery, was technically far milder; he spent only a single night in jail, "the only house in a slave state in which a free man can abide with honor." But its major consequence, his 1848 essay defining and defending "Civil Disobedience," has reverberated around the world ever since.

However, violation of a law to protest injustice guarantees neither exemption from the law nor the assurance that it will change. It is too easy to believe that the kind of discrimination Harriet Tubman experienced ended with the Emancipation Proclamation. But many twentieth-century black autobiographies bear painful, outraged witness to the humiliating discrimination that Martin Luther King, Jr., addresses in "Letter from Birmingham Jail." Because of the color of their skin, twenty million "black brothers and sisters" are subject to lynching, police brutality, discrimination in public schools and accommodations, segregated into the "airtight cage of poverty in the midst of an affluent society." King has learned from history that privileged groups seldom give up their privileges voluntarily, which is why he is impatient with pleas to "Wait." Civil disobedience, nonviolent refusal to obey the laws enforcing discrimination, is in King's view a last but inevitable resort in bringing about not only changes in the laws but also enforcement of them.

In "Civil Disobedience: Destroyer of Democracy," Lewis H. Van Dusen, Jr., takes issue with Dr. King's position. He distinguishes between Thoreau's civil disobedience, knowingly breaking the law from principles of moral righteousness, and Dr. King's conscientious testing of the law—violating one law while expecting support from a higher court.

Rhetorical Issues: Sources

There is no special or unique way to write about what one can learn from the past any more than there is a special way to write about any other subject. The nature of the topic, however, makes it particularly appropriate to consider the sources of our information about the past and to examine ways of using sources responsibly in our own writing.

Selecting Sources

Context: When psychologist Eliot Mishler titled his critique of psychological research in laboratories "Meaning In Context: Is There Any Other Kind?" he expected the answer to be an emphatic "No."

Isolated facts mean nothing without a context to help us determine which of the many possible interpretations is, or are, the best. "Best" interpretations usually mean those that accommodate all the available information and enhance our understanding of that information and the subject to which it pertains. Take for instance, the isolated facts that in 1960 the population of the Chesapeake Bay drainage area was 11 million people and that the "doubling rate," an annual 1.7 percent, was twice the national average. To make sense of this information we need to know the importance of the population figure, the meaning of the term "doubling rate," and the significance of the particular rate. In "The Islands of the Chesapeake Bay," William Warner explains that "doubling rate" is the rate at which the human population expands. This expansion effects an equivalent increase in the drainage of sewage, chemicals, and other pollutants into the Chesapeake Bay. Warner considers the significance of the doubling rate in absolute terms (the 1960 population will have tripled by the year 2000), in relation to the rate nationwide (twice the national average), and in terms of its consequences. "The great and noble" tributary rivers and the Bay itself serve as "natural sewers," turning the water into a slimy, pea-green, "horrid soup of sea that affronts all the senses." The Chesapeake Bay, he predicts, will soon die.

There are two categories of sources, primary (firsthand) and secondary (everything else). *Primary sources* include original documents by the people you are studying, such as manuscripts or books, interviews, diaries, and letters. Primary sources might also be by or about people who lived during the time period or participated in the event, activity, or other phenomenon under study. Pauli Murray consulted many such documents in writing her family's history, *Proud Shoes*. These sources pertained to life and history in and around Chapel Hill, North Carolina, from its founding to early twentieth century, including photographs, maps, documents (such as deeds, bills of sale of slaves, birth or marriage certificates) or records (financial statements, tax papers, court records, wills).

Secondary sources include everyone and everything else. Secondary sources may be people: descendants, friends, and acquaintances of your original subject; experts on the subject, whether formally trained or not, including scholars, researchers, police, physicians, folklorists, and statisticians. Secondary sources also include a host of reference materials (almanacs, data banks, statistical compilations, bibliographies) and written interpretations—scholarly articles and books, which are themselves based on a combination of primary and secondary sources.

As you evaluate your materials, both primary and secondary, you will need to consider:

- *The date.* For primary sources the date has to be contemporary with the subject. If you are looking for up-to-the-minute interpretations, the most recent secondary sources such as scholarly books, scientific data, or statistical compilations (identifiable by the copyright date) often supersede earlier information. But sometimes an earlier edition or work has set the standard—later editions often acknowledge their predecessors—and you will need to consult those as well. You might want to begin your study with current materials and work backward.

- *The authority of the source.* How reliable is the author? How well qualified is he or she in terms of background and experience? One way to tell is the extent to which a given scholar is cited or quoted in others' research.

- *Degree of generality or specialization.* How specialized is the source, and what degree of specialization do you want? If you are discussing civil disobedience in America, what will you use to supplement primary sources, such as, say, Thoreau's "Civil Disobedience" or writings of Martin Luther King, Jr.? Would a book discussing the history of American civil disobedience, or one focusing on the civil rights movement in the South in the 1960s, or on Vietnam War protests, be the most appropriate?

- *Is the source accurate,* as far as you can tell? Does the author document the evidence with reliable sources that readers can check? Is appropriate evidence used and interpreted fairly?

- *What biases does the source contain,* in the sense that it emphasizes one point of view over another? Can you recognize the viewpoint? All sources are biased in some ways; many American works, for instance, have a white, middle class, North American orientation. Your sources will not necessarily agree. If you are trying to interpret conflicting information, pick the least biased (most objective) sources, on the grounds that those who present or interpret the information have little or no vested interest in its use. If you are trying to interpret conflicting information from equally biased sources, rely most heavily on the source with the most authoritative reputation, the one you are most likely to trust. But you should be particularly careful not to rely uncritically, or too much, on any one source; then, you are likely to accept someone else's point of view as your own. You may well agree with one of your sources, but you need to use that source responsibly to show just how and why you agree.

Responsible Use of Sources

Suppose you are writing a paper on American civil disobedience. You are particularly interested in the relation between idealism and law-breaking. You decide that the following passage from Henry David Thoreau's essay in this chapter is relevant to your topic, and you want to use it as a source:

> Unjust laws exist: shall we be content to obey them, or shall we endeavor to amend them, and obey them until we have succeeded, or shall we transgress them at once? Men generally, under such a government as this, think that they ought to wait until they have persuaded the majority to alter them. They think that, if they should resist, the remedy would be worse than the evil. But it is the fault of the government itself that the remedy *is* worse than the evil. *It* makes it worse. Why is it not more apt to anticipate and provide for reform? Why does it not cherish its wise minority? Why does it cry and resist before it is hurt?

What Thoreau has to say is clearly useful for your topic. But how are you to use it? And how are you to avoid using it improperly?

Let's take a moment to look at the wrong ways to handle sources, for many students are nervous about falling into plagiarism—using sources as if they were your own idea—by mistake. Very few students will be deliberately dishonest and foolish enough to plan plagiarism, that is, to copy what Thoreau said word for word and hand it in as if it were original. But honest and sensible people still have trouble using sources properly and sometimes stumble unaware into plagiarism, unless they understand clearly how to incorporate other people's ideas into their own work.

For instance, one way to misuse Thoreau's material would be to copy what he says word for word and put a note at the end referring to the source of the quotation. Sometimes plagiarism happens if you take careless notes that fail to distinguish quotations from your summaries of what you have read. There is no intention to deceive, in this case, but plagiarism is still going on, since (without quotation marks) Thoreau's words and ideas are put forward as your own.

It is more responsible to put the quoted material in quotation marks, of course, but even that does not complete the job of using the source responsibly. Why is the quotation in your text? How does it relate to what *you* have to say?

The whole point of writing a paper using sources is not just to include relevant quotations and to cite sources, but rather to demonstrate that you have *thought about* your quotations and your sources in relation to your topic. If you just string together sources, quoted or paraphrased, with a bit of connection to hold them together, you are not accomplishing the inquiry that lies behind writing itself. Sources will help you demonstrate your ideas, but they cannot substitute for your ideas.

One way many students would use this source would be to figure out what Thoreau is saying and to put it into their own words:

> People suffering under unjust laws have to decide if they should obey the laws or not. Most people decide to obey them while they work for change, since breaking the law might be worse than the unjust law itself. But it is better to break the law, since the law itself should allow the best citizens to make changes.

But inserting this rewording of Thoreau's idea into your paper, while it shows that you understand his idea, is still not by itself a responsible use of the source, particularly if you fail to cite Thoreau at the end of the paraphrase. The *idea* is still his, even if the words are yours, and just placing someone else's ideas into your paper represents a failure to use the source properly. And even if you do cite Thoreau after the paraphrase, your reader will not know what the citation means. How much of what you say is yours, how much is Thoreau's, or is there any difference?

The problem you must handle as a writer using sources is not only to understand Thoreau, but also to come to some personal understanding of the material at hand (here, the moral and legal problem of either obeying or disobeying unjust laws). You must regard Thoreau critically; if you end up agreeing with him, you should say so, explicitly. If not, point out where and why you differ.

So we return once more to the topic. Is Thoreau's argument (those in "a wise minority" should break laws they feel to be unjust) an idea you wish to support, in whole or in part? What does your own experience say? What do other sources, for instance, Martin Luther King, Jr., or Lewis H. Van Dusen (in this chapter), say about the same subject? Does Thoreau's location in nineteenth-century New England in any way determine what he will see? How does Thoreau's view relate to your own?

To think this way is to come to terms with the problems of writing a paper using sources. If you decide to put the whole quotation into your paper, you will need to introduce it, analyze it, comment upon it, and relate it to your own ideas. You might begin, after the quotation, something like this:

When we look closely at what Thoreau has to say, we can argue that he oversimplifies the issue; as the last 150 years have made plain, it is hard to decide exactly what is an unjust law. Few of us today can be so certain that any law is wrong. But Thoreau's arrogant certainty has undeniable power. . . .

But perhaps you do not want to focus so heavily on Thoreau's views; in that case you may want to quote a small portion of what he says, as part of another argument:

Disobedience to law in our time has proven to be a powerful force for change. The idea that we should always obey laws while seeking to change them has repeatedly been shown to be the way governments perpetuate evil; they argue that breaking laws is worse than any evil the law may bring about. But I would argue, as does Thoreau, that "it is the fault of the government itself that the remedy *is* worse than the evil." A truly democratic government will provide ways for those who object to its laws to protest legally and effectively.

Or you may just want to allude to what Thoreau says as part of a survey of various ideas on your subject:

Among the most well-known proponents of disobeying laws they felt to be unjust are Thoreau (who briefly went to jail for opposing a government supporting slavery) and Dr. Martin Luther King, Jr., who . . .

There are many ways to use sources responsibly, but the important principle to keep in mind is that you must understand what the source is saying and how it relates to your own ideas. In using sources you must not simply be a sponge, soaking up uncritically everything you read. You must distinguish between the opinions of another and the opinion that you yourself, after careful consideration, come to hold. The quotation then becomes a fact, the fact that a particular writer has said something, which you as author of your own work must interpret as you would any other fact; you need to show how the evidence provided by the quotation relates to what you yourself have to say. Every writer has his or her own intellectual identity, though most ideas inevitably come from outside sources. A responsible use of sources recognizes that identity and distinguishes clearly between what you think and what the sources think. It is no sin to accept another person's idea: "But I would argue, as does Thoreau, that . . ." But you must interpose yourself between the sources and your writing, thus making other people's ideas your own through a process of critical scrutiny.

QUESTIONS FOR DISCOVERY AND DISCUSSION

1. Interview an elderly member of your family to find out what that person remembers of particular childhood traditions, stories, rituals, or customs. What can you discover about your family's past and how your parents carried on (or modified) family traditions? Can you find family photographs that reinforce the memories? How far back can you trace your roots?

2. What stories and traditions were influential in your own childhood? Think of experiences that show the power of the past. Did your parents read to you from books they themselves used as children? Were there old places or things that embodied important memories? Can you recall experiences that you had that were the same as those your parents, grandparents, or greatgrandparents had when they were children?

3. What values do you now hold that have been passed down to you from older generations? Where did they come from and what were their origins? Have you had to adjust these values to modern times, or do they still work as they did in the past?

4. To what degree did your previous schooling support or challenge the values and beliefs you received from your family? Explain to someone who does not know your family an incident that shows the way your schooling related to your family traditions.

Searching for Ancestors

BARRY LOPEZ

In "Searching for Ancestors," from his essay collection *Crossing Open Ground* (1988), Barry Lopez explores how and why he and two archaeologists went to northern Arizona to hunt for "tangible remains" of the Indian culture, generically called Anasazi. Throughout the essay, Lopez takes pains to dispel the notion that prehistoric means either "primitive" or "uncomplicated." When we search for ancestors, whether those of our family, clan, nation, or species, we need to be aware of the relation of the people to each other, the land, the times, and the climate—intellectual and geographical. As investigators of the past, "we are takers of notes, measurers of stone, examiners of fragments in the dust. We search for order in chaos wherever we go," but we need to beware of imposing our contemporary order, *ex post facto*. "In our best moments," says Lopez, "we remember to ask ourselves what it is we are doing, whom we are benefiting from these acts. One of the great dreams of man must be to find some place between the extremes of nature and civilization where it is possible to live without regret."

Lopez was born in New York in 1945. After earning degrees from Notre Dame in 1966 and 1968, he moved to rural Oregon, where he continues to live and write. Much of his writing presents sympathetic, sometimes poetic, interpretations of animal behavior in relation to other animals or humans. Among his books are *Desert Notes: Reflections in the Eye of a Raven* (1976); *River Notes: The Dance of Herons* (1979); *Of Wolves and Men* (1979), illustrated with his own photographs; and *Arctic Dreams: Imagination and Desire in a Northern Landscape* (1986), winner of the American Book Award.

I am lying on my back in northern Arizona. The sky above, the familiar arrangement of stars at this particular latitude on a soft June evening, is comforting. I reach out from my sleeping bag, waiting for sleep, and slowly brush the Kaibab Plateau, a grit of limestone 230 million years old. A slight breeze, the settling air at dusk, carries the pungent odor of blooming cliffrose. 1

Three of us sleep in this clearing, on the west rim of Marble 2 Canyon above the Colorado River. Two archaeologists and myself, out hunting for tangible remains of the culture called Anasazi. The Anasazi abandoned this particular area for good around A.D. 1150, because of drought, deteriorating trade alliances, social hostilities—hard to say now. But while they flourished, both here and farther to the east in the austere beauty of canyons called de Chelly and Chaco, they represented an apotheosis in North American culture, like the Hopewell of Ohio or the horse-mounted Lakota of the plains in the last century.

In recent years the Anasazi have come to signify prehistoric In- 3 dians in the same way the Lakota people have been made to stand for all historic Indians. Much has been made of the "mystery" of their disappearance. And perhaps because they seem "primitive," they are too easily thought of as an uncomplicated people with a comprehensible culture. It is not, and they are not. We know some things about them. From the start they were deft weavers, plaiting even the utensils they cooked with. Later they became expert potters and masons, strongly influencing cultures around them. They were clever floodwater farmers. And astronomers; not as sophisticated as the Maya, but knowledgeable enough to pinpoint the major celestial events, to plant and celebrate accordingly.

They were intimate with the landscape, a successful people. 4 Around A.D. 1300 they slipped through a historical crevice to emerge (as well as we know) as the people now called Hopi and Zuni, and the pueblo peoples of the Rio Grande Valley—Keres, Tiwa, Tewa.

On a long, dry June day like this, hundreds of tourists wander 5 in fascination at Mesa Verde and Pueblo Bonito; and I am out here on the land the Anasazi once walked—here with two people who squat down to look closely at the land itself before they say anything about its former inhabitants. Even then they are reticent. We are camped here amid the indigenous light siennas and dark umbers, the wild red of ripe prickly pear fruit, the dull silver of buffalo berry bushes, the dark, luminous green of a field of snakegrass.

We inquire after the Anasazi. Because we respect the spiritual 6 legacy of their descendants, the Hopi. Because of the contemporary allure of Taos. Because in our own age we are "killing the hidden waters" of the Southwest, and these were a people who took swift, resourceful advantage of whatever water they could find. Because of the compelling architecture of their cliff dwellings, the stunning placement of their homes in the stone walls of Betatakin, as if set in the mouth of an enormous wave or at the bottom of a towering cumulus cloud. We make the long automobile trip to Hovenweep or the hike into Tsegi Canyon to gaze at Keet Seel. It is as though we believed *here* is a good example, here are stories to get us through the night.

Some eight thousand years ago, after the decline of the Folsom 7 and Clovis hunters, whose spearpoints are still found in the crumbling arroyos of New Mexico, a culture we know very little about emerged in the Great Basin. Archaeologists call it simply the Desert Culture. Some two thousand years ago, while Rome was engaged in the Macedonian wars, a distinct group of people emerged from this complex. They were called Anasazi from the Navajo *anaasázi*, meaning "someone's ancestors." Their culture first appeared in the Four Corners country, where Utah, Arizona, New Mexico, and Colorado meet. By this time (A.D. 1) they were already proficient weavers and basket-makers, living a mixed agricultural hunter-gatherer life and dwelling in small groups in semisubterranean houses. Archaeologists call this period, up to about A.D. 700, the Basket Maker Period. It was followed by a Pueblo Period (A.D. 700–1598), during which time the Anasazi built the great cliff and pueblo dwellings by which most of us know them.

Archaeologists divide the Anasazi occupation geographically into 8 three contemporary traditions—Kayenta, Chaco, and Mesa Verde. Here, where I have rolled my sleeping bag out this June evening, Kayenta Anasazi lived, in an area of about ten thousand square miles bounded by the Henry Mountains in Utah, the Little Colorado River to the south, Grand Canyon to the west, and Chinle Wash, near the New Mexico border, to the east. This part of the Anasazi country has long been of interest to Robert Euler, the research anthropologist at Grand Canyon National Park. He lies quietly now a few yards away from me, in the night shadow of a large juniper tree. From here, at the lip of Marble Canyon and the old edge of Anasazi territory, amid the very same plants the Anasazi took such perceptive advantage of— threads of the yucca leaf to be made into snares; the soft, shreddy bark of the cliffrose to absorb the flow of blood; delicate black seeds of rice grass to eat—from here, with the aid of an observer like Euler, it is possible to imagine who these people might have been, to make some cautious surmise about them and the meaning they may have for us, who wistfully regard them now as mysterious and vanished, like the Eskimo curlew.

We go toward sleep this evening—Euler, a colleague named Trin- 9 kle Jones, and myself—restless with the bright, looming memory of a granary we have located today, a small storage structure below a cliff edge that has been visited only by violet-green swallows and pack rats since its Anasazi owners walked away some eight hundred years ago. It is like a piece of quartz in the mind.

In a quiet corner of the national park's health clinic on the south 10 rim of the Grand Canyon, an entire wall of Euler's modest office is covered by books. A small slip of paper there reads:

> These are not books, lumps of lifeless paper, but *minds* alive on the shelves. From each of them goes out its own voice, as inaudible as the streams of sound conveyed day and night by electric waves beyond the range of our physical hearing; and just as the touch of a

button on our set will fill the room with music, so by taking down one of these volumes and opening it, one can call into range the far distant voice in time and space, and hear it speaking to us, mind to mind, heart to heart.

GILBERT HIGHET

Highet was a classics scholar. The words reflect his respect for 11 the ideas of other cultures, other generations, and for the careful deliberations of trained minds. Euler is in this mold; keen and careful, expert in his field, but intent on fresh insight. At fifty-seven, with an ironic wit, willing to listen attentively to the ideas of an amateur, graciously polite, he is the sort of man you wish had taught you in college.

Of the Anasazi he says: "It is relatively easy to see *what* they did, 12 but why did they do these things? What were their values? What were the fundamental relationships between their institutions—their politics, economics, religion? All we can do is infer, from what we pick up on the ground."

To elucidate the Anasazi, Euler and his colleagues have taken 13 several ingenious steps in recent years. In the 1920s a man named Andrew Douglass pioneered a system of dating called dendrochronology. By comparing borings from timbers used in Anasazi dwellings, Douglass and his successors eventually constructed a continuous record of tree-ring patterns going back more than two thousand years. The measurements are so precise that archaeologists can, for instance, tell that a room in a particular dwelling in Chaco Canyon was roofed over in the spring or summer of 1040 with timbers cut in the fall or winter of 1039.

Using dendrochronology as a parallel guide in time, archaeolo- 14 gists have been able to corroborate and assemble long sequences of pottery design. With the aid of radiocarbon dating, obsidian hydration dating, and a technique called thermoluminescence, they have pinned down dates for cooking fires and various tools. By determining kinds of fossil pollens and their ratios to each other, palynologists have reconstructed former plant communities, shedding light on human diets at the time and establishing a history of weather patterns.

With such a convergence of dates and esoteric information, ar- 15 chaeologists can figure out when a group of people were occupying a certain canyon, what sort of meals they were eating, what kind of animals and plants were present there, and how they were adapting their farming methods and living patterns to cope with, say, several years of heavy rainfall. With more prosaic techniques—simple excavation and observation—much more becomes clear: details and artifacts of personal adornment; locally traded items (beans and squash for tanned deerskin) and distant trade patterns (turquoise for abalone shell beads from California or copper bells from Mexico); and prevalent infirmities and diseases (arthritis, iron-deficiency anemia).

As much as one can learn, however—the Anasazi were a short 16
people with straight black hair, who domesticated turkeys for a supply
of feathers, which they carefully wrapped around string and wove
together to make blankets—the information seems hollow when you
are standing in the cool silence of one of the great kivas at Mesa Verde.
Or staring at the stone that soars like a cathedral vault above White
House Ruin in Canyon de Chelly. Or turning an Anasazi flute over
in your hands. The analytic tools of science can obscure the fact that
these were a people. They had an obvious and pervasive spiritual and
aesthetic life, as well as clothing made of feathers and teeth worn
down by the grit in their cornmeal. Their abandoned dwellings and
ceremonial kivas would seem to make this clear. This belief by itself—
that they were a people of great spiritual strength—makes us want
to know them, to understand what they understood.

The day Euler and Jones discovered the intact granary, with its hand- 17
ful of tiny corncobs, I was making notes about the plants and animals
we had encountered and trying to envision how water fell and flowed
away over this parched land. Euler had told me the area we were
traversing was comparable to what the Anasazi had known when
they were here, though it was a little drier now. Here then was buffalo
berry, which must have irritated their flesh with the white powder
beneath its leaves, as it did mine. And apache plume, from whose
stout twigs the Anasazi made arrows. And a species of sumac, from
the fruits of which they made a sweet lemonade. Dogbane, from
whose fibrous stems they wove sandals, proof against scorpions, cactus spines, and the other sharp and pointed edges of this country.

One afternoon I came on the remains of a mule deer killed by a 18
mountain lion and thought the Anasazi, eminently practical, must
have availed themselves of such meat. And I considered the sheltered,
well-stocked dwellings of the pack rat, who may have indicated to the
newly arrived Anasazi the value of providence and storage.

Such wandering is like an interrogation of the landscape, trying 19
by means of natural history and analog to pry loose from it a sense
of a people who would be intimate with it—knowledgeable of the
behavior of its ground and surface water, its seven-year cycle of piñon
nut production, the various subtle euphonies of whirring insects,
bumblebees, and hummingbirds on a June afternoon—a people reflective of its order.

Euler stood by me at one point when I asked about a particular 20
plant—did they parch, very carefully, the tiny seeds of this desert
plume in fiber baskets over their fires?—and said that their botany

was so good they probably made use of everything they could digest.

They made mistakes, too, if you want to call them that: farmed   21
one area too intensively and ruined the soil; cut down too many trees
with their stone axes for housing and firewood and abetted erosion;
overhunted. But they survived. They lived through long droughts
and took advantage of years of wetness to secure their future. One
of the great lessons of the Anasazi is one of the great lessons of all
aboriginal peoples, of human ecology in general: Individuals die—of
starvation, disease, and injury; but the population itself—resourceful,
practical, determined—carries on through nearly everything. Their
indomitable fierceness is as attractive as the power we imagine concentrated in their kivas.

With the Anasazi, however, you must always turn back and look   22
at the earth—the earth they farmed and hunted and gathered fruits
and nuts and seeds upon—and to the weather. The Anasazi responded resourcefully and decisively to the earth and the weather
that together made their land. If they were sometimes victims of their
environment through drought or epidemic disease, they were more
often on excellent terms with it. Given a slight advantage, as they
were about A.D. 600 and again about A.D. 1150, when food was abundant at the peak of the Southwest's 550-year moisture cycle, their
culture flourished. Around A.D. 600 they developed pottery, the cultivated bean, and the bow and arrow. In the bean was an important
amino acid, lysine, not available in the corn they cultivated. Their diet
improved dramatically. By 1150 the Anasazi were building pueblos
with three-story, freestanding walls, and their crafts were resurgent
during this "classic" period. We can only wonder what might have
happened at the next climatic, in 1700—but by then the hostile Spanish were among them.

The rise and fall of Anasazi fortunes in time with the weather   23
patterns of the region is clear to most historians. What is not clear is
how much of a role weather played in the final retreat of the Anasazi
in A.D. 1300 from areas they had long occupied—Mesa Verde, southern Black Mesa, Chaco Canyon. Toward the end, the Anasazi were
building what seem to be defensive structures, but it is unclear against
whom they were defending themselves. A good guess is that they
were defending themselves against themselves, that this was a period
of intense social feuding. The sudden alteration of trading relationships, social and political realignment in the communities, drought—
whatever the reasons, the Anasazi departed. Their descendants took
up residence along the Rio Grande, near springs on the Hopi mesas,
and on tributaries of the Little Colorado where water was more dependable. Here, too, they developed farming techniques that were
not so harmful to the land.

For many in the Southwest today the Anasazi are a vague and 24
nebulous passage in the history of human life. For others, like Euler,
they are an intense reflection of the land, a puzzle to be addressed
the way a man might try to understand the now-departed curlew. For
still others they are a spiritual repository, a mysterious source of
strength both of their intimacy with the Colorado Plateau.

To wonder about the Anasazi today at a place like the Grand 25
Canyon is to be humbled—by space and the breadth of time—to find
the Anasazi neither remote nor primitive, but transcendent. The English novelist J. B. Priestley once said that if he were an American he
would make the final test of whatever men chose to do in art and
politics a comparison with this place. He believed that whatever was
cheap and ephemeral would be revealed for what it was when stood
up against it. Priestley was an intellectual, but he had his finger on
an abiding aboriginal truth: If something will not stand up in the
land, then it doesn't belong there. It is right that it should die. Most
of us are now so far removed from either a practical or an aesthetic
intimacy with North America that the land is no longer an arbiter for
us. And a haunting sense that this arrangement is somewhat dangerous brings us to stare into the Grand Canyon and to contemplate
the utter honesty of the Anasazi's life here.

In 1906, with some inkling that North America was slowly 26
being stripped of the evidence of its aboriginal life and that a knowledge of such life was valuable, Congress passed a protective Anti-
quities Act. The impulse in 1979 to pass a much stronger
Archaeological Resources Act was different. Spurred on by escalating
prices for Anasazi artifacts, thieves had been systematically looting
sites for commercial gain. The trend continues. A second serious
current threat to this human heritage is the small number of tourists
who, sometimes innocently, continue to destroy structures, walk off
with artifacts, and deface petroglyphs. More ominously, the national
parks and monuments where most Anasazi sites are now found operate on such restricted budgets that they are unable to adequately
inventory, let alone protect, these cultural resources.

Of the Grand Canyon's two thousand or more aboriginal sites 27
only three have been both excavated and stabilized. Of its 1.2 million
acres, 500,000 have never even been visited by an archaeologist or historian. In the summer of 1981 an unknown person or persons pushed
in the wall of an Anasazi granary on the Colorado River at the mouth
of Nankoweap Canyon, one of the most famous sites in the park.

The sites, which people come so far every year to visit, are more 28
vulnerable every year.

On a helicopter reconnaissance in September 1981, part of a long-   29
term project to locate and describe aboriginal sites in the park, Trinkle
Jones found what she thought was a set of untouched ruins in the
west rim of Marble Canyon. It was almost a year before she and Euler
could get there to record them, on a trip on which I accompanied
them.

Euler is glad to get out into the country, into the canyons that   30
have been the focus of his work since 1960. He moves easily through
the juniper-piñon savannahs, around the face of a cliff and along
narrow trails with a practiced stride, examining bits of stone and
brush. His blue eyes often fill with wonder when he relates bits of
Anasazi history, his right hand sometimes turning slowly in the air
as he speaks, as if he were showing you a rare fruit. He tells me one
night that he reveres the land, that he thinks about his own footprints
impressed in the soil and on the plants, how long before there will
be no trace.

Euler is a former college president, an author and editor, has been   31
on several university faculties and a codirector of the Black Mesa
Archaeological Project, working one step ahead of Peabody Coal's
drag buckets. The Park Service, so severely hampered by its humiliating lack of funds, is fortunate, at least, to be able to retain
such men.

The granaries Jones found prove, indeed, to be untouched. Over   32
a period of several days we map and describe nine new ruins. The
process is somewhat mechanical, but we each take pleasure in the
simple tasks. As the Anasazi had a complicated culture, so have we.
We are takers of notes, measurers of stone, examiners of fragments
in the dust. We search for order in chaos wherever we go. We worry
over what is lost. In our best moments we remember to ask ourselves
what it is we are doing, whom we are benefiting by these acts. One
of the great dreams of man must be to find some place between the
extremes of nature and civilization where it is possible to live without
regret.

I lie in my sleeping bag, staring up at the Big Dipper and other   33
familiar stars. It is surprisingly cool. The moon has risen over the
land of the Navajo nation to the east. Bats flutter overhead, swooping
after moths. We are the only people, I reflect, who go to such lengths
to record and preserve the past. In the case of the Anasazi it is not
even our own past. Until recently Indians distrusted this process.
When Andrew Douglass roamed the Southwest looking for house
timbers to core to establish his dendrochronologies, he was required
to trade bolts of velveteen for the privilege and to close off every drill
hole with a piece of turquoise.

I roll on my side and stare out into the canyon's abyss. I think of 34
the astonishing variety of insects and spiders I have seen today—
stinkbugs inverted in cactus flowers, butterflies, tiny biting gnats and
exotic red velvet ants, and on the ceiling of an Anasazi granary a very
poisonous brown recluse spider. For all the unrelieved tedium there
might seem to be in the miles of juniper-piñon savannah, for all the
cactus spines, sharp stones, strong light, and imagined strikes of
rattlesnakes, the land is replete with creatures, and there is a soft and
subtle beauty here. Turn an ash-white mule deer antler over, and its
underside, where it has lain against the earth, is flushed rose. Yellow
pollen clings to the backs of my hands. Wild grasses roll in the wind,
like the manes of horses. It is important to remember that the Anasazi
lived in a place, and that the place was very much like the place I lie
in tonight.

The Anasazi are a reminder: Human life is fundamentally diverse 35
and finally impenetrable. That we cannot do better than a crude reconstruction of their life on the Colorado Plateau a thousand years
ago is probably to our advantage, for it steers us away from presumption and judgment.

I roll over again and look at the brightening stars. How fortunate 36
we all are, I think, to have people like Euler among us, with their
long-lived inquiries; to have these bits of the Anasazi Way to provoke
our speculation, to humble us in this long and endless struggle to
find ourselves in the world.

The slow inhalation of light that is the fall of dusk is now complete. 37
The stars are very bright. I lie there recalling the land as if the Anasazi
were something that had once bloomed in it.

RESPONDING TO READING

Key words: community   discovery   identity   loss   nature
race   story

Rhetorical concepts: cause and effect   exploration   illustration
induction   myth   narrative/example   research report

1.   To what lengths is it appropriate to go "to record and preserve the past"
(paragraph 33)? By what means can we do so? For what purposes? Suppose
preserving the past conflicts with progress, what then?
2.   Why study history?
3.   What sorts of evidence do archaeologists use to understand and reconstruct past civilizations?
4.   "If something will not stand up in the land, then it doesn't belong there.
It is right that it should die" (paragraph 25). What does Lopez mean by that?
How could a natural terrain, or a species (such as buffalo, or the American

eagle), possibly protect itself against destruction by the forces of "civilization"? Yet surely Lopez does not mean that it is "right" that the land or particular species should die out. Discuss.

5. When you think of "ancestors," is your meaning the same as Lopez's? Define your meaning, and explain how you would go about studying ancestors, as you define them. What would you be looking for?

The Inheritance of Values

PAULI MURRAY

In searching for her ancestors when preparing to write *Proud Shoes* (1955), of which "The Inheritance of Values" is a chapter, Pauli Murray discovered her family's history to be a microcosm of the history of America, for better and for worse. "The ideals and influences within my own family had made me a life-long fighter against all forms of inequality and injustice," says Murray. Her research was complicated because of the difficulties in tracing blacks, particularly in the South, because "the experience of slavery . . . all but wiped out the identities of black ancestors." In census records before 1870, slaves were identified not by their own names, but by the names of their owners, and usually were not named at all in public records, such as deeds, wills, or bills of sale. After the Civil War, black families, scarcely literate, were scattered, so neither oral nor written traditions preserved their histories. Former slaves and their children were reluctant to talk about their bondage, "too painful to live with." When social taboos and miscegenation laws were broken, there was additional pressure to maintain silence. Murray's people included Cherokee Indians and a prominent, white slave-owning family, whose "deep sexual and emotional involvement with slaves" leapt racial and social barriers but created a further taboo of silence.

Despite these silences, Murray (1910–1985), a lawyer who had earned her degree from Howard University in 1944, persevered in her quest for information, as she was to do in every area of her life. She found in public archives "the records of obscure citizens and the country's leaders," documents "of a common humanity" that narrowed the distances between races, classes, and political positions. Her resourceful investigation provided the basis for both her family biography, *Proud Shoes*, and for her civil rights activities.

There was pride on both sides of the Fitzgerald family, but my 1 greatest inheritance, perhaps, was a dogged persistence, a granite quality of endurance in the face of calamity. There was pride in family background, of course, but my folks took greater pride in doing any kind of honest work to earn a living and remain independent. Some people thought this trait was peculiarly Grandfather's, that Grand-

mother was flighty and contentious. They did not know the inside
story: how she had struggled to keep her home together and bring
up six children with her husband going blind and losing ground most
of the way. Her tenacity, like that of Grandfather, sprang partly from
her deep religious faith and partly from a mulishness which refused
to countenance despair.

"There's more ways to kill a dog beside choking him on butter,"   2
she used to say.

She was remembering those uncertain years when the children   3
were growing up and Grandfather was fighting for his pension while
trying to build a home. He had bought an acre of ground in Durham,
planned his house on the edge of his line and used the rest of the
land to dig clay for his brickyard. He made bricks by hand, the hard
kind used for outer walls and guaranteed to withstand all kinds of
weather. It was a slow and costly process full of setbacks and failures.
His hired men were often careless and took advantage of his blind-
ness. They'd fire the kilns with raw green wood or go to sleep on the
job in the middle of a burning and let the fires go out. Grandfather's
bricks would come out crumbling and useless and he'd have to start
all over again.

Then there were his lonely pilgrimages from place to place, guided   4
only by his cane and a kind passerby, in search of old army comrades to help reconstruct his war record twenty years after his discharge. His search frequently ended in disappointment and he'd
come home discouraged to make bricks for a while before starting
out again. It took him almost ten years to prove his eligibility for
pension payments.

During those years Grandmother was trying to educate their chil-   5
dren. Fortunately, she came into a small inheritance when Mary Ruffin
Smith died around 1885. Miss Mary had not forgotten the four Smith
daughters. She left each of them one hundred acres of land with
provision that a house be built upon it not to cost more than $150.
To ensure that the land remained free from their husbands' debts or
control, she gave them only a life interest in it and provided that it
should pass to their children when they died. She also left her household goods and furnishings to be divided equally among the four.

Grandmother's hundred acres came out of the old Smith plan-   6
tation near Chapel Hill. She was never entirely satisfied with this
bequest; she felt Miss Mary had robbed her of the full inheritance
her father had intended for her, and the restrictions of "heir property"
which she did not own outright rankled. It served, however, as vindication of her own claims and was Miss Mary's backhanded recognition of their relationship. Aside from a twenty-five-acre gift to their

half-brother, Julius, who was not of Smith blood, and a few small cash bequests, the four Smith daughters and their children were the only individuals remembered in Mary Ruffin Smith's will.

Whatever Grandmother's dissatisfactions, which increased as years 7 passed, she made the most of her farm. She lived there with the children and worked the land while Grandfather was building his house in Durham. From time to time she sold off timber to help him in his brick business. She used whatever cash she could raise from her crops and fruit to send the children off to school. When she had no crops or fruit, she'd sell the chickens, the hogs or whatever else she could lay her hands on.

Aunt Sallie would never forget the time Grandmother sent Aunt 8 Maria to Hampton Institute to take up the tailoring trade. When time came for tuition, Grandmother had no money so she decided to sell her cow. Grandfather was away from home working on his pension, Aunt Pauline was off teaching and Uncle Tommie was away at school. Grandmother had no one to send to market except Sallie and Agnes, who were about twelve and eleven yars old at the time, but she was not dismayed.

"Children," she told them, "I want you to drive this cow down 9 to Durham and take her to Schwartz' market. Tell Mr. Schwartz that Cornelia Smith sent her and that she's a fine milk cow. I want a good price on her and I'm depending on you to get it."

It was a huge undertaking for two little girls—Durham was fifteen 10 miles away and the cow was none too manageable—but it would never have occurred to them that they could not deliver the cow. They started out early in the morning on a trip which took all day. The cow strayed off the road from time to time to graze in the meadows or lie down to rest and they had to pull and tug at her to get her started again. They arrived at the market in Durham near nightfall, somewhat frightened, their clothes torn and spattered with mud. When Mr. Schwartz heard all the commotion outside and came to find two bedraggled little girls standing guard over a huge cow, he listened to their story in disbelief.

"You don't mean to tell me you drove that cow all the way from 11 Chapel Hill?" he asked.

"Yes sir, we did." 12

"Well, I never. And you say you're Robert Fitzgerald's daugh- 13 ters?"

"Yes sir, we are." 14

"How do I know you didn't steal that cow?" 15

The little girls stood their ground. 16

"If you doubt our word, you send for our Uncle Richard Fitzger- 17 ald."

Mr. Schwartz finally sent for Uncle Richard, who came, took one 18
look at them and laughed.

"They're my brother's children all right, and if they say their 19
mother sent the cow to market, you can take their word for it," he
told Mr. Schwartz. So the butcher bought the cow on the spot and
Aunt Maria stayed in school another few months.

It was also part of Grandfather's creed not to coddle his daughters. 20
He expected them to make their way in life as he had done. I found
a letter he had written to Aunt Maria on September 25, 1895. She had
finished her work at Hampton and gone to Philadelphia to find employment as a dressmaker, without success. She wrote to Grandfather
for money to come home. He replied.

> You must not depend upon sewing. I'd go into service. You can get
> $12 to $15 per month and stick to work for two months without
> taking up your money, and you can come home independent. . . . I
> find many a fine mechanic tramping through the state because he
> cannot work at his trade. Too many people make this great mistake.
> You must do as I did when I first went to Philadelphia, then a boy
> 16. I couldn't get the kind of employment I sought so I took whatever
> I could get to do and stuck at it until I had accumulated enough to
> carry me where I wanted to go with money in my pocket. Now you
> are young and as able as you ever will be. You can live anywhere
> on the face of the earth as other people can. Take my advice, getting
> your board and lodging and $15 per month and you will soon be
> able to come home.

Thrift was another household god in Grandfather's home. It was 21
not only a strong ingredient of his own children's training but it was
expected of all prospective sons-in-law. When young Leon B. Jeffers
wrote my grandparents for consent to marry Aunt Maria in 1901, they
replied in the affirmative, saying, "From earliest acquaintance with
you, you have been held in highest esteem by us. Although you may
not have money and riches to bestow upon her now, if you have that
pure and undefiled love to present to her, with thrift and good management you can soon accumulate some property."

Only three of my grandparents' children were still living when I 22
was coming along—Aunt Pauline, Aunt Maria (who preferred to be
called Marie) and Aunt Sallie—all schoolteachers and all having a
hand in my upbringing. Their brother, Uncle Tommie, had left home
before he was twenty and was never heard from again. Some thought
he was lost at sea and others that he died of smallpox during the
Spanish-American War. The youngest sister, Roberta, succumbed to
typhoid fever when she was barely nineteen. My own mother, Agnes,
who had departed from the teaching tradition to become a registered
nurse, died suddenly when I was three, leaving six children and my

father, who was ill. I saw him only once after that before he died.

Having no parents of my own, I had in effect three mothers, each 23 trying to impress upon me those traits of character expected of a Fitzgerald—stern devotion to duty, capacity for hard work, industry and thrift, and above all honor and courage in all things. Grandfather, of course, was their standard bearer for most of the virtues, but sometimes they talked of my own mother, who was a woman of beauty and courage and whose spirit became a guiding force in my own life although I was too young to remember her.

What happened on my mother's wedding night seemed typical 24 of her courage. Her wedding to William H. Murray, a brilliant young schoolteacher from Baltimore, was scheduled for nine o'clock on the evening of July 1, 1903, at Emanuel A.M.E. Church on Chapel Hill Road in Durham, after which the reception was to be held at Grandfather's house. Engraved invitations were sent out to numerous relatives and friends and the five Fitzgerald daughters were as excited as if all of them were brides. Will Murray was the most popular of their brothers-in-law. He had come down from Baltimore in grand style, flanked by a troupe of young men to attend him.

Preparations were in full swing; everybody was scurrying about 25 all day long. There had never been such a big wedding in the Fitzgerald household. Aunt Marie Jeffers, who was expecting a child, was putting the finishing touches on my mother's wedding gown. As family modiste, she wouldn't think of letting Aggie get married until her skillful fingers had supervised each tuck and fold.

It had been a stiflingly hot day and toward evening a thunderstorm 26 threatened. The bride was almost ready and Aunt Marie stepped back to survey her handiwork when her face went deadly pale, she screamed and fell upon her knees in her first sharp labor pains. The wedding preparations were thrown into bedlam; everything came to a standstill. People gathered at the church and the groom was waiting impatiently, but there was no bride.

At Grandfather's house Aunt Marie's screams could be heard all 27 over the neighborhood. To add to the confusion the thunderstorm struck with terrifying intensity. It was the worst of all times for a child to be born in the Fitzgerald home, but if my mother was frightened she gave no sign. She slipped quietly out of her wedding clothes, put on her uniform and took her place beside the doctor who came to attend Aunt Marie. She was all nurse, coolheaded and composed. Childbirth was hazardous in those days and for a while it looked as if Aunt Marie would not make it. At the height of the storm, between sharp flashes of lightning and rolls of thunder which shook the house, the baby came. My mother's trained eye saw that the doctor's forceps were askew in the emergency and she quickly readjusted them, saving the baby's life. Even so, his head and neck were severely bruised and cut in the delivery and nobody expected him to live. He was thrown aside while doctor and nurse worked frantically to save the mother's life.

Somebody suggested that Agnes call off her wedding, but she 28 shook her head and stuck to her post. When it finally appeared that Aunt Marie would survive the crisis, my mother turned to the neglected infant, bathed and bandaged him, treated his wounds, hovered over him, smacked him and almost breathed life into him. She did not turn him loose until he let out a lusty cry and she felt that he would live. She then calmly washed her hands, put on her wedding dress once more and went out into a downpour to meet her groom. Everything went off as planned, except that it was several hours later and very much subdued. The reception was switched to Uncle Richard's house and the bride received her guests as graciously as if nothing untoward had happened. The baby, Gerald, celebrated his fifty-second birthday not long ago[1] and Aunt Marie reached eighty-one before she died.

It was through these homespun stories, each with its own moral, 29 that my elders sought to build their family traditions. In later years I realized how very much their wealth had consisted of intangibles. They had little of the world's goods and less of its recognition but they had forged enduring values for themselves which they tried to pass on to me. I would have need of these resources when I left the rugged security of Grandfather's house and found myself in a maze of terrifying forces which I could neither understand nor cope with. While my folks could not shield me from the impact of these forces, through their own courage and strength they could teach me to withstand them. My first experience with this outer world came the summer I was nearly seven.

RESPONDING TO READING

Key words: community discovery education family growing up identity memory minority power race rights story striving

Rhetorical concepts: anecdote autobiography illustration narrative/example

---

[1]He lived to be about 70.

1.   This memoir is organized simply: a series of abstractions (the inherited values) are given life through a series of family anecdotes that illustrate them. Pick one of the values and show how it is illustrated by several of the stories.
2.   Murray tells us that her inheritance was valuable, but not measurable in monetary terms: "In later years I realized how very much their wealth had consisted of intangibles." Describe the values she has inherited and explain how they can be considered "wealth."
3.   Murray could easily have treated this material with sentimentality and self-pity; she was orphaned early, her grandfather went blind, money was in short supply, racial prejudice was inescapable, and so on. Instead she focuses on the positive values of her inheritance. Examine the way Murray writes and show how her style and attitude relate to the values this essay celebrates. What has Murray learned from the past?
4.   Most families have a wealth of stories, though sometimes these are not well known to all the grandchildren. Interview one or two of your oldest relatives and ask them for some stories of their youth. Then write an essay in which you interpret two or three of these tales to bring out a family value or tradition.

Listening

EUDORA WELTY

Eudora Welty, unpretentious, unassuming, down-to-earth, is the grande dame of American writers. Her novel *The Optimist's Daughter* (1972) won the Pulitzer Prize. Nevertheless, she still lives, writes, and gardens in her hometown of Jackson, Mississippi, where she was born in 1909. Although she graduated from the University of Wisconsin in 1929 and studied advertising for a year at Columbia University, the Depression and her father's death in 1931 prompted her return to the South. Significant in her development as a writer were the three years she spent in the 1930s writing feature stories for the Works Progress Administration, based on her visits to Mississippi's eighty-two counties, where she met, photographed, and interpreted the lives of a great variety of people in small towns and rural areas. These individuals, communities, and landscapes fed her imagination for years, forming the basis of much of her fiction, including the short stories collected in *A Curtain of Green* (1941) and *The Wide Net* (1943), and her novels, *Delta Wedding* (1946), *The Ponder Heart* (1954), and *Losing Battles* (1970).

"Listening" is from Welty's most recent book, the autobiography *One Writer's Beginnings* (1983), derived from three lectures at Harvard that demonstrated the importance of "Listening," "Learning to See," and "Finding a Voice." Although in 1972 she was "discouraged at the very thought" of writing her autobiography because, she told an interviewer, "to me a writer's work should be everything. A writer's whole feeling, the force of his whole life, can go into a story. . . . [But one's] private life should be kept private. My own I don't think would particularly interest anybody." The appeal of Welty's endearing autobiography contradicts her modest assertion. Part of its charm derives from the sense of a strong, cohesive family that Welty conveys. Both parents consistently nurtured their young child, teaching her through their own example and through the shared activities of stargazing, playing with puzzles and toys, reading, and singing. No wonder the adult writer was content to live happily for decades with her widowed mother in the family home.

In our house on North Congress Street in Jackson, Mississippi,   1 where I was born, the oldest of three children, in 1909, we grew up to the striking of clocks. There was a mission-style oak grandfather clock standing in the hall, which sent its gong-like strokes through the livingroom, diningroom, kitchen, and pantry, and up the sounding board of the stairwell. Through the night, it could find its way into our ears; sometimes, even on the sleeping porch, midnight could wake us up. My parents' bedroom had a smaller striking clock that answered it. Though the kitchen clock did nothing but show the time, the dining room clock was a cuckoo clock with weights on long chains, on one of which my baby brother, after climbing on a chair to the top of the china closet, once succeeded in suspending the cat for a moment. I don't know whether or not my father's Ohio family, in having been Swiss back in the 1700s before the first three Welty brothers came to America, had anything to do with this; but we all of us have been time-minded all our lives. This was good at least for a future fiction writer, being able to learn so penetratingly, and almost first of all, about chronology. It was one of a good many things I learned almost without knowing it; it would be there when I needed it.

My father loved all instruments that would instruct and fascinate.   2 His place to keep things was the drawer in the "library table" where lying on top of his folded maps was a telescope with brass extensions, to find the moon and the Big Dipper after supper in our front yard, and to keep appointments with eclipses. There was a folding Kodak that was brought out for Christmas, birthdays, and trips. In the back of the drawer you could find a magnifying glass, a kaleidoscope, and a gyroscope kept in a black buckram box, which he would set dancing for us on a string pulled tight. He had also supplied himself with an assortment of puzzles composed of metal rings and intersecting links and keys chained together, impossible for the rest of us, however patiently shown, to take apart; he had an almost childlike love of the ingenious.

In time, a barometer was added to our diningroom wall; but we   3 didn't really need it. My father had the country boy's accurate knowledge of the weather and its skies. He went out and stood on our front steps first thing in the morning and took a look at it and a sniff. He was a pretty good weather prophet.

"Well, I'm *not*," my mother would say with enormous self-   4
satisfaction.

He told us children what to do if we were lost in a strange country.   5
"Look for where the sky is brightest along the horizon," he said. "That reflects the nearest river. Strike out for a river and you will find habitation." Eventualities were much on his mind. In his care for us children he cautioned us to take measures against such things as being struck by lightning. He drew us all away from the windows during the severe electrical storms that are common where we live. My mother stood apart, scoffing at caution as a character failing. "Why, I always loved a storm! High winds never bothered me in West Virginia! Just listen at that! I wasn't a bit afraid of a little lightning and thunder! I'd go out on the mountain and spread my arms wide and *run* in a good big storm!"

So I developed a strong meteorological sensibility. In years ahead   6
when I wrote stories, atmosphere took its influential role from the start. Commotion in the weather and the inner feelings aroused by such a hovering disturbance emerged connected in dramatic form. (I tried a tornado first, in a story called "The Winds.")

From our earliest Christmas times, Santa Claus brought us toys   7
that instruct boys and girls (separately) how to build things—stone blocks cut to the castle-building style, Tinker Toys, and Erector sets. Daddy made for us himself elaborate kites that needed to be taken miles out of town to a pasture long enough (and my father was not afraid of horses and cows watching) for him to run with and get up on a long cord to which my mother held the spindle, and then we children were given it to hold, tugging like something alive at our hands. They were beautiful, sound, shapely box kites, smelling delicately of office glue for their entire short lives. And of course, as soon as the boys attained anywhere near the right age, there was an electric train, the engine with its pea-sized working headlight, its line of cars, tracks equipped with switches, semaphores, its station, its bridges, and its tunnel, which blocked off all other traffic in the upstairs hall. Even from downstairs, and through the cries of excited children, the elegant rush and click of the train could be heard through the ceiling, running around and around its figure eight.

All of this, but especially the train, represents my father's fondest   8
beliefs—in progress, in the future. With these gifts, he was preparing his children.

And so was my mother with her different gifts.   9

I learned from the age of two or three that any room in our house,   10 at any time of day, was there to read in, or to be read to. My mother read to me. She'd read to me in the big bedroom in the mornings, when we were in her rocker together, which ticked in rhythm as we rocked, as though we had a cricket accompanying the story. She'd read to me in the dining room on winter afternoons in front of the coal fire, with our cuckoo clock ending the story with "Cuckoo," and at night when I'd got in my own bed. I must have given her no peace. Sometimes she read to me in the kitchen while she sat churning, and the churning sobbed along with *any* story. It was my ambition to have her read to me while *I* churned; once she granted my wish, but she read off my story before I brought her butter. She was an expressive reader. When she was reading "Puss in Boots," for instance, it was impossible not to know that she distrusted *all* cats.

It had been startling and disappointing to me to find out that 11 story books had been written by *people*, that books were not natural wonders, coming up of themselves like grass. Yet regardless of where they came from, I cannot remember a time when I was not in love with them—with the books themselves, cover and binding and the paper they were printed on, with their smell and their weight and with their possession in my arms, captured and carried off to myself. Still illiterate, I was ready for them, committed to all the reading I could give them.

Neither of my parents had come from homes that could afford to 12 buy many books, but though it must have been something of a strain on his salary, as the youngest officer in a young insurance company, my father was all the while carefully selecting and ordering away for what he and Mother thought we children should grow up with. They bought first for the future.

Besides the bookcase in the livingroom, which was always called 13 "the library," there were the encyclopedia tables and dictionary stand under windows in our dining room. Here to help us grow up arguing around the dining room table were the Unabridged Webster, the Columbia Encyclopedia, Compton's Pictured Encyclopedia, the Lincoln Library of Information, and later the Book of Knowledge. And the year we moved into our new house, there was room to celebrate it with the new 1925 edition of the Britannica, which my father, his face always deliberately turned toward the future, was of course disposed to think better than any previous edition.

In "the library," inside the mission-style bookcase with its three 14 diamond-latticed glass doors, with my father's Morris chair and the glass-shaded lamp on its table beside it, were books I could soon begin on—and I did, reading them all alike and as they came, straight down their rows, top shelf to bottom. There was the set of Stoddard's Lectures, in all its late nineteenth-century vocabulary and vignettes of peasant life and quaint beliefs and customs, with matching halftone illustrations: Vesuvius erupting, Venice by moonlight, gypsies glimpsed by their campfires. I didn't know then the clue they were to my father's longing to see the rest of the world. I read straight through his other love-from-afar: the Victrola Book of the Opera, with opera after opera in synopsis, with portraits in costume of Melba, Caruso, Galli-Curci, and Geraldine Farrar, some of whose voices we could listen to on our Red Seal records.

My mother read secondarily for information; she sank as a he- 15 donist into novels. She read Dickens in the spirit in which she would have eloped with him. The novels of her girlhood that had stayed on in her imgination, besides those of Dickens and Scott and Robert Louis Stevenson, were *Jane Eyre, Trilby, The Woman in White, Green Mansions, King Solomon's Mines.* Marie Corelli's name would crop up but I understood she had gone out of favor with my mother, who had only kept *Ardath* out of loyalty. In time she absorbed herself in Galsworthy, Edith Wharton, above all in Thomas Mann of the *Joseph* volumes.

St. Elmo was not in our house; I saw it often in other houses. This 16 wildly popular Southern novel is where all the Edna Earles in our population started coming from. They're all named for the heroine, who succeeded in bringing a dissolute, sinning roué and atheist of a lover (St. Elmo) to his knees. My mother was able to forgo it. But she remembered the classic advice given to rose growers on how to water their bushes long enough: "Take a chair and *St. Elmo*."

To both my parents I owe my early acquaintance with a beloved 17 Mark Twain. There was a full set of Mark Twain and a short set of Ring Lardner in our bookcase, and those were the volumes that in time united us all, parents and children.

Reading everything that stood before me was how I came upon 18 a worn old book without a back that had belonged to my father as a child. It was called *Sanford and Merton.* Is there anyone left who recognizes it, I wonder? It is the famous moral tale written by Thomas Day in the 1780s, but of him no mention is made on the title page of *this* book; here it is *Sanford and Merton in Words of One Syllable* by Mary Godolphin. Here are the rich boy and the poor boy and Mr. Barlow, their teacher and interlocutor, in long discourses alternating with dramatic scenes—danger and rescue allotted to the rich and the poor respectively. It may have only words of one syllable, but one of them is "quoth." It ends with not one but two morals, both engraved on rings: "Do what you ought, come what may," and "If we would be great, we must first learn to be good."

This book was lacking its front cover, the back held on by strips 19 of pasted paper, now turned golden, in several layers, and the pages stained, flecked, and tattered around the edges; its garish illustrations had come unattached but were preserved, laid in. I had the feeling even in my heedless childhood that this was the only book my father as a little boy had had of his own. He had held onto it, and might have gone to sleep on its coverless face: he had lost his mother when he was seven. My father had never made any mention to his own children of the book, but he had brought it along with him from Ohio to our house and shelved it in our bookcase.

My mother had brought from West Virginia that set of Dickens; those books looked sad, too—they had been through fire and water before I was born, she told me, and there they were, lined up—as I later realized, waiting for *me*.

I was presented, from as early as I can remember, with books of my own, which appeared on my birthday and Christmas morning. Indeed, my parents could not give me books enough. They must have sacrificed to give me on my sixth or seventh birthday—it was after I became a reader for myself—the ten-volume set of Our Wonder World. These were beautifully made, heavy books I would lie down with on the floor in front of the dining room hearth, and more often than the rest volume 5, *Every Child's Story Book*, was under my eyes. There were the fairy tales—Grimm, Andersen, the English, the French, "Ali Baba and the Forty Thieves"; and there was Aesop and Reynard the Fox; there were the myths and legends, Robin Hood, King Arthur, and St. George and the Dragon, even the history of Joan of Arc; a whack of *Pilgrim's Progress* and a long piece of *Gulliver*. They all carried their classic illustrations. I located myself in these pages and could go straight to the stories and pictures I loved; very often "The Yellow Dwarf" was first choice, with Walter Crane's Yellow Dwarf in full color making his terrifying appearance flanked by turkeys. Now that volume is as worn and backless and hanging apart as my father's poor *Sanford and Merton*. The precious page with Edward Lear's "Jumblies" on it has been in danger of slipping out for all these years. One measure of my love for Our Wonder World was that for a long time I wondered if I would go through fire and water for it is as my mother had done for Charles Dickens; and the only comfort was to think I could ask my mother to do it for me.

I believe I'm the only child I know of who grew up with this treasure in the house. I used to ask others, "Did you have Our Wonder World?" I'd have to tell them The Book of Knowledge could not hold a candle to it.

I live in gratitude to my parents for initiating me—and as early as I begged for it, without keeping me waiting—into knowledge of the word, into reading and spelling, by way of the alphabet. They taught it to me at home in time for me to begin to read before starting to school. I believe the alphabet is no longer considered an essential piece of equipment for traveling through life. In my day it was the keystone to knowledge. You learned the alphabet as you learned to count to ten, as you learned "Now I lay me" and the Lord's Prayer and your father's and mother's name and address and telephone number, all in case you were lost.

My love for the alphabet, which endures, grew out of reciting it 24 but, before that, out of seeing the letters on the page. In my own story books, before I could read them for myself, I fell in love with various winding, enchanted-looking initials drawn by Walter Crane at the heads of fairy tales. In "Once upon a time," an "O" had a rabbit running it as a treadmill, his feet upon flowers. When the day came, years later, for me to see the Book of Kells, all the wizardry of letter, initial, and word swept over me a thousand times over, and the illumination, the gold, seemed a part of the word's beauty and holiness that had been there from the start.

Learning stamps you with its moments. Childhood's learning is 25 made up of moments. It isn't steady. It's a pulse.

In a children's art class, we sat in a ring on kindergarten chairs 26 and drew three daffodils that had just been picked out of the yard; and while I was drawing, my sharpened yellow pencil and the cup of the yellow daffodil gave off whiffs just alike. That the pencil doing the drawing should give off the same smell as the flower it drew seemed part of the art lesson—as shouldn't it be? Children, like animals, use all their senses to discover the world. Then artists come along and discover it the same way, all over again. Here and there, it's the same world. Or now and then we'll hear from an artist who's never lost it.

In my sensory education I include my physical awareness of the 27 *word*. Of a certain word, that is; the connection it has with what it stands for. At around age six, perhaps, I was standing by myself in our front yard waiting for supper, just at that hour in a late summer day when the sun is already below the horizon and the risen full moon in the visible sky stops being chalky and begins to take on light. There comes the moment, and I saw it then, when the moon goes from flat to round. For the first time it met my eyes as a globe. The word "moon" came into my mouth as though fed to me out of a silver spoon. Held in my mouth the moon became a word. It had the roundness of a Concord grape Grandpa took off his vine and gave me to suck out of its skin and swallow whole, in Ohio.

This love did not prevent me from living for years in foolish error 28 about the moon. The new moon just appearing in the west was the rising moon to me. The new should be rising. And in early childhood the sun and moon, those opposite reigning powers, I just as easily assumed rose in east and west respectively in their opposite sides of the sky, and like partners in a reel they advanced, sun from the east, moon from the west, crossed over (when I wasn't looking) and went down on the other side. My father couldn't have known I believed that when, bending behind me and guiding my shoulder, he positioned me at our telescope in the front yard and, with careful adjustment of the focus, brought the moon close to me.

The night sky over my childhood Jackson was velvety black. I 29 could see the full constellations in it and call their names; when I could read, I knew their myths. Though I was always waked for eclipses, and indeed carried to the window as an infant in arms and shown Halley's Comet in my sleep, and though I'd been taught at our dining room table about the solar system and knew the earth revolved around the sun, and our moon around us, I never found out the moon didn't come up in the west until I was a writer and Herschel Brickell, the literary critic, told me after I misplaced it in a story. He said valuable words to me about my new profession: "Always be sure you get your moon in the right part of the sky."

My mother always sang to her children. Her voice came out just 30 a little bit in the minor key. "Wee Willie Winkie's" song was wonderfully sad when she sang the lullabies.

"Oh, but now there's a record. She could have her own record 31 to listen to," my father would have said. For there came a Victrola record of "Bobby Shafftoe" and "Rock-a-Bye Baby," all of Mother's lullabies, which could be played to take her place. Soon I was able to play her my own lullabies all day long.

Our Victrola stood in the dining room. I was allowed to climb onto 32 the seat of a dining room chair to wind it, start the record turning, and set the needle playing. In a second I'd jumped to the floor, to spin or march around the table as the music called for—now there were all the other records I could play too. I skinned back onto the chair just in time to lift the needle at the end, stop the record and turn it over, then change the needle. That brass receptacle with a hole in the lid gave off a metallic smell like human sweat, from all the hot needles that were fed it. Winding up, dancing, being cocked to start and stop the record, was of course all in one the act of *listening*—to "Overture to *Daughter of the Regiment*," "Selections from *The Fortune Teller*," "Kiss Me Again," "Gypsy Dance from *Carmen*," "Stars and Stripes Forever," "When the Midnight Choo-Choo Leaves for Alabam," or whatever came next. Movement must be at the very heart of listening.

Ever since I was first read to, then started reading to myself, there 33 has never been a line read that I didn't *hear*. As my eyes followed the sentence, a voice was saying it silently to me. It isn't my mother's voice, or the voice of any person I can identify, certainly not my own. It is human, but inward, and it is inwardly that I listen to it. It is to me the voice of the story or the poem itself. The cadence, whatever it is that asks you to believe, the feeling that resides in the printed word, reaches me through the reader-voice. I have supposed, but never found out, that this is the case with all readers—to read as listeners—and with all writers, to write as listeners. It may be part of the desire to write. The sound of what falls on the page begins the process of testing it for truth, for me. Whether I am right to trust so far I don't know. By now I don't know whether I could do either one, reading or writing, without the other.

My own words, when I am at work on a story, I hear too as they   34
go, in the same voice that I hear when I read in books. When I write and the sound of it comes back to my ears, then I act to make my changes. I have always trusted this voice.

RESPONDING TO READING

Key words: discovery education family growing up identity language memory reading story striving symbols talk writing

Rhetorical concepts: anecdote autobiography cause and effect illustration narrative/example

1.   This memoir, like Pauli Murray's, is a series of "scenes" from family history. But here the child herself is at the center of the stories and the essay has to do with the way childhood learning works: "Childhood's learning is made up of moments. It isn't steady. It's a pulse." Explain what Welty means by this "pulse" and show how "Listening" exemplifies it.
2.   "Listening" begins with the child listening to clocks and then presents a series of her other experiences as a listener. Identify them and explain why Welty finds listening to be a powerful, even central experience, in her own learning.
3.   Examine closely the passage in which the young Welty connects the sight of the moon and the word "moon" (paragraph 27). What does she mean when she says the word "had the roundness of a Concord grape"? What does the literary critic mean when he cautions her as an adult, "Always be sure you get your moon in the right part of the sky"? Find another passage in which a childhood scene resonates with meaning into adult life and show how it works.
4.   Tell the story of how you learned to read, or the first time you realized you could read. What were you reading, and how did you feel about your accomplishment? Be sure to characterize the person or people who taught you and the circumstances under which you learned; re-create a typical scene,

if you can. What does that scene, that experience mean to you now, as you reflect upon this as an adult?

5.   What, as a child, did you most enjoy doing with a parent, or grandparent, either on a single occasion or repeated over time? What ramifications has this experience for you now? When you explain this, try to re-create the experience, characterizing yourself and the other person through actions, thoughts, possibly dialogue, in the scene as you experienced it and as you see it again in your mind's eye.

The Inheritance of Tools

SCOTT RUSSELL SANDERS

Scott Russell Sanders derives his sense of the past from two locations. His early childhood was spent on "a scrape-dirt farm in Tennessee," where everything grew with beauty and vigor. For the next dozen years he lived on the grounds of a munitions factory in Ohio, a high security enclave of "dumps and man-made deserts, ponds once used for hatching fish and now smothered in oil, machine guns rusting in weeds." Ohio living taught him fear and the imminence of mortality. Country living taught him "not how to buy things but how to *do* things: carpentry, plumbing, grafting, gardening, pruning, sewing, making hay with or without sunshine, cooking, canning, felling and planting trees, feeding animals and fixing machines, electrical wiring, plastering, roofing."

In "The Inheritance of Tools," from his award-winning collection of personal essays, *The Paradise of Bombs* (1987), Sanders examines the creative, positive aspects of his heritage, showing how tools also become extensions of the human heart, as the knowledge of how to use and care for them is transmitted from generation to generation. The ways in which people use tools, and think about tools and care for them, reflect their values and personalities, "each hammer and level and saw . . . wrapped in a cloud of knowing."

At just about the hour when my father died, soon after dawn one   1
February morning when ice coated the windows like cataracts, I banged my thumb with a hammer. Naturally I swore at the hammer, the reckless thing, and in the moment of swearing I thought of what my father would say: "If you'd try hitting the nail it would go in a whole lot faster. Don't you know your thumb's not as hard as that hammer?" We both were doing carpentry that day, but far apart. He was building cupboards at my brother's place in Oklahoma; I was at home in Indiana, putting up a wall in the basement to make a bedroom for my daughter. By the time my mother called with news of his death—the long distance wires whittling her voice until it seemed too thin to bear the weight of what she had to say—my thumb was

swollen. A week or so later a white scar in the shape of a crescent moon began to show above the cuticle, and month by month it rose across the pink sky of my thumbnail. It took the better part of a year for the scar to disappear, and every time I noticed it I thought of my father.

The hammer had belonged to him, and to his father before him.   2
The three of us have used it to build houses and barns and chicken coops, to upholster chairs and crack walnuts, to make doll furniture and bookshelves and jewelry boxes. The head is scratched and pock-marked, like an old plowshare that has been working rocky fields, and it gives off the sort of dull sheen you see on fast creek water in the shade. It is a finishing hammer, about the weight of a bread loaf, too light, really, for framing walls, too heavy for cabinet work, with a curved claw for pulling nails, a rounded head for pounding, a fluted neck for looks, and a hickory handle for strength.

The present handle is my third one, bought from a lumberyard   3
in Tennessee, down the road from where my brother and I were helping my father build his retirement house. I broke the previous one by trying to pull sixteen-penny nails out of floor joists—a foolish thing to do with a finishing hammer, as my father pointed out. "You ever hear of a crowbar?" he said. No telling how many handles he and my grandfather had gone through before me. My grandfather used to cut down hickory trees on his farm, saw them into slabs, cure the planks in his hayloft, and carve handles with a drawknife. The grain in hickory is crooked and knotty, and therefore tough, hard to split, like the grain in the two men who owned this hammer before me.

After proposing marriage to a neighbor girl, my grandfather used   4
this hammer to build a house for his bride on a stretch of river bottom in northern Mississippi. The lumber for the place, like the hickory for the handle, was cut on his own land. By the day of the wedding he had not quite finished the house, and so right after the ceremony he took his wife home and put her to work. My grandmother had worn her Sunday dress for the wedding, with a fringe of lace tacked on around the hem in honor of the occasion. She removed this lace and folded it away before going out to help my grandfather nail siding on the house. "There she was in her good dress," he told me some fifty-odd years after that wedding day, "holding up them long pieces of clapboard while I hammered, and together we got the place covered up before dark." As the family grew to four, six, eight, and eventually thirteen, my grandfather used this hammer to enlarge his house room by room, like a chambered nautilus expanding its shell.

By and by the hammer was passed along to my father. One day   5 he was up on the roof of our pony barn nailing shingles with it, when I stepped out the kitchen door to call him for supper. Before I could yell, something about the sight of him straddling the spine of that roof and swinging the hammer caught my eye and made me hold my tongue. I was five or six years old, and the world's commonplaces were still news to me. He would pull a nail from the pouch at his waist, bring the hammer down, and a moment later the *thunk* of the blow would reach my ears. And that is what had stopped me in my tracks and stilled my tongue, that momentary gap between seeing and hearing the blow. Instead of yelling from the kitchen door, I ran to the barn and climbed two rungs up the ladder—as far as I was allowed to go—and spoke quietly to my father. On our walk to the house he explained that sound takes time to make its way through air. Suddenly the world seemed larger, the air more dense, if sound could be held back like any ordinary traveler.

6   By the time I started using this hammer, at about the age when I discovered the speed of sound, it already contained houses and mysteries for me. The smooth handle was one my grandfather had made. In those days I needed both hands to swing it. My father would start a nail in a scrap of wood, and I would pound away until it bent over.

7   "Looks like you got ahold of some of those rubber nails," he would tell me. "Here, let me see if I can find you some stiff ones." And he would rummage in a drawer until he came up with a fistful of more cooperative nails. "Look at the head," he would tell me. "Don't look at your hands, don't look at the hammer. Just look at the head of that nail and pretty soon you'll learn to hit it square."

8   Pretty soon I did learn. While he worked in the garage cutting dovetail joints for a drawer or skinning a deer or tuning an engine, I would hammer nails. I made innocent blocks of wood look like porcupines. He did not talk much in the midst of his tools, but he kept up a nearly ceaseless humming, slipping in and out of a dozen tunes in an afternoon, often running back over the same stretch of melody again and again, as if searching for a way out. When the humming did cease, I knew he was faced with a task requring great delicacy or concentration, and I took care not to distract him.

9   He kept scraps of wood in a cardboard box—the ends of two-by-fours, slabs of shelving and plywood, odd pieces of molding—and everything in it was fair game. I nailed scraps together to fashion what I called boats or houses, but the results usually bore only faint resemblance to the visions I carried in my head. I would hold up these constructions to show my father, and he would turn them over in his hands admiringly, speculating about what they might be. My

cobbled-together guitars might have been alien spaceships, my barns might have been models of Aztec temples, each wooden contraption might have been anything but what I had set out to make.

Now and again I would feel the need to have a chunk of wood shaped or shortened before I riddled it with nails, and I would clamp it in a vise and scrape at it with a handsaw. My father would let me lacerate the board until my arm gave out, and then he would wrap his hand around mine and help me finish the cut, showing me how to use my thumb to guide the blade, how to pull back on the saw to keep it from binding, how to let my shoulder do the work.

"Don't force it," he would say, "just drag it easy and give the teeth a chance to bite."

As the saw teeth bit down, the wood released its smell, each kind with its own fragrance, oak or walnut or cherry or pine—usually pine because it was the softest, easiest for a child to work. No matter how weathered and gray the board, no matter how warped and cracked, inside there was this smell waiting, as of something freshly baked. I gathered every smidgen of sawdust and stored it away in coffee cans, which I kept in a drawer of the workbench. When I did not feel like hammering nails, I would dump my sawdust on the concrete floor of the garage and landscape it into highways and farms and towns, running miniature cars and trucks along miniature roads. Looming as huge as a colossus, my father worked over and around me, now and again bending down to inspect my work, careful not to trample my creations. It was a landscape that smelled dizzyingly of wood. Even after a bath my skin would carry the smell, and so would my father's hair, when he lifted me for a bedtime hug.

I tell these things not only from memory but also from recent observation, because my own son now turns blocks of wood into nailed porcupines, dumps cans full of sawdust at my feet and sculpts highways on the floor. He learns how to swing a hammer from the elbow instead of the wrist, how to lay his thumb beside the blade to guide a saw, how to tap a chisel with a wooden mallet, how to mark a hole with an awl before starting a drill bit. My daughter did the same before him, and even now, on the brink of teenage aloofness, she will occasionally drag out my box of wood scraps and carpenter something. So I have seen my apprenticeship to wood and tools re-enacted in each of my children, as my father saw his own apprenticeship renewed in me.

The saw I use belonged to him, as did my level and both of my squares, and all four tools had belonged to his father. The blade of the saw is the bluish color of gun barrels, and the maple handle, dark from the sweat of hands, is inscribed with curving leaf designs. The level is a shaft of walnut two feet long, edged with brass and pierced by three round windows in which air bubbles float in oil-filled tubes of glass. The middle window serves for testing if a surface is horizontal, the others for testing if a surface is plumb or vertical. My grandfather used to carry this level on the gun rack behind the seat in his pickup, and when I rode with him I would turn around to watch the bubbles dance. The larger of the two squares is called a framing square, a flat steel elbow, so beat up and tarnished you can barely make out the rows of numbers that show how to figure the cuts on rafters. The smaller one is called a try square, for marking angles, with a blued steel blade for the shank and a brass-faced block of cherry for the head.

I was taught early on that a saw is not to be used apart from a 15 square: "If you're going to cut a piece of wood," my father insisted, "you owe it to the tree to cut it straight."

Long before studying geometry, I learned there is a mystical virtue 16 in right angles. There is an unspoken morality in seeking the level and the plumb. A house will stand, a table will bear weight, the sides of a box will hold together, only if the joints are square and the members upright. When the bubble is lined up between two marks etched in the glass tube of a level, you have aligned yourself with the forces that hold the universe together. When you miter the corners of a picture frame, each angle must be exactly forty-five degrees, as they are in the perfect triangles of Pythagoras, not a degree more or less. Otherwise the frame will hang crookedly, as if ashamed of itself and of its maker. No matter if the joints you are cutting do not show. Even if you are butting two pieces of wood together inside a cabinet, where no one except a wrecking crew will ever see them, you must take pains to ensure that the ends are square and the studs are plumb.

I took pains over the wall I was building on the day my father 17 died. Not long after that wall was finished—paneled with tongue-and-groove boards of yellow pine, the nail holes filled with putty and the wood all stained and sealed—I came close to wrecking it one afternoon when my daughter ran howling up the stairs to announce that her gerbils had escaped from their cage and were hiding in my brand new wall. She could hear them scratching and squeaking behind her bed. Impossible! I said. How on earth could they get inside my drum-tight wall? Through the heating vent, she answered. I went downstairs, pressed my ear to the honey-colored wood, and heard the *scritch scritch* of tiny feet.

"What can we do?" my daughter wailed. "They'll starve to death, 18 they'll die of thirst, they'll suffocate."

"Hold on," I soothed. "I'll think of something." 19

While I thought and she fretted, the radio on her bedside table 20 delivered us the headlines: Several thousand people had died in a city in India from a poisonous cloud that had leaked overnight from a chemical plant. A nuclear-powered submarine had been launched. Rioting continued in South Africa. An airplane had been hijacked in the Mediterranean. Authorities calculated that several thousand homeless people slept on the streets within sight of the Washington Monument. I felt my usual helplessness in the face of all these calamities. But here was my daughter, weeping because her gerbils were holed up in a wall. This calamity I could handle.

"Don't worry," I told her. "We'll set food and water by the heating 21 vent and lure them out. And if that doesn't do the trick, I'll tear the wall apart until we find them."

She stopped crying and gazed at me. "You'd really tear it apart? 22 Just for my gerbils? The *wall?*" Astonishment slowed her down only for a second, however, before she ran to the workbench and began tugging at drawers, saying, "let's see, what'll we need? Crowbar. Hammer. Chisels. I hope we don't have to use them—but just in case."

We didn't need the wrecking tools. I never had to assault my 23 handsome wall, because the gerbils eventually came out to nibble at a dish of popcorn. But for several hours I studied the tongue-and-groove skin I had nailed up on the day of my father's death, considering where to begin prying. There were no gaps in that wall, no crooked joints.

I had botched a great many pieces of wood before I mastered the 24 right angle with a saw, botched even more before I learned to miter a joint. The knowledge of these things resides in my hands and eyes and the webwork of muscles, not in the tools. There are machines for sale—powered miter boxes and radial-arm saws, for instance— that will enable any casual soul to cut proper angles in boards. The skill is invested in the gadget instead of the person who uses it, and this is what distinguishes a machine from a tool. If I had to earn my keep by making furniture or building houses, I suppose I would buy powered saws and pneumatic nailers; the need for speed would drive me to it. But since I carpenter only for my own pleasure or to help neighbors or to remake the house around the ears of my family, I stick with hand tools. Most of the ones I own were given to me by my father, who also taught me how to wield them. The tools in my workbench are a double inheritance, for each hammer and level and saw is wrapped in a cloud of knowing.

All of these tools are a pleasure to look at and to hold. Merchants 25 would never paste NEW! NEW! NEW! signs on them in stores. Their designs are old because they work, because they serve their purpose well. Like folk songs and aphorisms and the grainy bits of language, these tools have been pared down to essentials. I look at my claw hammer, the distillation of a hundred generations of carpenters, and consider that it holds up well beside those other classics—Greek vases, Gregorian chants, *Don Quixote,* barbed fish hooks, candles, spoons. Knowledge of hammering stretches back to the earliest humans who squatted beside fires, chipping flints. Anthropologists have a lovely name for those unworked rocks that served as the earliest hammers. "Dawn stones," they are called. Their only qualification for the work, aside from hardness, is that they fit the hand. Our ancestors used them for grinding corn, tapping awls, smashing bones. From dawn stones to the claw hammer is a great leap in time, but no great distance in design or imagination.

On that iced-over February morning when I smashed my thumb with 26 the hammer, I was down in the basement framing the wall that my daughter's gerbils would later hide in. I was thinking of my father, as I always did whenever I built anything, thinking how he would have gone about the work, hearing in memory what he would have said about the wisdom of hitting the nail instead of my thumb. I had the studs and plates nailed together all square and trim, and was lifting the wall into place when the phone rang upstairs. My wife answered, and in a moment she came to the basement door and called down softly to me. The stillness in her voice made me drop the framed wall and hurry upstairs. She told me my father was dead. Then I heard the details over the phone from my mother. Building a set of cupboards for my brother in Oklahoma, he had knocked off work early the previous afternoon because of cramps in his stomach. Early this morning, on his way into the kitchen of my brother's trailer, maybe going for a glass of water, so early that no one else was awake, he slumped down on the linoleum and his heart quit.

For several hours I paced around inside my house, upstairs and 27 down, in and out of every room, looking for the right door to open and knowing there was no such door. My wife and children followed me and wrapped me in arms and backed away again, circling and staring as if I were on fire. Where was the door, the door, the door? I kept wondering. My smashed thumb turned purple and throbbed, making me furious. I wanted to cut it off and rush outside and scrape away the snow and hack a hole in the frozen earth and bury the shameful thing.

I went down into the basement, opened a drawer in my work- 28 bench, and stared at the ranks of chisels and knives. Oiled and sharp, as my father would have kept them, they gleamed at me like teeth. I took up a clasp knife, pried out the longest blade, and tested the edge on the hair of my forearm. A tuft came away cleanly, and I saw my father testing the sharpness of tools on his own skin, the blades of axes and knives and gouges and hoes, saw the red hair shaved off in patches from his arms and the backs of hands. "That will cut bear," he would say. He never cut a bear with his blades, now my blades, but he cut deer, dirt, wood. I closed the knife and put it away. Then I took up the hammer and went back to work on my daughter's wall, snugging the bottom plate against a chalk line on the floor, shimming the top plate against the joists overhead, plumbing the studs with my level, making sure before I drove the first nail that every line was square and true.

RESPONDING TO READING

Key words: art discovery education family growing up identity loss memory

Rhetorical concepts: analogy anecdote autobiography metaphor narrative/example

1.   Show how Sanders characterizes his grandfather, his father, and himself through the continuity and transmission of their use of tools. Why does he focus on what these generations have in common and ignore any differences?
2.   How does "The Inheritance of Tools" demonstrate that knowledge and skill can be transmitted from one generation to the next? What is communicated along with the specific knowledge of how to use tools?
3.   Could readers who can't, don't, or won't use tools nevertheless appreciate this essay? Why or why not?
4.   Tell the story of your own experience of learning to use a particular tool or collection of tools (a computer, a sewing machine, a mountain bike, a power saw, an automobile). Your explanation, including your increasing skill and ability, should also delineate your relationship with the person (family member or other) and the way(s) in which the teaching and learning were accomplished. How many generations of learners does this cumulative process involve, including people you yourself may have taught?

The Obligation to Endure

RACHEL CARSON

Rachel Carson (1907–1964), a biologist, was also an ardent conservationist. In the Cold War era when threats of nuclear bombs and
promises of "better living through chemistry" were commonplace,
Carson took an environmentalist stance that at the time was considered radical and controversial. In "The Obligation to Endure," from
Silent Spring (1962), Carson attacked the "crusade to create a chemically sterile, insect-free world" in which "many specialists and most
of the so-called control [regulatory] agencies" were engaged.
Throughout *Silent Spring* she contended what has since been proven,
that there was an arsenal of widely used chemical pesticides and
herbicides that wrought far more destruction than they prevented.
Her earlier, less controversial, books were *Under the Sea Wind: A
Naturalist's Picture of Ocean Life* (1941); *The Sea Around Us* (1951),
winner of the National Book Award; and *The Edge of the Sea* (1955).
    Carson was strongly influenced by her mother who, she said,
embodied Albert Schweitzer's " 'reverence for life' more than anyone
I know." She earned a bachelor's degree in biology from the Pennsylvania College for Women in 1929 and a master's degree in biology
from Johns Hopkins in 1932. For fifteen years Carson edited publications for the U.S. Fish and Wildlife Service, until 1951 when her
books earned enough royalties to enable her to write full time. *Silent
Spring* spoke just in time, and Carson's legacy survives her. Since
her death, the federal government has passed the Endangered Species Preservation Act and other legislation requiring that all federal
departments protect endangered species and their habitats, forbidding trade in such species, and regulating the uses of pesticides.

The history of life on earth has been a history of interaction 1
between living things and their surroundings. To a large extent, the
physical form and the habits of the earth's vegetation and its animal
life have been molded by the environment. Considering the whole
span of earthly time, the opposite effect, in which life actually modifies
its surroundings, has been relatively slight. Only within the moment
of time represented by the present century has one species—man—
acquired significant power to alter the nature of his world.

During the past quarter century this power has not only increased 2
to one of disturbing magnitude but it has changed in character. The
most alarming of all man's assaults upon the environment is the
contamination of air, earth, rivers, and sea with dangerous and even

lethal materials. This pollution is for the most part irrecoverable; the chain of evil it initiates not only in the world that must support life but in living tissues is for the part irreversible. In this now universal contamination of the environment, chemicals are the sinister and little-recognized partners of radiation in changing the very nature of the world—the very nature of its life. Strontium 90, released through nuclear explosions into the air, comes to earth in rain or drifts down as fallout, lodges in soil, enters into the grass or corn or wheat grown there, and in time takes up its abode in the bones of a human being, there to remain until his death. Similarly, chemicals sprayed on crop-lands or forests or gardens lie long in soil, entering into living or-ganisms, passing from one to another in a chain of poisoning and death. Or they pass mysteriously by underground streams until they emerge and, through the alchemy of air and sunlight, combine into new forms that kill vegetation, sicken cattle, and work unknown harm on those who drink from once pure wells. As Albert Schweitzer has said, "Man can hardly even recognize the devils of his own creation."

It took hundreds of millions of years to produce the life that now 3 inhabits the earth—eons of time in which that developing and evolv-ing and diversifying life reached a state of adjustment and balance with its surroundings. The environment, rigorously shaping and di-recting the life it supported, contained elements that were hostile as well as supporting. Certain rocks gave out dangerous radiation; even within the light of the sun, from which all life draws its energy, there were shortwave radiations with power to injure. Given time—time not in years but in millennia—life adjusts, and a balance has been reached. For time is the essential ingredient; but in the modern world there is no time.

The rapidity of change and the speed with which new situations 4 are created follow the impetuous and heedless pace of man rather than the deliberate pace of nature. Radiation is no longer merely the background radiation of rocks, the bombardment of cosmic rays, the ultraviolet of the sun that have existed before there was any life on earth; radiation is now the unnatural creation of man's tampering with the atom. The chemicals to which life is asked to make its ad-justment are no longer merely the calcium and silica and copper and all the rest of the minerals washed out of the rocks and carried in rivers to the sea; they are the synthetic creations of man's inven-tive mind, brewed in his laboratories, and having no counterparts in nature.

To adjust to these chemicals would require time on the scale that 5 is nature's; it would require not merely the years of a man's life but the life of generations. And even this, were it by some miracle pos-sible, would be futile, for the new chemicals come from our laboratories in an endless stream; almost five hundred annually find their way into actual use in the United States alone. The figure is staggering and its implications are not easily grasped—500 new chemicals to which the bodies of men and animals are required somehow to adapt each year, chemicals totally outside the limits of biologic experience.

Among them are many that are used in man's war against nature. 6 Since the mid-1940s over 200 basic chemicals have been created for use in killing insects, weeds, rodents, and other organisms described in the modern vernacular as "pests"; and they are sold under several thousand different brand names.

These sprays, dusts, and aerosols are now applied almost uni- 7 versally to farms, gardens, forests, and homes—nonselective chemicals that have the power to kill every insect, the "good" and the "bad," to still the song of birds and the leaping of fish in the streams, to coat the leaves with a deadly film, and to linger on in soil—all this though the intended target may be only a few weeds or insects. Can anyone believe it is possible to lay down such a barrage of poisons on the surface of the earth without making it unfit for all life? They should not be called "insecticides," but "biocides."

The whole process of spraying seems caught up in an endless 8 spiral. Since DDT was released for civilian use, a process of escalation has been going on in which ever more toxic materials must be found. This has happened because insects, in a triumphant vindication of Darwin's principle of the survival of the fittest, have evolved super races immune to the particular insecticide used, hence a deadlier one has always to be developed—and then a deadlier one than that. It has happened because, for reasons to be described later, destructive insects often undergo a "flareback," or resurgence, after spraying, in numbers greater than before. Thus the chemical war is never won, and all life is caught in its violent crossfire.

Along with the possibility of the extinction of mankind by nuclear 9 war, the central problem of our age has therefore become the contamination of man's total environment with such substances of incredible potential for harm—substances that accumulate in the tissues of plants and animals and even penetrate the germ cells to shatter or alter the very material of heredity upon which the shape of the future depends.

Some would-be architects of our future look toward a time when 10 it will be possible to alter the human germ plasm by design. But we may easily be doing so now by inadvertence, for many chemicals, like radiation, bring about gene mutations. It is ironic to think that man might determine his own future by something so seemingly trivial as the choice of an insect spray.

All this has been risked—for what? Future historians may well 11 be amazed by our distorted sense of proportion. How could intelligent beings seek to control a few unwanted species by a method that contaminated the entire environment and brought the threat of disease and death even to their own kind? Yet this is precisely what we have done. We have done it, moreover, for reasons that collapse the moment we examine them. We are told that the enormous and expanding use of pesticides is necessary to maintain farm production. Yet is our real problem not one of *overproduction?* Our farms, despite measures to remove acreages from production and to pay farmers *not* to produce, have yielded such a staggering excess of crops that the American taxpayer in 1962 is paying out more than one billion dollars a year as the total carrying cost of the surplus-food storage program. And is the situation helped when one branch of the Agriculture Department tries to reduce production while another states, as it did in 1958, "It is believed generally that reduction of crop acreages under provisions of the Soil Bank will stimulate interest in use of chemicals to obtain maximum production on the land retained in crops."

All this is not to say there is no insect problem and no need of control. I am saying, rather, that control must be geared to realities, not to mythical situations, and that the methods employed must be such that they do not destroy us along with the insects.

The problem whose attempted solution has brought such a train 13 of disaster in its wake is an accompaniment of our modern way of life. Long before the age of man, insects inhabited the earth—a group of extraordinarily varied and adaptable beings. Over the course of time since man's advent, a small percentage of the more than half a million species of insects have come into conflict with human welfare in two principal ways: as competitors for the food supply and as carriers of human disease.

Disease-carrying insects become important where human beings 14 are crowded together, especially under conditions where sanitation is poor, as in time of natural diaster or war or in situations of extreme poverty and deprivation. Then control of some sort becomes necessary. It is a sobering fact, however, as we shall presently see, that the method of massive chemical control has had only limited success, and also threatens to worsen the very conditions it is intended to curb.

Under primitive agriculturel conditions the farmer had few insect 15 problems. These arose with the intensification of agriculture—the devotion of immense acreages to a single crop. Such a system set the stage for explosive increases in specific insect populations. Single-crop farming does not take advantage of the principles by which nature works; it is agriculture as an engineer might conceive it to be. Nature has introduced great variety into the landscape, but man has displayed a passion for simplifying it. Thus he undoes the built-in checks and balances by which nature holds the species within bounds. One important natural check is a limit on the amount of suitable habitat for each species. Obviously then, an insect that lives on wheat can build up its population to much higher levels on a farm devoted to wheat than on one in which wheat is intermingled with other crops to which the insect is not adapted.

The same thing happens in other situations. A generation or more 16 ago, the towns of large areas of the United States lined their streets with the noble elm tree. Now the beauty they hopefully created is threatened with complete destruction as disease sweeps through the elms, carried by a beetle that would have only limited chance to build up large populations and to spread from tree to tree if the elms were only occasional trees in a richly diversified planting.

Another factor in the modern insect problem is one that must be 17 viewed against a background of geologic and human history: the spreading of thousands of different kinds of organisms from their native homes to invade new territories. This worldwide migration has been studied and graphically described by the British ecologist Charles Elton in his recent book *The Ecology of Invasions*. During the Cretaceous Period, some hundred million years ago, flooding seas cut many land bridges between continents and living things found themselves confined in what Elton calls "colossal separate nature reserves." There, isolated from others of their kind, they developed many new species. When some of the land masses were joined again, about 15 million years ago, these species began to move out into new territories—a movement that is not only still in progress but is now receiving considerable assistance from man.

The importation of plants is the primary agent in the modern 18 spread of species, for animals have almost invariably gone along with the plants, quarantine being a comparatively recent and not completely effective innovation. The United States Office of Plant Introduction alone has introduced almost 200,000 species and varieties of plants from all over the world. Nearly half of the 180 or so major insect enemies of plants in the United States are accidental imports from abroad, and most of them have come as hitchhikers on plants.

In new territory, out of reach of the restraining hand of the 19 natural enemies that kept down its numbers in its native land, an invading plant or animal is able to become enormously abundant. Thus it is no accident that our most troublesome insects are introduced species.

These invasions, both the naturally occurring and those depen- 20 dent on human assistance, are likely to continue indefinitely. Quarantine and massive chemical campaigns are only extremely expensive ways of buying time. We are faced, according to Dr. Elton, "with a life-and-death need not just to find new technological means of suppressing this plant or that animal"; instead we need the basic knowledge of animal populations and their relations to their surroundings that will "promote an even balance and damp down the explosure power of outbreaks and new invasions."

Much of the necessary knowledge is now available but we do not 21 use it. We train ecologists in our universities and even employ them in our governmental agencies but we seldom take their advice. We allow the chemical death rain to fall as though there were no alternative, whereas in fact there are many, and our ingenuity could soon discover many more if given opportunity.

Have we fallen into a mesmerized state that makes us accept as 22 inevitable that which is inferior or detrimental, as though having lost the will or the vision to demand that which is good? Such thinking, in the words of the ecologist Paul Shepard, "idealizes life with only its head out of water, inches above the limits of toleration of the corruption of its own environment . . . Why should we tolerate a diet of weak poisons, a home in insipid surroundings, a circle of acquaintances who are not quite our enemies, the noise of motors with just enough relief to prevent insanity? Who would want to live in a world which is just not quite fatal?"

Yet such a world is pressed upon us. The crusade to create a 23 chemically sterile, insect-free world seems to have engendered a fanatic zeal on the part of many specialists and most of the so-called control agencies. On every hand there is evidence that those engaged in spraying operations exercise a ruthless power. "The regulatory entomologists . . . function as prosecutor, judge and jury, tax assessor and collector and sheriff to enforce their own orders," said Connecticut entomologist Neely Turner. The most flagrant abuses go unchecked in both state and federal agencies.

It is not my contention that chemical insecticides must never be 24 used. I do contend that we have put poisonous and biologically potent chemicals indiscriminately into the hands of persons largely or wholly ignorant of their potentials for harm. We have subjected enormous numbers of people to contact with these poisons, without their consent and often without their knowledge. If the Bill of Rights contains no guarantee that a citizen shall be secure against lethal poisons distributed either by private individuals or by public officials, it is surely only because our foreafathers, despite their considerable wisdom and foresight, could conceive of no such problem.

I contend, furthermore, that we have allowed these chemicals to 25 be used with little or no advance investigation of their effect on soil, water, wildlife, and man himself. Future generations are unlikely to condone our lack of prudent concern for the integrity of the natural world that supports all life.

There is still very limited awareness of the nature of the threat. 26 This is an era of specialists, each of whom sees his own problem and is unaware of or intolerant of the larger frame into which it fits. It is also an era dominated by industry, in which the right to make a dollar at whatever cost is seldom challenged. When the public protests, confronted with some obvious evidence of damaging results of pesticide applications, it is fed little tranquilizing pills of half truth. We urgently need an end to these false assurrances, to the sugar coating of unpalatable facts. It is the public that is being asked to assume the risks that the insect controllers calculate. The public must decide whether it wishes to continue on the present road, and it can do so only when in full possession of the facts. In the words of Jean Rostand, "The obligation to endure gives us the right to know."

RESPONDING TO READING

Key words: animals   community   discovery   loss   nature
power   science   transformation

Rhetorical concepts: anecdote   cause and effect   illustration   induction
process   research report

1.   Carson refers to "man's war against nature" (paragraph 6). Indeed, people use many metaphors of combat and aggression in discussing the relation of humans to the natural world. Why do they conceive of the relationship as adversarial? Is this inevitable?
2.   When she wrote "The Obligation to Endure" in 1962, Carson said, "The method of massive chemical control has had only limited success, and threatens to worsen the very conditions it is intended to curb" (paragraph 14). To what extent has her prediction come true?
3.   Carson says that the "United States Office of Plant Introduction alone has introduced almost 200,000 species and varieties of plants from all over the world" into the United States (paragraph 18). What advantages can you think of in importing plant species? What disadvantages are there?
4.   What are the advantages of trying to create "a chemically sterile, insect-free" world? What are the disadvantages?
5.   Write an essay in which you describe an ideal relationship of people and nature. You may focus on a particular aspect of nature, such as a specific species of animal or plant; or a particular type of setting (desert, ocean) or a specific location (your state, hometown, or own backyard); or on a natural phenomenon, such as the quality of air or water.

The Islands of Chesapeake Bay

WILLIAM WARNER

"The Islands of Chesapeake Bay" is from a chapter of William Warner's Pulitzer Prize-winning study of the life and lore of the Chesapeake Bay, *Beautiful Swimmers: Watermen, Crabs, and the Chesapeake
Bay* (1976). Warner was born in 1920, graduated form Princeton University in 1943, and for some twenty-five years worked as a writer
and research associate at the Smithsonian Institution. He writes from
the combined perspectives of the natural scientist, humanist, and
investigative journalist. *Beautiful Swimmers* reflects Warner's emphasis on the quality of life—human, plant, and animal—in the Chesapeake Bay region. He characterizes the two main crabbing islands,
Smith and Tangier, showing how their inhabitants, history, and
economy are intimately intertwined with the health of the crustacean
population—which in turn is affected by state fishing regulations.
Warner then moves to a discussion of the effects of environmental
pollution on the whole complex, delicate ecosystem. His book has
influenced a number of changes in legislation affecting pollutants
and fishing in the area.

   In this chapter and throughout the book, Warner uses a wide
variety of sources: research of marine biologists and engineers, in
technical reports, articles, interviews, and an inspection trip to the
nuclear power plants on the James River; state and interstate regulations governing fishing in the Chesapeake Bay; statistics on the
absorption of sewage drainage from the surrounding populations;
figures on boat registrations and ocean-going ship traffic to and from
Baltimore; and newspaper clippings, including letters from concerned citizens. He depends heavily on interviews—with seafood
processors, fish market managers, local historians, the blacksmith
"who alone manufactures the crab dredges," and most importantly,
with the watermen of the Chesapeake Bay themselves, who provide
information not only about their current fishing practices, but nature
lore, a sense of the history of the industry, a running commentary
on government regulations, hospitality—and a love of the place and
the process of crab fishing.[1]

Around noon every day of the week except Sunday, Crisfield goes   1
through a well-practiced ritual. Down at the County Dock at this hour
lies the gateway to "another world, a unique world where time holds
still and where Elizabethan speech may yet be heard," as legions of
hyperbolic travel writers have expressed it. The preparations for jour-
neying to this other world, at any rate, are certainly unique. Most
noticeably, they are attended by great commotion, out of which there

---

[1]Since *Beautiful Swimmers* was written, a number of changes have been written into the fishing
regulations, largely as a result of the book's influence in increasing public and official awareness
of the delicacy of the Bay's ecosystem. [Eds.]

eventually comes a reassuring sense of order and regularity. Cluttering the waterfront are cases of soft drinks, cartons of wholesale groceries and, in summer, towering stacks of soft crab boxes. Taxis race down to the foot of Main Street to deposit breathless housewives loaded down with the rewards of two hours of hurried shopping. People come and go with last-minute messages, exchanges of money, or diligences performed for third parties. At half past twelve—not precisely, but thereabouts—the passenger ferries that are the lifelines of the Chesapeake's two inhabited offshore islands will cast off. The *Dorolena*, Captain Rudy Thomas, goes to Virginia's Tangier; the *Island Belle*, Captain Frankie Dize, to Maryland's Smith.

Smith and Tangier Islands are both very important to the Chesapeake's blue crab fishery. The statement is reversible; it works either way. The islands could not exist economically without crabs, and the fishery would be much impoverished without the islanders' skill and industry in catching them. Earlier in this century finfish and oysters were the mainstays of Tangier's economy. "Don't say we didn't have fish traps!" says Tangier's ninety-one-year-old Captain Johnny Parks. "Whole Bay shore was full of them. Use to be one hundred and fifty between here and Tangier Light alone." 2

"But nary no more," he adds. 3

As happened with other Eastern Shore communities, Tangier's 4 pound fishery was done in during the years between the Great Depression and World War II. Tumbling wholesale fish prices and rising costs of maintaining and working the bit nets, as compared to gill netting[2] or trawling,[3] put an impossible squeeze on Tangier's fishermen. Only on the western shore, with its greater runs of river herring, could the pound netters hold out. But coincidental with the demise of Tangier's pound fishery was the introduction of the modern crab pot.[4] There is not a Tangierman who does not hail the latter event as the island's salvation. "Best thing that ever happened here" or "God's hand" are the expressions most frequently heard. Armed with this new device, the island's fishermen quickly became extraordinarily successful crabbers and have remained so ever since. Year round, one must also remember, since Tangier contributes some twenty-two ships to Virginia's winter crab dredging fleet down at the mouth of the Bay. Thanks to this advantage Tangier is responsible for more crabs than any other single locality in the Chesapeake Bay region, Crisfield and other larger communities included. Since the Chesa-

---

[2]*gill netting:* using a net, set upright in the water, which entangles the catch in its mesh [Eds.]

[3]*trawling:* using a boat to drag a large, baglike net along the bottom of the fishing bank [Eds.]

[4]*modern crab pot:* a cubical cage, 2 feet square top and bottom and 21 inches high, made of wire mesh, which is placed with bait under water to catch crabs [Eds.]

peake has long been and remains today the world's most intensive crab fishery, it is therefore quite accurate to say that Tangiermen catch more crabs than anyone else under the sun. One does not speak disparagingly, therefore, of *Callinectes sapidus* on Tangier Island.

Next in rank to the Tangiermen are the watermen of neighboring   5 Smith Island. There would be little difference in the crab catch of the two islands—indeed, Smith might easily surpass Tangier—except for the fact that the Smith Islanders (and all other Maryland watermen) are not allowed to cross the state water boundary and join Virginia's dredging fleet.[5] Winter on Smith Island thus means the oyster, and nothing else. But the disadvantage is balanced out in another season. Summer and the soft crab are Smith's glory. The island is surrounded by the best crab bottoms in the bay, has a larger scraping fleet[6] than Tangier and, as suggested elsewhere, goes all-out twelve hours a day every day of the season for the capture of peelers[7] and softs.[8] Although neither Maryland nor Virginia keeps accurate catch records by point of origin, there is little doubt that Smith Island is the champion of the Chesapeake in soft crab production. The packing plant managers know it and will tell you so. As far away as Fulton Market, too, you will hear the same opinion. If you want to know how the crop of big jumbos and whales is shaping up, the stand owners say, you get in touch with Smith Island. . . .

Smith Island may not be to everyone's liking, as I have ruefully   6 discovered from recommending visits to friends. But for those who want to see the water trades at their traditional best, Smith will never disappoint. Nor the naturalist, poking around the creeks and guts in the broad marshland north of the Big Thorofare, all of which has recently been set aside by the Department of Interior as the Glenn W. Martin National Wildlife Refuge. Those wishing to visit the refuge must simply bear in mind that it is not universally popular with the islanders, many of whom fondly recall the lethal punt guns and multi-cannoned batteries used when market gunning for waterfowl was a way of life and an important source of winter income. (Stanley Marshall, a native of Ewell, is the refuge manager; his brother has not spoken to him since he accepted the position.) But provided you can disavow any close association with conservation organizations or the federal government, a boat and friendly guide service can easily be

---

[5]This is no longer so. *Beautiful Swimmers* was introduced in a Maryland court case; the court ruled in favor of Maryland watermen, declaring that state boundaries do not hold for migrating species. [Eds.]

[6]*scraping fleet:* boats using long net bags to crop eelgrass where peelers and softs hide [Eds.]

[7]*peelers:* crabs showing signs of readiness to moult [Eds.]

[8]*softs:* crabs that have just moulted and whose new shells are still soft [Eds.]

secured from among the islanders. Late fall or winter is the time for waterfowl; spring and summer, for the heron rookeries. Hurry, too. Although Smith has not yet been discovered by tourists, at least on the Tangier scale, there is every sign that it may soon be.

For still others Smith Island's greatest fascination lies with the 7 memory of its older citizens, who enjoy telling how it was only thirty years ago living without electricity and working the water mainly by sail. To be sure, with the sole exception of Deal Island, there is no better place on the Bay to learn of forgotten craft and the skills required to take crabs and oysters under a full press of canvas. The older watermen like to talk most about the sporty little Smith Island crab skiffs—"dinkies" they were called locally—that went in flotillas to spend the week trotlining[9] or dipping for peelers up around Bloodsworth or South Marsh. Not much more than eighteen feet in length, the dinkies had a single large sprit-sail and carried one hundred pound sandbags as movable ballast, the dexterous placement of which was essential to maintaining an upright position. "Breeze up strong and didn't we go!" says William Wilson Sneade, seventy-three, who now occupies himself making fine buster floats[10] of cedar and spruce. "Just wicker [luff] the sail a little, move your bags around and you made out all right. But come squalls, you could capsize easy enough! Thing to do was head for the shallers, where you could get your feet on the bottom, unstep the mast and right your boat. Then step her up, set your spreet pole and off you go again!"

"That's right," laughs Omar Evans, the proprietor of Smith Is- 8 land's lone crab house. "Capsizing, it made you so mad you scooped out like half of the water and then drank the balance for cussedness."

Both men remember how bad the bugs were when they spent the 9 week in little shanties on the uninhabited islands up north. "You walked in the high grass," Evans recalls. "And the green flies carried you off." (They still do.) Sneade's memory of trotlining techniques is especially clear. "Tide up and a smart breeze, we put out our lines," he explains. "You set them fair with the wind, hoisted a little pink of sail, sailed downwind running the lines—you couldn't reach, that made the line too shaky for the crabs—and then you tacked back up and did it all over again. Tide down and slick pretty ca'm, we poled and dipped for peelers, standing right on the bow. Sometimes we took along a sharp-ended gunning skiff, also good for poling.[11]

Evans is an expert on the larger boats used in crab scraping. There 10

---

[9]*trotlining:* using long, bottom-resting pieces of line with multiple baits to catch crabs [Eds.]

[10]*buster floats:* containers built to rest in the water and hold female crabs ready to moult [Eds.]

[11]*poling:* using poles to maneuver small boats through eelgrass to catch peelers and softs [Eds.]

were the Jenkins Creek catboats, "one-sail bateaux," he calls them, and the bigger jib-headed sloops, out of which the skipjacks[12] probably evolved, that could pull three crab scrapes in a good breeze. "We built them good here," he says with pride. "Over in Crisfield they was boxy-stern and messy; they don't do anything right over there." Both recall that it was hard work hauling in the scrapes. "No winches, like they got later," Sneade reminds you. "You slacked off on the sail a bit and just pulled in your scrapes through main strength and awkwardness."

"Couldn't do that no more," he adds. "I'm all stove in. Ailing 11 more this year than the last ten. Age is coming to me, that's the thing."

Age is coming. To the islands as a whole, many observers believe. 12 Whether Tangier and Smith can in fact hold out is a question that is now sometimes raised. "Oh, no, the islands will never fail," an experienced picking plant owner in Crisfield recently reassured me. "Not as long as there are crabs in the Bay." He went on to explain very patiently that nobody in the Bay country caught more crabs, knew more about them, or went at it harder than the island people. "Why, they *study* crabs," he finished in tones of awe. "And the thing is they pass on all what they know to the young ones."

I think the Crisfield packer is right, at least on the subject of 13 generational succession. The blue crab holds great fascination for watermen of all ages. You've got to study him, the older ones say, because he's mean and ornery, very clever and always out to fool you. This is especially true during the long summer when there are erratic day-to-day shifts of the best thick of crabs which do not seem to correspond to the weather or other rational factors. The men talk of them continually, at home over the dinner table or in the general stores as they play checkers.

And the young listen and follow. True, many seem tempted to 14 go other ways. You see them around every crab house or shanty standing defiantly in the cockpit of their boats, alternately taciturn or shrill with complaint about the hard times of their profession. To reach them at all one must show some knowledge and appreciation of their work. It is almost as though they had a constant need for outsiders, for the strange persons, paradoxically, to remind them it is all right to be a waterman. I remember particularly a young scraper from Ewell . . . with whom I went to the Fox Islands on a beautiful September morning. As we crossed the Sound in the dark he railed bitterly against the water trades and all those who control them. The

---

[12]*skipjacks:* sailboats used for crab and oyster dredging [Eds.]

authorities in Annapolis were all politicians and crooks, he said. They had not done one single thing to help the watermen and never would. And the Baltimore newspapers print up a pack of lies, like it was the watermen who were the sole cause of everything that is wrong with the Bay. If he could only get those newspaper people out in the freeze of winter, he added, and then see what they say! But as dawn broke and the Foxes came in sight, he quietly bowed his head in prayer and said grace before eating a sandwich and drinking a last cup of coffee. Then, once on the crab grounds, he was a new man. Look here, he told me as we worked the scrapes, here were some egg cases[13] glued to the underside of a big Jimmy.[14] They are called blisters, he explained, and some watermen think they hold the eggs of the oyster toadfish. There was a shark fin cutting the water, right over there! Oh, yes, you often saw sharks around the Foxes. We should look over all the baby rockfish very carefully, too, he continued. They were tagging the little rocks and you could get a dollar for each recovered tag. He had found one from New Jersey, in fact, just a month ago. "Oh, I like this good enough," he said finally.

There are many like him in the younger generation. They may complain and they seem to want to carry a heavy chip on their shoulder. But the challenges and the independence of working on the water, trying to get the smart of it, continue to attract. If the price is fair, that is. And as long as there are crabs in the Bay.   15

Crisfield, Tangier, Smith, or most anywhere else in the Bay where men live from the water. As long as there are crabs to catch. The view presently is that there will be. And oysters and finfish, too, but only as long as people in other places do the necessary. The watermen know where the real danger lies. Regulation by Richmond or Annapolis is not going to avert it. All those laws, the watermen scoff. Half of them seem downright foolish. There is for example the matter of the width of the crab scrapes. Everyone knows that if you used a six-foot scrape instead of the prescribed three-and-a-half, it would take you twice as long to haul in and work over each lick and so the day's results would be pretty much the same. Or the much discussed history of the skipjacks. The Maryland law of 1865 requiring oysters to be dredged—taken in motion, that is, as opposed to at anchor— only by sailing craft is still in force. But in 1967 it was amended to allow the little engine-powered yawl or "push" boats carried in davits over skipjack sterns to provide powered dredging on Mondays and Tuesdays, with a daily catch limit of one hundred and fifty bushels.   16

---

[13]*egg cases:* protective structures that surround eggs until the larvae inside them are ready to hatch [Eds.]

[14]*big Jimmy:* a large male crab [Eds.]

(On "sailing days" during the rest of the week there have as yet been no limits, although the state has the authority to impose them whenever and to what degree it sees fit; tonging boats in recent years have generally been limited to twenty-five bushels per day per licensed tonger aboard.) This concession was made because of increasing costs in maintaining and operating the aging vessels, which have had a hard time competing with the highly efficient and less costly patent tonging boats. So, much as one hates to see the end of the celebrated skipjack fleet, now down to thirty-odd boats, the argument that powered dredging cleans off the oyster rocks too quickly has been broached and there are the daily catch limits in any case. "Let us all dredge," Maryland's three thousand tongers say. "All it means is that we get our limit quicker, so what is the sense in a man staying out in the cold any longer than he has to?" The propositon that all-out power dredging would create too many deep furrows in the bottom and smother too many oysters is not supported by the watermen. They could tow their dredges more smoothly and gently with power, they claim, and still make their jags in a shorter time. Besides, they have been doing it in Virginia for as long as anyone can remember.

But there is no argument the crabs have to be watched. Everyone 17 agrees that if ever the crab stocks bottom out at bad year levels and stay there, that will be the day to start worrying. The winter dredging must be closely reviewed—the season of 1974–75 was one of the poorest on record—and legislation barring this form of capture may soon be necessary. Similarly, although Virginia has established a 130-square-mile sanctuary for egg-bearing sponge crabs at the mouth of the Bay, it may some day be advisable for the state to prohibit the taking of sponges in all her waters, as Maryland has already done.

But none of these measures need be, the watermen insist, if the 18 Bay waters are kept healthy. They know precisely what is wrong. It is not so much the enormous Calvert Cliffs atomic energy plant sucking in bottom dwelling plankton, eggs and larvae at three million gallons per minute. Or the Army Corps of Engineers with its constant proposals to dredge new or deeper ship channels, the effects of which bury bottom dwelling organisms and reduce plankton photosynthesis. Or the proposed oil refinery in Norfolk, which will be dangerously close to the Bay's blue crab nursery. These things are bad enough. The public sees them and protests accordingly. The watermen on the other hand think the real problem is something harder to pinpoint. As they go out year after year, the water seems to be changing. It may be, they think, that it is everywhere getting a little tired. Each summer there are more fish kills and in winter you can sometimes see strange little red dots suspended in the water. Old, tired, and a little messy, you could even say. Age is coming to the Bay, too, perhaps. Simple as that.

I sometime have the feeling we're going to be another Lake Erie," says Vernon Bradshaw. Vernon should know. He has spent a long time watching the water, since the days his father was the keeper of Tangier Light and he and his sister went to live with him summers. "Oh, the Bay was pretty then," he says. "We fished or flew our kites, and all the boats sailed close by to speak us." 19

Some among the Chesapeake's marine biologists could not agree more strongly. The Bay is changing in ways that are very subtle. The agents of destruction take their toll stealthily, and in diffuse and complex patterns that are hard for the public to grasp. Scientists most commonly speak of them as "the doubling rate" and "oxygen deprivation." The doubling rate concerns human populations. In 1960 the population of the Chesapeake Bay drainage area was estimated at eleven million. This figure is expected to triple by the turn of the century. The average annual increase is 1.7 percent, or twice the national average. Significantly, the increase is not merely confined to the Baltimore, Washington and Norfolk metropolitan complexes, but is widely scattered and runs even higher around the Bay's immediate shoreline, where frenzied waterfront real estate development for leisure homes has almost reached Florida proportions in the last two decades. Down from cities large and small, then, come enormous quantities of sewage, some of it still raw and none of it fully processed for the removal of nitrogen and phosphorus. The great and noble rivers of the western shore—the Potomac and the James, especially— are in effect left to serve as the final treatment stages, natural sewers, in other words. And from the burgeoning waterfront resort developments comes more raw waste, how much no one exactly knows, since low water tables and shoddy planning in these communities frequently cause a high incidence of septic tank failure. To these must be added the 6,000 oceangoing ships that annually wind up the channel to Baltimore, dumping raw sewage equivalent to a town of 25,000. Even greater may be the waste that comes from the Bay's growing armada of pleasure craft, which now numbers over 175,000 licensed vessels. 20

As a result the Bay is receiving continually heavier loads of disease-producing bacteria, which cause frequent closings of shellfish beds, and of nitrogen and phosphorus, which have a far more devastating effect on water quality and marine resources in general. Again, accurate knowledge of how heavy the load may be in the Bay at large is lacking. But it is easy enough to sample and measure in certain of the tributaries. The District of Columbia offers one clear 21 example. Washington annually discharges into the Potomac River twenty-five million pounds of nitrogen and eight million pounds of phosphorus, the latter being a relative newcomer thanks to the increasing use of miracle-white detergents. These nitrates and phosphates are called "nutrients" by scientists. But the term may strike anyone hearing it for the first time as somewhat misleading, because what these nutrients principally nourish are harmful quantities of blue and green algae. The algae "blooms" or "explodes" in population by catastrophic quantum leaps, thanks to the abundance of the sewage-waste fertilizers. Then, enter oxygen deprivation. As the algae die and decompose, they take from the surrounding water nearly all of its oxygen. All forms of life around these blooms—fish, plants, mollusks and crustaceans—smother and die. You may see the process, if you wish, on the Potomac. Summer after summer, a few miles below Mount Vernon, there is a strange sea. It is slimy and pea-green in color, a horrid soup of a sea that affronts all the senses. To go through it in a small boat is a shocking experience. The same phenomenon, of course, occurs in many of the smaller tributaries, although less dramatically.

"The Patuxent River now receives sewage wastes from 78,000 22 people and some portions above the estuary show persistent low oxygen content, high fecal coliform bacteria counts and loss of as many as ten species of fish."

"Baltimore's Black River has in effect been sacrificed as a waste 23 treatment lagoon."

So read the technical reports. One tributary after another is 24 checked off as sacrificed or soon to be.

Down on the James River is the historic plantation of Shirley, 25 home of the Carters of Virginia since 1630. It has a simple utilitarian charm, not at all elegant like the bigger plantations near Williamsburg, and a ninth-generation Carter still works it as a farm. Looking out through Shirley's back windows you see a large and beautiful lawn, shaded by tall oak and elm, that extends to a bend in the river. But those who choose to walk the grounds must be prepared for certain shocks. Just around the bend on the other side of the river is a power plant, squat, monolithic and with tall stacks. It happens to be steam-powered, but down the river below Jamestown are two more plants. Nuclear-powered giants, they are, known locally as "Surry Number One" and "Surry Number Two." These three plants and the fact that the James receives the sewage of Richmond (and a host of lesser cities, much of it raw), is constantly being widened or rechanneled, and supports much heavy industry, have combined to alter very seriously the quality of the Chesapeake's most historic river. Walk down to the water's edge. There are no algal blooms, to be sure, but one senses that something is very much wrong. The water is highly turbid, almost opaque. Even in a bright sun the waves of the James are leaden and gray. The river seems to have lost some indefinable life force, its sparkle, if you prefer. Engineers assure us it is not yet sacrificed. But how well it will remain off the dead and dying list is a more troubling question.

"I can feel it, I can see it," says Dr. Willard Van Engel. "It's a great blanket of pollution—oil, detritus and just plain filth—slowly rolling down the Bay." Other biologists agree and go on to point out that this blanket has what they call a parallel doubling rate. As population doubles, they explain, so too does the nutrient load of nitrogen and phosphorus, inexorably and exactly, or on a one-to-one ratio. Meanwhile nothing new has been built in the way of tertiary sewage treatment or complete phosphate and nitrate removal in the Chesapeake drainage basin since 1960. Expensive as three-stage disposal may be, many scientists and administrators feel there is no other way. They argue that if the federal government can contribute over $926 million in a Great Lakes compact, no less attention is due what has been accurately called the nation's "most valuable and vulnerable large estuary" or "a spawning and juvenile growth area for marine organisms affecting all the Atlantic seaboard states." 26

"Yes, we discuss these matters forcefully with the federal and state agencies, and I am hopeful of some result," says Loren Sterling, president of the Milbourne Oyster Company, which is Crisfield's largest oyster and crab packing plant. Sterling is an experienced industry spokesman who, like many other Crisfielders, has been instrumental in extending the blue crab fishery to the southern states, as far as Florida, in fact, where he once ran a plant in Cedar Key. He finds the question of human population growth is at last being considered in the smaller towns and communities all around the Bay. "People are beginning to talk now of just how big they want to grow," he says. Sterling also places great faith in the Environmental Protection Agency, although he thinks the E.P.A. and other federal or state conservation agencies frequently put too much attention on small or easy targets. "If only they would work on the big people the way they work on the small," he reasons. "Then I think we'd be all right." 27

Others are less sanguine. Scientists at Johns Hopkins University's Chesapeake Bay Institute, the University of Maryland's Chesapeake Biological Laboratory and other centers of estuarine research have estimated that the Bay's nutrient load will double by 1995, unless extraordinary measures are taken, and that such ". . . doubling of present nitrogen and phosphorus loading would probably produce general eutrophication of the Upper Bay." 28

Eutrophication is defined as a body of water in which an increase 29 of mineral and organic nutrients has reduced dissolved oxygen to the point of causing imbalances among the various organisms inhabiting it. One is tempted to improve on the dictionary definition. A very one-sided imbalance, we could say, that produces a suffocating pea-green plant organism at the expense of nearly all others.

General eutrophication is Lake Erie. Simple as that.   30

RESPONDING TO READING

Key words: animals community discovery loss nature
power rights science transformation

Rhetorical concepts: analysis anecdote cause and effect illustration
induction narrative/example process research report

1.   Explain, using one or two examples, how Warner shows the intimate interrelationship of life in the Chesapeake Bay region—its people, history, economy, and marine life.
2.   What is the effect of including dialogue, character sketches, and personal experiences in a scientific and economic argument, as Warner does?
3.   Scientists and naturalists have been lamenting for decades the devastating effect of pollution on the quality of life—human, animal, and plant. Yet pollution escalates; its attendant problems continue, nationally and world-wide. Why don't private citizens, governments, and industries pay more attention to such advice?
4.   Identify a particular ecological problem with which you are familiar. Explain its causes, its history (over how long a time has the problem existed, and with what effects), and its present state. What could be done to solve the problem? What are the likely long-term consequences if the problem isn't solved?

Los Angeles Against the Mountains
JOHN MCPHEE

John McPhee was born in Princeton, New Jersey, in 1931. He graduated from Princeton University in 1953, and still lives, writes, and teaches in his home town. Eager to publish in the *New Yorker*, he submitted his work there for twelve years before his first essay was accepted, in 1964. Since then, nearly all of his writing has appeared there before being collected in books whose subject matter ranges from Florida (*Oranges*, 1967) to Alaska (*Coming into the Country*, 1977), New York (*Giving Good Weight*, 1979) to the Great Plains and the Rocky Mountains (*Basin and Range*, 1981).

"Los Angeles Against the Mountains" was published in *The Control of Nature* (1989), a book whose ambiguous title reflects its problematic subject. Here McPhee studies in characteristic detail people's all-out battles to force nature to accommodate—beyond its capacity—to high density population and industry. In the places he analyzes, overcrowding will destroy the very features that were initially attractive: the Mississippi Delta, the volcanic islands of Iceland and Hawaii, and the steep, mountainous hillsides of Los Angeles. In "Los Angeles Against the Mountains," he shows what happens when a population surrounds "the base of Mt. Olympus demanding and expecting the surrender of the gods," and instead finds a fragile terrain vulnerable to the effects of drought and flooding rains.

In Los Angeles versus the San Gabriel Mountains, it is not always 1 clear which side is losing. For example, the Genofiles, Bob and Jackie, can claim to have lost and won. They live on an acre of ground so high that they look across their pool and past the trunks of big pines at an aerial view over Glendale and across Los Angeles to the Pacific bays. The setting, in cool dry air, is serene and Mediterranean. It has not been everlastingly serene.

On a February night some years ago, the Genofiles were awakened 2 by a crash of thunder—lightning striking the mountain front. Ordinarily, in their quiet neighborhood, only the creek beside them was likely to make much sound, dropping steeply out of Shields Canyon on its way to the Los Angeles River. The creek, like every component of all the river systems across the city from mountains to ocean, had not been left to nature. Its banks were concrete. Its bed was concrete. When boulders were running there, they sounded like a rolling freight. On a night like this, the boulders should have been running. The creek should have been a torrent. Its unnatural sound was unnaturally absent. There was, and had been, a lot of rain.

The Genofiles had two teen-age children, whose rooms were on 3 the uphill side of the one-story house. The window in Scott's room looked straight up Pine Cone Road, a cul-de-sac, which, with hundreds like it, defined the northern limit of the city, the confrontation of the urban and the wild. Los Angeles is overmatched on one side by the Pacific Ocean and on the other by very high mountains. With respect to these principal boundaries, Los Angeles is done sprawling. The San Gabriels, in their state of tectonic youth, are rising as rapidly as any range on earth. Their loose inimical slopes flout the tolerance of the angle of repose. Rising straight up out of the megalopolis, they stand ten thousand feet above the nearby sea, and they are not kidding with this city. Shedding, spalling, self-destructing, they are disintegrating at a rate that is also among the fastest in the world. The phalanxed communities of Los Angeles have pushed themselves hard against these mountains, an aggression that requires a deep defense budget to contend with the results. Kimberlee Genofile called to her mother, who joined her in Scott's room as they looked up the street. From its high turnaround, Pine Cone Road plunges downhill like a ski run, bending left and then right and then left and then right in steep christiania turns for half a mile above a three-hundred-foot straightaway that aims directly at the Genofiles' house. Not far below the turnaround, Shields Creek passes under the street, and there a kink in its concrete profile had been plugged by a six-foot boulder. Hence the silence of the creek. The water was now spreading over the street. It descended in heavy sheets. As the young Genofiles and their mother glimpsed it in the all but total darkness, the scene was suddenly illuminated by a blue electrical flash. In the blue light they saw a massive blackness, moving. It was not a land-slide, not a mudslide, not a rock avalanche; nor by any means was it the front of a conventional flood. In Jackie's words, "It was just one big black thing coming at us, rolling, rolling with a lot of water in front of it, pushing the water, this big black thing. It was just one big black hill coming toward us."

In geology, it would be known as a debris flow. Debris flows 4 amass in stream valleys and more or less resemble fresh concrete. They consist of water mixed with a good deal of solid material, most of which is above sand size. Some of it is Chevrolet size. Boulders bigger than cars ride long distances in debris flows. Boulders grouped like fish eggs pour downhill in debris flows. The dark material coming toward the Genofiles was not only full of boulders; it was so full of automobiles it was like bread dough mixed with raisins. On its way down Pine Cone Road, it plucked up cars from driveways and the street. When it crashed into the Genofiles' house, the shattering of safety glass made terrific explosive sounds. A door burst open. Mud and boulders poured into the hall. We're going to go, Jackie thought. Oh, my God, what a hell of a way for the four of us to die together.

The parents' bedroom was on the far side of the house. Bob 5 Genofile was in there kicking through white satin draperies at the panelled glass, smashing it to provide an outlet for water, when the three others ran in to join him. The walls of the house neither moved nor shook. As a general contractor, Bob had built dams, department stores, hospitals, six schools, seven churches, and this house. It was made of concrete block with steel reinforcement, sixteen inches on center. His wife had said it was stronger than any dam in California. His crew had called it "the fort." In those days, twenty years before, the Genofiles' acre was close by the edge of the mountain brush, but a developer had come along since then and knocked down thousands of trees and put Pine Cone Road up the slope. Now Bob Genofile was thinking, I hope the roof holds. I hope the roof is strong enough to hold. Debris was flowing over it. He told Scott to shut the bedroom door. No sooner was the door closed than it was battered down and fell into the room. Mud, rock, water poured in. It pushed everybody against the far wall. "Jump on the bed," Bob said. The bed began to rise. Kneeling on it—on a gold velvet spread—they could soon press their palms against the ceiling. The bed also moved toward the glass wall. The two teen-agers got off, to try to control the motion, and were pinned between the bed's brass railing and the wall. Boulders went up against the railing, pressed it into their legs, and held them fast. Bob dived into the muck to try to move the boulders, but he failed. The debris flow, entering through windows as well as doors, continued to rise. Escape was still possible for the parents but not for the children. The parents looked at each other and did not stir. Each reached for and held one of the children. Their mother felt suddenly resigned, sure that her son and daughter would die and she and her husband would quickly follow. The house became buried to the eaves. Boulders sat on the roof. Thirteen automobiles were packed around the building, including five in the pool. A din of rocks kept banging against them. The stuck horn of a buried car was blaring. The family in the darkness in their fixed tableau watched one another by the light of a directional signal, endlessly blinking. The house had filled up in six minutes, and the mud stopped rising near the children's chins.

Stories like that do not always have such happy endings. A man   6
went outside to pick up his newspaper one morning, heard a sound, turned, and died of a heart attack as he saw his house crushed to pieces with his wife and two children inside. People have been buried alive in their beds. But such cases are infrequent. Debris flows generally are much less destructive of life than of property. People get out of the way.

If they try to escape by automobile, they have made an obvious   7
but imperfect choice. Norman Reid backed his Pontiac into the street one January morning and was caught from behind by rock porridge. It embedded the car to the chrome strips. Fifty years of archival news photograhs show cars of every vintage standing like hippos in chunky muck. The upper halves of their headlights peep above the surface. The late Roland Case Ross, an emeritus professor at California State University, told me of a day in the early thirties when he watched a couple rushing to escape by car. She got in first. While her husband was going around to get in his side, she got out and ran into the house for more silverware. When the car at last putt-putted downhill, a wall of debris was nudging the bumper. The debris stayed on the vehicle's heels all the way to Foothill Boulevard, where the car turned left.

Foothill Boulevard was U.S. Route 66—the western end of the   8
rainbow. Through Glendora, Azusa, Pasadena, it paralleled the mountain front. It strung the metropolitan border towns. And it brought
in emigrants to fill them up. The real-estate line of maximum advance
now averages more than a mile above Foothill, but Foothill receives
its share of rocks. A debris flow that passed through the Monrovia
Nursery went on to Foothill and beyond. With its twenty million
plants in twelve hundred varieties, Monrovia was the foremost con-
tainer nursery in the world, and in its recovery has remained so. The
debris flow went through the place picking up pots and cans. It got
into a greenhouse two hundred feet long and smashed out the southern wall, taking bougainvillea and hibiscus with it. Arby's, below
Foothill, blamed the nursery for damages, citing the hibiscus that had
come with the rocks. Arby's sought compensation, but no one was
buying beef that thin.

In the same storm, large tree trunks rode in the debris like javelins   9
and broke through the sides of houses. Automobiles went in through
picture windows. A debris flow hit the gym at Azusa Pacific College
and knocked a large hole in the upslope wall. In the words of Cliff
Hamlow, the basketball coach, "If we'd had students in there, it would
have killed them. Someone said it sounded like the roar of a jet engine.
It filled the gym up with mud, and with boulders two and three feet
in diameter. It went out through the south doors and spread all over
the football field and track. Chain-link fencing was sheared off—like
it had been cut with a welder. The place looked like a war zone."
Azusa Pacific College wins national championships in track, but
Coach Hamlow's basketball team (12–18), can't get the boulders out
of its game.

When a debris flow went through the Verdugo Hills Cemetery,   10
which is up a couple of switchbacks on the mountain front, two of
the central figures there, resting under impressive stones, were
"Hiram F. Hatch, 1st Lieut. 6th Mich. Inf., December 24, 1843–October
12, 1922," and "Henry J. Hatch, Brigadier General, United States
Army, April 28, 1869–December 31, 1931." The two Hatches held the
hill while many of their comrades slid below. In all, thirty-five coffins
came out of the cemetery and took off for lower ground. They went
down Hillrose Street and were scattered over half a mile. One came
to rest in the parking lot of a supermarket. Many were reburied by
debris and, in various people's yards, were not immediately found.
Three turned up in one yard. Don Sulots, who had moved into the
fallout path two months before, said, "It sounded like thunder. By
the time I made it to the front door and got it open, the muck was
already three feet high. It's quite a way to start off life in a new home—
mud, rocks, and bodies all around."

Most people along the mountain front are about as mindful of 11
debris flows as those corpses were. Here today, gone tomorrow. Those
who worry build barricades. They build things called deflection
walls—a practice that raises legal antennae and, when the caroming
debris breaks into the home of a neighbor, probes the wisdom of
Robert Frost. At least one family has experienced so many debris
flows coming through their back yard that they long ago installed
overhead doors in the rear end of their built-in garage. To guide the
flows, they put deflection walls in their back yard. Now when the
boulders come they open both ends of their garage, and the debris
goes through to the street.

Between Harrow Canyon and Englewild Canyon, a private street 12
called Glencoe Heights teased the mountain front. Came a time of
unprecedented rain, and the neighborhood grew ever more fearful—
became in fact so infused with catastrophic anticipation that it sought
the drastic sort of action that only a bulldozer could provide. A fire
had swept the mountainsides, leaving them vulnerable, dark, and
bare. Expecting floods of mud and rock, people had piled sandbags
and built heavy wooden walls. Their anxiety was continuous for many
months. "This threat is on your mind all the time," Gary Lukehart
said. "Every time you leave the house, you stop and put up another
sandbag, and you just hope everything will be all right when you get
back." Lukehart was accustomed to losing in Los Angeles. In the 1957
Rose Bowl, he was Oregon State's quarterback. A private street could
not call upon city or county for the use of heavy equipment, so in
the dead of night, as steady rain was falling, a call was put in to John
McCafferty—bulldozer for hire. McCafferty had a closeup knowledge
of the dynamics of debris flows: he had worked the mountain front
from San Dimas to Sierra Madre, which to him is Sarah Modri. ("In
those canyons at night, you could hear them big boulders comin'.
They sounded like thunder.") He arrived at Glencoe Heights within
the hour and set about turning the middle of the street into the Grand
Canal of Venice. His Cat was actually not a simple dozer but a 955
loader on tracks, with a two-and-a-quarter-yard bucket seven feet
wide. Cutting water mains, gas mains, and sewers, he made a ditch
that eventually extended five hundred feet and was deep enough to
take in three thousand tons of debris. After working for five hours,
he happened to be by John Caufield's place ("It had quit rainin', it
looked like the worst was over") when Caufield came out and said,
"Mac, you sure have saved my bacon."

McCafferty continues, "All of a sudden, we looked up at the 13
mountains—it's not too far from his house to the mountains, maybe
a hundred and fifty feet—and we could just see it all comin'. It seemed
the whole mountain had come loose. It flowed like cement." In the

ditch, he put the Cat in reverse and backed away from the oncoming debris. He backed three hundred feet. He went up one side of the ditch and was about halfway out of it when the mud and boulders caught the Cat and covered it over the hood. In the cab, the mud pushed against McCafferty's legs. At the same time, debris broke into Caufield's house through the front door and the dining-room window, and in five minutes filled it to the eaves.

Other houses were destroyed as well. A garage left the neighborhood with a car in it. One house was buried twice. (After McCafferty dug it out, it was covered again.) His ditch, however, was effective, and saved many places on slightly higher ground, among them Gary Lukehart's and the home of John Marcellino, the chief executive officer of Mackinac Island Fudge. McCafferty was promised a lifetime supply of fudge. He was on the scene for several days, and in one span worked twenty-four hours without a break. The people of the street brought him chocolate milkshakes. He had left his lowbed parked around the corner. When at last he returned to it and prepared to go home, he discovered that a cop had given him a ticket. 14

A metropolis that exists in a semidesert, imports water three hundred miles, has inveterate flash floods, is at the grinding edges of two tectonic plates, and has a microclimate tenacious of noxious oxides will have its priorities among the aspects of its environment that it attempts to control. For example, Los Angeles makes money catching water. In a few days in 1983, it caught twenty-eight million dollars' worth of water. In one period of twenty-four hours, however, the ocean hit the city with twenty-foot waves, a tornado made its own freeway, debris flows poured from the San Gabriel front, and an earthquake shook the region. Nature's invoice was forty million dollars. Later, twenty million more was spent dealing with the mountain debris. 15

There were those who would be quick—and correct—in saying that were it not for the alert unflinching manner and imaginative strategies by which Los Angeles outwits the mountains, nature's invoices at such times would run into the billions. The rear-guard defenses are spread throughout the city and include more than two thousand miles of underground conduits and concrete-lined open stream channels—a web of engineering that does not so much reinforce as replace the natural river systems. The front line of battle is where the people meet the mountains—up the steep slopes where the subdivisions stop and the brush begins. 16

Strung out along the San Gabriel front are at least a hundred and twenty bowl-shaped excavations that resemble football stadiums and are often as large. Years ago, when a big storm left back yards and 17 boulevards five feet deep in scree, one neighborhood came through amazingly unscathed, because it happened to surround a gravel pit that had filled up instead. A tungsten filament went on somewhere above Los Angeles. The county began digging pits to catch debris. They were quarries, in a sense, but exceedingly bizarre quarries, in that the rock was meant to come to them. They are known as debris basins. Blocked at their downstream ends with earthfill or concrete constructions, they are also known as debris dams. With clean spillways and empty reservoirs, they stand ready to capture rivers of boulders—these deep dry craters, lying close above the properties they protect. In the overflowing abundance of urban nomenclature, the individual names of such basins are obscure, until a day when they appear in a headline in the Los Angeles *Times:* Harrow, Englewild, Zachau, Dunsmuir, Shields, Big Dalton, Hog, Hook East, Hook West, Limekiln, Starfall, Sawpit, Santa Anita. For fifty miles, they mark the wild boundary like bulbs beside a mirror. Behind chain links, their idle ovate forms more than suggest defense. They are separated, on the average, by seven hundred yards. In aggregate, they are worth hundreds of millions of dollars. All this to keep the mountains from falling on Johnny Carson.

The principal agency that developed the debris basins was the 18 hopefully named Los Angeles County Flood Control District, known familiarly through the region as Flood Control, and even more intimately as Flood. ("when I was at Flood, one of our dams filled with debris overnight," a former employee remarked to me. "If any more rain came, we were going to have to evacuate the whole of Pasadena.") There has been a semantic readjustment, obviously intended to acknowledge that when a flood pours out of the mountains it might be half rock. The debris basins are now in the charge of the newly titled Sedimentation Section of the Hydraulic Division of the Los Angeles County Department of Public Works. People still call it Flood. By whatever name the agency is called, its essential tactic remains unaltered. This was summarized for me in a few words by an engineer named Donald Nichols, who pointed out that eight million people live below the mountains on the urban coastal plain, within an area large enough to accommodate Philadelphia, Detroit, Chicago, St. Louis, Boston, and New York. He said, "To make the area inhabitable, you had to put in lined channels on the plain and halt the debris at the front. If you don't take it out at the front, it will come out in the plain, filling up channels. A filled channel won't carry diddly-boo."

To stabilize mountain streambeds and stop descending rocks even 19 before they reach the debris basins, numerous crib structures (barriers made of concrete slats) have been emplaced in high canyons—the idea being to convert plunging streams into boulder staircases, and hypothetically cause erosion to work against itself. Farther into the mountains, a dozen dams of some magnitude were built in the nineteen-twenties and thirties to control floods and conserve water. Because they are in the San Gabriels, they inadvertently trap large volumes of debris. One of them—the San Gabriel Dam, in the San Gabriel River—was actually built as a debris-control structure. Its reservoir, which is regularly cleaned out, contained, just then, twenty million tons of mountain.

The San Gabriel River, the Los Angeles River, and the Big Tujunga 20 (Bigta Hung-ga) are the principal streams that enter the urban plain, where a channel that filled with rock wouldn't carry diddly-boo. Three colossal debris basins—as different in style as in magnitude from those on the mountain front—have been constructed on the plain to greet these rivers. Where the San Gabriel goes past Azusa on its way to Alamitos Bay, the Army Corps of Engineers completed in the late nineteen-forties a dam ninety-two feet high and twenty-four thousand feet wide—this to stop a river that is often dry, and trickles most of the year. Santa Fe Dam, as it is called, gives up at a glance its own story, for it is made of boulders that are shaped like potatoes and are generally the size of watermelons. They imply a large volume of water flowing with high energy. They are stream-propelled, stream-rounded boulders, and the San Gabriel is the stream. In Santa Fe Basin, behind the dam, the dry bed of the San Gabriel is half a mile wide. The boulder-strewn basin in its entirety is four times as wide as that. It occupies eighteen hundred acres in all, nearly three square miles, of what would be prime real estate were it not for the recurrent arrival of rocks. The scene could have been radioed home from Mars, whose cobbly face is in part the result of debris flows dating to a time when Mars had surface water.

The equally vast Sepulveda Basin is where Los Angeles receives 21 and restrains the Los Angeles River. In Sepulveda Basin are three golf courses, which lend ample support to the widespread notion that everything in Los Angeles is disposable. Advancing this national prejudice even further, debris flows, mudslides, and related phenomena have "provided literary minds with a ready-made metaphor of the alleged moral decay of Los Angeles." The words belong to Reyner Banham, late professor of the history of architecture at University College, London, whose passionate love of Los Angeles left him without visible peers. The decay was only "alleged," he said. Of such nonsense he was having none. With his "Los Angeles: The Architecture of Four Ecologies," Banham had become to this deprecated, defamed, traduced, and disparaged metropolis what Pericles was to Athens. Banham knew why the basins were there and what the people were defending. While all those neurasthenic literary minds are cow-ering somewhere in ethical crawl space, the quality of Los Angeles life rises up the mountain front. There is air there. Cool is the evening under the crumbling peaks. Cool descending air. Clean air. Air with a view. "The financial and topographical contours correspond almost exactly," Banham said. Among those "narrow, tortuous residential roads serving precipitous house-plots that often back up directly on unimproved wilderness" is "the fat life of the delectable mountains."

People of Gardena, Inglewood, and Watts no less than Azusa and 22 Altadena pay for the defense of the mountain front, the rationale being that debris trapped near its source will not move down and choke the channels of the inner city, causing urban floods. The political City of Los Angeles—in its vague and tentacular configuration—actually abuts the San Gabriels for twenty miles or so, in much the way that it extends to touch the ocean in widely separated places like Venice, San Pedro, and Pacific Palisades. Los Angeles County reaches across the mountains and far into the Mojave Desert. The words "Los Angeles" as generally used here refer neither to the political city nor to the county but to the multinamed urban integrity that has a street in it seventy miles long (Sepulveda Boulevard) and, from the Pacific Ocean at least to Pomona, moves north against the mountains as a comprehensive town.

The debris basins vary greatly in size—not, of course, in relation 23 to the populations they defend but in relation to the watersheds and washes above them in the mountains. For the most part, they are associated with small catchments, and the excavated basins are commensurately modest, with capacities under a hundred thousand cubic yards. In a typical empty reservoir—whatever its over-all dimensions may be—stands a columnar tower that resembles a campanile. Full of holes, it is known as a perforated riser. As the basin fills with a thick-flowing slurry of water, mud, and rock, the water goes into the tower, and is drawn off below. The county calls this water harvesting.

Like the freeways, the debris-control system ordinarily functions 24 but occasionally jams. When the Genofiles' swimming pool filled with cars, debris flows descended into other neighborhoods along that part of the front. One hit a culvert, plugged the culvert, crossed a road in a bouldery wave, flattened fences, filled a debris basin, went over the spillway, and spread among houses lying below, shoving them off their foundations. The debris basins have caught as much as six hundred thousand cubic yards in one storm. Over time, they have trapped some twenty million tons of mud and rock. Inevitably, sometimes something gets away.

At Devils Gate—just above the Rose Bowl, in Pasadena—a dam 25 was built in 1920 with control of water its only objective. Yet its reservoir, with a surface of more than a hundred acres, has filled to the

brim with four million tons of rock, gravel, and sand. A private operator has set up a sand-and-gravel quarry in the reservoir. Almost
exactly, he takes out what the mountains put in. As one engineer has
described it, "he pays Flood, and Flood makes out like a champ."

RESPONDING TO READING

Key words: community discovery loss memory nature
power striving transformation watershed

Rhetorical concepts: analogy analysis anecdote cause and effect
illustration induction narrative/example process research report

1.   How does the story of the Genofile house serve both to illustrate McPhee's
concerns and to organize the essay? Select another personal story in the essay
and show how it illustrates the conflict of people with nature. Whose side
are you on? Why?
2.   Compare and contrast the attempt to control Los Angeles floods with the
attempt to control insects that Rachel Carson describes. What motives led to
the actions that Carson and McPhee describe? What might be better courses
of action in each case? Should people ever interfere with nature? Why, or
why not?
3.   Describe what it was like to be caught up in some large event beyond
your control: a fire, riot, hurricane, ocean tide, downhill race, illness, accident,
for example. If no such event comes to mind, use an experience in which
you encountered nature and felt its force. Use the narrative and detail as a
way of illustrating your ideas about controlling nature.
4.   Why do people persist in building houses in the path of debris flows?
Select one or two other examples of people refusing to learn from the past,
imagining that they can conquer nature, and so repeating mistakes that lead
to serious trouble. Using these examples as your evidence, write an essay
on people and the ways they encounter, and should encounter, natural
forces.

Africa Daze Montana Knights

MARGARET KNOX

Margaret Knox (born 1954) earned a B.A. in history from the
University of California (1977), and a M.A. in journalism from the
University of Michigan (1983). After working at newspapers in Michigan and Atlanta, she and her husband, Dan Baum, opened a free-
lance news bureau in Zimbabwe, in an area of "substantial news
interest but few reporters." There they wrote from 1987–89 on a
variety of subjects, such as deforestation and illegal rhino hunting,

publishing their work internationally in newspapers, on radio, and in such environmental magazines as *Smithsonian, Sierra,* and *Nature Conservancy.*

Since 1990 the team, "each other's best—i.e. most severe—critics," has lived in Missoula, Montana, a good place to write amidst the environmental and social concerns on which Knox focuses. When *Buzzworm* (Western slang for "rattlesnake"), *The Environmental Journal,* asked her to combine a discussion of wildlife poaching and environmental destruction in Africa and the conflict between the timber industry and environmental preservationists in Montana, "I really tore my hair out over that article, it was so hard to do." Her successful blending of these complicated issues reveals, once again, that economic and environmental conflicts rage the world over; in the fate of one, animal, human, or nation, lies the fate of all.

Once upon a time, conservation was a gentleman's game. Over 1 stem-glasses of sherry and fat cigars, in the drawing rooms of Europe and New England, hunters and nature lovers lobbied for the preservation of Yellowstone National Park and claimed the vast Serengeti as a perpetual safari-land. They forged agreements, drafted laws and organized scientific expeditions. Their passions flowed eloquently through delicate quill pens. By and large, conservation work was a polite and decorous undertaking.

No more. As the globe shrinks and human populations explode, 2 conflicts over the last unpolluted, unpaved and untilled patches of soil are becoming ever more desperate and violent.

The conflicts aren't only between those who would leave nature 3 alone and those who would eat it, wear it, carve it or graze it. Even those who call themselves conservationists can't agree on the most fundamental questions: whether ranching is acceptable, whether hunting is appropriate, whether wildlife should be managed at all. People who have different ideas about how to protect nature are coming to blows. The language of preservation has become the language of war.

Fighting wars over scarce resources is not new: today, in a world 4 of five billion people, land is one of our scarcest. Most of us, when we think about it, would like to preserve vast tracts of pristine wilderness. Unfortunately, with so many people to feed, human needs for land often take precedence, especially in underdeveloped and developing countries. Overgrazing, deforestation and erosion result, tragically leaving ever less land for ever more people. People attack the earth with hoe and hoof and fire, and nature fights back with dust and flood and famine.

The warfare isn't just people fighting nature, but people fighting 5 people on behalf of nature. Helicopter-and-tommygun combat teams patrol through an African valley in search of poachers, and animal-rights activists physically assault hunters in Montana. Today's environmental crises push the conservation debate beyond the petition toward the tree spike. The rhetoric is heating up as well, to the point where even those who fundamentally share interests—loggers, say, and those who oppose rapacious, job-threatening clearcuts—are at each other's throats.

I am troubled. Part of me—my instinctively pacifist, consensus- 6 seeking side—recoils from seeing the movement to defend nature become shrill to the point of violence. But another voice tells me nature is in such peril that, to twist Barry Goldwater, extremism in defense of nature is no vice. And that scares me.

It is bad enough that the earth and its defenders are at war with 7 those who would rape it for profit. But even supposed allies, those fighting on the side of earth, are increasingly vicious with one another. Again and again conservation groups, each thinking it holds the franchise on ultimate wisdom, vilify and sabotage each other, fracturing the overall "environmental movement" and wasting precious energy that could better be spent working on the earth's behalf. The passions that have built up over the environment in the past few years give a sense of the magnitude of the crisis behind them.

The war between human and wildlife interests is being fought in 8 Zimbabwe with machine guns. The humans are by and large citizens of Zambia, which lies just north across the Zambezi River from Zimbabwe. If ever a people were economically desperate, it is the people of Zambia, whose monoproduct economy collapsed with copper prices in the 1970s and who have been driven to poverty so extreme that their *commercial export* farms have reverted to oxen. The Zambians are what we think of when we pity the destitution of the third world, enormously deserving of our sympathy.

Yet they are largely responsible for slaughtering the world's last 9 viable herd of black rhinoceros, which lives in the national park on Zimbabwe's side of the river. It's not that the Zambians are evil or vicious; they're hungry, and the proceeds from a single rhino horn can feed a family for months. What's more, the horns are easy to get. Rhino are curious and nearsighted, and it's a relatively simple matter to get close enough to drop one with a single shot. Once the animal is down, the horn—which isn't bone at all but rather densely packed hair—can be sheared off the nose in seconds with a knife and spirited across the river before daybreak.

To look at the rhino from the Zambians' perspective: here's an 10 animal walking around with thousands of dollars on its nose, an animal that doesn't do anybody any good anyway, except (again from the Zambians' perspective) as an attraction for rich tourists. Should Zambian families starve so tourists can take pictures of rhino?

Zimbabwe, which is relatively prosperous and can afford the "lux- 11 ury" of wilderness and wildlife, has moved many of the beasts out to the safety of game farms farther from the river. But ultimately President Robert Mugabe decided the rhino has a right to live where it lives and that it does Zimbabwe good to have wild rhino in the Zambezi Valley. In 1985 he ordered "Operation Stronghold," which is just as military as it sounds. Today, anyone found armed within the valley is considered a poacher and is shot on sight.

In the past five years, more than 60 poachers and at least one 12 scout of the Zimbabwe National Parks Department have been shot dead in firefights. "The poachers smear their bodies with juju (magic oils) to make themselves invisible," sighed Peter Matoka, when asked about it in his posh home in Zimbabwe's capital, Harare. Matoka, then Zambian High Commissioner to Zimbabwe, spent a good deal of his time repatriating the corpses of his countrymen killed in the rhino wars.

At first the Zambian parliament was outraged: Why should the 13 life of an animal take precedence over that of their people? Why was a misdemeanor like poaching being punished with death?

To answer that, you have to step back. We are in a crisis of ex- 14 tinctions. During the past 600 million years, the natural rate of extinction averaged one species a year. We now witness one to three extinctions every day. Scientists predict by the early 21st century we will be losing several hundred species a day. The rhino, a marvelously weird-looking beast, has become a symbol of the effort to slow the tide of extinctions. Its low-slung head, nose-mounted weaponry and armor of thick, nearly hairless, skin evolved 55 million years ago and is an exhilaratingly vivid link to prehistory. As many as 65,000 black rhino roamed the African bush in the early 1970s, but Middle Eastern and East Asian markets for rhino horn have whittled the species to about 600 wild beasts and their last remaining habitat to Zimbabwe's narrow and besieged Zambezi Valley.

After a few weeks of raucous protest on the part of his Parliament, 15 even Zambian President Kenneth Kaunda decided the Zimbabweans were right. Throughout Africa, every less extreme method of protecting the black rhino in its natural habitat has flopped. The Kenyans have resorted to electrified fences and round-the-clock guards to protect their last 200 black rhino. Even the Tanzanian government, which once forcibly moved several villages out of the path of a wildebeest migration, was unable to curb the rhino poaching.

The world pays lip service to its love of wildlife—at least the large, 16 spectacular mammals. But Asian pharmacists pay cash—astronomic prices for rhino horn to grind into medicine. Yemeni men lay out more than 1,000 [dollars] for a carved rhino-horn dagger.

Steve Edwards looks more like a green beret than a game warden. 17 At his Zambezi Valley base camp after a weekend patrol last year, his khaki chest was crisscrossed with web gear and his safari-vest pockets bulged with hand grenades. A battered automatic rifle was never far away. Edwards, a trained naturalist, wasn't in the mood to talk about the obsessive nesting habits of weaver birds or the water-retaining wonders of baobab trees. His thoughts ran to stalking human prey, ambushing the enemy and counting bodies—of rhino and Zambians. His stories balanced the gruesome details of rhino deaths against graphic accounts of victories over poaching gangs.

One hair-raising story sticks in my mind: An anti-poaching patrol 18 found a poachers' camp and planted a landmine under the fire ring. When the poachers returned and started a fire, the heat set off the mine. "We came back and found a biltong tree," chuckles Edwards. Biltong is beef jerky. Is this the modern environmentalist?

As a newcomer, it was difficult putting Edwards' fighting words 19 together with my Edenic surroundings. An orange sun was simmering into the river upstream from us. Two elephants splashed ashore on the bank nearby. Fireflies blinked. And we sat talking about triangulated gunfire, Claymore mines and the biltong tree. The wilderness has become an armed fortress.

Poaching, of course, isn't the only way human needs encroach 20 on the Zambezi Valley. There is a danger that this lush valley will be snatched out from under not only the rhino, but all its other wondrous inhabitants from the corn cricket to the elephant. The Zimbabwean government, continuously strapped for foreign exchange, last year gave Mobil Corp. exploration rights throughout the valley—including a national park and United Nations-designed World Heritage Site. On the other side of the country, Zimbabwe has thrown up a ten-foot storm fence at the Botswana border to keep wildebeest from spreading hoof-and-mouth disease to cattle. At the end of every drought, news photos show parched wildebeest dying against the fence just yards from a Zimbabwean water hole.

Wildlife and domestic livestock have hurled diseases back and 21 forth like spears since rinderpest brought by Indian cattle in the 1890s nearly wiped out the wildebeest. If hoof-and-mouth works against wildlife, another pest works in favor of the Zambezi Valley. When some Zimbabwe government officials see the Zambezi Valley, they see potential grazing land for thousands of families. Land-poor cattle grazers also are pressing their noses against these public lands. Their pleas for more range can't be ignored by a government whose revolutionary slogan 10 years ago was "Land for the People."

Right now, all that is preventing the human and bovine invasion 22 of the Zambezi Valley is the native tsetse fly, which is no trouble to thick-skinned wildlife, but whose diseased bite wreaks havoc on domestic livestock. The government is paradoxically willing to kill poachers in the valley but also experiments with tsetse fly traps to open it someday to grazing. So far, conservationists have managed to halt a full scale tsetse fly eradication program at the lip of the valley. But whenever Edwards finds traps, he destroys them for the same reason he hunts poachers—to preserve the Zambezi wilderness. "We can kill people all day long," he grins, "but the only thing that's really going to save this valley is the tsetse fly."

The Zimbabwean anti-poaching campaign may seem a far-off, dire 23 measure of a desperate third-world government. But human pressures on American wildlands are growing, too. And with it grows the intensity of rhetoric and action on nature's behalf. The pressures here come not from hungry peasants but from corporations promising people jobs, food and a fast fix for foreign debt.

Already, nearly three-quarters of our nation's forests are in pri- 24 vate hands; only 5 percent of native virgin forests remain. About 80 percent of all public lands in the west, including wilderness areas and national monuments, are leased for grazing. And while some conservationists continue ponderous legal efforts to protect these lands, others have lost patience. They see their cause—biological diversity for the long-term benefit of the earth—as too urgent and complex for easy persuasion.

In the name of the spotted owl, they have resorted to tree spiking 25 in the old-growth forests of the Northwest. In the name of streambanks, they have sabotaged ranch equipment in Nevada. Their violence—for there is no other word—is a double-edged sword. A tree spiking or a destructive protest makes the evening news in a way a march or a speech to the legislature doesn't. Issues that might otherwise be ignored by the media are thrust before the public for scrutiny. But as in Zimbabwe, the violence can repel people who might otherwise be sympathetic. The protests of Kenneth Kaunda's government to the shooting of Zambians sounded piteously feeble beside the uproar over eco-sabotage in this country. I got a fast lesson in the dangers of eco-polarization the night I first arrived in Montana.

My husband and I had stopped for the night at the Rocky Knob 26 Inn, a rustic logger's bar and motel far down the Bitterroot Valley at the bottom of Lost Trail Pass. It was snowy, and dark, and both of us were exhausted from wrestling our heavily-laden truck through the pass. We wanted only to have a quick dinner and go to bed.

At the bar stood a Central-Casting logger: six-foot-five and broad   27 as an old-growth redwood, he had a drooping mustache, sweat-stained Stetson and a red bandana around his neck. His voice was rough and his hands rougher: a toothpick danced at the corner of his mouth as he talked. He must have given us his name, but I remember him only as "Hoss," a cheerful, generous ambassador of Montanan goodwill.

We told him we were on our way to a new home in Missoula,   28 and he asked what brought us. I'm an environment writer, I told him, a mistake I won't make again.

"Environmentalist?" he snarled, his friendliness shattering at   29 once. "You a flower-sniffer? You a *tree*-spiker?" For him, environmentalist means tree-spiker, end of story.

And he isn't the only one. Throughout western Montana signs   30 are posted on houses and stores and bumpers: We Support the Timber Industry. Or, even more tragically, This Family Supported by Timber Dollars. To those families, anyone who questions the wisdom of clearcutting our national forests is a "flower-sniffer" or a "tree-spiker."

Yet if anyone should be making common cause with the "flower-   31 sniffers" who oppose clearcutting, it is the families who are supported by timber dollars. If the logging continues at its present pace, there won't be any timber dollars in Montana in a generation because there won't be any timber. The timber debate in Montana has grown too hot for its own good. Too much shouting is being done, and too much name calling. Tree spikes *have* saved stands of old-growth forest, and they *have* thrown the media spotlight on the rape of our forests. But they carry a price that the conservation community must consider, just as those dead Zambian poachers do.

In March, an incident of eco-sabotage both amplified and clouded   32 a complicated tug of war between natural and human imperatives. The setting was Hebgen Lake, just outside Yellowstone Park.

Within the park, the National Park Service can claim credit for   33 one of the century's great conservation victories: saving the bison. Only 500 remained after the carnage of the late 1800s; today more than 2,000 roam the park. So successful has the Park Service been that the herd regularly overflows Yellowstone. Through forests, down highways and along old railbeds, the shaggy humpbacked matriarchs annually lead their herds across the park's artificial boundary and toward an easier life on ancient grazing grounds claimed by cattle ranchers, the ground on which humans and nature today are clashing.

More than half of Yellowstone's bison are infected with a disease 34
called brucellosis, which causes abortions in cattle and a raging fever
in people who drink unpasteurized milk. Though it hasn't been con-
clusively proven, it is likely the bison can easily pass the disease to
their domesticated cousins. So as Montana ranchers—who have spent
more than $30 million ridding their herds of brucellosis—watch the
bison pouring out of the park, the human-versus-wilderness debate
stokes up as hot as in southern Africa.

The U.S. Department of Agriculture, whose mission is to protect 35
agricultural, not wildlife, interests, would like to inoculate the Yellowstone bison and sacrifice the park's essential wild nature to protect
the ranchers. The Park Service so far has refused, saying the bison
aren't a problem *inside* the park but only *outside*. Therefore, the Park
Service's reasoning goes, they should be dealt with outside the park.
Montana agreed to do just that, passing a law five years ago that
allows lottery-picked hunters to shoot the bison as they cross the line.

This year, enraged Earth First! and Fund for Animals protestors 36
tried to disrupt a hunt on Montana's Hebgen Lake, and by the time
it was over two of them were up on assault and other charges for
lashing one hunter with a ski pole and smearing bison blood on the
face of another. The newspapers and TV news had a field day.

The outcome: Montana's hunters have been conditioned to think 37
of anyone opposed to the bison shoot as a pole-wielding, blood-
smearing extremist. Those opposed to the hunt are confirmed in
considering the ranchers greedy spoilsports willing to contract-mur-
der defenseless bison. And almost everybody has one beef or another
with the state fish and wildlife department, the USDA or the Park
Service. Once again, anti-wilderness politicians such as Republican
Representative Ron Marlenee of Montana are trying to capitalize on
the public's image of "environmentalists" as a small bunch of shriek-
ing loonies. This time, the "flower sniffers" committed an unpardon-
able sin: They wrecked a good day's hunting for some red-blooded
Montanans.

In some ways, the real issue—what is the best way to balance 38
the interests of the bison and the ranchers—was lost amid the shouting. A rational solution seems further off than ever.

On the other hand, without such a dramatic, telegenic protest, 39
the public's interest might not have been aroused. Nobody will ever
shoot a bison in Montana again without raising public debate about
the wisdom of the hunt policy.

The new wave of high passions and dramatic acts has been un- 40
deniably useful in bringing our environmental crisis to the public eye
and holding it there. It's also clear now that militant actions should

be carefully chosen. Hot words and bursts of violence not only alienate the conservation community from those it would like to recruit, they also can fracture the community itself. If the rhino campaign in Zimbabwe falls apart, it won't be because the rest of the world objects to it. It will be because the agencies running it can't agree to get along with one another.

Nine rhino fell to poacher's guns over the Christmas holiday in 41 1988 when the anti-poaching campaign was effectively shut down by a turf war between the Zimbabwe national police and the parks department, both of which are ostensibly on the same side. The leader of the parks department's anti-poaching campaign and two of his men killed a poacher, who turned out to be the nephew of an important district official. The police, long bitter over their second-fiddle role in the anti-poaching campaign, seized the chance to arrest the parks men, and the anti-poaching war slid into a week of inaction. The charges against the parks men were finally dropped, but not before nine precious and unguarded rhino—1.5 percent of the total herd—were killed by poachers.

Perhaps no conservation organization has been as committed to 42 protecting endangered species as the Worldwide Fund for Nature, formerly the World Wildlife Fund. It provided the Zimbabwe rhino campaign's only helicopter, which the game wardens considered absolutely essential in the vast tangle of the Zambezi Valley. Yet in May 1989, the group yanked its funding for the chopper because it wasn't pleased with the Zimbabwe government's paperwork.

"The parks directorate is too bloody disorganized," said the 43 fund's ecologist Raoul du Toit. "The helicopter was a holding action until the agency could come up with a long-term approach."

At the present rate of poaching, the rhino population was barely 44 holding its own and the conservation group wanted the government to consider concentrating its meager forces on the densest herd. The government, bent on protecting the whole valley, never found time to plan alternative strategies. "It's such a shame," commented Dick Pitman of the Zambezi Valley Society, a conservation group. "We're losing the helicopter to what appears to be a personality conflict."

Although the hunting controversy in the United States can't quite 45 be described as a personality conflict, it does hinge on deeply personal moral issues not directly related to the cause of biodiversity and the survival of species. The hunting community can call up volumes of statistics on species they have helped save and land they have protected from development. Hunters were among the most vociferous advocates for setting aside Yellowstone in 1872. And though rapacious hide-hunters had by then nearly wiped out the bison, it was another hunter, Blackfoot Indian Walking Coyote, who saved the little herd that grew into today's Yellowstone bison.

But here, as in Zimbabwe, people who profess the same allegiance 46 to wilderness shriek at each other. To read pamphlets from hunting and anti-hunting lobbies is to read almost the exact same words. "We now know that the web of life is of enormous importance to our own existence and that there is an urgent need to preserve what is left of the natural world," says the anti-hunting group Friends of Animals.

"Wildlife conservation will not take care of itself. The daily loss 47 of habitat is still a constant threat," says the hunting advocacy group Wildlife Legislative Fund of America. Both sides decry the loss of natural habitat. Both sides profess an almost religious veneration and respect for wildlife. Both sides lobby hard to protect wildlands from development.

Yet with so much in common, the hunting and anti-hunting lob- 48 bies have deionized each other to the point where the differences in their philosophies, not their similarities, get all the attention, such as in a recent cover story on the hunting controversy in *U.S. News and World Report*. "These bloodthirsty nuts claim they provide a service for the environment. Nonsense!" Cleveland Amory of the New York-based Fund for Animals told *U.S. News*.

"The anti-hunters are invariably long on name calling and short 49 on scientifically based suggestions for solving complex wildlife conservation problems," countered George Reiger, conservation editor of the hunting and fishing magazine, *Field and Stream*. Hunters point to the Pitman-Robertson Act, which established an excise tax on guns in 1937 when frantic burning, draining, plowing and grazing were fast shrinking the habitats of birds and mammals. The tax has poured nearly $2 billion into training state fish and wildlife experts, counting animal populations and setting aside habitat. Some animals have their own fan clubs, private hunters' groups such as Ducks Unlimited and the Elk Foundation which donate millions to protect their chosen prey. Above all, hunters say their sport keeps thousands of people in touch with nature.

Dan Jacobs talks lovingly of the Montana back-country he hunts 50 and fishes, and of the sports he practices. Jacobs, a 39-year-old air-ambulance nurse, hand-loads his own bullets. He target shoots to keep up his skill—says he gave up bow hunting after badly wounding a bear and having to shoot it with a pistol. As much as anyone, he loathes the sight of careless, insensitive and drunken hunters who wound and lose animals. Jacobs earns his living, after all, relieving pain.

When Jacobs set out with two other hunters to kill a bison at 51
Hebgen Lake in March, he was wearing a t-shirt emblazoned "Keep
Montana Wild." To hear him talk about his role, he honestly thought
he was doing the beasts a favor. Hunting, to Jacobs, fills an important
ecological niche. "They starve up there," said Jacobs. "That's the
alternative."

Lee Dessaux was so enraged when Jacobs dropped a half-ton cow 52
bison, he whacked him again and again with a ski pole, then jabbed
Jacobs in the shoulder with its tip. "Compared to what happened to
the buffalo, pokin' that guy in the ribs was nothing," Dessaux, a 25-
year-old Earth First!er, said afterwards. "I think passionate expression
is quite appropriate in light of what happened."

Never mind Jacobs' t-shirt and eloquent waxing over the beauties 53
of wildlife. Hunters, to Dessaux, are just people who like to kill things.
And he isn't alone. According to one Yale University study, a third
of all Americans favors a total ban on hunting, and more than half
think hunting for sport and trophies is wrong. Anti-hunters and hunters don't yet go at it with nearly the ferocity or firepower of Zimbabwean game wardens and poachers. But officials in a wildlife refuge
in Connecticut recently canceled a hunt after an angry sportsman
loosed a load of birdshot toward a crowd of demonstrators.

Again, it's hard not to wish that the hunting and anti-hunting 54
camps—both of which have demonstrated their love of wildlife and
habitat—would advance their dialogue beyond the clamor of moral
outrage and consider the similarities of their positions. A lot of good
pro-environment energy is being spent backbiting within the broad
population of nature-lovers, while wetlands are draining, rainforests
are burning, auto-emissions standards are being relaxed and the atmosphere heats up.

It's unclear to me what was accomplished at Hebgen Lake. But 55
it's clear that the era that swelled Earth First!'s impatient membership
to 10,000 has been one of unparalleled greed in the United States and
unprecedented environmental degradation worldwide. When the
frockcoated conservationists of the past century were maneuvering
the first national parks through Congress, the South Pole hadn't even
been visited, much less an ozone hole discovered above it. The world's
population has tripled in the past century and industrial production
has grown fifty-fold. The desperation of Zambian peasants, the equal
desperation of the effort to save the rhino and the audacity of American eco-militants only reflect the level of crisis into which we have
plunged our earth. If we're surprised at how violent the struggle to
share and save the earth has become, we'd best remember: Tempers
rise with the stakes.

RESPONDING TO READING

Key words: animals class loss nature power rights
striving symbols transformation

Rhetorical concepts: analogy analysis anecdote cause and effect
comparison and contrast illustration meditation narrative/example
process

1.   Write an essay on the comparison/contrast given in the title. What is the
"daze" in the Zambian-Zimbabwe conflict? Who are the "knights" in Montana? What is implied by the days-nights pun? What do the African and
Montanan conflicts have in common? Are there important differences?
2.   Notice the series of arguments in defense of the earth that different groups
give (for example, the hunters vs. those opposed to hunting). Which of these
arguments do you find the most compelling? The least convincing? Why do
you think that there is such hostility between groups whose goals are apparently the same?
3.   Compare the approach Knox takes to her subject with that taken by the
other authors in this section. For example, do you see her as more or less
detached than Carson or Warner? McPhee uses much irony in his essay and
renders few judgments; how does his approach compare with that of Knox?
Select key sentences from the four essays and show how the authors' points
of view are made clear.
4.   Select an environmental issue that is important in your locality. Perhaps
you live, or go to school, near a nuclear power plant, or an endangered
wetland, or a threatened wildlife habitat; maybe there are pollution problems
with the water or the air. Describe the problem, using personal stories and
details, and examine the arguments of people who have attempted to deal
with the issue. Then, using what you know from the past, propose a solution
that might work.

Civil Disobedience

HENRY DAVID THOREAU

Henry David Thoreau (1817–1862), essayist, poet, and diarist, spent his life in Concord, Massachusetts. He graduated from Harvard in 1837, and thereafter worked at odd jobs while doing his real work as an original thinker. As a Transcendentalist, strongly influenced by the works of Kant, Coleridge, and Goethe, he believed that a certain kind of intuitive knowledge transcended the limits of human experience and the senses; for Thoreau, ideas and the natural world were more important and more powerful than material things. These views are reflected in his major works, *A Week on the Concord and Merrimack Rivers* (1849) and *Walden, or Life in the Woods* (1854), a record of the two years he spent at Walden Pond, in Concord. There he lived alone in a house he made and became the model of self-reliance, growing his own food, chopping his own wood, and living frugally while feasting on the bounty of nature and the cosmos.

But this self-reliance was not a means of separating himself from the pressing issues of his day; quite the reverse. As he makes clear in "Civil Disobedience," a democratic society that allows for freedom of expression embeds in that freedom the possibility of civil disobedience. He provided both inspiration and a theoretical rationale for the nonviolent protests of Gandhi in his quest to secure India's independence from British control and for the desegregation efforts of Pauli Murray and Martin Luther King, Jr.

From 1845 to 1848 the United States fought Mexico to secure annexation of Texas, a move intended to increase slave territory. Thoreau, an Abolitionist in a state where Abolitionists were harboring fugitive slaves and helping them to resettle, was profoundly committed to the position he articulates in "Civil Disobedience." He believed that any man more right than his neighbors is already a majority of one; God is a sufficient ally.

As a protest against the war, in July 1846, Thoreau refused to pay the Massachusetts poll tax, a per capita levy intended to raise money for the war, and he was jailed as a consequence. Although he spent only one night in jail, the experience moved him to examine its implications and to conclude that "Under a government which imprisons any unjustly, the true place for a just man is also a prison."

I heartily accept the motto, "That government is best which governs least;" and I should like to see it acted up to more rapidly and systematically. Carried out, it finally amounts to this, which also I believe—"That government is best which governs not at all;" and when men are prepared for it, that will be the kind of government which they will have. Government is at best but an expedient; but most governments are usually, and all governments are sometimes, inexpedient. The objections which have been brought against a standing army, and they are many and weighty, and deserve to prevail, may also at last be brought against a standing government. The standing army is only an arm of the standing government. The government itself, which is only the mode which the people have chosen to execute their will, is equally liable to be abused and perverted before the people can act through it. Witness the present Mexican war, the work of comparatively a few individuals using the standing government as their tool; for, in the outset, the people would not have consented to this measure.

This American government—what is it but a tradition, though a 2 recent one, endeavoring to transmit itself unimpaired to posterity, but each instant losing some of its integrity? It has not the vitality and force of a single living man; for a single man can bend it to his will. It is a sort of wooden gun to the people themselves. But it is not the less necessary for this; for the people must have some complicated machinery or other, and hear its din, to satisfy that idea of government which they have. Governments show thus how successfully men can be imposed on, even impose on themselves, for their own advantage. It is excellent, we must all allow. Yet this government never of itself furthered any enterprise, but by the alacrity with which it got out of its way. *It* does not keep the country free. *It* does not settle the West. *It* does not educate. The character inherent in the American people has done all that has been accomplished; and it would have done somewhat more, if the government had not sometimes got in its way. For government is an expedient by which men would fain succeed in letting one another alone; and, as has been said, when it is most expedient, the governed are most let alone by it. Trade and commerce, if they were not made of india-rubber, would never manage to bounce over the obstacles which legislators are continually putting in their way; and, if one were to judge these men wholly by the effects of their actions and not partly by their intentions, they would deserve to be classed and punished with those mischievous persons who put obstructions on the railroads.

But, to speak practically and as a citizen, unlike those who call 3 themselves no-government men, I ask for, not at once no government, but *at once* a better government. Let every man make known what kind of government would command his respect, and that will be one step toward obtaining it.

After all, the practical reason why, when the power is once in the 4 hands of the people, a majority are permitted, and for a long period continue, to rule is not because they are most likely to be in the right, nor because this seems fairest to the minority, but because they are physically the strongest. But a government in which the majority rule in all cases cannot be based on justice, even as far as men understand it. Can there not be a government in which majorities do not virtually decide right and wrong, but conscience?—in which majorities decide only those questions to which the rule of expediency is applicable? Must the citizen ever for a moment, or in the least degree, resign his conscience to the legislator? Why has every man a conscience, then? I think that we should be men first, and subjects afterwards. It is not desirable to cultivate a respect for the law, so much as for the right. The only obligation which I have a right to assume is to do at any time what I think right. It is truly enough said that a corporation has no conscience; but a corporation of conscientious men is a corporation *with* a conscience. Law never made men a whit more just; and, by means of their respect for it, even the well-disposed are daily made the agents of injustice. A common and natural result of an undue respect for law is, that you may see a file of soldiers, colonel, captain, corporal, privates, powder-monkeys, and all, marching in admirable order over hill and dale to the wars, against their wills, ay, against their common sense and consciences, which makes it very steep marching indeed, and produces a palpitation of the heart. They have no doubt that it is a damnable business in which they are concerned; they are all peaceably inclined. Now, what are they? Men at all? or small movable forts and magazines, at the service of some unscrupulous man in power? Visit the Navy-Yard, and behold a marine, such a man as an American government can make, or such as it can make a man with its black arts—a mere shadow and reminiscence of humanity, a man laid out alive and standing, and already, as one may say, buried under arms with funeral accompaniments, though it may be,—

> Not a drum was heard, not a funeral note,
>   As his corse to the rampart we hurried;
> Not a soldier discharged his farewell shot
>   O'er the grave where our hero was buried.[1]

The mass of men serve the state thus, not as men mainly, but as machines, with their bodies. They are the standing army, and the militia, jailers, constables, *posse comitatus,* etc. In most cases there is no free exercise whatever of the judgment or of the moral sense; but they put themselves on a level with wood and earth and stones; and

[1]Charles Wolfe, "Burial of Sir John Moore at Corunna" (1817). [Eds.]

wooden men can perhaps be manufactured that will serve the purpose as well. Such command no more respect than men of straw or a lump of dirt. They have the same sort of worth only as horses and dogs. Yet such as these even are commonly esteemed good citizens. Others—as most legislators, politicians, lawyers, ministers, and office-holders—serve the state chiefly with their heads; and, as they rarely make any moral distinctions, they are as likely to serve the devil, without *intending* it, as God. A very few—as heroes, patriots, martyrs, reformers in the great sense, and *men*—serve the state with their consciences also, and so necessarily resist it for the most part; and they are commonly treated as enemies by it. A wise man will only be useful as a man, and they will submit to be "clay," and "stop a hole to keep the wind away,"[2] but leave that office to his dust at least:—

> I am too high-born to be propertied,
> To be a secondary at control,
> Or useful serving-man and instrument
> To any sovereign state throughout the world.[3]

He who gives himself entirely to his fellow-men appears to them 6
useless and selfish; but he who gives himself partially to them is pronounced a benefactor and philanthropist.

How does it become a man to behave toward this American gov- 7
ernment today? I answer, that he cannot without disgrace be asso-ciated with it. I cannot for an instant recognize that political organi-zation as *my* government which is the *slave's* government also.

All men recognize the right of revolution; that is, the right to 8
refuse allegiance to, and to resist, the government, when its tyranny or its inefficiency are great and unendurable. But almost all say that such is not the case now. But such was the case, they think, in the Revolution of '75. If one were to tell me that his was a bad government because it taxed certain foreign commodities brought to its ports, it is most probable that I should not make an ado about it, for I can do without them. All machines have their friction; and possibly this does enough good to counter-balance the evil. At any rate, it is a great evil to make a stir about it. But when the friction comes to have its machine, and oppression and robbery are organized, I say, let us not have such a machine any longer. In other words, when a sixth of the population of a nation which has undertaken to be the refuge of liberty are slaves, and a whole country is unjustly overrun and conquered by a foreign

---

[2]*Hamlet*, V, i, II, 236–237. [Eds.]
[3]*King John*, V, ii, II, 79–82. [Eds.]

army, and subjected to military law, I think that it is not too soon for honest men to rebel and revolutionize. What makes this duty the more urgent is the fact that the country so overrun is not our own, but ours is the invading army.

Paley,[4] a common authority with many on moral questions, in his ⁹ chapter on the "Duty of Submission to Civil Government," resolves all civil obligation into expediency; and he proceeds to say that "so long as the interest of the whole society requires it, that is, so long as the established government cannot be resisted or changed without public inconveniency, it is the will of God . . . that the established government be obeyed—and no longer. This principle being admitted, the justice of every particular case of resistance is reduced to a computation of the quantity of the danger and grievance on the one side, and of the probability and expense of redressing it on the other." Of this, he says, every man shall judge for himself. But Paley appears never to have contemplated those cases to which the rule of expediency does not apply, in which a people, as well as an individual, must do justice, cost what it may. If I have unjustly wrested a plank from a drowning man, I must restore it to him though I drown myself.[5] This, according to Paley, would be inconvenient. But he that would save his life, in such a case, shall lose it.[6] This people must cease to hold slaves, and to make war on Mexico, though it cost them their existence as a people.

In their practice, nations agree with Paley; but does any one think ¹⁰ that Massachusetts does exactly what is right at the present crisis?

> A drab of state, a cloth-o'-silver slut,
> To have her train borne up, and her soul trail in the dirt.

Practically speaking, the opponents to a reform in Massachusetts are not a hundred thousand politicians at the South, but a hundred thousand merchants and farmers here, who are more interested in commerce and agriculture than they are in humanity, and are not prepared to do justice to the slave and to Mexico, *cost what it may.* I quarrel not with far-off foes, but with those who, near at home, coöperate with, and do the bidding of, those far away, and without whom the latter would be harmless. We are accustomed to say, that the mass of men are unprepared; but improvement is slow, because the few are not materially wiser or better than the many. It is not so important that

---

[4]Rev. William Paley, *Principles of Moral and Political Philosophy* (1785). [Eds.]

[5]Cited by Cicero, *De Officiis*, III. [Eds.]

[6]Luke IX: 24; Matthew X: 39. [Eds.]

many should be as good as you, as that there be some absolute goodness somewhere; for that will leaven the whole lump.[7] There are
thousands who are *in opinion* opposed to slavery and to the war, who
yet in effect do nothing to put an end to them; who, esteeming themselves children of Washington and Franklin, sit down with their hands
in their pockets, and say that they know not what to do, and do
nothing; who even postpone the question of freedom to the question
of free trade, and quietly read the prices-current along with the latest
advices from Mexico, after dinner, and, it may be, fall asleep over
them both. What is the price-current of an honest man and patriot
today? They hesitate, and they regret, and sometimes they petition;
but they do nothing in earnest and with effect. They will wait, well
disposed, for others to remedy the evil, that they may no longer have
it to regret. At most, they give only a cheap vote, and a feeble countenance and God-speed, to the right, as it goes by them. There are
nine hundred and ninety-nine patrons of virtue to one virtuous man.
But it is easier to deal with the real possessor of a thing than with
the temporary guardian of it.

All voting is a sort of gaming, like checkers or backgammon, with 11
a slight moral tinge to it, a playing with right and wrong, with moral
questions; and betting naturally accompanies it. The character of the
voters is not staked. I cast my vote, perchance, as I think right; but I
am not vitally concerned that that right should prevail. I am willing
to leave it to the majority. Its obligation, therefore, never exceeds that
of expediency. Even voting *for the right* is *doing* nothing for it. It is
only expressing to men feebly your desire that it should prevail. A
wise man will not leave the right to the mercy of chance, nor wish it
to prevail through the power of the majority. There is but little virtue
in the action of masses of men. When the majority shall at length
vote for the abolition of slavery, it will be because they are indifferent
to slavery, or because there is but little slavery left to be abolished by
their vote. *They* will then be the only slaves. Only *his* vote can hasten
the abolition of slavery who asserts his own freedom by his vote.

I hear of a convention to be held at Baltimore, or elsewhere, for 12
the selection of a candidate for the Presidency, made up chiefly of
editors, and men who are politicians by profession; but I think, what
is it to any independent, intelligent, and respectable man what decision they may come to? Shall we not have the advantage of his
wisdom and honesty, nevertheless? Can we not count upon some
independent votes? Are there not many individuals in the country
who do not attend conventions? But no: I find that the respectable

---

[7] I Corinthians V: 6. [Eds.]

man, so called, has immediately drifted from his position, and de-
spairs of his country, when his country has more reason to despair
of him. He forthwith adopts one of the candidates thus selected as
the only *available* one, thus proving that he is himself *available* for any
purposes of the demagogue. His vote is of no more worth than that
of any unprincipled foreigner or hireling native, who may have been
bought. O for a man who is a *man*, and, as my neighbor says, has a
bone in his back which you cannot pass your hand through! Our
statistics are at fault: the population has been returned too large. How
many *men* are there to a square thousand miles in this country? Hardly
one. Does not America offer any inducement for men to settle her?
The American has dwindled into an Odd Fellow—one who may be
known by the development of his organ of gregariousness, and a
manifest lack of intellect and cheerful self-reliance; whose first and
chief concern, on coming into the world, is to see that the almshouses
are in good repair; and, before yet he has lawfully donned the virile
garb, to collect a fund for the support of the windows and orphans
that may be; who, in short, ventures to live only by the aid of the
Mutual Insurance company, which has promised to bury him de-
cently.

It is not a man's duty, as a matter of course, to devote himself to 13
the eradication of any, even the most enormous, wrong; he may still
properly have other concerns to engage him; but it is his duty, at
least, to wash his hands of it and, if he gives it no thought longer,
not to give it practically his support. If I devote myself to other pursuits
and contemplations, I must first see, at least, that I do not pursue
them sitting upon another man's shoulders. I must get off him first,
that he may pursue his contemplations too. See what gross inconsis-
tency is tolerated. I have heard some of my townsmen say, "I should
like to have them order me out to help put down an insurrection of
the slaves, or to march to Mexico;—see if I would go"; and yet these
very men have each, directly by their allegiance, and so indirectly, at
least, by their money, furnished a substitute. The soldier is applauded
who refuses to serve in an unjust war by those who do not refuse to
sustain the unjust government which makes the war; is applauded
by those whose own act and authority he disregards and sets at
naught; as if the state were penitent to that degree that it hired one
to scourge it while it sinned, but not to that degree that it left off
sinning for a moment. Thus, under the name of Order and Civil
Government, we are all made at last to pay homage to and support
our own meanness. After the first blush of sin comes its indifference;
and from immoral it becomes, as it were, *un*moral, and not quite
unnecessary to that life which we have made.

The broadest and most prevalent error requires the most disin- 14 terested virtue to sustain it. The slight reproach to which the virtue of patriotism is commonly liable, the noble are most likely to incur. Those who, while they disapprove of the character and measures of a government, yield to it their allegiance and support are undoubtedly its most conscientious supporters, and so frequently the most serious obstacles to reform. Some are petitioning the State to dissolve the Union, to disregard the requisitions of the President. Why do they not dissolve it themselves—the union between themselves and the State—and refuse to pay their quota into its treasury? Do not they stand in the same relation to the State that the State does to the Union? And have not the same reasons prevented the State from resisting the Union which have prevented them from resisting the State?

How can a man be satisfied to entertain an opinion merely, and 15 enjoy *it*? Is there any enjoyment in it, if his opinion is that he is aggrieved? If you are cheated out of a single dollar by your neighbor, you do not rest satisfied with knowing that you are cheated, or with saying that you are cheated, or even with petitioning him to pay you your due; but you take effectual steps at once to obtain the full amount, and see that you are never cheated again. Action from principle, the perception and the performance of right, changes things and relations; it is essentially revolutionary, and does not consist wholly with anything which was. It not only divides States and churches, it divides families; ay, it divides the *individual*, separating the diabolical in him from the divine.

Unjust laws exist: shall we be content to obey them, or shall we 16 endeavor to amend them, and obey them until we have succeeded, or shall we transgress them at once? Men generally, under such a government as this, think that they ought to wait until they have persuaded the majority to alter them. They think that, if they should resist, the remedy would be worse than the evil. But it is the fault of the government itself that the remedy *is* worse than the evil. *It* makes it worse. Why is it not more apt to anticipate and provide for reform? Why does it not cherish its wise minority? Why does it cry and resist before it is hurt? Why does it not encourage its citizens to be on the alert to point out its faults, and *do* better than it would have them? Why does it always crucify Christ, and excommunicate Copernicus and Luther, and pronounce Washington and Franklin rebels?

One would think that a deliberate and practical denial of its au- 17 thority was the only offence never contemplated by a government; else, why has it not assigned its definite, its suitable and proportionate, penalty? If a man who has no property refuses but once to earn nine shillings for the State, he is put in prison for a period unlimited by any law that I know, and determined only by the discretion of those who placed him there; but if he should steal ninety times nine shillings from the State, he is soon permitted to go at large again.

If the injustice is part of the necessary friction of the machine of 18 government, let it go, let it go: perchance it will wear smooth—certainly the machine will wear out. If the injustice has a spring, or a pulley, or a rope, or a crank, exclusively for itself, then perhaps you may consider whether the remedy will not be worse than the evil; but if it is of such a nature that it requires you to be the agent of injustice to another, then, I say, break the law. Let your life be a counter friction to stop the machine. What I have to do is to see, at any rate, that I do not lend myself to the wrong which I condemn.

As for adopting the ways which the State has provided for reme- 19 dying the evil, I know not of such ways. They take too much time, and a man's life will be gone. I have other affairs to attend to. I came into this world, not chiefly to make this a good place to live in, but to live in it, be it good or bad. A man has not everything to do, but something; and because he cannot do *everything*, it is not necessary that he should do *something* wrong. It is not my business to be petitioning the Governor or the Legislature any more than it is theirs to petition me; and if they should not hear my petition, what should I do then? But in this case the State has provided no way: its very Constitution is the evil. This may seem to be harsh and stubborn and unconciliatory; but it is to treat with the utmost kindness and consideration the only spirit that can appreciate or deserves it. So is all change for the better, like birth and death, which convulse the body.

I do not hesitate to say, that those who call themselves Aboli- 20 tionists should at once effectually withdraw their support, both in person and property, from the government of Massachusetts, and not wait till they constitute a majority of one, before they suffer the right to prevail through them. I think that it is enough if they have God on their side, without waiting for that other one. Moreover, any man more right than his neighbors constitutes a majority of one already.

I meet the American government, or its representative, the State 21 government, directly, and face to face, once a year—no more—in the person of its tax-gatherer; this is the only mode in which a man situated as I am necessarily meets it; and it then says distinctly, Recognize me; and the simplest, the most effectual, and, in the present posture of affairs, the indispensablest mode of treating with it on this head, of expressing your little satisfaction with and love for it, is to deny it then. My civil neighbor, the tax-gatherer, is the very man I have to deal with—for it is, after all, with men and not with parchment that I quarrel—and he has voluntarily chosen to be an agent of the government. How shall he ever know well what he is and does as an officer of the government, or as a man, until he is obliged to consider whether he shall treat me, his neighbor, for whom he has respect, as a neighbor and well-disposed man, or as a maniac and disturber of the peace, and see if he can get over this obstruction to his neighborliness without a ruder and more impetuous thought or speech corresponding with his action. I know this well, that if one thousand, if one hundred, if ten men whom I could name—if ten *honest* men only—ay, if *one* HONEST man in this State of Massachusetts, *ceasing to hold slaves*, were actually to withdraw from this copartnership, and be locked up in the county jail therefor, it would be the abolition of slavery in America. For it matters not how small the beginning may seem to be: what is once well done is done forever. But we love better to talk about it: that we say is our mission. Reform keeps many scores of newspapers in its service, but not one man. If my esteemed neighbor, the State's ambassador,[8] who will devote his days to the settlement of the question of human rights in the Council Chamber, instead of being threatened with the prisons of Carolina, were to sit down the prisoner of Massachusetts, that State which is so anxious to foist the sin of slavery upon her sister—though at present she can discover only an act of inhospitality to be the ground of a quarrel with her— the Legislature would not wholly waive the subject the following winter.

Under a government which imprisons any unjustly, the true place 22 for a just man is also a prison. The proper place to-day, the only place which Massachusetts has provided for her freer and less desponding spirits, is in her prisons, to be put out and locked out of the State by her own act, as they have already put themselves out by their principles. It is there that the fugitive slave, and the Mexican prisoner on parole, and the Indian come to plead the wrongs of his race should find them; on that separate, but more free and honorable, ground, where the State places those who are not *with* her, but *against* her— the only house in a slave State in which a free man can abide with honor. If any think that their influence would be lost there, and their voices no longer afflict the ear of the State, that they would not be as an enemy within its walls, they do not know by how much truth is stronger than error, nor how much more eloquently and effectively he can combat injustice who has experienced a little in his own person. Cast your whole vote, not a strip of paper merely, but your whole influence. A minority is powerless while it conforms to the majority; it is not even a minority then; but it is irresistible when it clogs by its whole weight. If the alternative is to keep all just men in prison, or give up war and slavery, the State will not hesitate which to choose. If a thousand men were not to pay their tax-bills this year, that would

---

[8]Samuel Hoar, Concord statesman, was expelled from Charleston, South Carolina where he was sent on behalf of Massachusetts black seamen in 1844. [Eds.]

not be a violent and bloody measure, as it would be to pay them, and enable the State to commit violence and shed innocent blood. This is, in fact, the definition of a peaceable revolution, if any such is possible. If the tax-gatherer, or any public officer, asks me, as one has done, "But what shall I do?" my answer is, "If you really wish to do anything, resign your office." When the subject has refused allegiance, and the officer has resigned his office, then the revolution is accomplished. But even suppose blood should flow. Is there not a sort of blood shed when the conscience is wounded? Through this wound a man's real manhood and immortality flow out, and he bleeds to an everlasting death. I see this blood flowing now.

I have contemplated the imprisonment of the offender, rather than 23 the seizure of his goods—though both will serve the same purpose— because they who assert the purest right, and consequently are most dangerous to a corrupt State, commonly have not spent much time in accumulating property. To such the State renders comparatively small service, and a slight tax is wont to appear exorbitant, particularly if they are obliged to earn it by special labor with their hands. If there were one who lived wholly without the use of money, the State itself would hesitate to demand it of him. But the rich man—not to make any invidious comparison—is always sold to the institution which makes him rich. Absolutely speaking, the more money, the less virtue; for money comes between a man and his objects, and obtains them for him; and it was certainly no great virtue to obtain it. It puts to rest many questions which he would otherwise be taxed to answer; while the only new question which it puts is the hard but superfluous one, how to spend it. Thus his moral ground is taken from under his feet. The opportunities of living are diminished in proportion as what are called the "means" are increased. The best thing a man can do for his culture when he is rich is to endeavor to carry out those schemes which he entertained when he was poor. Christ answered the Herodians according to their condition. "Show me the tribute-money," said he;—and one took a penny out of his pocket;—if you use money which has the image of Caesar on it, and which he has made current and valuable, that is, *if you are men of the State*, and gladly enjoy the advantages of Caesar's government, then pay him back some of his own when he demands it. "Render therefore to Caesar that which is Caesar's, and to God those things which are God's"—leaving them no wiser than before as to which was which; for they did not wish to know.

When I converse with the freest of my neighbors, I perceive that, 24 whatever they may say about the magnitude and seriousness of the question, and their regard for the public tranquillity, the long and the short of the matter is, that they cannot spare the protection of the existing government, and they dread the consequences to their property and families of disobedience to it. For my own part, I should not like to think that I ever rely on the protection of the State. But, if I deny the authority of the State when it presents its tax-bill, it will soon take and waste all my property, and so harass me and my children without end. This is hard. This makes it impossible for a man to live honestly, and at the same time comfortably, in outward respects. It will not be worth the while to accumulate property; that would be sure to go again. You must hire or squat somewhere, and raise but a small crop, and eat that soon. You must live within yourself, and depend upon yourself always tucked up and ready for a start, and not have many affairs. A man may grow rich in Turkey even, if he will be in all respects a good subject of the Turkish government. Confucius said: "If a state is governed by the principles of reason, poverty and misery are subjects of shame; if a state is not governed by the principles of reason, riches and honors are the subjects of shame." No: until I want the protection of Massachusetts to be extended to me in some distant Southern port, where my liberty is endangered, or until I am bent solely on building up an estate at home by peaceful enterprise, I can afford to refuse allegiance to Massachusetts, and her right to my property and life. It costs me less in every sense to incur the penalty of disobedience to the State than it would to obey. I should feel as if I were worth less in that case.

Some years ago, the State met me in behalf of the Church, and 25 commanded me to pay a certain sum toward the support of a clergyman whose preaching my father attended, but never I myself. "Pay," it said, "or be locked up in the jail." I declined to pay. But, unfortunately, another man saw fit to pay it. I did not see why the schoolmaster should be taxed to support the priest, and not the priest the schoolmaster; for I was not the State's schoolmaster, but I supported myself by voluntary subscription. I did not see why the lyceum should not present its tax-bill, and have the State to back its demand, as well as the Church. However, at the request of the selectmen, I condescended to make some such statement as this in writing:—"Know all men by these presents, that I, Henry Thoreau, do not wish to be regarded as a member of any incorporated society which I have not joined." This I gave to the town clerk; and he has it. The State, having thus learned that I did not wish to be regarded as a member of that church, has never made a like demand on me since; though it said that it must adhere to its original presumption that time. If I had known how to name them, I should then have signed off in detail from all the societies which I never signed on to; but I did not know where to find a complete list.

I have paid no poll-tax for six years. I was put into a jail once on 26 this account, for one night; and, as I stood considering the walls of solid stone, two or three feet thick, the door of wood and iron, a foot thick, and the iron grating which strained the light, I could not help being struck with the foolishness of that institution which treated me as if I were mere flesh and blood and bones to be locked up. I wondered that it should have concluded at length that this was the best use it could put me to, and had never thought to avail itself of my services in some way. I saw that, if there was a wall of stone between me and my townsmen, there was a still more difficult one to climb or break through before they could get to be as free as I was. I did not for a moment feel confined, and the walls seemed a great waste of stone and mortar. I felt as if I alone of all my townsmen had paid my tax. They plainly did not know how to treat me, but behaved like persons who are underbred. In every threat and in every compliment there was a blunder; for they thought that my chief desire was to stand the other side of that stone wall. I could not but smile to see how industriously they locked the door on my meditations, which followed them out again without let or hindrance, and *they* were really all that was dangerous. As they could not reach me, they had resolved to punish my body; just as boys, if they cannot come at some person against whom they have a spite, will abuse his dog. I saw that the State was half-witted, that it was timid as a lone woman with her silver spoons, and that it did not know its friends from its foes, and I lost all my remaining respect for it, and pitied it.

Thus the State never intentionally confronts a man's sense, intellectual or moral, but only his body, his senses. It is not armed with superior wit or honesty, but with superior physical strength. I was not born to be forced. I will breathe after my own fashion. Let us see who is the strongest. What force has a multitude? They only can force me who obey a higher law than I. They force me to become like themselves. I do not hear of *men* being *forced* to live this way or that by masses of men. What sort of life were that to live? When I meet a government which says to me, "Your money or your life," why should I be in haste to give it my money? It may be in a great strait, and not know what to do: I cannot help that. It must help itself; do as I do. It is not worth the while to snivel about it. I am not responsible for the successful working of the machinery of society. I am not the son of the engineer. I perceive that, when an acorn and a chestnut fall side by side, the one does not remain inert to make way for the other, but both obey their own laws, and spring and grow and flourish as best they can, till one, perchance, overshadows and destroys the other. If a plant cannot live according to its nature, it dies; and so a man.

The night in prison was novel and interesting enough. The pris- 28
oners in their shirt-sleeves were enjoying a chat and the evening air
in the doorway, when I entered. But the jailer said, "Come, boys, it
is time to lock up"; and so they dispersed, and I heard the sound of
their steps returning into the hollow apartments. My room-mate was
introduced to me by the jailer as "a first-rate fellow and a clever man."
When the door was locked, he showed me where to hang my hat,
and how he managed matters there. The rooms were whitewashed
once a month; and this one, at least, was the whitest, most simply
furnished, and probably the neatest apartment in the town. He naturally wanted to know where I came from, and what brought me
there; and, when I had told him, I asked him in my turn how he came
there, presuming him to be an honest man, of course; and, as the
world goes, I believe he was. "Why," said he, "they accuse me of
burning a barn; but I never did it." As near as I could discover he
had probably gone to bed in a barn when drunk, and smoked his
pipe there; and so a barn was burnt. He had the reputation of being
a clever man, had been there some three months waiting for his trial
to come on, and would have to wait as much longer; but he was quite
domesticated and contented, since he got his board for nothing, and
thought that he was well treated.

He occupied one window, and I the other; and I saw that if one 29
stayed there long, his principal business would be to look out the
window. I had soon read all the tracts that were left there, and examined where former prisoners had broken out, and where a grate
had been sawed off, and heard the history of the various occupants
of that room; for I found that even here there was a history and a
gossip which never circulated beyond the walls of the jail. Probably
this is the only house in the town where verses are composed, which
are afterward printed in a circular form, but not published. I was
shown quite a long list of verses which were composed by some young
men who had been detected in an attempt to escape, who avenged
themselves by singing them.

I pumped my fellow-prisoner as dry as I could, for fear I should 30
never see him again; but at length he showed me which was my bed,
and left me to blow out the lamp.

It was like travelling into a far country, such as I had never ex- 31
pected to behold, to lie there for one night. It seemed to me that I
never had heard the town clock strike before, nor the evening sounds
of the village; for we slept with the windows open, which were inside
the grating. It was to see my native village in the light of the Middle
Ages, and our Concord was turned into a Rhine stream, and visions
of knights and castles passed before me. They were the voices of old

burghers that I heard in the streets. I was an involuntary spectator
and auditor of whatever was done and said in the kitchen of the
adjacent village inn—a wholly new and rare experience to me. It was
a closer view of my native town. I was fairly inside of it. I never had
seen its institutions before. This is one of its peculiar institutions; for
it is a shire town. I began to comprehend what its inhabitants were
about.

In the morning, our breakfasts were put through the hole in the   32
door, in small oblong-square tin pans, made to fit, and holding a pint
of chocolate, with brown bread, and an iron spoon. When they called
for the vessels again, I was green enough to return what bread I had
left; but my comrade seized it, and said that I should lay that up for
lunch or dinner. Soon after he was let out to work at haying in a
neighboring field, whither he went every day, and would not be back
till noon; so he bade me good-day, saying that he doubted if he should
see me again.

When I came out of prison—for some one interfered, and paid   33
that tax—I did not perceive that great changes had taken place on the
common, such as he observed who went in a youth and emerged a
tottering and gray-headed man; and yet a change had to my eyes
come over the scene—the town, and State, and country—greater than
any that mere time could effect. I saw yet more distinctly the State in
which I lived. I saw to what extent the people among whom I lived
could be trusted as good neighbors and friends; that their friendship
was for summer weather only; that they did not greatly propose to
do right; that they were a distinct race from me by their prejudices
and superstitions, as the Chinamen and Malays are; that in their
sacrifices to humanity they ran no risks, not even to their property;
that after all they were not so noble but they treated the thief as he
had treated them, and hoped, by a certain outward observance and
a few prayers, and by walking in a particular straight though useless
path from time to time, to save their souls. This may be to judge my
neighbors harshly; for I believe that many of them are not aware that
they have such an institution as the jail in their village.

It was formerly the custom in our village, when a poor debtor   34
came out of jail, for his acquaintances to salute him, looking through
their fingers, which were crossed to represent the grating of a jail
window, "How do ye do?" My neighbors did not thus salute me, but
first looked at me, and then at one another, as if I had returned from
a long journey. I was put into jail as I was going to the shoemaker's
to get a shoe which was mended. When I was let out the next morning,
I preceeded to finish my errand, and, having put on my mended
shoe, joined a huckleberry party, who were impatient to put them-

selves under my conduct; and in half an hour—for the house was soon tackled—was in the midst of a huckleberry field, on one of our highest hills, two miles off, and then the State was nowhere to be seen.

This is the whole history of "My Prisons."   35

I have never declined paying the highway tax, because I am as 36 desirous of being a good neighbor as I am of being a bad subject; and as for supporting schools, I am doing my part to educate my fellow-countrymen now. It is for no particular item in the tax-bill that I refuse to pay it. I simply wish to refuse allegiance to the State, to withdraw and stand aloof from it effectually. I do not care to trace the course of my dollar, if I could, till it buys a man or a musket to shoot one with—the dollar is innocent—but I am concerned to trace the effects of my allegiance. In fact, I quietly declare war with the State, after my fashion, though I will still make what use and get what advantage of her I can, as is usual in such cases.

If others pay the tax which is demanded of me, from a sympathy 37 with the State, they do but what they have already done in their own case, or rather they abet injustice to a greater extent than the State requires. If they pay the tax from a mistaken interest in the individual taxed, to save his property, to prevent his going to jail, it is because they have not considered wisely how far they let their private feelings interfere with the public good.

This, then, is my position at present. But one cannot be too much 38 on his guard in such a case, lest his action be biased by obstinacy or an undue regard for the opinions of men. Let him see that he does only what belongs to himself and to the hour.

I think sometimes, Why, this people mean well, they are only 39 ignorant; they would do better if they knew how: why give your neighbors this pain to treat you as they are not inclined to? But I think again, This is no reason why I should do as they do, or permit others to suffer much greater pain of a different kind. Again, I sometimes say to myself, When many millions of men, without heat, without ill will, without personal feeling of any kind, demand of you a few shillings only, without the possibility, such is their constitution, of retracting or altering their present demand, and without the possibility, on your side, of appeal to any other millions, why expose yourself to this overwhelming brute force? You do not resist cold and hunger, the winds and the waves, thus obstinately; you quietly submit to a thousand similar necessities. You do not put your head into the fire. But just in proportion as I regard this as not wholly a brute force, but partly a human force, and consider that I have relations to those millions as to so many millions of men, and not of mere brute or inanimate things, I see that appeal is possible, first and instanta-neoulsy, from them to the Maker of them, and secondly, from them to themselves. But if I put my head deliberately into the fire, there is no appeal to fire or to the Maker of fire, and I have only myself to blame. If I could convince myself that I have any right to be satisfied with men as they are, and to treat them accordingly, and not accord-ing, in some respects, to my requisitions and expectations of what they and I ought to be, then, like a good Mussulman and fatalist, I should endeavor to be satisfied with things as they are and say it is the will of God. And, above all, there is this difference between re-sisting this and a purely brute or natural force, that I can resist this with some effect; but I cannot expect, like Orpheus, to change the nature of the rocks and trees and beasts.

I do not wish to quarrel with any man or nation. I do not wish 40 to split hairs, to make fine distinctions, or set myself up as better than my neighbors. I seek rather, I may say, even an excuse for conforming to the laws of the land. I am but too ready to conform to them. Indeed, I have reason to suspect myself on this head; and each year, as the tax-gatherer comes round, I find myself disposed to review the acts and positions of the general and State governments, and the spirit of the people, to discover a pretext for conformity.

> We must affect our country as our parents,
> And if at any time we alienate
> Our love or industry from doing it honor,
> We must respect effects and teach the soul
> Matter of conscience and religion,
> And not desire of rule or benefit.

I believe that the State will soon be able to take all my work of this sort out of my hands, and then I shall be no better a patriot than my fellow-countrymen. Seen from a lower point of view, the Constitution, with all its faults, is very good; the law and the courts are very re-spectable; even this State and this American government are, in many respects, very admirable, and rare things, to be thankful for, such as a great many have described them; but seen from a point of view a little higher, they are what I have described them; seen from a higher still, and the highest, who shall say what they are, or that they are worth looking at or thinking of at all?

However, the government does not concern me much, and I shall 41 bestow the fewest possible thoughts on it. It is not many moments that I live under a government, even in this world. If a man is thought-free, fancy-free, imagination-free, that which *is not* never for a long time appearing *to be* to him, unwise rulers or reformers cannot fatally interrupt him.

I know that most men think differently from myself; but those 42 whose lives are by profession devoted to the study of these or kindred subjects content me as little as any. Statesmen and legislators, standing so completely within the institution, never distinctly and nakedly behold it. They speak of moving society, but have no resting-place without it. They may be men of a certain experience and discrimination, and have no doubt invented ingenious and even useful systems, for which we sincerely thank them; but all their wit and usefulness lie within certain not very wide limits. They are wont to forget that the world is not governed by policy and expediency. Webster never goes behind government, and so cannot speak with authority about it. His words are wisdom to those legislators who contemplate no essential reform in the existing government; but for thinkers, and those who legislate for all time, he never once glances at the subject. I know of those whose serene and wise speculations on this theme would soon reveal the limits of his mind's range and hospitality. Yet, compared with the cheap professions of most reformers, and the still cheaper wisdom and eloquence of politicians in general, his are almost the only sensible and valuable words, and we thank Heaven for him. Comparatively, he is always strong, original, and, above all, practical. Still, his quality is not wisdom, but prudence. The lawyer's truth is not Truth, but consistency or a consistent expediency. Truth is always in harmony with herself, and is not concerned chiefly to reveal the justice that may consist with wrong-doing. He well deserves to be called, as he has been called, the Defender of the Constitution. There are really no blows to be given by him but defensive ones. He is not a leader, but a follower. His leaders are the men of '87. "I have never made an effort," he says, "and never propose to make an effort; I have never countenanced an effort and never mean to countenance an effort, to disturb the arrangement as originally made, by which the various States came into the Union." Still thinking of the sanction which the Constitution gives to slavery, he says, "Because it was a part of the original compact—let it stand." Notwithstanding his special acuteness and ability, he is unable to take a fact out of its merely political relations, and behold it as it lies absolutely to be disposed of by the intellect—what, for instance, it behooves a man to do here in America today with regard to slavery—but ventures, or is driven, to make some such desperate answer as the following, while professing to speak absolutely, and as a private man—from which what new and similar code of social duties might be inferred? "The manner," says he, "in which the governments of those States where slavery exists are to regulate it is for their own consideration, under their responsibility to their consistuents, to the general laws of propriety, humanity, and justice, and to God. Associations formed elsewhere, springing from a feeling of humanity, or any other cause, have nothing whatever to do with it. They have never received any encouragement for me, and they never will."[9]

They who know of no purer sources of truth, who have traced 43 up its stream no higher, stand, and wisely stand, by the Bible and the Constitution, and drink at it there with reverence and humility; but they who behold where it comes trickling into this lake or that pool, gird up their loins once more, and continue their pilgrimage toward its fountain-head.

No man with a genius for legislation has appeared in America. 44 They are rare in the history of the world. There are orators, politicians, and eloquent men, by the thousand; but the speaker has not yet opened his mouth to speak who is capable of settling the much-vexed questions of the day. We love eloquence for its own sake, and not for any truth which it may utter, or any heroism it may inspire. Our legislators have not yet learned the comparative value of free trade and of freedom, of union, and of rectitude, to a nation. They have no genius or talent for comparatively humble questions of taxation and finance, commerce and manufactures and agriculture. If we were left solely to the wordy wit of legislators in Congress for our guidance, uncorrected by the seasonable experience and the effectual complaints of the people, America would not long retain her rank among the nations. For eighteen hundred years, though perchance I have no right to say it, the New Testament has been written; yet where is the legislator who has wisdom and practical talent enough to avail himself of the light which it sheds on the science of legislation?

The authority of government, even such as I am willing to submit 45 to—for I will cheerfully obey those who know and can do better than I, and in many things even those who neither know nor can do so well—is still an impure one: to be strictly just, it must have the sanction and consent of the governed. It can have no pure right over my person and property but what I concede to it. The progress from an absolute to a limited monarchy, from a limited monarchy to a democracy, is a progress toward a true respect for the individual. Even the Chinese philosopher was wise enough to regard the individual as the basis of the empire. Is a democracy, such as we know it, the last improvement possible in government? Is it not possible to take a step further towards recognizing and organizing the rights of man? There will never be a really free and enlightened State until the State comes to recognize the individual as a higher and independent power,

---

[9]These extracts have been inserted since the lecture was read.

from which all its own power and authority are derived, and treats him accordingly. I please myself with imagining a State at least which can afford to be just to all men, and to treat the individual with respect as a neighbor; which even would not think it inconsistent with its own repose if a few were to live aloof from it, not meddling with it, nor embraced by it, who fulfilled all the duties of neighbors and fellow-men. A State which bore this kind of fruit, and suffered it to drop off as fast as it ripened, would prepare the way for a still more perfect and glorious State, which also I have imagined, but not yet anywhere seen.

RESPONDING TO READING

Key words: community   freedom   identity   minority   power rights   striving

Rhetorical concepts: analysis   anecdote   cause and effect comparison and contrast   deduction   definition   explanation illustration   meditation   metaphor

1.   Thoreau is arguing against two political "evils": a state that endorses slavery and uses war, and rule by majority. What are his arguments against each? To what extent do you agree with his objections?

2.   To replace the rule of the state, and its majority, what does Thoreau propose as a guide? What are his arguments for relying upon that guide? What are some possible objections to using such a personal guide against the laws enacted legally? What are his replies to those arguments?

3.   What are Thoreau's arguments for refusing to pay taxes to support what he claims to be evil actions? What are his arguments for breaking the law, under certain circumstances? To what degree do you support or oppose these arguments? Explain.

4.   Describe Thoreau's attitude toward his night in jail. Notice his view of his cell mate, the jail routines, the effects on him of imprisonment, the moment of release. How does this attitude relate to the purpose of the essay?

5.   What does Thoreau mean when he says "any man more right than his neighbors constitutes a majority of one"? Describe an example of someone else who, convinced "they have God on their side," decided to break a law. Was the person you describe "a majority of one" or just a lawbreaker?

6.   The most famous sentence in this essay is "Under a government which imprisons any unjustly, the true place for a just man is also a prison." Explain what that means and consider why that sentence has been so frequently cited in the years since Thoreau. Look up the life of a prominent thinker (such as Mahatma Ghandi or Martin Luther King, Jr.), and describe how this idea has developed. Are there particular circumstances under which this idea is appropriate, or is it generally applicable?

I Like to Think of Harriet Tubman

SUSAN GRIFFIN

Susan Griffin (born 1943) identifies herself as a "radical feminist," a lesbian, and a mother who feels that "the mother/daughter relationship is . . . central to all women's lives." She attended Berkeley during the 1960s and earned two degrees from San Francisco State University, a B.A. in 1965 and an M.A. in 1973. Her numerous feminist writings draw on her experiences of having an abortion, being a welfare mother, and working at manual and clerical labor and as a teacher. Griffin sees her feminism and her writing as mutually reinforcing: "As a woman, I struggle to write from my life, to reflect all the difficulties, angers, joys of my existence in a culture that attempts to silence women, or that does not take our work, or words or our lives seriously." In precise, emphatic language Griffin expresses her views: in social commentary, *Woman and Nature: The Roaring Inside Her* (1978), *Rape: The Power of Consciousness* (1979), and *Pornography and Silence: Culture's Revenge against Nature* (1981); in radio drama, *Voices* (1975); and in poetry. Her poetry collections include *Like the Iris of an Eye* (1976), in which the poem "I Like to Think of Harriet Tubman" appears.

Harriet Tubman, a source of Griffin's inspiration, energy, and anger in the following poem, was born on a Maryland plantation around 1820 (slave births, marriages, and deaths were seldom recorded). Lines 3–6 and 63–64 refer to the fact that when she was thirteen, she was struck so hard by an overseer that she experienced the effects of the blows for the rest of her life. For a synopsis of her activities in masterminding the escapes of over three hundred fugitive slaves, see pages 439–440. Although slaveholders' rewards for her capture eventually totalled $40,000, she was never caught. During the Civil War, she served as a scout, a spy, a nurse, and a laundress for the Union forces in South Carolina and was finally granted a military pension about fifteen years before her death in 1913.

I like to think of Harriet Tubman.
Harriet Tubman who carried a revolver,
who had a scar on her head from a rock thrown
by a slave-master (because she
talked back), and who   5
had a ransom on her head
of thousands of dollars and who
was never caught, and who
had no use for the law
when the law was wrong,   10
who defied the law. I like
to think of her.
I like to think of her especially

when I think of the problem of
feeding children.   15

The legal answer
to the problem of feeding children
is ten free lunches every month,
being equal, in the child's real life,
to eating lunch every other day.   20
Monday but not Tuesday.
I like to think of the President
eating lunch Monday, but not
Tuesday.
And when I think of the President   25
and the law, and the problem of
feeding children, I like to
think of Harriet Tubman
and her revolver.

And then sometimes   30
I think of the President
and other men,
men who practice the law,
who revere the law,
who make the law,   35
who enforce the law,
who live behind
and operate through
and feed themselves
at the expense of   40
starving children
because of the law.

Men who sit in paneled offices
and think about vacations
and tell women   45
whose care it is
to feed children
not to be hysterical
not to be hysterical as in the word
hysterikos, the greek for   50
womb suffering,
not to suffer in their
wombs,
not to care,

not to bother the men   55
because they want to think
of other things
and do not want
to take the women seriously.
I want them   60
to take women seriously.

I want them to think about Harriet Tubman,
and remember,
remember she was beat by a white man
and she lived   65
and she lived to redress her grievances,
and she lived in swamps
and wore the clothes of a man
bringing hundreds of fugitives from
slavery, and was never caught,   70
and led an army,
and won a battle,
and defied the laws
because the laws were wrong, I want men
to take us seriously.   75
I am tired wanting them to think
about right and wrong.
I want them to fear.
I want them to feel fear now
as I have felt suffering in the womb, and   80
I want them
to know
that there is always a time
there is always a time to make right
what is wrong,   85
there is always a time
for retribution
and that time
is beginning.

RESPONDING TO READING

Key words: class community discovery freedom gender
identity language loss memory minority power race rights
striving symbols transformation

Rhetorical concepts: analogy anecdote biography metaphor poetry

1.   Do you read this as an angry poem? If so, find some words and lines that convey this anger to you and show how they function in the poem. At what and whom is the anger directed? Does the poem make you feel uncomfortable? If so, explain why; if not, explain why you think others are uncomfortable while you are not.

2.   Some of the lines of the poem are very short; two have only one word. Look at the short lines and consider why the poet has made them short. What effect do they have?

3.   To what degree does the Harriet Tubman of this poem carry out the ideas of Thoreau? To what degree does she take a different tack? What does the poet particularly admire about Tubman?

4.   Does Griffin intend Tubman to symbolize all women, or only some? Explain your answer.

5.   The poet wants men "to take women seriously." Does she mean all men, or certain kinds of men? Why does she feel this is not occurring and what evidence does she give? How does the figure of Tubman in the poem serve to make men take women seriously? What does the last quatrain of the poem suggest by saying that retribution is beginning? In your response, allude to other essays or poems in this book that speak to the same issues.

Letter from Birmingham Jail

MARTIN LUTHER KING, JR.

Just as Elie Wiesel writes to witness the Holocaust and to arouse public consciousness to prevent genocide and atrocities from ever occurring again (*see* "Why I Write" in Chapter 1), so Martin Luther King, Jr. (1929–1968) writes for the same moralistic reasons. As a witness to racial discrimination, in his own life and his own country, he wants his readers to put a stop to it, now and forever. In 1963 King wrote the "Letter from Birmingham Jail" while imprisoned for "parading without a permit" in a nonviolent civil rights demonstration. Though obstensibly replying to eight clergymen who feared violence in the Birmingham desegregation demonstrations and urged him to wait, King actually intended his letter for the worldwide audience his civil rights activities commanded. Warning that America had more to fear from passive moderates ("the appalling silence of good people") than from extremists, King defended his policy of nonviolent direct action and explained why he was compelled to disobey unjust laws, just as Thoreau did: "We should never forget that everything Adolf Hitler did in Germany was 'legal'," and that it was " 'illegal' to aid and comfort a Jew in Hitler's Germany."

"Letter from Birmingham Jail" reveals why its author was the most influential leader of the American civil rights movement in the 1950s and 1960s. A forceful and charismatic leader, Dr. King, was ordained Baptist clergyman educated at Morehouse College. In 1955 he became a national spokesperson for the civil rights movement when he led a successful boycott of the segregated bus system of Montgomery,

Alabama. He then became president of the Southern Christian Leadership Conference and led the sit-ins and demonstrations—including the 1964 march on Washington, D.C., where he gave his famous "I Have a Dream" speech—that helped to ensure passage of the 1964 Civil Rights Act and the Voting Rights Act of 1965. Dr. King received the Nobel Peace Prize in 1964. He was assassinated in 1968, a victim of violence during a nonviolent demonstration, but his legacy lives on.

April 16, 1963

My Dear Fellow Clergymen:

While confined here in the Birmingham city jail, I came across   1
your recent statement calling my present activities "unwise and untimely." Seldom do I pause to answer criticism of my work and ideas. If I sought to answer all the criticisms that cross my desk, my secretaries would have little time for anything other than such correspondence in the course of the day, and I would have no time for constructive work. But since I feel that you are men of genuine good will and that your criticisms are sincerely set forth, I want to try to answer your statement in what I hope will be patient and reasonable terms.[1]

I think I should indicate why I am here in Birmingham, since you   2
have been influenced by the view which argues against "outsiders coming in." I have the honor of serving as president of the Southern Christian Leadership Conference, an organization operating in every southern state, with headquarters in Atlanta, Georgia. We have some eighty-five affiliated organizations across the South, and one of them is the Alabama Christian Movement for Human Rights. Frequently we share staff, educational and financial resources with our affiliates. Several months ago the affiliate here in Birmingham asked us to be on call to engage in a nonviolent direct-action program if such were deemed necessary. We readily consented, and when the hour came we lived up to our promise. So I, along with several members of my staff, am here because I was invited here. I am here because I have organizational ties here.

But more basically, I am in Birmingham because injustice is here.   3
Just as the prophets of the eighth century B.C. left their villages and

---

[1]AUTHOR'S NOTE: This response to a published statement by eight fellow clergymen from Alabama (Bishop C. C. J. Carpenter, Bishop Joseph A. Durick, Rabbi Hilton L. Grafman, Bishop Paul Hardin, Bishop Holan B. Harmon, the Reverend George M. Murray, the Reverend Edward V. Ramage and the Reverend Earl Stallings) was composed under somewhat constricting circumstances. Begun on the margins of the newspaper in which the statement appeared while I was in jail, the letter was continued on scraps of writing paper supplied by a friendly Negro trusty, and concluded on a pad my attorneys were eventually permitted to leave me. Although the text remains in substance unaltered, I have indulged in the author's prerogative of polishing it for publication.

carried their "thus saith the Lord" far beyond the boundaries of their home towns, and, just as the Apostle Paul left his village of Tarsus and carried the gospel of Jesus Christ to the far corners of the Greco-Roman world, so am I compelled to carry the gospel of freedom beyond my own home town. Like Paul, I must constantly respond to the Macedonian call for aid.

Moreover, I am cognizant of the interrelatedness of all communities and states. I cannot sit idly by in Atlanta and not be concerned about what happens in Birmingham. Injustice anywhere is a threat to justice everywhere. We are caught in an inescapable network of mutuality, tied in a single garment of destiny. Whatever affects one directly, affects all indirectly. Never again can we afford to live with the narrow, provincial "outside agitator" idea. Anyone who lives inside the United States can never be considered an outsider anywhere within its bounds.

You deplore the demonstrations taking place in Birmingham. But your statement, I am sorry to say, fails to express a similar concern for the conditions that brought about the demonstrations. I am sure that none of you would want to rest content with the superficial kind of social analysis that deals merely with effects and does not grapple with underlying causes. It is unfortunate that demonstrations are taking place in Birmingham, but it is even more unfortunate that the city's white power structure left the Negro community with no alternative.

In any nonviolent campaign there are four basic steps: collection of the facts to determine whether injustices exist; negotiation; self-purification; and direct action. We have gone through all these steps in Birmingham. There can be no gainsaying the fact that racial injustice engulfs this community. Birmingham is probably the most thoroughly segregated city in the United States. An ugly record of brutality is widely known. Negroes have experienced grossly unjust treatment in the courts. There have been more unsolved bombings of Negro homes and churches in Birmingham than in any other city in the nation. These are the hard brutal facts of the case. On the basis of these conditions, Negro leaders sought to negotiate with the city fathers. But the latter consistently refused to engage in good-faith negotiation.

Then, last September, came the opportunity to talk with leaders of Birmingham's economic community. In the course of the negotiations, certain promises were made by the merchants—for example, to remove the stores' humiliating racial signs. On the basis of these promises, the Reverend Fred Shuttlesworth and the leaders of the Alabama Christian Movement for Human Rights agreed to a moratorium on all demonstrations. As the weeks and months went by, we realized that we were the victims of a broken promise. A few signs, briefly removed, returned; the others remained.

As in so many past experiences, our hopes had been blasted, and 8 the shadow of deep disappointment settled upon us. We had no alternative except to prepare for direct action, whereby we would present our very bodies as a means of laying our case before the conscience of the local and the national community. Mindful of the difficulties involved, we decided to undertake a process of self-purification. We began a series of workshops on nonviolence, and we repeatedly asked ourselves: "Are you able to accept blows without retaliating?" "Are you able to endure the ordeal of jail?" We decided to schedule our direct-action program for the Easter season, realizing that except for Christmas, this is the main shopping period of the year. Knowing that a strong economic-withdrawal program would be the by-product of direct action, we felt that this would be the best time to bring pressure to bear on the merchants for the needed change.

Then it occurred to us that Birmingham's mayoralty election was 9 coming up in March, and we speedily decided to postpone action until after election day. When we discovered that the Commissioner of Public Safety, Eugene "Bull" Connor, had piled up enough votes to be in the run-off, we decided again to postpone action until the day after the run-off so that the demonstrations could not be used to cloud the issues. Like many others, we waited to see Mr. Connor defeated, and to this end we endured postponement after postponement. Having aided in this community need, we felt that our direct-action program could be delayed no longer.

You may well ask "Why direct action? Why sit-ins, marches and 10 so forth? Isn't negotiation a better path?" You are quite right in calling for negotiation. Indeed, this is the very purpose of direct action. Nonviolent direct action seeks to create such a crisis and foster such a tension that a community which has constantly refused to negotiate is forced to confront the issue. It seeks so to dramatize the issue that it can no longer be ignored. My citing the creation of tension as part of the work of the nonviolent-resister may sound rather shocking. But I must confess that I am not afraid of the word "tension." I have earnestly opposed violent tension, but there is a type of constructive nonviolent tension which is necessary for growth. Just as Socrates felt that it was necessary to create a tension in the mind so that individuals could rise from the bondage of myths and half-truths to the unfettered realm of creative analysis and objective appraisal, so must we see the need for nonviolent gadflies to create the kind of tension in society that will help men rise from the dark depths of prejudice and racism to the majestic heights of understanding and brotherhood.

The purpose of our direct-action program is to create a situation 11 so crisis-packed that it will inevitably open the door to negotiation. I therefore concur with you in your call for negotiation. Too long has our beloved Southland been bogged down in a tragic effort to live in monologue rather than dialogue.

One of the basic points in your statement is that the action that 12 I and my associates have taken in Birmingham is untimely. Some have asked: "Why didn't you give the new city administration time to act?" The only answer that I can give to this query is that the new Birmingham administration must be prodded about as much as the outgoing one, before it will act. We are sadly mistaken if we feel that the election of Albert Boutwell as mayor will bring the millennium to Birmingham. While Mr. Boutwell is a much more gentle person than Mr. Connor, they are both segregationists, dedicated to maintenance of the status quo. I have hope that Mr. Boutwell will be reasonable enough to see the futility of massive resistance to desegregation. But he will not see this without pressure from devotees of civil rights. My friends, I must say to you that we have not made a single gain in civil rights without determined legal and nonviolent pressure. Lamentably, it is an historical fact that privileged groups seldom give up their privileges voluntarily. Individuals may see the moral light and voluntarily give up their unjust posture; but, as Reinhold Niebuhr has reminded us, groups tend to be more immoral than individuals.

We know through painful experience that freedom is never vol- 13 untarily given by the oppressor; it must be demanded by the oppressed. Frankly, I have yet to engage in a direct-action campaign that was "well-timed" in the view of those who have not suffered unduly from the disease of segregation. For years now I have heard the word "Wait!" It rings in the ear of every Negro with piercing familiarity. This "Wait" has almost always meant "Never." We must come to see, with one of our distinguished jurists, that "justice too long delayed is justice denied."

We have waited for more than 340 years for our constitutional and 14 Godgiven rights. The nations of Asia and Africa are moving with jetlike speed toward gaining political independence, but we still creep at horse-and-buggy pace toward gaining a cup of coffee at a lunch counter. Perhaps it is easy for those who have never felt the stinging darts of segregation to say, "Wait." But when you have seen vicious mobs lynch your mothers and fathers at will and drown your sisters and brothers at whim; when you have seen hate-filled policemen curse, kick and even kill your black brothers and sisters; when you see the vast majority of your twenty million Negro brothers smothering in an airtight cage of poverty in the midst of an affluent society; when you suddenly find your tongue twisted and your speech stammering as you seek to explain to your six-year-old daughter why she can't go to the public amusement park that has just been advertised on television, and see tears welling up in her eyes when she is told that Funtown is closed to colored children, and see ominous clouds of inferiority beginning to form in her little mental sky, and see her beginning to distort her personality by developing an unconscious bitterness toward white people; when you have to concoct an answer for a five-year-old son who is asking: "Daddy, why do white people treat colored people so mean?"; when you take a cross-country drive and find it necessary to sleep night after night in the uncomfortable corners of your automobile because no motel will accept you; when you are humiliated day in and day out by nagging signs reading "white" and "colored"; when your first name becomes "nigger," your middle name becomes "boy" (however old you are) and your last name becomes "John," and your wife and mother are never given the respected title "Mrs."; when you are harried by day and haunted by night by the fact that you are a Negro, living constantly at tiptoe stance, never quite knowing what to expect next, and are plagued with inner fears and outer resentments; when you are forever fighting a degenerating sense of "nobodiness"—then you will understand why we find it difficult to wait. There comes a time when the cup of endurance runs over, and men are no longer willing to be plunged into the abyss of despair. I hope, sirs, you can understand our legitimate and unavoidable impatience.

You express a great deal of anxiety over our willingness to break 15 laws. This is certainly a legitimate concern. Since we so diligently urge people to obey the Supreme Court's decision of 1954 outlawing segregation in the public schools, at first glance it may seem rather paradoxical for us consciously to break laws. One may well ask: "How can you advocate breaking some laws and obeying others?" The answer lies in the fact that there are two types of laws: just and unjust. I would be the first to advocate obeying just laws. One has not only a legal but a moral responsibility to obey just laws. Conversely, one has a moral responsibility to disobey unjust laws. I would agree with St. Augustine that "an unjust law is no law at all."

Now, what is the difference between the two? How does one 16 determine whether a law is just or unjust? A just law is a man-made code that squares with the moral law or the law of God. An unjust law is a code that is out of harmony with the moral law. To put it in the terms of St. Thomas Aquinas: An unjust law is a human law that is not rooted in eternal law and natural law. Any law that uplifts human personality is just. Any law that degrades human personality is unjust. All segregation statutes are unjust because segregation distorts the soul and damages the personality. It gives the segregator a false sense of superiority and the segregated a false sense of inferiority. Segregation, to use the terminology of the Jewish philosopher Martin Buber, substitutes an "I-it" relationship for an "I-thou" relationship and ends up relegating persons to the status of things. Hence segregation is not only politically, economically and sociologically unsound, it is morally wrong and sinful. Paul Tillich has said that sin is separation. Is not segregation an existential expression of man's tragic separation, his awful estrangement, his terrible sinfulness? Thus it is that I can urge men to obey the 1954 decision of the Supreme Court, for it is morally right; and I can urge them to disobey segregation ordinances, for they are morally wrong.

Let us consider a more concrete example of just and unjust laws. 17 An unjust law is a code that a numerical or power majority group compels a minority group to obey but does not make binding on itself. This is *difference* made legal. By the same token, a just law is a code that a majority compels a minority to follow and that it is willing to follow itself. This is *sameness* made legal.

Let me give another explanation. A law is unjust if it is inflicted 18 on a minority that, as a result of being denied the right to vote, had no part in enacting or devising the law. Who can say that the legislature of Alabama which set up that state's segregation laws was democratically elected? Throughout Alabama all sorts of devious methods are used to prevent Negroes from becoming registered voters, and there are some counties in which even though Negroes constitute a majority of the population, not a single Negro is registered. Can any law enacted under such circumstances be considered democratically structured?

Sometimes a law is just on its face and unjust in its application. 19 For instance, I have been arrested on a charge of parading without a permit. Now, there is nothing wrong in having an ordinance which requires a permit for a parade. But such an ordinance becomes unjust when it is used to maintain segregation and to deny citizens the First-Amendment privilege of peaceful assembly and protest.

I hope you are able to see the distinction I am trying to point out. 20 In no sense do I advocate evading or defying the law, as would the rabid segregationist. That would lead to anarchy. One who breaks an unjust law must do so openly, lovingly, and with a willingness to accept the penalty. I submit that an individual who breaks a law that conscience tells him is unjust, and who willingly accepts the penalty of imprisonment in order to arouse the conscience of the community over its injustice, is in reality expressing the highest respect for law.

Of course, there is nothing new about this kind of civil disobe- 21 dience. It was evidenced sublimely in the refusal of Shadrach, Meshach and Abednego to obey the laws of Nebuchadnezzar, on the ground that a higher moral law was at stake. It was practiced superbly by the early Christians, who were willing to face hungry lions and the excruciating pain of chopping blocks rather than submit to certain unjust laws of the Roman Empire. To a degree, academic freedom is a reality today because Socrates practiced civil disobedience. In our own nation, the Boston Tea Party represented a massive act of civil disobedience.

We should never forget that everything Adolf Hitler did in Ger- 22 many was "legal" and everything the Hungarian freedom fighters did in Hungary was "illegal." It was "illegal" to aid and comfort a Jew in Hitler's Germany. Even so, I am sure that, had I lived in Germany at the time, I would have aided and comforted my Jewish brothers. If today I lived in a Communist country where certain principles dear to the Christian faith are suppressed, I would openly advocate disobeying that country's anti-religious laws.

I must make two honest confessions to you, my Christian and 23 Jewish brothers. First, I must confess that over the past few years I have been gravely disappointed with the white moderate. I have almost reached the regrettable conclusion that the Negro's great stumbling block in his stride toward freedom is not the White Citizen's Counciler or the Ku Klux Klanner, but the white moderate, who is more devoted to "order" than to justice; who prefers a negative peace which is the absence of tension to a positive peace which is the presence of justice; who constantly says: "I agree with you in the goal you seek, but I cannot agree with your methods of direct action"; who paternalistically believes he can set the timetable for another man's freedom; who lives by a mythical concept of time and who constantly advises the Negro to wait for a "more convenient season." Shallow understanding from people of good will is more frustrating than absolute misunderstanding from people of ill will. Lukewarm acceptance is much more bewildering than outright rejection.

I had hoped that the white moderate would understand that law 24 and order exist for the purpose of establishing justice and that when they fail in this purpose they become the dangerously structured dams that block the flow of social progress. I had hoped that the white moderate would understand that the present tension in the South is a necessary phase of the transition from an obnoxious negative peace, in which the Negro passively accepted his unjust plight, to a substantive and positive peace, in which all men will respect the dignity and worth of human personality. Actually, we who engage in nonviolent direct action are not the creators of tension. We merely bring to the surface the hidden tension that is already alive. We bring it out in the open, where it can be seen and dealt with. Like a boil that can never be cured so long as it is covered up but must be opened with all its ugliness to the natural medicines of air and light, injustice must be exposed, with all the tension its exposure creates, to the light of human conscience and the air of national opinion before it can be cured.

In your statement you assert that our actions, even though peace- 25 ful, must be condemned because they precipitate violence. But is this a logical assertion? Isn't this like condemning a robbed man because his possession of money precipitated the evil act of robbery? Isn't this like condemning Socrates because his unswerving commitment to truth and his philosophical inquiries precipitated the act by the misguided populace in which they made him drink hemlock? Isn't this like condemning Jesus because his unique God-consciousness and never-ceasing devotion to God's will precipitated the evil act of crucifixion? We must come to see that, as the federal courts have consistently affirmed, it is wrong to urge an individual to cease his efforts to gain his basic constitutional rights because the quest may precipitate violence. Society must protect the robbed and punish the robber.

I had also hoped that the white moderate would reject the myth 26 concerning time in relation to the struggle for freedom. I have just received a letter from a white brother in Texas. He writes: "All Christians know that the colored people will receive equal rights eventually, but it is possible that you are in too great a religious hurry. It has taken Christianity almost two thousand years to accomplish what it has. The teachings of Christ take time to come to earth." Such an attitude stems from a tragic misconception of time, from the strangely irrational notion that there is something in the very flow of time that will inevitably cure all ills. Actually, time itself is neutral; it can be used either destructively or constructively. More and more I feel that the people of ill will have used time much more effectively than have the people of good will. We will have to repent in this generation not merely for the hateful words and actions of the bad people but for the appalling silence of the good people. Human progress never rolls in on wheels of inevitability; it comes through the tireless efforts of men willing to be coworkers with God, and without this hard work, time itself becomes an ally of the forces of social stagnation. We must use time creatively, in the knowledge that the time is always ripe to do right. Now is the time to make real the promise of democracy and transform our pending national elegy into a creative psalm of brotherhood. Now is the time to lift our national policy from the quicksand of racial injustice to the solid rock of human dignity.

You speak of our activity in Birmingham as extreme. At first I was 27 rather disappointed that fellow clergymen would see my nonviolent efforts as those of an extremist. I began thinking about the fact that

I stand in the middle of two opposing forces in the Negro community. One is a force of complacency, made up in part of Negroes who, as a result of long years of oppression, are so drained of self-respect and a sense of "somebodiness" that they have adjusted to segregation; and in part of a few middle-class Negroes who, because of a degree of academic and economic security and because in some ways they profit by segregation, have become insensitive to the problems of the masses. The other force is one of bitterness and hatred, and it comes perilously close to advocating violence. It is expressed in the various black nationalist groups that are springing up across the nation, the largest and best-known being Elijah Muhammad's Muslim movement. Nourished by the Negro's frustration over the continued existence of racial discrimination, this movement is made up of people who have lost faith in America, who have absolutely repudiated Christianity, and who have concluded that the white man is an incorrigible "devil."

I have tried to stand between these two forces, saying that we 28 need emulate neither the "do-nothingism" of the complacent nor the hatred and despair of the black nationalist. For there is the more excellent way of love and nonviolent protest. I am grateful to God that, through the influence of the Negro church, the way of non-violence became an integral part of our struggle.

If this philosophy had not emerged, by now many streets of the 29 South would, I am convinced, be flowing with blood. And I am further convinced that if our white brothers dismiss as "rabble-rousers" and "outside agitators" those of us who employ nonviolent direct action, and if they refuse to support our nonviolent efforts, millions of Negroes will, out of frustration and despair, seek solace and security in black-nationalist ideologies—a development that would inevitably lead to a frightening racial nightmare.

Oppressed people cannot remain oppressed forever. The yearning 30 for freedom eventually manifests itself, and that is what has happened to the American Negro. Something within has reminded him of his birthright of freedom, and something without has reminded him that it can be gained. Consciously or unconsciously, he has been caught up by the *Zeitgeist*, and with his black brothers of Africa and his brown and yellow brothers of Asia, South America and the Caribbean, the United States Negro is moving with a sense of great urgency toward the promised land of racial justice. If one recognizes this vital urge that has engulfed the Negro community, one should readily understand why public demonstrations are taking place. The Negro has many pent-up resentments and latent frustrations, and he must release them. So let him march; let him make prayer pilgrimages to the city hall; let him go on freedom rides—and try to understand why he must do so. If his repressed emotions are not released in nonviolent ways, they will seek expression through violence; this is not a threat but a fact of history. So I have not said to my people: "Get rid of your discontent." Rather, I have tried to say that this normal and healthy discontent can be channeled into the creative outlet of nonviolent direct action. And now this approach is being termed extremist.

But though I was initially disappointed at being categorized as an extremist, as I continued to think about the matter I gradually gained a measure of satisfaction from the label. Was not Jesus an extremist for love: "Love your enemies, bless them that curse you, do good to them that hate you, and pray for them which despitefully use you, and persecute you." Was not Amos an extremist for justice: "Let justice roll down like waters and righteousness like an ever-flowing stream." Was not Paul an extremist for the Christian gospel: "I bear in my body the marks of the Lord Jesus." Was not Martin Luther an extremist: "Here I stand; I cannot do otherwise, so help me God." And John Bunyan: "I will stay in jail to the end of my days before I make a butchery of my conscience." And Abraham Lincoln: "This nation cannot survive half slave and half free." And Thomas Jefferson: "We hold these truths to be self-evident, that all men are created equal. . . ." So the question is not whether we will be extremists, but what kind of extremists we will be. Will we be extremists for hate or for love? Will we be extremists for the preservation of injustice or for the extension of justice? In that dramatic scene on Calvary's hill three men were crucified. We must never forget that all three were crucified for the same crime—the crime of extremism. Two were extremists for immorality, and thus fell below their environment. The other, Jesus Christ, was an extremist for love, truth and goodness, and thereby rose above his environment. Perhaps the South, the nation and the world are in dire need of creative extremists.

I had hoped that the white moderate would see this need. Perhaps I was too optimistic; perhaps I expected too much. I suppose I should have realized that few members of the oppressor race can understand the deep groans and passionate yearnings of the oppressed race, and still fewer have the vision to see that injustice must be rooted out by strong, persistent and determined action. I am thankful, however, that some of our white brothers in the South have grasped the meaning of this social revolution and committed themselves to it. They are still all too few in quantity, but they are big in quality. Some—such as Ralph McGill, Lillian Smith, Harry Golden, James McBride Dabbs, Ann Braden and Sarah Patton Boyle—have written about our struggle in eloquent and prophetic terms. Others have marched with us down nameless streets of the South. They have languished in filthy, roach-infested jails, suffering the abuse and brutality of policemen who view them as "dirty nigger-lovers." Unlike so many of their moderate brothers and sisters, they have recognized the urgency of the moment and sensed the need for powerful "action" antidotes to combat the disease of segregation.

Let me take note of my other major disappointment. I have been 33 so greatly disappointed with the white church and its leadership. Of course, there are some notable exceptions. I am not unmindful of the fact that each of you has taken some significant stands on this issue. I commend you, Reverend Stallings, for your Christian stand on this past Sunday, in welcoming Negroes to your worship service on a nonsegregated basis. I commend the Catholic leaders of this state for integrating Spring Hill College several years ago.

But despite these notable exceptions, I must honestly reiterate 34 that I have been disappointed with the church. I do not say this as one of those negative critics who can always find something wrong with the church. I say this as a minister of the gospel, who loves the church; who was nurtured in its bosom; who has been sustained by its spiritual blessings and who will remain true to it as long as the cord of life shall lengthen.

When I was suddenly catapulted into the leadership of the bus 35 protest in Montgomery, Alabama, a few years ago, I felt we would be supported by the white church. I felt that the white ministers, priests and rabbis of the South would be among our strongest allies. Instead, some have been outright opponents, refusing to understand the freedom movement and misrepresenting its leaders; all too many others have been more cautious than courageous and have remained silent behind the anesthetizing security of stained-glass windows.

In spite of my shattered dreams, I came to Birmingham with the 36 hope that the white religious leadership of this community would see the justice of our cause and, with deep moral concern, would serve as the channel through which our just grievances could reach the power structure. I had hoped that each of you would understand. But again I have been disappointed.

I have heard numerous southern religious leaders admonish their 37 worshipers to comply with a desegregation decision because it is the law, but I have longed to hear white ministers declare: "Follow this decree because integration is morally right and because the Negro is your brother." In the midst of blatant injustices inflicted upon the Negro, I have watched white churchmen stand on the sideline and mouth pious irrelevancies and sanctimonious trivialities. In the midst of a mighty struggle to rid our nation of racial and economic injustice, I have heard many ministers say: "Those are social issues, with which the gospel has no real concern." And I have watched many churches commit themselves to a completely other-worldly religion which makes a strange, un-Biblical distinction between body and soul, between the sacred and the secular.

I have traveled the length and breadth of Alabama, Mississippi 38 and all the other southern states. On sweltering summer days and crisp autumn mornings I have looked at the South's beautiful churches with their lofty spires pointing heavenward. I have beheld the impressive outlines of her massive religious-education buildings. Over and over I have found myself asking: "What kind of people worship here? Who is their God? Where were their voices when the lips of Governor Barnett dripped with words of interposition and nullification? Where were they when Governor Wallace gave a clarion call for defiance and hatred? Where were their voices of support when bruised and weary Negro men and women decided to rise from the dark dungeons of complacency to the bright hills of creative protest?"

Yes, these questions are still in my mind. In deep disappointment 39 I have wept over the laxity of the church. But be assured that my tears have been tears of love. There can be no deep disappointment where there is not deep love. Yes, I love the church. How could I do otherwise? I am in the rather unique position of being the son, the grandson and the great-grandson of preachers. Yes, I see the church as the body of Christ. But, oh! How we have blemished and scarred that body through social neglect and through fear of being nonconformists.

There was a time when the church was very powerful—in the 40 time when the early Christians rejoiced at being deemed worthy to suffer for what they believed. In those days the church was not merely a thermometer that recorded the ideas and principles of popular opinion; it was a thermostat that transformed the mores of society. Whenever the early Christians entered a town, the people in power became disturbed and immediately sought to convict the Christians for being "disturbers of the peace" and "outside agitators." But the Christians pressed on, in the conviction that they were "a colony of heaven," called to obey God rather than man. Small in number, they were big in commitment. They were too God-intoxicated to be "astronomically intimidated." By their effort and example they brought an end to such ancient evils as infanticide and gladiatorial contests.

Things are different now. So often the contemporary church is a 41 weak, ineffectual voice with an uncertain sound. So often it is an archdefender of the status quo. Far from being disturbed by the presence of the church, the power structure of the average community is consoled by the church's silent—and often even vocal—sanction of things as they are.

But the judgment of God is upon the church as never before. If 42 today's church does not recapture the sacrificial spirit of the early church, it will lose its authenticity, forfeit the loyalty of millions, and be dismissed as an irrelevant social club with no meaning for the twentieth century. Every day I meet young people whose disappointment with the church has turned into outright disgust.

Perhaps I have once again been too optimistic. Is organized reli- 43 gion too inextricably bound to the status quo to save our nation and the world? Perhaps I must turn my faith to the inner spiritual church, the church within the church, as the true *ekklesia* and the hope of the world. But again I am thankful to God that some noble souls from the ranks of organized religion have broken loose from the paralyzing chains of conformity and joined us as active partners in the struggle for freedom. They have left their secure congregations and walked the streets of Albany, Georgia, with us. They have gone down the highways of the South on tortuous rides for freedom. Yes, they have gone to jail with us. Some have been dismissed from their churches, have lost the support of their bishops and fellow ministers. But they have acted in the faith that right defeated is stronger than evil triumphant. Their witness has been the spiritual salt that has preserved the true meaning of the gospel in these troubled times. They have carved a tunnel of hope through the dark mountain of disappointment.

I hope the church as a whole will meet the challenge of this 44 decisive hour. But even if the church does not come to the aid of justice, I have no despair about the future. I have no fear about the outcome of our struggle in Birmingham, even if our motives are at present misunderstood. We will reach the goal of freedom in Birmingham and all over the nation, because the goal of America is freedom. Abused and scorned though we may be, our destiny is tied up with America's destiny. Before the pilgrims landed at Plymouth, we were here. Before the pen of Jefferson etched the majestic words of the Declaration of Independence across the pages of history, we were here. For more than two centuries our forebears labored in this country without wages; they made cotton king; they built the homes of their masters while suffering gross injustice and shameful humiliation—and yet out of a bottomless vitality they continued to thrive and develop. If the inexpressible cruelties of slavery could not stop us, the opposition we now face will surely fail. We will win our freedom because the sacred heritage of our nation and the eternal will of God are embodied in our echoing demands.

Before closing I feel impelled to mention one other point in your 45 statement that has troubled me profoundly. You warmly commended the Birmingham police force for keeping "order" and "preventing violence." I doubt that you would have so warmly commended the police force if you had seen its dogs sinking their teeth into unarmed, nonviolent Negroes. I doubt that you would so quickly commend the policemen if you were to observe their ugly and inhumane treatment of Negroes here in the city jail; if you were to watch them push and curse old Negro women and young Negro girls; if you were to see them slap and kick old Negro men and young boys; if you were to observe them as they did on two occasions, refuse to give us food because we wanted to sing our grace together. I cannot join you in your praise of the Birmingham police department.

It is true that the police have exercised a degree of discipline in   46 handling the demonstrators. In this sense they have conducted themselves rather "nonviolently" in public. But for what purpose? To preserve the evil system of segregation. Over the past few years I have consistently preached that nonviolence demands that the means we use must be as pure as the ends we seek. I have tried to make clear that it is wrong to use immoral means to attain moral ends. But now I must affirm that it is just as wrong, or perhaps even more so, to use moral means to preserve immoral ends. Perhaps Mr. Connor and his policemen have been rather nonviolent in public, as was Chief Pritchett in Albany, Georgia, but they have used the moral means of nonviolence to maintain the immoral end of racial injustice. As T. S. Eliot has said: "The last temptation is the greatest treason: To do the right deed for the wrong reason."

I wish you had commended the Negro sit-inners and demon-   47 strators of Birmingham for their sublime courage, their willingness to suffer and their amazing discipline in the midst of great provocation. One day the South will recognize its real heroes. They will be the James Merediths, with the noble sense of purpose that enables them to face jeering and hostile mobs, and with the agonizing loneliness that characterizes the life of the pioneer. They will be old, oppressed, battered Negro women, symbolized in a seventy-two-year-old woman in Montgomery, Alabama, who rose up with a sense of dignity and with her people decided not to ride segregated buses, and who responded with ungrammatical profundity to one who inquired about her weariness: "My feet is tired, but my soul is at rest." They will be the young high school and college students, the young ministers of the gospel and a host of their elders, courageously and nonviolently sitting in at lunch counters and willingly going to jail for conscience' sake. One day the South will know that when these disinherited children of God sat down at lunch counters, they were in reality standing up for what is best in the American dream and for the most sacred values in our Judaeo-Christian heritage, thereby bringing our nation back to those great wells of democracy which were dug deep by the founding fathers in their formulation of the Constitution and the Declaration of Independence.

Never before have I written so long a letter. I'm afraid it is much   48
too long to take your precious time. I can assure you that it would
have been much shorter if I had been writing from a comfortable
desk, but what else can one do when he is alone in a narrow jail cell,
other than write long letters, think long thoughts and pray long
prayers?

If I have said anything in this letter that overstates the truth and   49
indicates an unreasonable impatience, I beg you to forgive me. If I
have said anything that understates the truth and indicates my having
a patience that allows me to settle for anything less than brotherhood,
I beg God to forgive me.

I hope this letter finds you strong in the faith. I also hope that   50
circumstances will soon make it possible for me to meet each of you,
not as an integrationist or a civil-rights leader but as a fellow clergyman and a Christian brother. Let us all hope that the dark clouds
of racial prejudice will soon pass away and the deep fog of misunderstanding will be lifted from our feardrenched communities, and
in some not too distant tomorrow the radiant stars of love and brotherhood will shine over our great nation with all their scintillating
beauty.

Yours for the cause of Peace and Brotherhood,
Martin Luther King, Jr.

RESPONDING TO READING

Key words: class community education freedom identity loss
minority power race rights striving transformation

Rhetorical concepts: analysis anecdote cause and effect explanation
illustration induction meditation narrative/example proclamation

1. Definitions are crucial to Martin Luther King, Jr.'s argument. Explain the
distinctions he makes between moral law and civil law, just and unjust law
(*see* paragraphs 16–17).
2. King grounds his argument in a long religious tradition. Why is it appropriate and necessary for him to do this? Why does he cite the theologians
Aquinas (a Catholic), Buber (a Jew), and Tillich (a Protestant) (paragraph 16)?
3. In what ways is this tradition relevant to the Civil Rights movement,
particularly as manifested in civil disobedience? See, for instance, King's
response to the argument that civil rights activists should go slow because
" 'It has taken Christianity almost two thousand years to accomplish what it
has' " (paragraph 26).
4. King's ostensible audience is the eight Alabama clergy to whom his "Letter from Birmingham Jail" is addressed. What evidence for this do you find,

besides the salutation? However, his real audience is far more extensive. Of whom is it composed? How can you tell? Do you see yourself as part of the intended audience? Why, or why not?

5.   On what grounds, under what circumstances would you be willing to go to jail? If the possibility of a prison record affected your opportunities for employment in some states (such as practicing medicine or law), would that deter you? Ultimately, what risks are you willing to take for a cause, and what price are you willing to pay?

Civil Disobedience: Destroyer of Democracy

LEWIS H. VAN DUSEN, JR.

"Civil Disobedience: Destroyer of Democracy" was originally published in the *American Bar Association Journal* in 1969, shortly after the Vietnam War protests and their accompanying civil disobedience disrupted the 1968 Democratic Convention in Chicago. Lewis H. Van Dusen, Jr., takes a predictable stance for a representative of the legal profession. He distinguishes "the conscientious law breaking of Socrates, Gandhi and Thoreau" from "the conscientious law testing" of Martin Luther King, Jr., who he claims "was not a civil disobedient." True civil disobedients, Van Dusen says, break the laws (such as by witholding taxes or violating state laws) knowing they are legally wrong, but believing they are morally right. In contrast, Dr. King's form of protest encourages the violation of one law in expectation of support from a higher jurisdictional body. Thus Dr. King encouraged civil rights protesters to violate state laws in order to challenge the Supreme Law of the Land, and unlike true civil disobedients, he did not expect to pay a penalty. Although Van Dusen is writing for lawyers, instead of being full of the predictable legal jargon, case references, and technical legal arguments, his essay is non-technical, an argument addressed more to general readers.

Van Dusen, born in 1910, is a graduate of Princeton and Oxford, where he was a Rhodes Scholar and earned a law degree in 1935. A lawyer in Philadelphia, he has been president and chancellor of the Philadelphia Bar Association. In the American Bar Association, he chaired the Committee on Ethics and Professional Responsibility, and served on the Committee on the Federal Judiciary.

As Charles E. Wyzanski, Chief Judge of the United States District 1
Court in Boston, wrote in the February, 1968, *Atlantic* [*Monthly*]: "Disobedience is a long step from dissent. Civil disobedience involves a deliberate and punishable breach of legal duty." Protesters might prefer a different definition. They would rather say that civil disobedience is the peaceable resistance of conscience.

The philosophy of civil disobedience was not developed in our 2

American democracy, but in the very first democracy of Athens. It was expressed by the poet Sophocles and the philosopher Socrates. In Sophocles's tragedy, Antigone chose to obey her conscience and violate the state edict against providing burial for her brother, who had been decreed a traitor. When the dictator Creon found out that Antigone had buried her fallen brother, he confronted her and reminded her that there was a mandatory death penalty for this deliberate disobedience of the state law. Antigone nobly replied, "Nor did I think your orders were so strong that you, a mortal man, could overrun the gods' unwritten and unfailing laws."

Conscience motivated Antigone. She was not testing the validity   3 of the law in the hope that eventually she would be sustained. Appealing to the judgment of the community, she explained her action to the chorus. She was not secret and surreptitious—the interment of her brother was open and public. She was not violent; she did not trespass on another citizen's rights. And finally, she accepted without resistance the death sentence—the penalty for violation. By voluntarily accepting the law's sanctions, she was not a revolutionary denying the authority of the state. Antigone's behavior exemplifies the classic case of civil disobedience.

Socrates believed that reason could dictate a conscientious diso-   4 bedience of state law, but he also believed that he had to accept the legal sanctions of the state. In Plato's *Crito,* Socrates from his hanging basket accepted the death penalty for his teaching of religion to youths contrary to state laws.

The sage of Walden, Henry David Thoreau, took this philosophy   5 of nonviolence and developed it into a strategy for solving society's injustices. First enunciating it in protest against the Mexican War, he then turned it to use against slavery. For refusing to pay taxes that would help pay the enforcers of the fugitive slave law, he went to prison. In Thoreau's words, "If the alternative is to keep all just men in prison or to give up slavery, the state will not hesitate which to choose."

Sixty years later, Gandhi took Thoreau's civil disobedience as his   6 strategy to wrest Indian independence from England. The famous salt march against a British imperial tax is his best-known example of protest.

But the conscientious law breaking of Socrates, Gandhi and Tho-   7 reau is to be distinguished from the conscientious law testing of Martin Luther King, Jr., who was not a civil disobedient. The civil disobedient withholds taxes or violates state laws knowing he is legally wrong, but believing he is morally right. While he wrapped himself in the mantle of Gandhi and Thoreau, Dr. King led his followers in violation of state laws he believed were contrary to the Federal Constitution. But since Supreme Court decisions in the end generally upheld his many actions, he should not be considered a true civil disobedient.

The civil disobedience of Antigone is like that of the pacifist who 8 withholds paying the percentage of his taxes that goes to the Defense Department, or the Quaker who travels against State Department regulations to Hanoi to distribute medical supplies, or the Vietnam war protester who tears up his draft card. This civil disobedient has been nonviolent in his defiance of the law; he has been unfurtive in his violation; he has been submissive to the penalties of the law. He has neither evaded the law nor interfered with another's rights. He has been neither a rioter nor a revolutionary. The thrust of his cause has not been the might of coercion but the martyrdom of conscience.

Was the Boston Tea Party Civil Disobedience?

Those who justify violence and radical action as being in the 9 tradition of our Revolution show a misunderstanding of the philosophy of democracy.

James Farmer, former head of the Congress of Racial Equality, in 10 defense of the mass action confrontation method, has told of a famous organized demonstration that took place in opposition to political and economic discrimination. The protesters beat back and scattered the law enforcers and then proceeded to loot and destroy private property. Mr. Farmer then said he was talking about the Boston Tea Party and implied that violence as a method for redress of grievances was an American tradition and a legacy of our revolutionary heritage. While it is true that there is no more sacred document than our Declaration of Independence, Jefferson's "inherent right of rebellion" was predicated on the tyrannical denial of democratic means. If there is no popular assembly to provide an adjustment of ills, and if there is no court system to dispose of injustices, then there is, indeed, a right to rebel.

The seventeenth century's John Locke, the philosophical father 11 of the Declaration of Independence, wrote in his *Second Treatise on Civil Government:* "Wherever law ends, tyranny begins . . . and the people are absolved from any further obedience. Governments are dissolved from within when the legislative [chamber] is altered. When the government [becomes] . . . arbitrary disposers of lives, liberties and fortunes of the people, such revolutions happen . . ."

But there are some sophisticated proponents of the revolutionary 12 redress of grievances who say that the test of the need for radical action is not the unavailability of democratic institutions but the ineffectuality of those institutions to remove blatant social inequalities.

If social injustice exists, they say, concerted disobedience is required against the constituted government, whether it be totalitarian or democratic in structure.

Of course, only the most bigoted chauvinist would claim that 13 America is without some glaring faults. But there has never been a utopian society on earth and there never will be unless human nature is remade. Since inequities will mar even the best-framed democracies, the injustice rationale would allow a free right of civil resistance to be available always as a shortcut alternative to the democratic way of petition, debate and assembly. The lesson of history is that civil insurgency spawns far more injustices than it removes. The Jeffersons, Washingtons and Adamses resisted tyranny with the aim of promoting the procedures of democracy. They would never have resisted a democratic government with the risk of promoting the techniques of tyranny.

Legitimate Pressures and Illegitimate Results

There are many civil rights leaders who show impatience with 14 the process of democracy. They rely on the sit-in, boycott or mass picketing to gain speedier solutions to the problems that face every citizen. But we must realize that the legitimate pressures that won concessions in the past can easily escalate into the illegitimate power plays that might extort demands in the future. The victories of these civil rights leaders must not shake our confidence in the democratic procedures, as the pressures of demonstration are desirable only if they take place within the limits allowed by law. Civil rights gains should continue to be won by the persuasion of Congress and other legislative bodies and by the decision of courts. Any illegal entreaty for the rights of some can be an injury to the rights of others, for mass demonstrations often trigger violence.

Those who advocate taking the law into their own hands should 15 reflect that when they are disobeying what they consider to be an immoral law, they are deciding on a possibly immoral course. Their answer is that the process for democratic relief is too slow, that only mass confrontation can bring immediate action, and that any injuries are the inevitable cost of the pursuit of justice. Their answer is, simply put, that the end justifies the means. It is this justification of any form of demonstration as a form of dissent that threatens to destroy a society built on the rule of law.

Our Bill of Rights guarantees wide opportunities to use mass 16 meetings, public parades and organized demonstrations to stimulate sentiment, to dramatize issues and to cause change. The Washington freedom march of 1963 was such a call for action. But the rights of free expression cannot be mere force cloaked in the garb of free speech. As the courts have decreed in labor cases, free assembly does not mean mass picketing or sit-down strikes. These rights are subject to limitations of time and place so as to secure the rights of others. When militant students storm a college president's office to achieve demands, when certain groups plan rush-hour car stalling to protest discrimination in employment, these are not dissent, but a denial of rights to others. Neither is it the lawful use of mass protest, but rather the unlawful use of mob power.

Justice Black, one of the foremost advocates and defenders of the   17
right of protest and dissent, has said:

> . . . Experience demonstrates that it is not a far step from what to many seems to be the earnest, honest, patriotic, kind-spirited multitude of today, to the fanatical, threatening, lawless mob of tomorrow. And the crowds that press in the streets for noble goals today can be supplanted tomorrow by street mobs pressuring the courts for precisely opposite ends.

Society must censure those demonstrators who would trespass   18
on the public peace, as it must condemn those rioters whose pillage would destroy the public peace. But more ambivalent is society's posture toward the civil disobedient. Unlike the rioter, the true civil disobedient commits no violence. Unlike the mob demonstrator, he commits no trespass on others' rights. The civil disobedient, while deliberately violating a law, shows an oblique respect for the law by voluntarily submitting to its sanctions. He neither resists arrest nor evades punishment. Thus, he breaches the law but not the peace.

But civil disobedience, whatever the ethical rationalization, is still   19
an assault on our democratic society, an affront to our legal order and an attack on our constitutional government. To indulge civil disobedience is to invite anarchy, and the permissive arbitrariness of anarchy is hardly less tolerable than the repressive arbitrariness of tyranny. Too often the license of liberty is followed by the loss of liberty, because into the desert of anarchy comes the man on horseback, a Mussolini or a Hitler.

Violations of Law Subvert Democracy

Law violations, even for ends recognized as laudable, are not only   20
assaults on the rule of law, but subversions of the democratic process. The disobedient act of conscience does not ennoble democracy; it erodes it.

First, it courts violence, and even the most careful and limited   21
use of nonviolent acts of disobedience may help sow the dragon-teeth

of civil riot. Civil disobedience is the progenitor of disorder, and disorder is the sire of violence.

Second, the concept of civil disobedience does not invite princi- 22 ples of general applicability. If the children of light are morally privileged to resist particular laws on grounds of conscience, so are the children of darkness. Former Deputy Attorney General Burke Marshall said: "If the decision to break the law really turned on individual conscience, it is hard to see in law how [the civil rights leader] is better off than former Governor Ross Barnett of Mississippi who also believed deeply in his cause and was willing to go to jail."

Third, even the most noble act of civil disobedience assaults the 23 rule of law. Although limited as to method, motive and objective, it has the effect of inducing others to engage in different forms of law breaking characterized by methods unsanctioned and condemned by classic theories of law violation. Unfortunately, the most patent lesson of civil disobedience is not so much nonviolence of action as defiance of authority.

Finally, the greatest danger in condoning civil disobedience as a 24 permissible strategy for hastening change is that it undermines our democratic processes. To adopt the techniques of civil disobedience is to assume that representative government does not work. To resist the decisions of courts and the laws of elected assemblies is to say that democracy has failed.

There is no man who is above the law, and there is no man who 25 has a right to break the law. Civil disobedience is not above the law, but against the law. When the civil disobedient disobeys one law, he invariably subverts all law. When the civil disobedient says that he is above the law, he is saying that democracy is beneath him. His disobedience shows a distrust for the democratic system. He is merely saying that since democracy does not work, why should he help make it work. Thoreau expressed well the civil disobedient's disdain for democracy:

> As for adopting the ways which the state has provided for remedying the evil, I know not of such ways. They take too much time and a man's life will be gone. I have other affairs to attend to. I came into this world not chiefly to make this a good place to live in, but to live in it, be it good or bad.

Thoreau's position is not only morally irresponsible but politically 26 reprehensible. When citizens in a democracy are called on to make a profession of faith, the civil disobedients offer only a confession of failure. Tragically, when civil disobedients for lack of faith abstain from democratic involvement, they help attain their own gloomy prediction. They help create the social and political basis for their own despair. By foreseeing failure, they help forge it. If citizens rely on antidemocratic means of protest, they will help bring about the undemocratic result of an authoritarian or anarchic state.

How far demonstrations properly can be employed to produce 27 political and social change is a pressing question, particularly in view of the provocations accompanying the National Democratic Convention in Chicago last August and the reaction of the police to them. A line must be drawn by the judiciary between the demands of those who seek absolute order, which can lead only to a dictatorship, and those who seek absolute freedom, which can lead only to anarchy. The line, wherever it is drawn by our courts, should be respected on the college campus, on the streets and elsewhere.

Undue provocation will inevitably result in overreaction, human 28 emotions being what they are. Violence will follow. This cycle undermines the very democracy it is designed to preserve. The lesson of the past is that democracies will fall if violence, including the intentional provocations that will lead to violence, replaces democratic procedures, as in Athens, Rome and the Weimar Republic. This lesson must be constantly explained by the legal profession.

We should heed the words of William James:

> Democracy is still upon its trial. The civic genius of our people is its only bulwark and . . . neither battleships nor public libraries nor great newspapers nor booming stocks: neither mechanical invention nor political adroitness, nor churches nor universities nor civil service examinations can save us from degeneration if the inner mystery be lost.
>
> That mystery, at once the secret and the glory of our English-speaking race, consists of nothing but two habits. . . . One of them is habit of trained and disciplined good temper towards the opposite party when it fairly wins its innings. The other is that of fierce and merciless resentment toward every man or set of men who break the public peace. (James, *Pragmatism* 1907, pages 127–128)

RESPONDING TO READING

Key words: community freedom loss minority power race rights striving transformation

Rhetorical concepts: analogy analysis cause and effect deduction definition process

1. Why does Van Dusen take pains to begin his argument by setting it in a long philosophical tradition and citing famous works on civil disobedience by Plato, Socrates, Sophocles, and Thoreau (paragraphs 2–6)?
2. Definitions are crucial to Van Dusen's argument. What distinctions does

he make between dissent and civil disobedience? Between the non-violent philosophy of Thoreau and Gandhi as "a strategy for solving society's injustices" (paragraph 6) and "the conscientious law testing of Martin Luther King, Jr., who was not a civil disobedient" (paragraphs 5–7)?

3.   On what grounds does Van Dusen distinguish between "legitimate" and "illegitimate" kinds of demonstrations (paragraphs 14–17)? Does he consider the Boston Tea Party and the American colonists' rebellion against England legitimate or illegitimate (paragraphs 110–13)? How does the authority for these differ, in Van Dusen's view, from protests against the Vietnam War (paragraphs 20–29)?

4.   What is the relation of civil disobedience to democracy? Does this relationship change if you take a long-range historical view rather than considering only a single incident? Do you agree or disagree with Van Dusen? In what ways have his arguments influenced your response?

QUESTIONS FOR REFLECTION AND WRITING

What Does Family History Mean?

1. Trace a particularly meaningful relationship—for better or for worse—between two or three people in your family, preferably of different generations. Examples might be the relationship between a set of your grandparents and one of your parents; or between your grandmother, your mother, and yourself; or between your father, your uncle, and yourself; or any other combination of people who have had an interesting relationship. Because your readers will not know any of the people, you will need to characterize each in sufficient detail to enable your reader to see them. Identify one or two of the major aspects of this relationship, illustrating it through a particular activity, such as Eudora Welty did with reading and Scott Russell Sanders did with tool using.

2. Return to the Questions for Discovery and Discussion at the end of the Introduction to this chapter. There, you were asked to interview an elderly member of your family and to accumulate such materials as family tales and old photographs. Using what you have discovered, write an essay on the ways the past of your family has affected who you are, what you value, and what you do. In the course of your essay, try to compare what you are saying about your own family history with what at least one of the authors in this section (Lopez, Murray, Welty, and Sanders) has had to say. Your goal will be to help yourself and your audience understand the way your family history has shaped who you are.

What Have We Done to the Earth?

1. Pick a current problem that results from environmental mistakes in the past that affect both society at large and you as an individual. You could elaborate on one of the issues discussed in this section (such as the threatened or actual destruction of a particular species of plant or animal, the pollution of a favorite beach or river, or the use of insecticides, or choose one that has special meaning for you. Analyze the problem and interpret its consequences in a way that might enable readers to prevent comparable problems in the future.)

2. Reflect upon what you know of the past in comparison with what the authors in this section have learned. Have you learned enough to help you in the present and future? If so, where have you learned it and how? If not, what went wrong? Then, write an essay about what you know, and wish you knew, of the past, and what its effects upon you are or might be.

How Does an Idea Evolve?

1. Compare Thoreau's "Civil Disobedience" to King's "Letter from Birmingham Jail." What do the two have in common? In what ways do they differ? Focus your essay on the ways that King develops ideas that Thoreau states.

2. Trace the evolution of an idea, from either its inception or some critical stage in its past to the present time. Identify one or two of its major proponents, and discuss several of its significant stages and changes. Among the many possibilities: representative government, women's suffrage, civil rights, the structure of the universe, capitalism, romantic love, and heroism.

What Can We Learn from the Past?

1. Write an essay in which you look closely at some aspect of the past, either in your family or in your reading; find appropriate primary sources (documents, photographs, etc.) and help your readers to discern the meaning of what you have come to know. Your goal will be to help an audience understand what it was really like and why it should be important to them.

2. Pick a problem in the present that only makes sense in terms of the past. Examples might be the conflict between the Jews and the Arabs in the Middle East, the debate over affirmative action hiring practices in the United States, or the quarrel with Japan over the import and export of automobiles. Write an essay in which you attempt to show those who are not aware of the past why a knowledge of it will help them understand what is going on and how to act more wisely in the present.

6

WHAT WILL THE FUTURE BE LIKE?

Time present and time past
Are both perhaps present in time future,
And time future contained in time past.

T. S. ELIOT

Why Consider This Question?

The future does not exist until it happens; one thing we have learned from the past is that we cannot know what the future will be like. Yet we continue to peer around the corner, hoping to find answers to what the future may hold. Why?

One reason is that by talking about the future we understand better what the present means. Serious science fiction writers have always known this. Ray Bradbury, imagining earth's colonization of Mars in *The Martian Chronicles,* presents the problem of humans encountering "the other," that is, those we do not understand: other species, other cultures, other social classes, or other people. Frank Herbert, in *Dune,* presents a world without water; Ursula LeGuin, in *The Left Hand of Darkness,* imagines a race without sex, or, more precisely, a world in which socially constructed meanings of sex are absurd. Margaret Atwood, in *The Handmaid's Tale,* presents a world dominated by a fierce and hypocritical religion. Such issues are likely to be of interest in the future, but we know that they are crucially important to consider in the present. Likewise, the popularity of both of the *Star Trek* series has more to do with the way they speak to the present than to the credibility of their views of the future. Imaginative writers have led the way into the future, but we do not judge their

567

work according to the way their predictions work out; we ask their futures to help us imagine today more creatively.

A second reason to concern ourselves with the future is to prepare ourselves for it. What will the jobs, the educational needs, and the physical demands of the future be like? Several predictions have been suggested, for example, that by the end of this century the United States will need more workers with Ph.D.s in all fields than we are likely to have under present policies. Such a prediction is immensely valuable for present college students thinking about going on to graduate school at a time when jobs are in short supply. If the prediction is sound—and this one is in some dispute—students can make plans wisely.

Despite our worries about whether even informed guesses about what is to come will work out, much about the future is predictable, or, at least probable. The odds are that the sun will rise tomorrow, and for many tomorrows after that; the physical laws of attraction and repulsion will not be repealed; the human race is likely to survive in something like its present state. While the course of human events is surely not as predictable as astronomical events, or perhaps even as predictable as the weather, we have learned some ways to make informed guesses about what may happen down the road. Just as imagining the future allows us to see the present more clearly, so our ability to look closely at the present suggests what the future may be like.

Much of our speculation about the future is based on the expectation that current trends and knowledge will continue; this is called *extrapolation,* that is, extending present lines into the future. We can sometimes "change" the future by changing the present, and extrapolation gives us the information we can use to make such changes. Thus, we know enough about the effects upon the earth's protective ozone layer of releasing certain chemicals into the atmosphere to know that all life on earth is threatened by solar radiation; most nations have now banned the use of these chemicals. Perhaps the two most powerful extrapolations in the twentieth century are represented in the readings in this book: Rachel Carson's *Silent Spring* (Chapter 5), which alerted the world to the dangers of indiscriminate use of insecticides, and Carl Sagan's essay, "Nuclear Winter" (in this Chapter), which predicted the devastating results of any nuclear weapons exchange upon the earth's climate and helped to halt talk of a "winnable" nuclear war. Both of these studies were based on the most careful accumulation of scientific evidence, with reasonable projections into the future.

We thus find ourselves speculating about the future for at least three reasons: we want to understand our present more fully, we want to see into the future to prepare ourselves for it, and we want to imagine possible futures so that we can choose a future we will want to inhabit or to have our children inhabit.

For many of us, the most immediate vision that we have of the future is indeed our children, or the children of those we love, even if they have not yet arrived. For this reason, the readings that follow begin with a consideration of the future of the family, the most personal and intimate location for shaping the future. But the family is not isolated; it exists within a society whose conflicts sometimes destroy families, or even (as Bettelheim argued in Chapter 3) render family values destructive to the individual. Thus the second section turns to the prospects of war or peace, an issue of enormous importance to all of our futures. The chapter concludes with a series of essays about the ways we can speak and think about the future, with a particular concern for the language of specialized communities (business and medicine are our examples) and of computers. The overriding question, however, remains: how can we most creatively, constructively, and coherently consider what the future will bring?

What Is the Future of the Family?

T. Berry Brazelton's "Issues for Working Parents," begins this section, a social scientist looking at the needs of children of working parents. The problem is severe: "The loss of the extended family has left the nuclear family unsupported." Without grandparents or other family caretakers, where are parents to turn if both work? What is the effect upon children, and hence the future, if others must play the traditional parental roles, particularly in babyhood? And what is the effect upon the family itself if children no longer are "seen as an opportunity for strengthening relationships within the family"? Deborah Fallows pursues the same questions, but from the perspective of a stay-at-home mother rather than a detached social scientist. Fallows speaks of the time she "dressed for motherhood rather than for success" and debates the meaning of progress and liberation for modern mothers.

Robert S. Weiss looks at the same situation from the male point of view in "Marriage As Partnership." Focusing on those he calls "occupationally successful men," Weiss tries to examine the values and attitudes they bring to their families with working wives. Perhaps it is no surprise that he finds that traditional values and traditional assumptions about family responsibilities continue to hold, despite "pride in their wives' achievements." Although some male behavior is changed, he finds that the male attitudes about marriage seem quite resistant to change. When we read this essay next to those by Brazelton and Fallows, we must puzzle about the future of the family.

Of course, one aspect of the future is sure: we are growing older and, if lucky enough, will one day be aged. Robert Butler, looking at the increasing numbers of older people in the American population, warns that the way we speak of them implies an entire complex of attitudes: "Those who think of older people as boobies, crones, witches, old biddies, old fogies, as out-to-pasture, boring, garrulous, pains-in-the-neck, as unproductive, worthless people, have another think coming." We need to come up with new language and new ways of thinking about the elderly, he argues, and the various myths of aging need to be replaced. After all, he points out, "old age is the only period of life with no future," and that perception presents unique possibilities for young and old alike. But an aside reminds us that "one fourth of older people have no family at all," an ominous reminder of the loneliness the future may hold.

Finally, Ellen Goodman asks us not to take the whole issue too seriously, particularly as she looks at the new version of the extended family in an age of multiple marriages. No longer does this family consist of grandparents, parents, uncles, aunts, cousins, sisters, and brothers, but such odd relatives as "stepaunt's husband's children by his first marriage." Our reality, she concludes, "is more flexible and our relationships more supportive than our language." The family, no doubt, has a future, and that future is different from the past. But that does not necessarily mean that the difference in family roles and functions represents a decline.

Will War Shape the Future?

War has a way of overturning planned futures; when it comes everyone's life changes. Margaret Mead opens this section with an argument that war is not necessary, is not built in to the biology of our species. The issue is significant, as she points out at the start, since some will argue that we have "such pugnacious instincts" that the best we can do is to "channel them in new directions." But Mead is more optimistic than that, and she bases her argument on anthropological knowledge of human cultures that do not practice war.

Mead's essay is more than fifty years old, and those fifty years have seen wars of every description. Czeslaw Milosz experienced some of that conflict and his gloomy essay, "American Ignorance of War," reflects that personal experience. The first encounter with war, he argues, upsets a person's belief that peace is natural: "His first stroll along a street littered with glass from bomb-shattered windows shakes his faith in the 'naturalness' of his world." Soon the conditions of war become natural, despite prior expectations that normal life is peaceful. Americans who believe that the future holds no war for them are, Milosz asserts, incredibly naive, for our turn will come.

If Milosz is right, and Mead's hopes for an invention to replace war turn out to be naive, Carl Sagan gives us a scenario for the future. In "The Nuclear Winter," he sets out the details of the "unprecedented human catastrophe" that a nuclear war would bring. Using the cool and detailed language of an observational scientist, he portrays a world of death and destruction almost beyond imagining. His purpose is clear; he thinks, with Mead, that we can prevent the catastrophe if we have the will: "Fortunately, it is not yet too late." Milosz views the situation differently.

Finally, John Lewis Gaddis, in "Coping with Victory," tries to assess the results of the conclusion of the Cold War. With the clear victory of the west, "we are at one of those rare points of leverage in history when familiar constraints have dropped away; what we do now could establish the framework within which events will play themselves out for decades to come." Unfortunately, Gaddis feels that "we are almost certainly not up to the task." Looking to his knowledge of history, he predicts "what we will probably do is fritter away the fruits of victory by failing to think through what it is we want victory to accomplish." Nonetheless, Gaddis proposes an explanation of what has occurred and a course of action that suggests cautious hope. We may, he suggests, actually be able to influence, if not control, the future, and war may not be inevitable.

How Can We Think and Speak About the Future?

Economist Robert B. Reich opens this section with a close look at the way the American corporation effects the American economy. The traditional belief that the corporation and the economy are linked in positive ways is no longer true, he asserts. If we are to see clearly into the future we must recognize that change: "What is good for the shareholders is not necessarily good for the nation." Furthermore, foreign ownership of American capital is continuing to increase rapidly and American corporations are now doing "all sorts of sophisticated work outside of the United States." The historic connection between corporations and the national interest is no longer valid and new ways of thinking about American business are necessary: "The struggle to define a new relationship between corporation and nation will be one of the central economic and political tasks of our era, and it will defy easy solutions." Reich proposes some of the outlines of the new thinking that such solutions will require, including a changed emphasis on education and on the interconnectedness of all people. But he suggests that a new way of thinking about American business, which includes new ways of speaking about business, is the first task.

The language of medicine is the subject of Perri Klass's essay, which argues that an important part of becoming a physician is mastering the special language of doctors. This "linguistic separation between doctors and patients" is what "Learning the Language" is all about; furthermore, the language helps to define the profession and those who "belong" to it. A way of speaking, Klass suggests, is an entire way of thinking and acting.

As some of us look into the future we see, for good or ill, the increasing presence of machines, particularly computers. When Gina Kolata asks "How Can Computers Get Common Sense?" she encounters many of the problems the field of Artificial Intelligence has found in trying to create machines that can think. Human reasoning turns out to be "a jumble of poorly understood mechanisms and methods" that computers are not well suited to reproduce. Human common sense, it turns out, is maddeningly complex and may not be possible for computers to duplicate. If computers could think the way we do, they might replace us, and "what will we do instead of work?" Well, Adrienne Rich proposes in her poetic response to these questions ("Artificial Intelligence"), we could play chess with our computers. But, as the computer coldly checkmates the speaker, who contemplates the poems the computer may someday write, we celebrate human reactions, human language.

Finally, Woody Allen, in his satiric "My Speech to the Graduates," pokes fun at all of our attempts to peer into the future. "More than any other time in history, mankind faces a crossroads. One path leads to despair and utter hopelessness. The other, to total extinction. Let us pray we have the wisdom to choose correctly." Allen poses dizzying moral problems which present experience deflates: "Am I my brother's keeper? Yes. Interestingly, in my case I share that honor with the Prospect Park Zoo." The future is a worry and a responsibility, but, meanwhile, we have the present to deal with: "Summing up, it is clear the future holds great opportunities. It also holds pitfalls. The trick is to avoid the pitfalls, seize the opportunities, and get back home by six o'clock."

Rhetorical Issues: Discourse Communities

Perri Klass puts the issue of discourse communities most clearly in "Learning the Language"; an essential part of learning to be a doctor is to learn to *talk* and *sound* like a doctor. The same goes for any profession. The first day in law school, a professor will tell the students that they have to learn how to "think like a lawyer," which means they have to stop thinking like a business or English or chemistry major; it also means that they have to learn the legal language which identifies them as lawyers, and they have to internalize that language, use it automatically. Specializing in a college major does not only mean taking advanced courses in a particular field; it means learning the way of speaking in that major, the way issues are defined, the way problems are approached. After a while, a psychology major ("Have you felt that way since you were a child?") just does not *sound* like a philosophy major ("What is the essential nature of being?").

Any group that has developed its own particular way of speaking can be called a "discourse community." We assert our belonging in that discourse community by speaking the language, by sounding the way a member of that community should. This is not merely a turn of phrase or a particular bit of jargon, though it may incidentally be one of those; basically, it is a sign of membership that indicates an awareness of the assumptions about the world that the group shares. Those in the baseball community, for example, know perfectly well what a "southpaw" is and why a "stolen base" is good rather than bad and why a "squeeze play" is not a sign of affection. Furthermore, such language is a way of identifying the insiders and keeping the outsiders out. When those not in the community complain that baseball is boring because there is so little action, those in the community smile conspiratorily and murmur about the intellectual duel between the pitcher and batter that only the cognoscenti can appreciate. Some linguists talk about the "codes" of discourse communities and call our ability to move from one community to another "code switching."

Most of us belong to a number of discourse communities and we switch codes effortlessly as we communicate our different memberships. Thus we sometimes speak in the language of college students and write papers in that language. At the same time, we may be members of a family, a work group, a sports team, a religious group, a community organization, and a club, each of which has its own language pattern. Some of us can belong to a dozen different discourse communities and switch codes so effortlessly that we are unaware of how differently we speak with different companions. Again, as we specialize in college, we start speaking and writing more and more as do those in our major field of study; if we become graduate students, we become even more "professional" in this way. We may even become so immersed in one discourse community that we forget to switch codes. If we talk to our family "like a psych major" or to our old school friends "like a grad student" we suffer ridicule. This ridicule has the same root as the low grades some students receive on papers because they write for college in informal language or write for history courses like chemistry majors. If we fail to switch codes when called for, we are insensitive to our audience and guilty of not understanding the limitations of our own language. However rich in special meanings, nuances, and metaphors our language may be *within* our community, we need to be aware that other communities may not share them.

Discourse communities not only share a common vocabulary, but also common ways of presenting what they communicate. A laboratory report not only tells about an experiment; it also tells how fully we have joined those who know how to complete laboratory reports. A personal essay not only recounts an experience but our membership in the community of those who tell and find meaning in stories about people. We show the habits of mind of our discourse communities as we speak and write; we know what we need to say and what we need not say—because everyone in our group already knows it. We know the patterns of language and organization that are expected. And, if we are fully part of the community, we do all of this without much thought: this is how things are *done.* In this way, our special language expresses what Kuhn in Chapter 2 called the "paradigm," the overall pattern of thought of our discourse community.

How do you become part of a discourse community? You pick it up the way you picked up the language you learned as an infant. You listen hard to those who have it mastered, ask questions, and read those adept at the language. It also means trying out the language to hear how you sound and taking correction. Freshman composition courses in college have many goals, but one consistent goal is to induct students into the college discourse community, to help them write "acceptable" papers. More advanced writing courses have a similar goal, though it becomes more complicated as students enter their major fields of study. This book, for example, seeks to bring together a wide range of college discourse communities to take advantage of the different ways they view common problems. This chapter gives you views of the future as seen by journalists, sociologists, an anthropologist, a physician, several poets, a physicist, an historian, an economist, and even a professional comedian.

Part of your job as a reader is to notice the discourse community of a writer. If you are not part of that discourse community, the writer must make some effort to include you rather than to exclude you. Notice how careful Perri Klass, a recent medical school graduate, is to enlist you as a reader on her side as she encounters and internalizes medical language. After introducing the special language of the doctors, she translates: "This means that our team (group of doctors and medical students) has already gotten one admission today." You might compare that article, written for the *New York Times*, with an article in a medical journal written exclusively for physicians. You might also compare the ways the *New York Times* distinguishes itself from local newspapers. (Notice, for example, that most newspapers use one- or two-sentence paragraphs.) If you read periodicals by specialists aiming at a general audience, such as *Scientific American, National Geographic, Psychology Today,* or *The New York Review of Books,* you encounter that same problem. Can you enter into the discourse community of the writer far enough to understand what is going on and why? If not, you have lost what the writer seeks to tell you, and the writer has lost a part of the audience.

Part of our job as writers is to communicate clearly with members of our discourse community and also with those who may not be. As we all become more specialized, it becomes harder to speak to each other or to hear what others are saying. We must speak professionally to our colleagues; we must also know how to communicate our special knowledge to those in other communities. As writers, we need to pay special attention to the problem of making contact with those outside our own discourse communities. Some of us will read our work out loud to real, or imaginary, audiences to see if we have established the right tone, reached the right listeners. Are special terms, or ordinary terms used in special ways, defined? Are we making the right assumptions about what the audience can be expected to know, and not know? Have we established our voice so that the audience will respect us and listen to what we have to say?

This rhetorical problem, like most of the problems raised in this book, is not subject to easy answers. It is a subject for inquiry, a matter to be considered, a question to be dealt with over and over again. Unlike some problems, however, it becomes harder rather than easier as we become better educated. A wit once described specialists as those who learn more and more about less and less until they know everything about nothing. The same wit described generalists as those who learn less and less about more and more until they know nothing about everything. In both cases, the scholar, whether specialist or generalist, becomes unable to communicate at all. A principal goal of this book is to urge you to become flexible and strong readers of work in many discourse communities, while you become inquiring writers able to communicate to a wide range of audiences.

QUESTIONS FOR DISCOVERY AND DISCUSSION

1. What will you be doing ten years from now? Consider your family life, your job, your location, your living quarters, your transportation, your financial situation, and so on. Will every social or occupational community be a different discourse community or will there be some overlap?

2. What assumptions have you made about the future of the country and the world in responding to the previous question?

3. Now imagine yourself at seventy years of age looking back at your life. Try to describe what happened to you and how it related to the hopes and dreams you had when you were younger, and to one or two major developments in science or society over your life span.

4. Consider the language you have been using as you have been thinking about the future. To what degree has this language helped determine what you can imagine?

What Is the Future of the Family?

Issues for Working Parents

T. BERRY BRAZELTON

Brazelton (born 1918) strongly resembles his predecessor, Dr. Benjamin Spock, in his medical career that combined pediatrics with psychiatry, in his unassuming but profound love for children and concern for their parents, and in his influence on American child-rearing practices through popular and professional publications. A graduate of Princeton (B.A., 1940) and Columbia (M.D., 1943), Brazelton has been in pediatric practice in Cambridge, Massachusetts since 1950, for much of that time engaged in research and teaching at Harvard Medical School. Among his numerous publications that combine solid research evidence with sane practical wisdom (the Brazeltons have four children) and a reassuring sense of humor are *Infants and Mothers: Individual Differences in Development* (1969), *Toddlers and Parents* (1974), *The Family: Can It Be Saved?* (1975), *To Listen to a Child* (1984), *Working and Caring* (1984), and *What Every Baby Knows* (1988).

"Issues for Working Parents" is more technical than many of Brazelton's books because, intended for a professional audience, it was published in the *American Journal of Orthopsychiatry* (1986). Here Brazelton addresses the realities, and difficulties, for working parents and their children in the 1990s, when some 70 percent of children over three months old have two working parents. He addresses such issues as parental leave, quality infant care, the necessity for infants to have numerous and continual opportunities for learning about themselves and their world, and key emotional factors in the early separation of parents and their infants. The national policy he proposes is costly: "We cannot tolerate ratios of more than one adult to every three infants, or one adult for every four toddlers," mature, well-trained, and well-paid. But would we not agree, given the current magnitude of social problems, that the consequences of not having quality child care available—whatever its source of funds—are far more costly, not only for the children of today but of the next century.

Not only are infants of working parents at risk if we do not provide optimal substitute care for them, their parents will suffer as well. The opportunity to strengthen the family, rather than weaken it, can be provided around a new baby if such issues as parental leave, quality infant care, and attention to key emotional factors in the early separation of parents and infants are addressed.

In 1981, more than half the mothers in the United States were employed outside the home.[29] By 1990, it is predicted that 70% of children will have two working parents. The number has been increasing each year since World War II, and ten times as many mothers of small children work now as did in 1945. No longer is it culturally unacceptable for mothers to have jobs. In fact, the practice has become so widespread that many mothers at home feel that they "should" be working. There is a general feeling that *a*) unless she works, a woman is missing out on an important part of life, and *b*) taking care of a home is not sufficiently rewarding work. These feelings create unspoken pressures on women today, making new mothers wonder when they should return to their job or begin to look or train for one. At each domestic frustration, at each spurt in their baby's independence, young mothers are apt to question whether their baby's need to have them at home still outweighs their own need for an occupation outside the home.

Countering these various pressures on women to work, there is   2
still a strong bias against mothers leaving their babies in substitute care unless it is absolutely necessary. Since society does not yet wholeheartedly support working mothers and their choices about substitute care, in the back of young mothers' minds a nagging question tends to persist: Is it really all right for mothers to work? Indeed, this troubling question may reflect the age-old, commonly cherished image of the "perfect mother"—at home taking care of her children.

In addition, the loss of the extended family has left the nuclear   3
family unsupported. Strong cultural values are no longer available to new parents, while broad social issues such as nuclear war, ecological misuse, and overpopulation parallel the more personal issue of changing roles for women and for men. As each sex begins to face squarely the unforeseen anxieties of dividing the self into two important roles—one geared toward the family, the other toward the world— the pressures on men and women are enormous and largely uncharted by past generations. It is no wonder that many new parents are anxiously overwhelmed by these issues as they take on the important new responsibility of creating and maintaining a stable world for their baby.

We do not have enough studies yet to know about the issues for   4
the infant. The studies we do have are likely to be biased, or based on experiences in special, often privileged populations.[19, 23] We need to know when it is safest for the child's future development to have to relate to two or three caregivers; what will be the effects on a baby's development of a group care situation; when babies are best able to find what they need from caregivers other than their parents; when parents are best able to separate from their babies without feeling too grieved at the loss. In a word, we need information on which to base general guidelines for parents. For it could be that the most subtle,

hard-to-deal-with pressure on young adults comes indirectly from society's ambivalent and discordant attitudes, which create a void of values in which the building and nurturing of a family becomes very difficult.

Another serious threat to the new family is posed by the very 5 instability of its future as a family. Largely because of divorce,[29] 58% of children in the U.S. will have spent a significant part of their lives in a single-parent home. Half of the marriages of the 1970s will split up in the 1980s. The U.S. family is in serious trouble.

A new baby can be seen as an opportunity for strengthening 6 relationships within the family. Because of the realignments that necessarily will occur around the advent of the new member, the old ties and the previous adjustments to the family's integrity are likely to be shaken—for better or for worse. The work of pregnancy for each parent has been documented by Bibring[5] and others.[9] The powerful ambivalence of pregnancy represents parental efforts to reshape their previous adjustment to their lives and to their partners. The self-questioning that leads to worry about having an impaired baby is common to women and represents the depth of their anxious ambivalence as they attempt to "make it" to the new level of nurturing and caring for the coming baby. This anxiety and the force of their ambivalence can, however, be channeled into a positive adjustment to accepting and nurturing the baby. Similarly, these forces can serve to strengthen relations with other members of the family. But this cannot be left to chance. Supportive, sensitive interventions during pregnancy must be offered to stressed, high-risk parents.

We have seen that relatively minor, relatively inexpensive adjust- 7 ments on the part of the medical system—such as prepared childbirth, father participation, presenting the baby to the mother and father at delivery[24]—can increase the opportunities for "bonding" to the baby. Although this is likely to be only a first step toward fostering attachment and significantly enhancing the possibilities for the baby's optimal development, it is a most important step. In my own work with the Newborn Behavioral Assessment,[8, 13] I have found that presenting a baby's behavior to eager parents gives them a better chance to understand their infant *and themselves* as nurturers at a sensitive point in their development as adults.[3] These simple interventions in an otherwise rather unwelcoming pathological medical system seem to enhance the parents' image of themselves as vital to their baby and to each other. Thus, they further the likelihood that the parents' positive self-image will be passed on to the baby.

In my work in pediatric primary care, the parents I see in a pre- 8 natal interview are generally predisposed to share their concerns about themselves and the well-being of their future baby. As they talk to me, they share the passion and the work of making the future adjustment to parenthood with either the hoped-for normal or the dreaded impaired infant. However, when both parents anticipate the pressures of having to return to work "too early" (in their own words, "before three months"), they seem to guard against talking about their future baby as a person and about their future role as parents. Instead, their concerns are expressed in terms of the instrumental work of adjusting to time demands, to schedules, to lining up the necessary substitute care. Very little can be elicited from them about their dreams of the baby or their vision of themselves as new parents. Perhaps they are already defending themselves against too intense an attachment in anticipation of the pain of separating prematurely from the new baby.

Efforts to involve the father in the birth process, to enhance his 9 sense of paternity and empowerment as he adjusts to his new role, should be increased. Having the father involved in labor and delivery can significantly increase his sense of himself as a person who is important to his child and to his mate. Several investigators have shown that increased participation of fathers in the care of their babies, increased sensitivity to their baby's cues at one month, and significantly increased support of their wives can result from the rather simple maneuver of sharing the newborn baby's behavior with the new father at three days, using the Neonatal Behavioral Assessment Scale (NBAS).[3] In light of these apparent gains, we would do well to consider a period of paid paternity leave, which might serve both symbolically and in reality as a means of stamping the father's role as critical to his family. Ensuring the father's active participation is likely to enhance his image of himself as a nurturing person and to assist him toward a more mature adjustment in his life as a whole.

Supporting the mother in her choices about delivery and in ad- 10 justing to the new baby seems even more critical for those new mothers who must return to work. If the mother can be awake and in control of delivery, if she can have the thrill of cuddling her new infant in the delivery room, if she can have the choice of rooming in with her baby and of sharing her baby's behavior with a supportive professional, she is likely to feel empowered as a new mother.

Work of Attachment

The efforts of the medical system to enhance parental "bonding" 11 to a new baby are certainly important to parents who must return to work. But bonding is not a magical assurance that the relationship will go well thereafter. The initial adjustment to the new baby at home is likely to be extremely stressful to any set of new parents. Most have had little or no prior experience with babies or with their own parents as they nurtured a smaller sibling. They come to this new role without enough knowledge or participational experience. The generation gap makes it difficult for them to turn back to parents or extended family for support. Professional support is expensive and difficult to locate. The mother (and father) is likely to be physically exhausted and emotionally depressed for a period after delivery. The baby is unpredictable and has not developed a reliable day-night cycle of states of sleep and waking. Crying at the end of the day often serves as a necessary outlet and discharge for a small baby's nervous system after an exciting but overwhelming day. This crying can easily be perceived as a sign of failure in parenting by harassed, inexperienced parents, and the crying that starts as a fussy period is then likely to become a colicky, inconsolable period at the end of every day over the next three months. Any mother is bound to feel inadequate and helpless at this time. She may wish to run away and to turn over her baby's care to a "more competent person." If she *must* go back to work in the midst of this trying period, she is unlikely to develop the same sense of understanding and competence with regard to her baby as she might if she had been able to stay at home and to "see it out." When this period of regular crying at the end of the day mercifully comes to an end at 12 weeks, coincident with further maturation of the nervous system, mothers tell me they feel relieved and as if they had finally "helped" the baby learn to adjust to its new environment. They claim to have a sense of having learned to cope with the baby's negativism over these months; their feelings of anger, frustration, and inadequacy during the infant's fussy period are replaced by a sense of mastery at this time. Since the baby is now vocalizing, smiling, and cooing responsively at this same time at the end of every day, they report that they feel they have "taught" the baby to socialize in more acceptable ways. They feel that "at last the baby is mine, and is smiling and vocalizing for *me*." There is likely to be a significant difference in a mother's feelings of personal achievement and intimacy with her baby if she has had to leave this adjustment to another caregiver in order to return to work before the end of the three-month transition.

In our own research on the development of reciprocal communication between parents and small babies, we have been impressed with the necessity for the development of a reciprocal understanding of each other's rhythms of attention and nonattention, which develops between a mother and her baby over the first four months. At least four levels of behavioral organization in the communication system between parents and their small infants develop at this time.[11] Based on a rhythmic interaction of attention and nonattention that is critical to the homeostatic controls necessary to the immature organism, parents and infant can learn to communicate more and more complex messages in clusters of behavior. Such behavior does not demand verbal communication, but involves important elements of affective and cognitive information and forms the base for the infant's learning about the world.[12] Thus, in an important period of intense communication between parent and infant, the parent provides the baby with affective and cognitive information, and with the opportunity to learn to exert controls over the internal homeostatic systems needed to pay attention to its surroundings. The four stages of learning about these controls provide infants with a source of learning about themselves and provide the mother or father with an important opportunity for learning the ingredients of a nurturant role with their baby. These early experiences of learning about each other are the basis for their shared emotional development in the future, and are critical as anlages for the infant's future ego.

Mother's Role

The most important role of the adult interactants seems to be that 13 of helping infants to form a regulatory base for their immature psychological and motor reactions.[2, 13]

The most important rule for maintaining an interaction seems to 14 be that a mother develop a sensitivity to her infant's capacity for attention and the infant's need for withdrawal—partial or complete— after a period of attending to her. Short cycles of attention and inattention seem to underlie all periods of prolonged interaction. Although in the laboratory setting we thought we were observing continuous attention to the mother on the part of the infant, stopframe analysis subsequently revealed the cyclical nature of the infant's looking and not-looking. Looking-away behavior reflects the need of infants to maintain some control over the amount of stimulation they can take in during such intense periods of interaction. This is a homeostatic model, similar to the type of model that underlies all the physiological reactions of the neonate, and it seems to apply to the immature organisms' capacity to attend to messages in a communication system.[12]

Basic to this regulatory system of reciprocal interaction between 15 parent and infant is the basic rhythm of attention-inattention that is set up between them.[12] A mother must respect her infant's needs for the regulation that this affords or she will overload the infant's immature psychophysiological system and the infant will need to protect itself by turning her off completely. Thus, she learns the infant's capacity for attention-inattention early, in order to maintain her infant's attention. Within this rhythmic, coherent configuration, mother and infant can introduce the mutable elements of communication.

Smiles, vocalizations, postures, and tactile signals all are such elements. They can be interchanged at will as long as they are based on the rhythmic structure.[13] The individual differences of the baby's needs for such a structure set the limits on it. The mother then has the opportunity to adapt her tempo within these limits. If she speeds up her tempo, she can reduce the baby's level of communication. If she slows down, she can expect a higher level of engagement and communicative behavior from her infant.[12, 28] Her use of tempo as a means of entraining the baby's response systems is probably the basis of the baby's learning about his* own control systems. In this process of variability, the baby learns the limits of his control systems. As the baby returns to a baseline, he learns about basic self-regulation. The feedback systems that are set up within this process afford the baby a kind of richness of self-regulation or adaptation.

Built on top of this base is the nonverbal message. By using a systems approach to understand this, we find that each behavioral message or cluster of behavior from one member of the dyad acts as a disruption of the system, which must then be reorganized. The process of reorganization affords the infant and the parent a model for learning—learning about the other as well as learning about oneself within this regulatory system. An "appropriate" or attractive stimulus creates a disruption and reorganization that is of a different nature from those that are the result of an intrusive or "inappropriate" stimulus. Each serves a purpose in this learning model.[9]   16

An inspection of the richness of such a homeostatic model, which provides each participant with an opportunity to turn off or on at any time in the interaction, demonstrates the fine-tuning available and necessary to each partner of the dyad for learning about "the other." The individual actions that may be introduced into the clusters of behavior that dominate the interaction become of real, if secondary, importance. A smile or a vocalization may be couched within several other actions to form a signaling cluster. But the individual piece of behavior is not the necessary requirement for a response: the cluster is. The basic rhythm, the "fit" of clusters of behavior, and the timing of appropriate clusters to produce responses in an expectable framework become the best prediction of real reciprocity in parent-infant interaction.[13]   17

Stages of Regulation

We have identified four stages of regulation and of learning within this system over the first four months of life:[11]   18

---

*"His" or "he" is used as a shortened form of his/her in referring to the baby.

1. Infants achieve homeostatic control over input and output systems (*i.e.*, they can both shut out and reach out for single stimuli, but then achieve control over their physiological systems and states).

2. Within this controlled system, infants can begin to attend to and use social cues to prolong their states of attention and to accept and incorporate more complex trains of messages.

3. Within such an entrained or mutual reciprocal feedback system, infants and parents begin to press the limits of *a*) infant capacity to take in and respond to information, and *b*) infant ability to withdraw to recover in a homeostatic system. Sensitive adults press infants to the limits of both of these and allow infants time and opportunity to realize that they have incorporated these abilities into their own repertoires. The mother-infant "games" described by Stern[28] are elegant examples of the real value of this phase as a system for affective and cognitive experiences at three and four months.

4. Within the dyad or triad, the baby is allowed to demonstrate and incorporate a sense of autonomy. (This phase is perhaps the real test of attachment.) At the point where the mother or nurturing parent can indeed permit the baby to be the leader or signal-giver, when the adult can recognize and encourage the baby's independent search for and response to environmental or social cues and games—to initiate them, to reach for and play with objects, etc.—the small infant's own feeling of competence and of voluntary control over its environment is strengthened. This sense of competence is at a more complex level of awareness and is constantly influenced by the baby's feedback systems. We see this at four to five months in normal infants during a feeding, when the infant stops to look around and to process the environment. When a mother can allow for this and even foster it, she and the infant become aware of the baby's burgeoning autonomy. In psychoanalytic terms, the infant's ego development is well on its way![9]

This model of development is a powerful one for understanding 19 the reciprocal bonds that are set up between parent and infant. The feedback model allows for flexibility, disruption, and reorganization. Within its envelope of reciprocal interaction, one can conceive of a rich matrix of different modalities for communication, individualized for each pair and critically dependent on the contribution of each member of the dyad or triad. There is no reason that each system cannot be shaped in different ways by the preferred modalities for interaction of each of its participants, but each *must* be sensitive and ready to adjust to the other member in the envelope. And at successive stages of development, the envelope will be different; richer, we would hope.

I regard these observations as evidence for the first stages of 20
emotional and cognitive awareness in the infant and in the nurturing
"other." A baby is learning about himself, developing an ego base.
The mother and father who are attached to and intimately involved
with this infant are both consciously and unconsciously aware of
parallel stages of their own development as nurturers.[9]

When parents are deprived too early of this opportunity to par- 21
ticipate in the baby's developing ego structure, they lose the opportunity to understand the baby intimately and to feel their own role
in development of these four stages. The likelihood that they will feel
cheated of the opportunity for their own development as nurturing
adults is great.

When a new mother must share her small baby with a secondary 22
caregiver, she will almost inevitably experience a sense of loss. Her
feelings of competition with the other caregiver may well be upper-
most in her consciousness. But beneath this conscious feeling of competition there is likely to be a less-than-conscious sense of grief.
Lindemann[25] described a syndrome, which he labeled a grief reaction,
that seems to fit the experiences that mothers of small babies describe
when they leave them in substitute care. They are apt to feel sad,
helpless, hopeless, inadequate to their babies. They feel a sense of
loneliness, of depression, of slowed down physical responses, and
even of somatic symptoms. To protect themselves from these feelings,
they are likely to develop three defenses.[10] These are healthy, normal,
and necessary defenses, but they can interfere with the mother's
attachment to her baby if they are not properly evaluated. The younger
the baby and the more inexperienced the mother, the stronger and
more likely are these defenses. They are correlated with the earliness
with which she returns to work:

1. *Denial.* A mother is likely to deny that her leaving has consequences—for the child or for herself. She will distort or ignore
   any signals in herself or in the baby to the contrary. Mothers who
   obviously know better will not visit their baby's day care center
   "because it is too painful." This denial may be a necessary defense
   against painful feelings but it may distort a mother's capacity to
   make proper decisions.

2. *Projection.* Working parents will have a tendency to project the
   important caregiving issues onto the substitute caregivers. Responsibility for both good and bad will be shifted, and often
   sidestepped.

3. *Detachment.* Not because she doesn't care but because it is painful
   to care and to be separated, the mother will tend to distance her
   feelings of responsibility and of intense attachment.

These three defenses are commonly necessary for mothers to   23
handle the new feelings engendered by separating from a small baby.
For example, imagine the feelings of a mother who returns to pick
her baby up from the day care center at the end of a working day.
The baby has saved up all his important feelings and now blows up
in a temper tantrum when the mother arrives. At that point, someone
in the day care center turns to her and says, "He never cries like that
with me, dear."

These conflicting emotions need to be faced by new parents and   24
understood by them in order to prevent costly adjustments which are
not in the family's best interests. We need to prepare working parents
for their roles in order to preserve the positive forces in strong attachments—to the baby and to each other. We certainly must protect
the period in which the attachment process is solidified and stabilized
by new parents. With the new baby, this is likely to demand at least
four months in which the new mother can feel herself free of competing demands of the workplace. Since most young families cannot
afford a period of unpaid leave, and since the workplace is not inclined
to provide such a period without sanctions against the new family,
it seems critical at this time to work toward a nationally subsidized
policy for paid leave at the time of a new baby. Such national recognition of the importance of the family could become symbolic recognition of the value of the family. It might serve to heighten the
emphasis on strong ties within the family, at a time when the national
trend toward divorce and instability of attachments has proven especially costly to our children.[21, 30] As a nation, we can no longer
afford to ignore our responsibilities toward children and their families.

Substitute Care

Obviously, it is critical that parents be provided the opportunity   25
for optimal substitute child care. If a mother is to be free emotionally
to realize her potential in the workplace, she must be confident that
her baby is in good hands. And, of course, it is critical for children
to grow and develop in a caring, stimulating environment. The
younger the child, the more critical is environment for the future of
his or her emotional and cognitive development.

Results of the research that has looked into outcomes for infants   26
and toddlers who have been in substitute care have ranged from citing
the dangers and potential emotional damage[1, 16–19, 27] to reporting potential emotional gains. Most studies to date have not found negative
consequences,[4, 14, 15, 22] but these studies tend to be biased in one of
several ways. They have investigated short-term outcomes, they have
studied middle-class, supervised day care, and their outcome meas-

ures may not have been aimed appropriately at the total child's development. Certainly, for millions of children, substitute care may not be optimal and we shall not understand fully the consequences for another generation.

We must have adults who can relate individually to each baby 27 with an appropriate amount of time and the energy to assure reciprocal, sensitive, caring responses. Safety and intellectual stimulation are elemental to such care. In order to provide this for each baby, we cannot tolerate ratios of more than one adult to every three infants, or one adult to every four toddlers.[22, 26] In addition, these adults need to be mature and well trained in such areas as the necessary requirements of social, intellectual, and physical parameters of infant development. The training for caregivers must be required and supervision for quality assurance be mandated at local, state, and national levels.[32, 33]

Optimal day care would include parents in the curriculum. Not 28 only could parents be urged to participate actively in their babies' care but the centers could provide opportunities for education, for peer support groups, and for the nurturing comforts for parenting that have been lost by nuclear families. Thus, with quality day care, both families and their small children could benefit.

Our future generations are at stake. Throughout the last 40 years, 29 Spitz, Bowlby, Harlow, and many subsequent researchers have pointed to the importance of providing a nurturing environment for small children. At present, infant caregivers are too often untrained, unsupervised, and grossly underpaid. But until we provide them with the salaries necessary for professionals, we cannot expect training or supervision to be successful. Even under the present conditions, the choices in child care for over 50% of working mothers are grossly inadequate. Poor, vulnerable people are unable to find care of any quality and must leave their small children in dangerously inadequate circumstances. Physical abuse and neglect, as well as sexual abuse, are inevitable under such conditions.

We must provide vital safeguards if we mean to protect the future 30 development of small children of working parents. These are costly, and cannot be paid for by parents alone. Our responsibility as mental health and child care professionals requires that we work toward development of a national policy with national subsidy.

References

1. Ainsworth, M. 1979. Attachment as related to mother-infant interaction. *In* Advances in the Study of Behavior, Vol. 9. J. Rosenblatt et al, eds. Academic Press, New York.

2. Als, H. 1978. Assessing an assessment. *In* Organization and Stability of Newborn Behavior: Commentary on the Brazelton Neonatal Behavioral Assessment Scale, A. Sameroff, ed. Mongr. Soc. Res. Child Devlpm. 43(177):14–29.

3. Beal, J. 1984. The effect of demonstration of the Brazelton Neonatal Assessment Scale on the father-infant relationship. Presented to the International Conference in Infant Studies, New York.

4. Belsky, J., Steinberg, L. and Walker, A. 1982. The ecology of day care. *In* Childrearing in Nontraditional Families. M. Lamb, ed. Erlbaum, Hillsdale, N.J.

5. Bibring, G., Dwyer, T. and Valenstein, A. 1961. A study of the psychological processes in pregnancy. Psychoanal. Stud. Child 16:9–72.

6. Bowlby, J. 1973. Attachment and Loss, Vol. 2. Basic Books, New York.

7. Braun, S. and Caldwell, B. 1973. Emotional adjustment of children in day care who enrolled prior to or after the age of three. Early Child Devlpm. Care 2:13–21.

8. Brazelton, T. 1973. The Neonatal Behavioral Assessment Scale. Spastics International Medical Publications, Heinemann, London. (Lippincott, Philadelphia, 1984)

9. Brazelton, T. 1983. Precursors for the development of emotions in early infancy. *In* Theory, Research and Experience, Vol. 2, R. Pluchik, ed. Academic Press, New York.

10. Brazelton, T. 1985. Working and Caring. Addison-Wesley, Boston.

11. Brazelton, T. and Als, H. 1979. Four early stages in the development of mother-infant interaction. Psychoanal. Stud. Child 34:349–369.

12. Brazelton, T., Koslowski B. and Main, M. 1974. The origins of reciprocity: the early mother-infant interaction. *In* The Effect of the Infant on Its Caregiver, M. Lewis and L. Rosenblum, eds., John Wiley, New York.

13. Brazelton, T. et al. 1975. Early mother-infant reciprocity. *In* Parent-Infant Interaction, Ciba Foundation Symposium 33. Elsevier, Amsterdam.

14. Caldwell, B. et al. 1970. Infant day care and attachment. Amer. J. Orthopsychiat. 40:397–412.

15. Clarke-Stewart, K. et al. 1980. Development and prediction of children's sociability from 1 to 2½ years. Devlpm. Psychol. 16:290–302.

16. Egelund, B. and Sroufe, L. 1981. Attachment and early maltreatment. Child Devlpm. 52:44–52.

17. Farber, E. and Egelund, B. 1982. Developmental consequences of out-of-home care for infants in a low income population. *In* Day Care: Scientific and Social Policy Issues, E. Zigler and E. Gordon, eds., Auburn House, Boston.

18. Fraiberg, S. 1977. Every Child's Birthright: In Defense of Mothering. Basic Books, New York.

19. Gamble, T. and Zigler, E. 1986. Effects of infant day care: another look at the evidence, Amer. J. Orthopsychiat. 56:26–42.

20. Greenacre, P. 1941. The Predisposition to Anxiety: Trauma, Growth, and Personality (Parts I and II). International Universities Press, New York.

21. Hetherington, M. 1981. Children and Divorce. *In* Parent-Child Interaction: Theory, Research, and Prospect, R. Henderson, ed. Academic Press, New York.

22. Kagan, J. 1982. Psychological Research on the Human Infant: An Evaluation Summary. W. T. Grant Foundation Publications, New York.

23. Kessen, W., Haith M. and Salapatek, P. 1970. Human infancy: a bibliography and guide. *In* Carmichael's Manual of Child Psychology (Vol. 1), W. Mussen, ed. John Wiley, New York.

24. Klaus, M. and Kennell, J. 1970. Mothers separated from their newborn infants. Pediat. Clin. N.A. 17:1015.

25. Lindemann, E. 1944. Grief. Amer. J. Psychiat. 101:141.

26. Rutter, M. 1981. Social-emotional consequences of day care for preschool children. Amer. J. Orthopsychiat. 51:4–28.

27. Schwartz, P. 1983. Length of day care attendance and attachment behavior in eighteen-month-old infants. Child Devlpm. 54:1073–1078.

28. Stern, D. 1974. The goal and structure of mother-infant play. J. Amer. Acad. Child Psychiat. 13:402–421.

29. U.S. Senate. 1982. American Families: Trends and Pressures. Joint Hearings before the Subcommittee on Children and Youth and the Committee on Labor and Public Welfare (Sept.).

30. Wallerstein, J. and Kelly, J. 1975. The effect of parental divorce: experiences of the preschool child. J. Amer. Acad. Child Psychiat. 14:600–616.

31. White, R. 1959. Motivation reconsidered: the concept of competence. Psychol. Rev. 66:297–333.

32. Zigler, E. and Butterfield, E. 1968. Motivational aspects of changes in IQ test performance of culturally deprived nursery school children. Child Devlpm. 39:1–14.

33. Zigler, E. and Trickett, P. 1978. IQ, social competence, and evaluation of early childhood intervention programs. Amer. Psychol. 33:789–798.

RESPONDING TO READING

Key words: community education family gender growing up identity striving

Rhetorical concepts: analysis cause and effect induction research report

1. Brazelton states flatly, "The U.S. family is in serious trouble." What evidence and what kinds of evidence does he present for that statement? How convincing is that evidence? Does your personal experience confirm or dispute his conclusion?

2. Brazelton does not hesitate to bring in his own experience working with families. But notice that the way he does this is very different from the way Fallows presents herself in the next essay. Compare and contrast the role of the writer (or the writer as character in the essay, a *persona*) in the two essays. Show how this difference relates to the different discourse communities to which the essays are directed.

3. List the problems new parents encounter, as Brazelton describes them. Why are these problems particularly severe for working parents and for women? What is the effect upon the children if the problems are handled badly?

4. Notice that Brazelton is as concerned about the development of the parents as the development of the child. Trace the development patterns he outlines and show how working parents can cope with the issues he sets out. Do you agree with his proposals for ways to meet these issues and for a national policy in this area? Why do we not yet have a national policy?

Why Mothers Should Stay Home

DEBORAH FALLOWS

Whether mothers should stay home and care for their young children
is not an option for millions of single or less affluent parents who
have to earn money to support their children. Yet for many middle-
class families, including most college graduates, the choices are not
as clear cut as they were a generation ago, when there was far greater
social pressure for mothers to stay home. Economist Barbara Bergmann explains, in *The Economic Emergence of Women* (1986), that until
relatively recently, biology did indeed determine the fate of urban
men and women. Men earned most of the money, often at hard
physical labor, but did relatively little housework or child care.
Women did the domestic tasks, but had more leisure time than
women who worked outside the home. Today, as both Bergmann
and Deborah Fallows point out, women who work outside the home
nevertheless do most of the housework and child care, running
errands and caring for dependent parents, unless they get additional
assistance from paid helpers or husbands who can be convinced to
assume more responsibilities than tradition and their culture have
decreed.

Fallows (born 1949) clearly has an upper-middle class, traditional
family in mind, and she uses herself—a well-educated (B.A. Radcliffe, 1971; Ph.D. University of Texas, 1977), talented, energetic,
eager parent—as the prime example of someone who decided to
stop working outside the home and stay at home with her two young
children. She has become a spokesperson for full-time mothers, asserting to an audience that ranges from radical feminists to conservative traditionalists that "the choice is *not* to be either a career
woman or a dumb housewife." She has expressed her views, which
she characterizes as the "radical middle," in articles in *Newsweek* and
Washington Monthly, and in her book, *A Mother's Work* (1985). Yet her
essay leaves a number of questions unanswered. Is her argument
applicable to less affluent families? To less capable, less engaged
parents? To families of non-Western culture? To single-parent and
nontraditional families, whose configurations are so varied and numerous as to outnumber the older traditional model? What indeed
will be the future of the family? And the future of the children of
these families?

About 18 months ago, when our first son was three years old and   1
our second was about to be born, I decided to stop working and stay
at home with our children. At the time, I wrote an article about the
myth of the superwoman, saying that contrary to the prevailing notion
of the day, it was not possible to be both a full-time career woman
and a full-fledged mother. I said that while everyone recognizes the
costs a stay-at-home mother pays in terms of power, prestige, money,
and advancement in traditional careers, we are not always aware of

or do not so readily admit what a full-time working woman loses and gives up in terms of mothering.

I've been at home with our children for almost a year and a half 2 now, and I've learned a number of things about my choice. My convictions about the importance of mothering, which were based more on intuition than experience at the time, run even deeper and stronger. Nothing means more to me now than the hours I spend with my children, but I find myself coping with a problem I hadn't fully foreseen. It is the task of regearing my life, of learning to live as a full-time mother without a professional career but still with many of the interests and ambitions that I had before I had children. And this is the hard part. It means unraveling those long-held life plans for a certain kind of career and deciding which elements are possible to keep and which I must discard. Perhaps even more important, it means changing the way I've been taught to think about myself and value the progress of my life.

My mother became a mother in 1946; she had gone to college, 3 studied music, and worked for a year at her father's office. Then she married and had my sister by the time she was 22. She wasn't expected to have a career outside the home, and she didn't. When I was growing up, the only mothers who worked were those who, as we whispered, "had to." Even the high school teachers, who we recognized probably weren't doing it just for the money, were slightly suspect.

But between my mother's time and our own, the climate of op- 4 portunity and expectations for women started to change. Betty Friedan and *The Feminine Mystique* came between all of those mothers and all of us daughters. The small town in northern Ohio where I grew up was not exactly a hotbed of feminist activity, but even there the signals for young women were changing in the mid-sixties. We were raised with a curious mixture of hope of becoming homecoming queen and pressure to run for student council president. When I was 11, the mothers in our neighborhood bundled off their awkward, preadolescent daughters to Saturday morning charm classes, where we learned how to walk on a straight line, one foot directly in front of the other, and the proper way to don a coat. We all felt a little funny and humiliated, but we didn't say anything. By the time we were 17, we were May Queens, princesses, head drum majorettes, and cheerleaders, but we were also class valedictorians, editors of the school paper and yearbook, student directors of the school band, and candidates for six-year medical programs, Seven Sisters colleges, and honors programs at the Big Ten universities. I admit with some embarrassment that my two most thrilling moments in high school were being chosen for the homecoming court and being named first-chair trumpet in the concert band.

This was the way we were supposed to achieve—to be both beau- 5
tiful and brilliant, charming and accomplished. It was one step beyond
what our mothers did: we were aiming to be class presidents, not
class secretaries; for medical school, not nursing school; we were
building careers, not just jobs to tide us over before we landed husbands and started raising babies.

When I made my decision to stop working and stay home with 6
our children, it was with a mixture of feelings. Part was defiance of
the background I've just described—how could feminism dare tell me
that I couldn't choose, with *pride*, motherhood alone? Part was anxiety—how could I keep some grasp on my extra-mothering self, on
the things I had really enjoyed doing before I had children? I didn't
want to become what the world kept telling me housewives are—
ladies whose interests are confined to soap operas and the laundry.
Certainly I knew from my own mother and from other women who
had spent their middle years as full-time mothers that it was possible
to be a thoughtful and sensitive person and still be a mother. But I
didn't know how, and I didn't know where to turn to ask. Even my
mother didn't have the answers. She was surprised when I told her
I wanted to stop working and stay home with my kids. "You young
women seem to handle everything so easily, so smoothly," she told
me. "I never knew you were so torn between being a mother and
being a professional."

The arrival of children in a woman's late twenties or early thirties 7
can be handy, of course, because it means you can finish your education and start a career before taking "time out" to start your family.
But it's also awkward.

At my tenth college reunion last June, I found that many of my 8
friends had just become partner or vice-president of one thing or
another, doctor-in-charge of some ward, tenured professor, editor-in-
chief, and so forth. In these moments, I feel as if everyone is growing
up around me. My reactions, though human, are not altogether
pretty. I feel sorry for myself—there but for two small children go I.
I feel frustrated in being passed over for things I know I could handle
as well as or better than the next person. I feel anxious, wondering
if I am going to "lose my touch," get rusty, boring, old, trivial too
quickly. And I am afraid that in putting aside my professional ambitions just now, I may be putting aside forever the chance to attain
the levels I once set for myself.

All of us, I think, spend time once in a while pondering the "what 9
ifs" of our lives, and we all experience momentary pangs of self-pity
over the course we've taken. I know I'm not an exception to this, but
I also know that when I add up the pluses and minuses my choice
was right for me, and it might be right for other women.

The Importance of "Quantity" Time

The first adjustment on that first morning that I dressed for moth- 10
erhood rather than for success was to believe intellectually in what I
felt emotionally: that it was as important, as worthy for me to spend
my time with my small children as to study, do research, try cases,
or invest a bank's money. Furthermore, I had to believe it was worth
it to the children to have me—not someone else—there most of the
time. There are a thousand small instances I have witnessed over the
past year and a half that illustrate this feeling. One that stays in my
mind happened last summer.

I had just dropped off our older son at the morning play camp 11
at the neighborhood school. I was about to drive off when a little boy
about eight years old burst out of the school and ran down the front
steps in tears. His mother was on her way down the walk and of
course she saw him. She led him over to the steps, took his hands in
hers, looked him directly in the eyes, and talked with him softly but
deliberately for a few minutes, calming him down so he could go
back inside happily and she could go on her way. What I recognized
in that instant was something I'd been trying to put my finger on for
months. I'd witnessed dozens of similar events, when a child was
simply overwhelmed by something, and I knew there was a difference—a distinct difference in the way parents respond at such moments from the way I had seen babysitters or maids act, however
loving and competent they may have been. Parents seem to have some
combination of self-assurance, completeness, deliberateness, and consistency. If that boy had been my son, I would have wanted to be
with him, too.

Perhaps this one episode was no more important than the many 12
reprimands or comforts I give my children during the day. But the
more I'm around my children, the more such instances I happen to
see and deal with. Perhaps a thousand of these episodes add up to
the values and security I want to give my children.

I spend a lot of time with my children at playgrounds. We often 13
go out on nice afternoons when our older son gets home from school,
sampling new ones or returning to old favorites. I particularly like
playgrounds because of the balance they afford: they encourage the
kids to strike out on their own but let me be there as a fallback. I've
watched my older son in his share of small fistfights and scuffles, and
I have been able to let him fight without intervening. He knows I'm
there and runs back as often for protection as for nice things like a
"Mom, see what I can do." Or our younger son toddles toward the
big slide and needs me to follow him up and hold him as we slide
down together. After so many hours, we've developed a style of play.

I think my children know what to expect of me and I have learned their limits. I've watched the styles of many mothers and children, and you often can see, after a time, a microcosm of their lives together. I've also seen plenty of children there with full-time maids. The maids have their own styles, which usually are different from the mothers'. I've never seen a maid slide down a slide with her small charge, but I have seen plenty scold children for climbing too high on the jungle gym, and I've seen plenty step in to stop the sandfights before anyone gets dirty or hurt. There's a reason for this, of course: a maid has a lot to explain if a youngster arrives home with a bloody nose, but a mother doesn't. Sometimes, I think, the nose is worth the lesson learned from it, yet that is something only a parent—not a maid or babysitter—can take the responsibility to decide.

It has taken me a few years to realize I have very high standards 14 for my role as a mother. I don't have to be a supermom who makes my children's clothes (I really can't sew), who does all the volunteer work at school (I do my share), or who cooks gourmet meals (we eat a lot of hamburgers). But I have to be around my children—a lot. I have to know them as well as I possibly can and see them in as many different environments and moods as possible in order to know best how to help them grow up—by comforting them, letting them alone, disciplining and enjoying them, being dependable but not stifling. What I need with them is time—in quantity, not quality.

I'm not talking about being with my children every minute of the 15 day. From the time they were several months old, we sent them out for short periods to the favorite neighborhood babysitter's. By the time he was two and a half, our older son was in a co-op nursery school (my husband and I would take turns doing parent duty for the 17 kids); now he's in pre-kindergarten for a full school day. These periods away from me are clearly important for my sanity, as well as for my children's socialization, their development of trust in people, and their ability to experience other ways of living. But there is a big difference between using childcare from 8 to 6, Monday through Friday, and using a babysitter or a nursery school three mornings a week.

I realize that not everyone enjoys the luxury of choice. Some of 16 my female friends work because it's the only way to make ends meet. But I think a lot of people pretend they have less room for choice than they really do. For some women, the reason may be the feeling— which is widespread among men—that their dignity and success are related to how much money they earn. For others, there is a sense of independence that comes with earning money that is hard to give up. (I know that I felt freer to buy things, especially for myself, or spend money on babysitters when I was contributing to the family income.) And still others define "necessities" in an expensive way: I've heard more than one woman say she "has to work" to keep up payments on the second house. Such a woman is the parallel to the government appointee who "has to resign" from his post to return to his former profession because he "can no longer afford government service."

Even though some women do have a choice, I am not suggesting 17 that all the responsibility for home and children should lie with the mother. While my husband and I are an example of a more traditional family, with a breadwinning father, a full-time mother, and two children, he shares with me many of the family responsibilities: night-tending, diapering, bathing, cooking, and playtime. A woman's decision to stay home or work is, at worst, a decision made by herself and, at best, a decision made with her spouse.

But with all these qualifications noted, I still know that my own 18 choice is to stay with my children. Why does this seem to be at odds with the climate of the times, especially among certain feminists? I think it is because of a confused sense of ambition—based, in turn, on a mistaken understanding of what being a housewife or mother actually means.

While the world's idea of the comparative importance of career 19 and motherhood may have changed a good deal since my mother's time, the general understanding of what motherhood means for those who choose it has not changed or advanced. And that may be the real problem for many women of my generation: who can blame them for shying away from a commitment to full-time motherhood if they're told, despite raising children, that motherhood is a vapid life of chores, routines, and TV? I couldn't stand motherhood myself if that were true. One of my many discoveries as a mother is that motherhood requires not the renunciation of my former ambitions but rather their refinement.

Even for those who intend to rush straight back to work, moth- 20 erhood involves some interruption in the normal career plan. Separating people, even temporarily, from their professional identities, can help them see the difference betwen the ambition to *be*—to have an impressive job title to drop at cocktail parties—and the ambition to *do* specific things that seem satisfying and rewarding. The ambition to be is often a casualty of motherhood; the ambition to do need not be.

I see many of my friends intensely driven to keep doing things, 21 to keep involved in their former interests, or to develop entirely new ones that they can learn from and grow with. In the free time they manage to set aside—thanks to babysitters, co-op babycare, naptimes, grandmothers' help, and husbands like mine who spend a lot of time with the children—they are thinking and doing.

Women I have talked to have described how, after some months   22 or years of settling into motherhood, their sense of what work is worth, and what they're looking for in work, has greatly changed. They are less tolerant, more selective, more demanding in what they do. One woman said that before she had children she would focus on a "cause," and was willing to do just about anything as her job toward that cause. Now she's still interested in advancing the cause, but she has no patience for busywork. In the limited time she can spare from her family, she wants to do things that really count, work in areas where her efforts make a difference. I'm not suggesting narcissism here but a clearer focus on a search for some long-range goal, some tangible accomplishment, a feeling so necessary during the season of child-raising when survival from one end of the day to the other is often the only achievement.

Each one's search is different, depending on factors like her hus-   23 band's job (if she has a husband) and the extent of his role as a caretaker, her children's needs, her family's financial situation, and her personal lifestyle.

One of my friends had taught English in public high schools for   24 the last ten years. She was the kind of teacher you remember fondly from your own childhood and hope your kids are lucky enough to have because she's dedicated, demanding, and creative. She expanded her subject to include other humanities, keeping herself several steps ahead of her students by reading and studying on her own, traveling to see museums and exhibits firsthand, collecting slides and books as she goes. She has a new baby daughter now and has stopped working to stay home with her child. She's decided to go back to school next fall, taking one or two courses at a time, to pursue a master's in fine arts—a chance to study formally what she's mostly taught herself and to return to her job someday with an even better background and more ideas for her teaching.

Going to school can be perfect for new mothers, as many in my   25 own mother's generation found. It requires very little time away from home, which means cutting down on time away from the children as well as on child-care costs. It can be cheap, as with my friend, who can attend a virtually tuition-free state university. You can pace your work to suit demands at home by carefully choosing the number of courses you take and the type of work required. And it's physically easy but intellectually challenging—the complement to the other demands of the early years of mothering.

Other mothers I know do different things with their time. One 26 friend, formerly a practicing lawyer and now a full-time mother, volunteers some of her time to advising the League of Women Voters on legal matters. Another, formerly a producer at a big radio station, now produces her own shows, albeit at a slower pace. A third quit her job to raise her daughter but spends a lot of time on artistic projects, which she sells.

But if there's no real blueprint for what a modern mother should 27 be, you wouldn't know it from what comes through in the media. On the *Today Show* last summer, for instance, Jane Pauley interviewed Felice Schwartz, the president of Catalyst, an organization that promotes career development for women. They were discussing women's changing life-styles. Ms. Schwartz said that now women are going back to work full-time four months after having children, while 15 years ago they were taking 20 years off to have them. "Isn't that fantastic progress?" she said. Fantastic it certainly is; progress it is not, except toward the narrowest and least generous notion of what achievement means for women or for humanity. Progress such as this is a step not toward "liberation" but toward the enslavement to career that has been the least attractive aspect of masculine success.

What is it really like to be a mother today seems to be a secret 28 that's kept from even my contemporaries who may be considering motherhood themselves. At a dinner recently, I sat near a young woman about my age, a New York television producer and recently anointed White House fellow. She and my husband and I were having a conversation about bureaucracy and what she found new or interesting or surprising about it in her new position. After several minutes, she turned away from my husband to me directly and said, "And how old are your children, Debbie?" It wasn't the question— not at all—but the tone that was revealing, the unattractive, condescending tone I've heard many older people use with youngsters, or doctors with patients. If I'd had her pegged as a fast-track superachiever, she had me pegged as little mother and lady of the house.

Hurt and anger were the wrong feelings at a moment like that, 29 although I felt them. Instead, I should have felt sorry for her, not because of her own choice but because she had no sense that a choice exists—waiting to be made by women like her and like me. The choice is *not* to be either a career woman or a dumb housewife. The issue is one that she, a woman at the age when careers take off and childbearing ability nears its eleventh hour, should be sensitive to and think about.

RESPONDING TO READING

Key words: community discovery education family gender
growing up   identity   striving   watershed

Rhetorical concepts: anecdote autobiography comparison and contrast
explanation   illustration   narrative/example

1.   In arguing that "it is not possible to be both a full-time career woman
and a full-fledged mother," Fallows is setting herself up for the difficult task
of intentionally challenging "the prevailing notion of the day" (paragraph 1).
What sorts of evidence does she use to support her argument? How convincing is she?
2.   To what extent can Fallows generalize from the examples she uses from
her own personal experience?
3.   Fallows argues her case on human terms, with little reference to the
economics of earning and spending money. Does this freedom from monetary
worry restrict her argument to the upper and upper-middle classes? How
relevant is her argument to single parents?
4.   Does Fallows's argument apply primarily to mothers of preschool children? Could an equivalent case be made for "Why Fathers Should Stay
Home"?
5.   What is or will your own family of the future be like? Incorporate a reply
to Fallows's argument, and define your role in this family as either the father
or mother of preschool children.

Marriage as Partnership

ROBERT S. WEISS

Weiss (born 1925), a sociologist, was educated at the University of
Buffalo (B.A. 1949) and the University of Michigan (Ph.D. 1955). He
has taught sociology at the University of Chicago, Harvard, Brandeis,
and MIT. Although Weiss's earlier publications included books on
Processes of Organization (1956) and *Institutions and the Person* (1968),
much of his recent research has focused on the relation of men's
work to the rest of their lives, as exemplified by his most recent book,
*Staying the Course: The Emotional and Social Lives of Men Who Do Well
at Work* (1990), in which "Marriage As Partnership" appears.
    Weiss's analysis of the work and lives of some seventy male Boston
area upper-middle-class managers, administrators, and professionals, between the ages of 35 and 55, dispels a number of myths about
such men—to the extent that one can generalize about an entire
society on the basis of such a sample. Unlike Thoreau's "mass of
men [who] lead lives of quiet desperation," Weiss's subjects "are
doing as well as they can to fashion satisfactory lives for themselves
and their families." They "keep society going," for they are good

workers, good citizens, and good husbands and fathers according
to their assumptions about marriage; they see themselves as the
financial mainstays and protectors of their households. Yet Weiss's
article also enables us to consider whether the traditional way is the
best way for every family member, irrespective of one's age, gender,
and class. What aspects of the traditional roles will be viable in the
future, and what should change with changing times? Why? In what
ways would you expect working wives and mothers to answer?

Most marital interaction deals with issues of partnership, large   1
and small: when to have children; whether to use the money in the
bank for a vacation; who will take the car in for servicing. Couples
raising children together may have few discussions not concerned
with partnership issues.

The understandings that inform the partnership aspect of mar-   2
riage are similar to those that would be found between business partners. True, a man's life is a larger and vaguer enterprise than a business. But the woman to whom the man is married contributes to life's
stability of purpose, works for its success, and so deserves a share of
its rewards, just as would a business partner.

Critical to the marital partnership is the decision of who does   3
what—what will be the contributions of the man and of his wife to
the joint enterprise that is the marital partnership?

The question of who does which of the chores required to keep   4
a house orderly, the children fed, and the bills paid has lately been
an area of skirmishing in that longest of wars, the War Between the
Sexes.[3] It was not, however, considered an especially troubling question by the men with whom we spoke. Virtually all of them believed
that they and their wives together had established a division of marital
labor that worked well enough; it was usually clear what each was to
do; there rarely were arguments over tasks left undone. Most indicated
that they and their wives were each grateful to the other for doing so
much. A few, to be sure, harbored resentments because their wives
weren't the housekeepers they thought they should be or because
their wives too infrequently consulted them about the children. And
at some earlier point in their marriages, several of the men seemed
to have engaged in sometimes tense negotiations with their wives
about how much the men were expected to help. But in most men's
marriages what seemed to exist now was a division of labor that
operated smoothly and with apparent acceptance by the men and
their wives.

The division of labor in childless marriages differed from that in   5
marriages with children. Couples without children tended to maintain
a division of labor somewhere between the "everybody does everything" of roommates or cohabitants and the sexual allocation of re-

sponsibility of a traditional married pair. The men might be more responsible for the heavy tasks, the wives for domestic arrangements, but there was a great deal of sharing. Especially for marriages in which the wives' earnings were comparable to the husbands', who did what seemed to be as much a matter of personal preference as of conformity to traditional expectations.

But couples whose division of household labor had been roughly 6 symmetric before the arrival of children witnessed an abrupt change once children were on the scene. The wives who had been working withdrew from the labor force so that they could look after the children. Most dropped out entirely, although a few kept some sort of part-time association, such as doing editing at home. The husbands, meanwhile, redoubled their efforts at work, since now they had a family to support.

Yet even after the arrival of children husbands did more than 7 "men's work" around the house, and women more than "women's work." Husbands sometimes cooked, often helped with cleaning, and looked after the children. Wives did yard work and, when the children were nursery school age, returned to paid employment.

Despite this flexibility, husbands and wives seemed to decide who 8 would do what on the basis of underlying principles. They might not themselves be able to say exactly what the principles were, but they seemed nevertheless to share belief in the principles and generally to agree on their application.

The Underlying Principles of the Marital Divison of Labor

All couples began their married lives with the recognition that 9 some tasks were traditionally "men's work" and others traditionally "women's work," an implication of principles that might be referred to as *the traditional principles* of the marital division of labor. Most couples used these principles to establish a basic pattern for their lives together. They might then modify the pattern, but often enough they acted on the principles without thinking much about the matter. Couples who were ideologically opposed to the traditional principles were likely nevertheless to act on them after they had children.

Whether or not they believe that their household is organized 10 along traditional lines, men know which tasks should be theirs, according to the traditional allocations, and which should be their wives'. They may have trouble, however, in developing an adequate formulation. Asked to say what makes something men's work and what makes something women's, they are likely to offer the rule that "Men are the breadwinners, and their wives take care of the house and the children." But they would agree that yardwork is men's work even though it is a part of home maintenance, as are household repairs and fixing the gutters. And they would agree that taking the children to a ballgame is something men should do, more than women, even though it involves child care. The traditional principles are not captured fully by "Men are breadwinners, women are homemakers and mothers."

More nearly fundamental, for the traditional view of the marital 11 division of labor, is that men provide the household with a structure within which to live and with the social place that comes with it. Men are responsible for supplying the household with money, as an expression of their responsibility for the standard of living of the household and the respect it commands in the community. They are also responsible for the integrity of the household, which is expressed as keeping the physical structure of the household in repair and protecting its occupants. And they have first responsibility for launching their children into adulthoods in which the children have a respectable place in the society.

In this traditional division of labor, men are responsible for much 12 of the household's relationships with the wider society. Their wives, then, are responsible for the internal functioning of the home; for child care and home maintenance; for relationships within the home; for the actual workings of the family.

The traditional principles were ordinarily augmented by an ad- 13 ditional principle, *the principle of helping out*. No matter who is supposed to do what, the other should be willing to help out if needed. If the man is not otherwise engaged and his wife needs help putting the children to bed, the man ought to pitch in. The responsibility, however, would remain his wife's.

The principle of helping out is entirely consistent with the tradi- 14 tional principles in that it does not lead to questioning the traditional allocation of responsibilities. Quite different is another principle often invoked in debates over the marital division of labor, *the principle of equity*. This is the principle that the work of the marriage should be divided fairly between the husband and wife.

The principle of equity can produce results different from those 15 of the traditional principles of the division of labor augmented by the principle of helping out. In application of the principle of equity, fairness is all. If neither the man nor his wife enjoys cleaning the house, then the husband should clean the house one week, the wife the next, or they should clean the house together, each doing half the work. Or the wife might be compensated elsewhere; perhaps the man should do some other task that neither enjoys, like laundry.

It is also not fair for one partner to use a labor-saving approach 16 that is not available to the other partner. If the man and his wife decide that they will share the cooking, it is not fair for the man to do his share by ringing up the neighborhood pizza parlor. Nor is it fair for one partner to perform child care by playing with the children when the other partner performs child care by preparing their food. Nor is it fair for one partner to claim press of work when the other partner works just as hard.

Sometimes a man will perform a chore that is based in none of 17 these principles. A husband will fix breakfast for his wife on a Sunday morning, although both agree that cooking is the wife's responsibility and there is no need for the husband to help or reason for him to believe that fixing her breakfast is only fair. Under such circumstances, his breakfast preparation is a gift to his wife, an expression of affection.

The Principles in Practice

In their division of marital labor, the men of this study largely 18 followed traditional principles augmented by the principle of helping out, even though they were also committed to the principle of equity. This was possible because the men felt that the arrangement they had established with their wives was fair.

With two exceptions, both in childless couples, one a man whose 19 wife earned as much as he did, the other a man whose wife earned more, the men of our sample understood themselves to be the marital partner in charge of assuring the family's income. That does not mean that they expected to be the sole earners of that income, but rather that they considered themselves to be the main earners, the partners who were ultimately responsible. The men might need their wives to help out if the household was to attain an aimed-at standard of living, but that did not diminish their responsibility for the domain. If a family's income should be too little for its bills, the fault would be the man's alone, not his wife's or his and his wife's together. He might perhaps argue that the bills were unjustified; that his wife, as the partner responsible for the family's spending, had overspent. But if he accepted that the family's income was inadequate, the failure would be entirely his.

Most men believed it was also they who were responsible for the 20 maintenance of the home and its grounds. In keeping with this, they were the ones to do whatever upkeep required building-trade skills, such as painting and carpentry, or to conduct the negotiations with the tradesmen who possessed such skills. However, maintenance of grounds, especially planting and gardening, could be assimilated to internal home care and become the woman's job, especially if the aim were decorative rather than functional. So could arranging for painting and carpentry. Indeed, men who felt they knew too little to hold their own with tradesmen, and so felt inadequate in an area that they believed to be theirs, could be relieved to have their wives take over. They could rationalize that it was easier for their wives to act as contractors because their wives were home during the day; and, in any event, their wives were only helping out.

Men believe without question that they are the ones to whom the 21 family should look for protection. It is they who should caution a daughter's boyfriend to drive carefully, should stand between an angry neighbor and one of their children who has infringed on that neighbor's territory, and, if no one else can do it, should be the one to send away a persistent door-to-door salesman. Couples so strongly committed to achieving equity that they try to ensure that the husband and wife perform the same tasks nevertheless consider it the husband's responsibility to check out a noise in the night.

Men felt strongly that it should be they who sponsored their sons 22 into the world of achievement: sports and, eventually, work. They also thought they should contribute to their daughter's movement into adulthood, but were less certain how this was to be done, especially after the daughters became adolescent. Sometimes they acted to support their older daughters' functioning at school or in work just as they might their sons', but at other times they seemed to feel that all they could offer was protection.

Men believed that their wives were responsible for the quality of 23 life inside their homes. This included all the activities necessary to the logistic support of the members of the household: keeping the household in provisions, producing meals and clean clothes, and when necessary driving the children to their various activities. It also included attending to the emotional climate of the household. The children's feelings of security, the ease with which people talked with each other, the household's sense of comfort—all these they saw as within their wives' domain. They looked to their wives for information about the emotional well-being of family members and, sometimes, for coaching in their own relationships with their children.

Men believed that as an extension of the wives' responsibility for 24 relationships within the home, their wives should manage the family's relationships with couples who were friends and with the family's kin, including the man's mother and sisters. The men, of course, did their own social arranging when it involved partners in sport or in leisure activities.

Men believed that they, rather than their wives, should interpret 25 the events of business and politics for the family. Managing the family's boundary with the political and economic world was in their domain of responsibility.

These principles of allocation of marital responsibilities are likely 26 to appear so natural to men—and to their wives—that they become the basis for the marital division of labor without discussion or thought.

> Subconsciously, I rely on my wife to run the house, keep things organized. And so far as our social schedule, she probably takes care of that in the sense of what we're going to be doing on Friday night or Wednesday or Sunday. And I suppose she relies on me to bring the bread home and put it on the table.

Mr. Powers, businessman

Mr. Abbott, a high-level technician, has been married almost 27 thirty years. His wife is in charge of patient information at a local hospital. Their two children are now grown. Mr. Abbott said:

> We've never officially worked it out, but I think that there are things that are categorized as the man type jobs such as painting the house, making repairs. She does a very good job with the house, keeps the house very clean. Shopping is her job, obviously. She doesn't mind. I let her pay most of the bills. She handles the budget in that sense. I take care of what I call the investing, whether it be savings or buying real estate or whatever. She won't interfere with that. We discuss major purchases. But I would have to say that she would probably leave that to me.
>
> I don't have a great deal of difficulty in explaining myself if I want to invest in some silly stock. I tell her it's really going to become great in a short while. She'll believe me and we'll go ahead and do it. Some of my ventures haven't been that good, either. Some have been quite good.

In recent years there has been a good deal of criticism of men for 28 insisting on a traditional division of labor within the home even when their wives work full time outside of the home. Men have been accused of using the power of their income (or of a supposed greater ability to make a life for themselves were the marriage to end) to require their wives to perform a disproportionate number of those tasks involved in running a home that are menial, repetitious, and degrading. However, this is not at all the way men feel about the traditional division of labor. Nor does it seem accurate to say that men smugly refuse to acknowledge that they have a good thing. Rather, men seem deeply invested in doing well at what they believe to be their responsibilities. Far from wanting to shirk their responsibility for income production, they will accept menial, repetitious, degrading, and dangerous work, if no better work is available. When they fail to meet what they believe to have been one of their responsibilties—providing an adequate income, protecting a child—their self-blame can be bottomless even if the fault was not theirs.

There is another reason men object, if only through passive re- 29 sistance, to sharing tasks traditional principles would say are their wives'. So long as they—and their wives—believe the tasks to be shared are in their wives' domains of responsibility, the men are answerable to their wives. Suppose a couple should decide that the husband will supervise the children's baths. The husband is asked by the children what toys they can take into the tub. Because the husband is functioning in his wife's domain—care of the children and their possessions—his response would be subject to overrule by her. If she said, "The boy shouldn't need to take toys into the tub any more," that would be it. Men accept that in their wives' domains of responsibility, their wives are the lead partner—not quite the boss, but certainly the partner with greater authority. It's hard for a man, when doing the dishes, not to feel subordinate to his wife.

> I tend to go along with the wife's beliefs and desires in terms of what the kids should have and what would be good for them and whether they can get along without something or not, that kind of thing. If I don't think that things are extremely wrong, and I don't find too many that are, or if I don't really feel all that strongly about them one way or the other, it's more comfortable for me to go along with it.
>
> ─────────────
>
> *Mr. Draper, executive and*
> *business owner*

One element of the traditional view of the family is that the man 30 is the family's "head." Yet the meaning of this status is by no means immediately apparent. One meaning it does not have is that he is the family's boss.

For several years, when teaching courses on the family or leading 31 workshops on family issues, I have asked people to role-play a family meeting. I cast a family of mother, father, twelve-year-old daughter, and ten-year-old son. I say that the family must work out how to arrange the family vacation. I tell the father that he is an avid fisherman and wants to vacation near a trout stream, and I tell the mother that she does not want to spend her vacation cleaning fish. I go on to tell the mother that she would prefer a beach setting where the children would have other children with whom to play, perhaps a cottage along a safe shore. And then I ask the family to resolve the dilemma.

Almost always when I have done this, the woman playing the 32 mother has taken the lead. She has asked the husband for his ideas, has elicited reactions from the children, has made her own suggestions and has piloted the way to compromise. She might first gain her husband's agreement to a plan that would provide something for everyone, would then turn to the children, inform them, listen to their objections, and gain their acquiescence by diplomacy, bribery, and firmness. Someimes the man held out stubbornly for the trout stream, but always the woman won him around. In one instance the man suggested going off by himself, but when the woman said that she wouldn't want him to do that, he immediately dropped the idea.

To this point the woman would be the marital partner who was 33 really running things in the family, though she would be doing so diplomatically, with deference to her husband. But now, with a decision agreed to, something noteworthy would occur. The man would turn to me and nod, to indicate that the family had come to a resolution. Though the woman had piloted the resolution, the man would assume responsibility for presenting it to me.

It happened once that the man and woman turned to me together 34 to say they had completed the exercise. I then sat stone-faced, refusing to respond. By doing this I manufactured an emergency: an instructor who seemed to have gone into a catatonic trance. Now, even though earlier it had not been the man alone who represented the family, it was the man who took charge and said again, a bit louder, that the group had completed the exercise.

In family life, the man is not head of the family in the sense that 35 he gets his way; often enough he ends by endorsing his wife's plans. He is family head in that he represents the family in its dealings with the world.

Men who adhere to traditional principles in the allocation of mar- 36 ital responsibilities almost uniformly also adhere to the principle of helping out, though with wide variation in the extent to which they are asked to help and actually do help. The assumption that each partner will help the other underlies much of what appears to be role sharing. Should the woman be overwhelmed by tasks within the home, the man may help out by vacuuming, doing dishes, or taking the kids for a ride in the car. Should the man be unable through his own income to meet the household's bills, then the woman may, in turn, help out. Should the man be made anxious by confrontations, then the woman can represent the household in a neighborhood conflict. And should the woman hate to cook, the man may do the cooking.

In all instances of helping out, both men and women are aware 37 of whose is the initial and formal responsibility. They understand that the one who helps out is doing something extra, and a partner may decline to help out if confronted by more urgent matters in his or her own domain. Men, especially, may give helping their wives lower priority than the demands of their work.

> Along with working, she keeps the house up and does the shopping and keeps everything rolling inside, and I try to get everything outside. She takes care of the household end, I take care of the other stuff, the outside, the repairs, things like that. Paying the bills and things like that. She takes care of the food and the wash and whatever needs to be cleaned. Even though I try to help her out once in a while, I haven't been successful lately.

> *Mr. Brewer, owner of a catering business*

As noted previously, one problem with helping out is that the 38 helper is in a subordinate position. The domain is, after all, the spouse's. So when wives help their husbands in their husbands' work, the wives are apt to be treated as subordinates rather than partners. And when men help their wives at home, their wives are apt to give them direction.

Reliance on traditional principles plus helping out is always sub- 39 ject to criticism from the standpoint of equity. "Yes," a woman may say, "in our parents' families our mothers did the cooking and cleaning. But they didn't also work full time and bring in almost half the income. It isn't fair for me not only to work but also to have responsibility for the home and the children."

The principle of equity can make men uncomfortable because it 40 implies that the men aren't meeting their obligations to their families through their work, their protectiveness, their captaining, and their helping out. Also, the men may anticipate becoming subordinates in their wives' domains of responsibility despite their wives' insistence that responsibility will be shared. The following scenario is one that some young couples report having followed.

> The wife argues, relying on the principle of equity: "You ought to share the work of the home. I work as hard at my job as you do at yours."
> The husband responds, rejecting the principle of equity, since he believes that he is already doing his share by meeting traditional expectations, and replacing it with the principle of helping out. "Tell me what to do and I'll do it."
> The wife returns to the principle of equity since use of the principle of helping out leaves her with unshared responsibility: "You live here too. You can see as well as I what has to be done. Why should I have to tell you what to do?"

The husband now reminds his wife that others are likely to see the domain as hers by threatening her with inferior performance. "Well, I know your standards are different, but you'll have to put up with the way I do it."

The husband has a good chance of winning, because his wife is 41 likely to agree that others will see her as the lead partner in home maintenance. In consequence it will be she who is embarrassed should a friend or relative visit and find the house scruffy.

Dual-Career Marriages

Mr. Foster is a former investment counselor who now, with part- 42 ners, manages a program of mutual funds. His income is large. Mrs. Foster has done graduate work in business management. She holds a responsible executive position in an accounting firm that pays her well, though her income does not match her husband's. Mr. Foster told us that he admired his wife for her success and fully supported her in her commitment to work.

The Fosters had three children, all at home, the youngest just 43 finishing primary school. Mr. Foster spent about as much time with the children as did his wife. When the children were smaller, Mrs. Foster had stayed at home with them. After about a year at home she had become deeply depressed, and her husband, searching for a remedy, had urged her to return to graduate school.

That time she was at home trying to deal with the kids, I think that was probably the hardest part of our marriage. She was just restless, very restless, and not feeling very accomplished. She was having a difficult time coping with being married and having kids and not having a career. At least that was my analysis.

I think that I would really say she was pretty disturbed. I remember now, the way she woke up crying a couple of times, like in bed, talking about her life. I used to get bored with it all. I'd say, "Just relax and go to sleep," that kind of thing. It was just sort of unarticulated anxiety on her part. It was a lot of self-doubt. She was not very confident, not as confident a person as she is now. And I remember it was very repetitive. It kept going around in circles. And she didn't quite know what was bugging her. But something sure as hell was bugging her. I was trying to be supportive. Trying to make it work.

What we did, she went back to school. It was a rallying point, an objective that was very definable. Everybody had a common goal to hold the thing together. And that was good. I was absolutely supportive of her going back to school. Absolutely! More than supportive, I pushed it. Because, why the hell shouldn't she? Why should she stay home? It's ridiculous.

Note how Mr. Foster applied the fundamental principles of the 44 division of labor to his marriage. He thought of his wife as the partner primarily responsible for the children and became irritated when she could not adapt to staying at home. But he also thought of himself as responsible for making the family work. When he became aware that staying home was depressing his wife, he saw it as his place to act.

With his wife working, Mr. Foster began to share tasks in the 45 home. He did some of the cooking (a bit less than his wife) and helped clean up after dinner. Most of the cooking and a good deal of child care was performed by a foreign student who acted as an au pair. While Mr. Foster's willingness to help at home was a critical element in freeing Mrs. Foster's time and energies for her job, having the foreign student may well have permitted the system to work.

Mr. Foster continued to define himself as the partner ultimately 46 responsible for the family's support. As one expression of this, he made his bank account available to his wife, although his wife kept her bank account entirely to herself.

> We've always had separate bank accounts, but I used to give Paula money before she went to work. Now Paula can sign on my account. I can't sign on hers.
> Certainly Paula's working has made a very big difference in what we could do. But I'm the court of last resort. I mean, I'm the backstop.

Mr. Foster did not pay for everything. Mrs. Foster paid for items 47 within the woman's domain: groceries and housekeeping services. Mr. Foster paid for the upkeep items, the items necessary to keep the house going. As Mr. Foster put it: "Paula runs much of the house and I run other things." Mr. Foster paid for evenings out—unless he was without cash, in which case he appealed to the principle of helping out:

> Paula buys the groceries. There's a guy who comes in here once a week, and the groceries, that's a pretty good bill. And she pays for the housekeeping. And I pay for essentially everything else. I pay for the telephone and the lights and tuitions and insurance. She buys a lot of stuff for the house that she wants to buy. Large furniture, that gets in a gray area. If we go out to dinner, I pay, generally. If I have money.

Mrs. Foster was highly successful in her work and became an 48 important member of her firm. Her contribution to the firm was not, in Mr. Foster's view, properly recognized. Mr. Foster became outraged on his wife's behalf.

After two years in the firm she believed she deserved a promotion and salary increase. They were refused. One reason given her was that she didn't need the status or the income since her husband was so successful.

This is a textbook case, what went on there. People who don't have daughters or wives, men who don't have daughters or wives who have gone through this, don't believe it goes on! This was so blatant it ought to be written up. I can't stand those people any more. I just absolutely see red! Just the hypocrisy! That's what it is, it's hypocrisy!

Mr. Foster's first thought, on hearing the story from his wife, was 49 to provide her with understanding and support. But this was *his wife* who was being misused, and he wanted to do battle for her. Again, a traditional principle: the husband's responsibility to protect the members of his household. Mr. Foster, insofar as he did not protect his wife, was failing to behave properly, in a way he could himself respect.

In another dual-career family, when the wife reported harsh and 50 unfair criticism from her boss, her husband felt almost impelled to call the boss and tell him off. The wife, alarmed, said, "Don't you dare! It means my career!" The husband reported the incident with full appreciation that his reaction had been misguided, but also with pride that he had been so strongly protective.

That the Fosters maintained a dual-career marriage does not mean 51 that Mr. Foster changed his understandings of his responsibilities in his family. Rather, he adapted his understandings to his special situation. He saw himself as behaving well—indeed, unselfishly.

I think men who aren't accepting of their wives' working are probably pretty selfish. I know there are a lot of people like that. We spent Saturday night with a couple like that. He wants his wife *there*. Why the hell *should* she be *there*? At his beck and call. Women are people.

Mr. Foster viewed his acceptance of his wife's working as some- 52 thing he was doing for her. (That was why he saw himself as unselfish.) Men can also, of course, understand their wives' working as helping out. Especially if their wives are not overburdened at home, and expenses have mounted—as with children at college—men may urge their wives to work.

We no longer have any children at home. And we will need money, at least for a couple of years, to pay two tuition bills. So those two things kind of came together at the same time. And she is going to be working and getting some money to help us over the hump with the tuition bills. After the tuition bills stop or maybe after we have only one child in school, if she wants to work, fine, if she doesn't, it is really up to her.

Mr. Ryder, department head

At no point do men understand themselves to be no longer re- 53 sponsible for income production, neither when they believe that their wives are working to help out nor when they believe their wives are working for self-realization. Nor do they stop considering their wives responsible for the domains that would be theirs were they not working.

Men are ordinarily willing to help working wives by contributing 54 to home maintenance and child care; even more, they are willing to accept that less will get done. They may, though, have moments when they regret having supported their wives' desire to work. Mr. Foster, for example, despite his insistence that he was willing to do dishes and to cook when the au pair was otherwise occupied, was irritated by evenings spent alone because his wife had to work. And though he said he didn't miss the social life that had been sacrificed to his wife's new priorities, he was thoroughly aware that it had been sacrificed.

Most of all, when men's wives work, men are likely to miss their 55 wives' solicitude should the men be stressed or fatigued by *their* work. Working wives are likely to be less attentive to careworn husbands than wives who believe their husbands to be engaged in a lone struggle for the family's subsistence. In one dual-career couple the husband and wife had agreed that neither of them would begin their evening together by burdening the other with the problems of the day. But the husband seemed wistfully to wish his wife had more tolerance for his job complaints.

RESPONDING TO READING

Key words: class   community   family   freedom   gender   identity power   rights

Rhetorical concepts: analysis   anecdote   explanation   illustration induction   narrative/example   research report

1.   Weiss looks at the same issue that Brazelton and Fallows have examined, but from a quite different perspective. What is his angle of vision? What does he see as the significant question to deal with? Why is this question important for the future of the family?
2.   Does the set of traditional assumptions about their marital responsibilities

made by the men in the interviews reflect your experience? What changes in husbands' assumptions, if any, occur when wives work? What evidence does Weiss give for these conclusions and how convincing are his data? Conduct two or three interviews of your own with married men of different ages and write an essay on the assumptions about marital responsibilities that emerge from your data; compare your conclusions to those Weiss asserts.

3.   Mr. Foster sees himself as very supportive of his wife as she returns to work. But Weiss sees this support rather differently: "Mr. Foster viewed his acceptance of his wife's working as something he was doing for her." How do you think Mrs. Foster saw the situation? What distinction is Weiss drawing here? Is it important?

4.   Weiss suggests that similar sets of motives lie beneath the problems that occur when wives work for their husbands and the problems that occur when husbands become protective of their wives at work. What are these motives and how do they relate to the "traditional assumptions" Weiss has defined.

5.   Elsewhere, Weiss has commented that, although "men's traditional understandings of marriage are in no way modified by wives working," men's behaviors "have changed greatly." Explain what Weiss means, giving examples from his essay and, if appropriate, from your own experience. To what degree do the essays by Brazelton and Fallows shed light on this interplay of traditional understandings and apparently untraditional behaviors?

Successful Aging

ROBERT N. BUTLER

Butler, a gerontologist and psychiatrist, is an expert on aging and a prominent advocate for the elderly, as implied by his coinage of the term "ageism" in 1968. His life reflects his personal credo: "To always stretch the limits of the possible through personal relationships, scholarship, science, writing, action and political activism. To work toward making life a work of art. To do no harm." Butler was trained at Columbia (B.A., 1949, M.D., 1953), with psychiatric residencies at the Langley Porter Institute and the National Institute of Mental Health. For twenty years he was on the faculty of the George Washington University Medical School; from 1976–82 he directed the National Institute of Aging; since then he has been a professor of geriatrics and adult development at New York's Mt. Sinai School of Medicine. He exerts a positive and forceful influence on public policy though service on a number of professional and governmental councils on aging, and through his books for both general and professional readers. *Why Survive? Being Old in America* (1975) received the Pulitzer Prize; among his other books are *Sex after Sixty* (1976), *Modern Biological Theories of Aging* (1987), and *The Promise of Productive Aging* (1990).

"Successful Aging," published in the popular journal *Mental Hygiene* (1974), is as characteristic of Butler's literary style as of his views on aging. Aging is not invariably tied to chronology, says

Butler; it is as variable among people as any other physiological, psychological, or social process. He is particularly eager to dispel ˎ the denigrating stereotypes of the aging as unproductive, disengaged, inflexible, and senile; in fact, only 5% of people over 65 are institutionalized. However, the future, anyone's future, is far from serene; older people experience more stresses than any other age group, including anxiety, depression, and grief, "either for one's own losses or for the ultimate loss of oneself." Yet there are positives; "only in old age can one experience a personal sense of the entire life cycle" through life review, aided by professionals or families who encourage recall and reminiscence. What kind of future can we expect as we age? What can we do, in a culture that denies death and denigrates old age, through facing the inevitable realistically, to make it the future that we want?

One of James Thurber's fables tells of a man who reported to his 1 wife that he saw a unicorn in his garden. Thinking her husband had lost his mind, she surreptitiously called the police and a psychiatrist. However, it was a setup, and they took her away instead. The husband tricked the police and the psychiatrist into thinking his wife had made it all up. The American humorist always offered morals at the conclusion of his fables, and in this case, it was: *Don't count your boobies before they are hatched.* Those who think of older people as boobies, crones, witches, old biddies, old fogies, as out-to-pasture, boring, garrulous, pains-in-the-neck, as unproductive, worthless people, have another thing coming. They had better not count their boobies before they are hatched. Great numbers of old people need not be and are not in institutions and, given a fighting chance in a society that has devalued them, can maintain a viable place in society. Indeed, at any one moment of time, 95 per cent of the persons over 65 live in the community. In our social policies and in our therapeutic programs we need, of course, to have in mind a basic standard of health and not have our thinking dominated by stereotypes of frailty, psychopathology, senility, confusion, decline, and institutionalization. However, there is, of course, no point to developing illusions concerning healthy, successful old age. Like all periods, it has its difficulties. There are problems to be dealt with. There are needs to be fulfilled. But old age can be an emotionally healthy and satisfying time of life, with a minimum of physical and mental impairments. Many older people have adapted well to their old age with a minimum of stress and a high level of morale.

Study of *normal* development has seldom gone beyond early adult 2 years, and the greatest emphasis has been on childhood. There have been realtively few centers for the study of adult human development. These centers have studied small population samples, usually of white, affluent middle-class people, composed about equally of men and women. This work at the University of Chicago, Duke University, the University of California and, for a brief period, at the National Institute of Mental Health has helped provide us with some understanding of successful mental health in aging.

In our culture few people think of old age as a time of potential   3
health and growth. This is partly realistic, considering the lot of so many older people who have been cast aside, become lonely, bitter, poor, and emotionally or physically ill. American society has not been generous or supportive of the *unproductive*—in this case, old people who have reached what is arbitrarily defined as the retirement period. But in a larger sense, the negative view of old age is a problem of Western civilization.

The Western concept of the life cycle is decidedly different from   4
that of the Orient, since it derives from an opposite view about what *self* means and what life is all about. Oriental philosophy places the individual self, his life span, and his death *within* the process of human experience. Life and death are familiar and equally acceptable parts of what self means. In the West, on the other hand, death is considered outside of the self. To be a self or person one must be alive, in control, and aware of what is happening.

The greater and more self-centered or narcissistic Western em-   5
phasis on individuality and control makes death an outrage—a tremendous affront to man rather than the logical and necessary process of old life making way for new. The opposite cultural views of East and West evolve to support two very different ways of life, each with its own merits. But the Western predilection for *progress*, conquest over nature, and personal self-realization has produced difficult problems for the elderly and for those preparing for old age.

This is particularly so when the national spirit of a nation and of   6
an historical period have emphasized and expanded the notion of measuring human worth in terms of individual productivity and power. Thus, old people are led to see themselves as *failing with age*— a phrase that refers as much to self-worth as it does to physical strength.

Religion has been the traditional solace by promising another   7
world wherein the self again springs to life, never to be further threatened by loss of its own integrity. Even though Western man's consummate dream of immortality is fulfilled by it, the integration of the aging experience to his life process still remains incomplete. Increasing secularization produces a frightening void that frequently is met by avoiding and denying the thought of one's own decline and death, and by forming self-protective prejudices against old people.

In some respects, we have come now to deal somewhat more   8
openly with death itself. But aging—that long prelude to death—has become a kind of obscenity, something to avoid.

Medicine and the behavioral sciences have mirrored social atti- 9
tudes by presenting old age as a grim litany of physical and emotional
ills. Decline of the individual has been the key concept; neglect, a
major treatment technique. Until about 1960 most of the medical,
psychological, psychiatric, and social work literature on the aging was
based on experience with the sick and the institutionalized, even
though only 5 per cent of the elderly were confined to institutions.*

The few research studies that have concentrated on the healthy 10
aged give indication of positive potential. But the general, almost
phobic, dislike of aging remains the norm, with healthy old people
being ignored and the chronically ill receiving half-hearted custodial
care. Only those elderly who happen to have exotic or *interesting*
diseases or emotional problems, or substantial financial resources ordinarily receive the research and treatment attention of the medical
and psychotherapeutic professions.

Health care is approaching a $100 billion-a-year business—second 11
only to the food industry. However, the health care industry does not
reflect the various human ills in due proportion. Although chronic
disease accounts for two-thirds of our nation's health costs, certainly
two-thirds of our medical school curriculum, medical manpower, intellectual emphasis, research, health delivery system are not devoted
to this important group of diseases. With the advent of a national
health insurance plan and the struggle that is now beginning to ensue
in Congress and in the Administration with respect to the character
of that insurance plan, it has to be recognized that none of the plans
under consideration face realistically the facts of life, disease, and
aging.

What is healthy old age? To begin with , one must remember that 12
science and medicine have historically been more concerned with
treating what goes wrong than with clarifying the complex interwoven
elements necessary to produce and support health. Typical of this is
the treatment of coronary attacks after the fact rather than prescribing
a preventive program involving diet, exercise, protection from stress,
and the absence of smoking. Most of the elderly's major disease could
be cited as examples of this same phenomenon. The tedious and less
dramatic process of prevention requires an understanding of what
supports or what interferes with healthy development throughout the
course of life. We spend only 4 cents of every health dollar on prevention.

In 1946 the World Health Organization defined health as *a state* 13

---

*This 5 per cent is a most significant minority, of course, with major needs. And,
ultimately, some 20 per cent of older people require institutional care, at least under the current
health care system that does not provide comprehensive home care.

of complete physical, mental, and social well-being and not merely the absence of disease or infirmity. This definition represents, of course, an ideal with many possible interpretations. But the three components of health—physical, emotional and social—compose the framework in which one can begin to analyze what is going well in addition to what is going wrong. The attempt must be made to locate those conditions that enable humans to thrive and not merely survive.

We cannot look at health simply as statistical or typical. If that   14 were the case, dental caries, which affects about 90 per cent of the population might be considered healthy. Moreover, health cannot be looked at simply as a state. It is a *process* of continuing change and growth. What may be apparent health at one moment in time may already contain the beginnings of illness to develop fully in still another moment.

Old age is a period where there is unique developmental work   15 to be accomplished. Childhood might be broadly defined as a period of gathering and enlarging strength and experience; whereas, the major developmental task in old age is to clarify, deepen, and find use for what one has already obtained in a lifetime of learning and adapting. The elderly must teach themselves to conserve their strength and resources where this is necessary, and to adjust in the best sense to those changes and losses that occur as part of the aging experience.

The ability of the elderly person to do this is contingent upon his   16 physical health, personality, earlier life experiences, and the societal supports (adequate finances, shelter, medical care, social roles, recreation) he receives. It is imperative that old people continue to develop and change in a flexible manner if health is to be promoted and maintained. Failure to adapt at any age, under any circumstances, can result in a physical or emotional illness. Optimum growth and adaptation may occur all along the course of life, when the individual's strengths and potentials are recognized, reinforced, and encouraged by the environment in which he lives.

To develop, then, a clear depiction of what old age can be like,   17 we must contrast the mythological with a realistic appraisal of old age. Let me present a sketch that I first gave in 1959 to a group of nursing home owners in Maryland. This is the stereotype of old age, and it hasn't changed much in the last 15 years.

> An older person thinks and moves slowly. He does not think as he used to, nor as creatively. He is bound to himself and to his past and can no longer change or grow. He can neither learn well nor swiftly, and even if he could, he would not wish to. Tied to his personal traditions and growing conservatism, he dislikes innovations and is not disposed to new ideas. Not only can he not move

forward, he often moves backwards. He enters a second childhood, caught often in increasing egocentricity and demanding more from his environment than he is willing to give to it. Sometimes he becomes more like himself, a caricature of a lifelong personality. He becomes irritable and cantankerous, yet shallow and enfeebled. He lives in his past. He is behind the times. He is aimless and wandering of mind, reminiscing and garrulous. Indeed, he is a study in decline. He is the picture of mental and physical failure. He has lost and cannot replace friends, spouse, jobs, status, power, influence, income. He is often stricken by diseases which in turn restrict his movement, his enjoyment of food, the pleasures of well-being. His sexual interest and activity decline. His body shrinks; so, too, does the flow of blood to his brain. His mind does not utilize oxygen and sugar at the same rate as formerly. Feeble, uninteresting, he awaits his death, a burden to society, to his family, and to himself.

There are certain major associated myths. There is *the myth of* 18 aging itself—the idea of chronological aging, measuring one's age by the number of years one has lived. It is clear that there are great differences in the rates of physiological, chronological, psychological, and social aging from person to person and also within each individual.

Then there is *the myth of unproductivity*. But in the absence of dis- 19 eases and social adversities, old people tend to remain productive and actively involved in life. There are dazzling examples like the 82-year-old Arturo Rubenstein working his hectic concert schedule; or of the 72-year-old Benjamin Dugger discovering the antibiotic aureomycin. Numbers of people become unusually creative for the first time in old age, when exceptional and inborn talents may be discovered and expressed. In fact, many old people continue to contribute usefully to their families and community in a variety of ways, including active employment.

Third, there is *the myth of disengagement* that older people prefer 20 to be disengaged from life, to withdraw into themselves, choosing to live alone or perhaps only with their own peers. Ironically, a few gerontologists hold these views. One study, *Growing Old, the Process of Disengagement*, presented a theory that mutual separation between the aged person and society is a natural part of the aging experience. There is no evidence to support this as a generalization. Disengagement is only one of the many patterns of reaction to old age.

Fourth is *the myth of inflexibility*. The ability to change and adapt 21 has little to do with one's age and more to do with one's lifelong character. But even this statement has to be qualified. One is not necessarily destined to one's character in earlier life. The endurance, strength, and stability in character structure are remarkable and protective, but most, if not all, people change and remain open to change throughout the course of life right up to its termination unless, of course, they are affected by major, massive destruction of brain tissue, illiteracy, or poverty.

Fifth is *the myth of senility*—the notion that old people are or 22 inevitably become senile, showing forgetfulness, confusional episodes, and reduced attention. This is widely accepted. Senility, in fact, is a layman's term—unfortunately used by doctors to categorize the behavior of the old. Some of what is called senile is the result of brain damage. But anxiety and depression are also frequently lumped in the same category of senility, even though they are treatable and reversible. Old people, like the young, experience a full range of emotions, including anxiety, grief, depression and paranoid states. It is all too easy to blame age and brain damage when accounting for the mental problems and emotional concerns of later life.

Drug tranquilization—much overused in the United States—is 23 another frequently misdiagnosed, but potentially reversible, cause of so-called senility. Malnutrition and unrecognized physical illnesses such as congestive heart failure and pneumonia may produce *senile behavior* by reducing the supply of blood, oxygen, and food to the brain. Alcoholism, often associated with bereavement, is another cause. Late-life alcoholism is a serious and common problem.

Now, of course, irreversible brain damage is no myth, and cerebral 24 arteriosclerosis or hardening of the arteries of the brain and so-called senile brain disease marked by the mysterious dissolution of brain cells are major and serious conditions that do impair human development in old age.

Sixth is *the myth of serenity*. In contrast to the previous myths that 25 view the elderly in a negative light, this myth portrays old age as a kind of adult fairyland. Old age is presented as a time of relative peace and serenity, when people can relax and enjoy the fruits of their labors after the storms of life are over. Visions of carefree, cookie-baking grandmothers and rocking-chair grandfathers are cherished by younger generations.

However, older persons experience more stresses than any other 26 age group, and these stresses are often devastating. Depression, anxiety, psychosomatic illnesses, paranoid states, garrulousness, and irritability are some of the internal reactions to them.

Depressive reactions are particularly widespread in late life. In 27 fact, *25 per cent of all suicides in the United States occur in people over 65.*

Another frequent companion of old age is grief, either for one's 28 own losses or for the ultimate loss of oneself. Apathy and emptiness are common sequels to the initial shock and sadness that follow the loss of close friends and relatives. Physical disease and social isolation can follow bereavement.

Anxiety is another common feature. There is much to be anxious 29
about, with poverty, loneliness and illness heading the list. Anxiety
may manifest itself in many forms—rigid patterns of thinking and
behavior, helplessness, manipulativeness, restlessness and suspi-
ciousness, sometimes to the point of paranoid states.

The stereotyping and myths surrounding old age can partly be 30
explained by lack of knowledge and by insuffcent daily and/or professional contact with varieties of older people. But there is another
powerful factor operating—a deep and profound prejudice against
the elderly, which is found to some degree in all of us.

In thinking about how to describe this, I coined the word *ageism* 31
in 1968:

> Ageism can be seen as a process of systematic stereotyping of and
> discrimination against people, because they are old—just as racism
> and sexism can accomplish this with skin color and gender. Old
> people are categorized as senile, rigid in thought and manner, old
> fashioned in morality and skills. Ageism allows the younger gen-
> erations to see older people as different from themselves. Thus, they
> subtly cease to identify with their elders as human beings.*

Over the years I have tried to enumerate certain characteristics 32
that help define tendencies to be observed in older people. They are
not inevitable nor are they found to the same degree in each person
who manifests them. They do show themselves regularly enough to
be considered typical of people who have lived a long time and are
viewing the world from the special vantage point of old age.

Old age is the only period of life with no future. Therefore a major 33
task in late life is learning not to think in terms of the future. Children
are extremely future-oriented and look forward to each birthday as a
sign of growing up. The middle aged, as Schopenhauer said, begin
to count the number of years they have left before death rather than
the number of years since birth. In old age, one's time perspective is
shortened even further as the end of life approaches. Some avoid
confronting this fact by retreating to the past. Others deny their age
and continue to be future-oriented. The latter are the people who fail
to make wills, leave important relationships unresolved, put off en-
joyments, and experience boredom.

A more satisfying resolution is found among those elderly who 34
begin to emphasize the quality of the present, of the time remaining,
rather than the quantity. When death becomes imminent, there tends

---

*Butler, R. N. "Ageism: Another Form of Bigotry." *The Gerontologist* 9:243–46, 1969.
Butler, R. N. and Lewis, Myrna I. *Aging and Mental Health*, St. Louis, Missouri: The C. V. Mosby
Company, 1973.

to be a sense of immediacy, of the here and now, of living in the moment.

Only in old age can one experience a personal sense of the entire 35 life cycle. This comes to its fullness with the awareness of death in the forefront. There is the unfolding process of change, the experiencing of a sense of time, the seasoning or sense of life experience with a broadening perspective and the accumulation of factual knowledge of what it is to be expected at the different points of the life cycle.

Old age inaugurates the process of the *life review*, promoted by 36 the realization of approaching dissolution and death. It is characterized by the progressive return to consciousness of past experience, in particular the resurgence of unresolved conflicts that can now be surveyed and integrated. The old are not only taking stock of themselves as they review their lives; they are trying to think and feel through what they will do with the time that is left and with whatever material and emotional legacies they may have to give to others.

They frequently experience grief. The death of others, often more 37 than their own death, concerns them. Perplexed, frightened at being alone and increasingly depressed, they at times become wary or cautious to the point of suspicion about the motivations of others. If unresolved conflicts and fears are successfully reintegrated, they can give new significance and meaning to an individual's life, in preparing for death and mitigating fears.

What can we do to help move society to a more balanced view of 38 older people, and how can we help older people to prevent problems in later life and to favor successful aging? How can we treat already troubled older people to help them successfully age? We cannot review all of the relevant factors, of course. They vary from preventive measures like a major attack on the known antecedents of arteriosclerosis that requires change in dietary habits and physical activity. We must certainly face the enormous problem of alcoholism in the United States. Many people with lifelong excessive alcoholic intake are now surviving into old age, and many older people are taking up alcohol following grief and loneliness.

There is the need for a major reformation of our culture's sensi- 39 bility toward old people through use of the media, which can help transform our views of what older people are really like and how to help them enhance their sense of themselves. There is also the political approach. Older people are learning to assert themselves for what they need, thereby winning self respect.

There are two forms of psychotherapy that can be helpful to older 40 people, from both the preventive and therapeutic perspectives. These two treatment forms I call *life review therapy* and *life cycle group therapy*.

Life review therapy includes the taking of an extensive autobiog- 41
raphy from the older person and from other family members. Such
memoirs can also be preserved by means of tape recordings, of value
to children in the family. In instances of persons of note, memoirs
have considerable historical importance and should be placed in archives for many reasons, including furthering our understanding of
creativity and improving the image of our elders. The use of the family
album, the scrapbook and other memorabilia, searching out of ge-
nealogies and pilgrimages back to places of emotional import evoke
crucial memories, responses and understanding in patients.

The consequences of these steps include expiation of guilt, ex- 42
orcism of problematic childhood identifications, resolution of intra-
psychic conflicts, reconciliation of family relationships, transmission
of knowledge and values to those who follow, and renewal of the
ideals of citizenship.

Such life review therapy can be conducted in a variety of settings 43
from outpatient, individual psychotherapy to counseling in senior
centers to skilled listening in nursing homes. Even non-professionals
can function as therapists by becoming trained listeners as older persons recount their lives. Many older people can be helped to conduct
their own life reviews. The process need not be expensive.

Reminiscence of the old has all too often been devalued—re- 44
garded as a symptom, usually of organic dysfunction and felt to
bespeak aimless wandering of the mind or living in the past. We
recognize, of course, the value of reminiscence as seen in the great
memoirs composed in old age, which may give fascinating accounts
of unusual and gifted people.

We see the role of the life review in film and fiction. Ingmar 45
Bergman's beautiful 1957 motion picture, *Wild Strawberries*, shows an
elderly physician whose dreams and visions concerned his past as he
changed from remoteness and selfishness to closeness and love. Literature is replete with examples of the life review. Ernest Hemingway's *The Snows of Kilimanjaro*, Samuel Beckett's *Krapp's Last Tape*, Leo
Tolstoy's *The Death of Ivan Ilych*.

Since 1970 Myrna I. Lewis, a social worker colleague of mine, and 46
myself have conducted four age-integrated psychotherapy groups of
about 8 to 10 members each with one contrasting middle-aged group.
We have integrated persons ranging from age 15 to over age 80 in
each of the four groups, based on the belief that age segregation as
practiced in our society leaves very little opportunity for the rich
exchange of feeling, experience, and support possible between the
generations.

The groups are oriented toward persons experiencing a crisis in 47
their life ranging from near normal to pathological reactions to ado-

lescence, education, marriage or single life, divorce, parenthood, work and retirement, widowhood, illness and impending death. Thus, such groups are concerned not only with intrinsic psychiatric disorders but with preventive and remedial treatment of people as they pass through the usual vicissitudes of the life cycle.

Criteria for membership include absence of active psychosis and 48 presence of life crisis, acute, subacute or chronic. Of course, reaction to life crises follow traditional diagnostic categories, including depression, anxiety states, hypochondriasis, alcoholism, drug misuse. Our groups are balanced for age, sex, and personality dynamics. We meet once a week for one-half hour. Individual membership in a group averages about 2 years. New group members are asked to participate for a minimum of 3 months.

The life cycle crises approach to group therapy is neither strictly 49 encounter nor strictly psychoanalytic. Rather, it can be equally concerned with the interaction among group members as determined by reality and the past histories and problems of each member. The goal is the amelioration of suffering, the overcoming of disability, and the opportunity for new experiences of intimacy and self fulfillment.

We believe that both forms of therapy can be very useful in the 50 nursing home, mental hospital and other institutions. Age integration helps to recapitulate the family—something woefully missing for many older people. The garrulousness of older people reflects a social symptom and an intense desire in the face of death to deal with one's individual life.

These are but two examples of how we can approach the older 51 patient in and out of institutions. Indeed, older persons' families— when they exist (and we must remember that one-fourth of older people have no family at all)—can themselves participate in therapeutic processes.

When older people look back on their lives, they regret more often 52 what they did not do rather than what they have done. Medicine should regret its failures to act responsibly in the health care—including mental health care—of older people. Physicians and psychotherapists should not assume that nothing can be done for older people. Nor should the public. No one should count older people as boobies before they are hatched.

RESPONDING TO READING

Key words: community   discovery   education   family   identity
loss   memory   power   rights

Rhetorical concepts: analysis   definition   explanation   illustration
induction   myth   process   research report

1. Butler is fighting against the traditional picture of old age. What are these stereotypes and myths? What evidence does he bring to support and to disprove them? What is the relation of these stereotypes to similar kinds of prejudice that various writers have been objecting to in this book? Using examples, write an essay comparing the relationship between stereotypes of aging to stereotypes of racial minorities or women.

2. What are the "opposite cultural views of East and West" on aging and death? How have medicine and the behavioral sciences "mirrored social attitudes"? Is it possible for the West to adopt the attitudes of the East?

3. What is healthy old age, as Butler defines it? What is the "unique developmental work to be accomplished"? What are the advantages of being old?

4. Interview two or three elderly people, including at least one who may be an example of successful aging. As you help your interviewees conduct "life reviews" you will be gathering much material for writing. What evidence have you found supporting the stereotypes and myths of aging? What evidence have you found denying them? To what extent do the concepts Butler has developed help you make sense of your interviews?

The Family That Stretches (Together)

ELLEN GOODMAN

Writing from a viewpoint that combines common sense and humanitarian values, Ellen Goodman addresses issues close to home, often matters particularly affecting families, working women, the poor, and the disadvantaged. "The Family That Stretches (Together)" attempts to define the meaning of *family*, through the conundrums of two children trying to identify who's who in their extended families, still in transition and flux. "We are in the same family," concludes the girl, specifying the essence of the relationship—family feeling—that defies biology and the law. The boy, however, cannot draw a traditional family tree, for it will not accommodate the step-grandfather or the ex-uncle with whom he feels a kindred spirit.

The technique in this essay is typical of the way Goodman (born 1941, B.A. Radcliffe, 1963), a columnist for the *Boston Globe* since 1971, writes her pieces, which are now syndicated in more than 400 newspapers and collected in three volumes, *Close to Home* (1979), *At Large* (1981), and *Keeping in Touch* (1985). Says Goodman:

> I never wanted to be a package-tour sort of columnist who covered thirteen countries in twenty-seven days. Nor do I want to write at arm's length about the Major Issues of Our Times. I think it's more important for all of us to make links between our personal lives and public issues. I don't want to present myself as a disembodied voice of authority, but as a woman, mother, vegetable gardener, failed jogger and expert on only one subject, the ambivalence of life.

From one or a combination of these identifiable personae, Goodman presents herself as a character in nearly every column, commenting in an engaged, human voice on the subject at hand. She often uses children (her own daughter is the likely source of the "ten-year-old researcher"), teenagers, or friends to provide a point of view that supplements, complements, or contradicts her own. The dialogues are intended to convince through their illustrations of contemporary life, rather than through elaborate analyses buttressed by facts and figures. This technique makes Goodman's work more commentary than analysis; in 1980 she received a Pulitzer Prize for distinguished commentary.

Casco Bay, Maine—The girl is spending the summer with her 1 extended family. She doesn't put it this way. But as we talk on the beach, the ten-year-old lists the people who are sharing the same house this month with the careful attention of a genealogist.

First of all there is her father—visitation rights awarded him the 2 month of August. Second of all there is her father's second wife and two children by her first marriage. All that seems perfectly clear. A step-mother and two stepbrothers.

Then there are the others, she slowly explains. There is her step- 3 mother's sister for example. The girl isn't entirely sure whether this makes the woman a stepaunt, or whether her baby is a stepcousin. Beyond that, the real puzzle is whether her stepaunt's husband's children by his first marriage have any sort of official relationship to her at all. It does, we both agree, seem a bit fuzzy.

Nevertheless, she concludes, with a certainty that can only be 4 mustered by the sort of ten-year-old who keeps track of her own Frequent Flier coupons, "We are in the same family." With that she closes the subject and focuses instead on her peanut butter and jelly.

I am left to my thoughts. My companion, in her own unself- 5 conscious way, is a fine researcher. She grasps the wide new family configurations that are neglected by census data takers and social scientists.

After all, those of us who grew up in traditional settings remember 6 families which extended into elaborate circles of aunts, uncles, and cousins. There were sides to this family, names and titles to be memorized. But they fit together in a biological pattern.

Now, as my young friend can attest, we have fewer children and 7 more divorces. We know that as many as 50 percent of recent marriages may end. About 75 percent of divorced women and 83 percent of divorced men then remarry. Of those marriages, 59 percent include a child from a former marriage.

So, our famlies often extend along lines that are determined by 8 decrees, rather than genes. If the nucleus is broken, there are still links forged in different directions.

The son of a friend was asked to produce a family tree for his 9 sixth-grade class. But he was dissatisfied with his oak. There was no

room on it for his stepgrandfather, though the man had married his
widowed grandmother years ago.

More to the point, the boy had to create an offshoot for his new   10
baby half-brother that seemed too distant. He couldn't find a proper
place for the uncle—the ex-uncle to be precise—whom he visited last
summer with his cousin.

A family tree just doesn't work, he complained. He would have   11
preferred to draw family bushes.

The reality is that divorce has created kinship ties that rival the   12
most complex tribe. These are not always easy relationships. The
children and even the adults whose family lives have been disrupted
by divorce and remarriage learn that people they love do not necessarily love each other. This extended family does not gather for re-
unions and Thanksgivings.

But when it works, it can provide a support system of sorts. I   13
have seen the nieces, nephews—even the dogs—of one marriage
welcomed as guests into another. There are all sorts of relationships
that survive the marital ones, though there are no names for these
kinfolk, no nomenclature for this extending family.

Not long ago, when living together first became a common pat-   14
tern, people couldn't figure out what to call each other. It was impossible to introduce the man you lived with as a "spouse equivalent."
It was harder to refer to the woman your son lived with as his lover,
mistress, housemate.

It's equally difficult to describe the peculiar membership of this   15
new lineage. Does your first husband's mother become a mother-out-
law? Is the woman no longer married to your uncle an ex-aunt? We
have nieces and nephews left dangling like participles from other lives
and stepfamilies entirely off the family tree.

Our reality is more flexible and our relationships more supportive   16
than our language. But for the moment, my ten-year-old researcher
is right. However accidentally, however uneasily, "We are in the same
family."

RESPONDING TO READING

Key words: community   discovery   family   growing up   identity
language

Rhetorical concepts: anecdote   definition   humor   illustration
narrative/example

1.   Brazelton, earlier in this chapter, said the family was in trouble. To what
degree does Goodman's essay show this trouble? To what degree does the
essay argue that the changes under way are not trouble but something else?

2.   What defines "family?" Write an essay showing the different definitions at work in this essay and in this chapter of *Inquiry*. Conclude with a definition of the term that is satisfying to you, and explain why.

3.   The boy in the essay finds that "a family tree just doesn't work," though "family bushes" might. What does this metaphor mean and suggest? What new terms might work for the "kinship relations" that conventional language cannot name? What does Goodman imply about the future of the family?

Warfare Is Only an Invention—Not a Biological Necessity

MARGARET MEAD

Margaret Mead (1901–1978) was a woman of enormous energy, stamina, and creativity. She has received numerous awards for her revolutionary anthropology, particularly for her pioneering field work in the ethnography of women and children. When Mead began her studies with Franz Boas at Columbia University in the 1920s (she earned a Ph.D. in 1929), anthropology was dependent on rigid, statistical analysis. But Boas, Mead, and other noted researchers between World Wars I and II regarded small, homogeneous, tribal societies as "natural laboratories," says anthropologist Clifford Geertz, and conceived of anthropology "as uniquely positioned to find out the essentials of social life that are disguised or covered over in complex, modern societies." Mead's method of understanding the Balinese, the Samoans, the New Guineans, and others was to learn the native language quickly and immerse herself in the society she was studying, using psychology, extensive interviews, and careful observation of the artifacts and customs of the culture to record (in copious notes) the tribal character. Then, to convey what she had learned to outsiders, she contextualized her information in a colorful, thickly descriptive style easy for general readers to understand.

Mead's prodigious effort resulted in thirty-nine books; the best known are *Coming of Age in Samoa* (1928), *Sex and Temperament in Three Primitive Societies* (1935), and her autobiography, *Blackberry Winter* (1972). In addition, she published nearly fourteen hundred other articles, interpreting and offering advice on an enormous range of issues in contemporary Western society, including cultural stability, adolescence, sex differences, education and culture, family life, child rearing, national character, international relationships, and cooperation and competition. The following article, originally published in *Asia* magazine (1940), illustrates both Mead's characteristic method of arguing—to use numerous parallel examples from diverse societies—and her anthropologist's justification for pacifism: "warfare is a defective social institution."

Is war a biological necessity, a sociological inevitability or just a bad invention? Those who argue for the first view endow man with such pugnacious instincts that some outlet in aggressive behavior is necessary if man is to reach full human stature. It was this point of view which lay back of William James's famous essay, "The Moral Equivalent of War," in which he tried to retain the warlike virtues and channel them in new directions. A similar point of view has lain back of the Soviet Union's attempt to make competition between groups rather than between individuals. A basic, competitive, aggressive, warring human nature is assumed, and those who wish to outlaw war or outlaw competitiveness merely try to find new and less socially destructive ways in which these biologically given aspects of man's nature can find expression. Then there are those who take the second view: warfare is the inevitable concomitant of the development of the state, the struggle for land and natural resources of class societies springing, not from the nature of man, but from the nature of history. War is nevertheless inevitable unless we change our social system and outlaw classes, the struggle for power, and possessions; and in the event of our success warfare would disappear, as a symptom vanishes when the disease is cured.

One may hold a sort of compromise position between these two extremes; one may claim that all aggression springs from the frustration of man's biologically determined drives and that, since all forms of culture are frustrating, it is certain each new generation will be aggressive and the aggression will find its natural and inevitable expression in race war, class war, nationalistic war, and so on. All three of these positions are very popular today among those who think seriously about the problems of war and its possible prevention, but I wish to urge another point of view, less defeatist perhaps than the first and third, and more accurate than the second: that is, that warfare, by which I mean recognized conflict between two groups *as groups*, in which each group puts an army (even if the army is only fifteen pygmies) into the field to fight and kill, if possible, some of the members of the army of the other group—that warfare of this sort is an invention like any other of the inventions in terms of which we order our lives, such as writing, marriage, cooking our food instead of eating it raw, trial by jury or burial of the dead, and so on. Some of this list any one will grant are inventions: trial by jury is confined to very limited portions of the globe; we know that there are tribes that do not bury their dead but instead expose or cremate them; and we know that only part of the human race has had the knowledge of writing as its cultural inheritance. But, whenever a way of doing things is found universally, such as the use of fire or the practice of some form of marriage, we tend to think at once that it is not an invention at all but an attribute of humanity itself. And yet even such universals as marriage and the use of fire are inventions like the rest, very basic ones, inventions which were perhaps necessary if human history was to take the turn that it has taken, but nevertheless inventions. At some point in his social development man was undoubtedly without the institution of marriage or the knowledge of the use of fire.

The case for warfare is much clearer because there are peoples 3 even today who have no warfare. Of these the Eskimos are perhaps the most conspicuous examples, but the Lepchas of Sikkim described by Geoffrey Gorer in *Himalayan Village* are as good. Neither of these peoples understands war, not even defensive warfare. The idea of warfare is lacking, and this idea is as essential to really carrying on war as an alphabet, or a syllabary is to writing. But whereas the Lepchas are a gentle, unquarrelsome people, and the advocates of other points of view might argue that they are not full human beings or that they had never been frustrated and so had no aggression to expand in warfare, the Eskimo case gives no such possibility of interpretation. The Eskimo are not a mild and meek people; many of them are turbulent and troublesome. Fights, theft of wives, murder, cannibalism, occur among them—all outbursts of passionate men goaded by desire or intolerable circumstance. Here are men faced with hunger, men faced with loss of their wives, men faced with the threat of extermination by other men, and here are orphan children, growing up miserably with no one to care for them, mocked and neglected by those about them. The personality necessary for war, the circumstances necessary to goad men to desperation are present, but there is no war. When a traveling Eskimo entered a settlement he might have to fight the strongest man in the settlement to establish his position among them, but this was a test of strength and bravery, not war. The idea of warfare, of one *group* organizing against another *group* to maim and wound and kill them was absent. And without that idea passions might rage but there was no war.

But, it may be argued, isn't this because the Eskimo have such a 4 low and undeveloped form of social organization? They own no land, they move from place to place, camping, it is true, season after season on the same site, but this is not something to fight for as the modern nations of the world fight for land and raw materials. They have no permanent possessions that can be looted, no towns that can be burned. They have no social classes to produce stress and strains within the society which might force it to go to war outside. Doesn't the absence of war among the Eskimo, while disproving the biological necessity of war, just go to confirm the point that it is the state of development of the society which accounts for war, and nothing else?

We find the answer among the pygmy peoples of the Andaman 5 Islands in the Bay of Bengal. The Andamans also represent an exceedingly low level of society; they are a hunting and food-gathering people; they live in tiny hordes without any class stratification; their houses are simpler than the snow houses of the Eskimo. But they knew about warfare. The army might contain only fifteen determined pygmies marching in a straight line, but it was the real thing none the less. Tiny army met tiny army in open battle, blows were exchanged, casualities suffered, and the state of warfare could only be concluded by a peacemaking ceremony.

Similarly, among the Australian aborigines, who built no permanent dwellings but wandered from water hole to water hole over their almost desert country, warfare—and rules of "international law"—were highly developed. The student of social evolution will seek in vain for his obvious causes of war, struggle for lands, struggle for power of one group over another, expansion of population, need to divert the minds of a populace restive under tyranny, or even the ambition of a successful leader to enhance his own prestige. All are absent, but warfare as a practice remained, and men engaged in it and killed one another in the course of a war because killing is what is done in wars. 6

From instances like these it becomes apparent that an inquiry into the cause of war misses the fundamental point as completely as does an insistence upon the biological necessity of war. If a people have an idea of going to war and the idea that war is the way in which certain situations, defined within their society, are to be handled, they will sometimes go to war. If they are a mild and unaggressive people, like the Pueblo Indians, they may limit themselves to defensive warfare; but they will be forced to think in terms of war because there are peoples near them who have warfare as a pattern, and offensive, raiding, pillaging warfare at that. When the pattern of warfare is known, people like the Pueblo Indians will defend themselves, taking advantage of their natural defenses, the *mesa* village site, and people like the Lepchas, having no natural defenses and no idea of warfare, will merely submit to the invader. But the essential point remains the same. There is a way of behaving which is known to a given people and labeled as an appropriate form of behavior; a bold and warlike people like the Sioux or the Maori may label warfare as desirable as well as possible; a mild people like the Pueblo Indians may label warfare as undesirable; but to the minds of both peoples the possibility of warfare is present. Their thoughts, their hopes, their plans are oriented about this idea, that warfare may be selected as the way to meet some situation. 7

So simple peoples and civilized peoples, mild peoples and violent, assertive peoples, will all go to war if they have the invention, just as those peoples who have the custom of dueling will have duels and peoples who have the pattern of vendetta will indulge in vendetta. And, conversely, peoples who do not know of dueling will not fight 8

duels, even though their wives are seduced and their daughters rav-
ished; they may on occasion commit murder but they will not fight
duels. Cultures which lack the idea of the vendetta will not meet
every quarrel in this way. A people can use only the forms it has. So
the Balinese have their special way of dealing with a quarrel between
two individuals: if the two feel that the causes of quarrel are heavy
they may go and register their quarrel in the temple before the gods,
and, making offerings, they may swear never to have anything to do
with each other again. Today they register such mutual "not-speak-
ing" with the Dutch government officials. But in other societies, although individuals might feel as full of animosity and as unwilling
to have any further contact as do the Balinese, they cannot register
their quarrel with the gods and go on quietly about their business
because registering quarrels with the gods is not an invention of which
they know.

Yet, if it be granted that warfare is after all an invention, it may   9
nevertheless be an invention that lends itself to certain types of personality, to the exigent needs of autocrats, to the expansionist desires
of crowded peoples, to the desire for plunder and rape and loot which
is engendered by a dull and frustrating life. What, then, can we say
of this congruence between warfare and its uses? If it is a form which
fits so well, is not this congruence the essential point? But even here
the primitive material causes us to wonder, because there are tribes
who go to war merely for glory, having no quarrel with the enemy,
suffering from no tyrant within their boundaries, anxious neither for
land nor loot nor women, but merely anxious to win prestige which
within that tribe has been declared obtainable only by war and without
which no young man can hope to win his sweetheart's smile of approval. But if, as was the case with the Bush Negroes of Dutch Guiana,
it is artistic ability which is necessary to win a girl's approval, the
same young man would have to be carving rather than going out on
a war party.

In many parts of the world, war is a game in which the individual   10
can win counters—counters which bring him prestige in the eyes of
his own sex or of the opposite sex; he plays for these counters as he
might, in our society, strive for a tennis championship. Warfare is a
frame for such prestige-seeking merely because it calls for the display
of certain skills and certain virtues; all of these skills—riding straight,
shooting straight, dodging the missiles of the enemy, and sending
one's own straight to the mark—can be equally well exercised in some
other framework, and, equally, the virtues—endurance, bravery, loyalty, steadfastness—can be displayed in other contexts. The tie-up
between proving oneself a man and proving this by a success in
organized killing is due to a defintion which many societies have made

of manliness. And often, even in those societies which counted success in warfare a proof of human worth, strange turns were given to the idea, as when the plains Indians gave their highest awards to the man who touched a live enemy rather than to the man who brought in a scalp—from a dead enemy—because the latter was less risky. Warfare is just an invention known to the majority of human societies by which they permit their young men either to accumulate prestige or avenge their honor or acquire loot or wives or slaves or sago lands or cattle or appease the blood lust of their gods or the restless souls of the recently dead. It is just an invention, older and more widespread than the jury system, but none the less an invention.

But, once we have said this, have we said anything at all? Despite 11 a few instances, dear to the hearts of controversialists, of the loss of the useful arts, once an invention is made which proves congruent with human needs or social forms, it tends to persist. Grant that war is an invention, that it is not a biological necessity nor the outcome of certain special types of social forms, still, once the invention is made, what are we to do about it? The Indian who had been subsisting on the buffalo for generations because with his primitive weapons he could slaughter only a limited number of buffalo did not return to his primitive weapons when he saw that the white man's more efficient weapons were exterminating the buffalo. A desire for the white man's cloth may mortgage the South Sea Islander to the white man's plantation, but he does not return to making bark cloth, which would have left him free. Once an invention is known and accepted, men do not easily relinquish it. The skilled workers may smash the first steam looms which they feel are to be their undoing, but they accept them in the end, and no movement which has insisted upon the mere abandonment of usable inventions has ever had much success. Warfare is here, as part of our thought; the deeds of warriors are immortalized in the words of our poets; the toys of our children are modeled upon the weapons of the soldier; the frame of reference within which our statesmen and our diplomats work always contains war. If we know that if is not inevitable, that it is due to historical accident that warfare is one of the ways in which we think of behaving, are we given any hope by that? What hope is there of persuading nations to abandon war, nations so thoroughly imbued with the idea that resort to war is, if not actually desirable and noble, at least inevitable whenever certain defined circumstances arise?

In answer to this question I think we might turn to the history 12 of other social inventions, and inventions which must once have seemed as firmly entrenched as warfare. Take the methods of trial which preceded the jury system: ordeal and trial by combat. Unfair, capricious, alien as they are to our feeling today, they were once the only methods open to individuals accused of some offense. The invention of trial by jury gradually replaced these methods until only witches, and finally not even witches, had to resort to the ordeal. And for a long time the jury system seemed the one best and finest method of settling legal disputes, but today new inventions, trial before judges only or before commissions, are replacing the jury system. In each case the old method was replaced by a new social invention; the ordeal did not go out because people thought it unjust or wrong, it went out because a method more congruent with the institutions and feelings of the period was invented. And, if we despair over the way in which war seems such an ingrained habit of most of the human race, we can take comfort from the fact that a poor invention will usually give place to a better invention.

For this, two conditions at least are necessary. The people must 13 recognize the defects of the old invention, and someone must make a new one. Propaganda against warfare, documentation of its terrible cost in human suffering and social waste, these prepare the ground by teaching people to feel that warfare is a defective social institution. There is further needed a belief that social invention is possible and the invention of new methods which will render warfare as out-of-date as the tractor is making the plow, or the motor car the horse and buggy. A form of behavior becomes out-of-date only when something else takes its place, and in order to invent forms of behavior which will make war obsolete, it is a first requirement to believe that an invention is possible.

RESPONDING TO READING

Key words: community loss power reality striving war watershed

Rhetorical concepts: analysis deduction definition illustration induction narrative example

1.   What are the logical consequences of each of the deterministic conclusions Mead summarizes in the first paragraph? What is the "sort of compromise position" that Mead proposes between them and what are the implications of that position? Why does Mead reject all three positions? Has new evidence appeared during the fifty or so years since the essay was written to support any of these positions?
2.   Why is it important to decide if war is biologically determined or only a human invention?
3.   How much and what kind of evidence is necessary or required to disprove assertions of biological necessity? What, for example, is shown by the contrast between the Eskimo and the pygmy people? Is Mead asserting that less well-

developed tribes do not know war or have the idea of war? Evaluate the evidence that Mead presents to see if it is sufficient to prove her argument.
4. List the various purposes for war which Mead cites. As the list accumulates, do you notice the author's attitude towards war? Describe Mead's view of war and of its goals. Why does she feel that people will not abandon this "invention" readily?
5. Give Mead's response to her own question, "What hope is there of persuading nations to abandon war?" Using your knowledge of all that has happened since 1940, evaluate her answer. Then speculate about the next fifty years: will war be replaced by a better invention or will it continue to exist?

American Ignorance of War

CZESLAW MILOSZ

Czeslaw Milosz (pronounced *Ches*-law *Mee*-wosh), poet, critic, novelist, essayist, and translator, was born in 1911 in Lithuania. During his first forty years he lived under three repressive political systems: as a child in Czarist Russia; in Poland as a member of the underground resistance during the Nazi occupation; and in Paris after World War II as a cultural attaché representing Communist Poland. He defected to the West in 1951 ("socialist realism is nothing more than a different name for a lie"), and has written ever since of the central issues of our time: the impact of history upon moral being, the search for ways to survive spiritual ruin in a ruined world. In 1960 he accepted a professorship at the University of California, Berkeley, where he has lived ever since, becoming an American citizen in 1970. His wide-ranging writings include *Native Realm: A Search for Self-Definition* (1968), *The History of Polish Literature* (1983), two novels, and eighteen volumes of poetry. His work was denied publication in his native land until he was awarded the Nobel Prize for Literature in 1980.

"American Ignorance of War," translated from the Polish by Jane Zielonko, is a section of Milosz's first American publication, *The Captive Mind* (1953), in which he examines the artist's life under Communism and explains why he defected. The book, praised as "a brilliant and original study of the totalitarian mentality," is still fresh and relevant forty years later. In "American Ignorance of War," Milosz warns his new fellow citizens to learn from the history of other countries. The current generations of Americans, having never experienced the mammoth upheaval of war on their own shores, regard their culture, their customs, their ways of thinking about life, as *natural*. Yet in a totalitarian regime, especially during wartime, all is utterly changed. What was once inconceivable—repression, humiliation, genocide—becomes the new norm, natural. Considering other major changes that have occurred in the past fifty years in our culture, among them atomic warfare and the AIDS epidemic, is it possible to deny that Milosz's bleak vision of the future cannot occur?

"Are Americans *really* stupid?" I was asked in Warsaw. In the   1
voice of the man who posed the question, there was despair, as well
as the hope that I would contradict him. This question reveals the
attitude of the average person in the people's democracies toward the
West: it is despair mixed with a residue of hope.

During the last few years, the West has given these people a   2
number of reasons to despair politically. In the case of the intellectual,
other, more complicated reasons come into play. Before the countries
of Central and Eastern Europe entered the sphere of the Imperium,
they lived through the Second World War. That war was much more
devastating there than in the countries of Western Europe. It destroyed not only their economies, but also a great many values which
had seemed till then unshakable.

Man tends to regard the order he lives in as *natural*. The houses   3
he passes on his way to work seem more like rocks rising out of the
earth than like products of human hands. He considers the work he
does in his office or factory as essential to the harmonious functioning
of the world. The clothes he wears are exactly what they should be,
and he laughs at the idea that he might equally well be wearing a
Roman toga or medieval armor. He respects and envies a minister of
state or a bank director, and regards the possession of a considerable
amount of money as the main guarantee of peace and security. He
cannot believe that one day a rider may appear on a street he knows
well, where cats sleep and children play, and start catching passersby
with his lasso. He is accustomed to satisfying those of his physiological needs which are considered private as discreetly as possible, without realizing that such a pattern of behavior is not common to all
human societies. In a word, he behaves a little like Charlie Chaplin
in *The Gold Rush*, bustling about in a shack poised precariously on
the edge of a cliff.

His first stroll along a street littered with glass from bomb-   4
shattered windows shakes his faith in the "naturalness" of his world.
The wind scatters papers from hastily evacuated offices, papers labeled "Confidential" or "Top Secret" that evoke visions of safes, keys,
conferences, couriers, and secretaries. Now the wind blows them
through the street for anyone to read; yet no one does, for each man
is more urgently concerned with finding a loaf of bread. Strangely
enough, the world goes on even though the offices and secret files
have lost all meaning. Farther down the street, he stops before a house
split in half by a bomb, the privacy of people's homes—the family
smells, the warmth of the beehive life, the furniture preserving the
memory of loves and hatreds—cut open to public view. The house
itself, no longer a rock, but a scaffolding of plaster, concrete, and
brick; and on the third floor, a solitary white bathtub, rain-rinsed of

all recollection of those who once bathed in it. Its formerly influential and respected owners, now destitute, walk the fields in search of stray potatoes. Thus overnight money loses its value and becomes a meaningless mass of printed paper. His walk takes him past a little boy poking a stick into a heap of smoking ruins and whistling a song about the great leader who will preserve the nation against all enemies. The song remains, but the leader of yesterday is already part of an extinct past.

He finds he acquires new habits quickly. Once, had he stumbled   5
upon a corpse on the street, he would have called the police. A crowd would have gathered, and much talk and comment would have ensued. Now he knows he must avoid the dark body lying in the gutter, and refrain from asking unnecessary questions. The man who fired the gun must have had his reasons; he might well have been executing an Underground sentence.

Nor is the average European accustomed to thinking of his native   6
city as divided into segregated living areas, but a single decree can force him to this new pattern of life and thought. Quarter A may suddenly be designated for one race; B, for a second; C, for a third. As the resettlement deadline approaches, the streets become filled with long lines of wagons, carts, wheelbarrows, and people carrying bundles, beds, chests, caldrons, and bird cages. When all the moves are effected, 2,000 people may find themselves in a building that once housed 200, but each man is at last in the proper area. Then high walls are erected around quarter C, and daily a given lot of men, women, and children are loaded into wagons that take them off to specially constructed factories where they are scientifically slaughtered and their bodies burned.

And even the rider with the lasso appears, in the form of a military   7
van waiting at the corner of a street. A man passing that corner meets a leveled rifle, raises his hands, is pushed into the van, and from that moment is lost to his family and friends. He may be sent to a concentration camp, or he may face a firing squad, his lips sealed with plaster lest he cry out against the state; but, in any case, he serves as a warning to his fellow men. Perhaps one might escape such a fate by remaining at home. But the father of a family must go out in order to provide bread and soup for his wife and children; and every night they worry about whether or not he will return. Since these conditions last for years, everyone gradually comes to look upon the city as a jungle, and upon the fate of twentieth-century man as identical with that of a caveman living in the midst of powerful monsters.

It was once thought obvious that a man bears the same name and   8
surname throughout his entire life; now it proves wiser for many reasons to change them and to memorize a new and fabricated bi-

ography. As a result, the records of the civilian state become completely confused. Everyone ceases to care about formalities, so that marriage, for example, comes to mean little more than living together.

Respectable citizens used to regard banditry as a crime. Today, 9 bank robbers are heroes because the money they steal is destined for the Underground. Usually they are young boys, mothers' boys, but their appearance is deceiving. The killing of a man presents no great moral problem to them.

The nearness of death destroys shame. Men and women change 10 as soon as they know that the date of their execution has been fixed by a fat little man with shiny boots and a riding crop. They copulate in public, on the small bit of ground surounded by barbed wire— their last home on earth. Boys and girls in their teens, about to go off to the barricades to fight against tanks with pistols and bottles of gasoline, want to enjoy their youth and lose their respect for standards of decency.

Which world is "natural"? That which existed before, or the world 11 of war? Both are natural, if both are within the realm of one's experience. All the concepts men live by are a product of the historic formation in which they find themselves. Fluidity and constant change are the characteristics of phenomena. And man is so plastic a being that one can even conceive of the day when a thoroughly self-respecting citizen will crawl on all fours, sporting a tail of brightly colored feathers as a sign of conformity to the order he lives in.

The man of the East cannot take Americans seriously because 12 they have never undergone the experiences that teach men how relative their judgements and thinking habits are. Their resultant lack of imagination is appalling. Because they were born and raised in a given social order and in a given system of values, they believe that any other order must be "unnatural," and that it cannot last because it is incompatible with human nature. But even they may one day know fire, hunger, and the sword. In all probability this is what will occur; for it is hard to believe that when one half of the world is living through terrible disasters, the other half can continue a nineteenth-century mode of life, learning about the distress of its distant fellow men only from movies and newspapers. Recent examples teach us that this cannot be. An inhabitant of Warsaw or Budapest once looked at newsreels of bombed Spain or burning Shanghai, but in the end he learned how these and many other catastrophes appear in actuality. He read a gloomy tales of the NKVD until one day he found he himself had to deal with it. *If something exists in one place, it will exist everywhere.* This is the conclusion he draws from his observations, and so he has no particular faith in the momentary prosperity of America. He suspects that the years 1933–1945 in Europe prefigure what will occur elsewhere. A hard school, where ignorance was punished not by bad marks but by death, has taught him to think sociologically and historically. But it has not freed him from irrational feelings. He is apt to believe in theories that foresee violent changes in the countries of the West, for he finds it unjust that they should escape the hardships he had to undergo.

RESPONDING TO READING

Key words: community   discovery   identity   loss   nature   power reality   rights   transformation   war

Rhetorical concepts: analogy   anecdote   cause and effect   illustration induction   metaphor   narrative/example

1.   Give the several definitions of "natural" that Milosz uses in this essay. How can he argue that war is natural? Why is it natural that Americans should be ignorant of war? Why does he argue that it is natural that war will come to America?
2.   Examine closely the details Milosz uses to support his argument. Notice the irony in the details, such as the "top secret" papers blowing in the street that nobody cares to read. Why does he select these details, why does he present them the way he does, and how do they affect you?
3.   Compare and contrast Milosz's essay with Mead's. Note the different experiences of the two writers, the dates of their essays, and the different examples they cite. Whose conclusions do you find most comfortable? Whose conclusions do you find most compelling?
4.   Will there be a war in America in your lifetime? Speculate about the possibilities. If so, what would be the causes, the forces in opposition, the results? If not, argue against Milosz's essay, particularly his assertion that "If something exists in one place, it will exist everywhere."

The Nuclear Winter

CARL SAGAN

Carl Sagan is a professor of astronomy and space sciences at Cornell University, where he also directs the Laboratory for Planetary Studies. Born in New York City in 1934, Sagan earned four degrees from the University of Chicago, including a Ph.D. in astronomy in 1960. He taught at Harvard from 1962 to 1968, before moving to Cornell, where he has worked on several space missions, including Mariner and Viking. He received the NASA Medal for Exceptional Scientific Achievement and the Joseph Priestly Prize "for distinguished contributions to the welfare of mankind." His numerous books include the popular *Broca's Brain: Reflections on the Romance of Science* (1979) and the Pulitzer-Prize-winning *The Dragons of Eden: Speculations on the Evolution of Human Intelligence* (1977).

"As long as there have been humans," says Sagan, "we have searched for our place in the cosmos. Where are we? Who are we? Sagan's exploration of these questions in his writings and the series *Cosmos*, on public television during the 1980s, have made him a popular spokesperson for both science and what some consider pseudo-science. Typical of many scientists with a following among the general public, Sagan is criticized by some of his peers for not exhibiting sufficient scientific rigor in his research. For instance, fellow astrophysicist Robert Jastrow says that despite the fact that Sagan is "capable of first-class reasoning" when he exercises sufficient discipline, he "soars all too often on flights of meaningless fancy," especially in his books on extraterrestrial intelligence and UFOs.

Sagan has become a major advocate of nuclear disarmament, and his speculative essay below, based on a mathematical model, first published in *Parade* (1983) and widely distributed by the antinuclear Council for a Livable World, shows the hypothetical and catastrophic consequences of a nuclear war. Through generating "an epoch of cold and dark," such a war would destroy our global civilization and reduce human population "to prehistoric levels or less," if not to extinction. In 1990 Sagan and Richard Turco published a sequel to these speculations, *A Path Where No Man Thought: Nuclear Winter and the End of the Arms Race*, received once again with characteristically mixed reactions.

"Into the eternal darkness, into fire, into ice."

DANTE, *The Inferno*

Except for fools and madmen, everyone knows that nuclear war   1
would be an unprecedented human catastrophe. A more or less typical strategic warhead has a yield of 2 megatons, the explosive equivalent of 2 million tons of TNT. But 2 million tons of TNT is about the same as all the bombs exploded in World War II—a single bomb with the explosive power of the entire Second World War but compressed into a few seconds of time and an area 30 or 40 miles across. . . .

In a 2-megaton explosion over a fairly large city, buildings would   2
be vaporized, people reduced to atoms and shadows, outlying structures blown down like matchsticks and raging fires ignited. And if the bomb were exploded on the ground, an enormous crater, like those that can be seen through a telescope on the surface of the Moon, would be all that remained where midtown once had been. There are now more than 50,000 nuclear weapons, more than 13,000 megatons of yield, deployed in the arsenals of the United States and the Soviet Union—enough to obliterate a million Hiroshimas.

But there are fewer than 3000 cities on the Earth with populations   3
of 100,000 or more. You cannot find anything like a million Hiroshimas

to obliterate. Prime military and industrial targets that are far from cities are comparatively rare. Thus, there are vastly more nuclear weapons than are needed for any plausible deterrence of a potential adversary.

Nobody knows, of course, how many megatons would be ex- 4 ploded in a real nuclear war. There are some who think that a nuclear war can be "contained," bottled up before it runs away to involve much of the world's arsenals. But a number of detailed analyses, war games run by the U.S. Department of Defense, and official Soviet pronouncements all indicate that this containment may be too much to hope for: Once the bombs begin exploding, communications failures, disorganization, fear, the necessity of making in minutes decisions affecting the fates of millions, and the immense psychological burden of knowing that your own loved ones may already have been destroyed are likely to result in a nuclear paroxysm. Many investigations, including a number of studies for the U.S. government, envision the explosion of 5000 to 10,000 megatons—the detonation of tens of thousands of nuclear weapons that now sit quietly, inconspicuously, in missile silos, submarines and long-range bombers, faithful servants awaiting orders.

The World Health Organization, in a recent detailed study chaired 5 by Sune K. Bergstrom (the 1982 Nobel laureate in physiology and medicine), concludes that 1.1 billion people would be killed outright in such a nuclear war, mainly in the United States, the Soviet Union, Europe, China and Japan. An additional 1.1 billion people would suffer serious injuries and radiation sickness, for which medical help would be unavailable. It thus seems possible that more than 2 billion people—almost half of all the humans on Earth—would be destroyed in the immediate aftermath of a global thermonuclear war. This would represent by far the greatest disaster in the history of the human species and, with no other adverse effects, would probably be enough to reduce at least the Northern Hemisphere to a state of prolonged agony and barbarism. Unfortunately, the real situation would be much worse.

In technical studies of the consequences of nuclear weapons ex- 6 plosions, there has been a dangerous tendency to underestimate the results. This is partly due to a tradition of conservatism which generally works well in science but which is of more dubious applicability when the lives of billions of people are at stake. In the Bravo test of March 1, 1954, a 15-megaton thermonuclear bomb was exploded on Bikini Atoll. It had about double the yield expected, and there was an unanticipated last-minute shift in the wind direction. As a result, deadly radioactive fallout came down on Rongelap in the Marshall Islands, more than 200 kilometers away. Almost all the children on

Rongelap subsequently developed thyroid nodules and lesions, and other long-term medical problems, due to the radioactive fallout.

Likewise, in 1973, it was discovered that high-yield airbursts will 7 chemically burn the nitrogen in the upper air, converting it into oxides of nitrogen; these, in turn, combine with and destroy the protective ozone in the Earth's atmosphere. The surface of the Earth is shielded from deadly solar ultraviolet radiation by a layer of ozone so tenuous that, were it brought down to sea level, it would be only 3 millimeters thick. Partial destruction of this ozone layer can have serious consequences for the biology of the entire planet.

These discoveries, and others like them, were made by chance. 8 They were largely unexpected. And now another consequence—by far the most dire—has been uncovered, again more or less by accident.

The U.S. Mariner 9 spacecraft, the first vehicle to orbit another 9 plant, arrived at Mars in late 1971. The planet was enveloped in a global dust storm. As the fine particles slowly fell out, we were able to measure temperature changes in the atmosphere and on the surface. Soon it became clear what had happened.

The dust, lofted by high winds off the desert into the upper 10 Martian atmosphere, had absorbed the incoming sunlight and prevented much of it from reaching the ground. Heated by the sunlight, the dust warmed the adjacent air. But the surface, enveloped in partial darkness, became much chillier than usual. Months later, after the dust fell out of the atmosphere, the upper air cooled and the surface warmed, both returning to their normal conditions. We were able to calculate accurately, from how much dust there was in the atmosphere, how cool the Martian surface ought to have been.

Afterwards, I and my colleagues, James B. Pollack and Brian Toon 11 of NASA's Ames Research Center, were eager to apply these insights to Earth. In a volcanic explosion, dust aerosols are lofted into the high atmosphere. We calculated by how much the Earth's global temperature should decline after a major volcanic explosion and found that our results (generally a fraction of a degree) were in good accord with actual measurements. Joining forces with Richard Turco, who has studied the effects of nuclear weapons for many years, we then began to turn our attention to the climatic implications of nuclear war. [The scientific paper, "Global Atmospheric Consequences of Nuclear War," is written by R. P. Turco, O. B. Toon, T. P. Ackerman, J. B. Pollack and Carl Sagan. From the last names of the authors, this work is generally referred to as "TTAPS."]

We knew that nuclear explosions, particularly groundbursts, 12 would lift an enormous quantity of fine soil particles into the atmosphere (more than 100,000 tons of fine dust for every megaton exploded in a surface burst). Our work was further spurred by Paul Crutzen of the Max Planck Institute for Chemistry in Mainz, West Germany, and by John Birks of the University of Colorado, who pointed out that huge quantities of smoke would be generated in the burning of cities and forests following a nuclear war.

Groundbursts—at hardened missile silos, for example—generate 13 fine dust. Airbusts—over cities and unhardened military installations—make fires and therefore smoke. The amount of dust and soot generated depends on the conduct of the war, the yields of the weapons employed and the ratio of groundbursts to airbusts. So we ran computer models for several dozen different nuclear war scenarios. Our baseline case, as in many other studies, was a 5000-megaton war with only a modest fraction of the yield (20 percent) expended on urban or industrial targets. Our job, for each case, was to follow the dust and smoke generated, see how much sunlight was absorbed and by how much the temperatures changed, figure out how the particles spread in longitude and latitude, and calculate how long before it all fell out of the air back onto the surface. Since the radioactivity would be attached to these same fine particles, our calculations also revealed the extent and timing of the subsequent radioactive fallout.

Some of what I am about to describe is horrifying. I know, because 14 it horrifies me. There is a tendency—psychiatrists call it "denial"— to put it out of our minds, not to think about it. But if we are to deal intelligently, wisely, with the nuclear arms race, then we must steel ourselves to contemplate the horrors of nuclear war.

The results of our calculations astonished us. In the baseline case, 15 the amount of sunlight at the ground was reduced to a few percent of normal—much darker, in daylight, than in a heavy overcast and too dark for plants to make a living from photosynthesis. At least in the Northern Hemisphere, where the great preponderance of strategic targets lies, a deadly gloom would persist for months.

Even more unexpected were the temperatures calculated. In the 16 baseline case, land temperatures, except for narrow strips of coastline, dropped to minus 25° Celsius (minus 13° Fahrenheit) and stayed below freezing for months—even for a summer war. (Because the atmospheric structure becomes much more stable as the upper atmosphere is heated and the lower air is cooled, we may have severely *under*estimated how long the cold and the dark would last.) The oceans, a significant heat reservoir, would not freeze, however, and a major ice age would probably not be triggered. But because the temperatures would drop so catastrophically, virtually all crops and farm animals, at least in the Northern Hemisphere, would be destroyed, as would most varieties of uncultivated or undomesticated food supplies. Most of the human survivors would starve.

In addition, the amount of radioactive fallout is much more than   17
expected. Many previous calculations simply ignored the intermediate
time-scale fallout. That is, calculations were made for the prompt
fallout—the plumes of radioactive debris blown downwind from each
target—and for the long-term fallout, the fine radioactive particles
lofted into the stratosphere that would descend about a year later,
after most of the radioactivity had decayed. However, the radioactivity
carried into the upper atmosphere (but not as high as the stratosphere)
seems to have been largely forgotten. We found for the baseline case
that roughly 30 percent of the land at northern midlatitudes could
receive a radioactive dose greater than 250 rads, and that about 50
percent of northern midlatitutudes could receive a dose greater than
100 rads. A 100-rad dose is the equivalent of about 1000 medical X-
rays. A 400-rad dose will, more likely than not, kill you.

The cold, the dark and the intense radioactivity, together lasting   18
for months, represent a severe assault on our civilization and our
species. Civil and sanitary services would be wiped out. Medical
facilities, drugs, the most rudimentary means for relieving the vast
human suffering, would be unavailable. Any but the most elaborate
shelters would be useless, quite apart from the question of what good
it might be to emerge a few months later. Synthetics burned in the
destruction of the cities would produce a wide variety of toxic gases,
including carbon monoxide, cyanides, dioxins and furans. After the
dust and soot settled out, the solar ultraviolet flux would be much
larger than its present value. Immunity to disease would decline.
Epidemics and pandemics would be rampant, especially after the
billion or so unburied bodies began to thaw. Moreover, the combined
influence of these severe and simultaneous stresses on life are likely
to produce even more adverse consequences—biologists call them
synergisms—that we are not yet wise enough to foresee.

So far, we have talked only of the Northern Hemisphere. But it   19
now seems—unlike the case of a single nuclear weapons test—that
in a real nuclear war, the heating of the vast quantities of atmospheric
dust and soot in northern midlatitudes will transport these fine particles toward and across the Equator. We see just this happening in
Martian dust storms. The Southern Hemisphere would experience
effects that, while less severe than in the Northern Hemisphere, are
nevertheless extremely ominous. The illusion with which some people
in the Northern Hemisphere reassure themselves—catching an Air
New Zealand flight in a time of serious international crisis, or the
like—is now much less tenable, even on the narrow issue of personal
survival for those with the price of a ticket.

But what if nuclear wars can be contained, and much less than   20

5000 megatons is detonated? Perhaps the greatest surprise in our work was that even small nuclear wars can have devastating climatic effects. We considered a war in which a mere 100 megatons were exploded, less than one percent of the world arsenals, and only in low-yield airbursts over cities. This scenario, we found, would ignite thousands of fires, and the smoke from these fires alone would be enough to generate an epoch of cold and dark almost as severe as in the 5000-megaton case. The threshold for what Richard Turco has called The Nuclear Winter is very low.

Could we have overlooked some important effect? The carrying 21 of dust and soot from the Northern to the Southern Hemisphere (as well as more local atmospheric circulation) will certainly thin the clouds out over the Northern Hemisphere. But, in many cases, this thinning would be insufficient to render the climatic consequences tolerable—and every time it got better in the Northern Hemisphere, it would get worse in the Southern.

Our results have been carefully scrutinized by more than 100 22 scientists in the United States, Europe and the Soviet Union. There are still arguments on points of detail. But the overall conclusion seems to be agreed upon: There are severe and previously unanticipated global consequences of nuclear war—subfreezing temperatures in a twilit radioactive gloom lasting for months or longer.

Scientists initially underestimated the effects of fallout, were 23 amazed that nuclear explosions in space disabled distant satellites, had no idea that the fireballs from high-yield thermonuclear explosions could deplete the ozone layer and missed altogether the possible climatic effects of nuclear dust and smoke. What else have we overlooked?

Nuclear war is a problem that can be treated only theoretically. 24 It is not amenable to experimentation. Conceivably, we have left something important out of our analysis, and the effects are more modest than we calculate. On the other hand, it is also possible—and, from previous experience, even likely—that there are further adverse effects that no one has yet been wise enough to recognize. With billions of lives at stake, where does conservatism lie—in assuming that the results will be better than we calculate, or worse?

Many biologists, considering the nuclear winter that these cal- 25 culations describe, believe they carry somber implications for life on Earth. Many species of plants and animals would become extinct. Vast numbers of surviving humans would starve to death. The delicate ecological relations that bind together organisms on Earth in a fabric of mutual dependency would be torn, perhaps irreparably. There is little question that our global civilization would be destroyed. The human population would be reduced to prehistoric levels, or less.

Life for any survivors would be extremely hard. And there seems to be a real possibility of the extinction of the human species.

It is now almost 40 years since the invention of nuclear weapons. 26 We have not yet experienced a global thermonuclear war—although on more than one occasion we have come tremulously close. I do not think our luck can hold forever. Men and machines are fallible, as recent events remind us. Fools and madmen do exist, and sometimes rise to power. Concentrating always on the near future, we have ignored the long-term consequences of our actions. We have placed our civilization and our species in jeopardy.

Fortunately, it is not yet too late. We can safeguard the planetary 27 civilization and the human family if we so choose. There is no more important or more urgent issue.

RESPONDING TO READING

Key words: community loss nature power reality science transformation war

Rhetorical concepts: analogy analysis cause and effect illustration induction narrative/example process research report

1. Sagan admits that "Nuclear war is a problem that can be treated only theoretically. It is not amenable to experimentation" (paragraph 24). To what extent is Sagan, or anyone, justified in making recommendations for national and international policies based on theory without experimentation?

2. Explain how Sagan uses the following types of evidence in making his argument that a "nuclear winter" is the inevitable consequence of a nuclear war:

 a. A "recent" study by the World Health Organization (paragraph 5)
 b. The Bravo test on Bikini Atoll (paragraph 6)
 c. A "global dust storm" on Mars (paragraphs 9–10)
 d. Computer calculations of the atmospheric effects of nuclear ground-bursts (paragraphs 1–17)
 e. Speculations on the long-term, interrelated consequences of an extended period of "cold, dark, and intense radioactivity" (paragraphs 18–25).

3. Why worry about nuclear war anymore? Is that concern obviated now that the Cold War with the former Soviet Union appears to be over?

4. In an essay or in discussion, amplify Sagan's conclusion, proposing a plan or a process through which "we can safeguard the planetary civilization and the human family" (paragraph 27). Although your subject might be nuclear warfare, you could also discuss a topic such as the worldwide AIDS epidemic, the disappearance of the rain forests, global warming, or other subjects on which you have sufficient information to present a convincing argument.

Coping with Victory

JOHN LEWIS GADDIS

Gaddis, an internationally recognized historian of U.S. foreign policy
during the Cold War, has never lacked for appropriate subjects. Born
in Texas (1941) and educated at the University of Texas, Austin (B.A.,
1963, Ph.D., 1968), Gaddis has been a professor of history at Ohio
University since 1976; he has also taught at the University of Helsinki
and the United States Naval War College. His first book, *The United
States and the Origins of the Cold War* (1972), won numerous awards
for distinguished history. He was also written *Strategies of Containment: A Critical Appraisal of American National Security Policy* (1982),
and edited *Containing the Soviet Union: A Critique of US Policy* (1987).
He is currently at work on a biography of George Kennan, architect
of much U.S.–Soviet foreign policy.

Thus Gaddis is well qualified to write "Coping with Victory,"
which was published in *The Atlantic Monthly* in May 1990. The author's focus derives from what he explains by analogy with the "dog-
and-car syndrome," the fact that dogs spend much time chasing cars
but very little time contemplating "what they would actually *do* with
a car" if they ever caught one. Thus for four decades American
leaders vigorously pursued victory in the Cold War—a new kind of
great-power rivalry kept in a state of perpetual tension by the threat
that the United States and the Soviet Union would go to war with
each other, though in fact they never did. What to do now that peace
has broken out is Gaddis's concern. "Victory," the end of the Cold
War, occurred as one consequence of Gorbachev's sweeping economic and political reforms in the Soviet Union in the late 1980s—
and ultimately resulted in the demise of the Soviet Union, which
was still intact as "Coping with Victory" went to press. The issues
Gaddis addresses here are pertinent not only to Soviet-American
relations, but to the relations among any nations involved in a major
political alteration and shift of power: Should we welcome the decline
and breakup of our erstwhile adversary? What is going to be left for
nuclear weapons to deter? How will other existing political align-
ments and treaties be affected? Should we help to repair the damage
caused by the system we have opposed?

One day in September of 1946 an as yet little-known George F.   1
Kennan found himself trying to explain to State Department colleagues what it was going to be like to deal with the Soviet Union as
the other great power in the postwar world. Traditional diplomacy
would not impress Stalin and his subordinates, Kennan insisted: "I
don't think we can influence them by reasoning with them, by arguing
with them, by going to them and saying, 'Look here, this is the way
things are.' " They weren't the sort to turn around and say, "By
George, I never thought of that before. We will go right back and
change our policies."

But by last year leaders of the Soviet Union and Eastern Europe 2
were saying something very much like that. Once confident of having
mastered the "science" of politics and history, the successors to Lenin
and Stalin have had to acknowledge that the system those "founding
fathers" imposed on Russia after the First World War and on its neighbors after the Second World War simply has not worked. They have
now in effect turned to the West and said, "Tell us what to do. We
will go right back and change our policies."

We have witnessed one of the most abrupt losses of ideological 3
self-confidence in modern history. The once impressive façade of
world communism no longer impresses anyone: those who lived for
so long under that system have at last, like Dorothy in *The Wizard of
Oz*, looked behind the curtain; they have found there, frantically pulling the levers, pumping the bellows, and pontificating into the speaking tubes, a few diminutive and frightened humbugs. As a result,
Eastern Europe has come to resemble the stage set for *Les Miserables*,
but with the revolutionaries this time winning. And most remarkably
of all, it is the leader of the Soviet Union itself—the current chief
wizard, if you will—who seems to be playing simultaneously the roles
of Dorothy and Jean Valjean.

The resulting situation leaves the United States and its allies— 4
preoccupied so recently with visions of American decline—in a position of great and unexpected influence. For not only have we prevailed, by peaceful means, over our old Cold War adversaries; it is
also the case that for the first time in more than a century there is no
clear challenger to the tradition of liberal democratic capitalism according to which this country and much of the rest of the West or-
ganizes itself. We are at one of those rare points of leverage in history
when familiar constraints have dropped away; what we do now could
establish the framework within which events will play themselves out
for decades to come.

Unfortunately we are almost certainly not up to this task. There 5
exists in the West something we might call the dog-and-car syndrome:
the name refers to the fact that dogs spend a great deal of time chasing
cars but very little time thinking about what they would actually *do*
with a car if they were ever to catch one. Our leaders are not all that
different: they pour their energy vigorously into the pursuit of victory,
whether in politics or in war, but when victory actually arrives, they
treat it as if it were an astonishing and wholly unforeseen development. They behave like the senator-elect in Robert Redford's movie
The Candidate when he takes an aide aside at the victory celebration
and asks incredulously, "What do we do now?"

If history is any guide, what we will probably do is fritter away 6
the fruits of victory by failing to think through what it is we want

victory to accomplish. The Athenians defeated the Persians in the fifth century B.C. only to defeat themselves through their own subsequent ambition and arrogance. The Turks spent centuries trying to take Constantinople for Islam only to see world power passing at the moment of their triumph, in 1453, to secular European states for whom the question of which faith ruled the "Eastern Rome" meant very little. The British drove the French from North America in 1763 but then alienated their own colonists, who in turn drove them out of their most valuable possessions on that continent. Victory in the First World War brought only dissension and disillusionment among the victors, and a purposeful urge for revenge among the vanquished. An even more decisive victory in the Second World War produced a long, costly, and nerve-wracking Cold War for those who won, and the mutually reinforcing benefits of peace and unprecedented prosperity for those who lost.

This depressing pattern of victories gone awry is almost enough 7 to make one wish we were commemorating Cold War defeat. It certainly ought to make us think seriously, and rather quickly, about how not to squander the opportunities that now lie before us.

We should begin by recalling that the Cold War was a new kind 8 of great-power rivalry, one in which the possibility of going to war always existed, but in which the necessity for doing so—at least in a form that would pit the Soviet Union and the United States *directly* against each other—never arose. As a result, that conflict took on the paradoxical character we associate with the name history has given it: the Cold War contained most of the anxieties, animosities, and apocalyptic exhortations that one tends to find in "hot" wars, but without the rubble or the body count. In time people became so used to this situation that some, myself included, began using the equally paradoxical term "long peace" to characterize it. Whatever the merits of the label, the importance of what it describes ought not to be minimized: a great-power competition carried on without great-power war is a distinct improvement over the way most such rivalries have been handled in the past.

But we also need to remember that the long peace grew out of a 9 relationship between two superpower adversaries. If they are no longer to be adversaries—or if one of them is no longer to be a superpower—then the conditions that gave us the long peace will change. We need to make sure as we put the Cold War behind us that we do not also jettison those principles and procedures that allowed it to evolve into the longest period of great-power rivalry without war in the modern era. If a long peace was in fact the offspring of the Cold War, then the last thing we should want to do, in tossing the parent onto the ash heap of history, is to toss the child as well.

We will need a strategy that does not waste time and energy trying 10 to turn back irreversible changes, but also one that is imaginative enough to find ways, within the limits of what is possible, to preserve the stability the Cold War has given us. The very concepts we employ in thinking about international affairs grew out of the now antiquated circumstances of superpower rivalry: if all we do is to apply old categories of thought to the new realities we confront—if we limit ourselves to trying to teach new dogs old tricks—we could find our approach to world politics to be as outdated as the approach that certain now-defunct Marxist regimes took toward their own internal affairs prior to 1989.

The following are some new issues we will face as we seek to 11 exend the long peace beyond a Cold War the West has now won. Old answers will not suffice in dealing with them.

Should We Welcome the Decline and Possible Breakup of the Soviet Union?

The most astonishing fact facing us as the 1990s begin is that we can no longer take for granted the continued existence of the USSR as the superpower we have known throughout the Cold War. Its economy is in ruins; its government is unsure of its own authority; its leaders confront nationalist pressures far more deeply rooted than the "socialist" values the Soviet state has been trying to implant for more than seven decades. There are those in the West who welcome these developments as the consummation of a wish long and devoutly held. Second thoughts, one hopes, will produce more-mature reflections.

Among them should be the realization that it takes two to tango, 13 and that the United States has no particular reason to want to conclude the bipolar superpower dance that has been going on since 1945. For by comparison with the multipolar international systems that preceded it, Cold War bipolarity has served the cause of peace remarkably well: the First and Second World Wars arose from failures of communication, cooperation, and common sense among several states of roughly equal strength, not from situations in which two clear antagonists confronted each other. The relative simplicity of postwar great-power relations may well have made possible their relative stability, and a situation in which the Soviet Union is no longer such a power would mean an end to that arrangement. War might not result, but instability, volatility, and unpedictability almost certainly would.

It is also worth noting that military hardware does not simply 14
vanish into thin air as a nation's position in the world declines, or as
its internal authority crumbles. The means by which a new war could
start—and indeed, with nuclear weapons, the means by which we
ourselves could be destroyed—will remain in the hands of whoever
rules the Soviet Union. If that country should break apart, these lethal
instruments might well come under the control of competing factions
whose caution with respect to their use might not exceed the intensity
of the rivalries that exist among them.

We confront, then, an apparent paradox: now that we have won 15
the Cold War, our chief interest may lie in the survival and successful
rehabilitation of the nation that was our principal adversary throughout that confict. But a historian would see nothing odd in this: Napoleon's conquerors moved quickly to reintegrate France into the
international community after 1815; Germany and Japan received similar treatment after their defeat in 1945. It was the failure to arrange
for Germany's reintegration after the First World War, some scholars
have argued, that led to the Second World War. Power vacuums are
dangerous things. Solicitude for a defeated adversary, therefore, is
not just a matter of charity or magnanimity; it also reflects the wise
victor's calculated self-interest, as confirmed by repeated historical
experience. . . .

If the Russian federal republic alone were all that survived under 16
Moscow's rule, it would still control 76 percent of the land area and
52 percent of the population of the present USSR. Bloated boundaries
have never provided very much security in a nuclear age in any event,
but with nationalism rampant and with the means of suppressing it no longer effective, they are certain in the future to provide
even less.

It would appear to make sense, therefore, for the United States 17
to favor as much of a breakup of the Soviet Union as would be necessary to leave it with a reasonably contented as opposed to a disaffected population, *precisely because we should want to see that state
survive as a great power.* And who knows: in a post–Cold War world
Kremlin leaders might actually acknowledge the sincerity of our motives in taking such a position (although we should probably not count
on that).

What Is Going to Be Left for Nuclear Weapons to Deter?

As areas of agreement in Soviet-American relations have ex- 18
panded, the occasions on which either side has felt the need to deter
the other have become rare, and that trend has in turn raised the
possibility of getting by with far fewer nuclear weapons and delivery

systems than each side has now. Reductions have already begun, and there is every reason to think that they will continue.

We and the Russians would do well, though, to resist the temptation to abolish nuclear weapons altogether, or even to reduce our stockpiles to a level approximating that of the next largest nuclear power. The reason for this is simple: nuclear weapons have played a major role in bringing about the evolution from Cold War to long peace. They have made each side think twice before taking action that might risk war; they have served as a kind of crystal ball into which statesmen can look to see what the consequences of a future conflict will be, and that vision has induced caution. 19

Nuclear weapons also sustained Soviet-American bipolarity beyond the time that it might otherwise have been expected to last. Given the Soviet Union's chronic economic difficulties, its claim to superpower status would have lost credibility long ago had that country not possessed a tremendous nuclear arsenal. But because of the stability that bipolarity brings, it is not at all clear that the world would have been a more peaceful place had the USSR become an "ordinary" power. . . . 20

It would be to the advantage of the United States and the Soviet Union, therefore, to retain their nuclear superiority over the rest of the world, albeit at much reduced levels, and with maximum cooperating to avoid surprises and accidents. But we might well rethink targeting doctrines, for as the physicist Freeman Dyson has wisely observed, just because a nation has nuclear weapons does not mean that it has to point them at anyone in particular. Their purpose, rather, should be to maintain a healthy fear of incautious action on the part of everyone, and a healthy respect for a major method by which we have achieved a long peace. If that fear and that respect come from the contemporary technological equivalent of rattling bones and chanting incantations around a campfire, then so be it. 21

How Will NATO, the Warsaw Pact, and a Reunified Germany Fit Together?

If the Soviet Union and the United States are no longer to confront each other as adversaries, then the original purpose of NATO and the Warsaw Pact—deterring military attack—will have passed away. It is worth recalling, though, that these alliances had secondary purposes as well: both were intended to overcome old nationalist rivalries in Europe; both were instruments by which the superpowers sought to integrate those portions of Germany that they controlled into those parts of Europe that fell within their influence. The two alliances served as stabilizers in that they brought a certain order and pre- 22 dictability to Europe; and although that stability was not always based on justice—witness Soviet behavior in Eastern Europe—it did secure peace for almost half a century on a previously war-prone continent. . . .

We should therefore seek to preserve the secondary stabilizing 23 functions of NATO and the Warsaw Pact, even as their original deterrent purposes disappear. It is always easier to modify existing institutions than to create new ones; preserving the Cold War alliances but shifting their roles could ensure that resurgent European nationalism does not, in these new and volatile circumstances, once again get out of control.

One way to accomplish this might be for a reunified Germany to 24 link itself to both alliances at the same time. Such a solution would have seemed ludicrous when NATO and the Warsaw Pact confronted each other as Cold War adversaries, but is it so implausible in a post–Cold War era? People have learned to live with stranger things: consider what happened to Germany itself, and to its former capital, in the years that followed the Second World War. If one keeps in mind that we are talking about a world in which once-competitive alliances have taken on the common task of preserving the stability Europe achieved during the Cold War—and if we remember that stability will be the prerequisite for any Europe-wide economic integration—then it might well be possible to persuade both East and West Germans that reunification would best proceed under the sponsorship of both alliances, and perhaps even with the continued stationing of at least a token number of Russian and American troops on German soil. . . .

The old meaning of sovereignty will not suffice in dealing with 25 the resurgence of nationalism in Europe: too many Europeans—and non-Europeans as well—have suffered from its excesses to be denied an interest in seeing to it that old evils do not return. The Cold War experience, for all its danger, illogic, and injustice, provided a valuable opportunity for Europeans to mature, to put away those irresponsible practices that dragged their continent into war twice during the first half of this century. Keeping NATO and the Warsaw Pact around for a while—even if their role resembles that of nursemaids more than that of warriors—might be the best way to reassure all concerned that this process of becoming wise will continue.

Should We Help to Repair the Damage Marxism Has Caused?

Economic distress obviously encourages political instability: as 26 Paul Kennedy, the Yale historian, has pointed out, uneven rates of economic and technological development are what cause great powers to rise and fall. If one accepts the argument that the United States and its allies should want Russia to remain a great power, then it would hardly make sense to welcome an economic collapse there or in Eastern Europe, however misguided the policies were that produced that prospect.

But the West has an ideological as well as a material interest in 27 wanting to see *perestroika* succeed: the cause of democracy throughout the world can only prosper if that ideology—and not Marxist authoritarianism—provides the means by which the USSR and its neighbors at last achieve economies capable of satisfying the needs of their peoples. And if the emergence of even partly democratic institutions inside the Soviet Union makes the prospect of war less likely—there is strong historical evidence that democracies tend not to fight each other—then that would be an important reinforcement for the role nuclear deterrence has already played in discouraging the incautious use of military force. . . .

One thing is apparent at the outset: any new aid program for the 28 Soviet Union and Eastern Europe will have to be multinational in character. The United States is well beyond the point at which it can take on a burden of this magnitude by itself, as it did in 1947. Fortunately, though, it can now enlist the very considerable resources and skills of former recipients of Marshall Plan aid in Europe, notably West Germany, and also those of Japan, another past beneficiary of American assistance. All these states have cause to welcome an integration of Soviet and Eastern European economies with those of the rest of the world; none of them has any good reason to want to see *perestroika* fail.

A multinational aid program would have several advantages over 29 older, unilateral forms of aid. It would maximize the resources available while minimizing the burden on an already overstretched American economy. It would be less susceptible than past foreign-aid programs to the charge that it serves the political interests of a particular state; it would also be less vulnerable to the volatility of domestic politics in any one state. It would soak up surplus products and capital from two large-scale exporters of these commodities—Germany and Japan—whose success in exporting has periodically strained their relationship with the United States. And such a program might also help to heal political differences that still exist between Japan and the Soviet Union and that might well exist between a reunified Germany and the Soviet Union.

We might also consider encouraging corporate rather than government sponsorship for at least a major portion of this assistance, 30 where profitability and propriety make it feasible. Corporate management could provide faster action and greater efficiency than would otherwise occur; it might also be more sensitive than official initiatives to those market forces in the Soviet Union and Eastern Europe whose emergence we want to encourage. Some such activity is already under way, most conspicuously with a project that surely marks a turning point of some kind in the history of our times: I refer to the recent and long-awaited opening of McDonald's in Moscow, a project that will be particularly interesting to watch because of the corporation's decision to develop its own network of farms, processing plants, and training centers inside the USSR. The resulting contest is sure to be a titanic one, and whether Russia will overwhelm McDonald's or McDonald's will overwhelm Russia is far from clear. But the fact that it is taking place at all can only warm the heart of anyone who has ever been to the Soviet Union and felt the urge to shout, out of sheer exasperation: "What this country needs is a good service economy!" . . .

The names that we attach to things—which in turn determine the 31 categories we use in thinking about them—are only representations of reality; they are not reality itself. Reality can shift, sometimes more rapidly than the names we have devised to characterize it. Concepts like "communism," "capitalism," "deterrence," "credibility," and "security" only approximate the conditions we confront; but words like these tend to take on a life of their own; thereby constraining imagination. One sees the argument made even today that Communist parties running command economies will never give up power, despite overwhelming evidence that this is exactly what is happening. We need to avoid letting the categories that exist in our minds blind us to what our eyes are seeing.

At the same time, though, there is at least one thing to be said 32 in favor of retaining old names, even as one accommodates to new realities. Cloaking change in the appearance of continuity is a time-honored technique of political leadership, for it allows those at the top to alter their thinking and shift their policies without seeming to be inconsistent. Cloaking change in the garb of continuity eases transitions; it can be a way of making revolution look like evolution, which is sometimes a useful thing to do. We should not, therefore, do away entirely with the terminology of the Cold War, or even with all the institutions that reflect that terminology; but we should welcome the opportunity slowly but steadily to shift the meanings we attach to them.

Who is it that we have defeated in the Cold War? It is not the 33 Russian People, whom we never saw as enemies, and toward whom we bear no ill will. It is not the Soviet Union, for we should want to see that state survive as a great power. It is not communism, because that doctrine has proved so malleable over the years that it has long since lost any precise meaning. It is certainly not Gorbachev and the current Soviet government, who have had the wisdom to recognize reality and the courage to adjust to it. It is not even the Cold War, because that experience brought us the long peace. Indeed, it is odd that there should be so much talk of victory and so little specificity as to at whose expense it actually came.

It might help clarify things if we recall what appears to be a 34 recurring competition in human affairs between coercive authority and individual autonomy, between what the sociologist John A. Hall has referred to as the forces of power and those of liberty. The tension is as old as recorded history, and it will no doubt be with us as long as history continues. But power and liberty are rarely precisely balanced: one or the other predominates most of the time, with only occasional shifts back and forth.

The century has not, on the whole, been kind to liberty. The 35 forces of authoritarianism overcame those of autonomy in most parts of the world most of the time during this period: witness the respective triumphs of fascism, communism, and all the varieties of dictatorship that lay between. It appeared until quite recently to be the fate of most people to have most of their lives managed for them, to lack the means of controlling their own affairs.

What happened in the revolutionary year 1989 was that liberty 36 suddenly found itself pushing against an open door. The balance swung away from power with breathtaking speed; the authoritarian alternatives that have dominated so much of twentieth-century history were revealed to be, for the most part, hollow shells. We have good reason to hope that liberty will flourish in the next few years as it has not in our lifetime; and it is in that context that the real nature of the West's "victory" in the Cold War becomes clear. For it was authoritarianism that suffered the real defeat, and in that sense all of us—including our old Cold War adversaries—have won.

But history will not stop with us, any more than it did with all 37 the others—Marx and Lenin among them—who thought they had mastered its secrets. The triumph of liberty will almost certainly be transitory; new forces will eventually arise that will swing the balance back to power once again. It is not clear at the moment, though, where they will come from, or when they will arrive. It would be prudent to be on the lookout for them; it would be wise to be prepared for their effects. But the fact that the forces of resurgent power are not yet in sight—that we have the luxury of at least some time to savor the liberties that all of us, Russians included, have won—ought to be an occasion for ecumenical, if wary, celebration.

RESPONDING TO READING

Key words: community   discovery   freedom   language   power
reality   transformation   war

Rhetorical concepts: analogy   analysis   anecdote   cause and effect
definition   induction   narrative/example

1.   Evaluate the description of recent history Gaddis gave in May 1990. Note, for example, his definition of the enemy that lost the Cold War. Have events since he wrote led to a change in the way we should see that history? How does his account of recent history address the expectations of Mead, Milosz, and Sagan as they looked to the future?

2.   Gaddis looks at the past with considerable optimism, for example, calling the Cold War the "long peace." But his view of the future is not nearly so optimistic: "If history is any guide, what we will probably do is fritter away the fruits of victory." What is his evidence for such a grim view of the future?

3.   Gaddis argues that the United States should take certain positions with regard to the former Soviet Union, nuclear weapons, and Europe in enlightened self-interest. Summarize these positions and consider the degree to which the United States has done what he suggested in the period since he wrote.

4.   "But history will not stop with us," Gaddis says, in his last paragraph. Basing your arguments on the essays in this seciton, which represent some fifty years of speculation on the subject, write an essay on the future of war and peace. What will happen next? And what will be the results?

How Can We Think and Speak

about the Future?

Corporation and Nation
ROBERT B. REICH

Reich (born 1946), is a political economist on the faculty of Harvard's
John F. Kennedy School of Government. After graduating from Dart-
mouth in 1968, Reich studied economics at Oxford as a Rhodes
scholar and earned a law degree from Yale in 1973. He served as
Assistant to the Solicitor General in the Ford administration and as
Director of Policy Planning for the Federal Trade Commission in the
Carter Administration. His engaging manner of speaking enlivens
"the dismal science" for the general audience of National Public
Radio and public television. With equal verve he writes for such
periodicals as *The New Republic, The New York Times Magazine,* and
The Atlantic Monthly—where "Corporation and Nation" was pub-
lished in May 1988. This essay anticipates the argument of *The
Work of Nations: Preparing Ourselves for 21st-Century Capitalism*
(1991). Among Reich's other books are *The Resurgent Liberal* (1989),
The Next American Frontier (1983), and *Minding America's Business*
(1982).

"Corporation and Nation" addresses a major economic transformation that has profound worldwide implications for the next century. The prevailing American concept, that what is "good for the
corporation is good for the nation" is not necessarily true, says Reich,
who explains how and why our nation's businesses—and legislators,
and citizens—need to take a global view of corporate enterprise in
the twenty-first century. As Reich explains in *The Work of Nations:*

> There will be no *national* products or technologies, no national corpora-
> tions, no national industries. There will no longer be national economies,
> at least as we have come to understand that concept. All that will remain
> rooted within national borders are the people who comprise a nation.
> Each nation's primary assets will be its citizens' skills and insights. Each
> nation's primary political task will be to cope with the centrifugal forces
> of the global economy which tear at the ties binding citizens together—
> bestowing ever greater wealth on the most skilled and insightful, while
> consigning the less skilled to a declining standard of living.

Thus, as Reich asserts in "Corporation and Nation," "America's
economic future depends not on the old jobs we used to do but on
the new contributions we can make to an increasingly integrated
world economy" (paragraph 35). Our economic survival as a nation
depends on our ability to conceive of the future in these terms.

If the corporations Americans own and work for succeed, the   1
American economy will too—or so we were brought up to believe.
This assumption was given its most brazen expression thirty-five years
ago, by Charles Erwin Wilson, who was then the president of General
Motors; he was nicknamed "Engine Charlie," in order to distinguish
him from another Charles E. Wilson, "Electric Charlie," who was the
president of General Electric through the 1940s. During the Senate
hearing on his confirmation as Eisenhower's nominee for Secretary
of Defense, Wilson was asked whether he could make a decision in
the interests of the United States that was adverse to the interests of
General Motors's shareholders. Wilson said that he could, but that
such a conflict would probably never arise. "I cannot conceive of one
because for years I thought what was good for our country was good
for General Motors, and vice versa. The difference did not exist."

Engine Charlie's statement was widely criticized at the time as   2
an example of corporate America's arrogance, but in fact it simply
expressed principles already codified in American law and policy: the
corporation existed for its shareholders, and as they prospered, so
would the nation.

This root principle of our political economy is no longer valid.   3
The corporations Americans own and work for are becoming disconnected from the national economy. The overall success of these corporations has less and less to do with America's continued growth
and prosperity. Corporation and nation are growing apart, and American law and politics must adapt to this new reality.

The Assertive Shareholder

When Engine Charlie uttered his dictum, it was easy to believe   4
that what was good for corporations and their shareholders was also
good for the national economy. At least, shareholders' interests were
not so narrowly defined as to seem inconsistent with the nation's
broader economic objectives. Shareholders were typically too widely
dispersed to exert any real control over the corporation. Most shareholders faithfully held on to their shares, treating them as long-term
investments, and trusting that share values would continue to rise
over time.

Top corporate executives thus enjoyed wide discretion to do what-   5
ever they pleased, including what they deemed to be socially responsible, as long as their expenditures could be justified as benefiting
shareholders over the long term. This rationalization was capacious
enough to encompass almost any activities that might improve the
corporation's image. In fact, some of the expenditures they made—
on basic research, the development of new products and technologies,

employee training, various educational and philanthropic activities—
had little positive effect on the corporation's bottom line, because the
new knowledge easily spread to other firms. But these activities did
help spur broader economic development within the regions the corporations inhabited. And many of the executives relished the role of
the "corporate statesman" who mobilized private resources for further
public gains.

These activities should not be romanticized. Managerial discretion   6
was not always put to such noble purposes. But it *could* be, and the
prevailing ideology held it to be an appropriate exercise of corporate
power.

In the past few years, however, the stock market has become far   7
more efficient at keeping the executives' attention fixed on the bottom
line. First, the dispersed individual shareholders of yore have largely
been replaced by a relatively few professional investment managers,
who are responsible for investing enough billions of dollars of pension
funds, mutual funds, and insurance funds to make up at least a third
of all the equity in corporate America. These investment managers
are responsible for some 70 percent of the trading on the New York
Stock Exchange. They compete against one another, and are quick to
shift funds from one corporation to another, depending on whose
share prices are rising or falling at the moment. Second, the dereg-
ulation of brokerage fees and new technologies linking computers to
trading floors have reduced the costs and increased the speed of such
transactions; the computer linkages also give investment managers
up-to-the-minute data on share prices. Third, financial entrepreneurs
have refined techniques for acquiring controlling blocks of shares,
sometimes even using the corporation's own assets as collateral. Because of these three developments, it has become relatively easy for
an aggressive company or a few audacious individuals to seize control
of even the largest of American corporations when they sense a failure
by the corporation's executives to exploit some opportunity for increasing the value of their shares.

To deter raiders, every major American corporation is busily "re-   8
structuring" itself, to use the Wall Street euphemism. This has required eliminating or drastically cutting back on discretionary spending. No longer are corporations investing in long-term development.
Even before last October's crash, research budgets had been slashed.
Investments in education and training were down. In 1986 the rate of
increase in corporate donations to charity dropped for the first time
in fifteen years. "There are very few corporate statesmen anymore,"
laments James Joseph, the president of the Council on Foundations,
which monitors corporate giving. "CEOs no longer want to spend
their time on social issues." As one executive put it recently, "It

becomes positively un-American to look at anything except their own bottom line."

Executives no longer argue that what is good for shareholders is 9 necessarily good for the nation. In fact, many are now insisting that the stock market's unrelenting demand for higher share value is actually harmful to the nation, and that raiders should be restrained. Their warnings are being heard. In one recent *Business Week*–Harris poll 64 percent of the people surveyed favored new government restrictions on hostile takeovers. States are taking the lead in protecting their corporations. Earlier this year Delaware—where almost half the firms on the New York Stock Exchange are incorporated—became the twenty-ninth state to limit takeovers, thus in one swoop effectively shielding half of corporate America. Congress is considering legislation to discourage hostile mergers nationwide.

What may have escaped notice by America's business leaders is 10 the logical consequence of their new argument. One of the great advantages of the Engine Charlie principle to American business was its implicit rejection of any formal means of holding corporations accountable for the nation's continued prosperity. In benefiting shareholders, the corporation would necessarily spur the economy forward. But once it is granted, even by business leaders, that this is not always the case—indeed, that too much attention to shareholders' demands may in fact detract from the nation's long-term vitality—then the presumptive link between corporate executives' responsibilities to their shareholders and to the nation is severed. What is good for the shareholders is not necessarily good for the nation.

The question that in Engine Charlie's day had been submerged 11 under the vague rubric of "long-term" shareholder interests thus arises: by what means should corporations be held accountable to the public for contributing to the nation's prosperity?

The Foreign Shareholder

As ever more of corporate America is bought by foreign nationals, 12 another divergence appears between the interests of the corporation and its shareholders and the interests of the nation.

In Engine Charlie's time virtually all major corporations doing 13 business in America were owned by Americans. Thirty years later this situation has changed. Other national economies are catching up with that of the United States; a few are on the verge of surpassing it. American-owned corporations are no longer the only global enterprises of significant power and scale, nor even the largest ones. And in historic reverse, foreign ownership of American capital now stands at over $200 billion, more than double what it was in 1980, and it is rising rapidly.

The low dollar has made bargains of American corporations, as 14 if corporate America were having a fire sale, with every company marked 35 to 50 percent off its regular price. The companies that have been bought include some sporting familiar names, like Doubleday, CBS Records, Purina Mills, Mack Truck, Allis-Chalmers, and Firestone. Foreign capital is also pouring into the American stock market, last October's crash notwithstanding. Indeed, the tenacity of foreign investors prevented the Dow Jones Industrial Average from falling even further. Major banks and investment houses—BankAmerica, Shearson Lehman, Paine Webber, and Goldman, Sachs—are now partly owned by Japanese banks intent on breaking into the American financial market.

The wave of foreign acquisition of corporate America is having 15 an effect in the United States similar to that felt in other nations when they faced American investment years ago—when charges of American "imperialism" were in the air and fears that American multinational corporations would exploit host nations were acute. Already a Republican administration in Washington, which is ideologically committed to free markets, has warned of the dangers of allowing foreigners to take over economically "strategic" American corporations. Meanwhile, would-be foreign buyers are coming under increasing scrutiny. A new trade bill recently passed by the House of Representatives would require foreign investors to report to the government any "significant" interest they had acquired in an American corporation. The version passed in the Senate would authorize the administration to review any proposed acquisition of an American corporation by foreigners. American business leaders, although delighted to have foreign investors bid up the prices of their own shares, have expressed mounting concern about the number of foreign-owned corporations popping up in their midst.

Here, too, the implication is that the interests of the shareholders 16 of the corporations in our midst are no longer the same as the nation's. In this instance, it is not enough that a corporation produces goods and services within the United States and employs American workers. To guarantee that corporate success will translate into national success, the corporation must also be firmly under the control of American citizens—so the argument goes. American shareholders and executives, it is assumed, can be trusted to act in the nation's interest under circumstances in which foreign shareholders and executives cannot be trusted. But a step is missing from this argument, just as a step was missing from the previous argument, that corporations protected from takeovers will act in the long-term interest of the economy. Here the unanswered question is, why and under what circumstances should American citizens be expected to forgo profits in pursuit of national goals?

The Cosmopolitan Shareholder

In Engine Charlie's time almost everything that American-owned 17 corporations sold here or abroad—particularly anything involving the slightest complexity in design or manufacturing—was produced in the United States. This is no longer the case. American-owned corporations are now doing all sorts of technologically sophisticated work outside the United States. A significant proportion of America's current trade imbalance is due to this tendency.

Look closely at almost any major American corporation that sells 18 complex gadgets and you are likely to see a foreign producer in disguise: in 1986 IBM imported $1.5 billion worth of data-processing equipment and General Electric half a billion dollars' worth of cassette recorders, microwave ovens, room air-conditioners, and telephones. Apple Computer's Asian plants make all Apple II computers, which in 1986 accounted for more than half of the company's sales. Eastman Kodak now sells, under its own name, Canon photocopiers, Matsushita video cameras, and TDK video tape, and it has farmed out the production of its 35-millimeter cameras to Haking Industries, in Hong Kong, and Chinon Industries, in Japan. And so on.

All such goods that American corporations buy or make abroad 19 and then sell in the United States are counted as American imports. The current frenzy in Washington over allegedly unfair foreign trade practices has obscured this reality. Consider Taiwan, which now exports some $19 billion more to the United States each year than it imports from the United States. The imbalance has provoked the indignation of American politicians, some of whom are demanding that Taiwan take steps to improve the balance or incur stiff penalties. But on closer examination the real culprit emerges. Several of Taiwan's top exporters are American-owned corporations—RCA, Texas Instruments, and General Instruments. All told, more than 30 percent of Taiwan's trade imbalance with the United States, and more than half of its imbalance in high-technology goods, is attributable to American-owned corporations' buying or making things in Taiwan and exporting them back to the United States. Taiwan's only sin is to have a highly skilled population that is willing to work for relatively low wages (Taiwanese engineers earn a quarter of the salary of American engineers, and Taiwanese technicians a fifth of their American counterparts' wages).

Even Japan's notorious trade surplus with the United States is in 20 substantial part the handiwork of American-owned corporations.

Fully $17 billion, or about 40 percent, of Japan's $39.5 billion trade surplus with the United States in 1985 (the last year for which such data are available) was the result of American corporations' buying or making things in Japan to be sold in the United States under their own brand names. One of the ironies of our age is that an American who buys a Ford automobile or an RCA television is likely to get *less* American workmanship than if he had bought a Honda or a Matshushita TV.

Americans who live and work in the United States continue to 21 consume more than they produce and to import more than they export—hardly the path to prosperity. But American-owned corporations are doing quite well, regardless. They are not only raking in nice profits by buying or making things abroad for sale here but also doing well by buying or making things abroad for sale everywhere else. In 1985 American-owned corporations sold the Japanese over $53 billion worth of goods that they made in Japan—a sum greater than the American trade deficit with Japan that year (Japanese companies, meanwhile, sold us only $15 billion worth of goods that they made in the United States). IBM Japan is huge and prosperous in its own right, with 18,000 employees, annual sales of $6 billion around the world, and research and production facilities that are among the most advanced anywhere.

In fact, American-owned corporations have remained competitive 22 worldwide. A recent study of Robert Lipsey and Irving Kravis, of the National Bureau of Economic Research, suggests that while the fraction of world markets held by U.S. corporations exporting from the United States has steadily dropped during the past twenty-five years, such losses have been offset by the gains of American-owned corporations exporting from other nations.

One conclusion that might be drawn from all this is that America's 23 competitive decline does not stem from any inherent deficiency in the top management of corporations. The stream of books exhorting managers toward excellence notwithstanding, American managers have done well by their shareholders (although *not* so well by America). Unsurprisingly, this insight has been welcomed by American business leaders eager to shift the blame for our competitive woes onto someone else. Mobil Oil Corporation made the argument succinctly in a recent pronouncement:

> American multinational companies can, and do, compete successfully all over the world. While the U.S. trade balance became a shambles, these companies continued to operate successfully in world markets. They did so by producing in those countries with the best business climates. . . .
> So to argue that American businessmen have lost their management and technological skills, or grown fat and lazy, is neither

true nor relevant. We should be looking to ourselves to learn why this country has provided a less favorable business environment than some of our trading partners. And then we should act to improve the climate.

Stripped to its brutal essentials, Mobil's message is this: American 24 corporations and their shareholders can now prosper by going wherever on the globe the costs of doing business are lowest—where wages, regulations, and taxes are minimal. Indeed, managers have a responsibility to their shareholders to seek out just such business climates. If America as a whole wants to be a successful exporter, it must compete with other nations to be the location where American corporations find it profitable to set up shop.

This lesson is well understood by state governments. Consider, 25 for example, the Hyster Company, an American-owned corporation that makes forklift trucks used to shuttle things around factories and warehouses. In 1982 Hyster informed public officials in five states and four nations where it built trucks that some Hyster plants would close. Operations would be retained wherever they were most generously subsidized. The bidding was ferocious. Within six months Hyster had collected $72.5 million in direct aid. Britain is reported to have offered $20 million to ransom fifteen hundred jobs in Irvine, Scotland. Several American towns—including Kewanee, Illinois; Sulligent, Alabama; and Berea, Kentucky—surrendered a total of $18 million in direct grants and subsidized loans to attract or preserve around two thousand jobs.

The same underlying problem emerges. Subsidies and tax breaks 26 are offered with no strings attached—no means of holding corporations accountable to the public. Executives of the Hyster Corporation are under no more legal obligation to direct corporate efforts toward spurring the American economy than are the executives of companies shielded from takeovers by recent state laws such as those passed by Delaware, or than are the executives of American-owned corporations in general. Hyster can take the subsidies and tax breaks and do with them whatever it wants. Indeed, just last August, Hyster announced another wave of closings. The Engine Charlie principle, as this example illustrates, is no longer valid, but nothing has replaced it to reestablish the link between corporation and nation.

Beyond Engine Charlie

The privileged place of the corporation in America has been jus- 27 tified for more than a century by the assumption that corporations automatically fuel the nation's economic growth—that what is good for shareholders is necessarily good for America. In the past few years, however, as corporate America has become simultaneously more attentive to the immediate demands of shareholders for high returns and more international in its ownership and operations, its links to the national economy have seriously weakened.

How *should* the corporation be bound to the nation in the future? 28 Should it be bound at all? The struggle to define a new relationship between corporation and nation will be one of the central economic and political tasks of our era, and it will defy easy solutions. Only the contours of the emerging debate can be seen.

On the one side will be those who argue that any divergence 29 between corporate strategies and national goals is perfectly okay. The world economy as a whole will be stronger if corporations are free to attract investors from anywhere and undertake production anywhere, with the sole objective of rewarding their shareholders with the highest possible returns. In this view, any special relationship between particular corporations and a particular nation will result in an inefficient use of resources overall. As the world economy grows ever more integrated, the nation-state is becoming outmoded and irrelevant anyway. A nation's only legitimate concern with corporations doing business within its borders should be to guard its citizens from harmful side effects of corporate activity, such as pollution, unsafe products, monopolization, and fraud.

But this view fails to take into account the positive side effects of 30 corporate activity for a nation—in particular, the training of a nation's work force in new skills applicable outside the company, and technological discoveries with broader potential. Such corporate investments in the skills and knowledge of a nation do not necessarily benefit shareholders, as has been noted, because the benefits often leak out of the company as the new knowledge spreads and as employees take their skills elsewhere. But they are critical for moving an economy forward. Positive side effects like these are as relevant to the welfare of a nation's citizens as are the potential harmful side effects. In a world in which nation-states continuously compete for economic power and the influence that flows from it, decisions about where investments are undertaken, by whom, and of what sort, can have profound political consequences as well.

On the other side of the debate will be those who argue that 31 corporations should be tightly bound to the nation. In this view, large corporations in particular should be firmly under public control. It will be urged, for example, that representatives of the public be placed on corporate boards; that some corporate shares be held by publicly appointed trustees or by public authorities; that American corporate investments in other nations, and foreign investments here, be reviewed to ensure compatibility with national economic goals; and that transfers of American capital or technology across the border be carefully monitored.

But this view suffers from the oppositve infirmity—it sacrifices 32 market efficiency for public accountability. Without the hope of maximizing profits, the spur of competition, and the fear of loss, enterprises have a tendency to stagnate. Too much of this, and entire economies can decline. There is a growing consensus, now apparently extending all the way to the Kremlin, that public ownership and centralized controls are not the path to progress either.

Recent efforts in the United States to deter hostile corporate take- 33 overs, limit foreign ownership of corporations, and improve the business climate through indiscrimiante tax breaks and subsidies represent the worst of both worlds—less efficiency and less accountability to the public. On the one hand, these initiatives can be costly: the regulation of takeovers may simply give job security to incompetent managers, limits in foreign ownership may only worsen our balance of payments, and tax breaks and subsidies thrown willy-nilly in the direction of corporations may induce them to do things they could do better and more cheaply elsewhere.

On the other hand, these initiatives offer no assurance that the 34 corporations that benefit from them will in turn help the broader economy. Indeed, they leave corporate executives free to do whatever they wish with the protections, tax breaks, and subsidies they receive. These measures are predicated on a blind trust that corporate executives shielded from takeovers will invest in the economy's long-term development, that American executives and shareholders will make sacrifices for the nation which foreign executives and shareholders will not, and that tax breaks and subsidies will automatically induce corporations to produce the kinds of goods in America that will strengthen the overall economy.

The best solution would be to focus specifically on what things 35 we want corporations to do that are apt to be unprofitable to shareholders, and then to induce corporations to do them. What is it we want corporations to do? Not to preserve jobs in the United States that can be done far more cheaply by foreign workers eager to do them. The costs of trying to keep such jobs here—as reflected in higher prices for consumers and onerous burdens on Third World workers deprived of work—would far exceed the benefits. We should ask corporations instead to help propel the American economy forward by training American workers in new skills and investing in new knowledge. America's economic future depends not on the old jobs we used to do but on the new contributions we can make to an increasingly integrated world economy.

Our overriding goal should be to ensure that America is a place 36
where enterprises of whatever nationality perform sophisticated
tasks, and thus give large numbers of Americans valuable experience.
There are several ways of inducing corporations to undertake complex
production in America. The first and most obvious is to ensure that
our citizens are capable of learning quickly on the job, so that Americans will be the kind of workers global corporations *want* to train.
This will require that we as a nation invest more than we do now in
education—in pre-school programs, in basic literacy and numeracy,
in scientific and technical competence, and in foreign-language training, to name only the most critical areas. Numerous recent studies
reveal the ignorance of American schoolchildren relative to those in
Japan and other industrialized nations, and the extent of illiteracy and
innumeracy in the society. In the past five years there has been much
handwringing over reading and math scores in certain locales, and
even some progress in raising them. The important point is that America's future productivity is directly related to our collective capacity
to learn on the job, which depends in turn on how well we are prepared to learn. No corporation, however well intentioned, can afford
to make up for a lack of basic education.

In addition to the general lure of a competent work force, however, 37
we will need more substantive inducements. They could take several
forms. We might, for example, subsidize corporations that do certain
kinds of advanced design and manufacturing in the United States,
with the amount of the subsidy depending upon the numbers of
employees so engaged. Or the inducement might take the form of a
tax credit, similarly structured. Or it might be a "domestic content"
rule, requiring that the highest-valued steps in the production of
certain goods sold here be undertaken in America.

Inducements like these would also be costly, resulting in higher 38
taxes or prices for most Americans. But unlike the open-ended initiatives now commonplace, these inducements would feature a quid
pro quo: corporations receiving them would be delivering benefits to
the American economy, through on-the-job training and new knowledge. And the greater the benefits to the economy, the greater the
inducements to the corporation.

These inducements would not hobble international trade or shel- 39
ter American corporations from competition. They would be made
available to *any* corporation—headquartered anywhere, owned by
anyone. Corporations would thus be held accountable for what we
as a public sought from them, yet would have a continued incentive
to allocate resources to their most profitable uses. Such inducements
would have the additional virtue of pushing us to clarify our long-

term development strategy—forcing our government representatives to define the categories of experience and skills we think will be most important to the nation's future.

The difficulties in the way of adminstering such inducements, or 40 even gaining sufficient political support to launch them, should not be underestimated. It has been hard enough to strengthen public education and ensure a minimal level of competence in the American work force; this program of on-the-job training and research is far more ambitious. Moreover, many Americans lack confidence in government's capacity to accomplish public purposes wisely and efficiently, and already feel overwhelmed and overtaxed by public needs.

But the alternatives are even less attractive. Our national strategy 41 for economic development clearly must be more than, and different from, the sum of the strategies used by the corporations our citizens own or work for. To repeat: this is not because these corporations are irresponsible or unpatriotic but because their widening global opportunities for making profits—and shareholders' mounting demands that they exploit such opportunities—are coming to have no direct or unique bearing on the nation's continued growth. The direction in which we are heading—blocking takeovers, hobbling foreign owners, and granting tax breaks and subsidies indiscriminately—seems far riskier and costlier than the direction I have proposed.

The growing divergence between corporation and nation is part 42 of a larger quandary. As our economy becomes so entwined with the world's that the nation's borders lose their commercial significance, Americans need to understand and recognize the subtle ways in which our citizens are connected to one another—not through the corporations we own but through the skills and knowledge we absorb. Without this understanding we cannot expect to elicit the sacrifices required to gain greater skills and knowledge. Corporations are no longer the building blocks of the U.S. econony; our citizens are.

RESPONDING TO READING

Key words: community power reality striving transformation

Rhetorical concepts: analysis cause and effect explanation illustration induction

1. Reich distinguishes between short-term (immediate profits) and long-term interests of corporations. Describe the differences he points out between them and why he thinks they have different implications for the good of the country. Include an explanation of how too much attention to "the bottom line" can damage the good of the country.

2. How do recent changes in the stock market (paragraph 7) affect the way corporation managers regard the bottom line, and short-term interests? How do these changes then affect the relationship between corporate and national goals? How has foreign investment and foreign production complicated this relationship? Should there be a public interest in these matters?

3. Consider the evidence Reich presents that American corporations are actually doing very well, even though the American economy is not. His conclusions contradict many popular notions about the position of American companies in relation to foreign ones. Is his argument convincing? If not, why not? If so, why do you think the popular notions he disputes persist so powerfully?

4. Consider the "debate" Reich presents between public accountability and market efficiency. What are the strengths and weaknesses of the arguments presented? What are the strengths and weaknesses of the compromise solutions that Reich proposes?

5. Notice how this debate echoes other debates you have seen in this book, such as Thoreau's denial of government power in "Civil Disobedience," Brazelton's call for governmental support for working parents, Culliton's welcome of a public voice in science research, or Bok's denial that lies should be used for the public good. Can you come up with ways to speak about the underlying conflict of private and public good, an issue which is sure to loom large in the future? Write an essay connecting the economic problem Reich defines to the social and moral problems that some other essay addresses. Be sure to consider the kinds of words the writers use, that is, the interplay of language and thought you see in the essays.

Learning the Language

PERRI KLASS

Although an American, Klass was born in Trinidad in 1958, where her father, an anthropologist, and her mother, a writer, were working at the time. These diverse and humanizing influences are reflected in the three major areas of Klass's life. Pediatrics: she earned an M.D. from Harvard in 1986, and has completed a pediatric residency at Boston Children's Hospital. Writing: Klass has published a novel, *Recombinations* (1985), a collection of short stories, *I Am Having an Adventure* (1986); a series of essays for the *New York Times*, and an autobiographical collection, *A Not Entirely Benign Procedure: Four Years as a Medical Student* (1987), of which "Learning the Language" is a chapter. Family: Klass's concern for children is reflected not only in her choice of medical specialty, but in the dovetailing of her two careers with the demands of motherhood. She planned her pregnancy to fit in with her second year medical school schedule, and she writes while her son naps.

Everyone new to a group (such as a family, a fraternity), an institution (such as college), a discipline or profession (each and every one), has to learn its code, in language and in behavior, as part of the initiation process. This is how we enter and become part of a discourse community. That this is "a not entirely benign procedure," as Klass's "Learning the Language" makes clear, is partly because of the dissonance between the codes of other groups of which the learner is already a part and the new codes the learner must master to succeed in the new context. However, the newness of a language, like the newness of a love affair, leaves the initiate acutely sensitive to shades of meanings and values that with greater familiarity go unnoticed. As a medical student learning the language, Klass is aware of the dehumanizing aspects of calling an infant a "brainstem preparation," or referring to a dying patient as "CTD" (circling the drain). Although specific meanings, perhaps even the vocabulary, for our language of the future may not yet exist we can be sure that they will emerge of necessity to accommodate the inevitable changes in our culture. Klass reminds us to be sensitive to the music, as well as the words.

"Mrs. Tolstoy is your basic LOL in NAD, admitted for a soft rule-   1
out MI," the intern announces. I scribble that on my patient list. In other words, Mrs. Tolstoy is a Little Old Lady in No Apparent Distress who is in the hospital to make sure she hasn't had a heart attack (rule out a Myocardial Infarction). And we think it's unlikely that she has had a heart attack (a *soft* rule-out).

If I learned nothing else during my first three months of working   2
in the hospital as a medical student, I learned endless jargon and abbreviations. I started out in a state of primeval innocence, in which I didn't even know that "s̄ CP, SOB, N/V" meant "without chest pain, shortness of breath, or nausea and vomiting." By the end I took the abbreviations so much for granted that I would complain to my mother the English professor, "And can you believe I had to put down *three* NG tubes last night?"

"You'll have to tell me what an NG tube is if you want me to sym-   3
pathize properly," my mother said. NG, nasogastric—isn't it obvious?

I picked up not only the specific expressions but also the patterns   4
of speech and the grammatical conventions; for example, you never say that a patient's blood pressure fell or that his cardiac enzymes rose. Instead, the patient is always the subject of the verb: "He dropped his pressure." "He bumped his enzymes." This sort of construction probably reflects the profound irritation of the intern when the nurses come in the middle of the night to say that Mr. Dickinson has disturbingly low blood pressure. "Oh, he's gonna hurt me bad tonight," the intern might say, inevitably angry at Mr. Dickinson for dropping his pressure and creating a problem.

When chemotherapy fails to cure Mrs. Bacon's cancer, what we   5
say is, "Mrs. Bacon failed chemotherapy."

"Well, we've already had one hit today, and we're up next, but at   6
least we've got mostly stable players on our team." This means that
our team (group of doctors and medical students) has already gotten
one new admission today, and it is our turn again, so we'll get whoever
is admitted next in emergency, but at least most of the patients we
already have are fairly stable, that is, unlikely to drop their pressures
or in any other way get suddenly sicker and hurt us bad. Baseball
metaphor is pervasive. A no-hitter is a night without any new ad-
missions. A player is always a patient—a nitrate player is a patient
on nitrates, a unit player is a patient in the intensive care unit, and
so on, until you reach the terminal player.

It is interesting to consider what it means to be winning, or doing   7
well, in this perennial baseball game. When the intern hangs up the
phone and announces, "I got a hit," that is not cause for congratu-
lations. The team is not scoring points; rather, it is getting hit, being
bombarded with new patients. The object of the game from the point
of view of the doctors, considering the players for whom they are
already responsible, is to get as few new hits as possible.

This special language contributes to a sense of closeness and   8
professional spirit among people who are under a great deal of stress.
As a medical student, I found it exciting to discover that I'd finally
cracked the code, that I could understand what doctors said and
wrote, and could use the same formulations myself. Some people
seem to become enamored of the jargon for its own sake, perhaps
because they are so deeply thrilled with the idea of medicine, with
the idea of themselves as doctors.

I knew a medical student who was referred to by the interns on   9
the team as Mr. Eponym because he was so infatuated with epony-
mous terminology, the more obscure the better. He never said "cap-
illary pulsations" if he could say "Quincke's pulses." He would
lovingly tell over the multinamed syndromes—Wolff-Parkinson-
White, Lown-Ganong-Levine, Schönlein-Henoch—until the temptation to suggest Schleswig-Holstein or Stevenson-Kefauver or Baskin-
Robbins became irresistible to his less reverent colleagues.

And there is the jargon that you don't ever want to hear yourself   10
using. You know that your training is changing you, but there are
certain changes you think would be going a little too far.

The resident was describing a man with devastating terminal pan-   11
creatic cancer. "Basically he's CTD," the resident concluded. I reminded myself that I had resolved not to be shy about asking when
I didn't understand things. "CTD?" I asked timidly.

The resident smirked at me. "Circling The Drain."   12

The images are vivid and terrible. "What happened to Mrs. Mel-   13
ville?"

"Oh, she boxed last night." To box is to die, of course.   14

Then there are the more pompous locutions that can make the   15
beginning medical student nervous about the effects of medical training. A friend of mine was told by his resident, "A pregnant woman
with sickle-cell represents a failure of genetic counseling."

Mr. Eponym, who tried hard to talk like the doctors, once ex-   16
plained to me, "An infant is basically a brainstem preparation." The
term "brainstem preparation," as used in neurological research, refers
to an animal whose higher brain functions have been destroyed so
that only the most primitive reflexes remain, like the sucking reflex,
the startle reflex, and the rooting reflex.

And yet at other times the harshness dissipates into a strangely   17
elusive euphemism. "As you know, this is a not entirely benign
procedure," some doctor will say, and that will be understood to
imply agony, risk of complications, and maybe even a significant
mortality rate.

The more extreme forms aside, one most important function of   18
medical jargon is to help doctors maintain some distance from their
patients. By reformulating a patient's pain and problems into a language that the patient doesn't even speak, I suppose we are in some
sense taking those pains and problems under our jurisdiction and
also reducing their emotional impact. This linguistic separation between doctors and patients allows conversations to go on at the bedside that are unintelligible to the patient. "Naturally, we're worried
about adeno-CA," the intern can say to the medical student, and lung
cancer need never be mentioned.

I learned a new language this past summer. At times it thrills me   19
to hear myself using it. It enables me to understand my colleagues,
to communicate effectively in the hospital. Yet I am uncomfortably
aware that I will never again notice the peculiarities and even atrocities
of medical language as keenly as I did this summer. There may be
specific expressions I manage to avoid, but even as I remark them,
promising myself I will never use them, I find that this language is
becoming my professional speech. It no longer sounds strange in my
ears—or coming from my mouth. And I am afraid that as with any
new language, to use it properly you must absorb not only the vocabulary but also the structure, the logic, the attitudes. At first you
may notice these new and alien assumptions every time you put
together a sentence, but with time and increased fluency you stop
being aware of them at all. And as you lose that awareness, for better
or for worse, you move closer and closer to being a doctor instead of
just talking like one.

RESPONDING TO READING

Key words: community discovery education identity language power science talk

Rhetorical concepts: analogy analysis anecdote autobiography definition illustration metaphor narrative/example process

1.   Klass presents several different reasons for the use of medical jargon. List these reasons and develop a paper that shows how they are related to each other.
2.   Klass sees value as well as danger in the use of language she presents. What is the value of this special language? What are its dangers? What does she mean when she says that absorbing a language means "you must absorb not only the vocabulary but also the structure, the logic, the attitudes." Write an essay in which you explain the structure, logic, and attitudes of the medical jargon Klass describes.
3.   Consider some other specialty (such as politics, the military, education, the law, or business) with a language of its own. You may want to consult one or more additional essays dealing with language in this book, such as those by Mairs, Rodriguez, Hampl, Langer, Conroy, Fussell, Murray, or Butler. Give examples of that specialized language and show how it implies the users' particular view of the world.
4.   If the future holds increasing specialization and increasing use of jargon, as many writers predict, what will future language be like and how will that language affect the way we relate to each other? Will physicians from different nations communicate with each other more or less efficiently than lawyers speaking English to plumbers? If English becomes the international language, what logic and attitudes will that bring into relations among nations? What difference would it make if Japanese were to become the international language? What form of language lies in your own future as you become specialized? Write an essay on your vision of language in the future and how it will affect human relationships.

How Computers Get Common Sense

GINA KOLATA

Kolata (born 1948) was educated at the University of Maryland (B.A., 1969, M.A., 1973, and did some graduate work at MIT, 1969–70. As a science columnist for *Science* 1973–87 and for the *New York Times* thereafter, Kolata has the ability to translate extremely complicated concepts of research in medicine, engineering, technology, and a variety of physical and national sciences into language that everyday readers can understand. Her award-winning books, *Combatting the*

Number One Killer: The Scientific Report on Heart Disease (1978) and *The High Blood Pressure Book* (1979), also reflect this rare talent.

"How Can Computers Get Common Sense?" was published in 1982 in *Science*. Here she deals with the perennial question of computer science embedded in the title; "Is it possible for computers to be programmed to think like human beings?" or is "artificial intelligence" a contradiction in terms? For instance, current computer programs that translate novels from one language to another get stuck on metaphors, for computers currently lack the "common sense" to understand that "In a pig's eye," for example, is a figurative expression of disbelief or derision, rather than an anatomical location. As computer scientists develop ever more ingenious applications with progressively more refinements, the question remains for the future to answer.

Despite all the marvelous things that computers can do today, they simply lack many of the qualities that are present in human intelligence—they don't even have common sense. And it is not at all clear how to program computers to give them common sense. Or, as experts in artificial intelligence put it, it is not clear how to represent common sense knowledge in a computer. "I think the AI [artificial intelligence] problem is one of the hardest science has ever undertaken," says Marvin Minsky of Massachussets Institute of Technology, who is one of the founders of the field of AI.   1

There are, of course, computer programs that frequently are described as possessing artificial intelligence. Such programs can perform medical diagnoses, for example, or can predict where mineral deposits lie. These so-called expert systems are developed by computer scientists who glean a list of rules and procedures from human experts, such as doctors or mineral prospectors. And often the systems are quite useful. But they also are quite limited. "Much of the ordinary common sense ability to predict the consequences of actions requires going beyond the rules present in expert systems," says John McCarthy of Stanford University.   2

Theoreticians, however, have reached no consensus on how to solve the AI problem—on how to make true thinking machines. Instead, there are two opposing philosphical viewpoints and a flurry of research activity along these two directions. The different viewpoints were represented at a recent meeting[1] of the American Association for Artificial Intelligence by Minsky and by McCarthy, who also is a founder of the AI field and is an inventor of the term "artificial intelligence."   3

---

[1]The National Conference on Artificial Intelligence, sponsored by the American Association for Artificial Intelligence, was held on 18 to 22 August at Carnegie-Mellon University and the University of Pittsburgh.

McCarthy believes that the way to solve the AI problem is to design computer programs to reason according to the well worked out languages of mathematical logic, whether or not that is actually the way people think. Minsky believes that a more fruitful approach is to try to get computers to imitate the way the human mind works which, he thinks, is almost certainly not with mathematical logic. 4

"I really think of myself as a psychologist," says Minsky, who reports that he gets his inspiration for attempting to represent knowledge in a computer by thinking about thinking, talking to psychologists and by going to playgrounds and questioning children who have not yet learned to conceal their thinking processes by couching their explanations in logical terms. From these investigations, he has become convinced that there is no single, simple way to explain human reasoning. "I think human intelligence is an accumulation of many different mechanisms and methods," he remarks. "I bet the human brain is a kludge." 5

So how do you put a jumble of poorly understood mechanisms and methods into a computer? Minsky believes that trying to represent the whole system with mathematical logic gets you into too many difficulties. "I've become convinced that the idea of 'fact' and the idea of 'truth' are no good. I think facts and truth are only good in mathemtics and that's an artificial system. Logical systems work very well in mathemetics, but that is a well-defined world. The only time when you can say something like, If a and b are integers, then a plus b always equals b plus a is in mathematics." 6

Minsky gives an example of the kind of difficulties that can occur if mathematical reasoning is applied to the real world. "Consider a fact like, 'Birds can fly.' If you think that common-sense reasoning is like logical reasoning then you believe there are general principles that state, 'If Joe is a bird and birds can fly then Joe can fly.' But we all know that there are exceptions. Suppose Joe is an ostrich or a penguin? Well, we can axiomatize and say if Joe is a bird and Joe is not an ostrich or a penguin, then Joe can fly. But suppose Joe is dead? Or suppose Joe has his feet set in concrete? The problem with logic is that once you deduce something you can't get rid of it. What I'm getting at is that there is a problem with exceptions. It is very hard to find things that are always true." 7

An alternative approach that Minsky developed is a system called frame (for framework) systems. It is a psychological approach. The idea is to put large collections of information into a computer—much more information than is ever needed to solve any particular problem—and then to define, in each particular situation, which details are optional and which are not. For example, a frame for "birds" might include feathers, wings, egg-laying, flying, and singing. In a 8 biological context, flying and singing are optional; feathers, wings and egg-laying are not.

In frame systems, there is a collection of frame definitions which 9 set the scene for common-sense reasoning. But the importance of the details in a frame can change if there is a change in purpose or goal. If you are walking in the woods, the importance of "flying" in your bird frame is substantial. If you are in Antarctica its importance is minimal. Or, in another type of example, you may have two different images of another person—one is as a business associate and the other is as a friend. If you cannot understand the person's behavior when you are viewing him as a business associate, you switch frames and try to understand his behavior by viewing him as a friend. In a sense, frame systems are like logic, but there is one important difference. Ordinarily, logic would not say which things are most important in which frame.

Minsky himself never actually sat down to program a computer 10 to use frame systems, but one of his students did. Ira Goldstein, who is now at Hewlett-Packard in Palo Alto, developed a computer language which he calls FRL, for frame representation language, which he and his colleagues use in developing expert systems.

Originally, FRL represented only static objects. But Steven Ro- 11 senberg at Hewlett-Packard recently began extending the language so that it also represents the rules people employ for reasoning. With Rosenberg's extension of FRL, says Goldstein, "You can tie rules of reasoning to a particular domain of discourse. With FRL, we emphasize more the use of specific knowledge to guide reasoning. We place less emphasis on general reasoning mechanisms devoid of heuristic guidance."

"Minsky never liked logic," says McCarthy. "When difficulties 12 with mathematical reasoning came up, he felt they killed off logic. Those of us who did like logic, and there weren't many, thought we should find a way of fixing the difficulties." Whether logical reasoning is really the way the brain works is beside the point, McCarthy says. "This is AI and so we don't care if it's psychologically real."

What McCarthy would like to do is to express common sense facts 13 in the language of first order mathematical logic, meaning a language consisting only of variables and relation symbols such as "less than" or "mother of." "A proper axiomatization is one in which a proof exists for all conclusions that are ordinarily drawn from these facts," McCarthy remarks. "But what we know now about common sense is that that's asking for too much. You need another kind of reasoning— nonmonotonic reasoning."

Ordinary mathematical reasoning is monotonic in that if you have 14 a set of premises and a set of conclusions, the set of conclusions is monotonic in the premises. If you add more facts, any conclusions you could draw without the addtional facts are still valid with them. But common sense reasoning is often quite different from this mathematical logic. McCarthy explains, "If you know I have a car, you may conclude that you can ask me for a ride. If I tell you the car is in the shop, you may conclude you can't ask me for a ride. If I tell you it will be out of the shop in 2 hours, you may conclude you can ask me." As more premises are added, the conclusion keeps changing. "What's new is the possibility of formalizing nonmonotonic reasoning." That is, the possibility of using rules like those of mathematical logic to represent even nonmonotonic reasoning in a computer.

McCarthy calls his version of nonmonotonic reasoning circum- 15 scription. Unlike frame systems, circumscription is not yet being applied. "Circumscription is new and is still changing continuously as a theoretical idea. There is still more theory to be done before it can be used in applications."

Circumscription is used to restrict a predicate as much as possible 16 compatible with the facts that are being taken into account. After this has been done, the desired conclusions may follow by mathematical logic. For example, in the "Birds can fly" problem, McCarthy would use a predicate called "prevented from flying." In it, he would put any facts preventing flying that were being taken into account. These could include, for example, birds that are penguins or ostriches, as well as dead birds, or birds with their feet in concrete. Then the computer would reason. "If Joe is a bird and Joe is not a member of the set 'prevented from flying' then Joe can fly."

But is this circumscription a substitute for common sense? If cer- 17 tainly cannot take into account every contingency. It is easy to think of examples of nonflying birds, such as a bird with a broken wing, that a person with common sense would recognize as unable to fly but the computer would not.

"The conclusions we draw are risky, bu that's inevitable," says 18 McCarthy. "We can't invent all the hypotheses that might come to mind although we would like to take into account all the obvious things or, if a nonobvious fact becomes apparent, to take it into account. There is no reason to suppose we can make an omniscient computer program. We only want to make it as good as people."

Yet, McCarthy observes, "I admit that there are difficulties with 19 circumscription. Suppose someone says, 'This bird is in a cage and is only prevented from flying on occasion.' That way lies madness. You can be forced to keep elaborating. The key thing about trying to formalize common sense is to avoid being forced to haggle."

Alternatives to logical reasoning also have their difficulties. Nils 20 Nilsson of SRI International, who is president elect of the American

Association for Artificial Intelligence, believes that "alternatives to logic all seem to be somewhat fuzzy and mushy. Some people think that's a virtue—they think that's what intelligence is all about. I don't see the evidence for that." In addition, says Nilsson, many of the people who try to develop systems that are alternatives to logic simply don't know much about logic. (Nilsson emphatically excludes Minsky from this group.) As a result, their alternative systems turn out to be mere subsets of logic. "Some of the things they invent are pale imitations of what logic can do," Nilsson remarks. "In some cases, there may be a little something extra, they may stick a little finger out. But the way to handle that is to extend logic. I think we should stand on the foundation that's been developed."

All efforts to solve the knowledge representation problem share 21 two major obstacles, McCarthy explains. "The preliminary problem is to decide what knowledge to represent. The key thing that we have not got formulated is the facts of the common sense world." Then, even if researchers do manage to represent knowledge in computers, they are still faced with the problem of getting answers out of the computer in a reasonable time.

It is both Minsky's and McCarthy's opinion that the problem of 22 common sense will need many new ideas to go further. But in the meantime, Minsky predicts, there will be immensely valuable spin-offs from attempts to solve the AI problem. This has been the pattern so far. Time sharing, word processing, the computer language LISP, symbolic manipulations by computers, all were developed by AI researchers in the course of their work on more basic problems. Minsky and McCarthy make an analogy with physics. As Minsky says, "It took 300 years from the time of Galileo to the discovery of quantum mechanics. You might ask, 'What took those guys so long?' " Yet all along there were important practical consequences of basic research in physics.

Of course, if the AI problem is solved, it will have enormous social 23 consequences which Minsky, for one, worries about. "Do we need AI? There certainly is a dark side to any kind of advance and that's the question of whether societies can tolerate new systems. One of the things that AI threatens to do is to make work unnecessary. The dark question is, what will we do instead of work?"

Is it even possible to solve the AI problem—to design a computer 24 that has common sense and intelligence? Minsky, McCarthy, and others in the field are convinced that the problem will be solved eventually. Asked why he holds this view, McCarthy answers, "The alternative is to say that there is an area of nature that is not reachable by science. And nothing in the history of science supports that hypothesis."

RESPONDING TO READING

Key words: discovery education identity language memory
power science transformation

Rhetorical concepts: analogy analysis cause and effect
comparison and contrast deduction definition explanation process
research report

1. What is an expert system? What can it do and what can it not do? Are
you an expert system?
2. What is intelligence? What is Artificial Intelligence? Is there a distinction
that matters? Minsky and McCarthy represent two views of the future of AI;
define these two views and evaluate them.
3. Distinguish between common-sense reasoning and logical reasoning.
Come up with examples that illustrate the difference. Why do computers
have such trouble developing common sense?
4. To what degree do you use frame representation language (FRL) when
you think? Give some examples of that kind of language. Could you call the
medical jargon that Klass describes in the previous essay a kind of FRL? What
problems do people have with FRL and how are these problems similar to
and different from the problems computers have?
5. "If the AI problem is solved, it will have enormous social consequences."
Write an essay describing these social consequences. What might the future
be like?

Artificial Intelligence

ADRIENNE RICH

The personal and professional life of Adrienne Rich (born 1929) has
altered considerably since the publication of her first three volumes
of poetry in the 1950s. After graduating from Radcliffe in 1951, Rich
married a Harvard economist in 1953 and bore three sons within the
next four years, "a radicalizing experience." Having tried, with progressive anger, to fill "the part of the Victorian Lady of Leisure, the Angel
in the House, and also of the Victorian cook, scullery maid, laundress, governess, and nurse," she broke out of her marriage in 1970.
   At the same time she was breaking away from the tight verse forms
and neat metrical patterns of her earlier poetry and writing more
freely, with the highly charged, emotional intensity characteristic of
Diving into the Wreck (1973)—awarded the National Book Award,
which Rich rejected as an individual but accepted "in the name of
all women." In "It Is the Lesbian in Us" (1976) she explains that
lesbianism, which she explored in *Twenty-one Love Poems* (1976), for
her, is "a sense of desiring oneself, choosing oneself. . . . It is the
lesbian in us who drives us to feel imaginatively, to render in lan-

guage, grasp, the full connection between woman and woman."
Since that time Rich has explored these connections, as well as issues
of racism, anti-Semitism, and other matters of social justice in articles, speeches, reviews—totalling five collections of prose and eighteen volumes of poetry.

"Artificial Intelligence" was published in *Snapshots of a Daughter-
in-Law* (1963), her volume that began to reflect what it meant to be
a female in a male-dominated society. "Artificial Intelligence" uses
the metaphor of a game of chess that pits an incandescent, wasteful,
emotional human being (perhaps female) against an impersonal,
efficient computer that forgets nothing, "has no dreams." In poems
that demonstrate conflict between humans and machines, the humans always win. Why is that so here? If a computer programmer
were to depict such opposition, in what ways would the argument
and the picture change? Since ours is becoming a computer-
dominated society, does the ascendancy of this technology doom
poetic expression to oblivion or to drastic change in the future?

Artificial Intelligence
—to GPS—

Over the chessboard now,
Your Artificiality concludes
a final check; rests; broods—
    no—sorts and stacks a file of memories,
while I   5
concede the victory, bow,
and slouch among my free associations.

You never had a mother,
let's say? no digital Gertrude
whom you'd as lief have seen   10
Kingless? So your White Queen
was just an "operator."
(My Red had incandescence,
ire, aura, flare,
and trapped me several moments in her stare.)   15

I'm sulking, clearly, in the great tradition
of human waste. Why not
dump the whole reeking snarl
and let you solve me once for all?
(*Parameter*: a black-faced Luddite   20
itching for ecstasies of sabotage.)

Still, when
they make you write your poems, later on,
who'd envy you, force-fed

on all those variorum   25
editions of our primitive endeavors,
those frozen pemmican language-rations
they'll cram you with? denied
our luxury of nausea, you
forget nothing, have no dreams.   30

RESPONDING TO READING

Key words: art discovery identity language loss memory
poetry power reading reality science symbols writing

Rhetorical concepts: analogy comparison and contrast definition
meditation metaphor poetry process

1.   This poem sets out a kind of comparison-contrast between the speaker
and the computer chess opponent. Write an essay on attributes the poem
gives to the computer and to the human speaker. In what ways are they alike
and in what ways are they different?
2.   What is the attitude of the speaker to the computer? Of the comptuer to
the speaker? What is suggested by calling the computer "Your Artificiality"?
What is suggested by calling humans "the whole reeking snarl"? What does
the reference to Luddites (British workers who destroyed machines in the
belief that machines would replace workers) say about those who see the
problem as a simple one? Write an essay on the poem's view of artificial and
human intelligence.
3.   The poem also contrasts the playing of chess with the writing of poetry
(Gertrude is the queen in Shakespeare's *Hamlet*). What do the playing of chess
and the writing of poetry have in common? How do they differ? Refer to the
previous essay, by Gina Kolata, and then write an essay on the computer as
chess player and poet.
4.   The poem concludes with a vision of the computer being programmed
with the language of poetry. Look at the words the poet uses to describe the
process; why is the language described as "frozen" and "primitive"? What
kind of poetry is this computer likely to turn out? To what degree do you
agree with the poet's view of AI? Write an essay about the language of the
future as it may emerge from an increasingly computerized world.

My Speech to the Graduates
WOODY ALLEN

The life of a serious professional, whatever the field, is dominated
by constant, thoughtful attention to the discipline in question.
Woody Allen, who writes and produces a film a year, may be even
more conscientious than most. As he says of his willingness to shoot

a scene forty times or more, he doesn't sleep well if "at the end of the day he knows a shot is less than what he was trying to do." "All this obsession," he says, "it isn't perfectionism—it's obsession, compulsion—and all of that is no guarantee that the film is going to be any better."

Woody Allen works in the improvisatory style of many great film director-writers, essentially writing his movies as he makes them, and rarely rehearsing the actors beforehand, for he relishes the spontaneity of their performance. Allen, born in Brooklyn in 1935 and educated—he says—at "a school for emotionally disturbed teachers," began writing for television stars such as Sid Caesar and Carol Channing when he was 17. Within a decade he had shifted to a career in films, as screenwriter, actor, and director. His twenty films include *Annie Hall* (1975), for which he won Academy Awards for directing and screenwriting, *Hannah and Her Sisters* (1986), and *Crimes and Misdemeanors* (1989). Collections of his parodies and other *New Yorker* pieces include *Getting Even* (1971), *Without Feathers* (1975), and *Side Effects* (1980).

Allen's most familiar comic figure in both his films and his writing is said to closely resemble himself—a well-intentioned, intellectual New Yorker ("I am at two with Nature," he once wrote), inept and highly neurotic, unsuccessful in love and business, getting by with a lot of help from his psychiatrist—despite a highly stable family life for over a decade. His "Speech to the Graduates" brings the cliches of the past to guide any graduates of any year, any place, any time, into an uncertain future.

More than any other time in history, mankind faces a crossroads. 1 One path leads to despair and utter hopelessness. The other, to total extinction. Let us pray we have the wisdom to choose correctly. I speak, by the way, not with any sense of futility, but with a panicky conviction of the absolute meaninglessness of existence which could easily be misinterpreted as pessimism. It is not. It is merely a healthy concern for the predicament of modern man. (Modern man is here defined as any person born after Nietzsche's edict that "God is dead," but before the hit recording "I Wanna Hold Your Hand.") This "predicament" can be stated one of two ways, though certain linguistic philosophers prefer to reduce it to a mathematical equation where it can be easily solved and even carried around in the wallet.

Put in its simplest form, the problem is: How is it possible to find 2 meaning in a finite world given my waist and shirt size? This is a very difficult question when we realize that science has failed us. True, it has conquered many diseases, broken the genetic code, and even placed human beings on the moon, and yet when a man of eighty is left in a room with two eighteen-year-old cocktail waitresses nothing happens. Because the real problems never change. After all, can the human soul be glimpsed through a microscope? Maybe—but you'd definitely need one of those very good ones with two eyepieces. We know that the most advanced computer in the world does not have a brain as sophisticated as that of an ant. True, we could say that of many of our relatives but we only have to put up with them at weddings or special occasions. Science is something we depend on all the time. If I develop a pain in the chest I must take an X-ray. But what if the radiation from the X-ray causes me deeper problems? Before I know it, I'm going in for surgery. Naturally, while they're giving me oxygen an intern decides to light up a cigarette. The next thing you know I'm rocketing over the World Trade Center in bed clothes. Is this science? True, science has taught us how to pasteurize cheese. And true, this can be fun in mixed company—but what of the H-bomb? Have you ever seen what happens when one of those things falls off a desk accidentally? And where is science when one ponders the eternal riddles? How did the cosmos originate? How long has it been around? Did matter begin with an explosion or by the word of God? And if by the latter, could He not have begun it just two weeks earlier to take advantage of some of the warmer weather? Exactly what do we mean when we say, man is mortal? Obviously it's not a compliment.

Religion too has unfortunately let us down. Miguel de Unamuno 3 writes blithely of the "eternal persistence of consciousness," but this is no easy feat. Particularly when reading Thackeray. I often think how comforting life must have been for early man because he believed in a powerful, benevolent Creator who looked after all things. Imagine his disappointment when he saw his wife putting on weight. Contemporary man, of course, has no such peace of mind. He finds himself in the midst of a crisis of faith. He is what we fashionably call "alienated." He has seen the ravages of war, he has known natural catastrophes, he has been to singles bars. My good friend Jacques Monod spoke often of the randomness of the cosmos. He believed everything in existence occurred by pure chance with the possible exception of his breakfast, which he felt certain was made by his housekeeper. Naturally belief in a divine intelligence inspires tranquillity. But this does not free us from our human responsibilities. Am I my brother's keeper? Yes. Interestingly, in my case I share that honor with the Prospect Park Zoo. Feeling godless then, what we have done is made technology God. And yet can technology really be the answer when a brand new Buick, driven by my close associate, Nat Zipsky, winds up in the window of Chicken Delight causing hundreds of customers to scatter? My toaster has never once worked properly in four years. I follow the instructions and push two slices of bread down in the slots and seconds later they rifle upward. Once they broke the nose of a woman I loved very dearly. Are we counting on nuts and bolts and electricity to solve our problems? Yes, the telephone is a good thing—and the refrigerator—and the air conditioner. But not every air conditioner. Not my sister Henny's, for instance. Hers makes a loud noise and still doesn't cool. When the man comes over to fix it, it gets worse. Either that or he tells her she needs a new one. When she complains, he says not to bother him. This man is truly alienated. Not only is he alienated but he can't stop smiling.

The trouble is, our leaders have not adequately prepared us for a mechanized society. Unfortunately our politicians are either incompetent or corrupt. Sometimes both on the same day. The Government is unresponsive to the needs of the little man. Under five-seven, it is impossible to get your Congressman on the phone. I am not denying that democracy is still the finest form of government. In a democracy at least, civil liberties are upheld. No citizen can be wantonly tortured, imprisoned, or made to sit through certain Broadway shows. And yet this is a far cry from what goes on in the Soviet Union. Under their form of totalitarianism, a person merely caught whistling is sentenced to thirty years in a labor camp. If, after fifteen years, he still will not stop whistling, they shoot him. Along with this brutal fascism we find its handmaiden, terrorism. At no other time in history has man been so afraid to cut into his veal chop for fear that it will explode. Violence breeds more violence and it is predicted that by 1990 kidnapping will be the dominant mode of social interaction. Overpopulation will exacerbate problems to the breaking point. Figures tell us there are already more people on earth than we need to move even the heaviest piano. If we do not call a halt to breeding, by the year 2000 there will be no room to serve dinner unless one is willing to set the table on the heads of strangers. Then they must not move for an hour while we eat. Of course energy will be in short supply and each car owner will be allowed only enough gasoline to back up a few inches.

Instead of facing these challenges we turn instead to distractions like drugs and sex. We live in far too permissive a society. Never before has pornography been this rampant. And those films are lit so badly! We are a people who lack defined goals. We have never learned to love. We lack leaders and coherent programs. We have no spiritual center. We are adrift alone in the cosmos wreaking monstrous violence on one another out of frustration and pain. Fortunately, we have not lost our sense of proportion. Summing up, it is clear the future holds great opportunities. It also holds pitfalls. The trick will be to avoid the pitfalls, seize the opportunities, and get back home by six o'clock.

RESPONDING TO READING

Key words: discovery   education   growing up   humor   language
reality   talk   writing

Rhetorical concepts: anecdote   humor   meditation   metaphor
narrative/example   parody   speech

1.   Part of the wit of this pretend speech has to do with the relation of the
speaker to the audience. Describe the rhetorical situation, that is, the attributes of the speaker and the audience. What does each of them expect of the
other? To what degree does the speaker carry out his end of the bargain?

2.   Another way to see how Allen has structured his parody is to compare
the speech with the typical graduation speech it makes fun of. Take a paragraph or two from this speech and modify it—write it the way it might have
been delivered at your actual graduation. Then show how Allen sets up
expectations and breaks them down. A parody is a form of critique; what is
Allen suggesting about the usual graduation speech?

3.   The speech keeps contrasting high-flown abstractions and ideals with
prosaic details. The deflation of the abstractions is part of the humor, but
does the speech affirm any abstractions at all? Would you call the parody
simply good fun, or is it in fact giving guidance to the graduates after all?
What will the future be like, according to Allen?

QUESTIONS FOR REFLECTION AND WRITING

What Is the Future of the Family?

1. Write an essay on the future of your family. Base your essay in part on your reading of the essays in the first section of this chapter and in part on your own knowledge of yourself and your family's past. How do you expect to resolve the family problems that will be part of the next generation's experience?

2. Authors in other chapters of this book have also dealt with family issues: Walker, Heath, Rodriguez, Bettelheim, Kozol, Olds, for example. Pick one or two of these that speak to special problems of interest to you (the Black or Latino family, sex and the family, the homeless family, etc.) and write an essay that looks at the future of the particular problem you have identified. What problems and possibilities lie ahead?

Will War Shape the Future?

1. Do you expect to see a war in your future? If not, on what sorts of evidence do you base your hopes? If so, what will it be like and who will participate? What are likely to be the consequences, both short term and long term?

2. Examine the arguments set out by Mead, and others, that humans are so aggressive by nature that war is inevitable. Mead goes on to refute these arguments, but others do not. Bring to bear upon the discussion whatever evidence you can find from your reading and experience. Then write an essay addressed to others in this class defending your conclusions. Finally, abstract and alter your argument so it would be suitable for a short "think piece" to be published in your local newspaper.

How Can We Think and Speak About the Future?

1. Write an essay on either business or medicine in the future, starting with either the Reich or Klass essays. Twenty years from now, will your subject be different from the way it is today? How and why, or why not?

2. Write an essay showing both the possibilities and problems with artificial intelligence. You will want to begin with the Kolata essay and the Rich poem, but the field changes so rapidly that you will also need to obtain some current articles. To what degree will computers be able to replace humans, and will that be desirable?

What Will the Future Be Like?

1. Create a dialogue about the past that you will have with your grandchildren someday. They will be asking about how you have come to know so much and about what caused you to do what you have done. You will probably exaggerate the degree of planning and logic that went into your life, but will want them to understand what happened. Since this scene is set in the distant future, imagine what your life will be (has been) like and what the family you establish will be like.

2. Write an essay about the future of this year's college graduates. Twenty years from now, what will be some of their major concerns? Their values? What are they likely to be doing, saying, thinking? Will they be working or replaced by computers? How will they communicate? What will they be telling their children about the past and about the future? What will their future be like?

3. Write an essay about the graduating class of twenty years from now. What will those graduates have studied and what will be some of their major concerns? Their values? What will their future be like?

Acknowledgments

WOODY ALLEN   "My Speech to the Graduates." From *Side Effects* by Woody Allen. Copyright © 1980 by Woody Allen. Reprinted by permission of Random House, Inc.

ISAAC ASIMOV   "Those Crazy Ideas." Reprinted by permission from *Fact and Fancy*. Copyright © 1962 by Isaac Asimov. Copyright 1958 by Strut and Smith Publishing Co. Copyright 1958, 1959, 1960, 1961 by Mercury Press, Inc.

MARGARET ATWOOD   "This Is a Photograph of Me." From *The Circle Game* by Margaret Atwood. © 1966, House of Ananci Press. Reprinted with the permission of Stoddard Publishing Co. Limited, 34 Lesmill Road, Don Mills, Ontario.

MARY BELENKY   " 'Just Knowing': The Inner Expert." Excerpt from *Women's Ways of Knowing* by Mary Field Belenky et al. Copyright © 1986 by Basic Books, Inc. Reprinted by permission of Basic Books, a division of HarperCollins Publishers Inc.

BRUNO BETTELHEIM   "The Ignored Lesson of Anne Frank." From *Surviving and Other Essays* by Bruno Bettelheim. Copyright © 1979 by Bruno Bettelheim and Trude Bettelheim. Reprinted by permission of Alfred A. Knopf, Inc

SISSELA BOK   "Lies for the Public Good." From *Lying: Moral Choice in Public and Private Life* by Sissela Bok. Copyright © 1978 by Sissela Bok. Reprinted by permission of Pantheon Books, a division of Random House, Inc.

T. BERRY BRAZELTON, M.D.   "Issues for Working Parents," *American Journal of Orthopsychiatry*, 56(1), January 1986. Copyright © 1986 by the American Orthopsychiatric Association, Inc. Reproduced by permission.

JACOB BRONOWSKI   "The Reach of Imagination." Delivered as the Blashfield Address May 1966. Reprinted by permission from the *Proceedings* of the American Academy of Arts and Letters and National Institute of Arts and Letters, Second Series #17, 1967.

ROBERT N. BUTLER   "Successful Aging," *Mental Hygiene* 58:3 (1974). Reprinted by permission of the National Mental Health Association, 1021 Prince St., Arlington, VA 22314-2971.

ALEXANDER CALANDRA   "Angels on a Pin," *Saturday Review*, December 25, 1968. Copyright © 1968 by Alexander Calandra. Reprinted by permission of Alexander Calandra, 829 Woodruff Drive, Ballwin, MO 63011.

ITALO CALVINO   "All at One Point" from *Cosmicomics* by Italo Calvino, copyright © 1965 by Giulio Einaudi editore s.p.a., Torino, English translation copyright © 1968 by Harcourt Brace Jovanovich, Inc. and Jonathan Cape Ltd., reprinted by permission of Harcourt Brace Jovanovich, Inc. and Wylie, Aitken & Stone, Inc.

RACHEL CARSON   "The Obligation to Endure" from *Silent Spring* by Rachel L. Carson. Copyright © 1962 by Rachel Carson. Copyright © renewed 1990 by Roger Christie. Reprinted by permission of Houghton Mifflin Company. All rights reserved.

SIV CEDERING   "Letter from Caroline Herschel (1750–1848)." This work originally appeared as "Caroline Herschel (1750–1848)," part IV of "Letters from the Astronomers" in *Letters from the Floating World*, by Siv Cedering. Reprinted by permission of the University of Pittsburgh Press. © 1984 by Siv Cedering.

FRANK CONROY   "Think About It." Copyright © 1988 by *Harper's Magazine*. All rights reserved. Reprinted from the November issue by special permission.

BARBARA J. CULLITON   "Science's Restive Public" by Barbara J. Culliton is reprinted from *Limits of Scientific Inquiry*, edited by Gerald Holton and Robert S. Morison, by permission of W. W. Norton & Company, Inc. Copyright © 1979, 1978 by the American Academy of Arts and Sciences.

JOAN DIDION   "On Self-Respect." From *Slouching Towards Bethlehem* by Joan Didion. Copyright © 1961, 1968 by Joan Didion. Reprinted by permission of Farrar, Straus & Giroux, Inc.

GRETEL EHRLICH   "Life at Close Range." Copyright © 1991 by Gretel Ehrlich. Reprinted from Janet Sternburg, ed., *The Writer on Her Work: New Essays in New Territory* by permission of the author.

DEBORAH FALLOWS   "Why Mothers Should Stay Home." Reprinted with permission from *The Washington Monthly*, January 1982. Copyright 1982 by The Washington Monthly Company, 1611 Connecticut Avenue, N.W., Washington, D.C. 20009. (202) 462-0128.

an imprint of Macmillan Publishing Company, from *Crossing Open Ground* by Barry Lopez. Copyright © 1983, 1988 Barry Holstun Lopez. First appeared in *Outside* magazine, April 1983.

NANCY MAIRS "On Being a Cripple." From *Plaintext* by Nancy Mairs. Copyright © 1986 The Arizona Board of Regents. Reprinted by permission of the University of Arizona Press.

JOHN MCPHEE Excerpt from "Los Angeles Against the Mountains" from *The Control of Nature* by John McPhee. Copyright © 1989 by John McPhee. Reprinted by permission of Farrar, Straus & Giroux, Inc.

MARGARET MEAD "Warfare Is Only an Invention—Not a Biological Necessity," *Asia*, Vol. 40, No. 8, August 1940. Reprinted by permission.

CZESLAW MILOSZ "American Ignorance of War." From *The Captive Mind* by Czeslaw Milosz, translated by J. Zielonko. Copyright 1951, 1953 by Czeslaw Milosz. Reprinted by permission of Alfred A. Knopf, Inc.

PAULI MURRAY "The Inheritance of Values." Excerpt from *Proud Shoes* by Pauli Murray. Copyright © 1956, 1978 by Pauli Murray. Reprinted by permission of HarperCollins Publishers.

SHARON OLDS "Sex Without Love." From *The Dead and the Living* by Sharon Olds. Copyright © 1983 by Sharon Olds. Reprinted by permission of Alfred A. Knopf, Inc.

ROBERT ORNSTEIN AND RICHARD THOMPSON "Learning and Brain Growth." From *The Amazing Brain* by Robert Ornstein and Richard F. Thompson. Text copyright © 1984 by Robert Ornstein and Richard F. Thompson. Reprinted by permission of Houghton Mifflin Company. All rights reserved.

PLATO "The Allegory of the Cave." Reprinted from *The Republic of Plato* translated by F. M. Conford (1941) by permission of Oxford University Press.

ROBERT B. REICH "Corporation and Nation," *The Atlantic*, May 1988. Reprinted by permission of the author.

ADRIENNE RICH "Artificial Intelligence" is reprinted from *The Fact of a Doorframe: Poems Selected and New, 1950–1984*, by Adrienne Rich, by permission of W. W. Norton & Company, Inc. Copyright © 1984 by Adrienne Rich. Copyright © 1975, 1978 by W. W. Norton & Company, Inc. Copyright © 1981 by Arienne Rich.

RICHARD RODRIGUEZ "Aria: Memoir of a Bilingual Childhood." From *Hunger of Memory* by Richard Rodriguez. Copyright © 1982 by Richard Rodriguez. Reprinted by permission of David R. Godine, Publisher.

MIKE ROSE " 'I Just Wanna Be Average' ." Reprinted with permission of The Free Press, a Division of Macmillan, Inc., from *Lives on the Boundary* by Mike Rose. Copyright © 1989 by Mike Rose.

CARL SAGAN "The Nuclear Winter." Copyright © 1983 Carl Sagan. All rights reserved. First published in *Parade*. Reprinted by permission of the author.

SCOTT RUSSELL SANDERS "The Inheritance of Tools." Copyright © 1986 by Scott Russell Sanders; first appeared in *The North American Review;* reprinted by permission of the author and Virginia Kidd, Literary Agent. "The Men We Carry in Our Minds." Copyright © 1984 by Scott Russell Sanders; first appeared in *Milkweed Chronicle;* reprinted by permission of the author and Virginia Kidd, Literary Agent.

LESLIE MARMON SILKO "Landscape, History, and the Pueblo Imagination." Copyright © 1986 by Leslie Marmon Silko. Reprinted by permission of Wylie, Aitken & Stone, Inc.

LINDA SIMON "The Naked Source," *Michigan Quarterly Review*, Vol. XXVII, No. 3, Summer 1988. Copyright © 1988 by Linda Simon. Reprinted by permission.

PAUL THEROUX "Being a Man" from *Sunrise with Seamonsters* by Paul Theroux. Copyright © 1985 by Cape Cod Scriveners Company. Reprinted by permission of Houghton Mifflin Company. All rights reserved.

JAMES THURBER "University Days." Copyright 1933, © 1961 James Thurber. From *My Life and Hard Times*, published by Harper & Row. Reprinted by permission.

LAUREL THATCHER ULRICH "Understanding Paternity." From *A Midwife's Tale* by Laurel Thatcher Ulrich. Copyright © 1990 by Laurel Thatcher Ulrich. Reprinted by permission of Alfred A. Knopf, Inc.

JOHN UPDIKE "At War with My Skin." From *Self-Consciousness* by John Updike. Copyright © 1989 by John Updike. Reprinted by permission of Alfred A. Knopf, Inc.

LEWIS H. VAN DUSEN, JR. "Civil Disobedience: Destroyer of Democracy," *ABA Journal*, February 1969. Reprinted by permission of the author.

ALICE WALKER "The Civil Rights Movement: What Good Was It?" from *In Search of Our Mothers' Gardens*, copyright © 1967 by Alice Walker, reprinted by permission of Harcourt Brace Jovanovich, Inc.

MARGARET WALKER "On Being Female, Black, and Free" by Margaret Walker is reprinted from *The Writer on Her Work*, edited by Janet Sternburg, by permission of W. W. Norton & Company, Inc. Copyright © 1980 by Janet Sternburg.

WILLIAM W. WARNER "The Islands of Chesapeake Bay." From *Beautiful Swimmers: Watermen, Crabs and the Chesapeake Bay* by William W. Warner. Copyright © 1976 by William W. Warner. By permission of Little, Brown and Company.

JAMES D. WATSON AND FRANCIS H. C. CRICK From "Molecular Structure of Nucleic Acids." Re-

Index by Field of Inquiry

693

Composition and the Arts

Computer Science

Economics and Business

Ethnic Studies

Fiction

Gender Studies

History

Rhetorical Index

697

Anecdote

Comparison and Contrast

Deduction

Definition

Explanation

Fiction

Index of Authors and Titles